OPPOSING VIEWPOINTS IN

American History

VOLUME II:
FROM RECONSTRUCTION TO
THE PRESENT

OPPOSING
VIEWPOINTS IN

American
History

VOLUME II:
FROM RECONSTRUCTION
TO THE PRESENT

David L. Bender, *Publisher*

Bruno Leone, *Executive Editor*

William Dudley, *Series Editor*

John C. Chalberg, Ph.D., Professor in American History,
Normandale Community College, Minneapolis,
Consulting Editor

GREENHAVEN PRESS, INC., SAN DIEGO, CALIFORNIA

Cover Photograph Credits:

Front Cover, clockwise from top

1. Atomic bomb explosion over Nagasaki, Japan, August 9, 1945 (Smithsonian); 2. Photograph of *Apollo 17* moonwalk, December 1972 (also on p. 247) (NASA); 3. Soup kitchen line in New York City during Great Depression (also on p. 167) (FDR Library); 4. Photograph of Martin Luther King Jr. and others in the March on Washington, August 28, 1963 (National Archives); 5. Photograph of women's suffrage demonstrator (also on p. 83) (The Bettmann Archive); 6. (center) Photograph of marines on Iwo Jima, February 23, 1945 (National Archives)

Back Cover, left to right

1. World War II poster of "Rosie the Riveter" (National Archives); 2. Photograph of steam railroad locomotive (also on p. 1) (Library of Congress); 3. Statue of Liberty

Library of Congress Cataloging-in-Publication Data

Opposing viewpoints in American history / William Dudley, book editor.
    p.   cm.
    Includes bibliographical references and indexes.
    Contents: v. 1. From colonial times to Reconstruction — v. 2. From Reconstruction to the present.
    ISBN 1-56510-348-3 (v. 1 : lib. bdg. : alk paper). — ISBN 1-56510-347-5 (v. 1 : pbk. : alk. paper). — ISBN 1-56510-350-5 (v. 2 : lib. bdg. : alk. paper). — ISBN 1-56510-349-1 (v. 2 : pbk. : alk. paper)
    1. United States—History—Sources. I. Dudley, William, 1964-   .
E173.07 1996   95-33446
973—dc20   CIP

FOREWORD

Educators have long sought ways to engage and interest students in American history. They have also endeavored to sharpen their students' critical thinking skills—to teach them how to effectively analyze and evaluate the material that they read. *Opposing Viewpoints in American History*, an offshoot of Greenhaven Press's acclaimed *American History Series*, has been designed with both these objectives in mind.

Opposing Viewpoints in American History is an anthology of primary documents—the speeches, letters, articles, and other writings that are the raw material from which historians seek to understand and reconstruct the past. Assembled in two volumes (*volume 1: From Colonial Times to Reconstruction* and *volume 2: From Reconstruction to the Present*), these viewpoints trace American social, political, and diplomatic history from the time of the earliest European contact through the end of the Cold War. Student interest will be sparked by a wide spectrum of American voices, both the famous and the unfamiliar, expressing in their own words their opinions on the critical issues of their times.

To help sustain student interest and stimulate critical thinking, *Opposing Viewpoints in American History*, unlike other primary readers, pairs these primary documents in a running debate format. The guiding philosophy behind this compilation is that by comparing and contrasting opposing viewpoints on an issue, students will be challenged to think critically about what they read. Thus, for example, readers can evaluate Thomas Paine's stirring call for American independence in *Common Sense* by comparing it to the tightly reasoned arguments of Loyalist Charles Inglis. Within these two volumes a white minister and an escaped slave differ on the evils of slavery; Chief Joseph and Theodore Roosevelt provide contrasting perspectives on the takeover of Indian land by whites; Franklin D. Roosevelt's call for a New Deal is complemented by Herbert Hoover's dire warnings about the harms of government meddling; and a nuclear physicist and a secretary of war differ on the merits of dropping the atomic bomb on Japan. The paired structuring of sources found in *Opposing Viewpoints in American History* also reflects the important reality that American history itself has been a story of conflict and controversy. The birth of the nation was the result of a hotly debated decision to break from Great Britain, and Americans have continued to debate the meaning and direction of their nation ever since.

Along with its primary documents, *Opposing Viewpoints in American History* includes several supplemental features intended to enhance the readers' understanding. Introductions and timelines supply basic historical background for each section of the book. In addition, prior to each viewpoint the editors have provided essential biographical information about the author; a brief overview of the issue being debated; and questions designed to stimulate interest, reinforce comprehension, and encourage critical thinking.

The combination of primary texts and background information make *Opposing Viewpoints in American History*, by itself or in conjunction with other American history textbooks, an effective way to teach and engage students in the study of American history. To further aid instructors, a test bank based on the materials in both volumes of *Opposing Viewpoints in American History* is available.

Thomas Jefferson once said that "difference of opinion leads to inquiry, and inquiry to truth"—a statement as valid today as in Jefferson's time. It is the editors' hope that this volume will challenge students to actively inquire into the "difference of opinion" found on the pages of America's history in order to better understand the nation's past and to see how that past helped largely shape the present.

John C. Chalberg
Consulting Editor

CONTENTS

Part II: The Progressive Era, 1895–1920

Part III: Prosperity, Depression, and War, 1920–1945

PART I:
REBUILDING AFTER THE CIVIL WAR, 1865–1895

Reconstruction

Twilight of the American Frontier

Industry, Agriculture, and Social Protest

1865
- Mar. 3 Freedman's Bureau established
- Apr. 9 Robert E. Lee surrenders to Ulysses S. Grant, ending Civil War
- Apr. 14 President Abraham Lincoln assassinated
- Nov. Mississippi enacts Black Code
- Dec. 18 Thirteenth Amendment, banning slavery, ratified
- Dec. 24 Ku Klux Klan founded in Tennessee

1867
- Mar. 1 Nebraska enters the Union
- Mar. 30 United States purchases Alaska from Russia

1869
- Mar. 15 Woman suffrage amendment to the Constitution proposed in Congress
- May 10 Nation's first transcontinental railroad completed
- Sept. 24 "Black Friday" financial panic on Wall Street
- Nov. 6 First intercollegiate football game played
- Dec. 10 Wyoming Territory grants women the right to vote

1871
- Mar. 3 Congress nullifies past treaties and makes Indians wards of the federal government
- Apr. 20 Ku Klux Klan Act passed by Congress
- Oct. 8–11 Great Chicago Fire
- Oct. 24 Race riot in Los Angeles, California, kills 15 Chinese immigrants

1873
- Mar. 3 Comstock Law bars obscenity (including birth control information) from the federal mails
- Sept. Wall Street Panic of 1873

1875
- Mar. 1 Civil Rights Act of 1875 forbids racial segregation in public places

1877
- Mar. 2 Rutherford B. Hayes declared winner of close and controversial presidential election
- Apr. Remaining federal troops are withdrawn from the South
- June–Oct. Nez Percé war
- July Railway workers stage first national strike

1878
- Aug. 21 American Bar Association founded

1865 **1870** **1875**

1866
- Apr. 9 Congress passes Civil Rights Act of 1866 over President Johnson's veto, nullifying state Black Codes
- July 24 Congress readmits the state of Tennessee to the Union
- July 30 Race riot in New Orleans; 200 casualties

1870
- Jan. 10 Standard Oil Company incorporated in Cleveland, Ohio
- Jan. 26 Virginia readmitted to the Union
- Feb. 23 Mississippi readmitted to the Union
- Feb. 25 Hiram R. Revels of Mississippi becomes nation's first black senator
- Mar. 30 Fifteenth Amendment, forbidding racial restrictions on suffrage, ratified

1872
- Mar. 1 Yellowstone National Park established by Congress
- June 19 Freedman's Bureau abolished
- Nov. 28 Susan B. Anthony arrested for attempting to vote
- Nov. 5 Grant reelected president

1879
- *Progress and Poverty* by Henry George published
- Feb. 15 Act of Congress permits women to argue cases before the U.S. Supreme Court
- Oct. 21 Thomas Edison invents the first practical incandescent light

1876
- Feb. 2 National League of baseball teams organized
- Mar. Alexander Graham Bell invents the telephone
- May–Nov. Centennial Exposition at Philadelphia
- June 25 George A. Custer's forces annihilated at the Battle of Little Big Horn
- Aug. 1 Colorado admitted to the Union

1868
- May President Andrew Johnson avoids impeachment by one vote
- June 22–24 Arkansas, Alabama, Florida, Louisiana, South Carolina, and North Carolina are readmitted to the Union
- July 21 Fourteenth Amendment, guaranteeing black civil rights, ratified
- July 28 Burlingame Treaty signed between China and the United States
- Nov. 3 Ulysses S. Grant elected president
- Dec. 25 President Johnson grants amnesty for all Confederate leaders

1880
- Nov. 2   James A. Garfield elected president

1882
- Jan. 2   Standard Oil Trust founded
- May 6   Chinese Exclusion Act passed

1883
- Jan. 16   Pendleton Act sets up Civil Service Commission
- May 24   Brooklyn Bridge opens
- July 4   Debut of "Buffalo Bill's Wild West Show"
- Oct. 15   Supreme Court in *Civil Rights Cases* declares Civil Rights Act of 1875 unconstitutional
- Nov. 18   Standard railway time zones adopted in United States

1887
- Feb. 4   Interstate Commerce Commission established by Congress
- Feb. 8   Dawes Severalty Act converts Indian tribal lands to individual ownership
- Mar. 3   Anti-immigrant American Protective Association (APA) founded

1889
- June   Andrew Carnegie's "Gospel of Wealth" article published
- Nov.   North Dakota, South Dakota, Montana, and Washington reach statehood

1892
- Jan. 1   Immigration receiving station in New York City transferred to Ellis Island
- July–Nov.   Homestead strike by steelworkers against the Carnegie Steel Company
- Sept.   First successful gas-powered automobile made in U.S.
- Nov. 8   Grover Cleveland elected president

1893
- Jan. 17   Queen Liliuokalani of Hawaii overthrown
- June 27   Crash of New York stock market begins four years of economic depression
- Nov. 7   Women's suffrage adopted in Colorado by popular vote

---

1880   **1885**   **1890**   **1895**

1881
- Feb. 19   Kansas adopts statewide prohibition
- May 21   American Red Cross founded
- July 2   President Garfield shot
- July 4   Booker T. Washington founds the Tuskegee Institute
- Sept. 19   Garfield dies; Vice President Chester A. Arthur becomes president

1884
- *Adventures of Huckleberry Finn* by Mark Twain published
- Nov. 4   Grover Cleveland elected president

1886
- Feb. 7   Anti-Chinese riots engulf Seattle
- May 4   Haymarket Square bombing and riot
- Sept. 4   Apache chief Geronimo captured, ending last major Indian war
- Oct. 28   Statue of Liberty dedicated
- Dec. 8   American Federation of Labor formed
- Dec. 22   Henry Grady's "New South" speech in New York

1888
- Feb.   First United States use of secret ballot at a public election, in Louisville, Kentucky
- Nov. 6   Benjamin Harrison elected president

1890
- Census Bureau declares the end of the frontier
- July   Idaho and Wyoming made states
- July 2   Passage of Sherman Antitrust Act outlawing monopolies
- Sept. 25   Yosemite National Park established
- Dec. 29   Wounded Knee massacre; 146 Sioux Indians killed by U.S. troops

1891
- Basketball invented by James Naismith
- May 19   Populist Party launched in Cincinnati, Ohio

1894
- July 2   President Cleveland sends in federal troops to enforce injunction against Pullman railway strike
- Aug. 27   Nation's first graduated income tax law passed by Congress

1895
- May 20   Supreme Court in *Pollock v. Farmer's Loan and Trust* declares income tax unconstitutional
- Sept. 18   Booker T. Washington's speech at the Atlanta Exposition

PART I:
REBUILDING AFTER THE
CIVIL WAR, 1865–1895

The Civil War had profound and lasting repercussions on the United States. No change was more dramatic than the death of the defining institution of the defeated Confederacy—slavery—which was abolished by constitutional amendment eight months after Robert E. Lee surrendered to Ulysses S. Grant at Appomattox in April 1865. Other significant changes took longer to materialize. For example, the military demands of war propelled advances in technology that laid the foundation for an explosion of industrial development in the victorious North. Still other transformations stemmed from wartime efforts by Congress to bind the far-flung nation together. Both the 1862 Homestead Act and the decision the same year to sponsor construction of a transcontinental railroad helped spur postwar westward migration—a development that transformed the western regions of the country.

The changes America underwent during the three decades following the war's end did not proceed without controversies and debates, as the following selection of opposing viewpoints illustrates. Some of the issues presented here were of special concern to specific regions of the country. Americans were frequently at odds over matters pertaining to the reconstruction of the South, the industrialization of the North, and the settlement of the West. Other issues, such as labor/management relations and immigration, were national in scope. But all of these disagreements took place in the context of a nation that was growing rapidly in population, wealth, and power.

The South and Reconstruction

Reconstruction (1865–1877) was dominated by two fundamental questions. One question concerned the manner in which the former Confederate states should be reintegrated into the Union. At issue was whether they should be permitted to regain their status as states quickly, as President Abraham Lincoln proposed before his April 1865 assassination, or whether they should be held as conquered provinces, as Radical Republicans in Congress argued. Closely related to this dilemma was a second question: How should the four million former slaves be reintegrated into what was no longer a slave society? Should they be granted the right to vote and otherwise participate in the political process? Or should their political and social rights be restricted, as many whites in both the North and the South believed? Radical Republicans insisted on federal control of Confederate states to ensure that the ex-slaves would soon be given political equality, economic opportunity, and full civil rights. Opponents of the Radical Republicans generally opposed federal control of state governments, in large part because they wanted to pass state laws that would limit the rights and powers of blacks (as many Southern states did after the Civil War by enacting special "Black Codes").

The Radical Republicans achieved mixed success in their goals. They passed federal laws that were designed to achieve a measure of integration throughout the South. Through the Fourteenth and Fifteenth Amendments, respectively, black Americans were granted citizenship and black men received the right to vote. But by 1877 all federal troops had been withdrawn from the former Confederate states, all eleven states had been readmitted to the Union, and political leadership in the South had returned to conservative whites. Three-quarters of the southern black population became sharecroppers, many of whom were so poor that their material welfare was not much better than it had been under slavery. During the 1880s southern writers and political leaders hailed the rise of a "New South" based on industrial renaissance and postwar reconciliation. But critics, both white and black, argued that whether the issue was race relations or economic development, the region still had a long way to go.

Immigration, Migration, and the American Frontier

The South was not the only region of the country divided along racial and ethnic lines. Blacks faced racial prejudice and discrimination in other parts of the nation. Moreover, the fears of some Americans were directed not only at blacks (who then constituted a relatively small portion of the population outside the South), but also at other minorities, including newly arrived immigrants and American Indians.

Between 1860 and 1890 more than ten million people immigrated to the United States. A large number of them came from Asia and southern and eastern Europe, areas that were previously not a major source of immigrants. While some settled in rural areas, many instead formed ethnic enclaves within America's cities. Some Americans encouraged immigration and praised immigrants' contributions to America, but others looked at the unfamiliar newcomers with suspicion. Some feared that immigrants would take jobs from native Americans or that the presence of large numbers of low-wage immigrant laborers in the workforce would depress wages. In California and other western states, Chinese immigrants and other minorities were often the victims of racial prejudice—and sometimes violence. On the local and national levels, debates began on whether the traditional American policy of open immigration should be abandoned.

Far away from America's cities and coastal regions, the areas affected by immigration, conflict arose between the Native American inhabitants of the western regions and the cowboys, pioneers, farmers, and other newcomers who sought Indian land. Conflicts between settlers and Indians often turned violent. In the 1870s and 1880s, partly in response to attacks by Native Americans and partly to secure the plains for settlement, the U.S. government launched numerous military campaigns to remove Native Americans to reservations. Many reformers argued that the reservations would provide Indians with a better, more secure way of life. They believed that Native Americans would benefit from learning modern agricultural methods, whites' social practices, and Christian religious beliefs. Although some whites decried the forced relocations, which they perceived as government abuses against American Indians, few advocated returning land to the Indian tribes or preserving Native American culture.

In addition to the Indian wars, the settlement of the West brought with it the destruction of the buffalo herds, the rise and fall of the open-range cattle system, and the joining of the East and the West by railroad. Between 1870 and 1890 the non-Indian population west of the Mississippi River grew from seven million to seventeen million. By 1890 the U.S. Census Bureau declared that the frontier, in the form of an unbroken line delineating an unsettled region, had all but disappeared. The prairies formerly populated by herds of buffalo and nomadic tribes of American Indians were now populated with farmers trying to earn a living from the land.

Agrarian Protest

The millions of people drawn west by the prospect of land to homestead faced a harsh life with numerous obstacles to success. Drought, locusts, and other natural disasters were a setback for some, but many farmers came to believe that their problems were the result of social inequities and faceless enemies, including banks, railroads, and corporations.

Previous generations of American farmers and settlers had been largely self-sufficient. They obtained their food, clothing, simple tools, and other necessities of life directly from their own land and toil or by trade in local markets. But in the years following the Civil War, farmers increasingly concentrated on raising cash crops, such as wheat, corn, or cotton. These crops were then shipped by rail to distant markets. Over time farmers grew dependent on railroad companies to market their products and on banks for working capital to buy needed land and farm machinery. Many farmers failed to break even due to the expensive shipping rates charged by railroads and the high interest rates of banks. The steady drop of prices for staple crops in the years following the Civil War, especially during the 1880s, worsened farmers' already bleak prospects.

Some farmers responded to economic distress by organizing among themselves. Their political efforts led to the formation of the Grange movement of the 1870s, the Farmers' Alliance network of the 1880s, and the Populist Party of the 1890s. All these movements called for greater regulation of banks and railroads; the Populist Party demanded outright government ownership of the railroads.

The Industrial North

While the frontier was being settled and the South was struggling to recover from the Civil War, the northern states led the nation in the most significant economic development of the era: the rapid rise and supremacy of industry, which by the 1890s had exceeded agriculture as a source of income for Americans. Advances in technology were a key factor in this industrial growth. Between 1860 and 1890, 440,000 patents were issued by the U.S. Patent Office. Among the inventions of the era were the telegraph, telephone, typewriter, and adding machine. The manufacture of steel, essential for railroad rails and skyscrapers, became a major American industry. With the growth of industry came controversies over the distribution of the wealth it produced.

Rich and Poor

The industrial age created an unprecedented gap between the rich and the poor. A few Americans were able to obtain great fortunes for themselves. The number of millionaires rose from around 20 in 1850 to more than 3,000 in 1900. Tycoons such as Andrew Carnegie (steel), John D. Rockefeller (oil), and J. Pierpont Morgan (banking and railroads) became dominant figures of the era, overshadowing in fame and power even presidents of the United States. Some praised these entrepreneurs as geniuses of business organization who helped to harness natural resources and to provide industrial products for American businesses and consumers. Others criticized them for using unethical methods to destroy competitors, for having little or no regard for the public good, and for underpaying and mistreating their workers.

At the other end of the economic scale were those who labored in the nation's factories, on the nation's rails, and in the nation's mines. These laborers typically worked at least sixty hours a week for low wages, often in hazardous conditions. The percentage of self-employed workers in America fell from about half of the workforce in 1860 to one-third by 1900; consequently, more workers than ever before were dependent on wages for a living. Their dependency on wages, combined with the fact that they could be laid off or fired at any time, created a perilous economic situation for many workers and their families. Some workers responded by forming labor unions and engaging in strikes. However, while they laid foundations for future labor movement successes, most of these efforts failed in the face of intense business and legal opposition.

The expansion of industry in these years had some positive results for American workers. The general decline in prices, while harmful for farmers dependent on crop sales, meant that workers with steady jobs enjoyed rising real incomes to help them purchase the increasing variety of consumer goods. The industrial revolution supported a growing middle class, provided work opportunities for America's immigrants, and allowed more women to find wage jobs outside the home. Many Americans viewed the growth of the middle class and the ascent of such figures as Carnegie, who rose from an impoverished immigrant to a steel magnate, as proof that in America anyone who worked hard could succeed and become rich. However, as the century drew to a close, some people were concerned that America's industrialization was not helping the nation as a whole, and that the widening divide between rich and poor Americans threatened national ideals of freedom and equality. These questions continued to be part of the American dialogue as the nation approached the twentieth century.

Reconstruction

VIEWPOINT 1A

Reconstruction Should Be Harsh (1865)

William Mason Grosvenor (1835–1900)

William Mason Grosvenor, an abolitionist prior to the Civil War, commanded one of the first units of black soldiers organized to fight for the North in that conflict. During the war he observed firsthand the relatively lenient reconstruction process by which the state government of Louisiana was re-created under Northern military occupation, with little change in the political or economic status of blacks beyond the abolition of legal slavery. In an article published in the *New Englander* magazine in 1865, Grosvenor criticizes the state and local governments

From William Mason Grosvenor, "The Law of Conquest the True Basis of Reconstruction," *New Englander*, vol. 29, January 1865.

established during the Civil War. He also takes issue with the "abeyance" theory of reconstruction—the idea that the Confederate states, never having legally seceded from the Union, still possessed all their constitutional privileges and prerogatives as member states of America, and should be restored these temporarily suspended rights as speedily as possible.

On what foundation does the North have the right to dictate social changes within the South, according to Grosvenor? What is the central question he posits as needing to be answered for reconstruction to be successful? Why is the time opportune for changes in the South, according to Grosvenor?

I t is fortunate that the political victory achieved in the re-election of President Lincoln is generally received, not with noisy exultation, but with calm and thoughtful thankfulness. It gives ground for hope that in rejoicing over triumphs gained and dangers escaped, the nation will not be blind to the severer trial yet to be met, and the fearful responsibilities that will attend it. . . .

There remains the . . . most serious test of all—the trial of wisdom and statesmanship. This is not merely a rebellion or a political contest with which we have to deal; it is a revolution. Our task is to obey and execute a fiat of the Almighty, written on the face of the Western hemisphere in the course of the Mississippi river: "There shall be, upon this broad domain, one nation and but one." The shock of arms revealed the fact that we had never been one people, and that a true nationality, embracing all States and sections, had never existed. Heterogeneous populations, hostile systems, and irreconcilable ideas had only been placed in contact, and held to bare juxta-position by a constitutional compact. No chemical union had ever taken place; for that the white-hot crucible of civil war was found necessary. To keep up the fire until antagonistic elements are refined away and a perfect union is effected is needful, and is the deliberate purpose of the nation, expressed in the late election; but that is not all. To direct the process of amalgamation, to determine the time for each step, and to give shape to the new substance, will demand the most exalted statesmanship. A single error may cause a flaw that shall send the whole work back to the furnace. . . .

A Higher Wisdom

To guide the resistless forces, and to shun dangers on either hand—as well the Scylla of a too timid conservatism as the Charybdis of an all-destroying radicalism—to settle the thousand questions and meet the thousand difficulties that will arise, will assuredly call for a higher wisdom, a wider knowledge, a profounder foresight than has yet been needed. If we were unused to war, and had to create an army and master the art; if we had hitherto found no need of self-sacrificing patriotism in the halcyon days when love of country was an undeveloped and untested force, so it may almost be said that no statesmanship yet made manifest among us is equal to the needs of the swiftly advancing emergency. All the maxims of the past are obsolete. The teachings of the great minds of other days will be, in this trial, of as little use as the old Constitution frigate with her carronades [short-range guns] in a battle of iron-clads. The machinery and framework of government may not improbably be found all too slender and weak for the mighty forces now evolved. A statesmanship will be needed that can steer by the compass instead of the lead-line, and can push boldly out of the narrow range of precedents and established forms into the deep water of first principles and permanent truths. It is work for a discoverer rather than for a pilot. . . .

But whether the future nationality shall be equal to the glorious possibilities of free government, whether the harmony of forces and homogeneity of elements shall be complete, will depend upon the measure of statesmanship that may guide the work now close at hand. Already a great constitutional reform is demanded; and we are but dull scholars if we have not learned through all the severe experiences of this war, that no work of human device is perfect, and that nations, like children, will outgrow their clothes. Already the financial problem calls for something more than temporary expedients. Already questions of a standing army, of a permanent revenue, and of tariff or direct taxation, require reëxamination by the light of new events and needs. Already the problem of the future of the negro race assumes the gravest importance, and can be deferred but a little longer. Questions of amnesty or punishment of public enemies already engage the attention of rulers and people. Behind these there throng in the anteroom whole troops of problems new and strange—of interests needing protection and claims clamoring for adjustment. The offing is full of questions, fast anchored once, but now cast adrift by the storm. The change to which we are called is radical. It is the new-birth of the nation.

In such a crisis it may be well to remember that the nation that governs itself has to pay for its blunders, and that it will not do to play at politics. . . .

———— • ————

"Punishment . . . shall be severe enough to prevent for all future time the recurrence of a crime so terribly destructive."

———— • ————

Of all the unsolved problems the most important, and the one that demands most urgently thorough examination and final settlement, is that which concerns the present status of the rebellious States and the proper mode of reconstruction. It is too momentous a subject to be left to chance. Future generations will consider with amazement that, instead of first ascertaining the true theory, and guiding by that the decisions that shall serve as precedents for the future, we permit local, temporary, and often personal considerations to determine the decisions. Thus blind and often conflicting precedents are established; and the theory is left to some era of leisure when the political geologist, by patient delving and much study of the fossil remains, may perhaps pick it out of the chaotic record. The organic law of ten future States ought to be arrived at in some different fashion. But this blindness of action, and the prevalence of views peculiarly chaotic and vague, are not without excuse. The question is one of no little difficulty; it goes deeper than all our statutes and deeper than the Constitution itself, and makes all precedents as useless as the trilobites. The very multitude of theories darkens counsel, and rarely, if ever, has the question been stripped of all extraneous matter and clearly stated. It has nothing to do with slavery or confiscation. It is simply this: "Do the civil rights under our government, once vested in certain States and the citizens of those States, still exist, and, if so, in whom are they vested?" To discuss particular measures of reconstruction and attempt partial reorganizations, without first giving to this question a final and formal answer, is to put up a frame and finish off a wing before the shape of the building is fixed or the foundation laid. . . .

It would surely be not a little to the credit of the nation to sweep away . . . all those paltry *simulacra* of elections and organizations which have hitherto started up like mushrooms in the track of our armies. . . . Have we not seen enough of these manufactured organizations, which "live, move and have their being" in the baggage wagons of our army? They afford excellent chances for political chicanery; nice honors and fat offices are recovered from "abeyance" by men whose surprising merit had not been discovered in times of peace; but is the Union cause materially helped or do the Union loving people of the South thereby obtain any substantial protection? Is it not time to ask if these sickly plants do not cost more than it is worth to rear them, and to look with favor on a theory, which, by removing all pretext for such premature growths, sweeps away the whole system of political jugglery so engendered?

Punishing Treason

Another consideration seems worthy of especial attention. Our law of treason is less effective or severe than that of other civilized nations. To the framers of the Constitution treason seemed a crime strangely horrid and improbable, and there doubtless appeared to be greater danger from an over rigorous loyalty, which, in times of excitement, might mistake reasonable freedom of thought and speech for hostility to the government. . . . But, were the South to lay down her arms to-day, and resume the rights which the abeyance theory concedes, there is no security that even these leaders would not find absolute immunity from punishment. Even the most notorious traitor could exercise every right of citizenship until he had been tried and convicted by a jury from his own State, and nothing in the laws of that State would exclude any other notorious traitor from the jury-box. What punishment would [Jefferson] Davis fear from a jury of Mississippians, of whom perhaps half had just laid aside smoking muskets and dripping swords to enter the panel? To

place such immunity within the reach of rebels, who may abandon the contest whenever they find it hopeless, is to put a premium on treason. We are cramped by no legal forms of constitutional obligations, unless we choose, in punishing this rebellion. Rising to the proportions of a civil war, it has placed in the hands of the nation not only the remedial agencies of the courts, but the torch and sword of the conqueror. Rebels are now not rebels only, but public enemies; Gettysburg's slaughter and Sherman's march have a broader sweep than any enacted penalties; and the right of conquest cuts deeper than any conceivable measure of confiscation. The law of war becomes supreme, and of that law *"Vae Victis"* ["Woe to the vanquished"] is the epitome. We have only to apply the principles of the decision above quoted to the work of reconstruction, to make sure that the punishment, for leaders at least, shall be severe enough to prevent for all future time the recurrence of a crime so terribly destructive to the national prosperity and the national honor. . . .

Schemes of reconstruction which make possible immunity for the great conspirators, or instant return to all political privileges for traitors as well as loyalists, will not be such as the people will approve or the nation can safely adopt. Nor will it answer, in overflowing leniency for past offenses, to neglect security for healthy political action in the future. Men who have deliberately betrayed trusts guarded by all the sanctity of an oath are not safely to be trusted as loyal and true citizens, whenever they may choose to renew an obligation once violated. But the state constitutions only can effectually debar any from suffrage, office, or trust; under the abeyance theory each State can demand recognition with her old constitution and laws; nor is it easy to find authority for requiring particular changes as conditions of recognition. Instead of retaining these old constitutions, redolent of the slave-pen, defiled in every part by the use of traitors, and infested in every joint and crevice by claims that loyal men must loathe but can never wholly extirpate, the erection and admission of new States demolishes all these relics of a shameful past, and secures new and spotless constitutions, each in harmony in every part with the spirit of the new era, and instinct and vital with freedom and loyalty.

VIEWPOINT 1B

Reconstruction Should Be Lenient (1866)

Herman Melville (1819–1891)

Northern-born writer Herman Melville, most famous for his novels including *Moby-Dick*, wrote a short collection of poems inspired by the Civil War that was published in 1866. In a companion essay to the poetry collection, the antiwar and antislavery Melville argues for a humane and revenge-free reconstruction policy toward the defeated South.

Why should Southern rebels not be viewed as vile traitors, according to Melville? How does he believe the nation should approach the question of the status of black ex-slaves? Is he more or less realistic than Grosvenor in his views of the South and its people?

———————

There seems no reason why patriotism and narrowness should go together, or why intellectual impartiality should be confounded with political trimming, or why serviceable truth should keep cloistered because not partisan. Yet the work of reconstruction, if admitted to be feasible at all, demands little but common sense and Christian charity. Little but these? These are much.

Southern Penitence

Some of us are concerned because as yet the South shows no penitence. But what exactly do we mean by this? Since down to the close of the war she never confessed any for braving it, the only penitence now left her is that which springs solely from the sense of discomfiture; and since this evidently would be a contrition hypocritical, it would be unworthy in us to demand it. Certain it is that penitence, in the sense of voluntary humiliation, will never be displayed. Nor does this afford just ground for unreserved condemnation. It is enough, for all practical purposes, if the South have been taught by the terrors of civil war to feel that secession, like slavery, is against destiny; that both now lie buried in one grave; that her fate is linked with ours; and that together we comprise the nation. . . .

Patriotism is not baseness, neither is it inhumanity. The mourners who this summer bear flowers to the mounds of the Virginian and Georgian dead are, in their domestic bereavement and proud affection, as sacred in the eye of heaven as are those who go with similar offerings of tender grief and love into the cemeteries of our Northern martyrs. And yet, in one aspect, how needless to point the contrast. . . .

There were excesses which marked the conflict, most of which are perhaps inseparable from a civil strife so intense and prolonged, and involving warfare in some border countries new and imperfectly civilized. Barbarities also there were, for which the Southern people collectively can hardly be held responsible, though perpetrated by ruffians in their name. But surely other qualities—exalted ones—

From Herman Melville, *Battle-Pieces and Aspects of War* (New York, 1866).

courage and fortitude matchless, were likewise displayed, and largely; and justly may these be held the characteristic traits, and not the former.

In this view, what Northern writer, however patriotic, but must revolt from acting on paper a part anyway akin to that of the live dog to the dead lion; and yet it is right to rejoice for our triumph, so far as it may justly imply an advance for our whole country and for humanity.

Let it be held no reproach to anyone that he pleads for reasonable consideration for our late enemies, now stricken down and unavoidably debarred, for the time, from speaking through authorized agencies for themselves. Nothing has been urged here in the foolish hope of conciliating those men— few in number, we trust—who have resolved never to be reconciled to the Union. On such hearts everything is thrown away except it be religious commiseration, and the sincerest. Yet let them call to mind that unhappy secessionist [Edmund Ruffin], not a military man, who, with impious alacrity, fired the first shot of the Civil War at Sumter, and a little more than four years afterward fired the last one into his own heart at Richmond.

Noble was the gesture into which patriotic passion surprised the people in a utilitarian time and country; yet the glory of the war falls short of its pathos— a pathos which now at last ought to disarm all animosity.

How many and earnest thoughts still rise, and how hard to repress them. We feel what past years have been, and years, unretarded years, shall come. May we all have moderation; may we all show candor. Though, perhaps, nothing could ultimately have averted the strife and though to treat of human actions is to deal wholly with second causes, nevertheless, let us not cover up or try to extenuate what, humanly speaking, is the truth; namely, that those unfraternal denunciations, continued through years, and which at last inflamed to deeds that ended in bloodshed, were reciprocal; and that, had the preponderating strength and the prospect of its unlimited increase lain on the other side, on ours might have lain those actions which now in our late opponents we stigmatize under the name of Rebellion.

As frankly let us own—what it would be unbecoming to parade were foreigners concerned—that our triumph was won not more by skill and bravery than by superior resources and crushing numbers; that it was a triumph, too, over a people for years politically misled by designing men, and also by some honestly erring men, who, from their position, could not have been otherwise than broadly influential; a people who, though, indeed, they sought to perpetuate the curse of slavery, and even extend it, were not the authors of it but (less fortunate, not less righteous than we) were the fated inheritors; a people who, having a like origin with ourselves, share essentially in whatever worthy qualities we may possess. No one can add to the lasting reproach which hopeless defeat has now cast upon secession by withholding the recognition of these verities.

———— • ————

"No consideration should tempt us to pervert the national victory into oppression for the vanquished."

———— • ————

Surely we ought to take it to heart that the kind of pacification, based upon principles operating equally all over the land, which lovers of their country yearn for, and which our arms, though signally triumphant, did not bring about, and which lawmaking, however anxious or energetic or repressive, never by itself can achieve, may yet be largely aided by generosity of sentiment public and private. Some revisionary legislation and adaptive is indispensable; but with this should harmoniously work another kind of prudence, not unallied with entire magnanimity. Benevolence and policy—Christianity and Machiavelli—dissuade from penal severities toward the subdued. Abstinence here is as obligatory as considerate care for our unfortunate fellowmen late in bonds, and, if observed, would equally prove to be wise forecast. The great qualities of the South, those attested in the war, we can perilously alienate, or we may make them nationally available at need.

The Place of Blacks

The blacks, in their infant pupilage to freedom, appeal to the sympathies of every humane mind. The paternal guardianship which, for the interval, government exercises over them was prompted equally by duty and benevolence. Yet such kindliness should not be allowed to exclude kindliness to communities who stand nearer to us in nature. For the future of the freed slaves we may well be concerned; but the future of the whole country, involving the future of the blacks, urges a paramount claim upon our anxiety. Effective benignity, like the Nile, is not narrow in its bounty, and true policy is always broad.

To be sure, it is vain to seek to glide, with molded words, over the difficulties of the situation. And for them who are neither partisans, nor enthusiasts, nor theorists, nor cynics, there are some doubts not readily to be solved. And there are fears. Why is not the cessation of war now at length attended with the settled calm of peace? Wherefore in a clear sky do we still turn our eyes toward the South, as the Neapoli-

tan, months after the eruption, turns his toward Vesuvius? Do we dread lest the repose may be deceptive? In the recent convulsion has the crater but shifted?

Let us revere that sacred uncertainty which forever impends over men and nations. Those of us who always abhorred slavery as an atheistical iniquity, gladly we join in the exulting chorus of humanity over its downfall. But we should remember that emancipation was accomplished not by deliberate legislation; only through agonized violence could so mighty a result be effected. In our natural solicitude to confirm the benefit of liberty to the blacks, let us forbear from measures of dubious constitutional rightfulness toward our white countrymen—measures of a nature to provoke, among other of the last evils, exterminating hatred of race toward race.

In imagination let us place ourselves in the unprecedented position of the Southerners—their position as regards the millions of ignorant manumitted slaves in their midst, for whom some of us now claim the suffrage. Let us be Christians toward our fellow whites, as well as philanthropists toward the blacks, our fellowmen. In all things and toward all, we are enjoined to do as we would be done by. Nor should we forget that benevolent desires, after passing a certain point, cannot undertake their own fulfillment without incurring the risk of evils beyond those sought to be remedied. Something may well be left to the graduated care of future legislation, and to heaven. . . .

But, so far as immediate measures looking toward permanent reestablishment are concerned, no consideration should tempt us to pervert the national victory into oppression for the vanquished. Should plausible promise of eventual good, or a deceptive or spurious sense of duty, lead us to essay this, count we must on serious consequences, not the least of which would be divisions among the Northern adherents of the Union. . . .

Let us pray that the terrible historic tragedy of our time may not have been enacted without instructing our whole beloved country through terror and pity; and may fulfillment verify in the end those expectations which kindle the bards of progress and humanity.

For Further Reading

LaWanda Cox and John H. Cox, *Politics, Principle, and Prejudice, 1865–1866: Dilemma of Reconstruction America.* Glencoe, IL: Free Press, 1963.

Stanton Garner, *The Civil War World of Herman Melville.* Lawrence: University Press of Kansas, 1993.

Harold M. Hyman, *A More Perfect Union: The Impact of the Civil War and Reconstruction upon the Constitution.* New York: Knopf, 1973.

VIEWPOINT 2A

The Fourteenth Amendment Violates States' Rights (1866)

Andrew J. Rogers (1828–1900)

The Thirteenth Amendment to the Constitution, banning slavery, was passed by Congress and ratified by the states in 1865. The following year, responding to "black codes" passed in several Southern states restricting the civil rights of blacks, Congress passed the 1866 Civil Rights Act, which protected black rights and citizenship. Many Radical Republican members of Congress believed that the act was insufficient; they argued that an amendment to the Constitution was needed to permanently secure citizenship and equality for the former slaves. On February 26, 1866, Representative John A. Bingham of Ohio proposed that Congress pass the following constitutional amendment:

> The Congress shall have the power to make all laws which shall be necessary and proper to secure to the citizens of each State all privileges and immunities of citizens in the several States, and to all persons in the several States equal protection in the rights of life, liberty, and property.

Immediately after Bingham introduced this proposed amendment, Andrew J. Rogers, a Democratic representative from New Jersey, rose to speak in opposition to it. The following viewpoint is excerpted from his remarks. Rogers argues that Bingham's proposed amendment makes the national government too powerful at the expense of the states. Such a change in the balance of power subverts what Rogers calls the "organic law" of America, including the U.S. Constitution as originally written. He contends that states have the sovereign right to determine whether to allow black suffrage, interracial marriage, and other matters. Congress eventually passed a constitutional amendment similar to Bingham's wording (see p.17).

Why is the proposed amendment in conflict with what the writers of the Constitution had in mind, according to Rogers? Does Rogers believe in black inferiority?

No resolution proposing an amendment to the Constitution of the United States had been offered to this Congress more dangerous to the liberties of the people and the foundations of this Government than the pending [Bingham] resolution. When sifted from top to bottom it will be found

From Andrew J. Rogers, *Congressional Globe*, 39th Cong., 1st sess., February 26, 1866, pp. 150–51.

to be the embodiment of centralization and the disfranchisement of the States of those sacred and immutable State rights which were reserved to them by the consent of our fathers in our organic law.

The Organic Law

When the gentleman [Ohio representative John A. Bingham] says the proposed amendment is intended to authorize no rights except those already embodied in the Constitution, I give him the plain and emphatic answer—if the Constitution provides the requirements contained in this amendment, why, in this time of excitement and public clamor, should we attempt to again ingraft upon it what is already in it? . . .

The gentleman takes the position that there is nothing in this proposed amendment with regard to privileges and immunities of citizens of the several States attempted to be ingrafted in the instrument, except those which already exist in it. If those rights already exist in the organic law of the land, I ask him, what is the necessity of so amending the Constitution as to authorize Congress to carry into effect a plain provision which now, according to his views, inheres in the very organic law itself?

I know what the gentleman will attempt to say in answer to that position: that because the Constitution authorizes Congress to carry the powers conferred by it into effect, privileges and immunities are not considered within the meaning of powers, and therefore Congress has no right to carry into effect what the Constitution itself intended when it provided that citizens of each State should have all privileges and immunities of citizens in the several States.

Congress Cannot Override a State

Now, sir, the answer to that argument is simply this: that when the Constitution was framed and ratified, its makers did not intend to lodge in the Congress of the United States any power to override a State and settle by congressional legislation the rights, privileges, and immunities of citizens in the several States. That matter was left entirely for the courts, to enforce the privileges and immunities of the citizens under that clause of the organic law. Although our forefathers, in their wisdom, after having exacted and wrested from Great Britain State rights, saw fit to incorporate in the Constitution such a principle in regard to citizens of the several States, yet they never intended to give to Congress the power, by virtue of that clause, to control the local domain of a State or the privileges and immunities of citizens in the State, even though they had come from another State. . . .

But this proposed amendment goes much further than the Constitution goes in the language which it uses with regard to the privileges and immunities of citizens in the several States. It proposes so to amend it that all persons in the several States shall by act of Congress have equal protection in regard to life, liberty, and property. If the bill to protect all persons in the United States in their civil rights and furnish the means of their vindication, which has just passed the Senate by almost the entire vote of the Republican party be constitutional, what, I ask, is the use of this proposed amendment? What is the use of authorizing Congress to do more than Congress has already done, so far as one branch is concerned, in passing a bill to guaranty civil rights and immunities to the people of the United States without distinction of race or color? If it is necessary now to amend the Constitution of the United States in the manner in which the learned gentleman [Bingham] who reported this amendment proclaims, then the vote of the Senate of the United States in passing that bill guarantying civil rights to all without regard to race or color was an attempt to project legislation that was manifestly unconstitutional, and which this proposed amendment is to make legal. . . .

Are Blacks Citizens?

My only hope for liberty is in the full restoration of all the States, with the rights of representation in the Congress of the United States upon no condition but to take the oath laid down in the Constitution. In the legislation by the States they should look to the protection, security, advancement, and improvement, physically and intellectually, of all classes, as well the blacks as the whites. Negroes should have the channels of education opened to them by the States, and by the States they should be protected in life, liberty, and property, and by the States should be allowed all the rights of being witnesses, of suing and being sued, of contracting, and doing every act or thing that a white man is authorized by law to do. But to give to them the right of suffrage, and hold office, and marry whites, in my judgment is dangerous and never ought to be extended to them by any State. However, that is a matter belonging solely to the sovereign will of the States. I have faith in the people, and dark and gloomy as the hour is, I do not despair of free government. I plant myself upon the will of God to work out a bright destiny for the American people. . . .

Who gave the Senate the constitutional power to pass that bill guarantying equal rights to all, if it is necessary to amend the organic law in the manner proposed by this joint resolution? This is but another attempt to consolidate the power of the States in the Federal Government. It is another step to an imperial despotism. It is but another attempt to blot out from that flag the eleven stars that represent the States of the South and to consolidate in the Federal Government, by the action of Congress, all the pow-

ers claimed by the Czar of Russia or the Emperor of the French. It provides that all persons in the several States shall have equal protection in the right of life, liberty, and property. Now, it is claimed by gentlemen upon the other side of the House [Republicans] that negroes are citizens of the United States. Suppose that in the State of New Jersey negroes are citizens, as they are claimed to be by the other side of the House, and they change their residence to the State of South Carolina, if this amendment be passed Congress can pass under it a law compelling South Carolina to grant to negroes every right accorded to white people there; and as white men there have the right to marry white women, negroes, under this amendment, would be entitled to the same right; and thus miscegenation and mixture of the races could be authorized in any State, as all citizens under this amendment are entitled to the same privileges and immunities, and the same protection in life, liberty, and property. . . .

The organic law says that no person but a natural-born citizen, or a citizen when it was made, shall be eligible to the office of President. This amendment would make all citizens eligible, negroes as well as whites. For if negroes are citizens, they are natural born, because they are the descendants of ancestors for several generations back, who were born here as well as themselves. The negroes cannot be citizens in a new State in which they may take up their residence unless they are entitled to the privileges and immunities of the citizens resident in that State. Most of the States make a distinction in the rights of married women. This would authorize Congress to repeal all such distinctions.

---•---

"This [proposed amendment] is but another attempt to consolidate the power of the States in the Federal Government. It is another step to an imperial despotism."

---•---

Marriage is a contract as set down in all the books from the Year-books down to the present time. A white citizen of any State may marry a white woman; but if a black citizen goes into the same State he is entitled to the same privileges and immunities that white citizens have, and therefore under this amendment a negro might be allowed to marry a white woman. I will not go for an amendment of the Constitution to give a power so dangerous, so likely to degrade the white men and women of this country, which would put it in the power of fanaticism in times of excitement and civil war to allow the people of any

State to mingle and mix themselves by marriage with negroes so as to run the pure white blood of the Anglo-Saxon people of the country into the black blood of the negro or the copper blood of the Indian.

Sovereignty of the States

Now, sir, the words "privileges and immunities" in the Constitution of the United States have been construed by the courts of the several States to mean privileges and immunities in a limited extent. . . . Those words, as now contained in the Constitution of the United States, were used in a qualified sense, and subject to the local control, dominion, and the sovereignty of the States. But this act of Congress proposes to amend the Constitution so as to take away the rights of the States with regard to the life, liberty, and property of the people, so as to enable and empower Congress to pass laws compelling the abrogation of all the statutes of the States which make a distinction, for instance, between a crime committed by a white man and a crime committed by a black man, or allow white people privileges, immunities, or property not allowed to a black man.

Take the State of Kentucky, for instance. According to her laws, if a negro commits a rape upon a white woman he is punished by death. If a white man commits that offense, the punishment is imprisonment. Now, according to this proposed amendment, the Congress of the United States is to have the right to repeal the law of Kentucky and compel that State to inflict the same punishment upon a white man for rape as upon a black man.

According to the organic law of Indiana a negro is forbidden to come there and hold property. This amendment would abrogate and blot out forever that law, which is valuable in the estimation of the sovereign people of Indiana.

In the State of Pennsylvania there are laws which make a distinction with regard to the schooling of white children and the schooling of black children. It is provided that certain schools shall be designated and set apart for white children, and certain other schools designated and set apart for black children. Under this amendment, Congress would have power to compel the State to provide for white children and black children to attend the same school, upon the principle that all the people in the several States shall have equal protection in all the rights of life, liberty, and property, and all the privileges and immunities of citizens in the several States.

The effect of this proposed amendment is to take away the power of the States; to interfere with the internal police and regulations of the States; to centralize a consolidated power in this Federal Government which our fathers never intended should be exercised by it.

The Fourteenth Amendment Does Not Violate States' Rights (1866)

John A. Bingham (1815–1900)

John A. Bingham, a Republican representative from Ohio, was a leader of the Radical Republicans who dominated Congress in the early years of Reconstruction. A member of the Joint Committee on Reconstruction, Bingham was involved in the preparation of what would become the Fourteenth Amendment to the Constitution.

On February 26, 1866, Bingham introduced to Congress a draft of a constitutional amendment that would give Congress the power to make laws ensuring the civil rights of all citizens. (Bingham's proposal, with slightly different wording, would later be included in the Fourteenth Amendment.) The following viewpoint is excerpted from arguments Bingham made in Congress defending his draft amendment against criticism by Democratic representative Andrew J. Rogers (see viewpoint 2A). Bingham argues that the amendment is necessary to give the federal government enforcement power over civil rights legislation. Without such power, he argues, states would be free to violate the constitutional and civil rights of blacks with impunity.

What are the main arguments of the "gentlemen of Congress" who oppose his amendment, according to Bingham? How does he answer their objections? Why was the express authority to enforce the protection of civil rights not given to Congress in the original Constitution, according to Bingham?

The people of the United States have intrusted to the present Congress in some sense the care of the Republic, not only for the present, but for all the hereafter. [The Joint Committee on Reconstruction] would not have sent to this House for its consideration this proposition [Fourteenth Amendment] but for the conviction that its adoption by Congress and its ratification by the people of the United States is essential to the safety of all the people of every State. I repel the suggestion made here in the heat of debate, that the committee or any of its members who favor this proposition seek in any form to mar the Constitution of the country, or take away from any state any right that belongs to it, or from any citizen of any State any right that belongs to him

From John A. Bingham, *Congressional Globe*, 39th Cong., 1st sess., February 28, 1866, pp. 157–60.

under that Constitution. The proposition pending before the House is simply a proposition to arm the Congress of the United States, by the consent of the people of the United States, with the power to enforce the bill of rights as it stands in the Constitution today. . . .

Gentlemen admit the force of the provisions in the bill of rights, that the citizens of the United States shall be entitled to all the privileges and immunities of citizens of the United States in the several States, and that no person shall be deprived of life, liberty, or property without due process of law; but they say, "We are opposed to its enforcement by act of Congress under an amended Constitution, as proposed." That is the sum and substance of all the argument that we have heard on this subject. Why are gentlemen opposed to the enforcement of the bill of rights, as proposed? Because they aver it would interfere with the reserved rights of the States! Who ever before heard that any State had reserved to itself the right, under the Constitution of the United States, to withhold from any citizen of the United States within its limits, under any pretext whatever, any of the privileges of a citizen of the United States, or to impose upon him, no matter from what State he may have come, any burden contrary to that provision of the Constitution which declares that the citizen shall be entitled in the several States to all the immunities of a citizen of the United States?

Enforcing the Constitution

What does the word immunity in your Constitution mean? Exemption from unequal burdens. Ah! say gentlemen who oppose this amendment, we are not opposed to equal rights; we are not opposed to the bill of rights that all shall be protected alike in life, liberty, and property; we are only opposed to enforcing it by national authority, even by the consent of the loyal people of all the States. . . .

Why, I ask, should not the "injunctions and prohibitions," addressed by the people in the Constitution to the States and the Legislatures of States, be enforced by the people through the proposed amendment? By the decisions read the people are without remedy. It is admitted . . . that the State Legislatures may by direct violations of their duty and oaths avoid the requirements of the Constitution, and thereby do an act which would break up any government.

Those oaths have been disregarded; those requirements of our Constitution have been broken; they are disregarded to-day in Oregon; they are disregarded to-day, and have been disregarded for the last five, ten, or twenty years in every one of the eleven States recently in insurrection.

The question is, simply, whether you will give by this amendment to the people of the United States the power, by legislative enactment, to punish officials of States for violation of the oaths enjoined upon them by their Constitution? That is the question, and the whole question. The adoption of the proposed amendment will take from the States no rights that belong to the States. They elect their Legislatures; they enact their laws for the punishment of crimes against life, liberty, or property; but in the event of the adoption of this amendment, if they conspire together to enact laws refusing equal protection to life, liberty, or property, the Congress is thereby vested with power to hold them to answer before the bar of the national courts for the violation of their oaths and of the rights of their fellow-men. Why should it not be so? That is the question. Why should it not be so? Is the bill of rights to stand in our Constitution hereafter, as in the past five years within eleven States, a mere dead letter? It is absolutely essential to the safety of the people that it should be enforced.

Unity of the People

Mr. Speaker, it appears to me that this very provision of the bill of rights brought in question this day, upon this trial before the House, more than any other provision of the Constitution, makes that unity of government which constitutes us one people, by which and through which American nationality came to be, and only by the enforcement of which can American nationality continue to be.

The imperishable words of [George] Washington ought to be in the minds of all of us touching this great question whether the unity of the Government shall be enforced hereafter by just penal enactments when the Legislatures of States refuse to do their duty or keep inviolate their oath. Washington, speaking to you and to me and to the millions who are to come after us, says:

> The unity of the Government which constitutes you one people is a main pillar in the edifice of your real independence, the support of your tranquillity at home, your peace abroad, of your safety, or your prosperity, of that very liberty which you so highly prize.

Is it not essential to the unity of the people that the citizens of each State shall be entitled to all the privileges and immunities of citizens in the several States? Is it not essential to the unity of the Government and the unity of the people that all persons, whether citizens or strangers, within this land, shall have equal protection in every State in this Union in the rights of life and liberty and property?

Why, sir, what an anomaly is presented today to the world! We have the power to vindicate the personal liberty and all the personal rights of the citizen on the remotest sea, under the frowning batteries of the remotest tyranny on this earth, while we have not the power in time of peace to enforce the citizens' rights to life, liberty, and property within the limits of South Carolina after her State government shall be recognized and her constitutional relations restored. . . .

As the whole Constitution was to be the supreme law in every State, it therefore results that the citizens of each State, being citizens of the United States, should be entitled to all the privileges and immunities of citizens of the United States in every State, and all persons, now that slavery has forever perished, should be entitled to equal protection in the rights of life, liberty, and property.

———— • ————

"The adoption of the proposed amendment will take from the States no rights that belong to the States."

———— • ————

As a further security for the enforcement of the Constitution, and especially of this sacred bill of rights, to all the citizens and all the people of the United States, it is further provided that the members of the several State Legislatures and all executive and judicial officers, both of the United States and of the several States, shall be bound by oath or affirmation to support this Constitution. The oath, the most solemn compact which man can make with his Maker, was to bind the State Legislatures, executive officers, and judges to sacredly respect the Constitution and all the rights secured by it. And yet there is still another provision lest a State Legislature, with the approval of a State Executive, should, in disregard of their oath, invade the rights of any citizen or person by unjust legislation, violative alike of the Constitution and the rights secured by it, which is very significant and not to be overlooked, which is,

> And the judges of every State shall be bound by the Constitution of the United States, anything in the constitution and laws of any State to the contrary notwithstanding.

With these provisions in the Constitution for the enforcement in every State of its requirements, is it surprising that the framers of the Constitution omitted to insert an express grant of power in Congress to enforce by penal enactment these great canons of the supreme law, securing to all the citizens in every State all the privileges and immunities of citizens, and to all the people all the sacred rights of person—those rights dear to freemen and formidable only to tyrants—and of which the fathers of the Republic spoke, after God had given them the victory, in that memorable address in which they declared, "Let it be

remembered that the rights for which America has contended were the rights of human nature"? Is it surprising that essential as they held the full security to all citizens of all the privileges and immunities of citizens, and to all the people the sacred rights of person, that having proclaimed them they left their lawful enforcement to each of the States, under the solemn obligation resting upon every State officer to regard, respect, and obey the constitutional injunction?

Protection of Rights

What more could have been added to that instrument to secure the enforcement of these provisions of the bill of rights in every State, other than the additional grant of power which we ask this day? Nothing at all. And I am perfectly confident that that grant of power would have been there but for the fact that its insertion in the Constitution would have been utterly incompatible with the existence of slavery in any State; for although slaves might not have been admitted to be citizens they must have been admitted to be persons. That is the only reason why it was not there. There was a fetter upon the conscience of the nation; the people could not put it there and permit slavery in any State thereafter. Thank God, that fetter has been broken; it has turned to dust before the breath of the people, speaking as the voice of God and solemnly ordaining that slavery is forever prohibited everywhere within the Republic except as punishment for crime on due conviction. Even now for crimes men may be enslaved in States, notwithstanding the new amendment.

As slaves were not protected by the Constitution, there might be some color of excuse for the slave States in their disregard for the requirement of the bill of rights as to slaves and refusing them protection in life or property; though, in my judgment, there could be no possible apology for reducing men made like themselves, in the image of God, to a level with the brutes of the field, and condemning them to toil without reward, to live without knowledge, and die without hope.

But, sir, there never was even colorable excuse, much less apology, for any man North or South claiming that any State Legislature or State court, or State Executive, has any right to deny protection to any free citizen of the United States within their limits in the rights of life, liberty, and property. Gentlemen who oppose this amendment oppose the grant of power to enforce the bill of rights. Gentlemen who oppose this amendment simply declare to these rebel States, go on with your confiscation statutes, your statutes of banishment, your statues of unjust imprisonment, your statutes of murder and death against men because of their loyalty to the Constitution and Government of the United States. . . .

I speak in behalf of this amendment in no party spirit, in no spirit of resentment toward any State or the people of any State, in no spirit of innovation, but for the sake of a violated Constitution and a wronged and wounded country whose heart is now smitten with a strange, great sorrow. I urge the amendment for the enforcement of these essential provisions of your Constitution, divine in their justice, sublime in their humanity, which declare that all men are equal in the rights of life and liberty before the majesty of American law.

Representatives, to you I appeal, that hereafter, by your act and the approval of the loyal people of this country, every man in every State of the Union, in accordance with the written words of your Constitution, may, by the national law, be secured in the equal protection of his personal rights. Your Constitution provides that no man, no matter what his color, no matter beneath what sky he may have been born, no matter in what disastrous conflict or by what tyrannical hand his liberty may have been cloven down, no matter how poor, no matter how friendless, no matter how ignorant, shall be deprived of life or liberty or property without due process of law—law in its highest sense, that law which is the perfection of human reason, and which is impartial, equal, exact justice; that justice which requires that every man shall have his right; that justice which is the highest duty of nations as it is the imperishable attribute of the God of nations.

For Further Reading

Alfred Avins, ed., *The Reconstruction Amendments' Debates: The Legislative History and Contemporary Debates in Congress on the 13th, 14th, and 15th Amendments*. Richmond: Virginia Commission on Constitutional Government, 1967.

Joseph B. Bliss, *The Framing of the Fourteenth Amendment*. Urbana: University of Illinois Press, 1956.

William R. Brock, *An American Crisis: Congress and Reconstruction, 1865–1867*. New York: St. Martin's Press, 1963.

Eric Foner, *Reconstruction: America's Unfinished Revolution, 1863–1877*. New York: Harper & Row, 1988.

William Edward Nelson, *The Fourteenth Amendment: From Political Principle to Judicial Doctrine*, Cambridge, MA: Harvard University Press, 1988.

David A. J. Richards, *Conscience and the Constitution: History, Theory, and Law of the Reconstruction Amendments*. Princeton, NJ: Princeton University Press, 1993.

The Fourteenth Amendment (Adopted 1868)

SECTION 1. All persons born or naturalized in the United States, and subject to the jurisdiction thereof, are citizens of the United States and of the State wherein they reside. No State shall make or enforce any law which shall abridge the privileges or immunities of citizens of the United States; nor shall any State deprive any person of life, liberty, or property, without due process of law; nor deny to any person within its jurisdiction the equal protection of the laws. . . .

SECTION 5. The Congress shall have the power to enforce, by appropriate legislation, the provisions of this article.

VIEWPOINT 3A

Blacks Are Capable of Holding Public Office (1868)

Henry McNeal Turner (1834–1915)

In July 1868 the Georgia state legislature debated whether to expel twenty-seven black state congressmen because of their race. The action was one of several taken by white southerners in response to the unprecedented participation in political affairs by blacks during the early years of Reconstruction. Henry McNeal Turner, a freeborn South Carolina native who became the first black chaplain in the United States Army during the Civil War, was one of the black representatives facing expulsion. In a September 3, 1868, speech, he defends the right of blacks to hold public office and their effectiveness as legislators.

How, according to Turner, have blacks contributed to Georgia's rehabilitation and readmission to the Union? What advice does he give to fellow blacks? What importance does he attach to racial questions dividing blacks and whites, as opposed to North/ South divisions?

Before proceeding to argue this question upon its intrinsic merits, I wish the Members of this House to understand the position that I take. I hold that I am a member of this body. Therefore, sir, I shall neither fawn nor cringe before any party, nor stoop to *beg* them for my rights. Some of my colored fellow-members, in the course of their remarks, took occasion to appeal to the *sympathies* of Members on the opposite side, and to eulogize their character for magnanimity. It reminds me very much, sir, of slaves begging under the lash. I am here to demand my rights, and to hurl thunderbolts at the men who would dare to cross the threshold of my manhood. There is an old aphorism which says, "Fight the Devil with fire," and if I should observe the rule in this instance, I wish gentlemen to understand that it is but fighting them with their own weapon.

The scene presented in this House, today, is one unparalleled in the history of the world. From this

From Henry McNeal Turner, *On the Eligibility of Colored Members to Seats in the Georgia Legislature* (Atlanta, 1868).

day, back to the day when God breathed the breath of life into Adam, no analogy for it can be found. Never, in the history of the world, has a man been arraigned before a body clothed with legislative, judicial or executive functions, charged with the offence of being of a darker hue than his fellow-men. I know that questions have been before the Courts of this country, and of other countries, involving topics not altogether dissimilar to that which is being discussed here today. But, sir, never, in all the history of the great nations of this world—never before—has a man been arraigned, charged, with an offence committed by the God of Heaven himself. Cases may be found where men have been deprived of their rights for crimes and misdemeanors; but it has remained for the State of Georgia, in the very heart of the nineteenth century, to call a man before the bar, and there charge him with an act for which he is no more responsible than for the head which he carries up on his shoulders. The Anglo-Saxon race, sir, is a most surprising one. No man has ever been more deceived in that race than I have been for the last three weeks. I was not aware that there was in the character of that race so much cowardice, or so much pusillanimity. The treachery which has been exhibited by gentlemen belonging to that race has shaken my confidence in it more than anything that has come under my observation from the day of my birth. . . .

Whose Legislature is this? Is it a white man's Legislature, or is it a black man's Legislature? Who voted for a Constitutional Convention, in obedience to the mandate of the Congress of the United States? Who first rallied around the standard of Reconstruction? Who set the ball of loyalty rolling in the State of Georgia? And whose voice was heard on the hills and in the valleys of this State? It was the voice of the brawny-armed negro, with the few humanitarian-hearted white men who came to our assistance. I claim the honor, sir, of having been the instrument of convincing hundreds—yea, thousands—of white men, that to reconstruct under the measures of the United States Congress was the safest and the best course for the interest of the State.

A Monopoly of Power

Let us look at some facts in connection with this matter. Did half the white men of Georgia vote for this Legislature? Did not the great bulk of them fight, with all their strength, the Constitution under which we are acting? And did they not fight against the organization of this Legislature? And further, sir, did they not *vote* against it? Yes, sir! And there are persons in this Legislature, today, who are ready to spit their poison in my face, while they themselves opposed, with all their power, the ratification of this Constitution. They question my right to a seat in this body, to represent the people whose legal votes elected me. This objection, sir, is an unheard of monopoly of power. No analogy can be found for it, except it be the case of a man who should go into my house, take possession of my wife and children, and then tell me to walk out. I stand very much in the position of a criminal before your bar, because I dare to be the exponent of the views of those who sent me here. Or, in other words, we are told that if black men want to speak, they must speak through white trumpets; if black men want their sentiments expressed, they must be adulterated and sent through white messengers, who will quibble, and equivocate, and evade, as rapidly as the pendulum of a clock. If this be not done, then the black men have committed an outrage, and their Representatives must be denied the right to represent their constituents.

———— • ————

"How can a white man represent a colored constituency, if a colored man cannot do it?"

———— • ————

The great question, sir, is this: Am I a man? If I am such, I claim the rights of a man. Am I not a man, because I happen to be of a darker hue than honorable gentlemen around me? Let me see whether I am or not. I want to convince the House, today, that I am entitled to my seat here. A certain gentleman has argued that the negro was a mere development similar to the orangutan or chimpanzee, but it so happens that, when a negro is examined, physiologically, phrenologically and anatomically, and, I may say, physiognomically, he is found to be the same as persons of different color. I would like to ask any gentleman on this floor, where is the analogy? Do you find me a quadruped, or do you find me a man? Do you find three bones less in my back than in that of the white man? Do you find less organs in the brain? If you know nothing of this, I do; for I have helped to dissect fifty men, black and white, and I assert that by the time you take off the mucous pigment—the color of the skin—you cannot, to save your life, distinguish between the black man and the white. Am I a man? Have I a soul to save, as you have? Am I susceptible of eternal development, as you are? Can I learn all the arts and sciences that you can—has it ever been demonstrated in the history of the world? Have black men ever exhibited bravery, as white men have done? Have they ever been in the professions? Have they not as good articulative organs as you? Some people argue that there is a very close similarity between the larynx of the negro and that of the orangutan. Why, sir, there is not so much similarity between them as there is between the larynx of the man and that of the dog, and this fact I dare any Member of this House to dispute. God saw fit to vary everything in Nature. There are no two men alike—no two voices alike—no two trees alike. God has weaved and tissued variety and versatility throughout the boundless space of His creation. Because God saw fit to make some red, and some white, and some black, and some brown, are we to sit here in judgment upon what God has seen fit to do? As well might one play with the thunderbolts of heaven as with that creature that bears God's image—God's photograph. . . .

The negro is here charged with holding office. Why, sir, the negro never wanted office. I recollect that when we wanted candidates for the Constitutional Convention, we went from door to door in the "negro belt," and begged white men to run. Some promised to do so; and yet, on the very day of election, many of them *first* made known their determination not to comply with their promises. They told black men, everywhere, that they would rather see *them* run; and it was this encouragement of the white men that induced the colored man to place his name upon the ticket as a candidate for the Convention. In many instances, these white men voted for us. We did not want them, nor ask them, to do it. All we wanted them to do was, to stand still and allow us to walk up to the polls and deposit our ballots. They would not come here themselves, but would insist upon sending us. . . . Now, however, a change has come over the spirit of their dream. They want to turn the "nigger" out; and, to support their argument, they say that the black man is debarred from holding office by the Reconstruction measures of Congress. Let me tell them one thing for their information. Black men have held office, and are now holding office, under the United States Government. Andrew Johnson, President of the United States, in 1865, commissioned me as United States Chaplain, and I would have been Chaplain today, had I not resigned—not desiring to hold office any longer. Let the Democratic party, then, go to Mr. Johnson, and ask him why he commissioned a negro to that position? And if they inquire further, they will ascertain that black men have been commissioned as Lieutenants, Captains, Majors, Brevet Colonels, Surgeons, and other offices of trust and responsibility, under the United States Government. . . .

The honorable gentleman from Whitfield (Mr. Shumate), when arguing this question, a day or two ago, put forth the proposition that to be a Representative was not to be an officer—"it was a privilege that citizens had a right to enjoy." These are his words. It was not an office; it was a "privilege." Every gentleman here knows that he denied that to be a Representative was to be an officer. Now, he is recognized as a leader of the Democratic party in this House, and generally cooks victuals for them to eat; makes that remarkable declaration, and how are you, gentlemen on the other side of the House, to ignore that declaration? Are you going to expel me from this House, because I am an officer, when one of your great lights says that I am *not* an officer? If you deny my right—the right of my constituents to have representation here—because it is a "privilege," then, sir, I will show you that I have as many privileges as the whitest man on this floor. If I am not permitted to occupy a seat here, for the purpose of representing my constituents, I want to know how white men can be permitted to do so? How can a white man represent a colored constituency, if a colored man cannot do it? The great argument is: "Oh, we have inherited" this, that and the other. Now, I want gentlemen to come down to cool, common sense. Is the created greater than the Creator? Is man greater than God? It is very strange, if a white man can occupy on this floor *a seat created by colored votes*, and a black man cannot do it. Why, gentlemen, it is the most short-sighted reasoning in the world. A man can see better than that with half an eye. . . .

A Political Slave

It is said that Congress never gave us the right to hold office. I want to know, sir, if the Reconstruction measures did not base their action on the ground that no distinction should be made on account of race, color, or previous condition! Was not that the grand fulcrum on which they rested? And did not every reconstructed State have to reconstruct on the idea that no discrimination, in any sense of the term, should be made? There is not a man here who will dare say, "No." If Congress has simply given me merely sufficient civil and political rights to make me a mere political slave for Democrats, or anybody else—giving them the opportunity of jumping on my back, in order to leap into political power—I do not thank Congress for it. Never, so help me, God, shall I be a political slave. I am not now speaking for those colored men who sit with me in this House, nor do I say that they endorse my sentiments [cries from the colored Members, "We do!"], but I am speaking simply and solely for myself. Congress, after assisting Mr. Lincoln to take me out of servile slavery, did not intend to put me and my race into *political* slavery. If they did, let them take away my ballot—I do not want it, and shall not have it. [Several colored Members: "Nor we!"] I don't want to be a mere tool of that sort. I have been a slave long enough already.

I tell you what I would be willing to do: I am willing that the question should be submitted to Congress for an explanation as to what was meant in the passage of these Reconstruction measures, and of the [Fourteenth] Constitutional Amendment. Let the Democratic party in this House pass a Resolution giving this subject that direction, and I shall be content. I dare you, gentlemen, to do it. Come up to the question openly, whether it meant that the negro might hold office, or whether it meant that he should merely have the right to vote. If you are honest men, you will do it. If, however, you will not do that, I would make another proposition: Call together, again, the Convention that framed the Constitution under which we are acting; let them take a vote upon the subject, and I am willing to abide their decision. . . .

But, Mr. Speaker, I do not regard this movement as a thrust at me. It is a thrust at the Bible—a thrust at the God of the Universe, for making a man and not finishing him; it is simply calling the Great Jehovah a fool. Why, sir, though we are not white, we have accomplished much. We have pioneered civilization here; we have built up your country; we have worked in your fields, and garnered your harvests, for two hundred and fifty years! And what do we ask of you in return? Do we ask you for compensation for the sweat our fathers bore for you—for the tears you have caused, and the hearts you have broken, and the lives you have curtailed, and the blood you have spilled? Do we ask retaliation? We ask it not. We are willing to let the dead past bury its dead; but we ask you, now, for our RIGHTS. You have all the elements of superiority upon your side; you have our money and your own; you have our education and your own; and you have our land and your own, too. We, who number hundreds of thousands in Georgia, including our wives and families, with not a foot of land to call our own—strangers in the land of our birth; without money, without education, without aid, without a roof to cover us while we live, nor sufficient clay to cover us when we die! It is extraordinary that a race such as yours, professing gallantry, and chivalry, and education, and superiority, living in a land where ringing chimes call child and sire to the Church of God—a land where Bibles are read and Gospel truths are spoken, and where courts of justice are presumed to exist; it is extraordinary, I say, that, with all these advantages on your side, you can make war upon the poor defenceless black man. You know we have no money, no railroads, no telegraphs, no advantages of any sort, and yet all manner of injustice is placed upon us. You know that the black people of this country acknowledge you as their superiors, by virtue of your education and advantages.

There was a Resolution passed here at the early part of this session stating that all persons who were in their seats were eligible thereto. What are gentle-men going to do, with that Resolution staring them in the face? Your children and my children will read that Resolution, and they will be astonished that persons, claiming to be men, with souls and consciences, should, contrary to the express provision of that Resolution, turn the colored man out of his seat in this Hall. . . .

You may expel us, gentlemen, but I firmly believe that you will some day repent it. The black man cannot protect a country, if the country doesn't protect him; and if, tomorrow, a war should arise, I would not raise a musket to defend a country where my manhood is denied. The fashionable way in Georgia, when hard work is to be done, is, for the white man to sit at his ease, while the black man does the work; but, sir, I will say this much to the colored men of Georgia, as, if I should be killed in this campaign, I may have no opportunity of telling them at any other time: Never lift a finger nor raise a hand in defence of Georgia, unless Georgia acknowledges that you are men, and invests you with the rights pertaining to manhood. Pay your taxes, however, obey all orders from your employers, take good counsel from friends, work faithfully, earn an honest living, and show, by your conduct, that you can be good citizens. . . .

Where have you ever heard of four millions of freemen being governed by laws, and yet have no hand in their making? Search the records of the world, and you will find no example. "Governments derive their just powers from the consent of the governed." How dare you to make laws by which to try me and my wife and children, and deny me a voice in the making of these laws? I know you can establish a monarchy, an autocracy, an oligarchy, or any other kind of an "ocracy" that you please; and that you can declare whom you please to be sovereign; but tell me, sir, how you can clothe me with more power than another, where all are sovereigns alike? How can you say you have a Republican form of Government, when you make such distinction and enact such proscriptive laws? . . .

Everlasting Shame

We are a persecuted people. Luther was persecuted; Galileo was persecuted; good men in all nations have been persecuted; but the persecutors have been handed down to posterity with shame and ignominy. If you pass this Bill, you will never get Congress to pardon or enfranchise another rebel in your lives. You are going to fix an everlasting disfranchisement upon Mr. [Robert A.] Toombs and the other leading men of Georgia. You may think you are doing yourselves honor by expelling us from this House; but when we go, we will . . . light a torch of truth that will never be extinguished—the impression that will run through the country, as people picture in their mind's eye these poor black men, in all parts of this Southern country, pleading for their rights. When you expel us, you make us forever your political foes, and you will never find a black man to vote a Democratic ticket again; for so help me God I will go through all the length and breadth of the land, where a man of my race is to be found, and advise him to beware of the Democratic party. Justice is the great doctrine taught in the Bible. God's Eternal Justice is founded upon Truth and the man who steps from Justice steps from Truth, and cannot make his principles to prevail.

VIEWPOINT 3B

Blacks Are Not Capable of Holding Public Office (1873)

James S. Pike (1811–1882)

A less-than-flattering view of black participation in state government during Reconstruction invests the following excerpts from the 1873 book *The Prostrate State* by James S. Pike. The book's contents originally appeared as newspaper articles written by Pike for the *New York Tribune* while on a reporting tour of South Carolina (one of several former Confederate states with black politicians in its government, and the only one in which blacks formed a majority in the state legislature). Although Pike was hailed by contemporaries as a longtime abolitionist and an objective northern witness to southern developments, the Maine Republican was no advocate of equal rights for blacks. A critic of President Ulysses S. Grant and the Radical Reconstruction agenda, he once suggested that free slaves be deported or placed on a reservation.

What racial attitudes does Pike reveal? Does he make any positive comments on black legislators? Why do you think his book became so popular and influential in the North when it was first published in 1873? How might Henry McNeal Turner, author of the opposing viewpoint, respond to Pike's arguments?

Columbia, the capital of South Carolina, is charmingly situated in the heart of the upland country, near the geographical centre of the State. It has broad, open streets, regularly laid out, and fine, shady residences in and about the town. . . .

Yesterday, about 4 p.m., the assembled wisdom of the State, whose achievements are illustrated on that theatre, issued forth from the State-House. About three-quarters of the crowd belonged to the African race. They were of every hue, from the light octoroon to the deep black. They were such a look-

From James S. Pike, *The Prostrate State* (New York, 1873).

ing body of men as might pour out of a market-house or a court-house at random in any Southern State. Every negro type and physiognomy was here to be seen, from the genteel serving-man to the rough-hewn customer from the rice or cotton field. Their dress was as varied as their countenances. There was the second-hand black frock-coat of infirm gentility, glossy and threadbare. There were the stove-pipe hat of many ironings and departed styles. There were also to be seen a total disregard of the proprieties of costume in the coarse and dirty garments of the field; the stub-jackets and slouch hats of soiling labor. In some instances, rough woolen comforters embraced the neck and hid the absence of linen. Heavy brogans, and short, torn trousers, it was impossible to hide. The dusky tide flowed out into the littered and barren grounds, and, issuing through the coarse wooden fence of the inclosure, melted away into the street beyond. These were the legislators of South Carolina. . . .

"I tremble," wrote [Thomas] Jefferson, when depicting the character of Southern slavery, "I tremble when I reflect that God is just." But did any of that old band of Southern Revolutionary patriots who wrestled in their souls with the curse of slavery ever contemplate such a descent into barbarism as this spectacle implied and typified? "My God, look at this!" was the unbidden ejaculation of a low-country planter, clad in homespun, as he leaned over the rail inside the House, gazing excitedly upon the body in session. "This is the first time I have been here. I thought I knew what we were doing when we consented to emancipation. I knew the negro, and I predicted much that has happened, but I never thought it would come to this. Let me go."

Here, then, is the outcome, the ripe, perfected fruit of the boasted civilization of the South, after two hundred years of experience. A white community, that had gradually risen from small beginnings, till it grew into wealth, culture, and refinement, and became accomplished in all the arts of civilization; that successfully asserted its resistance to a foreign tyranny by deeds of conspicuous valor, which achieved liberty and independence through the fire and tempest of civil war, and illustrated itself in the councils of the nation by orators and statesmen worthy of any age or nation—such a community is then reduced to this. It lies prostrate in the dust, ruled over by this strange conglomerate, gathered from the ranks of its own servile population. It is the spectacle of a society suddenly turned bottomside up. The wealth, the intelligence, the culture, the wisdom of the State, have broken through the crust of that social volcano on which they were contentedly reposing, and have sunk out of sight, consumed by the subterranean fires they had with such temerity braved and defied.

The New Government

In the place of this old aristocratic society stands the rude form of the most ignorant democracy that mankind ever saw, invested with the functions of government. It is the dregs of the population habilitated in the robes of their intelligent predecessors, and asserting over them the rule of ignorance and corruption, through the inexorable machinery of a majority of numbers. It is barbarism overwhelming civilization by physical force. It is the slave rioting in the halls of his master, and putting that master under his feet. And, though it is done without malice and without vengeance, it is nevertheless none the less completely and absolutely done. Let us approach nearer and take a closer view. We will enter the House of Representatives. Here sit one hundred and twenty-four members. Of these, twenty-three are white men, representing the remains of the old civilization. These are good-looking, substantial citizens. They are men of weight and standing in the communities they represent. They are all from the hill country. The frosts of sixty and seventy winters whiten the heads of some among them. There they sit, grim and silent. They feel themselves to be but loose stones, thrown in to partially obstruct a current they are powerless to resist. They say little and do little as the days go by. They simply watch the rising tide, and mark the progressive steps of the inundation. They hold their places reluctantly. They feel themselves to be in some sort martyrs, bound stoically to suffer in behalf of that still great element in the State whose prostrate fortunes are becoming the sport of an unpitying Fate. Grouped in a corner of the commodious and well-furnished chamber, they stolidly survey the noisy riot that goes on in the great black Left and Centre, where the business and debates of the House are conducted, and where sit the strange and extraordinary guides of the fortunes of a once proud and haughty State. In this crucial trial of his pride, his manhood, his prejudices, his spirit, it must be said of the Southern Bourbon of the Legislature that he comports himself with a dignity, a reserve, and a decorum, that command admiration. He feels that the iron hand of Destiny is upon him. He is gloomy, disconsolate, hopeless. The gray heads of this generation openly profess that they look for no relief. They see no way of escape. The recovery of influence, of position, of control in the State, is felt by them to be impossible. They accept their position with a stoicism that promises no reward here or hereafter. They are the types of a conquered race. They staked all and lost all. Their lives remain, their property and their children do not. War, emancipation, and grinding taxation, have consumed them. Their struggle now is against complete confiscation.

They endure, and wait for the night.

This dense negro crowd they confront do the debating, the squabbling, the law-making, and create all the clamor and disorder of the body. These twenty-three white men are but the observers, the enforced auditors of the dull and clumsy imitation of a deliberative body, whose appearance in their present capacity is at once a wonder and a shame to modern civilization.

———— • ————

"It is the dregs of the population habilitated in the robes of their intelligent predecessors, and asserting over them the rule of ignorance and corruption."

———— • ————

Deducting the twenty-three members referred to, who comprise the entire strength of the opposition, we find one hundred and one remaining. Of this one hundred and one, ninety-four are colored, and seven are their white allies. Thus the blacks outnumber the whole body of whites in the House more than three to one. On the mere basis of numbers in the State the injustices of this disproportion is manifest, since the black population is relatively four to three of the whites. A just rectification of the disproportion, on the basis of population merely, would give fifty-four whites to seventy black members. And the line of race very nearly marks the line of hostile politics. As things stand, the body is almost literally a Black Parliament, and it is the only one on the face of the earth which is the representative of a white constituency and the professed exponent of an advanced type of modern civilization. But the reader will find almost any portraiture inadequate to give a vivid idea of the body, and enable him to comprehend the complete metamorphosis of the South Carolina Legislature, without observing its details. The Speaker is black, the Clerk is black, the door-keepers are black, the little pages are black, the chairman of the Ways and Means is black, and the chaplain is coal-black. At some of the desks sit colored men whose types it would be hard to find outside of Congo; whose costume, visages, attitudes, and expression, only befit the forecastle of a buccaneer. It must be remembered, also, that these men, with not more than half a dozen exceptions, have been themselves slaves, and that their ancestors were slaves for generations. Recollecting the report of the famous schooner Wanderer, fitted out by a Southern slave-holder twelve or fifteen years ago, in ostentatious defiance of the laws against the slave-trade, and whose owner and master boasted of having brought a cargo of slaves from Africa and safely landed them in South Carolina and Georgia, one thinks it must be true, and that some of these representatives are the very men then stolen from their African homes. If this be so, we will not now quarrel over their presence. It would be one of those extraordinary coincidences that would of itself almost seem to justify the belief of the direct interference of the hand of Providence in the affairs of men. . . .

Disorder in the House

One of the things that first strike a casual observer in this negro assembly is the fluency of debate, if the endless chatter that goes on there can be dignified with this term. The leading topics of discussion are all well understood by the members, as they are of a practical character, and appeal directly to the personal interests of every legislator, as well as to those of his constituents. When an appropriation bill is up to raise money to catch and punish the Ku-klux, they know exactly what it means. They feel it in their bones. So, too, with educational measures. The free school comes right home to them; then the business of arming and drilling the black militia. They are eager on this point. Sambo can talk on these topics and those of a kindred character, and their endless ramifications, day in and day out. There is no end to his gush and babble. The intellectual level is that of a bevy of fresh converts at a negro camp-meeting. Of course this kind of talk can be extended indefinitely. It is the doggerel of debate, and not beyond the reach of the lowest parts. Then the negro is imitative in the extreme. He can copy like a parrot or a monkey, and he is always ready for a trial of his skill. He believes he can do any thing, and never loses a chance to try, and is just as ready to be laughed at for his failure as applauded for his success. He is more vivacious than the white, and, being more volatile and good-natured, he is correspondingly more irrepressible. His misuse of language in his imitations is at times ludicrous beyond measure. He notoriously loves a joke or an anecdote, and will burst into a broad guffaw on the smallest provocation. He breaks out into an incoherent harangue on the floor just as easily, and being without practice, discipline, or experience, and wholly oblivious of Lindley Murray, or any other restraint on composition, he will go on repeating himself, dancing as it were to the music of his own voice, forever. He will speak half a dozen times on one question, and every time say the same things without knowing it. He answers completely to the description of a stupid speaker in Parliament, given by Lord Derby on one occasion. It was said of him that he did not know what he was going to say when he got up; he did not know what he was saying while he was speaking, and he did not know what he

had said when he sat down.

But the old stagers admit that the colored brethren have a wonderful aptness at legislative proceedings. They are "quick as lightning" at detecting points of order, and they certainly make incessant and extraordinary use of their knowledge. No one is allowed to talk five minutes without interruption, and one interruption is the signal for another and another, until the original speaker is smothered under an avalanche of them. Forty questions of privilege will be raised in a day. At times, nothing goes on but alternating questions of order and of privilege. The inefficient colored friend who sits in the Speaker's chair cannot suppress this extraordinary element of the debate. Some of the blackest members exhibit a pertinacity of intrusion in raising these points of order and questions of privilege that few white men can equal. Their struggles to get the floor, their bellowings and physical contortions, baffle description. The Speaker's hammer plays a perpetual tattoo all to no purpose. The talking and the interruptions from all quarters go on with the utmost license. Every one esteems himself as good as his neighbor, and puts in his oar, apparently as often for love of riot and confusion as for any thing else. It is easy to imagine what are his ideas of propriety and dignity among a crowd of his own color, and these are illustrated without reserve. The Speaker orders a member whom he has discovered to be particularly unruly to take his seat. The member obeys, and with the same motion that he sits down, throws his feet on to his desk, hiding himself from the Speaker by the soles of his boots. In an instant he appears again on the floor. After a few experiences of this sort, the Speaker threatens, in a laugh, to call "the gemman" to order. This is considered a capital joke, and a guffaw follows. The laugh goes round, and then the peanuts are cracked and munched faster than ever; one hand being employed in fortifying the inner man with this nutriment of universal use, while the other enforces the views of the orator. This laughing propensity of the sable crowd is a great cause of disorder. They laugh as hens cackle—one begins and all follow.

Good Intentions

But underneath all this shocking burlesque upon legislative proceedings, we must not forget that there is something very real to this uncouth and untutored multitude. It is not all sham, nor all burlesque. They have a genuine interest and a genuine earnestness in the business of the assembly which we are bound to recognize and respect, unless we would be accounted shallow critics. They have an earnest purpose, born of a conviction that their position and condition are not fully assured, which lends a sort of dignity to their proceedings. The barbarous, animated jargon in which they so often indulge is on occasion seen to be so transparently sincere and weighty in their own minds that sympathy supplants disgust. The whole thing is a wonderful novelty to them as well as to observers. Seven years ago these men were raising corn and cotton under the whip of the overseer. Today they are raising points of order and questions of privilege. They find they can raise one as well as the other. They prefer the latter. It is easier, and better paid. Then, it is the evidence of an accomplished result. It means escape and defense from old oppressors. It means liberty. It means the destruction of prison-walls only too real to them. It is the sunshine of their lives. It is their day of jubilee. It is their long-promised vision of the Lord God Almighty.

Shall we, then, be too critical over the spectacle? Perhaps we might more wisely wonder that they can do so well in so short a time. The barbarians overran Rome. The dark ages followed. But then the day finally broke, and civilization followed. The days were long and weary; but they came to an end at last. Now we have the printing-press, the railroad, the telegraph; and these denote an utter revolution in the affairs of mankind. Years may now accomplish what it formerly took ages to achieve. Under the new lights and influences shall not the black man speedily emerge? Who knows? We may fear, but we may hope. Nothing in our day is impossible. Take the contested supposition that South Carolina is to be Africanized. We have a Federal Union of great and growing States. It is incontestably white at the centre. We know it to possess vital powers. It is well abreast of all modern progress in ideas and improvements. Its influence is all-pervading. How can a State of the Union escape it? South Carolina alone, if left to herself, might fall into midnight darkness. Can she do it while she remains an integral part of the nation?

But will South Carolina be Africanized? That depends. Let us hear the judgment of an intelligent foreigner who has long lived in the South, and who was here when the war began. He does not believe it. White people from abroad are drifting in, bad as things are. Under freedom the blacks do not multiply as in slavery. The pickaninnies die off from want of care. Some blacks are coming in from North Carolina and Virginia, but others are going off farther South. The white young men who were growing into manhood did not seem inclined to leave their homes and migrate to foreign parts. There was an exodus after the war, but it has stopped, and many have come back. The old slave-holders still hold their lands. The negroes were poor and unable to buy, even if the land-owners would sell. This was a powerful impediment to the development of the negro into a controlling force in the State. His whole power was in his

numbers. The present disproportion of four blacks to three whites in the State he believed was already decreasing. The whites seemed likely to more than hold their own, while the blacks would fall off. Cumulative voting would encourage the growth and add to the political power of the whites in the Legislature, where they were at present over-slaughed.

For Further Reading

Lerone Bennett, *Black Power, U.S.A.: The Human Side of Reconstruction, 1867–1877.* Chicago: Johnson Publishing, 1967.

Robert Franklin Durden, *James Shepherd Pike: Republicanism and the American Negro, 1850–1882.* Durham, NC: Duke University Press, 1957.

Annjennette Sophie McFarlin, ed., *Black Congressional Reconstruction Orators and Their Orations, 1869–1879.* Metuchen, NJ: Scarecrow Press, 1976.

Mungo Melanchthon Ponton, *Life and Times of Henry M. Turner.* New York: Negro Universities Press, 1970.

Joel Williamson, *After Slavery: The Negro in South Carolina During Reconstruction, 1861–1877.* Chapel Hill: University of North Carolina Press, 1965.

Forrest G. Wood, *Black Scare: The Racist Response to Emancipation and Reconstruction.* Berkeley: University of California Press, 1968.

VIEWPOINT 4A

The Ku Klux Klan Is a Peacekeeping Organization (1872)

John Brown Gordon (1823–1904)

In 1871 the U.S. Congress established the Joint Select Committee to Inquire into the Condition of Affairs in the Late Insurrectionary States. The primary purpose of this committee was to investigate the rise of white secret societies in the South, such as the Ku Klux Klan, that used vigilante violence and terrorism to keep newly enfranchised blacks in "their place."

The following viewpoint is drawn from testimony given by John Brown Gordon, one of the people questioned by the committee. Gordon had been a lieutenant general in the Confederate army; after Reconstruction ended in 1877 he entered Georgia politics, eventually serving as governor of Georgia and in the U.S. Senate. In response to questions by the committee, Gordon denies specific knowledge about the Ku Klux Klan, but argues that white groups are being formed in the South for the purpose of peacekeeping and self-protection against the threat of black violence. He specifically cites the Union League, a political group organized by north-

John Brown Gordon, from *Testimony Taken by the Joint Select Committee to Inquire into the Condition of Affairs in the Late Insurrectionary States: Alabama*, vol. 1, Washington, DC: Government Printing Office, 1872.

ern Republicans, as a potential source of black-on-white violence.

What evidence does Gordon use to argue that blacks were threatening to whites? What does Gordon criticize about "radicals"? Ralph Lowell Eckert and other historians now believe Gordon was a prominent member of the Georgia Klan; how does this revelation affect his credibility?

Q*uestion.* What do you know of any combinations in Georgia, known as Ku-Klux, or by any other name, who have been violating the law?

Answer. I do not know anything about any Ku Klux organization, as the papers talk about it. I have never heard of anything of that sort except in the papers and by general report; but I do know that an organization did exist in Georgia at one time. I know that in 1868—I think that was the time—I was approached and asked to attach myself to a secret organization in Georgia. I was approached by some of the very best citizens of the State—some of the most peaceable, law-abiding men, men of large property, who had large interests in the State. The object of this organization was explained to me at the time by these parties; and I want to say that I approved of it most heartily. I would approve again of a similar organization, under the same state of circumstances.

Question. Tell us about what that organization was.

Answer. The organization was simply this—nothing more and nothing less: it was an organization, a brotherhood of the property-holders, the peaceable, law-abiding citizens of the State, for self-protection. The instinct of self-protection prompted that organization; the sense of insecurity and danger, particularly in those neighborhoods where the negro population largely predominated. The reasons which led to this organization were three or four. The first and main reason was the organization of the Union League, as they called it, about which we knew nothing more than this: that the negroes would desert the plantations, and go off at night in large numbers; and on being asked where they had been, would reply, sometimes, "We have been to the muster"; sometimes, "We have been to the lodge"; sometimes, "We have been to the meeting." Those things were observed for a great length of time. We knew that the "carpet-baggers," as the people of Georgia called these men who came from a distance and had no interest at all with us; who were unknown to us entirely; who from all we could learn about them did not have any very exalted position at their homes—these men were organizing the colored people. We knew that beyond all question. We knew of certain

instances where great crimes had been committed; where overseers had been driven from plantations, and the negroes had asserted their right to hold the property for their own benefit. Apprehension took possession of the entire public mind of the State. Men were in many instances afraid to go away from their homes and leave their wives and children, for fear of outrage. Rapes were already being committed in the country. There was this general organization of the black race on the one hand, and an entire disorganization of the white race on the other hand. We were afraid to have a public organization; because we supposed it would be construed at once, by the authorities at Washington, as an organization antagonistic to the Government of the United States. It was therefore necessary, in order to protect our families from outrage and preserve our own lives, to have something that we could regard as a brotherhood—a combination of the best men of the country, to act purely in self-defense, to repel the attack in case we should be attacked by these people. That was the whole object of this organization. I never heard of any disguises connected with it; we had none, very certainly. This organization, I think, extended nearly all over the State. It was, as I say, an organization purely for self-defense. It had no more politics in it than the organization of the Masons. I never heard the idea of politics suggested in connection with it.

A Peace Police Organization

Question. Did it have any antagonism toward either the State or the Federal Government?

Answer. None on earth—not a particle. On the contrary, it was purely a peace police organization, and I do know of some instances where it did prevent bloodshed on a large scale. I know of one case in Albany, Georgia, where, but for the instrumentality of this organization, there would have been, beyond all doubt, a conflict, growing out of a personal difficulty between a black man and a white man. The two races gathered on each side, but this organization quelled the trouble easily and restored peace, without any violence to anybody, and without a particle of difficulty with either the black race or the white. They stopped one just as much as they did the other. This society was purely a police organization to keep the peace, to prevent disturbances in our State. That was the motive that actuated me in going into it, and that was the whole object of the organization, as explained to me by these persons who approached me. I approved of the object.

Question. You had no riding about at nights?

Answer. None on earth. I have no doubt that such things have occurred in Georgia. It is notoriously stated—I have no personal knowledge of anything of the kind, but I have reason to believe it—that disguised parties have committed outrages in Georgia; but we have discovered in some cases that these disguised parties did not belong to any particular party. We have demonstrated that beyond all question in some cases, by bringing to trial and conviction parties who belonged, for instance, to the radical [Republican] party, who had in disguise committed outrages in the State. There is not a good man in Georgia who does not deplore that thing just as much as any radical deplores it. When I use the term "radical," I do not mean to reflect upon the republican party generally; but in our State a republican is a very different sort of a man from a republican generally in the Northern States. In our State republicanism means nothing in the world but creating disturbance, riot, and animosity, and filching and plundering. That is what it means in our State— nothing else; there is no politics in it. In the North the thing is very different. There men can differ in politics, and yet have the kindliest relations; in Georgia we cannot do it unless we are willing to countenance all sorts of outrages upon our people. There are genteel republicans in Georgia, who are just as safe as any one else; who travel all over the State; who occupy high positions, and are never insulted in the street, the cars, or anywhere else. If there is any organization in Georgia for the purpose of putting down republicanism there, why does it not attack the leaders of that party? It strikes me as the very highest commentary upon the law-abiding spirit of the people of Georgia that such men as I could name— men in high position who have plundered our people by the million—still live and are countenanced on the streets, have no insults offered to them. The truth is simply this: that individuals in Georgia of all parties and all colors have, I suppose, committed outrage; but such affairs have been purely personal, just as they are when they occur anywhere else in the United States. I do not believe any more crimes have been committed in Georgia than in any other community of the same number anywhere else in the country. That is my honest conviction. I do not believe that any crime has ever been committed by this organization of which I have spoken, and of which I was a member. I believe it was purely a peace police—a law-abiding concern. That was its whole object, and it never would have existed but for the apprehension in the minds of our people of a conflict in which we would have had no sympathy and no protection. We apprehended that the sympathy of the entire Government would be against us; and nothing in the world but the instinct of self-protection prompted that organization. We felt that we must at any cost protect ourselves, our homes, our wives and children from outrage. We would have preferred death rather than to have submitted to

what we supposed was coming upon us. At this time I do not believe any such organization exists, or has existed for a long time. I have not heard of it for two years, I am certain.

Self-Protection Is No Longer Needed

Question. Why did it cease to exist; why did it pass away?

Answer. Well, sir, it just dissolved because the courts became generally established; and though the courts were in the hands of the opposite party, our people believed they were trying to do justice; that a general protection was extended over us. Our people thought we could get justice at the hands of these judges; though they were of the opposite party, and though negroes were on the juries, we were satisfied that in the existing condition of things we were safe. Since Governor [Rufus] Bullock's election [in 1868] I have not heard anything of that organization. I am not sure that it did not pass away with his election. It certainly has not existed since within my knowledge; and I think I would have known it if it had. I think that my position would have brought it to my knowledge if any such organization had existed for several years past. As I have stated, the only reason it has passed away is, I think, because the people felt safe. Courts were established and police regulations were generally instituted.

———— • ————

"This society was purely a police organization to keep the peace, to prevent disturbances in our State."

———— • ————

You must remember that we were in a state of anarchy there for a long time. We had no law but drum-head courts-martial. Our people were entirely powerless to do anything. We always felt that if the Federal troops were kept in our midst we would be protected. I want to state that with great emphasis. Our people have always felt that if the white troops of the Federal Army could have been stationed in our midst in those negro belts we would have been safe. But the troops were perhaps two hundred miles away; and before they could have been brought to our relief the whole neighborhood might have been slaughtered. We then believed that such a thing might occur on almost any night. Such was the condition of things in Georgia at that time. I do not believe that it exists now, or has existed for two years. To my certain knowledge this organization never did exist as a political organization. I do not know what may have been the case elsewhere; but very certainly there was no politics in this thing in Georgia, so far as I had anything to do with it; and I think that the organization was of the same character all over the State—probably over the South wherever it existed. We never called it Ku-Klux, and therefore I do not know anything about Ku-Klux.

VIEWPOINT 4B

The Ku Klux Klan Is a Terrorist Organization (1872)

The Federal Grand Jury

In October 1871 violence in South Carolina—the state where the Ku Klux Klan was most active—became so rampant that President Ulysses S. Grant sent federal troops to occupy nine counties to keep the peace. Shortly thereafter, a federal grand jury was established to investigate activities by the Ku Klux Klan in that state. The following viewpoint is excerpted from the jury's report to the judges of the U.S. circuit court in Columbia, South Carolina.

What do the jurors conclude about the Ku Klux Klan? In their view, what might happen if the federal government does not intervene against the Klan? What elements of the Klan's oath quoted here do you find particularly revealing about the purpose of the Klan?

I n closing the labors of the present term, the grand jury beg leave to submit the following presentment.

During the whole session we have been engaged in investigations of the most grave and extraordinary character—investigations of the crimes committed by the organization known as the Ku Klux Klan. The evidence elicited has been voluminous, gathered from the victims themselves and their families, as well as those who belong to the Klan and participated in its crimes. The jury has been shocked beyond measure at the developments which have been made in their presence of the number and character of the atrocities committed, producing a state of terror and a sense of utter insecurity among a large portion of the people, especially the colored population. The evidence produced before us has established the following facts:

1. That there has existed since 1868, in many counties of the state [South Carolina], an organization known as the "Ku Klux Klan," or "Invisible Empire of the South," which embraces in its membership a

From the House of Representatives, *Report of the Federal Grand Jury to the Judges of the U.S. Circuit Court, Columbia, S.C.*, 42nd Cong., 2nd sess., H. Rept. 22, pt. 1, 48–49.

large proportion of the white population of every profession and class.

2. That this Klan [is] bound together by an oath, administered to its members at the time of their initiation into the order, of which the following is a copy:

OBLIGATION

I [name], before the immaculate Judge of Heaven and earth, and upon the Holy Evangelists of Almighty God, do, of my own free will and accord, subscribe to the following sacredly binding obligation:

1. We are on the side of justice, humanity, and constitutional liberty, as bequeathed to us in its purity by our forefathers.

2. We oppose and reject the principles of the Radical Party.

3. We pledge mutual aid to each other in sickness, distress, and pecuniary embarrassment.

4. Female friends, widows, and their households shall ever be special objects of our regard and protection.

Any member divulging, or causing to be divulged, any of the foregoing obligations, shall meet the fearful penalty and traitor's doom, which is Death! Death! Death!

That, in addition to this oath, the Klan has a constitution and bylaws, which provide, among other things, that each member shall furnish himself with a pistol, a Ku Klux gown, and a signal instrument. That the operations of the Klan were executed in the night, and were invariably directed against members of the Republican Party by warnings to leave the country, by whippings, and by murder.

"The Klan, in carrying out the purposes for which it was organized and armed, inflicted summary vengeance on the colored citizens."

---

3. That in large portions of the counties of York, Union, and Spartanburgh, to which our attention has been more particularly called in our investigations during part of the time for the last eighteen months, the civil law has been set at defiance and ceased to afford any protection to the citizens.

4. That the Klan, in carrying out the purposes for which it was organized and armed, inflicted summary vengeance on the colored citizens of these counties by breaking into their houses at the dead of night, dragging them from their beds, torturing them in the most inhuman manner, and in many instances

murdering them; and this, mainly, on account of their political affiliations. Occasionally, additional reasons operated, but in no instance was the political feature wanting.

5. That for this condition of things, for all these violations of law and order and the sacred rights of citizens, many of the leading men of those counties were responsible. It was proven that large numbers of the most prominent citizens were members of the order. Many of this class attended meetings of the Grand Klan. At a meeting of the Grand Klan held in Spartanburgh County, at which there were representatives from the various dens of Spartanburgh, York, Union, and Chester counties, in this state, besides a number from North Carolina, a resolution was adopted that no raids should be undertaken or anyone whipped or injured by members of the Klan without orders from the Grand Klan. The penalty for violating this resolution was 100 lashes on the bare back for the first offense; and for the second, death.

This testimony establishes the nature of the discipline enforced in the order, and also the fact that many of the men who were openly and publicly speaking against the Klan, and pretending to deplore the work of this murderous conspiracy, were influential members of the order and directing its operations, even in detail.

Whippings and Murders

The jury has been appalled as much at the number of outrages as at their character, it appearing that 11 murders and over 600 whippings have been committed in York County alone. Our investigation in regard to the other counties named has been less full; but it is believed, from the testimony, that an equal or greater number has been committed in Union, and that the number is not greatly less in Spartanburgh and Laurens.

We are of the opinion that the most vigorous prosecution of the parties implicated in these crimes is imperatively demanded; that without this there is great danger that these outrages will be continued, and that there will be no security to our fellow citizens of African descent.

We would say further that unless the strong arm of the government is interposed to punish these crimes committed upon this class of citizens, there is every reason to believe that an organized and determined attempt at retaliation will be made, which can only result in a state of anarchy and bloodshed too horrible to contemplate.

For Further Reading

Ralph Lowell Eckert, *John Brown Gordon: Soldier, Southerner, American*. Baton Rouge: Louisiana University Press, 1989.

Proceedings in the Ku Klux Trials at Columbia, S.C., in the United States Circuit Court, November Term, 1871. New York: Negro Universities Press, 1969.

George Rable, *But There Was No Peace: The Role of Violence in the Politics of Reconstruction*. Athens: University of Georgia Press, 1984.

Everette Swinney, *Suppressing the Ku Klux Klan*. New York: Garland, 1987.

Allan W. Trelease, *White Terror: The Ku Klux Klan Conspiracy and Southern Reconstruction*. New York: Harper & Row, 1971.

United States Congress, *Affairs in the Late Insurrectionary States*. New York: Arno Press, 1969.

Wyn Craig Wade, *The Fiery Cross: The Ku Klux Klan in America*. New York: Simon and Schuster, 1987.

Twilight of the American Frontier

VIEWPOINT 5A

The Takeover of Indian Land: A White Man's View (1889)

Theodore Roosevelt (1858–1919)

Future president of the United States Theodore Roosevelt first gained national attention as the author of several noted books, including the three-volume study *The Winning of the West*. In writing this and other books Roosevelt drew on his own experiences living and working on a North Dakota cattle ranch in the 1880s. In the following excerpt from the first volume of *The Winning of the West*, published in 1889, Roosevelt summarizes his positions on the white settlement on land previously occupied by American Indians, and the warfare and violence that marked their displacement.

How would you summarize Roosevelt's attitude toward American Indians? What objections does Roosevelt have to "sentimentalists" and their portrayal of the Indian? Do you agree with Roosevelt that the Indians' displacement was inevitable? Why or why not?

Border warfare . . . was a war waged by savages against armed settlers, whose families followed them into the wilderness. Such a war is inevitably bloody and cruel; but the inhuman love of cruelty for cruelty's sake, which marks the red Indian above all other savages, rendered these wars more terrible than any others. For the hideous, unnamable, unthinkable tortures practised by the red men on their captured foes, and on their foes' tender

From Theodore Roosevelt, *The Winning of the West*, vol. 1 (New York: Knickerbocker Press, 1889).

women and helpless children, were such as we read of in no other struggle, hardly even in the revolting pages that tell the deeds of the Holy Inquisition. It was inevitable—indeed it was in many instances proper—that such deeds should awake in the breasts of the whites the grimmest, wildest spirit of revenge and hatred.

The history of the border wars, both in the ways they were begun and in the ways they were waged, makes a long tale of injuries inflicted, suffered, and mercilessly revenged. It could not be otherwise when brutal, reckless, lawless borderers, despising all men not of their own color, were thrown in contact with savages who esteemed cruelty and treachery as the highest of virtues, and rapine and murder as the worthiest of pursuits. Moreover, it was sadly inevitable that the law-abiding borderer as well as the white ruffian, the peaceful Indian as well as the painted marauder, should be plunged into the struggle to suffer the punishment that should only have fallen on their evil-minded fellows.

Looking back, it is easy to say that much of the wrong-doing could have been prevented; but if we examine the facts to find out the truth, not to establish a theory, we are bound to admit that the struggle was really one that could not possibly have been avoided. The sentimental historians speak as if the blame had been all ours, and the wrong all done to our foes, and as if it would have been possible by any exercise of wisdom to reconcile claims that were in their very essence conflicting; but their utterances are as shallow as they are untruthful. Unless we were willing that the whole continent west of the Alleghanies should remain an unpeopled waste, the hunting-ground of savages, war was inevitable; and even had we been willing, and had we refrained from encroaching on the Indians' lands, the war would have come nevertheless, for then the Indians themselves would have encroached on ours. Undoubtedly we have wronged many tribes; but equally undoubtedly our first definite knowledge of many others has been derived from their unprovoked outrages upon our people. The Chippewas, Ottawas, and Pottawatamies furnished hundreds of young warriors to the parties that devastated our frontiers generations before we in any way encroached upon or wronged them.

Mere outrages could be atoned for or settled; the question which lay at the root of our difficulties was that of the occupation of the land itself, and to this there could be no solution save war. The Indians had no ownership of the land in the way in which we understand the term. The tribes lived far apart; each had for its hunting-grounds all the territory from which it was not barred by rivals. Each looked with jealousy upon all interlopers, but each was prompt to act as an interloper when occasion offered. Every good hunting-ground was claimed by many nations. It was rare, indeed, that any tribe had an uncontested title to a large tract of land; where such title existed, it rested, not on actual occupancy and cultivation, but on the recent butchery of weaker rivals. For instance, there were a dozen tribes, all of whom hunted in Kentucky, and fought each other there, all of whom had equally good titles to the soil, and not one of whom acknowledged the right of any other; as a matter of fact they had therein no right, save the right of the strongest. The land no more belonged to them than it belonged to Boon [Daniel Boone] and the white hunters who first visited it.

On the borders there are perpetual complaints of the encroachments of whites upon Indian lands; and naturally the central government at Washington, and before it was at Washington, has usually been inclined to sympathize with the feeling that considers the whites the aggressors, for the government does not wish a war, does not itself feel any land hunger, hears of not a tenth of the Indian outrages, and knows by experience that the white borderers are not easy to rule. As a consequence, the official reports of the people who are not on the ground are apt to paint the Indian side in its most favorable light, and are often completely untrustworthy, this being particularly the case if the author of the report is an eastern man, utterly unacquainted with the actual condition of affairs on the frontier.

Indians Have No True Title to the Land

Such a man, though both honest and intelligent, when he hears that the whites have settled on Indian lands, cannot realize that the act has no resemblance whatever to the forcible occupation of land already cultivated. The white settler has merely moved into an uninhabited waste; he does not feel that he is committing a wrong, for he knows perfectly well that the land is really owned by no one. It is never even visited, except perhaps for a week or two every year, and then the visitors are likely at any moment to be driven off by a rival hunting-party of greater strength. The settler ousts no one from the land; if he did not chop down the trees, hew out the logs for a building, and clear the ground for tillage, no one else would do so. He drives out the game, however, and of course the Indians who live thereon sink their mutual animosities and turn against the intruder. The truth is, the Indians never had any real title to the soil; they had not half as good a claim to it, for instance, as the cattlemen now have to all eastern Montana, yet no one would assert that the cattlemen have a right to keep immigrants off their vast unfenced ranges. The settler and pioneer have at bottom had justice on their side; this great continent could not have been kept as nothing but a game preserve for squalid savages. Moreover, to the most oppressed Indian nations the whites often acted as a protection, or, at least, they deferred instead of hastening their fate. But for the interposition of the whites it is probable that the Iroquois would have exterminated every Algonquin tribe before the end of the eighteenth century; exactly as in recent time the Crows and Pawnees would have been destroyed by the Sioux, had it not been for the wars we have waged against the latter.

Again, the loose governmental system of the Indians made it as difficult to secure a permanent peace with them as it was to negotiate the purchase of the lands. The sachem, or hereditary peace chief, and the elective war chief, who wielded only the influence that he could secure by his personal prowess and his tact, were equally unable to control all of their tribesmen, and were powerless with their confederated nations. If peace was made with the Shawnees, the war was continued by the Miamis; if peace was made with the latter, nevertheless perhaps one small band was dissatisfied, and continued the contest on its own account; and even if all the recognized bands were dealt with, the parties of renegades or outlaws had to be considered; and in the last resort the full recognition accorded by the Indians to the right of private warfare, made it possible for any individual warrior who possessed any influence to go on raiding and murdering unchecked. Every tribe, every sub-tribe, every band of a dozen souls ruled over by a petty chief, almost every individual warrior of the least importance, had to be met and pacified. Even if peace were declared, the Indians could not exist long without breaking it. There was to them no temptation to trespass on the white man's ground for the purpose of settling; but every young brave was brought up to regard scalps taken and horses stolen, in war or peace, as the highest proofs and tokens of skill and courage, the sure means of attaining glory and honor, the admiration of men and the love of women. Where the young men thought thus, and the chiefs had so little real control, it was inevitable that there should be many unprovoked forays for scalps, slaves, and horses made upon the white borderers.

White Atrocities

As for the whites themselves, they too have many and grievous sins against their red neighbors for which to answer. They cannot be severely blamed for trespassing upon what was called the Indian's land; for let sentimentalists say what they will, the man who puts the soil to use must of right dispossess the man who does not, or the world will come to a standstill; but for many of their other deeds there can be no pardon. On the border each man was a law unto himself, and good and bad alike were left in perfect

freedom to follow out to the uttermost limits their own desires; for the spirit of individualism so characteristic of American life reached its extreme of development in the backwoods. The whites who wished peace, the magistrates and leaders, had little more power over their evil and unruly fellows than the Indian sachems had over the turbulent young braves. Each man did what seemed best in his own eyes, almost without let or hindrance; unless, indeed, he trespassed upon the rights of his neighbors, who were ready enough to band together in their own defence, though slow to interfere in the affairs of others.

———— • ————

"The settler and pioneer have at bottom had justice on their side; this great continent could not have been kept as nothing but a game preserve for squalid savages."

———— • ————

Thus the men of lawless, brutal spirit who are found in every community and who flock to places where the reign of order is lax, were able to follow the bent of their inclinations unchecked. They utterly despised the red man; they held it no crime whatever to cheat him in trading, to rob him of his peltries or horses, to murder him if the fit seized them. Criminals who generally preyed on their own neighbors, found it easier, and perhaps hardly as dangerous, to pursue their calling at the expense of the redskins, for the latter, when they discovered that they had been wronged, were quite as apt to vent their wrath on some outsider as on the original offender. If they injured a white, all the whites might make common cause against them; but if they injured a red man, though there were sure to be plenty of whites who disapproved of it, there were apt to be very few indeed whose disapproval took any active shape.

Each race stood by its own members, and each held all of the other race responsible for the misdeeds of a few uncontrollable spirits; and this clannishness among those of one color, and the refusal or the inability to discriminate between the good and the bad of the other color were the two most fruitful causes of border strife. When, even if he sought to prevent them, the innocent man was sure to suffer for the misdeeds of the guilty, unless both joined together for defence, the former had no alternative save to make common cause with the latter. Moreover, in a sparse backwoods settlement, where the presence of a strong, vigorous fighter was a source of safety to the whole community, it was impossible to expect that he would be punished with severity for offences which, in their hearts, his fellow townsmen could not help regarding as in some sort a revenge for the injuries they had themselves suffered. Every quiet, peaceable settler had either himself been grievously wronged, or had been an eye-witness to wrongs done to his friends; and while these were vivid in his mind, the corresponding wrongs done the Indians were never brought home to him at all. If his son was scalped or his cattle driven off, he could not be expected to remember that perhaps the Indians who did the deed had themselves been cheated by a white trader, or had lost a relative at the hands of some border ruffian, or felt aggrieved because a hundred miles off some settler had built a cabin on lands they considered their own. When he joined with other exasperated and injured men to make a retaliatory inroad, his vengeance might or might not fall on the heads of the real offenders; and, in any case, he was often not in the frame of mind to put a stop to the outrages sure to be committed by the brutal spirits among his allies—though these brutal spirits were probably in a small minority.

The excesses so often committed by the whites, when, after many checks and failures, they at last grasped victory, are causes for shame and regret; yet it is only fair to keep in mind the terrible provocations they had endured. Mercy, pity, magnanimity to the fallen, could not be expected from the frontiersmen gathered together to war against an Indian tribe. Almost every man of such a band had bitter personal wrongs to avenge. He was not taking part in a war against a civilized foe; he was fighting in a contest where women and children suffered the fate of the strong men, and instead of enthusiasm for his country's flag and a general national animosity towards its enemies, he was actuated by a furious flame of hot anger, and was goaded on by memories of which merely to think was madness. His friends had been treacherously slain while on messages of peace; his house had been burned, his cattle driven off, and all he had in the world destroyed before he knew that war existed and when he felt quite guiltless of all offence; his sweetheart or wife had been carried off, ravished, and was at the moment the slave and concubine of some dirty and brutal Indian warrior; his son, the stay of his house, had been burned at the stake with torments too horrible to mention; his sister, when ransomed and returned to him, had told of the weary journey through the woods, when she carried around her neck as a horrible necklace the bloody scalps of her husband and children; seared into his eyeballs, into his very brain, he bore ever with him, waking or sleeping, the sight of the skinned, mutilated, hideous body of the baby who had just grown old enough to recognize him and to crow and laugh when taken in his arms. Such incidents as these were not exceptional; one or more, and often all of them, were the invariable attendants of every one of the countless Indian inroads that took place during the long generations of forest warfare. It was small wonder that men who had thus lost everything should sometimes be fairly crazed by their wrongs. Again and again on the frontier we hear of some such unfortunate who has devoted all the remainder of his wretched life to the one object of taking vengeance on the whole race of the men who had darkened his days forever. Too often the squaws and pappooses fell victims of the vengeance that should have come only on the warriors; for the whites regarded their foes as beasts rather than men, and knew that the squaws were more cruel than others in torturing the prisoner, and that the very children took their full part therein, being held up by their fathers to tomahawk the dying victims at the stake.

Thus it is that there are so many dark and bloody pages in the book of border warfare, that grim and iron-bound volume, wherein we read how our forefathers won the wide lands that we inherit. It contains many a tale of fierce heroism and adventurous ambition, of the daring and resolute courage of men and the patient endurance of women; it shows us a stern race of freemen who toiled hard, endured greatly, and fronted adversity bravely, who prized strength and courage and good faith, whose wives were chaste, who were generous and loyal to their friends. But it shows us also how they spurned at restraint and fretted under it, how they would brook no wrong to themselves, and yet too often inflicted wrong on others; their feats of terrible prowess are interspersed with deeds of the foulest and most wanton aggression, the darkest treachery, the most revolting cruelty; and though we meet with plenty of the rough, strong, coarse virtues, we see but little of such qualities as mercy for the fallen, the weak, and the helpless, or pity for a gallant and vanquished foe.

Viewpoint 5B

The Takeover of Indian Land: An Indian's View (1879)

Chief Joseph (1840?–1904)

Chief Joseph was one of the leaders of the Nez Percé, a tribe of American Indians who in 1877 were expelled from their homeland in the area where Washington, Oregon, and Idaho meet. Refusing to be sent to a reservation, the Nez Percé tried to escape to Canada while fighting off and eluding a U.S. military campaign to capture them. The retreat

From Chief Joseph, "An Indian's Views of Indian Affairs," *North American Review*, April 1879.

gained national attention and almost succeeded in its goal before Chief Joseph finally surrendered to General Nelson Miles on October 5, 1877 (stating, in a famous speech, "I will fight no more forever"). In betrayal of Miles's promise that Joseph and his followers would be sent to ancestral lands in Idaho, the Nez Percé were instead sent to a reservation in present-day Oklahoma. In January 1879 Chief Joseph visited Washington, D.C., to meet with President Rutherford B. Hayes and to plead for the return of his people to the Lapwai Indian Reservation in Idaho. On January 14 he gave a speech to Congress and cabinet members. The (translated) speech was published in the April 1879 issue of the *North American Review* and is excerpted here.

What laws and values does Joseph describe as important? How different or similar are they to the values expressed in the selection by Roosevelt? What does Joseph's account reveal about the clash of civilizations between white settlers and American Indians? What does it reveal about divisions within the Nez Percé? About the U.S. government? Does the story described by Chief Joseph strengthen or weaken the argument that violent clashes between whites and Indians were inevitable?

––––––––––––

My friends, I have been asked to show you my heart. I am glad to have a chance to do so. I want the white people to understand my people. Some of you think an Indian is like a wild animal. This is a great mistake. I will tell you all about our people, and then you can judge whether an Indian is a man or not. I believe much trouble and blood would be saved if we opened our hearts more. I will tell you in my way how the Indian sees things. The white man has more words to tell you how they look to him, but it does not require many words to speak the truth. What I have to say will come from my heart, and I will speak with a straight tongue. Ah-cum-kin-i-ma-me-hut (the Great Spirit) is looking at me, and will hear me.

My name is In-mut-too-yah-lat-lat (Thunder traveling over the Mountains). I am chief of the Wal-lam-wat-kin band of Chute-pa-lu, or Nez Percés (nose-pierced Indians). I was born in eastern Oregon, thirty-eight winters ago. My father was chief before me. When a young man, he was called Joseph by Mr. Spaulding, a missionary. He died a few years ago. There was no stain on his hands of the blood of a white man. He left a good name on the earth. He advised me well for my people.

Our fathers gave us many laws, which they had learned from their fathers. These laws were good. They told us to treat all men as they treated us; that we should never be the first to break a bargain; that

it was a disgrace to tell a lie; that we should speak only the truth; that it was a shame for one man to take from another his wife, or his property without paying for it. We were taught to believe that the Great Spirit sees and hears everything, and that he never forgets; that hereafter he will give every man a spirit-home according to his deserts: if he has been a good man, he will have a good home; if he has been a bad man, he will have a bad home. This I believe, and all my people believe the same.

We Met the First White Men

We did not know there were other people besides the Indian until about one hundred winters ago, when some men with white faces came to our country. They brought many things with them to trade for furs and skins. They brought tobacco, which was new to us. They brought guns with flint stones on them, which frightened our women and children. Our people could not talk with these white-faced men, but they used signs which all people understand. These men were Frenchmen, and they called our people "Nez Percés," because they wore rings in their noses for ornaments. Although very few of our people wear them now, we are still called by the same name. These French trappers said a great many things to our fathers, which have been planted in our hearts. Some were good for us, but some were bad. Our people were divided in opinion about these men. Some thought they taught more bad than good. An Indian respects a brave man, but he despises a coward. He loves a straight tongue, but he hates a forked tongue. The French trappers told us some truths and some lies.

The first white men of your people who came to our country were named Lewis and Clarke. They also brought many things that our people had never seen. They talked straight, and our people gave them a great feast, as a proof that their hearts were friendly. These men were very kind. They made presents to our chiefs and our people made presents to them. We had a great many horses, of which we gave them what they needed, and they gave us guns and tobacco in return. All the Nez Percés made friends with Lewis and Clarke, and agreed to let them pass through their country, and never to make war on white men. This promise the Nez Percés have never broken. No white man can accuse them of bad faith, and speak with a straight tongue. It has always been the pride of the Nez Percés that they were the friends of the white men. When my father was a young man there came to our country a white man (Rev. Mr. Spaulding) who talked spirit law. He won the affections of our people because he spoke good things to them. At first he did not say anything about white men wanting to settle on our lands. Nothing was said about that until about twenty winters ago, when a number of white people came into our country and built houses and made farms. At first our people made no complaint. They thought there was room enough for all to live in peace, and they were learning many things from the white men that seemed to be good. But we soon found that the white men were growing rich very fast, and were greedy to possess everything the Indian had. My father was the first to see through the schemes of the white men, and he warned his tribe to be careful about trading with them. He had suspicion of men who seemed so anxious to make money. I was a boy then, but I remember well my father's caution. He had sharper eyes than the rest of our people.

Next there came a white officer (Governor Stevens), who invited all the Nez Percés to a treaty council. After the council was opened he made known his heart. He said there were a great many white people in the country, and many more would come; that he wanted the land marked out so that the Indians and white men could be separated. If they were to live in peace it was necessary, he said, that the Indians should have a country set apart for them, and in that country they must stay. My father, who represented his band, refused to have anything to do with the council, because he wished to be a free man. He claimed that no man owned any part of the earth, and a man could not sell what he did not own.

"The white man has no right to come here and take our country."

Mr. Spaulding took hold of my father's arm and said, "Come and sign the treaty." My father pushed him away, and said: "Why do you ask me to sign away my country? It is your business to talk to us about spirit matters, and not to talk to us about parting with our land." Governor Stevens urged my father to sign his treaty, but he refused. "I will not sign your paper," he said; "you go where you please, so do I; you are not a child, I am no child; I can think for myself. No man can think for me. I have no other home than this. I will not give it up to any man. My people would have no home. Take away your paper. I will not touch it with my hand."

My father left the council. Some of the chiefs of the other bands of the Nez Percés signed the treaty, and then Governor Stevens gave them presents of blankets. My father cautioned his people to take no presents, for "after a while," he said, "they will claim that you have accepted pay for your country." Since

that time four bands of the Nez Percés have received annuities from the United States. My father was invited to many councils, and they tried hard to make him sign the treaty, but he was firm as the rock, and would not sign away his home. His refusal caused a difference among the Nez Percés.

Eight years later (1863) was the next treaty council. A chief called Lawyer, because he was a great talker, took the lead in this council, and sold nearly all the Nez Percés country. My father was not there. He said to me: "When you go into council with the white man, always remember your country. Do not give it away. The white man will cheat you out of your home. I have taken no pay from the United States. I have never sold our land." In this treaty Lawyer acted without authority from our band. He had no right to sell the Wallowa (winding water) country. That had always belonged to my father's own people, and the other bands had never disputed our right to it. No other Indians ever claimed Wallowa.

In order to have all people understand how much land we owned, my father planted poles around it and said:

"Inside is the home of my people—the white man may take the land outside. Inside this boundary all our people were born. It circles around the graves of our fathers, and we will never give up these graves to any man."

The United States claimed they had bought all the Nez Percés country outside of Lapwai Reservation, from Lawyer and other chiefs, but we continued to live on this land in peace until eight years ago, when white men began to come inside the bounds my father had set. We warned them against this great wrong, but they would not leave our land, and some bad blood was raised. The white men represented that we were going upon the war-path. They reported many things that were false.

The United States Government again asked for a treaty council. My father had become blind and feeble. He could no longer speak for his people. It was then that I took my father's place as chief. In this council I made my first speech to white men. I said to the agent who held the council:

"I did not want to come to this council, but I came hoping that we could save blood. The white man has no right to come here and take our country. We have never accepted any presents from the Government. Neither Lawyer nor any other chief had authority to sell this land. It has always belonged to my people. It came unclouded to them from our fathers, and we will defend this land as long as a drop of Indian blood warms the hearts of our men."

The agent said he had orders, from the Great White Chief at Washington, for us to go upon the Lapwai Reservation, and that if we obeyed he would help us in many ways. "You *must* move to the agency," he said. I answered him: "I will not. I do not need your help; we have plenty, and we are contented and happy if the white man will let us alone. The reservation is too small for so many people with all their stock. You can keep your presents; we can go to your towns and pay for all we need; we have plenty of horses and cattle to sell, and we won't have any help from you; we are free now; we can go where we please. Our fathers were born here. Here they lived, here they died, here are their graves. We will never leave them." The agent went away, and we had peace for a little while.

A Man Must Love His Father's Grave

Soon after this my father sent for me. I saw he was dying. I took his hand in mine. He said: "My son, my body is returning to my mother earth, and my spirit is going very soon to see the Great Spirit Chief. When I am gone, think of your country. You are the chief of these people. They look to you to guide them. Always remember that your father never sold his country. You must stop your ears whenever you are asked to sign a treaty selling your home. A few years more, and white men will be all around you. They have their eyes on this land. My son, never forget my dying words. This country holds your father's body. Never sell the bones of your father and your mother." I pressed my father's hand and told him I would protect his grave with my life. My father smiled and passed away to the spirit-land.

I buried him in that beautiful valley of winding waters. I love that land more than all the rest of the world. A man who would not love his father's grave is worse than a wild animal.

For a short time we lived quietly. But this could not last. White men had found gold in the mountains around the land of winding water. They stole a great many horses from us, and we could not get them back because we were Indians. The white men told lies for each other. They drove off a great many of our cattle. Some white men branded our young cattle so they could claim them. We had no friend who would plead our cause before the law councils. It seemed to me that some of the white men in Wallowa were doing these things on purpose to get up a war. They knew that we were not strong enough to fight them. I labored hard to avoid trouble and bloodshed. We gave up some of our country to the white men, thinking that then we could have peace. We were mistaken. The white man would not let us alone. We could have avenged our wrongs many times, but we did not. Whenever the Government has asked us to help them against other Indians, we have never refused. When the white men were few and we were strong we could have killed them all off,

but the Nez Percés wished to live at peace.

If we have not done so, we have not been to blame. I believe that the old treaty has never been correctly reported. If we ever owned the land we own it still, for we never sold it. In the treaty councils the commissioners have claimed that our country had been sold to the Government. Suppose a white man should come to me and say, "Joseph, I like your horses, and I want to buy them." I say to him, "No, my horses suit me, I will not sell them." Then he goes to my neighbor, and says to him: "Joseph has some good horses. I want to buy them, but he refuses to sell." My neighbor answers, "Pay me the money, and I will sell you Joseph's horses." The white man returns to me, and says, "Joseph, I have bought your horses, and you must let me have them." If we sold our lands to the Government, this is the way they were bought.

On account of the treaty made by the other bands of the Nez Percés, the white men claimed my lands. We were troubled greatly by white men crowding over the line. Some of these were good men, and we lived on peaceful terms with them, but they were not all good.

Nearly every year the agent came over from Lapwai and ordered us on to the reservation. We always replied that we were satisfied to live in Wallowa. We were careful to refuse the presents or annuities which he offered.

Deer and Grizzly Bears

Through all the years since the white men came to Wallowa we have been threatened and taunted by them and the treaty Nez Percés. They have given us no rest. We have had a few good friends among white men, and they have always advised my people to bear these taunts without fighting. Our young men were quick-tempered, and I have had great trouble in keeping them from doing rash things. I have carried a heavy load on my back ever since I was a boy. I learned then that we were but few, while the white men were many, and that we could not hold our own with them. We were like deer. They were like grizzly bears. We had a small country. Their country was large. We were contented to let things remain as the Great Spirit Chief made them. They were not; and would change the rivers and mountains if they did not suit them.

Year after year we have been threatened, but no war was made upon my people until General Howard came to our country two years ago and told us that he was the white war-chief of all that country. He said: "I have a great many soldiers at my back. I am going to bring them up here, and then I will talk to you again. I will not let white men laugh at me the next time I come. The country belongs to the Government, and I intend to make you go upon the reservation.". . .

General Howard sent out runners and called all the Indians in to a grand council. I was in that council. I said to General Howard, "We are ready to listen." He answered that he would not talk then, but would hold a council next day, when he would talk plainly. I said to General Howard: "I am ready to talk to-day. I have been in a great many councils, but I am no wiser. We are all sprung from a woman, although we are unlike in many things. We can not be made over again. You are as you were made, and as you were made you can remain. We are just as we were made by the Great Spirit, and you can not change us; then why should children of one mother and one father quarrel—why should one try to cheat the other? I do not believe that the Great Spirit Chief gave one kind of men the right to tell another kind of men what they must do."

General Howard replied: "You deny my authority, do you? You want to dictate to me, do you?"

Then one of my chiefs—Too-hool-hool-suit—rose in the council and said to General Howard: "The Great Spirit Chief made the world as it is, and as he wanted it, and he made a part of it for us to live upon. I do not see where you get authority to say that we shall not live where he placed us."

General Howard lost his temper and said: "Shut up! I don't want to hear any more of such talk. The law says you shall go upon the reservation to live, and I want you to do so, but you persist in disobeying the law" (meaning the treaty). "If you do not move, I will take the matter into my own hand, and make you suffer for your disobedience."

Too-hool-hool-suit answered: "Who are you, that you ask us to talk, and then tell me I sha'n't talk? Are you the Great Spirit? Did you make the world? Did you make the sun? Did you make the rivers to run for us to drink? Did you make the grass to grow? Did you make all these things, that you talk to us as though we were boys? If you did, then you have the right to talk as you do."

General Howard replied, "You are an impudent fellow, and I will put you in the guard-house," and then ordered a soldier to arrest him.

Too-hool-hool-suit made no resistance. He asked General Howard: "Is that your order? I don't care. I have expressed my heart to you. I have nothing to take back. I have spoken for my country. You can arrest me, but you can not change me or make me take back what I have said."

The soldiers came forward and seized my friend and took him to the guard-house. My men whispered among themselves whether they should let this thing be done. I counseled them to submit. I knew if we resisted that all the white men present, including General Howard, would be killed in a moment, and we would be blamed. If I had said

nothing, General Howard would never have given another unjust order against my men. I saw the danger, and, while they dragged Too-hool-hool-suit to prison, I arose and said: "*I am going to talk now. I don't care whether you arrest me or not.*" I turned to my people and said: "The arrest of Too-hool-hool-suit was wrong, but we will not resent the insult. We were invited to this council to express our hearts, and we have done so." Too-hool-hool-suit was prisoner for five days before he was released.

The council broke up for that day. On the next morning General Howard came to my lodge, and invited me to go with him and White-Bird and Looking-Glass, to look for land for my people. As we rode along we came to some good land that was already occupied by Indians and white people. General Howard, pointing to this land, said: "If you will come on to the reservation, I will give you these lands and move these people off."

I replied: "No. It would be wrong to disturb these people. I have no right to take their homes. I have never taken what did not belong to me. I will not now."

We rode all day upon the reservation, and found no good land unoccupied. . . .

In the council, next day, General Howard informed me, in a haughty spirit, that he would give my people *thirty days* to go back home, collect all their stock, and move on to the reservation, saying, "If you are not here in that time, I shall consider that you want to fight, and will send my soldiers to drive you on.". . .

I knew I had never sold my country, and that I had no land in Lapwai; but I did not want bloodshed. I did not want my people killed. I did not want anybody killed. Some of my people had been murdered by white men, and the white murderers were never punished for it. I told General Howard about this, and again said I wanted no war. I wanted the people who lived upon the lands I was to occupy at Lapwai to have time to gather their harvest.

I said in my heart that, rather than have war, I would give up my country. I would give up my father's grave. I would give up everything rather than have the blood of white men upon the hands of my people.

General Howard refused to allow me more than thirty days to move my people and their stock. I am sure that he began to prepare for war at once.

When I returned to Wallowa I found my people very much excited upon discovering that the soldiers were already in the Wallowa Valley. We hold a council, and decided to move immediately, to avoid bloodshed.

Too-hool-hool-suit, who felt outraged by his imprisonment, talked for war, and made many of my young men willing to fight rather than be driven like dogs from the land where they were born. He declared that blood alone would wash out the disgrace General Howard had put upon him. It required a strong heart to stand up against such talk, but I urged my people to be quiet, and not to begin a war.

No Way to Avoid War

We gathered all the stock we could find, and made an attempt to move. We left many of our horses and cattle in Wallowa, and we lost several hundred in crossing the river. All of my people succeeded in getting across in safety. Many of the Nez Percés came together in Rocky Cañon to hold a grand council. I went with all my people. This council lasted ten days. There was a great deal of war-talk, and a great deal of excitement. There was one young brave present whose father had been killed by a white man five years before. This man's blood was bad against white men, and he left the council calling for revenge.

Again I counseled peace, and I thought the danger was past. We had not complied with General Howard's order because we could not, but we intended to do so as soon as possible. I was leaving the council to kill beef for my family, when news came that the young man whose father had been killed had gone out with several other hot-blooded young braves and killed four white men. He rode up to the council and shouted: "Why do you sit here like women? The war has begun already." I was deeply grieved. All the lodges were moved except my brother's and my own. I saw clearly that the war was upon us when I learned that my young men had been secretly buying ammunition. I heard then that Too-hool-hool-suit, who had been imprisoned by General Howard, had succeeded in organizing a war-party. I knew that their acts would involve all my people. I saw that the war could not then be prevented. The time had passed. I counseled peace from the beginning. I knew that we were too weak to fight the United States. We had many grievances, but I knew that war would bring more. We had good white friends, who advised us against taking the war-path. . . .

There were bad men among my people who had quarreled with white men, and they talked of their wrongs until they roused all the bad hearts in the council. Still I could not believe that they would begin the war. I know that my young men did a great wrong, but I ask, Who was first to blame? They had been insulted a thousand times; their fathers and brothers had been killed; their mothers and wives had been disgraced; they had been driven to madness by whisky sold to them by white men; they had been told by General Howard that all their horses and cattle which they had been unable to drive out of Wallowa were to fall into the hands of white men; and, added to all this, they were homeless and desperate.

I would have given my own life if I could have undone the killing of white men by my people. I blame my young men and I blame the white men. I blame General Howard for not giving my people time to get their stock away from Wallowa. I do not acknowledge that he had the right to order me to leave Wallowa at any time. I deny that either my father or myself ever sold that land. It is still our land. It may never again be our home, but my father sleeps there, and I love it as I love my mother. I left there, hoping to avoid bloodshed.

If General Howard had given me plenty of time to gather up my stock, and treated Too-hool-hool-suit as a man should be treated, there *would have been no war*. . . .

I could see no other way to avoid a war. We moved over to White Bird Creek, sixteen miles away, and there encamped, intending to collect our stock before leaving; but the soldiers attacked us, and the first battle was fought. We numbered in that battle sixty men, and the soldiers a hundred. The fight lasted but a few minutes, when the soldiers retreated before us for twelve miles. They lost thirty-three killed, and had seven wounded. When an Indian fights, he only shoots to kill; but soldiers shoot at random. None of the soldiers were scalped. We do not believe in scalping, nor in killing wounded men. Soldiers do not kill many Indians unless they are wounded and left upon the battle-field. Then they kill Indians. . . .

Battles and Retreats

Finding that we were outnumbered, we retreated to Bitter Root Valley. Here another body of soldiers came upon us and demanded our surrender. We refused. They said, "You can not get by us." We answered, "We are going by you without fighting if you will let us, but we are going by you anyhow." We then made a treaty with these soldiers. We agreed not to molest any one, and they agreed that we might pass through the Bitter Root country in peace. We bought provisions and traded stock with white men there.

We understood that there was to be no more war. We intended to go peaceably to the buffalo country, and leave the question of returning to our country to be settled afterward.

With this understanding we traveled on for four days, and, thinking that the trouble was all over, we stopped and prepared tent-poles to take with us. We started again, and at the end of two days we saw three white men passing our camp. Thinking that peace had been made, we did not molest them. We could have killed or taken them prisoners, but we did not suspect them of being spies, which they were.

That night the soldiers surrounded our camp. About daybreak one of my men went out to look after his horses. The soldiers saw him and shot him down like a coyote. I have since learned that these soldiers were not those we had left behind. They had come upon us from another direction. The new white war chief's name was Gibbon. He charged upon us while some of my people were still asleep. We had a hard fight. Some of my men crept around and attacked the soldiers from the rear. In this battle we lost nearly all our lodges, but we finally drove General Gibbon back.

Finding that he was not able to capture us, he sent to his camp a few miles away for his big guns (cannons), but my men had captured them and all the ammunition. We damaged the big guns all we could, and carried away the powder and lead. In the fight with General Gibbon we lost fifty women and children and thirty fighting men. We remained long enough to bury our dead. The Nez Percés never make war on women and children; we could have killed a great many women and children while the war lasted, but we would feel ashamed to do so cowardly an act. . . .

We retreated as rapidly as we could toward the buffalo country. After six days General Howard came close to us, and we went out and attacked him, and captured nearly all his horses and mules (about two hundred and fifty head). We then marched on to the Yellowstone Basin.

On the way we captured one white man and two white women. We released them at the end of three days. They were treated kindly. The women were not insulted. Can the white soldiers tell me of one time when Indian women were taken prisoners, and held three days and then released without being insulted? Were the Nez Percés women who fell into the hands of General Howard's soldiers treated with as much respect? I deny that a Nez Percé was ever guilty of such a crime. . . .

Nine days' march brought us to the mouth of Clarke's Fork of the Yellowstone. We did not know what had become of General Howard, but we supposed that he had sent for more horses and mules. He did not come up, but another new war-chief (General Sturgis) attacked us. We held him in check while we moved all our women and children and stock out of danger, leaving a few men to cover our retreat.

Several days passed, and we heard nothing of General Howard, or Gibbon, or Sturgis. We had repulsed each in turn, and began to feel secure, when another army, under General Miles, struck us. This was the fourth army, each of which outnumbered our fighting force, that we had encountered within sixty days. . . .

We lost, the first day and night, eighteen men and three women. General Miles lost twenty-six killed and forty wounded. The following day General Miles

sent a messenger into my camp under protection of a white flag. . . .

The Decision to Surrender

I could not bear to see my wounded men and women suffer any longer; we had lost enough already. General Miles had promised that we might return to our own country with what stock we had left. I thought we could start again. I believed General Miles, or *I never would have surrendered.* I have heard that he has been censured for making the promise to return us to Lapwai. He could not have made any other terms with me at that time. I would have held him in check until my friends came to my assistance, and then neither of the generals nor their soldiers would have ever left Bear Paw Mountain alive.

On the fifth day I went to General Miles and gave up my gun, and said, "From where the sun now stands I will fight no more." My people needed rest—we wanted peace.

I was told we could go with General Miles to Tongue River and stay there until spring, when we would be sent back to our country. Finally it was decided that we were to be taken to Tongue River. We had nothing to say about it. After our arrival at Tongue River, General Miles received orders to take us to Bismarck. The reason given was, that subsistence would be cheaper there.

General Miles was opposed to this order. He said: "You must not blame me. I have endeavored to keep my word, but the chief who is over me has given the order, and I must obey it or resign. That would do you no good. Some other officer would carry out the order."

I believe General Miles would have kept his word if he could have done so. I do not blame him for what we have suffered since the surrender. I do not know who is to blame. We gave up all our horses—over eleven hundred—and all our saddles—over one hundred—and we have not heard from them since. Somebody has got our horses.

General Miles turned my people over to another soldier, and we were taken to Bismarck. Captain Johnson, who now had charge of us, received an order to take us to Fort Leavenworth. At Leavenworth we were placed on a low river bottom with no water except river-water to drink and cook with. We had always lived in a healthy country, where the mountains were high and the water was cold and clear. Many of my people sickened and died, and we buried them in this strange land. I can not tell how much my heart suffered for my people while at Leavenworth. The Great Spirit Chief who rules above seemed to be looking some other way, and did not see what was being done to my people.

During the hot days (July, 1878) we received notice that we were to be moved farther away from our own country. We were not asked if we were willing to go. We were ordered to get into the railroad-cars. Three of my people died on the way to Baxter Springs. It was worse to die there than to die fighting in the mountains.

We were moved from Baxter Springs (Kansas) to the Indian Territory, and set down without our lodges. We had but little medicine, and we were nearly all sick. Seventy of my people have died since we moved there.

We have had a great many visitors who have talked many ways. Some of the chiefs (General Fish and Colonel Stickney) from Washington came to see us, and selected land for us to live upon. We have not moved to that land, for it is not a good place to live.

The Commissioner Chief (E.A. Hayt) came to see us. I told him, as I told every one, that I expected General Miles's word would be carried out. He said it "could not be done; that white men now lived in my country and all the land was taken up; that, if I returned to Wallowa, I could not live in peace; that law-papers were out against my young men who began the war, and that the Government could not protect my people." This talk fell like a heavy stone upon my heart. I saw that I could not gain anything by talking to him. Other law chiefs (Congressional Committee) came to see me and said they would help me to get a healthy country. I did not know who to believe. The white people have too many chiefs. They do not understand each other. They do not all talk alike. . . .

I Cannot Understand So Many Chiefs

At last I was granted permission to come to Washington and bring my friend Yellow Bull and our interpreter with me. I am glad we came. I have shaken hands with a great many friends, but there are some things I want to know which no one seems able to explain. I can not understand how the Government sends a man out to fight us . . . and then breaks his word. Such a Government has something wrong about it. I can not understand why so many chiefs are allowed to talk so many different ways, and promise so many different things. I have seen the Great Father Chief (the President), the next Great Chief (Secretary of the Interior), the Commissioner Chief (Hayt), the Law Chief (General Butler), and many other law chiefs (Congressmen), and they all say they are my friends, and that I shall have justice, but while their mouths all talk right I do not understand why nothing is done for my people. I have heard talk and talk, but nothing is done. Good words do not last long unless they amount to something. Words do not pay for my dead people. They do not pay for my

country, now overrun by white men. They do not protect my father's grave. They do not pay for all my horses and cattle. Good words will not give me back my children. Good words will not make good the promise of your War Chief General Miles. Good words will not give my people good health and stop them from dying. Good words will not get my people a home where they can live in peace and take care of themselves. I am tired of talk that comes to nothing. It makes my heart sick when I remember all the good words and all the broken promises. There has been too much talking by men who had no right to talk. Too many misrepresentations have been made, too many misunderstandings have come up between the white men about the Indians. If the white man wants to live in peace with the Indian he can live in peace. There need be no trouble. Treat all men alike. Give them all the same law. Give them all an even chance to live and grow. All men were made by the same Great Spirit Chief. They are all brothers. The earth is the mother of all people, and all people should have equal rights upon it. You might as well expect the rivers to run backward as that any man who was born a free man should be contented when penned up and denied liberty to go where he pleases. If you tie a horse to a stake, do you expect he will grow fat? If you pen an Indian up on a small spot of earth, and compel him to stay there, he will not be contented, nor will he grow and prosper. I have asked some of the great white chiefs where they get their authority to say to the Indian that he shall stay in one place, while he sees white men going where they please. They can not tell me.

Treat Us Like All Other Men

I only ask of the Government to be treated as all other men are treated. If I can not go to my own home, let me have a home in some country where my people will not die so fast. I would like to go to Bitter Root Valley. There my people would be healthy; where they are now they are dying. Three have died since I left my camp to come to Washington.

When I think of our condition my heart is heavy. I see men of my race treated as outlaws and driven from country to country, or shot down like animals.

I know that my race must change. We can not hold our own with the white men as we are. We only ask an even chance to live as other men live. We ask to be recognized as men. We ask that the same law shall work alike on all men. If the Indian breaks the law, punish him by the law. If the white man breaks the law, punish him also.

Let me be a free man—free to travel, free to stop, free to work, free to trade where I choose, free to choose my own teachers, free to follow the religion of my fathers, free to think and talk and act for myself—

and I will obey every law, or submit to the penalty.

Whenever the white man treats the Indian as they treat each other, then we will have no more wars. We shall all be alike—brothers of one father and one mother, with one sky above us and one country around us, and one government for all. Then the Great Spirit Chief who rules above will smile upon this land, and send rain to wash out the bloody spots made by brothers' hands from the face of the earth. For this time the Indian race are waiting and praying. I hope that no more groans of wounded men and women will ever go to the ear of the Great Spirit Chief above, and that all people may be one people.

In-mut-too-yah-lat-lat has spoken for his people.

For Further Reading

Michael Gibson, *The American Indians: From Colonial Times to the Present.* New York: G. P. Putnam's Sons, 1974.

Jason Hook, *Chief Joseph: Guardian of the Nez Percé.* New York: Sterling, 1989.

Oliver O. Howard, *Nez Percé Joseph.* Boston: Lee & Shepard, 1881.

Alvin M. Josephy Jr., *The Nez Percé Indians and the Opening of the Northwest.* New Haven, CT: Yale University Press, 1971.

Francis P. Prucha, *The Great Father: The United States Government and the American Indian.* 2 vols. Lincoln: University of Nebraska Press, 1984.

Theodore Roosevelt, *Hunting Trips of a Ranchman.* New York: G. P. Putnam's Sons, 1885.

Robert M. Utley, *Frontier Regulars: The United States Army and the Indian, 1866–1891.* New York: Macmillan, 1974.

Wilcomb E. Washburn, *The Indian in America.* New York: Harper & Row, 1975.

VIEWPOINT 6A

Excluding Chinese Immigrants Runs Counter to the Spirit of America (1882)

George F. Hoar (1826–1904)

The first significant law restricting immigration into the United States was the Chinese Exclusion Act of 1882. The law suspended all immigration of Chinese workers for ten years and barred Chinese immigrants then living in the United States (mostly in California) from applying for U.S. citizenship. George F. Hoar, a Republican senator from Massachusetts from 1877 to 1904, was one of the outspoken opponents of this legislation. In the following viewpoint, taken from remarks made during the Senate debate on the 1882 Chinese Exclusion Act, Hoar opposes the bill as a violation of American ideals and

From George F. Hoar, *Congressional Record*, 47th Cong., 1st sess., 1882, vol. 13, pp. 1515–23.

as an unworthy expression of racial fears.

Why is the bill in fundamental conflict with the ideals of the nation's founders, according to Hoar? What comparisons does he make between blacks and Chinese immigrants? Are his arguments expressed here devoid of racial or national prejudice? How does his view of America's place in the world affect his arguments?

Mr. President, a hundred years ago the American people founded a nation upon the moral law. They overthrew by force the authority of their sovereign, and separated themselves from the country which had planted them, alleging as their justification to mankind certain propositions which they held to be self-evident.

They declared—and that declaration is the one foremost action of human history—that all men equally derive from their Creator the right to the pursuit of happiness; that equality in the right to that pursuit is the fundamental rule of the divine justice in its application to mankind; that its security is the end for which governments are formed, and its destruction good cause why governments should be overthrown. For a hundred years this principle has been held in honor. Under its beneficent operation we have grown almost twentyfold. Thirteen States have become thirty-eight; three million have become fifty million; wealth and comfort and education and art have flourished in still larger proportion. Every twenty years there is added to the valuation of this country a wealth enough to buy the whole German Empire, with its buildings and its ships and its invested property. This has been the magnet that has drawn immigration hither. The human stream, hemmed in by banks invisible but impassable, does not turn toward Mexico, which can feed and clothe a world, or South America, which can feed and clothe a hundred worlds, but seeks only that belt of States where it finds this law in operation. The marvels of comfort and happiness it has wrought for us scarcely surpass what it has done for other countries. The immigrant sends back the message to those he has left behind. There is scarcely a nation in Europe west of Russia which has not felt the force of our example and whose institutions are not more or less slowly approximating to our own. . . .

Racial Distinctions Are Unconstitutional

Nothing is more in conflict with the genius of American institutions than legal distinctions between individuals based upon race or upon occupation. The framers of our Constitution believed in the safety and wisdom of adherence to abstract principles. They meant that their laws should make no distinction between men except such as were required by personal conduct and character. The prejudice of race, the last of human delusions to be overcome, has been found until lately in our constitutions and statutes, and has left its hideous and ineradicable stains on our history in crimes committed by every generation. The negro, the Irishman, and the Indian have in turn been its victims here, as the Jew and the Greek and the Hindoo in Europe and Asia. But it is reserved for us at the present day, for the first time, to put into the public law of the world and into the national legislation of the foremost of republican nations a distinction inflicting upon a large class of men a degradation by reason of their race and by reason of their occupation. . . .

———— • ————

"What argument can be urged against the Chinese which was not heard against the negro within living memory?"

———— • ————

Here is a declaration made by a compact between the two greatest nations of the Pacific [China and the United States], and now to be re-enforced by a solemn act of legislation, which places in the public law of the world and in the jurisprudence of America the principle that it is fit that there should hereafter be a distinction in the treatment of men by governments and in the recognition of their rights to the pursuit of happiness by a peaceful change of their homes, based not on conduct, not on character, but upon race and upon occupation. You may justly deny to the Chinese what you may not justly deny to the Irishman. You may deny to the laborer what you may not deny to the scholar or to the idler. And this declaration is extorted from unwilling China by the demand of America. With paupers, lazzaroni, harlots, persons afflicted with pestilential disease, laborers are henceforth to be classed in the enumerations of American public law. . . .

See also, Mr. President, how this class of immigrants, diminishing in itself, diminishes still more in its proportion to the rapidly increasing numbers who come from other lands. Against 22,943 Asiatic immigrants in 1876, there are but 5,802 in 1880. In 1878 there were 9,014 from Asia, in a total of 153,207, or one in seventeen of the entire immigration; and this includes all persons who entered the port of San Francisco to go to any South American country. In 1879 there were 9,604 from China in a total of 250,565, or one in twenty-six. In 1880 there were 5,802 from China in a total immigration of 593,359, or one in one hundred and two. The whole Chinese population, then, when the census of 1880 was

taken, was but one in five hundred of our people. The whole Chinese immigration was but one in one hundred and two of the total immigration; while the total annual immigration quadrupled from 1878 to 1880, the Chinese was in 1880 little more than one-half what it was in 1878, and one-fourth what it was in 1876.

The number of immigrants of all nations was 720,045 in 1881. Of these 20,711 were Chinese. There is no record in the Bureau of Statistics of the number who departed within the year. But a very high anti-Chinese authority places it above 10,000. Perhaps the expectation that the hostile legislation under the treaty would not affect persons who entered before it took effect stimulated somewhat their coming. But the addition to the Chinese population was less than one seventy-second of the whole immigration. All the Chinese in the country do not exceed the population of its sixteenth city. All the Chinese in California hardly surpass the number which is easily governed in Shanghai by a police of one hundred men. There are as many pure blooded Gypsies wandering about the country as there are Chinese in California. What an insult to American intelligence to ask leave of China to keep out her people, because this little handful of almond-eyed Asiatics threaten to destroy our boasted civilization. We go boasting of our democracy, and our superiority, and our strength. The flag bears the stars of hope to all nations. A hundred thousand Chinese land in California and everything is changed. God has not made of one blood all the nations any longer. The self-evident truth becomes a self-evident lie. The golden rule does not apply to the natives of the continent where it was first uttered. The United States surrender to China, the Republic to the despot, America to Asia, Jesus to Joss.

Base Motives for the Exclusion Act

The advocates of this legislation appeal to a twofold motive for its support.

First. They invoke the old race prejudice which has so often played its hateful and bloody part in history.

Second. They say that the Chinese laborer works cheap and lives cheap, and so injures the American laborer with whom he competes.

The old race prejudice, ever fruitful of crime and of folly, has not been confined to monarchies or to the dark ages. Our own Republic and our own generation have yielded to this delusion, and have paid the terrible penalty. I do not mean to go over the ground which Mr. Sumner, with his accustomed industry and learning, so thoroughly traversed in his lecture upon caste. But I wish to plant myself upon the greatest authority in modern science, himself perhaps the most perfect example of the greatness of the capacity of the human intellect under the most favorable conditions. Listen to Alexander von Humboldt, as quoted by Mr. Sumner:

> While we maintain the unity of the human species, we at the same time repel the depressing assumption of superior and inferior races of men. There are nations more susceptible of cultivation, more highly civilized, more ennobled by mental cultivation, than others, but none in themselves nobler than others.—*Alexander von Humboldt, quoted in Sumner's Works*, volume 13, page 157.

What argument can be urged against the Chinese which was not heard against the negro within living memory? . . .

Who is now so bold as to deny to the colored race fitness for citizenship? Twenty years have not passed by since the children of the African savage were emancipated from slavery. In that brief space they have vindicated their title to the highest privileges and their fitness for the highest duties of citizenship. These despised savages have sat in the House and in the Senate. I have served with them for twelve years in both branches. Can you find an equal number, chosen on any principle of selection, whose conduct has been marked by more uniform good sense and propriety? . . .

It is scarcely forty years since the Irishman, who has been such a source of wealth and strength to America, began his exodus across the sea. There are men in this body, whose heads are not yet gray, who can remember how the arguments now used against the Chinese filled the American mind with alarm when used against the Irishman. He comes, said the honest bigotry of that day, only to get the means of living, and then to return; he will drive the American to starvation by the competition of his cheap labor; he lives in squalor and filth; he wants only a few potatoes for food; he is blindly attached to the Popish religion; he owes allegiance to a foreign potentate; he is incapable of intelligent citizenship. . . .

Even the humane and liberal John Stuart Mill says:

> If there were no other escape from that fatal immigration of the Irish—which has done and is doing so much to degrade the condition of our agricultural and some classes of our town population—I should see no injustice and the greatest possible expediency in checking that destructive inroad by prohibitive laws.

In the early edition of his *Political Economy*, Mr. Bowen, the learned and able professor at Harvard, expresses the same fear for America. He says the annual addition to our population of 400,000 foreigners, of whom one-fourth are Irish, is likely to effect a general and great depreciation in the price of labor.

> Throw down the little that is left of our protective system—

He proceeds—

> and let the emigration from Great Britain and Ireland to our shores increase to half a million annually, and within the lifetime of the present generation the laborer's hire in our Atlantic States will be as low as it is in England. This we should regard as the greatest calamity which the folly of men or the wrath of Heaven could bring upon the land.

These are but temperate expressions of opinions which drove less intelligent persons to frenzy and crime. The streets of Baltimore and of New Orleans ran with Irish blood. A great party was founded, and swept some States, on a platform of opposition to foreigners.

I suppose no person now would like to repeat the arguments which were addressed to the Know-Nothing party in 1855. The Irishman has contributed by his labor to cover our land with railroads, which in their turn create cities, give value to land, and open new opportunities for labor. His sons and daughters are found in large numbers in our factories. He is acquiring land. He is a large depositor in our savings banks. He rendered indispensable service in war. More and more every year he ceases to be the dupe of demagogues, and is learning the higher duties of citizenship. Meantime, the wage of the American workman is higher and not lower for his presence. While he has bettered his own condition he has raised to a higher grade of social life and wealth the American laborer whose place he has taken. . . .

The Chinese Character

An argument is based on the character of the Chinese. You should take a race at its best, and not at its worst, in looking for its possibilities under the influence of freedom. The Chinese are in many particulars far superior to our own ancestors as they were when they first came forth into the light of history. Our British forefathers, at a time far within the historic period, remained in a degradation of superstition and a degradation of barbarism to which China never descended. Centuries after the Chinese philosopher had uttered the golden rule, and had said, "I like life and I like righteousness; if I cannot keep the two together I will let life go; and choose righteousness," the Druids of Britain were offering human sacrifices to pagan deities. We must take a race at its best in determining its capacity for freedom. This race can furnish able merchants, skillful diplomatists, profound philosophers, faithful servants, industrious and docile laborers. An eminent member of the other House told me that he had dealt with Chinese merchants to the amount of hundreds of thousands, perhaps millions, and that they had never deceived him. . . .

One of the ablest of the writers against the Chinese, Mr. James A. Whitney, sums up his opinion thus:

The Chinese intellect, the Chinese character, is strong, vigorous, patient, and far-sighted. As diplomates, the statesmen of China have held their own with those of every nation in the world.

Indeed, a large part of the argument of the Senator from California is based, not on Chinese inferiority, but on his dread of Chinese superiority in most of the occupations of life. Their civilization, he says, will be too strong for ours, if the two come in conflict in a fair field. . . .

Now I wish to read a sentence or two from the report of Senator Morton, the last dying legacy of this great Senator and lover of human liberty, published since his death and left by him unfinished as his last public work. He says:

> If the Chinese in California were white people, being in all other respects what they are, I do not believe that the complaints and warfare made against them would have existed to any considerable extent. Their difference in color, dress, manners, and religion has, in my judgment, more to do with this hostility than their alleged vices or any actual injury to the white people of California. . . .
>
> As a rule, they are industrious, temperate, and honest in their dealings. Some thousands of them are employed as household servants in the cities and in the country. In this capacity the testimony generally concurs in giving them a high character. They very readily learn to perform all kinds of household duty, are devoted to their employment, and soon become exceedingly skillful. The testimony proved that they went to all parts of the State to serve in that capacity, when other servants or help of that kind could not be obtained from the cities, and that if they were banished it would be very hard, in fact, as many of the witnesses said, impossible to supply their places. As laborers upon the farms and in the gardens and vineyards nearly all of the witnesses speak of them in the highest terms. . . .
>
> In the construction of railroads and other public works of California the Chinese have been of the greatest service and have performed the largest part of the labor. . . .

It is said that two races have been side by side for thirty years and no step taken toward assimilation. It is admitted that they have learned our industries rapidly and intelligently. That they do not incline to become Christians or republicans may perhaps be accounted for by the treatment they have received. They are excluded by statute from the public schools. They have no honest trial by jury. Judge Blake, of the San Francisco criminal court, testifies:

> It is true that as a rule when a Chinaman's case goes to a jury there is no help about it, the jury must convict him. . . .

What special inducements have the Chinese to

become republicans in a State which has established a constitution which in article 2, section 1, says:

> Every native male citizen of the United States, every male person who shall have acquired the rights of citizenship under or by virtue of the treaty of Queretaro, and every male naturalized citizen thereof, who shall have become such ninety days prior to any election, of the age of twenty-one years, who shall have been a resident of the State one year next preceding the election, and of the county in which he claims his vote ninety days, and in the election precinct thirty days, shall be entitled to vote at all elections which are now or may hereafter be authorized by law: *Provided*, No native of China, no idiot, insane person, or person convicted of any infamous crime, and no person hereafter convicted of the embezzlement or misappropriation of public money, shall ever exercise the privileges of an elector in this State. . . .

An eminent and learned judge of the Supreme Court of the United States gave a judgment on an ordinance of the city of San Francisco directing that the head of every person convicted of crime should be shaved, should be "cut or clipped to a uniform length of one inch from the scalp thereof"—an ordinance directed against the Chinese only, intended to impose upon them cruel and degrading punishments. Judge Field says, after pointing out the iniquity of this ordinance:

> It is not creditable to the humanity and civilization of our people, much less to their Christianity, that an ordinance of this character was possible. . . .

There is a mass of evidence on this point. I might present many extracts from the report of the Congressional committee of 1876, but I will not, in order to save the time of the Senate. I wish, however, to read one statement of Mr. Pixley, who represented the anti-Chinese side. After summing up the qualities of the men such as he has described, he says:

> In other words, I believe . . . that the Chinese have no souls to save, and if they have they are not worth the saving.

But it is urged, and this, in my judgment, is the greatest argument for the bill, that the introduction of the labor of the Chinese reduces the wages of the American laborer. "We are ruined by Chinese cheap labor" is a cry not limited to the class to whose representative the brilliant humorist of California first ascribed it. I am not in favor of lowering anywhere the wages of any American labor, skilled or unskilled. On the contrary, I believe the maintenance and the increase of the purchasing power of the wages of the American workingman should be the one principal object of our legislation. The share in the product of agriculture or manufacture which goes to labor should, and I believe will, steadily increase. For that, and for that only, exists our protective system. The acquisition of wealth, national or individual, is to be desired only for that. The statement of the accomplished Senator from California on this point meets my heartiest concurrence. I have no sympathy with any men, if such there be, who favor high protection and cheap labor.

But I believe that the Chinese, to whom the terms of the California Senator attribute skill enough to displace the American in every field requiring intellectual vigor, will learn very soon to insist on his full share of the product of his work. But whether that be true or not, the wealth he creates will make better and not worse the condition of every higher class of labor. There may be trouble or failure in adjusting new relations. But sooner or later every new class of industrious and productive laborers elevates the class it displaces. The dread of an injury to our labor from the Chinese rests on the same fallacy that opposed the introduction of labor-saving machinery, and which opposed the coming of the Irishman and the German and the Swede. Within my memory in New England all the lower places in factories, all places of domestic service, were filled by the sons and daughters of American farmers. The Irishmen came over to take their places; but the American farmer's son and daughter did not suffer; they were only elevated to a higher plane. In the increased wealth of the community their share is much greater. The Irishman rose from the bog or the hovel of his native land to the comfort of a New England home and placed his children in a New England school. The Yankee rises from the loom and the spinning-jenny to be the teacher, the skilled laborer in the machine shop, the inventor, the merchant, or the opulent landholder and farmer of the West.

I wish also to read in this connection what Mr. Morton says as his conclusion:

> That they have injuriously interfered with the white people of California, or have done them a serious injury, may well be doubted. The great fact is that there is to-day and always has been a scarcity of labor on the Pacific coast. There is work for all who are there, both white and Mongolian, and the State would undoubtedly develop much more rapidly were there more and cheaper labor. There was much intelligent testimony to the fact that the Chinese by their labor opened up large avenues and demand for white labor. The Chinese performed the lowest kind, while the whites monopolized that of a superior character. This was well stated by Mr. Crocker, a very intelligent witness, largely interested in the Central Pacific and Southern California Railroads. In answer to a question as to what was the effect of Chinese upon white labor, and whether it was to deprive white men of employment, or had that effect at any time, he said: "I think that they

afford white men labor. I think that their presence here affords to white men a more elevated class of labor. As I said before, if you should drive these 75,000 Chinamen off you would take 75,000 white men from an elevated class of work and put them down to doing this low class of labor that the Chinamen are now doing, and instead of elevating you would degrade the white labor to that extent."

Then again:

> For any man to ride through California, from one end of this State to the other, and see the miles upon miles of uncultivated land, and in the mountains millions of acres of timber, and the foothills waiting for some one to go and cultivate them, and then talk about there being too much labor here in the country, is simply nonsense, in my estimation. There is labor for all, and the fact that the Chinamen are here gives an opportunity to white men to go in and cultivate this land where they could not cultivate it otherwise. Other evidence showed that by Chinese labor over 1,000,000 acres of tule lands have been reclaimed. This was work of the hardest and most unhealthy character, requiring them to work for a large part of the time in mud and water; but the lands, when reclaimed, were occupied and cultivated by white men, furnishing a great many homes, and were in fact the richest and most productive in California. They also chiefly performed the work in constructing irrigating canals for farming purposes, and dams and canals for supplying the mines with water, by which a very large extent of country was made exceedingly productive, furnishing homes and employment for thousands of white men, and by which, also, the mines were made profitable, and created a large demand for white labor. The evidence further showed that the railroads, chiefly constructed by these people, were the pioneers in settlement and agriculture; that the settlements followed the railroads; that wherever a railroad was constructed the lands were taken up and converted into farms and homesteads. While there was complaint that the Chinese, by their cheap labor, took it from white people, inquiry failed to show that there was any considerable number of white people in California out of employment, except those who were willfully idle; that there was work, and remunerative work, for all who chose to perform it.

California has a population of 700,000. She can support seventeen million. Will it be claimed that these seventeen million will not be better off by finding there the wealth and the improvements which Chinese labor will prepare for their possession; by finding the railroad built, the swamp drained, the highway smoothed, the harbor dredged?

Will it be maintained that if California could have for nothing what she gets cheaply from Chinese labor, she would not be better off? If the swamp lands had been made prairie lands by nature; if the ravines had been filled and mountains tunneled by nature, so that the road-bed was ready for the rail; if every man, instead of buying shoes from Massachusetts, had a pair left gratis at his door, that the State would not be better off? Is barren land or productive land best for a State? Then surely the laborer who does these things at least cost does most for the community, and gives the people who occupy the State opportunity for better profit in other fields of industry. . . .

The Laws of the Universe

Humanity, capable of infinite depths of degradation, is capable also of infinite heights of excellence. The Chinese, like all other races, has given us its examples of both. To rescue humanity from this degradation is, we are taught to believe, the great object of God's moral government on earth. It is not by injustice, exclusion, caste, but by reverence for the individual soul that we can aid in this consummation. It is not by Chinese policies that China is to be civilized. I believe that the immortal truths of the Declaration of Independence came from the same source with the Golden Rule and the Sermon on the Mount. We can trust Him who promulgated these laws to keep the country safe that obeys them. The laws of the universe have their own sanction. They will not fail. The power that causes the compass to point to the north, that dismisses the star on its pathway through the skies, promising that in a thousand years it shall return again true to its hour, and keeps His word, will vindicate His own moral law. As surely as the path on which our fathers entered a hundred years ago led to safety, to strength, to glory, so surely will the path on which we now propose to enter bring us to shame, to weakness, and to peril.

VIEWPOINT 6B

Chinese Immigrants Should Be Excluded (1882)

James Harvey Slater (1826–1899)

In 1882 Congress debated and passed the Chinese Exclusion Act—legislation restricting Chinese immigration. The act voided the 1868 Burlingame Treaty with China, which had guaranteed unrestricted immigration between the two nations, as well as an 1880 treaty that regulated but did not end Chinese immigration. The following viewpoint is a speech by Senator James Harvey Slater of Oregon in favor of the Chinese Exclusion Act. Slater refutes the arguments of Senator George F. Hoar (see viewpoint 6A) and others who charged that the immigration restriction ran counter to American ideals.

From James Harvey Slater, *Congressional Record*, 47th Cong., 1st sess., 1882, vol. 13, pp. 1635–36.

What reasons does Slater provide for opposing Chinese immigration? How does his comparison of Chinese and blacks differ from that of Hoar? Does Slater's speech indicate significant divisions between eastern and western states?

I am in hearty accord with the promoters of this bill, and trust that it may pass substantially as it came from the hands of the committee. The only fear that I have is that it may not prove as effectual in checking the influx of Chinese laborers as its promoters hope and expect it will. It may turn out after a time that its provisions can be systematically evaded, but this will come not so much from the bill itself as from the provisions of the treaty under which it is drawn, the defect being one difficult to meet with legislative provisions.

Treaty Considerations

The bill is drawn in accord with the provisions of the treaty, and whatever of defects there may prove to be in its provisions when it shall go into operation will have to be referred to the narrowness of the treaty stipulations in conformity with which it is constructed. It cannot be disguised that the treaty of 1880 is so constructed that there is danger that no legislation, however carefully prepared, if kept strictly within its provisions, will be certain to save it from proving to be a snare and a delusion. Under the treaty we may suspend for a limited period the coming of laborers from China to the United States, but the coming of other classes for other purposes is unrestricted, and the rights which they may enjoy are made even greater than they were under the Burlingame treaty. They may come without limit as teachers, professors, traders, and merchants, and when here are to enjoy all the privileges of the citizens and subjects of the most favored nation, and being lawfully within the United States under treaty stipulations may they not change their vocations and become laborers? As citizens and subjects of other nations they would certainly have this right.

Possibly the treaty carries with it the power to extend legislation to the prohibiting of any Chinese other than laborers from engaging in the labor avocations of the country during the suspension of the coming of Chinese laborers, but the difficulty of enforcing such a provision would in my judgment render it of little value. It may be humiliating to confess, but the facts are, our commissioners who negotiated the late Chinese treaty were unequal to their task, and failed to properly accomplish, or even to comprehend, the work assigned to them. And I fear, sir, that we of the Pacific coast will yet regret that we ever consented that this treaty might be finally consummated. But, like drowning men who catch at anything which promises the possibility of escape from peril, we were unwilling to make opposition to this treaty, fearing that nothing better might be obtained in any reasonable time, and also hoping that legislation under its provisions might be so framed as to check the tide of Chinese immigration to our coast until such time as the morbid and unnatural, though prevailing, craze about the universal brotherhood of man might in some degree subside and wiser counsels prevail.

The Right to Control Immigration

What was needed was the assertion authoritatively of our absolute right to control this immigration in our own way and in our own good time—the assertion of our right to terminate Chinese immigration absolutely and unconditionally when and as we please; and above and over all the assertion of our right as a nation to do just what China has always done under the Burlingame treaty as respects citizens of the United States traveling or residing in China, and that is the right to prohibit Chinese residing or traveling in the United States from engaging in any of the labor avocations of the country. That is what was needed and what should have been insisted upon, and if we had had a foreign policy worthy a nation of fifty million people it is what would have been exacted, not as a concession from China but as a right belonging to us as a people and nation and as inhering to our sovereignty.

It is humiliating to an American to read this later treaty and find from its terms and provisions that the United States is placed in the attitude of a recipient of favors from the hands and by the gracious benignity of the imperial Government of China, as if this country was a dependency. By its terms and provisions we are restricted in the exercise of rights which pertain to our Government as a sovereign State and which are important and necessary to the protection of the interests of our own citizens and to the preservation of the very form and substance of our own Government.

Since the promulgation of the Burlingame treaty the subjects of China have come to the United States and passed freely through every part of it. They have traveled upon our stages, steamboats, and railroads; they have gone singly and in small numbers into any and every part of it without molestation and in perfect safety; they have worked in our mines, as servants, as cooks, as common laborers, as mechanics and artisans, and have been allowed to engage in any business they desired to; and, with rare exceptions, have been unmolested, and always found protection when protection was needed. How has it been during all that time with the citizens of the United States in China? Have they been allowed to enter China at any and all points or to engage in any of the labor avocations of the country? No, sir. Only in certain cities have they been permitted to come, and these have been limited in number, and even in those cities our citizens have been restricted to defined and designated limits, and they are not permitted to engage in any of the labor avocations of the country, but are restricted to commercial business, and not even permitted to engage in the internal trade of the country. If they venture out of the prescribed limits for foreigners in the cities where they are permitted to come, or if they venture into the country beyond the distance allowed, they do it at the peril of their lives.

The Burlingame treaty was very unequal in its terms, and in its practical operation it was still more so. The commission sent to negotiate the new treaty seem to have overlooked these inequalities, and yet the agitation which led to their being sent out ought to have been a sufficient notice to them of these matters. Evidently, however, they and the power that sent them on their mission were so fully imbued with that theory of the modern philanthropist which takes to its embrace "all the world and the rest of mankind" without regard "to previous condition of servitude," and makes but little inquiry as to the degree of development reached by its *protegés* in the process of evolution from lower forms, that the most important part of their mission, the assertion of the inherent right of a nation or people to control in its own way the admission into its own territory and among its own people of foreign elements, incongruous with and dangerous to the peace, happiness, and good order of its own community, was overlooked or subordinated to mere idea.

———— • ————

"It will be a serious mistake to allow this tide of immigration to continue without restriction."

———— • ————

The advocates and promoters of this bill are met with the objection that the principles upon which it rests are violative of the right of expatriation which we as a people have so long and so persistently proclaimed. Why, Mr. President [of the Senate], this is strange reasoning; the application of these principles can have no kind of application here. The circumstances under which we have so often asserted the fundamental right of every man to sever his relation with his native country does not and cannot apply to the relation the Chinese immigrant seeks to maintain in this country. We have asserted the right of expatriation in behalf of our adopted citizens when and wherever the governments from whence they came sought to enforce upon them obligations supposed and claimed to exist by reason of their having been born within their jurisdiction. We asserted the principle because we had taken upon ourselves the obligation of giving them protection for their allegiance—correlative obligations assumed when we received them into our political community. Certainly, sir; the Chinaman, according to our theories which we have made the basis of our political structure, has a right to expatriate himself from his native country and abjure the authority of his emperor and government, but does that clothe him with the right to demand admission into the social compact of any other country or community without the consent of such community?

Why, sir, the mere statement of such a proposition carries with it its own refutation. No principle is better settled in international law than that aliens can acquire no other or greater right in or among a people to whom they would attach themselves than such people may or will accord them. The very right to come at all is derived not from the alien himself nor yet from the country whence he comes, but from the people with whom he would form new relations.

The Pursuit of Happiness

Again, sir, we are told that in this legislation we are treading backward and forsaking the principles and traditions upon which our fathers one hundred years ago laid the foundations of government, and the Declaration of Independence is invoked as a sufficient argument and showing of this statement. The right to the pursuit of happiness is asserted as conclusive of the whole question. No one will deny the axiomatic and self-evident truths of the Declaration of Independence respecting human rights, but that they apply in this case may well be denied. The pursuit of happiness is certainly the inalienable right of every human being, but that pursuit must be regulated by human society and by human laws. It might be a great source of happiness to the highwayman to meet the honorable Senator from Massachusetts [Mr. Hoar] upon the highway and forcibly take from his possession his purse. Necessitous hunger and privation might impel to such an act, and the gold or currency that purse might be expected to contain would bring numberless benefits and blessings, not only to the highwayman, but also to those who might be dependent upon him; but the law of society steps in to protect the citizen in his right to go unmolested about his pursuits, and pronounces such acts criminal and affixes severe penalties to their commission.

So it is daily demonstrated in a thousand ways that the pursuit of happiness is circumscribed and limited by the laws and necessities of organized society. What is true of the individual members of a community in this respect is equally true of nations and peoples, and also true of individuals leaving their native land in search of happiness and to better their own condition among another people in another country. They have no right in the pursuit of their own happiness to inflict injury upon the people of other communities. To assert the right of aliens to impose themselves upon or into communities to which they are alien without their consent and to their detriment, is to assert a principle, when carried to its logical consequences, subversive of all human government. Such a principle leads inevitably to anarchy. The law of life and self-preservation is as important and necessary to communities as to individuals, and is as inalienable and inherent in the one case as in the other; and no principle is more firmly imbedded in the ethics of international law than that it is both the right and the duty of the paramount authority in every state, in whatever form that authority may be vested, and however it may be exercised, to protect the state and the people of the state from all and every evil that may threaten its safety or menace the interests, prosperity, or happiness of its people, be they few or many, and herein alone can be found justification for a resort to the arbitrament of war.

Teeming Hordes

Disguise it as we may we cannot longer fail to recognize the fact that western civilization has met the eastern upon the shores of the Pacific. The westward march of the Caucasian has there met the same teeming hordes that generations ago gave a westward direction to his tireless energy by imposing on his east a living wall of Asiatics, impossible to pass or overcome. The Pacific Ocean until recently had proved an impassable barrier and no Mongolian had ever passed to its eastward shore. But recent developments in steamships and the establishment of lines of steam communication between San Francisco and the open ports of China and Japan have practically connected the two continents and bridged the intervening sea. So that for a few dollars a Chinese immigrant can come from any of the ports of China to San Francisco. At first but few came, some returned, and a larger number followed, and in that way the tide of immigrants swelled to considerable proportions. Almost from the first their coming was objected to, and as its effects became more and more apparent this opposition became more and more pronounced, until within the last seven or eight years it has been greatly intensified, and by its universality as well as intensity has served to hold in check and to keep down and diminish the number of Chinese coming to the United States.

From 1850 to 1880 more than 200,000 Chinese landed on the Pacific coast. The census of 1880 shows that there were in that year 105,000 remaining in this country; but persons well informed in the customs and manners of the Chinese affirm that this is far below the correct figures. The smallness of their present numbers as compared to the total population of the country has been strongly contrasted and urged as a reason for discrediting the earnest statements of the people of the Pacific States and Territories that this Chinese population is a menace to good order and good government and the best interest of the people there. But the fact is overlooked that even according to the census there are 75,000 in the State of California, and some ten thousand in the State of Oregon, while the appeal of the Trades Assembly of California, quoted by the honorable Senator from Delaware [Mr. Bayard] on last Friday, estimates, after investigation, the Chinese population of California at 150,000, or 20 per cent, greater than the male whites capable of bearing arms. From this it would seem that the adult Chinese male laboring element in California was very nearly equal to the adult white laboring element. If, however, the census report be taken, then they constitute something like one-half of the male laboring element in that State.

But we are told by the honorable Senator from Massachusetts that the Chinese are the most easily governed race in the world; that every Chinaman in America has four hundred and ninety-nine Americans to control him. But the honorable Senator omitted to state that of the four hundred and ninety-nine Americans four hundred and eighty-seven of them were from one thousand to three thousand miles away from where the evils of Chinese emigration are being felt. Why, sir, in the Pacific States and Territories beyond Utah there are, according to the census reports, one Chinaman to every twelve of the white population, and I have no doubt that if the exact numbers of the Chinese population could be ascertained that the ratio would be one to every eight or ten of the white population. Carry this ratio throughout the United States and there would be a Chinese population of adult male laborers of near 5,000,000 to compete with white labor, to depress and demoralize it by underbidding and bringing it down to starvation prices. Let me bring it a little closer, Mr. President. Massachusetts has a population of 1,758,000. Now let the Senators of that State add to that population 175,000 adult Chinese laborers to compete with and underbid the working classes and they may be able to form some just conceptions of the condition of the poor laboring classes in the Pacific States and Territories. My impression is that there would be a small-sized bedlam in Massachusetts under such a

state of facts. Pennsylvania has 4,282,000 population. I ask her Senators what effect it would have upon the laboring population of the great State to send into it 400,000 able-bodied laboring Chinese to depress the labor market in the struggle and competition that would ensue. The State of New York has a population of over 5,000,000; let the Senators of that State reflect what would be the effect of letting in 500,000 Chinese laborers to compete with their laboring population. If Senators will but reflect upon these facts they can readily comprehend how it is that there is such a wonderful unanimity in sentiment in every locality where the blight of this immigration has been felt; they will no longer be surprised at the steady and growing opposition to that class of immigrants, an opposition so universal that in a secret vote by concealed ballots no more than 800 votes were given favoring this immigration to 150,000 against it.

Aliens from an Alien Culture

Mr. President, the honorable Senator from Massachusetts [Mr. Hoar] asked "What argument can be urged against the Chinese which was not heard against the negro within living memories?" I do not suppose that I can satisfy the honorable Senator of the fallacy of his reasoning, but I may call attention to the utter want of any parallelism between the relations of the negro to the people of the United States and that of the Chinese, who desire to come among us as immigrants. The negro was native to the soil, born and bred within our jurisdiction, speaking our language, having, in a large degree, our civilization, and adhering to our religion. He was with us, if not of us; his ancestors were brought here against their will, and the generation with which we had to deal had no land, clime, or country to call their own except the land in which they were born, and no ties with any people or race except those with whom they had been reared. From necessity they were to remain with and of us; the only question, was what should be the relation.

The Chinese are aliens, born in a foreign land, speak a foreign tongue, owe allegiance to a foreign government, are idolaters in religion, have a different civilization from ours, do not and will not assimilate with our people, come only to get money, and return; and they are inimical to our laws, evade them whenever and wherever they can. So numerous are they at home in their own country that existence among the lower orders of their people is, and has been for centuries, a struggle for existence, and through this ceaseless struggle they have developed into a race of people of such character and physical qualities as to be able to exist and thrive where and under conditions the white man would perish and die out. They bring their customs with them, and persistently adhere to and retain them. Having the protection of our laws they systematically evade and violate them. They persistently and secretly maintain a code of laws and a form of government of their own, which they enforce with seeming certainty and effectiveness. Those who come as immigrants are of the lowest orders of the Chinese population, largely criminal. They bring with them their filth and frightful and nameless diseases and contagions. They bring no families as a general rule, but numbers of their country women are brought for purposes of prostitution, and are bought and sold among themselves as slaves, and our laws and courts are powerless to prevent it. They enhance the cost of government, and increase the burdens of taxation, while they contribute practically nothing in the way of taxes. Their labor is essentially servile, and is demoralizing to every class of white labor with which it comes in competition.

Hordes of Heathens

These, sir, are the people for whom the honorable Senator would open wide the door of admission, or, being open, would refuse to close it, but rather invites these hordes of heathens that swarm like rats in a cellar and live in filth and degradation along the sea-coast of China to come and compete with and degrade American labor, and compares them to the colored people born and reared in America. The negro is thoroughly American, if he is not Caucasian; the Chinese are neither Caucasian nor American, but are alien to our race, customs, religion, and civilization. The bill is not directed against those already here, but against the hordes that threaten to come. The terms of the treaty place those here beyond the reach of legislative enactment, and effort is now being made to bring in a large number of Chinese laborers before legislation can be had. Last year's immigration was over 20,000. This fact sufficiently demonstrates their purpose to come.

Mr. President, thirty-two years ago last September I camped on the banks of the Sacramento River, where the city of that name now stands, then a city of tents. There I first met the Mongolian; from that date to the present time I have been familiar with them. I have seen them singly and in crowds as they passed through the country from one section to another, traveling on foot with their bamboo sticks and baggage; have seen them in the mines by tens and by hundreds, and in the towns and cities, where they congregate at times in great numbers; have seen them on the witness stand, in the courts as litigants and criminals; have prosecuted them and have defended them in the courts. From this experience and observation I have formed the deliberate judgment that it will be a serious mistake to allow this tide of immigration to continue without restriction. After careful and thoughtful study of this whole matter I have settled down in the conviction that they should be prohibited from entering the labor avocations of the country, leaving them the right to come for commercial purposes, for travel or curiosity, as the Burlingame treaty left them.

I hope, Mr. President, the bill will pass substantially as reported.

For Further Reading

George F. Hoar, *Autobiography of Seventy Years*. New York: Charles Scribner's Sons, 1903.

Stuart C. Miller, *The Unwelcome Immigrant*. Berkeley: University of California Press, 1969.

Elmer Clarence Sandmeyer, *The Anti-Chinese Movement in California*. Urbana: University of Illinois Press, 1991.

Alexander Saxton, *The Indispensable Enemy*. Berkeley: University of California Press, 1971.

Henry Shih-shan Tsai, *The Chinese Experience in America*. Bloomington: University of Indiana Press, 1986.

Richard E. Welch, *George Frisbie Hoar and the Half-Breed Republicans*. Cambridge, MA: Harvard University Press, 1971.

Industry, Agriculture, and Social Protest

VIEWPOINT 7A

Concentrations of Wealth Harm America (1883)

Henry George (1839–1897)

Henry George was a social reformer whose prolific writings on American social and economic conditions, especially his 1879 book *Progress and Poverty*, were widely read. George's prescription of a "single tax" on property to replace all other taxes was never enacted by the states or by Congress, but he remained an influential critic of America until his death. In the following selection from his 1883 book *Social Problems*, George condemns the growing inequality between the wealthy few and the impoverished many as one of the harmful developments of America's new industrial age.

What does George consider to be the true sources of the great business fortunes being made around him? How do his views on the attainment of wealth differ from those of Andrew Carnegie, author of the opposing viewpoint? What signs of George's evangelical family upbringing are evident in this viewpoint?

From Henry George, *Social Problems* (New York, 1883).

There is in all the past nothing to compare with the rapid changes now going on in the civilized world. It seems as though in the European race, and in the nineteenth century, man was just beginning to live—just grasping his tools and becoming conscious of his powers. The snail's pace of crawling ages has suddenly become the headlong rush of the locomotive, speeding faster and faster. This rapid progress is primarily in industrial methods and material powers. But industrial changes imply social changes and necessitate political changes. Progressive societies outgrow institutions as children outgrow clothes. Social progress always requires greater intelligence in the management of public affairs; but this the more as progress is rapid and change quicker. . . .

Wealth and Civilization

A civilization which tends to concentrate wealth and power in the hands of a fortunate few, and to make of others mere human machines, must inevitably evolve anarchy and bring destruction. But a civilization is possible in which the poorest could have all the comforts and conveniences now enjoyed by the rich; in which prisons and almshouses would be needless, and charitable societies unthought of. Such a civilization waits only for the social intelligence that will adapt means to ends. Powers that might give plenty to all are already in our hands. Though there is poverty and want, there is, yet, seeming embarrassment from the very excess of wealth-producing forces. "Give us but a market," say manufacturers, "and we will supply goods without end!" "Give us but work!" cry idle men. . . .

The progress of civilization requires that more and more intelligence be devoted to social affairs, and this not the intelligence of the few, but that of the many. We cannot safely leave politics to politicians, or political economy to college professors. The people themselves must think, because the people alone can act.

In a "journal of civilization" a professed teacher declares the saving word for society to be that each shall mind his own business. This is the gospel of selfishness, soothing as soft flutes to those who, having fared well themselves, think everybody should be satisfied. But the salvation of society, the hope for the free, full development of humanity, is in the gospel of brotherhood—the gospel of Christ. Social progress makes the well-being of all more and more the business of each; it binds all closer and closer together in bonds from which none can escape. He who observes the law and the proprieties, and cares for his family, yet takes no interest in the general weal, and gives no thought to those who are trodden under foot, save now and then to bestow alms, is not a true Christian. Nor is he a good citizen. The duty of the citizen is more and harder than this. . . .

There is a suggestive fact that must impress any one who thinks over the history of past eras and preceding civilizations. The great, wealthy and powerful nations have always lost their freedom; it is only in small, poor and isolated communities that Liberty has been maintained. So true is this that the poets have always sung that Liberty loves the rocks and the mountains; that she shrinks from wealth and power and splendor, from the crowded city and the busy mart. . . .

The mere growth of society involves danger of the gradual conversion of government into something independent of and beyond the people, and the gradual seizure of its powers by a ruling class—though not necessarily a class marked off by personal titles and a hereditary status, for, as history shows, personal titles and hereditary status do not accompany the concentration of power, but follow it. The same methods which, in a little town where each knows his neighbor and matters of common interest are under the common eye, enable the citizens freely to govern themselves, may, in a great city, as we have in many cases seen, enable an organized ring of plunderers to gain and hold the government. So, too, as we see in Congress, and even in our State legislatures, the growth of the country and the greater number of interests make the proportion of the votes of a representative, of which his constituents know or care to know, less and less. And so, too, the executive and judicial departments tend constantly to pass beyond the scrutiny of the people.

But to the changes produced by growth are, with us, added the changes brought about by improved industrial methods. The tendency of steam and of machinery is to the division of labor, to the concentration of wealth and power. Workmen are becoming massed by hundreds and thousands in the employ of single individuals and firms; small storekeepers and merchants are becoming the clerks and salesmen of great business houses; we have already corporations whose revenues and pay rolls belittle those of the greatest States. And with this concentration grows the facility of combination among these great business interests. How readily the railroad companies, the coal operators, the steel producers, even the match manufacturers, combine, either to regulate prices or to use the powers of government! The tendency in all branches of industry is to the formation of rings against which the individual is helpless, and which exert their power upon government whenever their interests may thus be served.

It is not merely positively, but negatively, that great aggregations of wealth, whether individual or corporate, tend to corrupt government and take it out of the control of the masses of the people. "Nothing is more timorous than a million dollars—except two million dollars." Great wealth always supports the party in power, no matter how corrupt it may be. It never exerts itself for reform, for it instinctively fears change. It never struggles against misgovernment. When threatened by the holders of political power it does not agitate, nor appeal to the people; it buys them off. It is in this way, no less than by its direct interference, that aggregated wealth corrupts government, and helps to make politics a trade. Our organized lobbies, both legislative and Congressional, rely as much upon the fears as upon the hopes of moneyed interests. When "business" is dull, their resource is to get up a bill which some moneyed interest will pay them to beat. So, too, these large moneyed interests will subscribe to political funds, on the principle of keeping on the right side of those in power, just as the railroad companies deadhead [transport for free] President [Chester A.] Arthur when he goes to Florida to fish.

The more corrupt a government the easier wealth can use it. Where legislation is to be bought, the rich make the laws; where justice is to be purchased, the rich have the ear of the courts. And if, for this reason, great wealth does not absolutely prefer corrupt government to pure government, it becomes none the less a corrupting influence. A community composed of very rich and very poor falls an easy prey to whoever can seize power. The very poor have not spirit and intelligence enough to resist; the very rich have too much at stake

Developments in America

The rise in the United States of monstrous fortunes, the aggregation of enormous wealth in the hands of corporations, necessarily implies the loss by the people of governmental control. Democratic forms may be maintained, but there can be as much tyranny and misgovernment under democratic forms as any other—in fact, they lend themselves most readily to tyranny and misgovernment. Forms count for little. The Romans expelled their kings, and continued to abhor the very name of king. But under the name of Caesars and Imperators, that at first meant no more than our "Boss," they crouched before tyrants more absolute than kings. We have already, under the popular name of "bosses," developed political Caesars in municipalities and states. If this development continues, in time there will come a national boss. We are young; but we are growing. The day may arrive when the "Boss of America" will be to the modern world what Caesar was to the Roman world. This, at least, is certain: Democratic government in more than name can exist only where wealth is distributed with something like equality—where the great mass of citizens are personally free and inde-

pendent, neither fettered by their poverty nor made subject by their wealth. There is, after all, some sense in a property qualification. The man who is dependent on a master for his living is not a free man. To give the suffrage to slaves is only to give votes to their owners. That universal suffrage may add to, instead of decreasing, the political power of wealth we see when mill-owners and mine operators vote their hands. The freedom to earn, without fear or favor, a comfortable living, ought to go with the freedom to vote. Thus alone can a sound basis for republican institutions be secured. How can a man be said to have a country where he has no right to a square inch of soil; where he has nothing but his hands, and, urged by starvation, must bid against his fellows for the privilege of using them? When it comes to voting tramps, some principle has been carried to a ridiculous and dangerous extreme. I have known elections to be decided by the carting of paupers from the almshouse to the polls. But such decisions can scarcely be in the interest of good government.

Beneath all political problems lies the social problem of the distribution of wealth. This our people do not generally recognize, and they listen to quacks who propose to cure the symptoms without touching the disease. "Let us elect good men to office," say the quacks. Yes; let us catch little birds by sprinkling salt on their tails!

It behooves us to look facts in the face. The experiment of popular government in the United States is clearly a failure. Not that it is a failure everywhere and in everything. An experiment of this kind does not have to be fully worked out to be proved a failure. But speaking generally of the whole country, from the Atlantic to the Pacific, and from the Lakes to the Gulf, our government by the people has in large degree become, is in larger degree becoming, government by the strong and unscrupulous.

People Losing Power

The people, of course, continue to vote; but the people are losing their power. Money and organization tell more and more in elections. In some sections bribery has become chronic, and numbers of voters expect regularly to sell their votes. In some sections large employers regularly bulldoze their hands into voting as *they* wish. In municipal, State and Federal politics the power of the "machine" is increasing. In many places it has become so strong that the ordinary citizen has no more influence in the government under which he lives than he would have in China. He is, in reality, not one of the governing classes, but one of the governed. He occasionally, in disgust, votes for "the other man," or "the other party;" but, generally, to find that he has effected only a change of masters, or secured the same masters under different names. And he is beginning to accept the situation, and to leave politics to politicians, as something with which an honest, self-respecting man cannot afford meddle. . . .

As for the great railroad managers, they may well say, "The people be d—d!" When they want the power of the people they buy the people's masters. The map of the United States is colored to show States and Territories. A map of real political powers would ignore State lines. Here would be a big patch representing the domains of Vanderbilt; there Jay Gould's dominions would be brightly marked. In another place would be set off the empire of Stanford and Huntington; in another the newer empire of Henry Villard. The States and parts of States that own the sway of the Pennsylvania Central would be distinguished from those ruled by the Baltimore and Ohio; and so on. In our National Senate, sovereign members of the Union are supposed to be represented; but what are more truly represented are railroad kings and great moneyed interests, though occasionally a mine jobber from Nevada or Colorado, not inimical to the ruling powers, is suffered to buy himself a seat for glory. And the Bench as well as the Senate is being filled with corporation henchmen. A railroad king makes his attorney a judge of last resort, as the great lord used to make his chaplain a bishop. . . .

The people are largely conscious of all this, and there is among the masses much dissatisfaction. But there is a lack of that intelligent interest necessary to adapt political organization to changing conditions. The popular idea of reform seems to be merely a change of men or a change of parties, not a change of system. Political children, we attribute to bad men or wicked parties what really springs from deep general causes. . . .

Can Anyone Be Rich?

The comfortable theory that it is in the nature of things that some should be poor and some should be rich, and that the gross and constantly increasing inequalities in the distribution of wealth imply no fault in our institutions, pervades our literature, and is taught in the press, in the church, in school and in college.

This is a free country, we are told—every man has a vote and every man has a chance. The laborer's son may become President; poor boys of to-day will be millionaires thirty or forty years from now, and the millionaire's grandchildren will probably be poor. What more can be asked? If a man has energy, industry, prudence and foresight, he may win his way to great wealth. If he has not the ability to do this he must not complain of those who have. If some enjoy much and do little, it is because they, or their par-

ents, possessed superior qualities which enabled them to "acquire property" or "make money." If others must work hard and get little, it is because they have not yet got their start, because they are ignorant, shiftless, unwilling to practise that economy necessary for the first accumulation of capital; or because their fathers were wanting in these respects. The inequalities in condition result from the inequalities of human nature, from the difference in the powers and capacities of different men. If one has to toil ten or twelve hours a day for a few hundred dollars a year, while another, doing little or no hard work, gets an income of many thousands, it is because all that the former contributes to the augmentation of the common stock of wealth is little more than the mere force of his muscles. He can expect little more than the animal, because he brings into play little more than animal powers. He is but a private in the ranks of the great army of industry, who has but to stand still or march, as he is bid. The other is the organizer, the general, who guides and wields the whole great machine, who must think, plan and provide; and his larger income is only commensurate with the far higher and rarer powers which he exercises, and the far greater importance of the function he fulfils. Shall not education have its reward, and skill its payment? What incentive would there be to the toil needed to learn to do anything well were great prizes not to be gained by those who learn to excel? It would not merely be gross injustice to refuse a Raphael or a Rubens more than a house-painter, but it would prevent the development of great painters. To destroy inequalities in condition would be to destroy the incentive to progress. To quarrel with them is to quarrel with the laws of nature. We might as well rail against the length of the days or the phases of the moon; complain that there are valleys and mountains; zones of tropical heat and regions of eternal ice. And were we by violent measures to divide wealth equally, we should accomplish nothing but harm; in a little while there would be inequalities as great as before.

This, in substance, is the teaching which we constantly hear. It is accepted by some because it is flattering to their vanity, in accordance with their interests or pleasing to their hope; by others, because it is dinned into their ears. Like all false theories that obtain wide acceptance, it contains much truth. But it is truth isolated from other truth or alloyed with falsehood.

To try to pump out a ship with a hole in her hull would be hopeless; but that is not to say that leaks may not be stopped and ships pumped dry. It is undeniable that, under present conditions, inequalities in fortune would tend to reassert themselves even if arbitrarily leveled for a moment; but that does not prove that the conditions from which this tendency to inequality springs may not be altered. Nor because there are differences in human qualities and powers does it follow that existing inequalities of fortune are thus accounted for. I have seen very fast compositors and very slow compositors, but the fastest I ever saw could not set twice as much type as the slowest, and I doubt if in other trades the variations are greater. Between normal men the difference of a sixth or seventh is a great difference in height—the tallest giant ever known was scarcely more than four times as tall as the smallest dwarf ever known, and I doubt if any good observer will say that the mental differences of men are greater than the physical differences. Yet we already have men hundreds of millions of times richer than other men.

That he who produces should have, that he who saves should enjoy, is consistent with human reason and with the natural order. But existing inequalities of wealth cannot be justified on this ground. As a matter of fact, how many great fortunes can be truthfully said to have been fairly earned? How many of them represent wealth produced by their possessors or those from whom their present possessors derived them? Did there not go to the formation of all of them something more than superior industry and skill? Such qualities may give the first start, but when fortunes begin to roll up into millions there will always be found some element of monopoly, some appropriation of wealth produced by others. Often there is a total absence of superior industry, skill or self-denial, and merely better luck or greater unscrupulousness.

Sources of Great Wealth

An acquaintance of mine died in San Francisco recently, leaving $4,000,000, which will go to heirs to be looked up in England. I have known many men more industrious, more skilful, more temperate than he—men who did not or who will not leave a cent. This man did not get his wealth by his industry, skill or temperance. He no more produced it than did those lucky relations in England who may now do nothing for the rest of their lives. He became rich by getting hold of a piece of land in the early days, which, as San Francisco grew, became very valuable. His wealth represented not what he had earned, but what the monopoly of this bit of the earth's surface enabled him to appropriate of the earnings of others.

A man died in Pittsburgh, the other day, leaving $3,000,000. He may or may not have been particularly industrious, skilful and economical, but it was not by virtue of these qualities that he got so rich. It was because he went to Washington and helped lobby through a bill which, by way of "protecting American workmen against the pauper labor of Europe," gave him the advantage of a sixty-per-cent.

tariff. To the day of his death he was a stanch protectionist, and said free trade would ruin our "infant industries." Evidently the $3,000,000 which he was enabled to lay by from his own little cherub of an "infant industry" did not represent what he had added to production. It was the advantage given him by the tariff that enabled him to scoop it up from other people's earnings.

"Beneath all political problems lies the social problem of the distribution of wealth."

This element of monopoly, of appropriation and spoliation will, when we come to analyze them, be found largely to account for all great fortunes. . . .

Take the great Vanderbilt fortune. The first Vanderbilt was a boatman who earned money by hard work and saved it. But it was not working and saving that enabled him to leave such an enormous fortune. It was spoliation and monopoly. As soon as he got money enough he used it as a club to extort from others their earnings. He ran off opposition lines and monopolized routes of steamboat travel. Then he went into railroads, pursuing the same tactics. The Vanderbilt fortune no more comes from working and saving than did the fortune that Captain Kidd buried.

Or take the great Gould fortune. Mr. Gould might have got his first little start by superior industry and superior self-denial. But it is not that which has made him the master of a hundred millions. It was by wrecking railroads, buying judges, corrupting legislatures, getting up rings and pools and combinations to raise or depress stock values and transportation rates.

So, likewise, of the great fortunes which the Pacific railroads have created. They have been made by lobbying through profligate donations of lands, bonds and subsidies, by the operations of Crédit Mobilier and Contract and Finance Companies, by monopolizing and gouging. And so of fortunes made by such combinations as the Standard Oil Company, the Bessemer Steel Ring, the Whisky Tax Ring, the Lucifer Match Ring, and the various rings for the "protection of the American workman from the pauper labor of Europe."

Or take the fortunes made out of successful patents. Like that element in so many fortunes that comes from the increased value of land, these result from monopoly, pure and simple. And though I am not now discussing the expediency of patent laws, it may be observed, in passing, that in the vast majority of cases the men who make fortunes out of patents are not the men who make the inventions.

Through all great fortunes, and, in fact, through nearly all acquisitions that in these days can fairly be termed fortunes, these elements of monopoly, of spoliation, of gambling run. The head of one of the largest manufacturing firms in the United States said to me recently, "It is not on our ordinary business that we make our money; it is where we can get a monopoly." And this, I think, is generally true.

The Evils of Monopolists

Consider the important part in building up fortunes which the increase of land values has had, and is having, in the United States. This is, of course, monopoly, pure and simple. When land increases in value it does not mean that its owner has added to the general wealth. The owner may never have seen the land or done aught to improve it. He may, and often does, live in a distant city or in another country. Increase of land values simply means that the owners, by virtue of their appropriation of something that existed before man was, have the power of taking a larger share of the wealth produced by other people's labor. Consider how much the monopolies created and the advantages given to the unscrupulous by the tariff and by our system of internal taxation—how much the railroad (a business in its nature a monopoly), telegraph, gas, water and other similar monopolies, have done to concentrate wealth; how special rates, pools, combinations, corners, stock-watering and stock-gambling, the destructive use of wealth in driving off or buying off opposition which the public must finally pay for, and many other things which these will suggest, have operated to build up large fortunes, and it will at least appear that the unequal distribution of wealth is due in great measure to sheer spoliation; that the reason why those who work hard get so little, while so many who work little get so much, is, in very large measure, that the earnings of the one class are, in one way or another, filched away from them to swell the incomes of the other.

That individuals are constantly making their way from the ranks of those who get less than their earnings to the ranks of those who get more than their earnings, no more proves this state of things right than the fact that merchant sailors were constantly becoming pirates and participating in the profits of piracy, would prove that piracy was right and that no effort should be made to suppress it.

I am not denouncing the rich, nor seeking, by speaking of these things, to excite envy and hatred; but if we would get a clear understanding of social problems, we must recognize the fact that it is due to monopolies which we permit and create, to advantages which we give one man over another, to methods of extortion sanctioned by law and by public opinion, that some men are enabled to get so enormously rich while others remain so miserably poor. If we look around us and note the elements of monopoly, extortion and spoliation which go to the building up of all, or nearly all, fortunes, we see on the one hand how disingenuous are those who preach to us that there is nothing wrong in social relations and that the inequalities in the distribution of wealth spring from the inequalities of human nature; and on the other hand, we see how wild are those who talk as though capital were a public enemy, and propose plans for arbitrarily restricting the acquisition of wealth. Capital is a good; the capitalist is a helper, if he is not also a monopolist. We can safely let any one get as rich as he can if he will not despoil others in doing so.

There are deep wrongs in the present constitution of society, but they are not wrongs inherent in the constitution of man nor in those social laws which are as truly the laws of the Creator as are the laws of the physical universe. They are wrongs resulting from bad adjustments which it is within our power to amend. The ideal social state is not that in which each gets an equal amount of wealth, but in which each gets in proportion to his contribution to the general stock. And in such a social state there would not be less incentive to exertion than now; there would be far more incentive. Men will be more industrious and more moral, better workmen and better citizens, if each takes his earnings and carries them home to his family, than where they put their earnings in a "pot" and gamble for them until some have far more than they could have earned, and others have little or nothing.

VIEWPOINT 7B

Concentrations of Wealth Help America (1889)
Andrew Carnegie (1835–1919)

Andrew Carnegie was one of the leading industrialists of the Gilded Age. His business ventures, first in railroads and subsequently in steel, enabled this immigrant from a poor Scottish family to amass a fortune estimated at one point to be over half a billion dollars. Carnegie, unlike most of his business peers, was a frequent commentator on economic and social issues; he contributed articles to various journals and wrote several books. One of the most famous of his articles first appeared in the June 1889 issue of the

From Andrew Carnegie, "Wealth," *North American Review*, June 1889.

North American Review. In the essay, portions of which appear below, Carnegie defends the creation of concentrations of wealth as an inevitable and necessary part of industrial progress, and prescribes how affluent people should use their riches. The essay has become popularly known as "The Gospel of Wealth."

Why does Carnegie consider concentrations of wealth inevitable? How does Carnegie distinguish between mere charity and what he called "scientific philanthropy"? Do Carnegie and Henry George, author of the opposing viewpoint, have totally incompatible views on the industrialization of America? Why might Carnegie's opinions expressed here have drawn criticism from both the right and the left of the political spectrum?

The problem of our age is the proper administration of wealth, that the ties of brotherhood may still bind together the rich and poor in harmonious relationship. The conditions of human life have not only been changed, but revolutionized, within the past few hundred years. In former days there was little difference between the dwelling, dress, food, and environment of the chief and those of his retainers. The Indians are today where civilized man then was. When visiting the Sioux, I was led to the wigwam of the chief. It was like the others in external appearance, and even within the difference was trifling between it and those of the poorest of his braves. The contrast between the palace of the millionaire and the cottage of the laborer with us today measures the change which has come with civilization. This change, however, is not to be deplored, but welcomed as highly beneficial. It is well, nay, essential, for the progress of the race that the houses of some should be homes for all that is highest and best in literature and the arts, and for all the refinements of civilization, rather than that none should be so. Much better this great irregularity than universal squalor. Without wealth there can be no Maecenas [a generous patron of the arts]. The "good old times" were not good old times. Neither master nor servant was as well situated then as today. A relapse to old conditions would be disastrous to both—not the least so to him who serves—and would sweep away civilization with it. But whether the change be for good or ill, it is upon us, beyond our power to alter, and, therefore, to be accepted and made the best of. It is a waste of time to criticize the inevitable.

It is easy to see how the change has come. One illustration will serve for almost every phase of the cause. In the manufacture of products we have the whole story. It applies to all combinations of human industry, as stimulated and enlarged by the inventions of this scientific age. Formerly, articles were manufactured at the domestic hearth, or in small shops which formed part of the household. The master and his apprentices worked side by side, the latter living with the master, and therefore subject to the same conditions. When these apprentices rose to be masters, there was little or no change in their mode of life, and they, in turn, educated succeeding apprentices in the same routine. There was, substantially, social equality, and even political equality, for those engaged in industrial pursuits had then little or no voice in the State.

The inevitable result of such a mode of manufacture was crude articles at high prices. Today the world obtains commodities of excellent quality at prices which even the preceding generation would have deemed incredible. In the commercial world similar causes have produced similar results, and the race is benefited thereby. The poor enjoy what the rich could not before afford. What were the luxuries have become the necessaries of life. The laborer has now more comforts than the farmer had a few generations ago. The farmer has more luxuries than the landlord had, and is more richly clad and better housed. The landlord has books and pictures rarer and appointments more artistic than the king could then obtain.

The price we pay for this salutary change is, no doubt, great. We assemble thousands of operatives in the factory, and in the mine, of whom the employer can know little or nothing, and to whom he is little better than a myth. All intercourse between them is at an end. Rigid castes are formed, and, as usual, mutual ignorance breeds mutual distrust. Each caste is without sympathy with the other, and ready to credit anything disparaging in regard to it. Under the law of competition, the employer of thousands is forced into the strictest economies, among which the rates paid to labor figure prominently, and often there is friction between the employer and the employed, between capital and labor, between rich and poor. Human society loses homogeneity.

Concentrations of Wealth Are Essential

The price which society pays for the law of competition, like the price it pays for cheap comforts and luxuries, is also great; but the advantages of this law are also greater still than its cost—for it is to this law that we owe our wonderful material development, which brings improved conditions in its train. But, whether the law be benign or not, we must say of it, as we say of the change in the conditions of men to which we have referred: It is here; we cannot evade it; no substitutes for it have been found; and while the law may be sometimes hard for the individual, it is best for the race, because it insures the survival of the fittest in every department. We accept and welcome, therefore, as conditions to which we must accommodate ourselves, great inequality of environment; the concentration of business, industrial and commercial, in the hands of a few; and the law of competition between these, as being not only beneficial, but essential to the future progress of the race. Having accepted these, it follows that there must be great scope for the exercise of special ability in the merchant and in the manufacturer who has to conduct affairs upon a great scale. That this talent for organization and management is rare among men is proved by the fact that it invariably secures enormous rewards for its possessor, no matter where or under what laws or conditions. The experienced in affairs always rate the MAN whose services can be obtained as a partner as not only the first consideration, but such as render the question of his capital scarcely worth considering: for able men soon create capital; in the hands of those without the special talent required, capital soon takes wings. Such men become interested in firms or corporations using millions; and, estimating only simple interest to be made upon the capital invested, it is inevitable that their income must exceed their expenditure and that they must, therefore, accumulate wealth. Nor is there any middle ground which such men can occupy, because the great manufacturing or commercial concern which does not earn at least interest upon its capital soon becomes bankrupt. It must either go forward or fall behind; to stand still is impossible. It is a condition essential to its successful operation that it should be thus far profitable, and even that, in addition to interest on capital, it should make profit. It is a law, as certain as any of the others named, that men possessed of this peculiar talent for affairs, under the free play of economic forces must, of necessity, soon be in receipt of more revenue than can be judiciously expended upon themselves, and this law is as beneficial for the race as the others.

Objections to the foundations upon which society is based are not in order, because the condition of the race is better with these than it has been with any other which has been tried. Of the effect of any new substitutes proposed we cannot be sure. The Socialist or Anarchist who seeks to overturn present conditions is to be regarded as attacking the foundation upon which civilization itself rests, for civilization took its start from the day when the capable, industrious workman said to his incompetent and lazy fellow, "If thou dost not sow, thou shalt not reap," and thus ended primitive Communism by separating the drones from the bees. One who studies this subject will soon be brought face to face with the conclusion that upon the sacredness of property civilization itself depends—the right of the laborer to his hundred dollars in the savings-bank, and equally the legal right of the millionaire to his millions. Every man must be allowed "to sit under his own vine and fig-tree, with none to make afraid," if human society is to advance, or even to remain so far advanced as it is. To those who propose to substitute Communism for this intense Individualism, the answer therefore is: The race has tried that. All progress from that barbarous day to the present time has resulted from its displacement. Not evil, but good, has come to the race from the accumulation of wealth by those who have had the ability and energy to produce it. But even if we admit for a moment that it might be better for the race to discard its present foundation, Individualism—that it is a nobler ideal that man should labor, not for himself alone, but in and for a brotherhood of his fellows, and share with them all in common, realizing Swedenborg's idea of heaven, where, as he says, the angels derive their happiness, not from laboring for self, but for each other—even admit all this, and a sufficient answer is, This is not evolution, but revolution. It necessitates the changing of human nature itself—a work of eons, even if it were good to change it, which we cannot know.

---•---

"Not evil, but good, has come to the race from the accumulation of wealth by those who have had the ability and energy to produce it."

---•---

It is not practicable in our day or in our age. Even if desirable theoretically, it belongs to another and long-succeeding sociological stratum. Our duty is with what is practicable now—with the next step possible in our day and generation. It is criminal to waste our energies in endeavoring to uproot, when all we can profitably accomplish is to bend the universal tree of humanity a little in the direction most favorable to the production of good fruit under existing circumstances. We might as well urge the destruction of the highest existing type of man because he failed to reach our ideal as to favor the destruction of Individualism, Private Property, the Law of Accumulation of Wealth, and the Law of Competition; for these are the highest result of human experience, the soil in which society, so far, has produced the best fruit. Unequally or unjustly, perhaps, as these laws sometimes operate, and imperfect as they appear to the Idealist, they are, nevertheless, like the highest type of man, the best and most valuable of all that humanity has yet accomplished.

We start, then, with a condition of affairs under

which the best interests of the race are promoted, but which inevitably gives wealth to the few. Thus far, accepting conditions as they exist, the situation can be surveyed and pronounced good. The question then arises—and if the foregoing be correct, it is the only question with which we have to deal—What is the proper mode of administering wealth after the laws upon which civilization is founded have thrown it into the hands of the few? And it is of this great question that I believe I offer the true solution. It will be understood that fortunes are here spoken of, not moderate sums saved by many years of effort, the returns from which are required for the comfortable maintenance and education of families. This is not wealth, but only competence, which it should be the aim of all to acquire, and which it is for the best interests of society should be acquired.

Disposing of Surplus Wealth

There are but three modes in which surplus wealth can be disposed of. It can be left to the families of the decedents; or it can be bequeathed for public purposes; or, finally, it can be administered by its possessors during their lives. Under the first and second modes most of the wealth of the world that has reached the few has hitherto been applied. Let us in turn consider each of these modes. The first is the most injudicious. In monarchical countries, the estates and the greatest portion of the wealth are left to the first son, that the vanity of the parent may be gratified by the thought that his name and title are to descend unimpaired to succeeding generations. The condition of this class in Europe today teaches the failure of such hopes or ambitions. The successors have become impoverished through their follies, or from the fall in the value of land. Even in Great Britain the strict law of entail has been found inadequate to maintain an hereditary class. Its soil is rapidly passing into the hands of the stranger. Under republican institutions the division of property among the children is much fairer; but the question which forces itself upon thoughtful men in all lands is, Why should men leave great fortunes to their children? If this is done from affection, is it not misguided affection? Observation teaches that, generally speaking, it is not well for the children that they should be so burdened. Neither is it well for the State. Beyond providing for the wife and daughters moderate sources of income, and very moderate allowances indeed, if any, for the sons, men may well hesitate; for it is no longer questionable that great sums bequeathed often work more for the injury than for the good of the recipients. Wise men will soon conclude that, for the best interests of the members of their families, and of the State, such bequests are an improper use of their means.

It is not suggested that men who have failed to educate their sons to earn a livelihood shall cast them adrift in poverty. If any man has seen fit to rear his sons with a view to their living idle lives, or, what is highly commendable, has instilled in them the sentiment that they are in a position to labor for public ends without reference to pecuniary considerations, then, of course, the duty of the parent is to see that such are provided for in moderation. There are instances of millionaires' sons unspoiled by wealth, who, being rich, still perform great services to the community. Such are the very salt of the earth, as valuable as, unfortunately, they are rare. It is not the exception, however, but the rule, that men must regard; and, looking at the usual result of enormous sums conferred upon legatees, the thoughtful man must shortly say, "I would as soon leave to my son a curse as the almighty dollar," and admit to himself that it is not the welfare of the children, but family pride, which inspires these legacies.

As to the second mode, that of leaving wealth at death for public uses, it may be said that this is only a means for the disposal of wealth, provided a man is content to wait until he is dead before he becomes of much good in the world. Knowledge of the results of legacies bequeathed is not calculated to inspire the brightest hopes of much posthumous good being accomplished by them. The cases are not few in which the real object sought by the testator is not attained, nor are they few in which his real wishes are thwarted. In many cases the bequests are so used as to become only monuments of his folly. It is well to remember that it requires the exercise of not less ability than that which acquired it, to use wealth so as to be really beneficial to the community. Besides this, it may fairly be said that no man is to be extolled for doing what he cannot help doing, nor is he to be thanked by the community to which he only leaves wealth at death. Men who leave vast sums in this way may fairly be thought men who would not have left it at all had they been able to take it with them. The memories of such cannot be held in grateful remembrance, for there is no grace in their gifts. It is not to be wondered at that such bequests seem so generally to lack the blessing.

The growing disposition to tax more and more heavily large estates left at death is a cheering indication of the growth of a salutary change in public opinion. The State of Pennsylvania now takes—subject to some exceptions—one tenth of the property left by its citizens. The budget presented in the British Parliament the other day proposes to increase the death duties; and, most significant of all, the new tax is to be a graduated one. Of all forms of taxation this seems the wisest. Men who continue hoarding great sums all their lives, the proper use of which for public ends would work good to the community from which it chiefly came, should be made to feel that the community, in the form of the State, cannot thus be deprived of its proper share. By taxing estates heavily at death the State marks its condemnation of the selfish millionaire's unworthy life. . . .

The Solution

There remains, then, only one mode of using great fortunes; but in this we have the true antidote for the temporary unequal distribution of wealth, the reconciliation of the rich and the poor—a reign of harmony, another ideal, differing, indeed, from that of the Communist in requiring only the further evolution of existing conditions, not the total overthrow of our civilization. It is founded upon the present most intense Individualism, and the race is prepared to put it in practice by degrees whenever it pleases. Under its sway we shall have an ideal State, in which the surplus wealth of the few will become, in the best sense, the property of the many, because administered for the common good; and this wealth, passing through the hands of the few, can be made a much more potent force for the elevation of our race than if distributed in small sums to the people themselves. Even the poorest can be made to see this, and to agree that great sums gathered by some of their fellow-citizens and spent for public purposes, from which the masses reap the principal benefit, are more valuable to them than if scattered among themselves in trifling amounts through the course of many years.

If we consider the results which flow from the Cooper Institute [an adult education institute founded by industrialist and philanthropist Peter Cooper], for instance, to the best portion of the race in New York not possessed of means, and compare these with those which would have ensued for the good of the masses from an equal sum distributed by Mr. Cooper in his lifetime in the form of wages, which is the highest form of distribution, being for work done and not for charity, we can form some estimate of the possibilities for the improvement of the race which lie embedded in the present law of the accumulation of wealth. Much of this sum, if distributed in small quantities among the people, would have been wasted in the indulgence of appetite, some of it in excess, and it may be doubted whether even the part put to the best use, that of adding to the comforts of the home, would have yielded results for the race, as a race, at all comparable to those which are flowing and are to flow from the Cooper Institute from generation to generation. Let the advocate of violent or radical change ponder well this thought. . . .

This, then, is held to be the duty of the man of wealth: To set an example of modest, unostentatious living, shunning display or extravagance; to provide moderately for the legitimate wants of those dependent upon him; and, after doing so, to consider all surplus revenues which come to him simply as trust funds, which he is called upon to administer, and strictly bound as a matter of duty to administer in the manner which, in his judgment, is best calculated to produce the most beneficial results for the community—the man of wealth thus becoming the mere trustee and agent for his poorer brethren, bringing to their service his superior wisdom, experience, and ability to administer, doing for them better than they would or could do for themselves. . . .

The best uses to which surplus wealth can be put have already been indicated. Those who would administer wisely must, indeed, be wise; for one of the serious obstacles to the improvement of our race is indiscriminate charity. It were better for mankind that the millions of the rich were thrown into the sea than so spent as to encourage the slothful, the drunken, the unworthy. Of every thousand dollars spent in so-called charity today, it is probable that nine hundred and fifty dollars is unwisely spent—so spent, indeed, as to produce the very evils which it hopes to mitigate or cure. . . .

In bestowing charity, the main consideration should be to help those who will help themselves; to provide part of the means by which those who desire to improve may do so; to give those who desire to rise the aids by which they may rise; to assist, but rarely or never to do all. Neither the individual nor the race is improved by almsgiving. Those worthy of assistance, except in rare cases, seldom require assistance. The really valuable men of the race never do, except in case of accident or sudden change. Every one has, of course, cases of individuals brought to his own knowledge where temporary assistance can do genuine good, and these he will not overlook. But the amount which can be wisely given by the individual for individuals is necessarily limited by his lack of knowledge of the circumstances connected with each. He is the only true reformer who is as careful and as anxious not to aid the unworthy as he is to aid the worthy, and, perhaps, even more so, for in almsgiving more injury is probably done by rewarding vice than by relieving virtue.

The rich man is thus almost restricted to following the examples of Peter Cooper, Enoch Pratt of Baltimore, . . . and others, who know that the best means of benefiting the community is to place within its reach the ladders upon which the aspiring can rise—free libraries, parks, and means of recreation, by which men are helped in body and mind; works of art, certain to give pleasure and improve the public taste; and public institutions of various kinds, which will improve the general condition of the people; in this manner returning their surplus wealth to the mass of their fellows in the forms best calculated to do them lasting good.

Thus is the problem of rich and poor to be solved. The laws of accumulation will be left free, the laws of distribution free. Individualism will continue, but the millionaire will be but a trustee for the poor, intrusted for a season with a great part of the increased wealth of the community, for administering it for the community far better than it could or would have done for itself. The best minds will thus have reached a stage in the development of the race in which it is clearly seen that there is no mode of disposing of surplus wealth creditable to thoughtful and earnest men into whose hands it flows, save by using it year by year for the general good. This day already dawns. Men may die without incurring the pity of their fellows, still sharers in great business enterprises from which their capital cannot be or has not been withdrawn, and which is left chiefly at death for public uses; yet the day is not far distant when the man who dies leaving behind him millions of available wealth, which was free for him to administer during life, will pass away "unwept, unhonored, and unsung," no matter to what uses he leaves the dross which he cannot take with him. Of such as these the public verdict will then be "The man who dies thus rich dies disgraced."

Such, in my opinion, is the true gospel concerning wealth, obedience to which is destined some day to solve the problem of the rich and the poor, and to bring "Peace on earth, among men good will."

For Further Reading

Samuel P. Hays, *The Response to Industrialism*. Chicago: University of Chicago Press, 1957.

Harold C. Livesay, *Andrew Carnegie and the Rise of Big Business*. Boston: Little, Brown, 1975.

John L. Thomas, *Alternative America: Henry George, Edward Bellamy, Henry Demarest Lloyd and the Adversary Tradition*. Cambridge, MA: Belknap Press, 1983.

John Ord Tipple, *Andrew Carnegie/Henry George: The Problems of Progress*. Cleveland: H. Allen, 1960.

Joseph Frazier Wall, ed., *The Andrew Carnegie Reader*. Pittsburgh: University of Pittsburgh Press, 1992.

VIEWPOINT 8A

The Organizing of Labor into Unions Is Dangerous (1886)

Henry Clews (1834–1923)

Henry Clews was a leading financier and investor during and after the Civil War, and served as an economic adviser to President Ulysses S. Grant. In the following viewpoint, taken from an article originally published in the June 1886 issue of the *North American Review*, Clews denounces what he sees as a clear danger to America—the growth of unionism in the American labor force. He specifically attacks the Knights of Labor, the leading U.S. national organization of workers during the 1880s. He cites a May 1886 general strike that was held in Chicago (the strike ended in violence with fatalities suffered by both police and strikers) as an example of the problems unions create.

What individual rights does Clews emphasize? What significance does Clews see in the number of immigrants entering America? Why does he believe that laborers have "no ground for complaint"?

———————

T he Knights of Labor have undertaken to test, upon a large scale, the application of compulsion as a means of enforcing their demands. The point to be determined is whether capital or labor shall, in future, determine the terms upon which the invested resources of the nation are to be employed.

To the employer, it is a question whether his individual rights as to the control of his property shall be so far overborne as to not only deprive him of his freedom but also expose him to interferences seriously impairing the value of his capital. To the employees, it is a question whether, by the force of coercion, they can wrest, to their own profit, powers and control which, in every civilized community, are secured as the most sacred and inalienable rights of the employer.

This issue is so absolutely revolutionary of the normal relations between labor and capital, that it has naturally produced a partial paralysis of business, especially among industries whose operations involve contracts extending into the future. There has been at no time any serious apprehension that such an utterly anarchical movement could succeed so long as American citizens have a clear perception of their rights and their true interests; but it has been distinctly perceived that this war could not fail to create a divided if not hostile feeling between the two great classes of society; that it must hold in check not only a large extent of ordinary business operations but also the undertaking of those new enterprises which contribute to our national progress, and that the commercial markets must be subjected to serious embarrassments.

From the nature of the case, however, this labor disease must soon end one way or another; and there is not much difficulty in foreseeing what its termination will be. The demands of the Knights and their sympa-

Henry Clews, "The Folly of Organized Labor," *North American Review*, June 1886.

thizers, whether openly expressed or temporarily concealed, are so utterly revolutionary of the inalienable rights of the citizen and so completely subversive of social order that the whole community has come to a firm conclusion that these pretensions must be resisted to the last extremity of endurance and authority; and that the present is the best opportunity for meeting the issue firmly and upon its merits.

"[Labor organizations] stand discredited and distrusted before the community at large as impracticable, unjust, and reckless."

The organizations have sacrificed the sympathy which lately was entertained for them on account of inequities existing in certain employments; they stand discredited and distrusted before the community at large as impracticable, unjust, and reckless; and, occupying this attitude before the public, their cause is gone and their organization doomed to failure. They have opened the floodgates to the immigration of foreign labor, which is already pouring in by the thousands; and they have set a premium on nonunion labor, which will be more sought for than ever, and will not be slow to secure superior earnings by making arrangements with employers upon such terms and for such hours as may best suit their interests. Thus, one great advantage will incidentally come out of this crisis beneficial to the workingman, who, by standing aloof from the dead-level system of the unions, will be enabled to earn according to his capacity and thereby maintain his chances for rising from the rank of the employee to that of the employer.

This result cannot be long delayed; because not only is loss and suffering following close upon the heels of the strikers, but the imprudences of their leaders are breeding dissatisfaction among the rank and file of the organizations, which, if much further protracted, will gravely threaten their cohesion. It is by no means certain that we may not see a yet further spread of strikes, and possibly with even worse forms of violence than we have yet witnessed; but, so long as a way to the end is seen, with a chance of that end demonstrating to the organizations that their aspirations to control capital are impossible dreams, the temporary evils will be borne with equanimity. The coolness with which the past phases of the strikes have been endured shows that the steady judgment of our people may be trusted to keep them calm under any further disturbance that may arise.

It is quite evident that the backbone of the strike is broken and that the worst is past, and that a general recovery of trade will assert itself, more or less, in spite of whatever obstacles may be raised by the labor organizations.

The labor movement inaugurated as a stupendous undertaking and announced to come off on the 1st of May, now past, has been a signal failure. The cause of justice and peace has achieved for itself new prestige sufficient to give it longevity, for the reason that the strike movement has been deprived of justification and right of existence. . . .

The timely and forcible action of Mayor Harrison, of Chicago, will put dynamiters and rioters where they belong, and thus divide the sheep from the goats in a very short time. If officials would sink political bias, the country would soon be rid of lawbreakers and disturbers of the peace. As this plan has now been adopted, it will be far-reaching in its effect, and stop mob gatherings, riotous speechmaking, and other such bad incentives which recently have been so conspicuous in Chicago, Milwaukee, St. Louis, and elsewhere. The laboring classes, who are parties to the strike, will now have an opportunity to retire to their homes, where there will be more safety than in the streets—which will bring to them reflection; they will then soon become satisfied that they are the aggrieved parties; and the not-unlikely result will be their turning upon the leaders who have deceived them.

Labor and Immigration

There have been numerous vacancies created by the strikers voluntarily resigning. There has been no difficulty in filling these vacancies by those that are equally capable, if not more so, from other countries flocking to our shores. The steam ferry which connects this country and Europe has demonstrated this by the steamer that arrived in six days and ten hours' time from European shores to our own. As the interval between the downtrodden and oppressed operatives of the Old World and America is thus reduced to hours, Europe will quickly send to us all the labor we need to meet the emergency. Mrs. Gray, the Third Avenue Railroad Company, and the Missouri Pacific are the generals that have won the victory. Strikes may have been justifiable in other nations but they are not justifiable in our country, and there is where the mistake was in organizing such a movement. The Almighty has made this country for the oppressed of other nations, and therefore this is the land of refuge for the oppressed, and the hand of the laboring man should not be raised against it.

The laboring man in this bounteous and hospitable country has no ground for complaint. His vote is potential and he is elevated thereby to the position of man. Elsewhere he is a creature of circumstance, which is that of abject depression. Under the government of this nation, the effort is to elevate the standard of the human race and not to degrade it. In all other nations it is the reverse. What, therefore, has the laborer to complain of in America? By inciting strikes and encouraging discontent, he stands in the way of the elevation of his race and of mankind.

The tide of emigration to this country, now so large, makes peaceful strikes perfectly harmless in themselves, because the places of those who vacate good situations are easily filled by the newcomers. When disturbances occur under the cloak of strikes, it is a different matter, as law and order are then set at defiance. The recent disturbances in Chicago, which resulted in the assassination of a number of valiant policemen through some cowardly Polish nihilist firing a bomb of dynamite in their midst, was the worst thing that could have been done for the cause of the present labor agitation, as it alienates all sympathy from them. It is much to the credit, however, of Americans and Irishmen that, during the recent uprising of the labor classes, none of them have taken part in any violent measures whatsoever, nor have they shown any sympathy with such a policy.

If the labor troubles are to be regarded as only a transient interruption of the course of events, it is next to be asked: What may be anticipated when those obstructions disappear? We have still our magnificent country, with all the resources that have made it so prosperous and so progressive beyond the record of all nations. There is no abatement of our past ratio of increase of population; no limitation of the new sources of wealth awaiting development; no diminution of the means necessary to the utilization of the unbounded riches of the soil, the mine, and the forest. Our inventive genius has suffered no eclipse. In the practical application of what may be called the commercial sciences, we retain our lead of the world. As pioneers of new sources of wealth, we are producing greater results than all the combined new colonizing efforts which have recently excited the ambitions of European governments. To the overcrowded populations of the Old World, the United States still presents attractions superior to those of any other country; as is evidenced by the recent sudden revival of emigration from Great Britain and the Continent to our shores.

VIEWPOINT 8B

Labor Unions Are Essential (1894)

Samuel Gompers (1850–1924)

One of America's most prominent labor leaders was Samuel Gompers, who cofounded the American Federation of Labor in 1886 and served as the AFL's

president almost continuously thereafter until his death. The following viewpoint is taken from an 1894 open letter by Gompers to Peter Grosscup, a judge in the U.S. District Court of Illinois. During a strike against the Pullman Company in 1894, Grosscup had presided over the indictment of American Railway Union president Eugene V. Debs for violating a court injunction against strikes (such injunctions were frequently used by the courts to stifle labor activities), and in his charge to the jury made the then-common argument that union organizing constituted an illegal conspiracy. Gompers in the viewpoint below defends the right and necessity of laborers to organize and bargain collectively.

How have changes in industrial technology affected the plight of laborers, according to Gompers? What might Gompers find most objectionable about the arguments of Henry Clews, author of the opposing viewpoint? Is Gompers for or against laissez-faire economics, given his comments on trusts? What role does Gompers see for the government in helping the working class?

Y ou say that, as you stated in your charge to the grand jury, you believe in labor organizations within such lawful and reasonable limits as will make them a service to the laboring man and not a menace to the lawful institutions of the country. I have had the pleasure of reading your charge to the grand jury, and have only partially been able to discover how far you believe in labor organizations.

What Workers Can Discuss

You would certainly have no objection officially or personally to workingmen organizing, and in their meetings discuss perhaps "the origin of man," benignly smiling upon each other and declaring that all existing things are right, going to their wretched homes to find some freedom in sleep from gnawing hunger. You would have them extol the virtues of monopolists and wreckers of the people's welfare. You would not have them consider seriously the fact that more than 2 million of their fellows are unemployed, and though willing and able, cannot find the opportunity to work in order that they may sustain themselves, their wives, and their children. You would not have them consider seriously the fact that [George] Pullman who has grown so rich from the toil of his workmen that he can riot in luxury, while he heartlessly turns these very workmen out of their tenements into the streets and leave to the tender mercies of corporate greed. Nor would you have them ponder upon the hundreds of other Pullmans

From a letter of Samuel Gompers, reprinted in the *American Federationist*, vol. 1., September 1894.

of different names.

You know, or ought to know, that the introduction of machinery is turning into idleness thousands faster than new industries are founded, and yet, machinery certainly should not be either destroyed or hampered in its full development. The laborer is a man, he is made warm by the same sun and made cold—yes, colder—by the same winter as you are. He has a heart and brain, and feels and knows the human and paternal instinct for those depending upon him as keenly as do you.

What shall the workers do? Sit idly by and see the vast resources of nature and the human mind be utilized and monopolized for the benefit of the comparative few? No. The laborers must learn to think and act, and soon, too, that only by the power of organization and common concert of action can either their manhood be maintained, their rights to life (work to sustain it) be recognized, and liberty and rights secured.

Since you say that you favor labor organizations within certain limits, will you kindly give to thousands of your anxious fellow citizens what you believe the workers could and should do in their organizations to solve this great problem? Not what they should not do. You have told us that.

The National Wealth

I am not one of those who regards the entire past as a failure. I recognize the progress made and the improved conditions of which nearly the entire civilized world are the beneficiaries. I ask you to explain, however, that if the wealth of the whole world is, as you say, "preeminently and beneficially the nation's wealth," how is it that thousands of able-bodied, willing, earnest men and women are suffering the pangs of hunger? We may boast of our wealth and civilization, but to the hungry man and woman and child our progress is a hollow mockery, our civilization a sham, and our "national wealth" a chimera.

You recognize that the industrial forces set in motion by steam and electricity have materially changed the structure of our civilization. You also admit that a system has grown up where the accumulations of the individual have passed from his control into that of representative combinations and trusts, and that the tendency in this direction is on the increase. How, then, can you consistently criticize the workingmen for recognizing that as individuals they can have no influence in deciding what the wages, hours of toil, and conditions of employment shall be?

You evidently have observed the growth of corporate wealth and influence. You recognize that wealth, in order to become more highly productive, is concentrated into fewer hands, and controlled by representatives and directors, and yet you sing the old siren song that the workingman should depend entirely upon his own "individual effort."

The school of laissez-faire, of which you seem to be a pronounced advocate, has produced great men in advocating the theory of each for himself and his Satanic majesty taking the hindermost, but the most pronounced advocates of your school of thought in economics have, when practically put to the test, been compelled to admit that combination and organization of the toiling masses are essential both to prevent the deterioration and to secure an improvement in the condition of the wage earners.

If, as you say, the success of commercial society depends upon the full play of competition, why do not you and your confreres turn your attention and direct the shafts of your attacks against the trusts and corporations, business wreckers and manipulators in the food products—the necessities of the people. Why garland your thoughts in beautiful phrase when speaking of these modern vampires, and steep your pen in gall when writing of the laborers' efforts to secure some of the advantages accruing from the concentrated thought and genius of the ages? . . .

Progress and Poverty

One becomes enraptured in reading the beauty of your description of modern progress. Could you have had in mind the miners of Spring Valley or Pennsylvania, or the clothing workers of the sweatshops of New York or Chicago when you grandiloquently dilate,

> Who is not rich today when compared with his ancestors of a century ago? The steamboat and the railroad bring to his breakfast table the coffees of Java and Brazil, the fruits from Florida and California, and the steaks from the plains. The loom arrays him in garments and the factories furnish him with a dwelling that the richest contemporaries of his grandfather would have envied. With health and industry he is a prince.

Probably you have not read within the past year of babes dying of starvation at their mothers' breasts. More than likely the thousands of men lying upon the bare stones night after night in the City Hall of Chicago last winter escaped your notice. You may not have heard of the cry for bread that was sounded through this land of plenty by thousands of honest men and women. But should these and many other painful incidents have passed you by unnoticed, I am fearful that you may learn of them with keener thoughts with the coming sleets and blasts of winter.

You say that "labor cannot afford to attack capital." Let me remind you that labor has no quarrel with capital, as such. It is merely the possessors of capital who refuse to accord to labor the recognition, the right, the justice which is the laborers' due with whom we contend.

See what is implied by your contemptuous reference to the laborer when you ask, "Will the conqueror destroy his trophy?" Who ever heard of a conqueror marching unitedly with his *trophy*, as you would have them? But if by your comparison you mean that the conqueror is the corporation, the trust, the capitalist class, and ask then whether they would destroy their *trophy*, I would have you ask the widows and orphans of the thousands of men killed annually through the avarice of railroad corporations refusing to avail themselves of modern appliances in coupling and other improvements on their railroads.

Inquire from the thousands of women and children whose husbands or fathers were suffocated or crushed in the mines through the rapacious greed of stockholders clamoring for more dividends. Investigate the sweating dens of the large cities. Go to the mills, factories, through the country. Visit the modern tenement houses or hovels in which thousands of workers are compelled to eke out an existence. Ask these whether the conqueror (monopoly) cares whether his trophy (the laborers) is destroyed or preserved. Ascertain from employers whether the laborer is not regarded the same as a machine, thrown out as soon as all the work possible has been squeezed out of him.

Labor Legislation

Are you aware that all the legislation ever secured for the ventilation or safety of mines, factory, or workshop is the result of the efforts of organized labor? Do you know that the trade unions were the shield for the seven-year-old children from being the conqueror's trophy until they become somewhat older? And that the reformatory laws now on the statute books protecting or defending the trophies of both sexes, young and old from the fond care of the conquerors were wrested from congresses, legislatures, and parliaments despite the Pullmans, the Jeffries, the Ricks, the Tafts, the Williams, the Woods, or the Grosscups.

By what right, sir, do you assume that the labor organizations do not conduct their affairs within lawful limits, or that they are a menace to the lawful institutions of the country? Is it because some thoughtless or overzealous member at a time of great excitement and smarting under a wrong may violate under a law or commit an improper act? Would you apply the same rule to the churches, the other moral agencies and organizations that you do to the organizations of labor? If you did, the greatest moral force of life today, the trade unions, would certainly stand out the clearest, brightest, and purest. Because a certain class (for which you and a number of your col-

leagues on the bench seem to be the special pleaders) have a monopoly in their lines of trade, I submit that this is no good reason for their claim to have a monopoly on true patriotism or respect for the lawful institutions of the country.

———— • ————

"The labor movement as represented by the trades unions stands for right, for justice, for liberty."

———— • ————

But speaking of law reminds me of the higher law of the land. The Constitution prescribes that all rights not specifically granted to the general government are reserved to the states. There is another provision prohibiting the President from sending armed forces into any state except for the purpose of maintaining "a republican form of government," and then only upon the requisition of the legislature of the state, or of the governor when the legislature is not in session. Yet when, during the recent [1894 Pullman] railroad strike, the President [Grover Cleveland] sent the troops into Illinois, it was not in compliance with the request of the legislature of that state, nor of the governor, but in spite of his protest. Yes, even when the governor remonstrated he was practically told by the President to stop arguing the law upon the question. Pardon the simplicity of my inquiry, but does not the law require that its limits shall be observed by a president, a judge, equally as by a labor organization?

The Interstate Commerce Law

If I remember aright you based the injunctions recently issued by you upon the provisions of the [1887] Interstate Commerce Law, a law enacted by Congress upon the demand of the farmers and shippers of our country to protect them against the unjust and outrageous discriminations imposed by the railroads. Where in the law can you find one word to justify your course applying to workingmen organized and engaged in a strike?

Read the discussions in Congress when that law was under consideration. You will not find a remote reference to the application of the laws as you construe it. In fact, I am informed upon excellent authority that when the law was before the Senate in the form of a bill, Senator Morgan, of Alabama, proposed an amendment which, if adopted, would have had the effect of empowering judges to issue an order of the nature you have in the recent railroad strike; but it was not adopted; it was defeated. How then in the face of this you can issue your omnibus restraining order passes the comprehension of ordinary men. . . .

Year by year man's liberties are trampled underfoot at the bidding of corporations and trusts, rights are invaded, and law perverted. In all ages, wherever a tyrant has shown himself, he has always found some willing judge to clothe that tyranny in the robes of legality, and modern capitalism has proven no exception to the rule.

You may not know that the labor movement as represented by the trades unions stands for right, for justice, for liberty. You may not imagine that the issuance of an injunction depriving men of a legal as well as a natural right to protect themselves, their wives, and little ones must fail of its purpose. Repression or oppression never yet succeeded in crushing the truth or redressing a wrong.

In conclusion let me assure you that labor will organize and more compactly than ever and upon practical lines; and despite relentless antagonism, achieve for humanity a nobler manhood, a more beautiful womanhood, and a happier childhood.

For Further Reading

John Avrich, *The Haymarket Tragedy.* Princeton, NJ: Princeton University Press, 1984.

Leon Fink, *Workingmen's Democracy: The Knights of Labor and American Politics.* Urbana: University of Illinois Press, 1983.

Samuel Gompers, *Seventy Years of Life and Labor.* Ithaca, NY: ILR Press, 1984.

Harold C. Livesay, *Samuel Gompers and Organized Labor in America.* Boston: Little, Brown, 1978.

Philip Taft, *The A.F. of L. in the Time of Gompers.* New York: Harper & Row, 1957.

VIEWPOINT 9A

A New Industrial South of Racial Harmony Is Rising (1887)

Henry W. Grady (1850–1889)

Henry W. Grady was editor of the *Atlanta Constitution* in Georgia and a noted public speaker. He gained nationwide attention as a spokesman for the "New South," a term he helped popularize in the United States in a famous 1886 address in New York. Grady and members of his generation of southern leaders envisioned a post-Reconstruction South reconciled to the Union, devoted to white supremacy, and diversified in its economy beyond growing a few staple crops such as cotton. In the following viewpoint, taken from a speech made at a Texas state fair in Dallas on October 26, 1887, Grady summarizes

From Joel Chandler Harris, *Life of Henry W. Grady, Including His Writings and Speeches* (New York: Cassell Publishing, 1890).

his views on race, industry, and the future of the South.

How does Grady contrast the situation of blacks before and after the end of slavery? Why must whites maintain political supremacy over blacks, in his view? Does Grady make any links between the two problems of race relations and economic development in the South? What evidence does he provide for his optimistic outlook on the South's economic future?

I shall be pardoned for . . . adhering to-day to blunt and rigorous speech—for there are times when fine words are paltry, and this seems to me to be such a time. So I shall turn away from the thunders of the political battle upon which every American hangs intent, and repress the ardor that at this time rises in every American heart—for there are issues that strike deeper than any political theory has reached, and conditions of which partisanry has taken, and can take, but little account. Let me, therefore, with studied plainness, and with such precision as is possible—in a spirit of fraternity that is broader than party limitations, and deeper than political motive—discuss with you certain problems upon the wise and prompt solution of which depends the glory and prosperity of the South. . . .

The future holds a problem, in solving which the South must stand alone; in dealing with which, she must come closer together than ambition or despair have driven her, and on the outcome of which her very existence depends. This problem is to carry within her body politic two separate races, and nearly equal in numbers. . . .

What shall the South do to be saved? Through what paths shall she reach the end? Through what travail, or what splendors, shall she give to the Union this section, its wealth garnered, its resources utilized, and its rehabilitation complete—and restore to the world this problem solved in such justice as the finite mind can measure, or finite hands administer?

In dealing with this I shall dwell on two points.

First, the duty of the South in its relation to the race problem.

Second, the duty of the South in relation to its no less unique and important industrial problem. . . .

Views on Former Slaves

What of the negro? This of him. I want no better friend than the black boy who was raised by my side, and who is now trudging patiently with downcast eyes and shambling figure through his lowly way in life. I want no sweeter music than the crooning of my old "mammy," now dead and gone to rest, as I heard it when she held me in her loving arms, and bending her old black face above me stole the cares from my brain, and led me smiling into sleep. I want no truer soul than that which moved the trusty slave, who for four years while my father fought with the armies that barred his freedom, slept every night at my mother's chamber door, holding her and her children as safe as if her husband stood guard, and ready to lay down his humble life on her threshold. History has no parallel to the faith kept by the negro in the South during the war. Often five hundred negroes to a single white man, and yet through these dusky throngs the women and children walked in safety, and the unprotected homes rested in peace. . . . A thousand torches would have disbanded every Southern army, but not one was lighted. When the master going to a war in which slavery was involved said to his slave, "I leave my home and loved ones in your charge," the tenderness between man and master stood disclosed. And when the slave held that charge sacred through storm and temptation, he gave new meaning to faith and loyalty. I rejoice that when freedom came to him after years of waiting, it was all the sweeter because the black hands from which the shackles fell were stainless of a single crime against the helpless ones confided to his care.

From this root, imbedded in a century of kind and constant companionship, has sprung some foliage. As no race had ever lived in such unresisting bondage, none was ever hurried with such swiftness through freedom into power. Into hands still trembling from the blow that broke the shackles, was thrust the ballot. In less than twelve months from the day he walked down the furrow a slave, the negro dictated in legislative halls from which [Jefferson] Davis and [John C.] Calhoun had gone forth, the policy of twelve commonwealths. When his late master protested against his misrule, the federal drum beat rolled around his strongholds, and from a hedge of federal bayonets he grinned in good-natured insolence. From the proven incapacity of that day has he far advanced? Simple, credulous, impulsive—easily led and too often easily bought, is he a safer, more intelligent citizen now than then? Is this mass of votes, loosed from old restraints, inviting alliance or a waiting opportunity, less menacing than when its purpose was plain and its way direct?

My countrymen, right here the South must make a decision on which very much depends. Many wise men hold that the white vote of the South should divide, the color line be beaten down, and the southern states ranged on economic or moral questions as interest or belief demands. I am compelled to dissent from this view. The worst thing in my opinion that could happen is that the white people of the South should stand in opposing factions, with the vast mass of ignorant or purchasable negro votes

between. Consider such a status. If the negroes were skillfully led,—and leaders would not be lacking,—it would give them the balance of power—a thing not to be considered. If their vote was not compacted, it would invite the debauching bid of factions, and drift surely to that which was the most corrupt and cunning. With the shiftless habit and irresolution of slavery days still possessing him, the negro voter will not in this generation, adrift from war issues, become a steadfast partisan through conscience or conviction. In every community there are colored men who redeem their race from this reproach, and who vote under reason. Perhaps in time the bulk of this race may thus adjust itself. But, through what long and monstrous periods of political debauchery this status would be reached, no tongue can tell. . . .

A Question of Race

One thing further should be said in perfect frankness. Up to this point we have dealt with ignorance and corruption—but beyond this point a deeper issue confronts us. Ignorance may struggle to enlightenment, out of corruption may come the incorruptible. God speed the day when,—every true man will work and pray for its coming,— the negro must be led to know and through sympathy to confess that his interests and the interests of the people of the South are identical. The men who, from afar off, view this subject through the cold eye of speculation or see it distorted through partisan glasses, insist that, directly or indirectly, the negro race shall be in control of the affairs of the South. We have no fears of this; already we are attaching to us the best elements of that race, and as we proceed our alliance will broaden; external pressure but irritates and impedes. Those who would put the negro race in supremacy would work against infallible decree, for the white race can never submit to its domination, because the white race is the superior race. But the supremacy of the white race of the South must be maintained forever, and the domination of the negro race resisted at all points and at all hazards—because the white race is the superior race. This is the declaration of no new truth. It has abided forever in the marrow of our bones, and shall run forever with the blood that feeds Anglo-Saxon hearts. . . .

It is a race issue. Let us come to this point, and stand here. Here the air is pure and the light is clear, and here honor and peace abide. Juggling and evasion deceives not a man. Compromise and subservience has carried not a point. There is not a white man North or South who does not feel it stir in the gray matter of his brain and throb in his heart. Not a negro who does not feel its power. It is not a sectional issue. It speaks in Ohio, and in Georgia. It speaks wherever the Anglo-Saxon touches an alien race. It has just spoken in universally approved legislation [the 1882 Chinese Exclusion Act] in excluding the Chinaman from our gates, not for his ignorance, vice or corruption, but because he sought to establish an inferior race in a republic fashioned in the wisdom and defended by the blood of a homogeneous people. . . .

All this is no unkindness to the negro—but rather that he may be led in equal rights and in peace to his uttermost good. Not in sectionalism—for my heart beats true to the Union, to the glory of which your life and heart is pledged. Not in disregard of the world's opinion—for to render back this problem in the world's approval is the sum of my ambition, and the height of human achievement. Not in reactionary spirit—but rather to make clear that new and grander way up which the South is marching to higher destiny. . . . Not in passion, my countrymen, but in reason—not in narrowness, but in breadth—that we may solve this problem in calmness and in truth, and lifting its shadows let perpetual sunshine pour down on two races, walking together in peace and contentment. Then shall this problem have proved our blessing, and the race that threatened our ruin work our salvation as it fills our fields with the best peasantry the world has ever seen. Then the South—putting behind her all the achievements of her past—and in war and in peace they beggar eulogy—may stand upright among the nations and challenge the judgment of man and the approval of God, in having worked out in their sympathy, and in His guidance, this last and surpassing miracle of human government.

Industry in the South

What of the South's industrial problem? When we remember that amazement followed the payment by thirty-seven million Frenchmen of a billion dollars indemnity to Germany, that the five million whites of the South rendered to the torch and sword three billions of property—that thirty million dollars a year, or six hundred million dollars in twenty years, has been given willingly of our poverty as pensions for Northern soldiers, the wonder is that we are here at all. There is a figure with which history has dealt lightly, but that, standing pathetic and heroic in the genesis of our new growth, has interested me greatly—our soldier-farmer of '65. What chance had he for the future as he wandered amid his empty barns, his stock, labor, and implements gone—gathered up the fragments of his wreck—urging kindly his borrowed mule—paying sixty per cent. for all that he bought, and buying all on credit—his crop mortgaged before it was planted—his children in want, his neighborhood in chaos—working under new conditions and retrieving every error by a costly year—plodding all day down the furrow, hopeless

and adrift, save when at night he went back to his broken home, where his wife, cheerful even then, renewed his courage, while she ministered to him in loving tenderness. Who would have thought as during those lonely and terrible days he walked behind the plow, locking the sunshine in the glory of his harvest, and spreading the showers and the verdure of his field—no friend near save nature that smiled at his earnest touch, and God that sent him the message of good cheer through the passing breeze and the whispering leaves—that he would in twenty years, having carried these burdens uncomplaining, make a crop of $800,000,000. Yet this he has done, and from his bounty the South has rebuilded her cities, and recouped her losses. While we exult in his splendid achievement, let us take account of his standing.

Whence this enormous growth? For ten years the world has been at peace. The pioneer has now replaced the soldier. Commerce has whitened new seas, and the merchant has occupied new areas. Steam has made of the earth a chess-board, on which men play for markets. Our western wheat-grower competes in London with the Russian and the East Indian. The Ohio wool grower watches the Australian shepherd, and the bleat of the now historic sheep of Vermont is answered from the steppes of Asia. The herds that emerge from the dust of your amazing prairies might hear in their pauses the hoofbeats of antipodean herds marching to meet them. Under Holland's dykes, the cheese and butter makers fight American dairies. The hen cackles around the world. California challenges vine-clad France. The dark continent is disclosed through meshes of light. There is competition everywhere. The husbandman, driven from his market, balances price against starvation, and undercuts his rival. This conflict often runs to panic, and profit vanishes. The Iowa farmer burning his corn for fuel is not an unusual type.

Amid this universal conflict, where stands the South? While the producer of everything we eat or wear, in every land, is fighting through glutted markets for bare existence, what of the southern farmer? In his industrial as in his political problem he is set apart—not in doubt, but in assured independence. Cotton makes him king. Not the fleeces that Jason sought can rival the richness of this plant, as it unfurls its banners in our fields. . . .

Not alone in cotton, but in iron, does the South excel. . . . Having ores and coal stored in exhaustless quantity, in such richness, and in such adjustment, that iron can be made and manufacturing done cheaper than elsewhere on this continent, is to now command, and at last control, the world's market for iron. . . . In 1880 the South made 212,000 tons of iron. In 1887, 845,000 tons. She is now actually building, or has finished this year, furnaces that will produce more than her entire product of last year. Birmingham alone will produce more iron in 1889 than the entire South produced in 1887. Our coal supply is exhaustless, Texas alone having 6,000 square miles. In marble and granite we have no rivals, as to quantity or quality. In lumber our riches are even vaster. More than fifty per cent. of our entire area is in forests, making the South the best timbered region of the world. We have enough merchantable yellow pine to bring, in money, $2,500,000,000—a sum the vastness of which can only be understood when I say it nearly equaled the assessed value of the entire South, including cities, forests, farms, mines, factories and personal property of every description whatsoever. Back of this our forests of hard woods, and measureless swamps of cypress and gum. Think of it. In cotton a monopoly. In iron and coal establishing swift mastery. In granite and marble developing equal advantage and resource. In yellow pine and hard woods the world's treasury. Surely the basis of the South's wealth and power is laid by the hand of the Almighty God, and its prosperity has been established by divine law which works in eternal justice and not by taxes levied on its neighbors through human statutes. Paying tribute for fifty years that under artificial conditions other sections might reach a prosperity impossible under natural laws, it has grown apace—and its growth shall endure if its people are ruled by two maxims, that reach deeper than legislative enactment, and the operation of which cannot be limited by artificial restraint, and but little hastened by artificial stimulus.

Perils of the Single Crop

First. No one crop will make a people prosperous. If cotton held its monopoly under conditions that made other crops impossible—or under allurements that made other crops exceptional—its dominion would be despotism.

Whenever the greed for a money crop unbalances the wisdom of husbandry, the money crop is a curse. When it stimulates the general economy of the farm, it is the profiting of farming. In an unprosperous strip of Carolina, when asked the cause of their poverty, the people say, "Tobacco—for it is our only crop." In Lancaster, Pa., the richest American county by the census, when asked the cause of their prosperity, they say, "Tobacco—for it is the golden crown of a diversified agriculture." The soil that produces cotton invites the grains and grasses, the orchard and the vine. Clover, corn, cotton, wheat, and barley thrive in the same inclosure; the peach, the apple, the apricot, and the Siberian crab in the same orchard. Herds and flocks graze ten months every year in the meadows

over which winter is but a passing breath, and in which spring and autumn meet in summer's heart. Sugar-cane and oats, rice and potatoes, are extremes that come together under our skies. To raise cotton and send its princely revenues to the west for supplies, and to the east for usury, would be misfortune if soil and climate forced such a curse. When both invite independence, to remain in slavery is a crime. To mortgage our farms in Boston for money with which to buy meat and bread from western cribs and smokehouses, is folly unspeakable. I rejoice that Texas is less open to this charge than others of the cotton States. With her eighty million bushels of grain, and her sixteen million head of stock, she is rapidly learning that diversified agriculture means prosperity. Indeed, the South is rapidly learning the same lesson; and learned through years of debt and dependence it will never be forgotten. . . .

———— • ————

"The South, under the rapid diversification of crops and diversification of industries, is thrilling with new life."

———— • ————

But agriculture alone—no matter how rich or varied its resources—cannot establish or maintain a people's prosperity. There is a lesson in this that Texas may learn with profit. No commonwealth ever came to greatness by producing raw material. Less can this be possible in the future than in the past. The Comstock lode [a rich deposit of gold and silver ore in Nevada] is the richest spot on earth. And yet the miners, gasping for breath fifteen hundred feet below the earth's surface, get bare existence out of the splendor they dig from the earth. It goes to carry the commerce and uphold the industry of distant lands, of which the men who produce it get but dim report. Hardly more is the South profited when, stripping the harvest of her cotton fields, or striking her teeming hills, or leveling her superb forests, she sends the raw material to augment the wealth and power of distant communities. . . .

The most prosperous section of this world is that known as the Middle States of this republic. With agriculture and manufacturers in the balance, and their shops and factories set amid rich and ample acres, the result is such deep and diffuse prosperity as no other section can show. Suppose those States had a monopoly of cotton and coal so disposed as to command the world's markets and the treasury of the world's timber, I suppose the mind is staggered in contemplating the majesty of the wealth and power they would attain. What have they that the South lacks?—and to her these things were added, and climate, ampler acres and rich soil. It is a curious fact that three-fourths of the population and manufacturing wealth of this country is comprised in a narrow strip between Iowa and Massachusetts, comprising less than one-sixth of our territory, and that this strip is distant from the source of raw materials on which its growth is based, of hard climate and in a large part of sterile soil. Much of this forced and unnatural development is due to slavery, which for a century fenced enterprise and capital out of the South. . . .

The New South

With amazing rapidity she [the South] has moved away from the one-crop idea that was once her curse. In 1880 she was esteemed prosperous. Since that time she has added 393,000,000 bushels to her grain crops, and 182,000,000 head to her live stock. This has not lost one bale of her cotton crop, which, on the contrary, has increased nearly 200,000 bales. With equal swiftness has she moved away from the folly of shipping out her ore at $2 a ton and buying it back in implements from $20 to $100 per ton; her cotton at 10 cents a pound and buying it back in cloth at 20 to 80 cents per pound; her timber at $8 per thousand and buying it back in furniture at ten to twenty times as much. In the past eight years $250,000,000 have been invested in new shops and factories in her States; 225,000 artisans are now working that eight years ago were idle or worked elsewhere, and these added $227,000,000 to the value of her raw material—more than half the value of her cotton. Add to this the value of her increased grain crops and stock, and in the past eight years she has grown in her fields or created in her shops manufactures more than the value of her cotton crop. The incoming tide has begun to rise. Every train brings manufacturers from the East and West seeking to establish themselves or their sons near the raw material and in this growing market. Let the fullness of the tide roll in.

It will not exhaust our materials, nor shall we glut our markets. When the growing demand of our southern markets, feeding on its own growth, is met, we shall find new markets for the South. . . . Our neighbors to the south need nearly every article we make; we need nearly everything they produce. Less than 2,500 miles of road must be built to bind by rail the two American continents. When this is done, and even before, we shall find exhaustless markets to the south. Texas shall command, as she stands in the van of this new movement, its richest rewards.

The South, under the rapid diversification of crops and diversification of industries, is thrilling with new life. As this new prosperity comes to us, it will bring no sweeter thought to me, and to you, my country-

men, I am sure, than that it adds not only to the comfort and happiness of our neighbors, but that it makes broader the glory and deeper the majesty, and more enduring the strength, of the Union which reigns supreme in our hearts. In this republic of ours is lodged the hope of free government on earth. Here God has rested the ark of his covenant with the sons of men. Let us—once estranged and thereby closer bound,—let us soar above all provincial pride and find our deeper inspirations in gathering the fullest sheaves into the harvest and standing the staunchest and most devoted of its sons as it lights the path and makes clear the way through which all the people of this earth shall come in God's appointed time. . . .

A Vision

As I think of it, a vision of surpassing beauty unfolds to my eyes. I see a South, the home of fifty millions of people, who rise up every day to call from blessed cities, vast hives of industry and of thrift; her countrysides the treasures from which their resources are drawn; her streams vocal with whirring spindles; her valleys tranquil in the white and gold of the harvest; her mountains showering down the music of bells, as her slow-moving flocks and herds go forth from their folds; her rulers honest and her people loving, and her homes happy and their hearthstones bright, and their waters still, and their pastures green, and her conscience clear; her wealth diffused and poorhouses empty, her churches earnest and all creeds lost in the gospel. Peace and sobriety walking hand in hand through her borders; honor in her homes; uprightness in her midst; plenty in her fields; straight and simple faith in the hearts of her sons and daughters; her two races walking together in peace and contentment; sunshine everywhere and all the time, and night falling on her generally as from the wings of the unseen dove.

VIEWPOINT 9B

A New Industrial South Cannot Be Built on Racial Inequality (1889)

Lewis H. Blair (1834–1916)

Lewis H. Blair, following service as a Confederate soldier in the Civil War, established himself as a successful businessman in Richmond, Virginia. He also wrote several books and articles on social and economic problems of the South. In *A Southern Prophe-*

Excerpted from Lewis H. Blair, *A Southern Prophecy*, 1889. The text reprinted here is from the 1964 Little, Brown & Co. edition edited by Prof. C. Vann Woodward and is used with his permission.

cy, an 1889 book that is excerpted in this viewpoint, Blair attacks the views of Henry W. Grady and other promoters of the "New South." He argues that the South, far from enjoying an economic and industrial renaissance, is still lagging far behind other regions of the United States. Blair maintains that the continuing degradation of blacks in the South is the primary cause of the region's poverty, and urges an end to racial prejudice and segregation.

What flaws does Blair find in written reports of the South's new prosperity? What two future scenarios of race relations in the South does he describe? What does this viewpoint reveal about Blair's attitudes toward blacks? How do they differ from those of Grady, author of the opposing viewpoint?

The real question before us is: Is the South prosperous? If the correct answer be in the affirmative, then this proposed inquiry is altogether fruitless; but if in the negative, then this proposed inquiry into the prosperity of the South becomes the most momentous that can engage our attention. Judging by the glowing reports in the newspapers for the past three years, we must conclude that the South is enjoying a veritable deluge of prosperity, and that both individually and as states it is surpassing even the Eastern states, those petted children of legislation since the foundation of the Union. Judging by these sheets, one would naturally imagine that the South is a region where poverty is unknown and where everybody is industriously and successfully laying up wealth; where manufacturing sites are engrossing arable lands; where cotton, so long king, is tottering on his throne, and where manufactures are about to usurp his scepter. Seen through newspaper lenses, the South is indeed a happy Arcadia.

Exaggerating Southern Prosperity

Just here it may be well to say a few words about so-called *Manufacturers' Records* [a trade journal published in Baltimore, Maryland] which are circulating a vast amount of misinformation about the growth and prosperity of the South, and misleading multitudes on this point.

Such journals proceed on the same plan as would the Superintendent of the Census in 1890, should he, instead of actually enumerating the people, start with the population of 1880, and add thereto not only all the births, but also all the stillbirths, all the miscarriages, and all the abortions since that year, and deduct nothing for deaths in the meanwhile. Of course such a computation would be utterly absurd, and could only lead to ridiculous conclusions. But so it is with the computations of the so-called *Manufacturers' Records*. In arriving at their aggregates of

additional manufactures they write to the proprietors of every scheme they see noticed in their local exchanges, and they include not only concerns that have actually begun operations, but also all projected and even all suggested enterprises, all of which they capitalize at the highest authorized amount; and to make their calculations all the more mischievous and misleading they deduct nothing for the many hundreds or many thousands of manufacturing concerns that annually fail or retire from business.

Thus in the census of 1880 the South is credited with $133,240,000 manufacturing capital, but for the last eight years these reliable records have, by including actual, probable, and possible manufacturing enterprises, by capitalizing them at their maximum and by deducting nothing for failures and retirements, added not less than $1,000,000,000 to the manufacturing capital of the South, or nearly eight times as much as the South started with in 1865 and had succeeded in gathering together during the subsequent fifteen years. The impression is sought to be conveyed that while the South had $133,240,000 employed in manufactures in 1880, she has in 1888 $1,133,240,000 so employed. This is entirely false, because the South has lost since 1880 quite as much as she has gained in manufactures, or at the very best no one at all familiar with the South doubts that the census will show no greater increase of manufactures than it does population. The writer lives in one of the principal manufacturing cities of the South, and he observes therein no great increase of manufactures, the failures having almost if not quite offset the increase. In the mineral regions there has been some increase, but it is pretty certain that this growth has been fully offset by decadence in the South at large. . . .

A few words also as to the glowing reports of the prosperity of the South as set forth by [northern writers] Colonel Alex. K. McClure, Hon. Wm. D. Kelley, and others. These gentlemen occupy pretty much the position of kings who, surrounded by ministers and courtiers whose interest it is to keep them in darkness, rarely if ever know the true state of affairs, and their opinions are of as little value. These gentlemen who undertake to learn the condition of affairs by a hurried trip in palace cars are usually taken in charge and coached by interested parties, who carry them to a few selected spots like Birmingham and Chattanooga, where there is much life, activity and growth, and are told exultingly, "There! Look! Does not this remind you of Pennsylvania?" etc., etc. These gentlemen are thus placed in the attitude of envoys in olden times to an enemy's camp. The envoys were led blindfolded through the camp, and their eyes were unbandaged only when they reached the royal headquarters, where everything had been prearranged to impress them with the power and magnificence of the army or sovereign. So these gentlemen, having been hurried through hundreds of miles in luxurious palace coaches, have practically been blindfolded as to the condition of the country passed through, and not having their eyes unbandaged until in the midst of furnaces, rolling mills, and all the activities of a manufacturing center, they are dazzled by what they see, and they at once jump to the conclusion that what they behold is merely a type of the whole South, and that as there is great prosperity before their eyes, so there is great prosperity in the South.

These gentlemen altogether forget, most likely, listening to the brilliant conversation of their chaperons about the new South—have not seen the hundreds and hundreds of miles of poor country passed through, with its fenceless plantations, its unpainted and dilapidated homesteads, its small proportion of cultivated fields and its large proportion of lands returning and returned to a state of nature, its patches instead of its fields of crops, the scarcity of stock of all kinds, and the thriftless and idle groups found at almost every depot. They lose sight of the real South—that is to say, of ninety-five per cent thereof, but seeing the other five per cent concentrated in two or three active, stirring, and busy cities they erroneously conclude that the ninety-five per cent which they do not and cannot see is like the five per cent which they have been invited to inspect. Reversing the process of the tiny fragment held close to the eye hiding the sun, and holding these bits of sunshine close to the eye, the South at large, great though its poverty actually is, is made to appear as bright and as prosperous as these bits of sunshine.

If, instead of this process, these gentlemen would visit the farming and planting community, whether cotton, tobacco, sugar, grain, or whatnot be raised, which is the real South, and if they were brought into actual business contact with the people themselves, they would soon see, even leaving out the six millions of Negroes who are in the depths of indigence, that fully ninety-five per cent of the whites would at death leave their families, after debts were paid, with scarcely more than a roof to cover them, and that for every ten living in any degree of ease and comfort there were ninety who had nothing beyond the commonest necessaries of life. Yes, there shall be a new South, and prominent men from the North must be brought to testify to it, even though their testimony must in the nature of the case be untrustworthy and valueless.

To doubt is to be damned, is true in other things besides religion, and so to doubt the current charming presentations of Southern growth and prosperity is to bring down anathemas upon one's head. What! the South not prosperous? Impossible, they cry; and the individual who questions is an idiot.

Would that the South were rich, because numberless blessings follow in the train of wealth, just as numberless evils follow in the trail of poverty. To be rich is to be great, mighty and powerful, to be feared, honored and respected, like the United States, like Great Britain, like Germany; to be poor is to be weak, wretched and miserable, to be despised, plundered and imposed upon, like Spain, Turkey, or Mexico. If claiming to be rich could make the South rich, none could make louder or more vehement claims than myself, and a rejuvenated giant South should ever be on my tongue; but claims and boasts are vain in the face of nature, which demands deeds and not sentiments, but deeds in accordance with principles of well-established economic laws.

Prosperity is an inestimable blessing, and to obtain it we must, like the husbandman in Scripture who sold everything to purchase one field, make every sacrifice, and be deterred by no difficulties; but like all other good things prosperity has its price, and we must pay the full price or must go without, and the greater the good the greater the cost. We all desire prosperity, and we have been sighing for it for years, and yet prosperity lags; but if we have it not it is because we have not sought aright—that is, not in accordance with the laws of nature.

In order for success one must understand fully his position as well as be willing to take all necessary steps to secure success, for his measures cannot be appropriate if this knowledge be lacking. . . .

Causes of Poverty

As many streams are required to make the river, so many causes are required to produce prosperity, and as the river is great in proportion to the number of streams flowing together, so prosperity is great in proportion to the number of causes harmoniously cooperating.

There are many causes conspiring to the poverty or lack of prosperity of the South, the principal of which are a general prevalence of ignorance, a general disregard of human life, a general lack of economy and self-denial; but great as these causes are, a greater and more far-reaching cause of all is the degradation of the Negro, who, being our principal source of labor, is our principal dependence for prosperity.

Each of these causes would greatly retard the prosperity of the South, or indeed of any country, but all of them combined, destructive as they would necessarily be to prosperity, are not as serious and as fatal as the last cause, namely: the degradation of the Negro. Like a malignant cancer which poisons the whole system, this degradation seems to intensify all the other drawbacks under which we labor. Thus general ignorance is intensified by the gross ignorance of all the blacks and of the whites nearest them in social and financial condition; the general disregard of human life is intensified by the slight regard in which a Negro's life is held, and the whites, regarding the Negro's life of little sanctity, naturally regard all life as of little value, and therefore freely take each other's life; and the general lack of economy and self-denial is naturally intensified by the careless, wasteful and negligent manner in which the Negro, upon whom we are mainly dependent for labor, usually does his work. The Negro is an extremely defective tool, and no man, whether planter, carpenter, or whatnot, can continue constantly to use wretched implements without becoming wasteful and negligent himself, and without disregarding economy. We may remove all the other hindrances to prosperity; the whites may become well educated; we may hold human life in scrupulous regard and may become models of economy and self-denial, but if the blacks are to be left to grovel in their present degraded condition, even then prosperity would be measurably in default, because the six million Negroes, remaining degraded, would prove an incubus upon the whites, who would be in imminent danger of impoverishment by the thieving of such multitudes, whose highest and only ambition would be to live without work at the expense of those who were responsible for their degradation. . . .

Although justice—and we should always bear in mind that justice is a stern virtue that will sooner or later avenge herself upon her violators, though at the same time she never fails to honor and reward those who respect her requirements—although justice demands that the whites elevate the Negroes, for in the light of morality we stand responsible for their welfare, their elevation will not be advocated on any such ground, nor on the ground of religion either, but simply on economic grounds, on the ground of advantage to the whites. Just as we would urge the South to improve its animals, tools, methods of planting, etc., so that it may derive the more good from their labor and capital, so we urge the elevation of the Negroes, because the better men and citizens they are the more we, the whites, can in the end make out of them. . . .

The South Should Be Rich

That the South ought to be the richest section of the United States goes without saying, for it occupies not only a broad and fertile territory, but it lies beneath a sun that produces in abundance many of the most valuable productions of commerce. In addition to the great staff of life—bread—tobacco and cotton flourish here as nowhere else, and rice, sugar, and naval stores [turpentine and other products obtained from evergreen trees] add millions annual-

ly to its wealth; but although this production has been going on uninterruptedly for more than twenty years her people are not rich, but on the contrary are very poor. They are not only burdened with debt up to their full capacity for borrowing, but much, if not the greatest part, of their crops is made by loans, beginning with the time of planting. Their homes are not only unsupplied with many of the most essential comforts, but their plantations are ill supplied with stock and implements, their cribs and smokehouses are mostly empty, their fences have disappeared, and their dwellings and farm buildings are not only indifferent, but they present a general appearance of neglect and too often of dilapidation. The want of accumulated capital is extreme, and for at least six months of the year money, instead of being a reality, is rather a thing of memory and of hope, or of the past and the future, with the greater part of the people. But as an ounce of prevention is worth a pound of cure, so well-attested facts, even though they be few, are worth libraries of speculations and assertion. We will therefore bid adieu to assertions which are of no authority, and will resort to facts to substantiate our statements. . . .

Banks are . . . evidence of prosperity, for the accumulations of prosperity naturally seek investment in banks. The following is the report of the United States Comptroller of the Currency, December 4, 1886:

	Southern States	Other States
Capital stock paid in	$31,065,450.00	$517,175,280.00
Surplus fund	8,262,139.00	148,987,051.00
Undivided profits	4,483,274.00	62,020,200.00
Total	$43,810,863.00	$728,182,531.00

Banks are not only evidences of prosperity, but they are in turn causes of prosperity. What shall we say, then, of the prosperity of the South when it possesses six per cent of banking capital for twenty-six per cent of population? . . .

Manufacturing

Manufactures are other evidences of wealth, and what is their report? Here we have to go back some years to the United States census of 1880, but this evidence will probably be demurred to by devout believers in a new South, for they will say manufactures have made wonderful strides since then. Such objectors may be correct, but it is extremely doubtful, because except in Birmingham, Chattanooga and a few other localities an observer can behold few material evidences of increase of manufactures; certainly nothing commensurate with the growth of manufactures in most of the other states. The last census reports: manufactures in the South, $240,444,295; in all other, $5,129,223,411; which is not quite five per cent, against twenty-six per cent of population. Bearing in mind that Southern manufactures were mostly of the coarsest character, requiring the least skill and therefore earning the least profit, the poverty of the South under this head is all the more striking and lamentable; and to show this, the following digest is made from the report:

ELEVEN SOUTHERN STATES

Cotton manufactures 16,165,607
Woolen manufactures. 2,336,597
Flour and grist mills 63,803,041
Foundry products 7,091,959
Iron and steel products 7,836,653
Lumber products 31,620,878
Naval stores. 5,871,983
Tobacco 20,138,340

$154,865,058

Observe that $63,803,041 is credited to flour and grist mills, which are mostly small neighborhood affairs, and most of this amount is as fairly credited to manufactures as if we credited to bakeries the subsequent labors of the women in converting the flour and the meal into loaf-bread, biscuits, ashcake and pone. To the credit of lumber is passed $31,620,878. This is one of the crudest of manufactures, and instead of classing sawmills under the head of wealth-producers, we should rather class them under the head of bankruptcy-breeders. Only $18,502,204 goes to the credit of textiles, and only $14,928,612 to iron and steel and their varied products.

The difference, according to the census, between cost of manufactures and what the manufactures sell for is twenty per cent. Therefore, in the census year seventy-four per cent of population added about $1,000,000,000 to their wealth, while the twenty-six per cent of Southern population added only $48,000,000.

This was in 1880, and probably we may hear a chorus of "patriotic" Southerners and enthusiastic believers in a new South scornfully exclaim, "1880! oh, yes, 1880!" and most probably these gentlemen will exclaim, "Talk at this stage of the world, when the South is taking such giant strides, of 1880; you had as well talk to us about the time when Captain John Smith was having his romantic adventure with old Powhatan and his lovely Pocahontas."

The Iron Industry

But although we have no late census to refer to, we have official figures of the iron industry, the one in which the South is said to have accomplished most, so let us see what these figures say:

| | 1880 | | |
| | South | Whole country | Percentage |
	Tons	Tons	South
Production pig iron	207,798	4,295,414	5
	1887		
Production pig iron	767,791	7,187,206	10
Production steel, all kinds		3,739,760	0

Here is a wonderful progress, worthy of being celebrated with a full band of Jew's harps. Here is the South with enough coal and iron, almost locked in each other's embrace, to supply the world with iron at the very lowest cost, and yet in seven years she has added 560,000 tons to her product, or an additional five per cent on the total production of the whole country. While the South was adding 560,000 tons the rest of the country added 2,900,000 tons. Observe that the South is not credited with a pound of the 3,739,760 tons of steel produced in 1887. . . .

"Patriotism" would say hide all these uncomplimentary facts, but common sense says it is better to look our deficiencies squarely in the face, for we will never overcome our shortcomings until we are convinced of their existence. Common sense beats "patriotism" every time, and while things frequently go backwards under the lead of "patriotism," which is only a longer word for "gush," they are always pushing forward under the guidance of common sense. "Know thyself" is not only essential for the individual, but also for the state. . . .

Having sufficiently demonstrated, it is thought, not only the comparative, but also the positive, poverty of the South, which ought in many respects to be the richest section, let us now proceed to point out some of the causes of this poverty, or at all events of this want of prosperity.

One Primary Cause

As already stated, these causes are many, the chief of which are illiteracy, disregard of human life, lack of economy and self-denial, and degradation of the Negro—already mentioned—and vicious economic legislation, one of the most insidious, because generally unsuspected, of all the causes sapping our prosperity. For want of space only one of these causes will be treated, except incidentally, but as this cause is the greatest of all, and in a measure underlies all but the last cause, by handling this cause properly, the whole field affecting our prosperity will have been gone over. This cause is the degradation of the Negro.

But the question really to be considered is not the degradation of the Negro, for that is patent to all, but the elevation of the Negro, since it is by his elevation alone that we are to secure prosperity; for elevate him and the other evils will be cured during the process of his elevation.

But the question will be very generally asked, Why elevate the Negro at all? Is he not now good enough to obey us obsequiously, and to make our corn, our cotton, our tobacco, our rice, and our sugar? What more do we want of him? The reply is that if the Negro is forever to remain simply the instrument for doing our menial and manual work, for plowing and sowing, for driving mules, for worming tobacco and picking cotton, he is already too elevated, and he should be still further humbled and degraded. In his present condition he has some of the ideas and aspirations of a freeman, some desires for education, and he has almost entire control of his personal movements. He works when it suits him, but then he may idle at the crisis of a crop; but as we cannot compel him with the lash to work, he is on the whole not a profitable laborer either for himself or for an employer. To make him efficient, and to make him work the crop at the proper time, in spite of the attractions of political and religious gatherings, the overseer with the lash must be ever before his eyes. To allow the Negro to remain as he is, is for him a still "lower deep" in the social scale, and in his descent he drags us down with him.

But if the Negro is to become an intelligent voter, is to be a citizen capable of taking a sensible part in the affairs of his community, and to be a valuable coworker in adding to the wealth of the State, then we have a vast deal to do in order to elevate him. To make him *our* assistant in the production of wealth, the Negro must be made to work, or he must be induced by ambition, by the hope of enjoying in full the fruits of his labors, to work steadily and intelligently. If we are not willing to elevate him, we should set to work resolutely and deliberately to manacle both his mind and limbs, and to cow him, so that a little white child shall control a thousand. We will then at least get enough out of him to supply his few physical wants and to enable us to live in idleness and comparative comfort, which is not now the case. But if there is no hope of our ever being able to do this, what is the next best thing for us to do for our own good? Make a man of him. But this can be done only by means of education and other fostering influences, by cultivating his self-respect, by inspiring his hope, by letting him see that the land of his birth is as much his country as it is that of the wealthiest and haughtiest white. Now he is not only an alien, but an inferior—in reality a serf, in the land of his nativity.

We must trample, or we must elevate; to maintain the *status quo* is impossible. To trample is to perpetuate and intensify the poverty and stagnation under which we groan; to elevate is to make the South rich, happy and strong. . . .

Three Principal Things

Before we can make men of depraved and degraded human beings, be they Negro, Semite, or even Caucasian, and therefore efficient producers of wealth, there are three principal things to be done. They must be inspired with self-respect, their hope must be stimulated and their intelligence must be cultivated, and especially so with the Negro, for his self-respect is feeble, his hope faint, and his intelligence slight; he must economically, morally, and socially be born again, and self-respect, hope and intelligence are the trinity that will work out his elevation, and they are also the rule of three to work out our own material regeneration.

Self-respect is, in general terms, that quality that prevents our stealing, lying, drunkenness, idling, neglecting family, etc., and the man that is materially lacking in self-respect is generally little better than rotten driftwood, and incapable of accomplishing any good for the society in which he lives. . . .

Hope is, in general terms, that sentiment that leads us to expect rewards from our exertions, and that stimulates us to effort. When hope is faint we can accomplish little, and when hope is extinct we slavishly submit to fate and sheepishly yield all that we have, even our lives, to the first comer. But where hope is strong, and where we can reasonably expect an adequate return for our labor, there we witness abounding prosperity, as in the commercial and manufacturing sections of our country, and indeed in all new countries. . . .

Intelligence is, in general terms, that fruit of the training of the nervous system, of which the brain is merely the crown, which enables us to perceive objects and situations in their true light and relationship; which enables us to grasp and avail ourselves of attending circumstances that will assist us to accomplish our object with the least expenditure, and which enables us to perceive and to avoid those difficulties and impediments that will thwart us altogether, or that will cause us to expend unnecessary effort.

The Negro is greatly deficient in all these cardinal qualifications. His self-respect is so small he pays little regard to chastity or the marriage vow, and bastardy is very general; he pays little regard to honesty, and when his necessities or his inclinations combine with opportunity, the difference between *meum et tuum* [mine and yours] is reduced to its least expression; and he pays little regard for truth, for he looks upon lying and deceit as very venial faults, if indeed they be faults at all.

And what hope has the Negro, and what stimulus does it exert upon him? Alas, in the present attitude of public sentiment he can have but little hope, and hope can supply him with small incentive. And why? Because he is looked upon with contempt as a degraded inferior simply by virtue of having a black skin. A Negro may be learned, pious or distinguished; he may have rendered great services to his country or to humanity; he may be honored in England, France and Germany; but when he comes among us who are so superior to the flower of Europe, he is at once sent to Coventry [i.e., ostracized]. If he should obtain accommodation at hotels he receives it surreptitiously, and if any family, be it clerical, professional or mercantile, should receive him except as an inferior and as an act of condescension, as we sometimes invite inferiors to take a seat in our presence, that family is at once, or would be, put under the social ban. Not only if one is a Negro, but if he has, or is even suspected to have, one drop of Negro blood, he is placed under almost every disadvantage, and he can never feel safe from snubs, insults, or even kicks from the superior whites. In other words, the Negro is the victim of caste.

———— • ————

"The South can never become prosperous, with its laboring population bereft of hope."

———— • ————

In countries where caste prevails, there is little hope of progress for the inferior castes, and none at all for the lowest caste of all. In such countries, if people are born in a stable, they and their descendants are doomed to remain forever in a stable, and if they happen to be born in a higher station, there they remain perpetually. . . .

The South . . . is a veritable land of caste, and its chains hang heavily upon those of the lowest caste. In the palmy days of slavery, when one man held in his hand the lives of a thousand, there were several castes; but now, though there are still many social and other gradations, there are primarily only two castes.

Then there was first in rank and influence the caste of educated and wealthy planters, who assumed the airs and imitated the manners of the most exclusive aristocracy of England and France, whence their families had immigrated. In Virginia, Louisiana and South Carolina, but especially in the last state, many were highly cultivated and intellectual, were polished and refined to a high degree, the men being elegant and chivalric, and the women charming and beautiful. In them we beheld all that was noble and attractive in the system of caste. Next came an intermediate caste of planters. They were frequently men of wealth, but without education and of little refinement, and though they met the first caste on nearly equal but yet deferential terms on the hustings and court green, the families of the two castes never thought of visiting socially. Then came the overseer caste. This caste, usually hard and heartless, was composed mainly of men who had been overseers, but who had acquired a few slaves, and had set up for themselves. Although the men mingled on semi-equal terms with those next above them, they were generally looked down upon, if not despised; and their families, as a rule, never thought of visiting socially the families of those above them. Finally came the "poor white" caste, possessed of no Negroes, but of a few acres, and despised alike by whites and blacks.

The Negroes, of course, were lower still, but they were hardly considered as human beings. They were regarded pretty much like horses and cattle, simply as instruments like them, to enable the other castes to live, some in elegance, some in ease, but all in comfort without thought and without toil. They were treated, too, pretty much as cattle; many, when the masters were kind, treated mildly and their physical necessities carefully provided for; and many, when the masters were harsh and brutal, treated with cruelty and sometimes worked or beaten to death, it being a maxim with some cotton planters that it was cheaper to work a Negro to death and buy another than to work him reasonably and prolong his life.

But now, in the new order of things, all these castes have become amalgamated into one, and a new caste has been formed of those who were formerly considered too low to form a caste at all, and Southern society is now virtually divided into two castes. In the first caste are merged indiscriminately gentleman, farmer, overseer, poor white, and each and every one of these, regardless of education, worth, refinement, decency or morality, belongs to this class simply by reason of a white skin. The second caste is composed promiscuously of all who have a black skin and all related to them, however remotely; and all who are thus marked, however cultured and refined they may be, however able and however excellent, are confined as by fate to this caste, and are not permitted to throw off its galling chains; and society, by its inexorable verdict, decrees that the meanest, lowest, and most degraded of the first caste are, *ipso facto*, the irreversible and perpetual superiors of the best, highest and ablest of the second caste.

Hope cannot exist, certainly cannot flourish, under such a weight. If he is to remain forever a "nigger," an object of undisguised contempt, even to the lowest whites, the Negro will naturally say to himself, Why strive, why labor, why practice painful self-denial in order to rise, if I am to derive no good from my effort? On the contrary, he will not exert himself, but will sink into despondency, and instead of becoming a net producer, and thus an instrument of our own prosperity, he will continue as he is, a depredator upon others' industry and a consumer of wealth. The South can never become prosperous, with its laboring population bereft of hope. Without hope the proudest Anglo-Saxon sinks into despair—much more the helpless Negro, who is little more than a child. . . .

The South *must* do something; it can't say, I won't do anything, or, I will fold my hands and see what will happen. The South, impelled by the current of events, has done a great deal, and it is still doing much, but a vast deal yet remains to be done, and the point is to prove to the South that it is in its interest to do this great deal more, and to do it without unnecessary delay. . . .

Race Prejudice

The most important and the most difficult step to take is to mollify and finally to obliterate race and color prejudice, a prejudice by no means peculiar to the South or to white and black races, for until very recent years the Frenchman had neither charity nor justice for the Englishman, though separated only by a narrow strip of water, and the Englishman reciprocated in kind and with usurious interest; and although divided by only an imaginary line, the prejudices between Englishman and Scotchman were notorious; and even today the Englishman is ruled by prejudice when Ireland and her claims are in question. But these race prejudices have now measurably disappeared, and they will finally become practically extinct as intercourse, commercial and otherwise, makes nations mutually acquainted. And not only national but personal prejudices of all kinds also disappear as intelligence is disseminated. Prejudice against color itself has quite disappeared among Latin nations, and is quite unknown in Great Britain, our worthy exemplar in so many respects, where a Negro stands on his merits like other people.

But a general exclamation will arise that prejudice against color is ineradicable, and that we can never, never overcome it. Such a confession involves two contradictory assertions, both of which are equally erroneous. It implies that we are superior to the great European nations, and in the same breath that we are inferior to them—superior in that we are too wise to follow their example and divest ourselves of prejudice against color, and inferior in that we are unwilling or unable to do so. Neither is true; and if European nations have found it wise to break down

the prejudice against color it will not be wise, but foolish, for us not to follow their example; and if they have been able and willing to throw off the shackles of prejudice, we are dishonoring ourselves to say or to think that we cannot do so likewise. Many glory in prejudice, foolishly thinking it a mark of superiority, but prejudice is always a weakness, and when it is extreme it is a badge of dishonor. The prejudiced are as they are because they do not see things in their true light, and are like a horse that shies and throws its rider to death because it sees in the simple clod, stone or stump a frightful specter about to spring upon and devour it. The clearer one sees and the more enlightened he is, the freer he is from prejudice, which may be termed seeing things in a false light. And for so many generations past we have been looking upon the Negro in a false light that we cannot see him and his rights in their true light, and we shy violently and run the risk of wrecking our whole material welfare at the ideas of elevation, equality, manhood, etc., for the Negro. Southerners cannot be true to their lofty character if either unwilling or incapable of overcoming color prejudice, nor true to their interests either.

For Further Reading

Harold E. Davis, *Henry Grady's New South*. Tuscaloosa: University of Alabama Press, 1990.

Paul M. Gaston, *The New South Creed: A Study in Southern Mythmaking*. New York: Knopf, 1970.

Raymond B. Nixon, *Henry W. Grady, Spokesman of the New South*. New York: Russell & Russell, 1969.

Jonathan M. Wiener, *Social Origins of the New South*. Baton Rouge: Louisiana State University Press, 1978.

Joel Williamson, *The Crucible of Race: Black/White Relations in the American South Since Emancipation*. New York: Oxford University Press, 1984.

C. Vann Woodward, *Origins of the New South, 1877–1913*. Baton Rouge: Louisiana State University Press, 1951.

Gavin Wright, *Old South, New South: Revolutions in the Southern Economy Since the Civil War*. New York: Basic Books, 1986.

VIEWPOINT 10A

A Populist Prescription for Social Reform (1892)

People's Party Platform of 1892

The People's Party (or Populist Party) was organized in 1892; its presidential nominee, James Weaver, polled more than one million votes (out of eleven million cast) and won 5 states (out of 44) in the 1892 elections. Many of its participants and their ideas can be traced back to the Farmers' Alliance

From Edward McPherson, *A Handbook of Politics for 1892* (Washington, DC: Chapman, 1892).

and other agrarian movements and organizations of the 1870s and 1880s. Populist writers and speakers argued that farmers were being left behind in the industrial revolution and that the government should actively intervene in the economy to assure the welfare of farmers and workers. The following viewpoint—a preamble, policy platform, and supplementary resolutions adopted by the People's Party at its July 1892 convention in Omaha, Nebraska—provides a concise summary of what Populists believed was wrong with America and what should be done to fix it. Much of the viewpoint's writing is attributed to Ignatius Donnelly, a radical newspaper editor and future congressman from Minnesota.

What were the main causes of social ills in America, according to Donnelly and the Populists? What do the Populists assert about the Republican and Democratic parties? What do they see as the proper role of government?

Assembled upon the one hundred and sixteenth anniversary of the Declaration of Independence, the People's Party of America in their first National Convention, invoking upon their action the blessing of Almighty God, puts forth, in the name and on behalf of the people of this country, the following preamble and declaration of principles:

Preamble

The conditions which surround us best justify our co-operation. We meet in the midst of a nation brought to the verge of moral, political and material ruin. Corruption dominates the ballot box, the Legislatures, the Congress, and touches even the ermine of the Bench. The people are demoralized; most of the States have been compelled to isolate the voters at the polling places to prevent universal intimidation or bribery. The newspapers are largely subsidized or muzzled, public opinion silenced, business prostrated, our homes covered with mortgages, labor impoverished, and the land concentrating in the hands of the capitalists. The urban workmen are denied the right of organization for self-protection; imported pauperized labor beats down their wages; a hireling standing army, unrecognized by our laws, is established to shoot them down, and they are rapidly degenerating into European conditions. The fruits of the toil of millions are boldly stolen to build up colossal fortunes for a few, unprecedented in the history of mankind, and the possessors of these in turn despise the Republic and endanger liberty. From the same prolific womb of governmental injustice we breed the two great classes—tramps and millionaires.

The national power to create money is appropriated to enrich bond-holders; a vast public debt, payable in legal tender currency, has been funded into gold-bearing bonds, thereby adding millions to the burdens of the people.

Silver, which has been accepted as coin since the dawn of history, has been demonetized to add to the purchasing power of gold by decreasing the value of all forms of property as well as human labor, and the supply of currency is purposely abridged to fatten usurers, bankrupt enterprise and enslave industry.

A vast conspiracy against mankind has been organized on two continents, and it is rapidly taking possession of the world. If not met and overthrown at once, it forebodes terrible social convulsions, the destruction of civilization, or the establishment of an absolute despotism.

We have witnessed, for more than a quarter of a century, the struggles of the two great political parties for power and plunder, while grievous wrongs have been inflicted upon the suffering people. We charge that the controlling influences dominating both these parties have permitted the existing dreadful conditions to develop without serious effort to prevent or restrain them.

Neither do they now promise us any substantial reform. They have agreed together to ignore, in the coming campaign, every issue but one. They propose to drown the outcries of a plundered people with the uproar of a sham battle over the tariff, so that capitalists, corporations, national banks, rings, trusts, watered stock, the demonetization of silver and the oppressions of the usurers may all be lost sight of. They propose to sacrifice our homes, lives and children, on the altar of mammon; to destroy the multitude in order to secure corruption funds from the millionaires.

Assembled on the anniversary of the birthday of the nation, and filled with the spirit of the grand general and chieftain who established our independence, we seek to restore the Government of the Republic to the hands of the "plain people" with whose class it originated. We assert our purposes to be identical with the purposes of the National Constitution, to form a more perfect Union and establish justice, insure domestic tranquility, provide for the common defense, promote the general welfare and secure the blessings of liberty for ourselves and our posterity.

We declare that this Republic can only endure as a free government while built upon the love of the whole people for each other and for the nation; that it cannot be pinned together by bayonets; that the civil war is over and that every passion and resentment which grew out of it must die with it, and that we must be in fact, as we are in name, one united brotherhood of freedom.

Our country finds itself confronted by conditions for which there is no precedent in the history of the world; our annual agricultural productions amount to billions of dollars in value, which must within a few weeks or months be exchanged for billions of dollars' worth of commodities consumed in their production; the existing currency supply is wholly inadequate to make this exchange; the results are falling prices, the formation of combines and rings, the impoverishment of the producing class. We pledge ourselves that, if given power, we will labor to correct these evils by wise and reasonable legislation, in accordance with the terms of our platform.

———— • ————

"The powers of government . . . should be expanded . . . to the end that oppression, injustice and poverty, shall eventually cease."

———— • ————

We believe that the powers of government—in other words, of the people—should be expanded (as in the case of the postal service) as rapidly and as far as the good sense of an intelligent people and the teachings of experience shall justify, to the end that oppression, injustice and poverty, shall eventually cease in the land.

While our sympathies as a party of reform are naturally upon the side of every proposition which will tend to make men intelligent, virtuous and temperate, we nevertheless regard these questions—important as they are—as secondary to the great issues now pressing for solution, and upon which not only our individual prosperity, but the very existence of free institutions depend; and we ask all men to first help us to determine whether we are to have a Republic to administer, before we differ as to the conditions upon which it is to be administered; believing that the forces of reform this day organized will never cease to move forward, until every wrong is righted, and equal rights and equal privileges securely established for all the men and women of this country. We declare, therefore,

First.—That the union of the labor forces of the United States this day consummated shall be permanent and perpetual; may its spirit enter into all hearts for the salvation of the Republic, and the uplifting of mankind.

Second.—Wealth belongs to him who creates it, and every dollar taken from industry without an equivalent is robbery. "If any will not work, neither shall he eat." The interests of rural and civic labor are the same; their enemies are identical.

Third.—We believe that the time has come when the railroad corporations will either own the people

or the people must own the railroads; and should the Government enter upon the work of owning and managing all railroads, we should favor an amendment to the Constitution by which all persons engaged in the Government service shall be placed under a civil service regulation of the most rigid character, so as to prevent the increase of the power of the national administration by the use of such additional Government employes.

FINANCE.—We demand a national currency, safe, sound and flexible, issued by the General Government only [replacing notes issued by private banks], a full legal tender for all debts public and private. . . .

(A) We demand free and unlimited coinage of silver and gold at the present legal ratio of 16 to 1.

(B) We demand that the amount of circulating medium [money] be speedily increased to not less than $50 per capita.

(C) We demand a graduated income tax.

(D) We believe that the money of the country should be kept as much as possible in the hands of the people, and hence we demand that all State and National revenues shall be limited to the necessary expenses of the Government, economically and honestly administered.

(E) We demand that Postal Savings Banks be established by the Government for the safe deposit of the earnings of the people and to facilitate exchange.

TRANSPORTATION.—Transportation being a means of exchange and a public necessity, the government should own and operate the railroads in the interest of the people.

The telegraph and telephone, like the post office system, being a necessity for the transmission of news, should be owned and operated by the Government in the interest of the people.

LAND.—The land, including all the natural sources of wealth, is the heritage of the people and should not be monopolized for speculative purposes, and alien ownership of land should be prohibited. All land now held by railroads and other corporations in excess of their actual needs, and all lands now owned by aliens should be reclaimed by the Government and held for actual settlers only.

Supplementary Resolutions

The following supplementary resolutions, not to be incorporated in the platform, came from the Committee on Resolutions and were adopted, as follows:

Whereas, Other questions having been presented for our consideration, we hereby submit the following, not as a part of the platform of the People's Party, but as resolutions expressive of the sentiment of this Convention:

1. *Resolved,* That we demand a free ballot and a fair count in all elections, and pledge ourselves to

secure it to every legal voter without Federal intervention, through the adoption by the States of the unperverted Australian or secret ballot system.

2. That the revenue derived from a graduated income tax should be applied to the reduction of the burden of taxation now resting upon the domestic industries of this country.

3. That we pledge our support to fair and liberal pensions to ex-Union soldiers and sailors.

4. That we condemn the fallacy of protecting American labor under the present system, which opens our ports to the pauper and criminal classes of the world, and crowds out our wage-earners; and we denounce the present ineffective laws against contract labor [for immigrants], and demand the further restriction of undesirable immigration.

5. That we cordially sympathize with the efforts of organized workingmen to shorten the hours of labor, and demand a rigid enforcement of the existing eight-hour law on Government work, and ask that a penalty clause be added to the said law.

6. That we regard the maintenance of a large standing army of mercenaries, known as the Pinkerton system, as a menace to our liberties, and we demand its abolition. [Private security forces, including the Pinkerton agency, were often used to break strikes.] . . .

7. That we commend to the favorable consideration of the people and to the reform press the legislative system known as the initiative and referendum.

8. That we favor a constitutional provision limiting the office of President and Vice-President to one term, and providing for the election of Senators of the United States by a direct vote of the people.

9. That we oppose any subsidy or national aid to any private corporation for any purpose.

10. That this convention sympathizes with the Knights of Labor [a labor organization], and their righteous contest with the tyrannical combine of clothing manufacturers of Rochester, and declare it to be the duty of all who hate tyranny and oppression, to refuse to purchase the goods made by the said manufacturers, or to patronize any merchants who sell such goods.

VIEWPOINT 10B

A Social Darwinist View of Social Reform (1894)

William Graham Sumner (1840–1910)

Those who opposed the Populist Party and other movements calling for radical changes in American

William Graham Sumner, "The Absurd Effort to Make the World Over," *Forum*, March 1894.

society often applied the ideas of the British naturalist Charles Darwin. Darwin developed the theories of natural selection and "survival of the fittest" to account for the development of biological species; "Social Darwinists" applied similar ideas to economic conditions in America and other nations to explain the social and economic inequality. One such theorist was William Graham Sumner, a former Episcopal clergyman who was a professor of political and social science at Yale University from 1872 to 1909. Sumner's writings and speeches, in which he argued that all attempts to reform society were doomed because they flew in the face of nature itself, made him one of the leading defenders of the status quo during the Gilded Age. The following viewpoint, taken from an article published in *Forum* magazine in March 1894, is a classic summation of his philosophy.

How does Sumner defend concentrations of wealth? What significance does he attach to democracy over the course of America's history? What elements of Sumner's arguments presented here could most readily be classified as Social Darwinism? Which parts of the People's Party platform would Sumner oppose? Which might he accept?

———

It will not probably be denied that the burden of proof is on those who affirm that our social condition is utterly diseased and in need of radical regeneration. My task at present, therefore, is entirely negative and critical: to examine the allegations of fact and the doctrines which are put forward to prove the correctness of the diagnosis and to warrant the use of the remedies proposed.

The propositions put forward by social reformers nowadays are chiefly of two kinds. There are assertions in historical form, chiefly in regard to the comparison of existing with earlier social states, which are plainly based on defective historical knowledge, or at most on current stock historical dicta which are uncritical and incorrect. Writers very often assert that something never existed before because they do not know that it ever existed before, or that something is worse than ever before because they are not possessed of detailed information about what has existed before. The other class of propositions consists of dogmatic statements which, whether true or not, are unverifiable. This class of propositions is the pest and bane of current economic and social discussion. Upon a more or less superficial view of some phenomenon a suggestion arises which is embodied in a philosophical proposition and promulgated as a truth. From the form and nature of such propositions they can always be brought under the head of "ethics." This word at least gives them an air of elevated sentiment and purpose, which is the only warrant they possess. It is impossible to test or verify them by any investigation or logical process whatsoever. It is therefore very difficult for anyone who feels a high responsibility for historical statements, and who absolutely rejects any statement which is unverifiable, to find a common platform for discussion or to join issue satisfactorily in taking the negative.

When anyone asserts that the class of skilled and unskilled manual laborers of the United States is worse off now in respect to diet, clothing, lodgings, furniture, fuel, and lights; in respect to the age at which they can marry; the number of children they can provide for; the start in life which they can give to their children, and their chances of accumulating capital, than they ever have been at any former time, he makes a reckless assertion for which no facts have been offered in proof. Upon an appeal to facts, the contrary of this assertion would be clearly established. It suffices, therefore, to challenge those who are responsible for the assertion to make it good.

Industrial Organization

If it is said that the employed class are under much more stringent discipline than they were thirty years ago or earlier, it is true. It is not true that there has been any qualitative change in this respect within thirty years, but it is true that a movement which began at the first settlement of the country has been advancing with constant acceleration and has become a noticeable feature within our time. This movement is the advance in the industrial organization. The first settlement was made by agriculturists, and for a long time there was scarcely any organization. There were scattered farmers, each working for himself, and some small towns with only rudimentary commerce and handicrafts. As the country has filled up, the arts and professions have been differentiated and the industrial organization has been advancing. This fact and its significance has hardly been noticed at all; but the stage of the industrial organization existing at any time, and the rate of advance in its development, are the absolutely controlling social facts. Nine-tenths of the socialistic and semi-socialistic, and sentimental or ethical, suggestions by which we are overwhelmed come from failure to understand the phenomena of the industrial organization and its expansion. It controls us all because we are all in it. It creates the conditions of our existence, sets the limits of our social activity, regulates the bonds of our social relations, determines our conceptions of good and evil, suggests our life-philosophy, molds our inherited political institutions, and reforms the oldest and toughest customs, like marriage and property. I repeat that the turmoil of heterogeneous and antagonistic social whims and speculations in which we live is due to the failure to understand what the industrial organization

is and its all-pervading control over human life, while the traditions of our school of philosophy lead us always to approach the industrial organization, not from the side of objective study, but from that of philosophical doctrine. Hence it is that we find that the method of measuring what we see happening by what are called ethical standards, and of proposing to attack the phenomena by methods thence deduced, is so popular.

The advance of a new country from the very simplest social coordination up to the highest organization is a most interesting and instructive chance to study the development of the organization. It has of course been attended all the way along by stricter subordination and higher discipline. All organization implies restriction of liberty. The gain of power is won by narrowing individual range. The methods of business in colonial days were loose and slack to an inconceivable degree. The movement of industry has been all the time toward promptitude, punctuality, and reliability. It has been attended all the way by lamentations about the good old times; about the decline of small industries; about the lost spirit of comradeship between employer and employee; about the narrowing of the interests of the workman; about his conversion into a machine or into a "ware," and about industrial war. These lamentations have all had reference to unquestionable phenomena attendant on advancing organization. In all occupations the same movement is discernible—in the learned professions, in schools, in trade, commerce, and transportation. It is to go on faster than ever, now that the continent is filled up by the first superficial layer of population over its whole extent and the intensification of industry has begun. The great inventions both make the intension of the organization possible and make it inevitable, with all its consequences, whatever they may be. I must expect to be told here, according to the current fashions of thinking, that we ought to control the development of the organization. The first instinct of the modern man is to get a law passed to forbid or prevent what, in his wisdom, he disapproves. A thing which is inevitable, however, is one which we cannot control. We have to make up our minds to it, adjust ourselves to it, and sit down to live with it. Its inevitableness may be disputed, in which case we must reexamine it; but if our analysis is correct, when we reach what is inevitable we reach the end, and our regulations must apply to ourselves, not to the social facts.

Now the intensification of the social organization is what gives us greater social power. It is to it that we owe our increased comfort and abundance. We are none of us ready to sacrifice this. On the contrary, we want more of it. We would not return to the colonial simplicity and the colonial exiguity if we could. If not, then we must pay the price. Our life is bounded on every side by conditions. We can have this if we will agree to submit to that. In the case of industrial power and product the great condition is combination of force under discipline and strict coordination. Hence the wild language about wage-slavery and capitalistic tyranny.

———— • ————

"It is the greatest folly of which a man can be capable, to sit down with a slate and pencil to plan out a new social world."

———— • ————

In any state of society no great achievements can be produced without great force. Formerly great force was attainable only by slavery aggregating the power of great numbers of men. Roman civilization was built on this. Ours has been built on steam. It is to be built on electricity. Then we are all forced into an organization around these natural forces and adapted to the methods of their application; and although we indulge in rhetoric about political liberty, nevertheless we find ourselves bound tight in a new set of conditions, which control the modes of our existence and determine the directions in which alone economic and social liberty can go.

If it is said that there are some persons in our time who have become rapidly and in a great degree rich, it is true; if it is said that large aggregations of wealth in the control of individuals is a social danger, it is not true.

The movement of the industrial organization which has just been described has brought out a great demand for men capable of managing great enterprises. Such have been called "captains of industry." The analogy with military leaders suggested by this name is not misleading. The great leaders in the development of the industrial organization need those talents of executive and administrative skill, power to command, courage, and fortitude, which were formerly called for in military affairs and scarcely anywhere else. The industrial army is also as dependent on its captains as a military body is on its generals. One of the worst features of the existing system is that the employees have a constant risk in their employer. If he is not competent to manage the business with success, they suffer with him. Capital also is dependent on the skill of the captain of industry for the certainty and magnitude of its profits. Under these circumstances there has been a great demand for men having the requisite ability for this function. As the organization has advanced, with more impersonal bonds of coherence and wider scope of opera-

tions, the value of this functionary has rapidly increased. The possession of the requisite ability is a natural monopoly. Consequently, all the conditions have concurred to give to those who possessed this monopoly excessive and constantly advancing rates of remuneration.

Another social function of the first importance in an intense organization is the solution of those crises in the operation of it which are called the conjuncture of the market. It is through the market that the lines of relation run which preserve the system in harmonious and rhythmical operation. The conjuncture is the momentary sharper misadjustment of supply and demand which indicates that a redistribution of productive effort is called for. The industrial organization needs to be insured against these conjunctures, which, if neglected, produce a crisis and catastrophe; and it needs that they shall be anticipated and guarded against as far as skill and foresight can do it. The rewards of this function for the bankers and capitalists who perform it are very great. The captains of industry and the capitalists who operate on the conjuncture, therefore, if they are successful, win, in these days, great fortunes in a short time. There are no earnings which are more legitimate or for which greater services are rendered to the whole industrial body. The popular notions about this matter really assume that all the wealth accumulated by these classes of persons would be here just the same if they had not existed. They are supposed to have appropriated it out of the common stock. This is so far from being true that, on the contrary, their own wealth would not be but for themselves; and besides that, millions more of wealth, many-fold greater than their own, scattered in the hands of thousands, would not exist but for them.

Within the last two years I have traveled from end to end of the German Empire several times on all kinds of trains. I reached the conviction, looking at the matter from the passenger's standpoint, that, if the Germans could find a Cornelius Vanderbilt [an American railroad tycoon] and put their railroads in his hands for twenty-five years, letting him reorganize the system and make twenty-five million dollars out of it for himself in that period, they would make an excellent bargain.

Wealth and Society

But it is repeated until it has become a commonplace which people are afraid to question, that there is some social danger in the possession of large amounts of wealth by individuals. I ask, Why? I heard a lecture two years ago by a man who holds perhaps the first chair of political economy in the world. He said, among other things, that there was great danger in our day from great accumulations; that this danger ought to be met by taxation, and he referred to the fortune of the Rothschilds and to the great fortunes made in America to prove his point. He omitted, however, to state in what the danger consisted or to specify what harm has ever been done by the Rothschild fortunes or by the great fortunes accumulated in America. It seemed to me that the assertions he was making, and the measures he was recommending, ex-cathedra, were very serious to be thrown out so recklessly. It is hardly to be expected that novelists, popular magazinists, amateur economists, and politicians will be more responsible. It would be easy, however, to show what good is done by accumulations of capital in a few hands—that is, under close and direct management, permitting prompt and accurate application; also to tell what harm is done by loose and unfounded denunciations of any social component or any social group. In the recent debates on the income tax the assumption that great accumulations of wealth are socially harmful and ought to be broken down by taxation was treated as an axiom, and we had direct proof how dangerous it is to fit out the average politician with such unverified and unverifiable dogmas as his warrant for his modes of handling the direful tool of taxation.

Great figures are set out as to the magnitude of certain fortunes and the proportionate amount of the national wealth held by a fraction of the population, and eloquent exclamation-points are set against them. If the figures were beyond criticism, what would they prove? Where is the rich man who is oppressing anybody? If there was one, the newspapers would ring with it. The facts about the accumulation of wealth do not constitute a plutocracy, as I will show below. Wealth, in itself considered, is only power, like steam, or electricity, or knowledge. The question of its good or ill turns on the question how it will be used. To prove any harm in aggregations of wealth it must be shown that great wealth is, as a rule, in the ordinary course of social affairs, put to a mischievous use. This cannot be shown beyond the very slightest degree, if at all.

Therefore, all the allegations of general mischief, social corruption, wrong, and evil in our society must be referred back to those who make them for particulars and specifications. As they are offered to us we cannot allow them to stand, because we discern in them faulty observation of facts, or incorrect interpretation of facts, or a construction of facts according to some philosophy, or misunderstanding of phenomena and their relations, or incorrect inferences, or crooked deductions.

Assuming, however, that the charges against the existing "capitalistic"—that is, industrial—order of things are established, it is proposed to remedy the ill by reconstructing the industrial system on the principles of democracy. Once more we must untangle the snarl of half ideas and muddled facts.

Defining Democracy

Democracy is, of course, a word to conjure with. We have a democratic-republican political system, and we like it so well that we are prone to take any new step which can be recommended as "democratic" or which will round out some "principle" of democracy to a fuller fulfillment. Everything connected with this domain of political thought is crusted over with false historical traditions, cheap philosophy, and undefined terms, but it is useless to try to criticize it. The whole drift of the world for five hundred years has been toward democracy. That drift, produced by great discoveries and inventions, and by the discovery of a new continent, has raised the middle class out of the servile class. In alliance with the crown they crushed the feudal classes. They made the crown absolute in order to do it. Then they turned against the crown and, with the aid of the handicraftsmen and peasants, conquered it. Now the next conflict which must inevitably come is that between the middle capitalist class and the proletariat, as the word has come to be used. If a certain construction is put on this conflict, it may be called that between democracy and plutocracy, for it seems that industrialism must be developed into plutocracy by the conflict itself. That is the conflict which stands before civilized society to-day. All the signs of the times indicate its commencement, and it is big with fate to mankind and to civilization.

Although we cannot criticise democracy profitably, it may be said of it, with reference to our present subject, that up to this time democracy never has done anything, either in politics, social affairs, or industry, to prove its power to bless mankind. If we confine our attention to the United States, there are three difficulties with regard to its alleged achievements, and they all have the most serious bearing on the proposed democratization of industry.

1. The time during which democracy has been tried in the United States is too short to warrant any inferences. A century or two is a very short time in the life of political institutions, and if the circumstances change rapidly during the period the experiment is vitiated.

2. The greatest question of all about American democracy is whether it is a cause or a consequence. It is popularly assumed to be a cause, and we ascribe to its beneficent action all the political vitality, all the easiness of social relations, all the industrial activity and enterprise which we experience and which we value and enjoy. I submit, however, that, on a more thorough examination of the matter, we shall find that democracy is a consequence. There are eco-

nomic and sociological causes for our political vitality and vigor, for the ease and elasticity of our social relations, and for our industrial power and success. Those causes have also produced democracy, given it success, and have made its faults and errors innocuous. Indeed, in any true philosophy, it must be held that in the economic forces which control the material prosperity of a population lie the real causes of its political institutions, its social class-adjustments, its industrial prosperity, its moral code, and its world-philosophy. If democracy and the industrial system are both products of the economic conditions which exist, it is plainly absurd to set democracy to defeat those conditions in the control of industry. If, however, it is not true that democracy is a consequence, and I am well aware that very few people believe it, then we must go back to the view that democracy is a cause. That being so, it is difficult to see how democracy, which has had a clear field here in America, is not responsible for the ills which Mr. [Edward] Bellamy [author of a utopian novel, *Looking Backward*] and his comrades in opinion see in our present social state, and it is difficult to see the grounds of asking us to intrust it also with industry. The first and chief proof of success of political measures and systems is that, under them, society advances in health and vigor and that industry develops without causing social disease. If this has not been the case in America, American democracy has not succeeded. Neither is it easy to see how the masses, if they have undertaken to rule, can escape the responsibilities of ruling, especially so far as the consequences affect themselves. If, then, they have brought all this distress upon themselves under the present system, what becomes of the argument for extending the system to a direct and complete control of industry?

3. It is by no means certain that democracy in the United States has not, up to this time, been living on a capital inherited from aristocracy and industrialism. We have no pure democracy. Our democracy is limited at every turn by institutions which were developed in England in connection with industrialism and aristocracy, and these institutions are of the essence of our system. While our people are passionately democratic in temper and will not tolerate a doctrine that one man is not as good as another, they have common sense enough to know that he is not; and it seems that they love and cling to the conservative institutions quite as strongly as they do to the democratic philosophy. They are, therefore, ruled by men who talk philosophy and govern by the institutions. Now it is open to Mr. Bellamy to say that the reason why democracy in America seems to be open to the charge made in the last paragraph, of responsibility for all the ill which he now finds in our society, is because it has been infected with industri-

alism (capitalism); but in that case he must widen the scope of his proposition and undertake to purify democracy before turning industry over to it. The socialists generally seem to think that they make their undertakings easier when they widen their scope, and make them easiest when they propose to remake everything; but in truth social tasks increase in difficulty in an enormous ratio as they are widened in scope.

Unintended Consequences

The question, therefore, arises, if it is proposed to reorganize the social system on the principles of American democracy, whether the institutions of industrialism are to be retained. If so, all the virus of capitalism will be retained. It is forgotten, in many schemes of social reformation in which it is proposed to mix what we like with what we do not like, in order to extirpate the latter, that each must undergo a reaction from the other, and that what we like may be extirpated by what we do not like. We may find that instead of democratizing capitalism we have capitalized democracy—that is, have brought in plutocracy. Plutocracy is a political system in which the ruling force is wealth. The denunciation of capital which we hear from all the reformers is the most eloquent proof that the greatest power in the world to-day is capital. They know that it is, and confess it most when they deny it most strenuously. At present the power of capital is social and industrial, and only in a small degree political. So far as capital is political, it is on account of political abuses, such as tariffs and special legislation on the one hand and legislative strikes on the other. These conditions exist in the democracy to which it is proposed to transfer the industries. What does that mean except bringing all the power of capital once for all into the political arena and precipitating the conflict of democracy and plutocracy at once? Can anyone imagine that the masterfulness, the overbearing disposition, the greed of gain, and the ruthlessness in methods, which are the faults of the master of industry at his worst, would cease when he was a functionary of the State, which had relieved him of risk and endowed him with authority? Can anyone imagine that politicians would no longer be corruptly fond of money, intriguing, and crafty when they were charged, not only with patronage and government contracts, but also with factories, stores, ships, and railroads? Could we expect anything except that, when the politician and the master of industry were joined in one, we should have the vices of both unchecked by the restraints of either? In any socialistic state there will be one set of positions which will offer chances of wealth beyond the wildest dreams of avarice; *viz.*, on the governing committees. Then there will be rich men whose wealth will indeed be a menace to social interests, and instead of industrial peace there will be such war as no one has dreamed of yet: the war between the political ins and outs—that is, between those who are on the committee and those who want to get on it.

We must not drop the subject of democracy without one word more. The Greeks already had occasion to notice a most serious distinction between two principles of democracy which lie at its roots. Plutarch says that Solon got the archonship in part by promising equality, which some understood of esteem and dignity, others of measure and number. There is one democratic principle which means that each man should be esteemed for his merit and worth, for just what he is, without regard to birth, wealth, rank, or other adventitious circumstances. The other principle is that each one of us ought to be equal to all the others in what he gets and enjoys. The first principle is only partially realizable, but, so far as it goes, it is elevating and socially progressive and profitable. The second is not capable of an intelligible statement. The first is a principle of industrialization. It proceeds from and is intelligible only in a society built on the industrial virtues, free endeavor, security of property, and repression of the baser vices; that is, in a society whose industrial system is built on labor and exchange. The other is only a rule of division for robbers who have to divide plunder or monks who have to divide gifts. If, therefore, we want to democratize industry in the sense of the first principle, we need only perfect what we have now, especially on its political side. If we try to democratize it in the sense of the other principle, we corrupt politics at one stroke; we enter upon an industrial enterprise which will waste capital and bring us all to poverty, and we set loose greed and envy as ruling social passions.

The Limits of Human Reform

If this poor old world is as bad as they say, one more reflection may check the zeal of the headlong reformer. It is at any rate a tough old world. It has taken its trend and curvature and all its twists and tangles from a long course of formation. All its wry and crooked gnarls and knobs are therefore stiff and stubborn. If we puny men by our arts can do anything at all to straighten them, it will only be by modifying the tendencies of some of the forces at work, so that, after a sufficient time, their action may be changed a little and slowly the lines of movement may be modified. This effort, however, can at most be only slight, and it will take a long time. In the meantime spontaneous forces will be at work, com-

pared with which our efforts are like those of a man trying to deflect a river, and these forces will have changed the whole problem before our interferences have time to make themselves felt. The great stream of time and earthly things will sweep on just the same in spite of us. It bears with it now all the errors and follies of the past, the wreckage of all the philosophies, the fragments of all the civilizations, the wisdom of all the abandoned ethical systems, the debris of all the institutions, and the penalties of all the mistakes. It is only in imagination that we stand by and look at and criticize it and plan to change it. Everyone of us is a child of his age and cannot get out of it. He is in the stream and is swept along with it. All his sciences and philosophy come to him out of it. Therefore the tide will not be changed by us. It will swallow up both us and our experiments. It will absorb the efforts at change and take them into itself as new but trivial components, and the great movement of tradition and work will go on unchanged by our fads and schemes. The things which will change it are the great discoveries and inventions, the new reactions inside the social organism, and the changes in the earth itself on account of changes in the cosmical forces. These causes will make it just what, in fidelity to them, it ought to be. The men will be carried along with it and be made by it. The utmost they can do by their cleverness will be to note and record their course as they are carried along, which is what we do now, and is that which leads us to the vain fancy that we can make or guide the movement. That is why it is the greatest folly of which a man can be capable, to sit down with a slate and pencil to plan out a new social world.

For Further Reading

David D. Anderson, *Ignatius Donnelly*. Boston: Twayne Publishers, 1980.

John G. Cawelti, *Apostles of the Self-Made Man*. Chicago: University of Chicago Press, 1965.

Gene Clanton, *Populism: The Humane Preference in America, 1890–1900*. Boston: Twayne Publishers, 1991.

Bruce Curtis, *William Graham Sumner*. Boston: Twayne Publishers, 1981.

Lawrence Goodwyn, *Democratic Promise: The Populist Movement in America*. New York: Oxford University Press, 1976.

Robert Green McCloskey, *American Conservatism in the Age of Enterprise: A Study of William Graham Sumner, Stephen J. Field, and Andrew Carnegie*. New York: Harper & Row, 1964.

George B. Tindall, ed., *A Populist Reader*. New York: Harper Torchbooks, 1966.

PART II:
THE PROGRESSIVE ERA,
1895–1920

Jim Crow and Black Response

American Empire: Debate over the Philippines

Social Issues of the Progressive Era

New Nationalism vs. New Freedom

World War I and the League of Nations

1895
- July   United States intervenes in Great Britain/Venezuela boundary dispute
- February 24   Rebellion against Spanish rule breaks out in Cuba
- September 18   Booker T. Washington's speech at the Atlanta Exposition

1897
- January Gold rush starts in Klondike, Alaska

1899
- February 4   Filipino rebels under Emilio Aguinaldo attack American troops in Manila, starting rebellion that lasts three years
- September 6   United States proposes "Open Door" policy toward China

1901
- January 10   First great oil strike in Texas
- February 25   U.S. Steel Corporation founded; nation's first billion-dollar corporation
- March 2   Congress passes Platt Amendment making Cuba a quasi-protectorate of the United States
- September 14   McKinley dies eight days after assassination attempt; Roosevelt takes office
- November 9   Northern Securities Company, a railroad holding company controlled by J.P. Morgan, is incorporated

1903
- Ford Motor Company formed
- *The Souls of Black Folk* by W.E.B. Du Bois published
- May 23   Wisconsin is first state to adopt direct primary for party elections
- October   Baseball holds first World Series
- November   United States secures rights to Panama Canal route after Panama, with assistance from the U.S. Navy, secedes from Colombia
- December 17   Wilbur and Orville Wright achieve world's first successful airplane flight

1907
- Peak year of immigration: 1,285,349 immigrants
- October Panic of 1907 reveals pitfalls of U.S. monetary system
- November 16   Oklahoma enters the Union

1895 · 1900 · 1905

1896
- January 4   Utah becomes the 45th state
- April 23   Demonstration of Thomas Edison's motion picture invention
- May 18   Supreme Court in *Plessy v. Ferguson* legalizes segregation
- November 3 William McKinley elected president

1898
- February 15   The U.S. battleship *Maine* sunk in Havana Harbor in Cuba after mysterious explosion
- April 21–December 10   Spanish-American War results in U.S. victory and acquisition of Guam, Puerto Rico, and the Philippines; Cuba gains independence from Spain
- July 28   Hawaii annexed by the United States

1900
- March 6   Social Democratic (later Socialist) Party founded by Eugene Debs
- September 18   First direct primary election in nation held in Hennepin County, Minnesota
- November 6 McKinley reelected president; Theodore Roosevelt elected vice president; noted Progressive Robert M. La Follette elected governor of Wisconsin

1902
- *McClure's* magazine begins to publish articles by Lincoln Steffens, Ida M. Tarbell, and other "muckrackers"
- March 10 Roosevelt sues Northern Securities Company in first "trust-busting" suit
- May 12   United Mine Workers strike idles 140,000 workers; President Roosevelt intervenes in October; strikers end walkout on October 21

1904
- March 14 Supreme Court orders dissolution of Northern Securities Company for violating antitrust laws
- December 6 Pronouncement of the "Roosevelt Corollary" to the Monroe Doctrine

1905
- January 4 U.S. takes over customs and international debt of the Dominican Republic
- June   Industrial Workers of the World (IWW) founded

1906
- Upton Sinclair's *The Jungle* published
- April 18–19   Great San Francisco Earthquake
- June 30   Pure Food and Drug Act and Meat Inspection Act passed by Congress
- April 17   In *Lochner v. New York* Supreme Court finds state law limiting maximum working hours unconstitutional
- September 29   U.S. troops occupy Cuba

1908

•February 24 Supreme Court in *Muller v. Oregon* upholds Oregon's law mandating ten-hour maximum workday for women

•October 1 Henry Ford's Model T automobile goes on the market

•November 3 William Howard Taft elected president

1912

•Massachusetts becomes first state to adopt minimum wage legislation for women and children

•January 6 New Mexico becomes the 47th state

•February 14 Arizona admitted as 48th state

•April 15 SS *Titanic* disaster

•August U.S. Marines land in Nicaragua

•August 24 Alaska receives territorial status

•November 5 Woodrow Wilson elected president

1910

•March 26 United States forbids immigration of criminals, paupers, and anarchists

•August 31 Theodore Roosevelt's "New Nationalism" speech

1914

•January 5 Henry Ford perfects assembly line; announces adoption of five-dollar minimum daily wage for his workers

•August World War I begins in Europe; President Wilson proclaims U.S. neutrality and offers to mediate the conflict

•August 15 Panama Canal opens

•September 26 Federal Trade Commission established

1916

•March Clashes between U.S. troops and Mexican guerrilla leader "Pancho" Villa

•May 4 Germany pledges to restrict its submarine warfare and not to attack merchant ships without warning

•October 16 Margaret Sanger opens nation's first birth control clinic

•November 7 Woodrow Wilson reelected president

1920

•March 19 A final attempt to ratify the Treaty of Versailles fails in the Senate

•August 26 Nineteenth Amendment, guaranteeing women the right to vote, added to Constitution

•November 2 Warren G. Harding elected president

1910   **1915**   **1920**

1909

•June 1 National Association for the Advancement of Colored People (NAACP) founded

1911

•March 25 Triangle Shirtwaist factory fire kills 141 trapped workers in New York City

•May 15 Supreme Court orders dissolution of Standard Oil Company

1913

•Congress passes Hetch Hetchy dam bill

•February 25 Sixteenth Amendment added to Constitution

•May 31 Seventeenth Amendment added to Constitution

•December 13 Federal Reserve System established

1915

•January 25 First transcontinental telephone call

•May 7 British passenger liner *Lusitania* sunk by a German submarine; 114 Americans drowned

•December 4 Ku Klux Klan revived in Georgia

1917

•February 3 United States severs diplomatic relations with Germany after it resumes submarine attacks on U.S. ships

•March 2 Puerto Rico made a U.S. territory

•April 2 Wilson asks Congress for declaration of war against Germany; Jeannette Rankin of Montana, Congress's first woman, is one of the 50 representatives to vote no

•October First U.S. detachments arrive at military front lines in France

•November Bolshevist revolution in Russia; United States refuses to recognize new regime

1918

•January 8 Wilson's "Fourteen Points" speech to Congress outlines U.S. war aims

•May 16 Sedition Act passed outlawing speech critical of the war effort

•November 11 World War I ends

1919

•January 29 Eighteenth Amendment added to Constitution; its prohibition of alcohol is to take effect January 16, 1920

•June 28 Treaty of Versailles signed; includes Wilson's proposal for a League of Nations

PART II:
THE PROGRESSIVE ERA,
1895–1920

Between 1895 and 1920 the United States witnessed significant developments in both domestic and foreign affairs. In the domestic sphere the country debated and enacted numerous social, economic, and political reforms that have become known collectively as progressivism. In foreign affairs the United States participated in two wars that signified the country's emergence as a world power. By 1920, however, the American people were reacting against both domestic reform and foreign entanglements.

The Progressive Movement

The progressive movement was a response to trends in the country's social and economic conditions since the Civil War—trends many Americans found disturbing. These changes included the rise of big business and the formation of monopolies; corruption in local, state, and federal governments; the widening of class divisions; and the growing numbers of poor people in the nation's cities. Progressives believed that all of these developments threatened American ideals of fairness and equal opportunity. To counter this threat they sponsored numerous reform efforts (although most progressives rejected radical changes such as those prescribed by socialism). While not all Americans agreed with progressives on the need for change, the reforms that were proposed, debated, and in many cases enacted during this time had a lasting impact on American society.

Progressivism had much in common with the agrarian-based Populist movement that peaked in the early and mid-1890s. Populists, like progressives, decried the unequal distribution of wealth and power in the nation. (At the turn of the century, 2 percent of the nation's population controlled 60 percent of its wealth.) Both movements condemned the power of large business corporations and trusts that controlled whole industries, and they called for greater government regulation of the economy. Both movements also advocated reformed and stronger governments to protect the public interest. Some former Populists played major roles in the progressive movement itself. Important differences between the two movements existed, however. Progressivism differed from Populism in that it had an urban rather than a rural base of support. Progressivism also had greater appeal among the educated middle class and therefore attracted the support of more writers, academics, and intellectuals than did the Populist movement. The progressives also opted to work within the two major political parties rather than try to repeat the Populist attempt to create a new third party.

Those who called themselves progressives varied widely in occupation and in their beliefs. They included politicians, preachers, social welfare workers, academics, business owners, journalists, and others. They often disagreed on particular issues or on which cause or reform was most important. Some progressives believed that the main problem to be addressed was the dominance of business monopolies; others believed it to be the unequal status of women. Some focused on the conservation of natural resources, while others focused on corruption in city government or the influx of immigrants. In many respects, progressivism can be considered an aggregate of causes rather than one cohesive movement.

Progressive Reforms and Reformers

In its infancy, the progressive movement was most active at the state and local levels. Mayors such as Hazen Pingree of Detroit and Tom Johnson of Cleveland forcefully attacked urban poverty and municipal corruption. Governors such as Robert La Follette of Wisconsin and Hiram Johnson of California capitalized on reformist sentiment to break the control of business over their respective state governments. La Follette and other governors then helped create new laws regulating railroads and utilities, setting minimum wages and maximum hours for workers, abolishing child labor, and ensuring more democratic participation in the nomination and election of public officials.

Notable progressives worked outside of politics as well. Jane Addams founded Hull House in Chicago in 1889 and began a lifelong career of helping poor residents of urban slums. Journalist "muckrakers" such as Upton Sinclair, Ida Tarbell, and Lincoln Steffens exposed shady business practices and political scandals in widely read books and magazine articles. Scholars such as John Dewey and Charles A. Beard applied progressive ideas to the study of philosophy, history, and economics.

Three of the leading figures of the Progressive Era were U.S. presidents: Theodore Roosevelt, William H. Taft, and Woodrow Wilson. Roosevelt became president in 1901 following the assassination of William McKinley. The former New York governor immediately began to use his office (which he called his "bully pulpit") to give progressivism a place on the national agenda. Roosevelt was particularly concerned about environmental issues, but he also lent his support to strengthening antitrust laws and regulating business, including the railroad, meatpacking, and oil industries. Taft, president from 1909 to 1913, carried forward many of Roosevelt's policies (although by the end of his term many progressives were clamoring for a new president). Wilson, president from 1913 to 1921 and leader of the progressive wing of the Democratic Party, accomplished numerous government reforms, including the creation of the Federal Reserve System to manage the nation's currency and the Federal Trade Commission, a government agency with broad powers to regulate business practices.

The Progressive Era produced four constitutional amendments, each of which addressed a major progressive concern. The Sixteenth Amendment authorized a federal income tax, which was intended in part to ensure a greater measure of economic equality among American citizens. The Seventeenth Amendment established popular elections for U.S. senators (who had previously been selected by state legislators), advancing the progressive goal of increasing citizens' participation in the election of their representatives. Many progressives viewed alcohol consumption as a major social problem; the Eighteenth Amendment, which banned the "manufacture, sale, or transportation of intoxicating liquors," ushered in the era of Prohibition. Finally, the Nineteenth Amendment extended the right to vote to women, a victory for the woman's suffrage movement, which was the leading feminist cause of the Progressive Era.

Blacks and Other Minorities

Blacks fared poorly during the Progressive Era. In the southern states, where most blacks lived, white-dominated state and local governments enforced the segregation of the races in schools, public buildings, and virtually all other areas of life. White politicians devised numerous mechanisms, such as literacy tests and poll taxes, designed to deny blacks the right to vote. Lynch mobs killed hundreds of blacks. Many southern blacks migrated to northern cities, hoping to find better jobs and more equal treatment. Those who moved north did find that jobs were plentiful (especially after the United States entered World War I), but gains in employment were offset by continued racial discrimination and poor living conditions in urban slums. The black community was divided over how best to respond to the continued denial of equal rights in American society.

Although a few progressives supported equal rights for blacks, many did not. President Woodrow Wilson, for example, formally segregated federal government employees. Other minorities were also adversely affected by some of the policies advocated by progressive reformers, many of whom believed that the quality of American life was threatened as much by unfamiliar immigrants as by corrupt politicians. Progressives in California supported the passage of laws restricting the ability of Japanese immigrants and other noncitizens to lease land. Many progressives advocated immigration restrictions to reduce America's intake of foreigners not of a northern European background. In his 1916 book *The Passing of the Great Race*, prominent progressive Madison Grant wrote in favor of immigration restrictions, racial segregation, and forced sterilization of "worthless race types" (which he defined to include blacks, Jews, and southern and eastern Europeans).

The United States Becomes a World Power

Along with domestic reforms, significant developments in foreign affairs affected the United States during the Progressive Era. During the decades following the Civil War, most Americans paid relatively little attention to the world beyond America's shores. However, by the 1890s several trends came together to draw Americans' attention to international issues. One development was the growing importance of trade and investment in America's economy. Another was the increasing international competition for colonies. With Great Britain, France, Germany, and other European nations jockeying for colonies in Asia and Africa, some Americans worried that the United States was missing out on a potential source of wealth and international stature. They believed that in order to be recognized as a great nation, the United States needed an overseas empire. Other Americans sharply criticized such beliefs, arguing that a colonial empire was unworthy of America's heritage as a nation founded on an anticolonial statement, the Declaration of Independence.

America's first significant venture into colonialism followed the 1898 Spanish-American War. The war ended with the United States' taking the Philippines, Guam, and Puerto Rico from the defeated Spanish. This decision to acquire colonies, especially the Philippines (the largest and most remote of the acquired territories), signaled a new American commitment to imperialism—a commitment that was further demonstrated by America's three-year war to put down a Filipino rebellion for independence. Under Presidents McKinley, Roosevelt, Taft, and Wilson, the United States undertook several ventures to expand and protect what were deemed to be America's strategic and economic interests abroad, especially in the Western Hemisphere. Between 1900 and 1914 American troops intervened repeatedly in Cuba, Panama, Nicaragua, the Dominican Republic, Haiti, and Mexico. Americans took over the customs houses and supervised elections of a number of these countries. One of the most celebrated—and criticized—foreign policy undertakings of the United States was its support of Panama's revolution from Colombia in 1903 in order to gain control of a site to build the Panama Canal, which was completed in 1914.

The progressive movement assumed no single position on foreign affairs or on American imperialism. Some progressives argued that imperialism betrayed American ideals of equality and self-government. Others held that America was in a good position to improve life in other countries by remaking their economies and governments in the image of the United States. "I will teach those Latin American countries to elect good men," said progressive president Woodrow Wilson near the start of his administration.

World War I

Progressives were equally divided on the merits and drawbacks of entering World War I. When war began in Europe in 1914, few Americans, progressive or otherwise, favored taking sides in the conflict. However, in May 1915, when a German submarine sank the British passenger liner *Lusitania*, killing 128 Americans and hundreds of other people, ex-president Theodore Roosevelt and others argued that the United States should enter the war against Germany, or at least undergo a massive military "preparedness" program. But other notable progressives, including social reformer Jane Addams and Wisconsin leader Robert La Follette (by then a U.S. senator), argued that America should remain neutral in the war. They worried that domestic reforms would be sacrificed if the United States plunged into war. President Wilson himself struggled to maintain "peace with honor" for three years before finally asking Congress for a declaration of war against Germany on April 2, 1917, citing German submarine attacks on U.S. ships as the primary reason for his decision. America would subsequently send 2 million soldiers to fight in Europe, of which 112,000 would perish.

Both during and after the war, Wilson tried to preserve his progressive ideals by arguing that the United States, through its military and diplomatic interventions in Europe, sought to establish a world "safe for democracy" and to end the era of colonialism and power politics. The League of Nations, an international organization of member nations created by Woodrow Wilson during the 1919 peace talks in Europe, was to be the centerpiece of his vision of a progressive new world. However, the mood of the nation was changing. After long and acrimonious debate the Senate rejected U.S. membership in the League of Nations. Running for president in 1920, Republican Warren G. Harding promised a return to "normalcy," a word that to many Americans signified the rejection both of drastic domestic reforms and involvement in world affairs. Harding's 1920 election victory marked the end of the Progressive Era.

Jim Crow and Black Response

VIEWPOINT 11A

Blacks Should Stop Agitating for Political Equality (1895)

Booker T. Washington (1856–1915)

Born a slave shortly before the Civil War, Booker T. Washington received his education at the Hampton Institute, an industrial school founded by Samuel C. Armstrong, a former Union general, for the education of freed blacks. After teaching at Hampton for a time, in 1881 Washington founded the Tuskegee Institute in Alabama, a vocational institute for blacks, which under his leadership grew into one of the leading centers of black education in the United States. Washington's national prominence was assured by his speech at the 1895 Atlanta Exposition, reprinted here, and for the next twenty years he was considered by white America to be the preeminent spokesman for the country's blacks. Those years were marked by the growth of "Jim Crow" laws and other measures that disenfranchised blacks and increased racial segregation. Washington advocated a policy of accommodation on civil rights issues, arguing that blacks should concentrate on economic self-improvement rather than changes in political laws.

What are the sources of Washington's optimism about race relations? What elements of Washington's speech might account for his popularity with white establishment leaders (including then-president Grover Cleveland, who in a letter to Washington wrote that the address "cannot fail to delight and encourage all who wish well for your race")?

M r. President and Gentlemen of the Board of Directors and Citizens:

One-third of the population of the South is of the Negro race. No enterprise seeking the material, civil, or moral welfare of this section can disregard this element of our population and reach the highest success. I but convey to you, Mr. President and Directors, the sentiment of the masses of my race when I say that in no way have the value and manhood of the American Negro been more fittingly and generously recognized than by the managers of this magnificent exposition at every stage of its progress. It is a recognition that will do more to cement the friendship of

From Booker T. Washington's speech at the Atlanta Exposition, September 18, 1895; reprinted in his book *Up from Slavery* (Doubleday, 1901).

the two races than any occurrence since the dawn of our freedom.

Not only this, but the opportunity here afforded will awaken among us a new era of industrial progress. Ignorant and inexperienced, it is not strange that in the first years of our new life we began at the top instead of at the bottom; that a seat in Congress or the state legislature was more sought than real estate or industrial skill; that the political convention or stump speaking had more attractions than starting a dairy farm or truck garden.

A ship lost at sea for many days suddenly sighted a friendly vessel. From the mast of the unfortunate vessel was seen a signal: "Water, water; we die of thirst!" The answer from the friendly vessel at once came back: "Cast down your bucket where you are." A second time the signal, "Water, water, send us water!" ran up from the distressed vessel, and was answered: "Cast down your bucket where you are." And a third and fourth signal for water was answered: "Cast down your bucket where you are." The captain of the distressed vessel, at last heeding the injunction, cast down his bucket, and it came up full of fresh, sparkling water from the mouth of the Amazon River.

"The wisest among my race understand that the agitation of questions of social equality is the extremest folly."

To those of my race who depend on bettering their condition in a foreign land or who underestimate the importance of cultivating friendly relations with the Southern white man, who is their next-door neighbor, I would say: Cast down your bucket where you are; cast it down in making friends, in every manly way, of the people of all races by whom we are surrounded. Cast it down in agriculture, mechanics, in commerce, in domestic service, and in the professions. And in this connection it is well to bear in mind that whatever other sins the South may be called to bear, when it comes to business, pure and simple, it is in the South that the Negro is given a man's chance in the commercial world, and in nothing is this exposition more eloquent than in emphasizing this chance.

Our greatest danger is that, in the great leap from slavery to freedom, we may overlook the fact that the masses of us are to live by the productions of our hands and fail to keep in mind that we shall prosper in proportion as we learn to dignify and glorify common labor, and put brains and skill into the common occupations of life; shall prosper in proportion as we learn to draw the line between the superficial and the substantial, the ornamental gewgaws of life and the useful. No race can prosper till it learns that there is as much dignity in tilling a field as in writing a poem. It is at the bottom of life we must begin, and not at the top. Nor should we permit our grievances to overshadow our opportunities.

To those of the white race who look to the incoming of those of foreign birth and strange tongue and habits for the prosperity of the South, were I permitted I would repeat what I say to my own race, "Cast down your bucket where you are." Cast it down among the 8 million Negroes whose habits you know, whose fidelity and love you have tested in days when to have proved treacherous meant the ruin of your firesides. Cast down your bucket among these people who have, without strikes and labor wars, tilled your fields, cleared your forests, builded your railroads and cities, and brought forth treasures from the bowels of the earth and helped make possible this magnificent representation of the progress of the South. Casting down your bucket among my people, helping and encouraging them as you are doing on these grounds, and, with education of head, hand, and heart, you will find that they will buy your surplus land, make blossom the waste places in your fields, and run your factories.

While doing this, you can be sure in the future, as in the past, that you and your families will be surrounded by the most patient, faithful, law-abiding, and unresentful people that the world has seen. As we have proved our loyalty to you in the past, in nursing your children, watching by the sickbed of your mothers and fathers, and often following them with tear-dimmed eyes to their graves, so in the future, in our humble way, we shall stand by you with a devotion that no foreigner can approach, ready to lay down our lives, if need be, in defense of yours; interlacing our industrial, commercial, civil, and religious life with yours in a way that shall make the interests of both races one. In all things that are purely social we can be as separate as the fingers, yet one as the hand in all things essential to mutual progress.

Development for All

There is no defense or security for any of us except in the highest intelligence and development of all. If anywhere there are efforts tending to curtail the fullest growth of the Negro, let these efforts be turned into stimulating, encouraging, and making him the most useful and intelligent citizen. Effort or means so invested will pay a thousand percent interest. These efforts will be twice blessed—"blessing him that gives and him that takes."

There is no escape, through law of man or God, from the inevitable:

The laws of changeless justice bind
Oppressor with oppressed;
And close as sin and suffering joined
We march to fate abreast

Nearly 16 millions of hands will aid you in pulling the load upward, or they will pull against you the load downward. We shall constitute one-third and more of the ignorance and crime of the South, or one-third its intelligence and progress; we shall contribute one-third to the business and industrial prosperity of the South, or we shall prove a veritable body of death, stagnating, depressing, retarding every effort to advance the body politic.

Gentlemen of the exposition, as we present to you our humble effort at an exhibition of our progress, you must not expect overmuch. Starting thirty years ago with ownership here and there in a few quilts and pumpkins and chickens (gathered from miscellaneous sources), remember: the path that has led from these to the invention and production of agricultural implements, buggies, steam engines, newspapers, books, statuary, carving, paintings, the management of drugstores and banks, has not been trodden without contact with thorns and thistles. While we take pride in what we exhibit as a result of our independent efforts, we do not for a moment forget that our part in this exhibition would fall far short of your expectations but for the constant help that has come to our educational life, not only from the Southern states but especially from Northern philanthropists who have made their gifts a constant stream of blessing and encouragement.

The wisest among my race understand that the agitation of questions of social equality is the extremest folly, and that progress in the enjoyment of all the privileges that will come to us must be the result of severe and constant struggle rather than of artificial forcing. No race that has anything to contribute to the markets of the world is long in any degree ostracized. It is important and right that all privileges of the law be ours, but it is vastly more important that we be prepared for the exercise of these privileges. The opportunity to earn a dollar in a factory just now is worth infinitely more than the opportunity to spend a dollar in an opera house.

In conclusion, may I repeat that nothing in thirty years has given us more hope and encouragement and drawn us so near to you of the white race as this opportunity offered by the exposition; and here bending, as it were, over the altar that represents the results of the struggles of your race and mine, both starting practically empty-handed three decades ago, I pledge that, in your effort to work out the great and intricate problem which God has laid at the doors of the South, you shall have at all times the patient, sympathetic help of my race; only let this be constantly in mind that, while from representations in these buildings of the product of field, of forest, of mine, of factory, letters, and art, much good will come—yet far above and beyond material benefits will be that higher good, that let us pray God will come, in a blotting out of sectional differences and racial animosities and suspicions, in a determination to administer absolute justice, in a willing obedience among all classes to the mandates of law. This, coupled with our material prosperity, will bring into our beloved South a new heaven and a new earth.

VIEWPOINT 11B

A Critique of
Booker T. Washington (1903)

W.E.B. Du Bois (1868–1963)

From 1895 until his death twenty years later, the most famous leader of black America was Booker T. Washington, a political moderate who advocated a policy of economic self-improvement and political accommodation. An early critique of Washington's views comes from this excerpted passage from *The Souls of Black Folk*, a noted 1903 study of black life written by W.E.B. Du Bois. Du Bois, the first black granted a doctorate at Harvard University in Massachusetts, later helped found the National Association for the Advancement of Colored People (NAACP) and was for many years America's leading black intellectual and civil rights activist.

What connection does Du Bois see between Washington's successes and popularity and potential problems for blacks in America? Could Du Bois be considered more or less realistic about civil rights than Washington? Why or why not?

E asily the most striking thing in the history of the American Negro since 1876 is the ascendancy of Mr. Booker T. Washington. It began at the time when war memories and ideals were rapidly passing; a day of astonishing commercial development was dawning; a sense of doubt and hesitation overtook the freedmen's sons,—then it was that his leading began. Mr. Washington came, with a single definite programme, at the psychological moment when the nation was a little ashamed of having bestowed so much sentiment on Negroes, and was concentrating its energies on Dollars. His programme of industrial education, conciliation of the South, and submission and silence as to civil and

From W.E.B. Du Bois, *The Souls of Black Folk* (Chicago: A.C. McClurg, 1903).

political rights, was not wholly original; the Free Negroes from 1830 up to wartime had striven to build industrial schools, and the American Missionary Association had from the first taught various trades; and [Joseph C.] Price and others had sought a way of honorable alliance with the best of the Southerners. But Mr. Washington first indissolubly linked these things; he put enthusiasm, unlimited energy, and perfect faith into this programme, and changed it from a by-path into a veritable Way of Life. And the tale of the methods by which he did this is a fascinating study of human life.

It startled the nation to hear a Negro advocating such a programme after many decades of bitter complaint: it startled and won the applause of the South, it interested and won the admiration of the North; and after a confused murmur of protest, it silenced if it did not convert the Negroes themselves.

To gain the sympathy and coöperation of the various elements comprising the white South was Mr. Washington's first task; and this, at the time Tuskegee was founded, seemed, for a black man, well-nigh impossible. And yet ten years later it was done in the word spoken at Atlanta: "In all things purely social we can be as separate as the five fingers, and yet one as the hand in all things essential to mutual progress." This "Atlanta Compromise" is by all odds the most notable thing in Mr. Washington's career. The South interpreted it in different ways: the radicals received it as a complete surrender of the demand for civil and political equality; the conservatives, as a generously conceived working basis for mutual understanding. So both approved it, and to-day its author is certainly the most distinguished Southerner since Jefferson Davis, and the one with the largest personal following.

Next to this achievement comes Mr. Washington's work in gaining place and consideration in the North. Others less shrewd and tactful had formerly essayed to sit on these two stools and had fallen between them; but as Mr. Washington knew the heart of the South from birth and training, so by singular insight he intuitively grasped the spirit of the age which was dominating the North. And so thoroughly did he learn the speech and thought of triumphant commercialism, and the ideals of material prosperity, that the picture of a lone black boy poring over a French grammar amid the weeds and dirt of a neglected home soon seemed to him the acme of absurdities. One wonders what Socrates and St. Francis of Assisi would say to this.

And yet this very singleness of vision and thorough oneness with his age is a mark of the successful man. It is as though Nature must needs make men narrow in order to give them force. So Mr. Washington's cult has gained unquestioning followers, his work has wonderfully prospered, his friends are legion, and his enemies are confounded. To-day he stands as the one recognized spokesman of his ten million fellows, and one of the most notable figures in a nation of seventy millions. One hesitates, therefore, to criticise a life which, beginning with so little, has done so much. And yet the time is come when one may speak in all sincerity and utter courtesy of the mistakes and shortcomings of Mr. Washington's career, as well as of his triumphs, without being thought captious or envious, and without forgetting that it is easier to do ill than well in the world.

The criticism that has hitherto met Mr. Washington has not always been of this broad character. In the South especially has he had to walk warily to avoid the harshest judgments,—and naturally so, for he is dealing with the one subject of deepest sensitiveness to that section. Twice—once when at the Chicago celebration of the Spanish-American War he alluded to the color-prejudice that is "eating away the vitals of the South," and once when he dined with President Roosevelt—has the resulting Southern criticism been violent enough to threaten seriously his popularity. In the North the feeling has several times forced itself into words, that Mr. Washington's counsels of submission overlooked certain elements of true manhood, and that his educational programme was unnecessarily narrow. Usually, however, such criticism has not found open expression, although, too, the spiritual sons of the Abolitionists have not been prepared to acknowledge that the schools founded before Tuskegee, by men of broad ideals and self-sacrificing spirit, were wholly failures or worthy of ridicule. While, then, criticism has not failed to follow Mr. Washington, yet the prevailing public opinion of the land has been but too willing to deliver the solution of a wearisome problem into his hands, and say, "If that is all you and your race ask, take it."

Among his own people, however, Mr. Washington has encountered the strongest and most lasting opposition, amounting at times to bitterness, and even to-day continuing strong and insistent even though largely silenced in outward expression by the public opinion of the nation. Some of this opposition is, of course, mere envy; the disappointment of displaced demagogues and the spite of narrow minds. But aside from this, there is among educated and thoughtful colored men in all parts of the land a feeling of deep regret, sorrow, and apprehension at the wide currency and ascendancy which some of Mr. Washington's theories have gained. These same men admire his sincerity of purpose, and are willing to forgive much to honest endeavor which is doing something worth the doing. They coöperate with Mr. Washington as far as they conscientiously can; and, indeed, it is no ordinary tribute to this man's tact and

power that, steering as he must between so many diverse interests and opinions, he so largely retains the respect of all.

But the hushing of the criticism of honest opponents is a dangerous thing. It leads some of the best of the critics to unfortunate silence and paralysis of effort, and others to burst into speech so passionately and intemperately as to lose listeners. Honest and earnest criticism from those whose interests are most nearly touched,—criticism of writers by readers, of government by those governed, of leaders by those led,—this is the soul of democracy and the safeguard of modern society. If the best of the American Negroes receive by outer pressure a leader whom they had not recognized before, manifestly there is here a certain palpable gain. Yet there is also irreparable loss,—a loss of that peculiarly valuable education which a group receives when by search and criticism it finds and commissions its own leaders. The way in which this is done is at once the most elementary and the nicest problem of social growth. History is but the record of such group-leadership; and yet how infinitely changeful is its type and character! And of all types and kinds, what can be more instructive than the leadership of a group within a group?—that curious double movement where real progress may be negative and actual advance be relative retrogression. All this is the social student's inspiration and despair.

Now in the past the American Negro has had instructive experience in the choosing of group leaders, founding thus a peculiar dynasty which in the light of present conditions is worth while studying. When sticks and stones and beasts form the sole environment of a people, their attitude is largely one of determined opposition to and conquest of natural forces. But when to earth and brute is added an environment of men and ideas, then the attitude of the imprisoned group may take three main forms,—a feeling of revolt and revenge; an attempt to adjust all thought and action to the will of the greater group; or, finally, a determined effort at self-realization and self-development despite environing opinion. . . .

Mr. Washington represents in Negro thought the old attitude of adjustment and submission; but adjustment at such a peculiar time as to make his programme unique. This is an age of unusual economic development, and Mr. Washington's programme naturally takes an economic cast, becoming a gospel of Work and Money to such an extent as apparently almost completely to overshadow the higher aims of life. Moreover, this is an age when the more advanced races are coming in closer contact with the less developed races, and the race-feeling is therefore intensified; and Mr. Washington's programme practically accepts the alleged inferiority of the Negro races. In our own land, the reaction from the sentiment of war time has given impetus to race-prejudice against Negroes, and Mr. Washington withdraws many of the high demands of Negroes as men and American citizens. In other periods of intensified prejudice all the Negro's tendency to self-assertion has been called forth; at this period a policy of submission is advocated. In the history of nearly all other races and peoples the doctrine preached at such crises has been that manly self-respect is worth more than lands and houses, and that a people who voluntarily surrender such respect, or cease striving for it, are not worth civilizing.

Washington's Prescription

In answer to this, it has been claimed that the Negro can survive only through submission. Mr. Washington distinctly asks that black people give up, at least for the present, three things,—

First, political power,

Second, insistence on civil rights,

Third, higher education of Negro youth,—

and concentrate all their energies on industrial education, the accumulation of wealth, and the conciliation of the South. This policy has been courageously and insistently advocated for over fifteen years, and has been triumphant for perhaps ten years. As a result of this tender of the palm-branch, what has been the return? In these years there have occurred:

1. The disfranchisement of the Negro
2. The legal creation of a distinct status of civil inferiority for the Negro
3. The steady withdrawal of aid from institutions for the higher training of the Negro

These movements are not, to be sure, direct results of Mr. Washington's teachings; but his propaganda has, without a shadow of doubt, helped their speedier accomplishment. The question then comes: Is it possible, and probable, that nine millions of men can make effective progress in economic lines if they are deprived of political rights, made a servile caste, and allowed only the most meager chance for developing their exceptional men? If history and reason give any distinct answer to these questions, it is an emphatic *No*. And Mr. Washington thus faces the triple paradox of his career:

1. He is striving nobly to make Negro artisans business men and property-owners; but it is utterly impossible, under modern competitive methods, for workingmen and property-owners to defend their rights and exist without the right of suffrage.
2. He insists on thrift and self-respect, but at the same time counsels a silent submission to civic inferiority such as is bound to sap the manhood of any race in the long run.

3. He advocates common-school and industrial training, and depreciates institutions of higher learning; but neither the Negro common-schools, nor Tuskegee itself, could remain open a day were it not for teachers trained in Negro colleges, or trained by their graduates.

This triple paradox in Mr. Washington's position is the object of criticism by two classes of colored Americans. One class is spiritually descended from Toussaint the Savior [Haitian rebellion leader Toussaint L'Ouverture], through Gabriel, Vesey, and Turner [Gabriel Prosser, Denmark Vesey, Nat Turner], and they represent the attitude of revolt and revenge; they hate the white South blindly and distrust the white race generally, and so far as they agree on definite action, think that the Negro's only hope lies in emigration beyond the borders of the United States. And yet, by the irony of fate, nothing has more effectually made this programme seem hopeless than the recent course of the United States toward weaker and darker peoples in the West Indies, Hawaii, and the Philippines,—for where in the world may we go and be safe from lying and brute force?

The other class of Negroes who cannot agree with Mr. Washington has hitherto said little aloud. They deprecate the sight of scattered counsels, of internal disagreement; and especially they dislike making their just criticism of a useful and earnest man an excuse for a general discharge of venom from small-minded opponents. Nevertheless, the questions involved are so fundamental and serious that it is difficult to see how men like . . . Kelly Miller, J.W.E. Bowen, and other representatives of this group, can much longer be silent. Such men feel in conscience bound to ask of this nation three things:

1. The right to vote
2. Civic equality
3. The education of youth according to ability

They acknowledge Mr. Washington's invaluable service in counselling patience and courtesy in such demands; they do not ask that ignorant black men vote when ignorant whites are debarred, or that any reasonable restrictions in the suffrage should not be applied; they know that the low social level of the mass of the race is responsible for much discrimination against it, but they also know, and the nation knows, that relentless color-prejudice is more often a cause than a result of the Negro's degradation; they seek the abatement of this relic of barbarism, and not its systematic encouragement and pampering by all agencies of social power from the Associated Press to the Church of Christ. They advocate, with Mr. Washington, a broad system of Negro common schools supplemented by thorough industrial training; but they are surprised that a man of Mr. Washington's insight cannot see that no such educational system ever has rested or can rest on any other basis than that of the well-equipped college and university, and they insist that there is a demand for a few such institutions throughout the South to train the best of the Negro youth as teachers, professional men, and leaders.

This group of men honor Mr. Washington for his attitude of conciliation toward the white South; they accept the "Atlanta Compromise" in its broadest interpretation; they recognize, with him, many signs of promise, many men of high purpose and fair judgment, in this section; they know that no easy task has been laid upon a region already tottering under heavy burdens. But, nevertheless, they insist that the way to truth and right lies in straightforward honesty, not in indiscriminate flattery; in praising those of the South who do well and criticising uncompromisingly those who do ill; in taking advantage of the opportunities at hand and urging their fellows to do the same, but at the same time in remembering that only a firm adherence to their higher ideals and aspirations will ever keep those ideals within the realm of possibility. They do not expect that the free right to vote, to enjoy civic rights, and to be educated, will come in a moment; they do not expect to see the bias and prejudices of years disappear at the blast of a trumpet; but they are absolutely certain that the way for a people to gain their reasonable rights is not by voluntarily throwing them away and insisting that they do not want them; that the way for a people to gain respect is not by continually belittling and ridiculing themselves; that, on the contrary, Negroes must insist continually, in season and out of season, that voting is necessary to modern manhood, that color discrimination is barbarism, and that black boys need education as well as white boys.

———— • ————

"By every civilized and peaceful method we must strive for the rights which the world accords to men."

———— • ————

In failing thus to state plainly and unequivocally the legitimate demands of their people, even at the cost of opposing an honored leader, the thinking classes of American Negroes would shirk a heavy responsibility,—a responsibility to themselves, a responsibility to the struggling masses, a responsibility to the darker races of men whose future depends so largely on this American experiment, but especially a responsibility to this nation,—this common Fatherland. It is wrong to encourage a man or a people in evil-doing; it is wrong to aid and abet a national crime simply because it is unpopular not to do so. The growing spirit of kindliness and reconciliation between the North and South after the frightful difference of a generation ago ought to be a source of deep congratulation to all, and especially to those whose mistreatment caused the war; but if that reconciliation is to be marked by the industrial slavery and civic death of those same black men, with permanent legislation into a position of inferiority, then those black men, if they are really men, are called upon by every consideration of patriotism and loyalty to oppose such a course by all civilized methods, even though such opposition involves disagreement with Mr. Booker T. Washington. We have no right to sit silently by while the inevitable seeds are sown for a harvest of disaster to our children, black and white.

First, it is the duty of black men to judge the South discriminatingly. The present generation of Southerners are not responsible for the past, and they should not be blindly hated or blamed for it. Furthermore, to no class is the indiscriminate endorsement of the recent course of the South toward Negroes more nauseating than to the best thought of the South. The South is not "solid"; it is a land in the ferment of social change, wherein forces of all kinds are fighting for supremacy; and to praise the ill the South is to-day perpetrating is just as wrong as to condemn the good. Discriminating and broadminded criticism is what the South needs,—needs it for the sake of her own white sons and daughters, and for the insurance of robust, healthy mental and moral development.

To-day even the attitude of the Southern whites toward the blacks is not, as so many assume, in all cases the same; the ignorant Southerner hates the Negro, the workingmen fear his competition, the money-makers wish to use him as a laborer, some of the educated see a menace in his upward development, while others—usually the sons of the masters— wish to help him to rise. National opinion has enabled this last class to maintain the Negro common schools, and to protect the Negro partially in property, life, and limb. Through the pressure of the money-makers, the Negro is in danger of being reduced to semi-slavery, especially in the country districts; the workingmen, and those of the educated who fear the Negro, have united to disfranchise him, and some have urged his deportation; while the passions of the ignorant are easily aroused to lynch and abuse any black man. To praise this intricate whirl of thought and prejudice is nonsense; to inveigh indiscriminately against "the South" is unjust; but to use the same breath in praising Governor [Charles B.] Aycock, exposing Senator [John T.] Morgan, arguing with Mr. Thomas Nelson Page, and denouncing Senator Ben

Tillman, is not only sane, but the imperative duty of thinking black men.

Half-Truths

It would be unjust to Mr. Washington not to acknowledge that in several instances he has opposed movements in the South which were unjust to the Negro; he sent memorials to the Louisiana and Alabama constitutional conventions, he has spoken against lynching, and in other ways has openly or silently set his influence against sinister schemes and unfortunate happenings. Notwithstanding this, it is equally true to assert that on the whole the distinct impression left by Mr. Washington's propaganda is, first, that the South is justified in its present attitude toward the Negro because of the Negro's degradation; secondly, that the prime cause of the Negro's failure to rise more quickly is his wrong education in the past; and, thirdly, that his future rise depends primarily on his own efforts. Each of these propositions is a dangerous half-truth. The supplementary truths must never be lost sight of first, slavery and race-prejudice are potent if not sufficient causes of the Negro's position; second, industrial and common-school training were necessarily slow in planting because they had to await the black teachers trained by higher institutions,—it being extremely doubtful if any essentially different development was possible, and certainly a Tuskegee was unthinkable before 1880; and, third, while it is a great truth to say that the Negro must strive and strive mightily to help himself, it is equally true that unless his striving be not simply seconded, but rather aroused and encouraged, by the initiative of the richer and wiser environing group, he cannot hope for great success.

In his failure to realize and impress this last point, Mr. Washington is especially to be criticised. His doctrine has tended to make the whites, North and South, shift the burden of the Negro problem to the Negro's shoulders and stand aside as critical and rather pessimistic spectators; when in fact the burden belongs to the nation, and the hands of none of us are clean if we bend not our energies to righting these great wrongs.

The South ought to be led, by candid and honest criticism, to assert her better self and do her full duty to the race she has cruelly wronged and is still wronging. The North—her co-partner in guilt—cannot salve her conscience by plastering it with gold. We cannot settle this problem by diplomacy and suaveness, by "policy" alone. If worse comes to worst, can the moral fibre of this country survive the slow throttling and murder of nine millions of men?

The black men of America have a duty to perform, a duty stern and delicate,—a forward movement to oppose a part of the work of their greatest leader. So far as Mr. Washington preaches Thrift, Patience, and Industrial Training for the masses, we must hold up his hands and strive with him, rejoicing in his honors and glorying in the strength of this Joshua called of God and of man to lead the headless host. But so far as Mr. Washington apologizes for injustice, North or South, does not rightly value the privilege and duty of voting, belittles the emasculating effects of caste distinctions, and opposes the higher training and ambition of our brighter minds,—so far as he, the South, or the Nation, does this,—we must unceasingly and firmly oppose them. By every civilized and peaceful method we must strive for the rights which the world accords to men, clinging unwaveringly to those great words which the sons of the Fathers would fain forget: "We hold these truths to be self-evident: That all men are created equal; that they are endowed by their Creator with certain unalienable rights; that among these are life, liberty, and the pursuit of happiness."

For Further Reading

W.E.B. Du Bois, *The Souls of Black Folk*. New York: Crest, 1961.

Louis R. Harlan, *Booker T. Washington*. 2 vols. New York: Oxford University Press, 1972, 1983.

Augustine Meier, *Negro Thought in America, 1880–1915*. Ann Arbor: University of Michigan Press, 1963.

Elliot M. Rudwick, *W.E.B. Du Bois*. New York: Atheneum, 1969.

Booker T. Washington, *Up from Slavery*. New York: Doubleday, 1901.

VIEWPOINT 12A

Racial Segregation Is Constitutional (1896)

Henry B. Brown (1836–1913)

In 1890 the state of Louisiana passed a law requiring the segregation of white and colored races on passenger trains (many states passed similar laws at this time). Homer A. Plessy, a person of mixed racial background, was forcibly ejected from a train, arrested, and tried for breaking the law after attempting to sit in a whites-only passenger coach. He challenged the constitutionality of the state law, and his case made it to the U.S. Supreme Court. The Court ruled 8–1 in 1896 to uphold the state law, arguing that state-imposed racial segregation laws were constitutional as long as equal facilities were provided for whites and blacks. The following viewpoint is taken from the majority opinion, written by Henry B. Brown, an associate justice of the Supreme Court from 1890 to 1906. The opinion established the "sep-

From the majority opinion in *Plessy v. Ferguson*, 163 U.S. 537 (1896).

arate but equal" standard, which was the law of the land until the Supreme Court overturned it in 1954 in the case of *Brown v. Board of Education.*

How does Brown distinguish between political and social equality, and what importance does this distinction have in his argument? How does he respond to the claim that segregation creates a "badge of inferiority" on blacks? Does the result of *Plessy v. Ferguson* seem to vindicate either the arguments of Booker T. Washington or of W.E.B. Du Bois found in viewpoints 11A and 11B?

This case turns upon the constitutionality of an act of the General Assembly of the State of Louisiana, passed in 1890, providing for separate railway carriages for the white and colored races. . . .

The first section of the statute enacts "that all railway companies carrying passengers in their coaches in this State, shall provide equal but separate accommodations for the white, and colored races, by providing two or more passenger coaches for each passenger train, or by dividing the passenger coaches by a partition so as to secure separate accommodations: *Provided*, That this section shall not be construed to apply to street railroads. No person or persons, shall be admitted to occupy seats in coaches, other than, the ones, assigned, to them on account of the race they belong to."

By the second section it was enacted "that the officers of such passenger trains shall have power and are hereby required to assign each passenger to the coach or compartment used for the race to which such passenger belongs; any passenger insisting on going into a coach or compartment to which by race he does not belong, shall be liable to a fine of twenty-five dollars, or in lieu thereof to imprisonment for a period of not more than twenty days in the parish prison, and any officer of any railroad insisting on assigning a passenger to a coach or compartment other than the one set aside for the race to which said passenger belongs, shall be liable to a fine of twenty-five dollars, or in lieu thereof to imprisonment for a period of not more than twenty days in the parish prison; and should any passenger refuse to occupy the coach or compartment to which he or she is assigned by the officer of such railway, said officer shall have power to refuse to carry such passenger on his train, and for such refusal neither he nor the railway company which he represents shall be liable for damages in any of the courts of this State."

The third section provides penalties for the refusal or neglect of the officers, directors, conductors and employés of railway companies to comply with the act, with a proviso that "nothing in this act shall be construed as applying to nurses attending children of the other race." The fourth section is immaterial.

Homer A. Plessy's Case

The information filed in the criminal District Court charged in substance that Plessy, being a passenger between two stations within the State of Louisiana, was assigned by officers of the company to the coach used for the race to which he belonged, but he insisted upon going into a coach used by the race to which he did not belong. Neither in the information nor plea was his particular race or color averred.

The petition for the writ of prohibition averred that petitioner was seven eighths Caucasian and one eighth African blood; that the mixture of colored blood was not discernible in him, and that he was entitled to every right, privilege and immunity secured to citizens of the United States of the white race; and that, upon such theory, he took possession of a vacant seat in a coach where passengers of the white race were accommodated, and was ordered by the conductor to vacate said coach and take a seat in another assigned to persons of the colored race, and having refused to comply with such demand he was forcibly ejected with the aid of a police officer, and imprisoned in the parish jail to answer a charge of having violated the above act.

The constitutionality of this act is attacked upon the ground that it conflicts both with the Thirteenth Amendment of the Constitution, abolishing slavery, and the Fourteenth Amendment, which prohibits certain restrictive legislation on the part of the States.

The Thirteenth Amendment

1. That it does not conflict with the Thirteenth Amendment, which abolished slavery and involuntary servitude, except as a punishment for crime, is too clear for argument. Slavery implies involuntary servitude—a state of bondage; the ownership of mankind as a chattel, or at least the control of the labor and services of one man for the benefit of another, and the absence of a legal right to the disposal of his own person, property and services. This amendment was said in the [1873] *Slaughter-house cases . . .* to have been intended primarily to abolish slavery, as it had been previously known in this country, and that it equally forbade Mexican peonage or the Chinese coolie trade, when they amounted to slavery or involuntary servitude, and that the use of the word "servitude" was intended to prohibit the use of all forms of involuntary slavery, of whatever class or name. It was intimated, however, in that case that this amendment was regarded by the statesmen of that day as insufficient to protect the colored race from certain laws which had been enacted in the

Southern States, imposing upon the colored race onerous disabilities and burdens, and curtailing their rights in the pursuit of life, liberty and property to such an extent that their freedom was of little value; and that the Fourteenth Amendment was devised to meet this exigency.

So, too, in the *Civil Rights cases* [referring to an 1883 Supreme Court decision that collectively ruled on several challenges to the 1875 Civil Rights Act, including *United States v. Stanley*, and that declared sections of that national civil rights law unconstitutional], . . . it was said that the act of a mere individual, the owner of an inn, a public conveyance or place of amusement, refusing accommodations to colored people, cannot be justly regarded as imposing any badge of slavery or servitude upon the applicant, but only as involving an ordinary civil injury, properly cognizable by the laws of the State, and presumably subject to redress by those laws until the contrary appears. "It would be running the slavery argument into the ground," said Mr. Justice [Joseph P.] Bradley, "to make it apply to every act of discrimination which a person may see fit to make as to the guests he will entertain, or as to the people he will take into his coach or cab or car, or admit to his concert or theatre, or deal with in other matters of intercourse or business."

A statute which implies merely a legal distinction between the white and colored races—a distinction which is founded in the color of the two races, and which must always exist so long as white men are distinguished from the other race by color—has no tendency to destroy the legal equality of the two races, or reëstablish a state of involuntary servitude. Indeed, we do not understand that the Thirteenth Amendment is strenuously relied upon by the plaintiff in error in this connection.

The Fourteenth Amendment

2. By the Fourteenth Amendment, all persons born or naturalized in the United States, and subject to the jurisdiction thereof, are made citizens of the United States and of the State wherein they reside; and the States are forbidden from making or enforcing any law which shall abridge the privileges or immunities of citizens of the United States, or shall deprive any person of life, liberty or property without due process of law, or deny to any person within their jurisdiction the equal protection of the laws.

The proper construction of this amendment was first called to the attention of this court in the *Slaughter-house cases*, . . . which involved, however, not a question of race, but one of exclusive privileges. The case did not call for any expression of opinion as to the exact rights it was intended to secure to the colored race, but it was said generally that its main purpose was to establish the citizenship of the negro; to give definitions of citizenship of the United States and of the States, and to protect from the hostile legislation of the States the privileges and immunities of citizens of the United States, as distinguished from those of citizens of the States.

The object of the amendment was undoubtedly to enforce the absolute equality of the two races before the law, but in the nature of things it could not have been intended to abolish distinctions based upon color, or to enforce social, as distinguished from political equality, or a commingling of the two races upon terms unsatisfactory to either. Laws permitting, and even requiring, their separation in places where they are liable to be brought into contact do not necessarily imply the inferiority of either race to the other, and have been generally, if not universally, recognized as within the competency of the state legislatures in the exercise of their police power. The most common instance of this is connected with the establishment of separate schools for white and colored children, which has been held to be a valid exercise of the legislative power even by courts of States where the political rights of the colored race have been longest and most earnestly enforced.

State Precedents

One of the earliest of these cases is that of *Roberts v. City of Boston*, . . . in which the Supreme Judicial Court of Massachusetts held that the general school committee of Boston had power to make provision for the instruction of colored children in separate schools established exclusively for them, and to prohibit their attendance upon the other schools. "The great principle," said Chief Justice [Lemuel] Shaw, p. 206, "advanced by the learned and eloquent advocate for the plaintiff," (Mr. Charles Sumner,) "is, that by the constitution and laws of Massachusetts, all persons without distinction of age or sex, birth or color, origin or condition, are equal before the law. . . . But, when this great principle comes to be applied to the actual and various conditions of persons in society, it will not warrant the assertion, that men and women are legally clothed with the same civil and political powers, and that children and adults are legally to have the same functions and be subject to the same treatment; but only that the rights of all, as they are settled and regulated by law, are equally entitled to the paternal consideration and protection of the law for their maintenance and security." It was held that the powers of the committee extended to the establishment of separate schools for children of different ages, sexes and colors, and that they might also establish special schools for poor and neglected children, who have become too old to attend the primary school, and yet have not acquired the rudiments of learning, to enable them to enter the ordinary schools. Similar laws have been enacted by Congress under its general power of legislation over the District of Columbia, . . . as well as by the legislatures of many of the States, and have been generally, if not uniformly, sustained by the courts. . . .

Laws forbidding the intermarriage of the two races may be said in a technical sense to interfere with the freedom of contract, and yet have been universally recognized as within the police power of the State. . . .

The distinction between laws interfering with the political equality of the negro and those requiring the separation of the two races in schools, theatres and railway carriages has been frequently drawn by this court. Thus in *Strauder v. West Virginia,* . . . it was held that a law of West Virginia limiting to white male persons, 21 years of age and citizens of the State, the right to sit upon juries, was a discrimination which implied a legal inferiority in civil society, which lessened the security of the right of the colored race, and was a step toward reducing them to a condition of servility. Indeed, the right of a colored man that, in the selection of jurors to pass upon his life, liberty and property, there shall be no exclusion of his race, and no discrimination against them because of color, has been asserted in a number of cases. . . .

•

"If one race be inferior to the other socially, the Constitution of the United States cannot put them upon the same plane."

•

In the [1883 Supreme Court] *Civil Rights case,* . . . it was held that an act of Congress, entitling all persons within the jurisdiction of the United States to the full and equal enjoyment of the accommodations, advantages, facilities and privileges of inns, public conveyances, on land or water, theatres and other places of public amusement, and made applicable to citizens of every race and color, regardless of any previous condition of servitude, was unconstitutional and void, upon the ground that the Fourteenth Amendment was prohibitory upon the States only, and the legislation authorized to be adopted by Congress for enforcing it was not direct legislation on matters respecting which the States were prohibited from making or enforcing certain laws, or doing certain acts, but was corrective legislation, such as might be necessary or proper for counteracting and redressing the effect of such laws or acts. In delivering the opinion of the court Mr. Justice Bradley observed that the Fourteenth Amendment "does not invest

Congress with power to legislate upon subjects that are within the domain of state legislation; but to provide modes of relief against state legislation, or state action, of the kind referred to. It does not authorize Congress to create a code of municipal law for the regulation of private rights; but to provide modes of redress against the operation of state laws, and the action of state officers, executive or judicial, when these are subversive of the fundamental rights specified in the amendment. Positive rights and privileges are undoubtedly secured by the Fourteenth Amendment; but they are secured by way of prohibition against state laws and state proceedings affecting those rights and privileges, and by power given to Congress to legislate for the purpose of carrying such prohibition into effect; and such legislation must necessarily be predicated upon such supposed state laws or state proceedings, and be directed to the correction of their operation and effect.". . .

While we think the enforced separation of the races, as applied to the internal commerce of the State, neither abridges the privileges or immunities of the colored man, deprives him of his property without due process of law, nor denies him the equal protection of the laws, within the meaning of the Fourteenth Amendment, we are not prepared to say that the conductor, in assigning passengers to the coaches according to their race, does not act at his peril, or that the provision of the second section of the act, that denies to the passenger compensation in damages for a refusal to receive him into the coach in which he properly belongs, is a valid exercise of the legislative power. Indeed, we understand it to be conceded by the State's attorney, that such part of the act as exempts from liability the railway company and its officers is unconstitutional. The power to assign to a particular coach obviously implies the power to determine to which race the passenger belongs, as well as the power to determine who, under the laws of the particular State, is to be deemed a white, and who a colored person. This question, though indicated in the brief of the plaintiff in error [Plessy], does not properly arise upon the record in this case, since the only issue made is as to the unconstitutionality of the act, so far as it requires the railway to provide separate accommodations, and the conductor to assign passengers according to their race.

It is claimed by the plaintiff in error that, in any mixed community, the reputation of belonging to the dominant race, in this instance the white race, is *property*, in the same sense that a right of action, or of inheritance, is property. Conceding this to be so, for the purposes of this case, we are unable to see how this statute deprives him of, or in any way affects his right to, such property. If he be a white man and assigned to a colored coach, he may have his action for damages against the company for being deprived of his so called property. Upon the other-hand, if he be a colored man and be so assigned, he has been deprived of no property, since he is not law-fully entitled to the reputation of being a white man.

In this connection, it is also suggested by the learned counsel for the plaintiff in error that the same argument that will justify the state legislature in requiring railways to provide separate accommoda-tions for the two races will also authorize them to require separate cars to be provided for people whose hair is of a certain color, or who are aliens, or who belong to certain nationalities, or to enact laws requiring colored people to walk upon one side of the street, and white people upon the other, or requiring white men's houses to be painted white, and colored men's black, or their vehicles or business signs to be of different colors, upon the theory that one side of the street is as good as the other, or that a house or vehicle of one color is as good as one of another color. The reply to all this is that every exercise of the police power must be reasonable, and extend only to such laws as are enacted in good faith for the promotion for the public good, and not for the annoyance or oppression of a particular class. Thus in *Yick Wo v. Hopkins*, . . . it was held by this court that a munici-pal ordinance of the city of San Francisco, to regulate the carrying on of public laundries within the limits of the municipality, violated the provisions of the Constitution of the United States, if it conferred upon the municipal authorities arbitrary power, at their own will, and without regard to discretion, in the legal sense of the term, to give or withhold con-sent as to persons or places, without regard to the competency of the persons applying, or the propriety of the places selected for the carrying on of the busi-ness. It was held to be a covert attempt on the part of the municipality to make an arbitrary and unjust dis-crimination against the Chinese race. While this was the case of a municipal ordinance, a like principle has been held to apply to acts of a state legislature passed in the exercise of the police power. . . .

So far, then, as a conflict with the Fourteenth Amendment is concerned, the case reduces itself to the question whether the statute of Louisiana is a reasonable regulation, and with respect to this there must necessarily be a large discretion on the part of the legislature. In determining the question of rea-sonableness it is at liberty to act with reference to the established usages, customs and traditions of the people, and with a view to the promotion of their comfort, and the preservation of the public peace and good order. Gauged by this standard, we cannot say that a law which authorizes or even requires the separation of the two races in public conveyances is unreasonable, or more obnoxious to the Fourteenth Amendment than the acts of Congress requiring sep-arate schools for colored children in the District of Columbia, the constitutionality of which does not seem to have been questioned, or the corresponding acts of state legislatures.

We consider the underlying fallacy of the plaintiff's argument to consist in the assumption that the enforced separation of the two races stamps the col-ored race with a badge of inferiority. If this be so, it is not by reason of anything found in the act, but solely because the colored race chooses to put that construction upon it. The argument necessarily assumes that if, as has been more than once the case, and is not unlikely to be so again, the colored race should become the dominant power in the state leg-islature, and should enact a law in precisely similar terms, it would thereby relegate the white race to an inferior position. We imagine that the white race, at least, would not acquiesce in this assumption. The argument also assumes that social prejudices may be overcome by legislation, and that equal rights cannot be secured to the negro except by an enforced com-mingling of the two races. We cannot accept this proposition. If the two races are to meet upon terms of social equality, it must be the result of natural affinities, a mutual appreciation of each other's mer-its and a voluntary consent of individuals. As was said by the Court of Appeals of New York in *People v. Gallagher*, . . . "this end can neither be accomplished nor promoted by laws which conflict with the gener-al sentiment of the community upon whom they are designed to operate. When the government, there-fore, has secured to each of its citizens equal rights before the law and equal opportunities for improve-ment and progress, it has accomplished the end for which it was organized and performed all of the functions respecting social advantages with which it is endowed." Legislation is powerless to eradicate racial instincts or to abolish distinctions based upon physical differences, and the attempt to do so can only result in accentuating the difficulties of the pre-sent situation. If the civil and political rights of both races be equal one cannot be inferior to the other civilly or politically. If one race be inferior to the other socially, the Constitution of the United States cannot put them upon the same plane.

It is true that the question of the proportion of col-ored blood necessary to constitute a colored person, as distinguished from a white person, is one upon which there is a difference of opinion in the different States, some holding that any visible admixture of black blood stamps the person as belonging to the colored race; . . . others that it depends upon the pre-ponderance of blood; . . . and still others that the pre-dominance of white blood must only be in the pro-portion of three fourths. . . . But these are questions to be determined under the laws of each State and are not properly put in issue in this case. Under the allegations of his petition it may undoubtedly become a question of importance whether, under the laws of Louisiana, the petitioner belongs to the white or colored race.

The judgment of the court below is, therefore,

Affirmed.

VIEWPOINT 12B

Racial Segregation Is Unconstitutional (1896)

John Marshall Harlan (1833–1911)

In 1896 the U.S. Supreme Court in the case of *Plessy v. Ferguson* upheld a Louisiana state law requiring the racial segregation of train passengers. The sole dissenter was John Marshall Harlan, who served as an associate justice of the Supreme Court from 1877 to 1911. Portions of his dissenting opinion appear below. A Kentuckian and former slaveholder, Harlan is best remembered today for his dissents in this and other cases in which the Supreme Court upheld racial segregation and limited black civil rights.

How important in Harlan's arguments is his opinion on the proper duties of the Supreme Court? How does Harlan respond to the argument that the Louisiana law applies to both races equally?

B y the Louisiana statute, the validity of which is here involved, all railway companies (other than street railroad companies) carrying passengers in that State are required to have separate but equal accommodations for white and colored persons, "by providing two or more passenger coaches for each passenger train, *or* by dividing the passenger coaches by a *partition* so as to secure separate accommodations." Under this statute, no colored person is permitted to occupy a seat in a coach assigned to white persons; nor any white person, to occupy a seat in a coach assigned to colored persons. The managers of the railroad are not allowed to exercise any discretion in the premises, but are required to assign each passenger to some coach or compartment set apart for the exclusive use of his race. If a passenger insists upon going into a coach or compartment not set apart for persons of his race, he is subject to be fined, or to be imprisoned in the parish jail. Penalties are prescribed for the refusal or neglect of the officers, directors, conductors and

From John Marshall Harlan's dissenting opinion in *Plessy v. Ferguson* 163 U.S. 537 (1896).

employés of railroad companies to comply with the provisions of the act.

Only "nurses attending children of the other race" are excepted from the operation of the statute. No exception is made of colored attendants travelling with adults. A white man is not permitted to have his colored servant with him in the same coach, even if his condition of health requires the constant, personal assistance of such servant. If a colored maid insists upon riding in the same coach with a white woman whom she has been employed to serve, and who may need her personal attention while travelling, she is subject to be fined or imprisoned for such an exhibition of zeal in the discharge of duty.

While there may be in Louisiana persons of different races who are not citizens of the United States, the words in the act, "white and colored races," necessarily include all citizens of the United States of both races residing in that State. So that we have before us a state enactment that compels, under penalties, the separation of the two races in railroad passenger coaches, and makes it a crime for a citizen of either race to enter a coach that has been assigned to citizens of the other race.

Thus the State regulates the use of a public highway by citizens of the United States solely upon the basis of race.

However apparent the injustice of such legislation may be, we have only to consider whether it is consistent with the Constitution of the United States.

That a railroad is a public highway, and that the corporation which owns or operates it is in the exercise of public functions, is not, at this day, to be disputed. Mr. Justice [Samuel] Nelson, speaking for this court in *New Jersey Steam Navigation Co. v. Merchants' Bank*, . . . said that a common carrier was in the exercise "of a sort of public office, and has public duties to perform, from which he should not be permitted to exonerate himself without the assent of the parties concerned." Mr. Justice [William] Strong, delivering the judgment of this court in *Olcott v. The Supervisors*, . . . said: "That railroads, though constructed by private corporations and owned by them, are public highways, has been the doctrine of nearly all the courts ever since such conveniences for passage and transportation have had any existence.". . .

Civil Rights and the Constitution

In respect of civil rights, common to all citizens, the Constitution of the United States does not, I think, permit any public authority to know the race of those entitled to be protected in the enjoyment of such rights. Every true man has pride of race, and under appropriate circumstances when the rights of others, his equals before the law, are not to be affected, it is his privilege to express such pride and to take such action based upon it as to him seems proper. But I deny that any legislative body or judicial tribunal may have regard to the race of citizens when the civil rights of those citizens are involved. Indeed, such legislation, as that here in question, is inconsistent not only with that equality of rights which pertains to citizenship, National and State, but with the personal liberty enjoyed by every one within the United States.

The Thirteenth Amendment does not permit the withholding or the deprivation of any right necessarily inhering in freedom. It not only struck down the institution of slavery as previously existing in the United States, but it prevents the imposition of any burdens or disabilities that constitute badges of slavery or servitude. It decreed universal civil freedom in this country. This court has so adjudged. But that amendment having been found inadequate to the protection of the rights of those who had been in slavery, it was followed by the Fourteenth Amendment, which added greatly to the dignity and glory of American citizenship, and to the security of personal liberty, by declaring that "all persons born or naturalized in the United States, and subject to the jurisdiction thereof, are citizens of the United States and of the State wherein they reside," and that "no State shall make or enforce any law which shall abridge the privileges or immunities of citizens of the United States; nor shall any State deprive any person of life, liberty or property without due process of law, nor deny to any person within its jurisdiction the equal protection of the laws." These two amendments, if enforced according to their true intent and meaning, will protect all the civil rights that pertain to freedom and citizenship. Finally, and to the end that no citizen should be denied, on account of his race, the privilege of participating in the political control of his country, it was declared by the Fifteenth Amendment that "the right of citizens of the United States to vote shall not be denied or abridged by the United States or by any State on account of race, color or previous condition of servitude."

These notable additions to the fundamental law were welcomed by the friends of liberty throughout the world. They removed the race line from our governmental systems. They had, as this court has said, a common purpose, namely, to secure "to a race recently emancipated, a race that through many generations have been held in slavery, all the civil rights that the superior race enjoy." They declared, in legal effect, this court has further said, "that the law in the States shall be the same for the black as for the white; that all persons, whether colored or white, shall stand equal before the laws of the States, and, in regard to the colored race, for whose protection the amendment was primarily designed, that no discrimination

shall be made against them by law because of their color." We also said: "The words of the amendment, it is true, are prohibitory, but they contain a necessary implication of a positive immunity, or right, most valuable to the colored race—the right to exemption from unfriendly legislation against them distinctively as colored—exemption from legal discriminations, implying inferiority in civil society, lessening the security of their enjoyment of the rights which others enjoy, and discriminations which are steps towards reducing them to the condition of a subject race." It was, consequently, adjudged that a state law that excluded citizens of the colored race from juries, because of their race and however well qualified in other respects to discharge the duties of jurymen, was repugnant to the Fourteenth Amendment.... At the present term, referring to . . . previous adjudications, this court [in *Gibson v. Mississippi*] declared that "underlying all of those decisions is the principle that the Constitution of the United States, in its present form, forbids, so far as civil and political rights are concerned, discrimination by the General Government or the States against any citizen because of his race. All citizens are equal before the law.". . .

The decisions referred to show the scope of the recent amendments of the Constitution. They also show that it is not within the power of a State to prohibit colored citizens, because of their race, from participating as jurors in the administration of justice.

The Louisiana Law

It was said in argument that the statute of Louisiana does not discriminate against either race, but prescribes a rule applicable alike to white and colored citizens. But this argument does not meet the difficulty. Every one knows that the statute in question had its origin in the purpose, not so much to exclude white persons from railroad cars occupied by blacks, as to exclude colored people from coaches occupied by or assigned to white persons. Railroad corporations of Louisiana did not make discrimination among whites in the matter of accommodation for travellers. The thing to accomplish was, under the guise of giving equal accommodation for whites and blacks, to compel the latter to keep to themselves while travelling in railroad passenger coaches. No one would be so wanting in candor as to assert the contrary. The fundamental objection, therefore, to the statute is that it interferes with the personal freedom of citizens. "Personal liberty," it has been well said, "consists in the power of locomotion, of changing situation, or removing one's person to whatsoever places one's own inclination may direct, without imprisonment or restraint, unless by due course of law." . . . If a white man and a black man choose to occupy the same public conveyance on a public highway, it is their right to do so, and no government, proceeding alone on grounds of race, can prevent it without infringing the personal liberty of each.

It is one thing for railroad carriers to furnish, or to be required by law to furnish, equal accommodations for all whom they are under a legal duty to carry. It is quite another thing for government to forbid citizens of the white and black races from travelling in the same public conveyance, and to punish officers of railroad companies for permitting persons of the two races to occupy the same passenger coach. If a State can prescribe, as a rule of civil conduct, that whites and blacks shall not travel as passengers in the same railroad coach, why may it not so regulate the use of the streets of its cities and towns as to compel white citizens to keep on one side of a street and black citizens to keep on the other? Why may it not, upon like grounds, punish whites and blacks who ride together in street cars or in open vehicles on a public road or street? Why may it not require sheriffs to assign whites to one side of a court-room and blacks to the other? And why may it not also prohibit the commingling of the two races in the galleries of legislative halls or in public assemblages convened for the consideration of the political questions of the day? Further, if this statute of Louisiana is consistent with the personal liberty of citizens, why may not the State require the separation in railroad coaches of native and naturalized citizens of the United States, or of Protestants and Roman Catholics?

The answer given at the argument to these questions was that regulations of the kind they suggest would be unreasonable, and could not, therefore, stand before the law. Is it meant that the determination of questions of legislative power depends upon the inquiry whether the statute whose validity is questioned is, in the judgment of the courts, a reasonable one, taking all the circumstances into consideration? A statute may be unreasonable merely because a sound public policy forbade its enactment. But I do not understand that the courts have anything to do with the policy or expediency of legislation. . . . There is a dangerous tendency in these latter days to enlarge the functions of the courts, by means of judicial interference with the will of the people as expressed by the legislature. Our institutions have the distinguishing characteristic that the three departments of government are coördinate and separate. Each must keep within the limits defined by the Constitution. And the courts best discharge their duty by executing the will of the law-making power, constitutionally expressed, leaving the results of legislation to be dealt with by the people through their representatives. Statutes must always have a reasonable construction. Sometimes they are to be construed strictly; sometimes, liberal-ly, in order to carry out the legislative will. But however construed, the intent of the legislature is to be respected, if the particular statute in question is valid, although the courts, looking at the public interests, may conceive the statute to be both unreasonable and impolitic. If the power exists to enact a statute, that ends the matter so far as the courts are concerned. The adjudged cases in which statutes have been held to be void, because unreasonable, are those in which the means employed by the legislature were not at all germane to the end to which the legislature was competent.

The Color-Blind Constitution

The white race deems itself to be the dominant race in this country. And so it is, in prestige, in achievements, in education, in wealth and in power. So, I doubt not, it will continue to be for all time, if it remains true to its great heritage and holds fast to the principles of constitutional liberty. But in view of the Constitution, in the eye of the law, there is in this country no superior, dominant, ruling class of citizens. There is no caste here. Our Constitution is color-blind, and neither knows nor tolerates classes among citizens. In respect of civil rights, all citizens are equal before the law. The humblest is the peer of the most powerful. The law regards man as man, and takes no account of his surroundings or of his color when his civil rights as guaranteed by the supreme law of the land are involved. It is, therefore, to be regretted that this high tribunal, the final expositor of the fundamental law of the land, has reached the conclusion that it is competent for a State to regulate the enjoyment by citizens of their civil rights solely upon the basis of race.

In my opinion, the judgment this day rendered will, in time, prove to be quite as pernicious as the decision made by this tribunal in the [1857] *Dred Scott case*. It was adjudged in that case that the descendants of Africans who were imported into this country and sold as slaves were not included nor intended to be included under the word "citizens" in the Constitution, and could not claim any of the rights and privileges which that instrument provided for and secured to citizens of the United States; that at the time of the adoption of the Constitution they were "considered as a subordinate and inferior class of beings, who had been subjugated by the dominant race, and, whether emancipated or not, yet remained subject to their authority, and had no rights or privileges but such as those who held the power and the government might choose to grant them.". . . The recent amendments of the Constitution, it was supposed, had eradicated these principles from our institutions. But it seems that we have yet, in some of the States, a dominant race—a superior class of citizens, which assumes to regulate the enjoyment of civil rights, common to all citizens, upon the basis of race. The present decision, it may well be apprehended, will not only stimulate aggressions, more or less brutal and irritating, upon the admitted rights of colored citizens, but will encourage the belief that it is possible, by means of state enactments, to defeat the beneficent purposes which the people of the United States had in view when they adopted the recent amendments of the Constitution, by one of which the blacks of this country were made citizens of the United States and of the States in which they respectively reside, and whose privileges and immunities, as citizens, the States are forbidden to abridge. Sixty millions of whites are in no danger from the presence here of eight millions of blacks. The destinies of the two races, in this country, are indissolubly linked together, and the interests of both require that the common government of all shall not permit the seeds of race hate to be planted under the sanction of law. What can more certainly arouse race hate, what more certainly create and perpetuate a feeling of distrust between these races, than state enactments, which, in fact, proceed on the ground that colored citizens are so inferior and degraded that they cannot be allowed to sit in public coaches occupied by white citizens? That, as all will admit, is the real meaning of such legislation as was enacted in Louisiana.

———— • ————

"Our Constitution is color-blind, and neither knows nor tolerates classes among citizens."

———— • ————

The sure guarantee of the peace and security of each race is the clear, distinct, unconditional recognition by our governments, National and State, of every right that inheres in civil freedom, and of the equality before the law of all citizens of the United States without regard to race. State enactments, regulating the enjoyment of civil rights, upon the basis of race, and cunningly devised to defeat legitimate results of the war, under the pretence of recognizing equality of rights, can have no other result than to render permanent peace impossible, and to keep alive a conflict of races, the continuance of which must do harm to all concerned. This question is not met by the suggestion that social equality cannot exist between the white and black races in this country. That argument, if it can be properly regarded as one, is scarcely worthy of consideration; for social equality no more exists between two races when

travelling in a passenger coach or a public highway than when members of the same races sit by each other in a street car or in the jury box, or stand or sit with each other in a political assembly, or when they use in common the streets of a city or town, or when they are in the same room for the purpose of having their names placed on the registry of voters, or when they approach the ballot-box in order to exercise the high privilege of voting.

There is a race so different from our own that we do not permit those belonging to it to become citizens of the United States. Persons belonging to it are, with few exceptions, absolutely excluded from our country. I allude to the Chinese race. But by the statute in question, a Chinaman can ride in the same passenger coach with white citizens of the United States, while citizens of the black race in Louisiana, many of whom, perhaps, risked their lives for the preservation of the Union, who are entitled, by law, to participate in the political control of the State and nation, who are not excluded, by law or by reason of their race, from public stations of any kind, and who have all the legal rights that belong to white citizens, are yet declared to be criminals, liable to imprisonment, if they ride in a public coach occupied by citizens of the white race. It is scarcely just to say that a colored citizen should not object to occupying a public coach assigned to his own race. He does not object, nor, perhaps, would he object to separate coaches for his race, if his rights under the law were recognized. But he objects, and ought never to cease objecting to the proposition, that citizens of the white and black races can be adjudged criminals because they sit, or claim the right to sit, in the same public coach on a public highway.

A Badge of Servitude

The arbitrary separation of citizens, on the basis of race, while they are on a public highway, is a badge of servitude wholly inconsistent with the civil freedom and the equality before the law established by the Constitution. It cannot be justified upon any legal grounds.

If evils will result from the commingling of the two races upon public highways established for the benefit of all, they will be infinitely less than those that will surely come from state legislation regulating the enjoyment of civil rights upon the basis of race. We boast of the freedom enjoyed by our people above all other peoples. But it is difficult to reconcile that boast with a state of the law which, practically, puts the brand of servitude and degradation upon a large class of our fellow-citizens, our equals before the law. The thin disguise of "equal" accommodations for passengers in railroad coaches will not mislead any one, nor atone for the wrong this day done.

The result of the whole matter is, that while this court has frequently adjudged, and at the present term has recognized the doctrine, that a State cannot, consistently with the Constitution of the United States, prevent white and black citizens, having the required qualifications for jury service, from sitting in the same jury box, it is now solemnly held that a State may prohibit white and black citizens from sitting in the same passenger coach on a public highway, or may require that they be separated by a "partition," when in the same passenger coach. May it not now be reasonably expected that astute men of the dominant race, who affect to be disturbed at the possibility that the integrity of the white race may be corrupted, or that its supremacy will be imperilled, by contact on public highways with black people, will endeavor to procure statutes requiring white and black jurors to be separated in the jury box by a "partition," and that, upon retiring from the court room to consult as to their verdict, such partition, if it be a moveable one, shall be taken to their consultation room, and set up in such way as to prevent black jurors from coming too close to their brother jurors of the white race. If the "partition" used in the court room happens to be stationary, provision could be made for screens with openings through which jurors of the two races could confer as to their verdict without coming into personal contact with each other. I cannot see but that, according to the principles this day announced, such state legislation, although conceived in hostility to, and enacted for the purpose of humiliating citizens of the United States of a particular race, would be held to be consistent with the Constitution.

I do not deem it necessary to review the decisions of state courts to which reference was made in argument. Some, and the most important, of them are wholly inapplicable, because rendered prior to the adoption of the last amendments of the Constitution, when colored people had very few rights which the dominant race felt obliged to respect. Others were made at a time when public opinion, in many localities, was dominated by the institution of slavery; when it would not have been safe to do justice to the black man; and when, so far as the rights of blacks were concerned, race prejudice was, practically, the supreme law of the land. Those decisions cannot be guides in the era introduced by the recent amendments of the supreme law, which established universal civil freedom, gave citizenship to all born or naturalized in the United States and residing here, obliterated the race line from our systems of governments, National and State, and placed our free institutions upon the broad and sure foundation of the equality of all men before the law.

I am of opinion that the statute of Louisiana is inconsistent with the personal liberty of citizens, white and black, in that State, and hostile to both the spirit and letter of the Constitution of the United States. If laws of like character should be enacted in the several States of the Union, the effect would be in the highest degree mischievous. Slavery, as an institution tolerated by law would, it is true, have disappeared from our country, but there would remain a power in the States, by sinister legislation, to interfere with the full enjoyment of the blessings of freedom; to regulate civil rights, common to all citizens, upon the basis of race; and to place in a condition of legal inferiority a large body of American citizens, now constituting a part of the political community called the People of the United States, for whom, and by whom through representatives, our government is administered. Such a system is inconsistent with the guarantee given by the Constitution to each State of a republican form of government, and may be stricken down by Congressional action, or by the courts in the discharge of their solemn duty to maintain the supreme law of the land, anything in the constitution or laws of any State to the contrary notwithstanding.

For the reasons stated, I am constrained to withhold my assent from the opinion and judgment of the majority.

For Further Reading

Loren P. Beth, *John Marshall Harlan: The Last Whig Justice.* Lexington: University of Kentucky Press, 1992.

Charles A. Lofgren, *The Plessy Case: A Legal-Historical Interpretation.* New York: Oxford University Press, 1987.

I.A. Newby, *Jim Crow's Defense: Anti-Negro Thought in America, 1900–1930.* Baton Rouge: Louisiana University Press, 1965.

Otto H. Olsen, *The Thin Disguise: Turning Point in Negro History; Plessy v. Ferguson: A Documentary Presentation, 1864–1896.* New York: Humanities Press, 1967.

C. Vann Woodward, *The Strange Career of Jim Crow.* 3rd rev. ed. New York: Oxford University Press, 1974.

American Empire: Debate over the Philippines

VIEWPOINT 13A

America Should Retain the Philippines (1900)

Albert J. Beveridge (1862–1937)

America's victory in the Spanish-American War in 1898 left the United States in possession of former

From Albert J. Beveridge, *Congressional Record*, 56th Cong., 1st sess., 1900, pp. 704–12.

Spanish colonies Puerto Rico, Guam, and the Philippine Islands. Some Americans, known as anti-imperialists, were disturbed by the idea of their country's holding foreign colonies, and the treaty with Spain was ratified by the Senate in February 1899 by only a one-vote margin. The Philippine Islands, located across the Pacific Ocean from the United States, were the central focus of American anti-imperialist sentiment, which intensified in 1899 when Filipino nationalists, led by Emilio Aguinaldo, engaged in guerrilla warfare against U.S. soldiers in the Philippines.

One of the leading opponents of the anti-imperialist movement was Albert J. Beveridge, author of the following viewpoint. Elected by the state of Indiana to the U.S. Senate in 1899 at the age of 36, Beveridge toured the Philippines just prior to taking office, and was in favor of their annexation by the United States. On January 9, 1900, he addressed the Senate in support of the following proposition: "*Resolved . . . that the Philippine Islands are territory belonging to the United States; that it is the intention of the United States to retain them as such and to establish and maintain such governmental control throughout the archipelago as the situation may demand.*"

Are the reasons for retaining the Philippines primarily economic, moral, or both, according to Beveridge? Does racial prejudice provide the foundation for his arguments? Beveridge is considered one of the most Progressive senators of his era. What does this say about progressivism?

I address the Senate at this time because Senators and Members of the House on both sides have asked that I give to Congress and the country my observations in the Philippines and the far East, and the conclusions which those observations compel; and because of hurtful resolutions introduced and utterances made in the Senate, every word of which will cost and is costing the lives of American soldiers.

The times call for candor. The Philippines are ours forever, "territory belonging to the United States," as the Constitution calls them. And just beyond the Philippines are China's illimitable markets. We will not retreat from either. We will not repudiate our duty in the archipelago. We will not abandon our opportunity in the Orient. We will not renounce our part in the mission of our race, trustee, under God, of the civilization of the world. And we will move forward to our work, not howling out regrets like slaves whipped to their burdens, but with gratitude for a task worthy of our strength, and thanksgiving to Almighty God that He has marked us as His chosen people, henceforth to lead in the regeneration of the world.

This island empire is the last land left in all the oceans. If it should prove a mistake to abandon it,

the blunder once made would be irretrievable. If it proves a mistake to hold it, the error can be corrected when we will. Every other progressive nation stands ready to relieve us.

But to hold it will be no mistake. Our largest trade henceforth must be with Asia. The Pacific is our ocean. More and more Europe will manufacture the most it needs, secure from its colonies the most it consumes. Where shall we turn for consumers of our surplus? Geography answers the question. China is our natural customer. She is nearer to us than to England, Germany, or Russia, the commercial powers of the present and the future. They have moved nearer to China by securing permanent bases on her borders. The Philippines give us a base at the door of all the East.

Lines of navigation from our ports to the Orient and Australia; from the [proposed Central American] Isthmian Canal to Asia; from all Oriental ports to Australia, converge at and separate from the Philippines. They are a self-supporting, dividend-paying fleet, permanently anchored at a spot selected by the strategy of Providence, commanding the Pacific. And the Pacific is the ocean of the commerce of the future. Most future wars will be conflicts for commerce. The power that rules the Pacific, therefore, is the power that rules the world. And, with the Philippines, that power is and will forever be the American Republic. . . .

The Philippines command the commercial situation of the entire East. Can America best trade with China from San Francisco or New York? From San Francisco, of course. But if San Francisco were closer to China than New York is to Pittsburgh, what then? And Manila is nearer Hongkong than Habana [Havana] is to Washington. And yet American statesmen plan to surrender this commercial throne of the Orient where Providence and our soldiers' lives have placed us. When history comes to write the story of that suggested treason to American supremacy and therefore to the spread of American civilization, let her in mercy write that those who so proposed were merely blind and nothing more.

Resources of the Islands

But if they did not command China, India, the Orient, the whole Pacific for purposes of offense, defense, and trade, the Philippines are so valuable in themselves that we should hold them. I have cruised more than 2,000 miles through the archipelago, every moment a surprise at its loveliness and wealth. I have ridden hundreds of miles on the islands, every foot of the way a revelation of vegetable and mineral riches. . . .

Luzon is larger and richer than New York, Pennsylvania, Illinois, or Ohio. Mindanao is larger and richer than all New England, exclusive of Maine. Manila, as a port of call and exchange, will, in the time of men now living, far surpass Liverpool. Behold the exhaustless markets they command. It is as if a half dozen of our States were set down between Oceania [islands of the South Pacific] and the Orient, and those States themselves undeveloped and unspoiled of their primitive wealth and resources.

Nothing is so natural as trade with one's neighbors. The Philippines make us the nearest neighbors of all the East. Nothing is more natural than to trade with those you know. This is the philosophy of all advertising. The Philippines bring us permanently face to face with the most sought-for customers of the world. National prestige, national propinquity, these and commercial activity are the elements of commercial success. The Philippines give the first; the character of the American people supply the last. It is a providential conjunction of all the elements of trade, of duty, and of power. If we are willing to go to war rather than let England have a few feet of frozen Alaska, which affords no market and commands none, what should we not do rather than let England, Germany, Russia, or Japan have all the Philippines? And no man on the spot can fail to see that this would be their fate if we retired. . . .

The Character of the People

It will be hard for Americans who have not studied them to understand the people. They are a barbarous race, modified by three centuries of contact with a decadent race. The Filipino is the South Sea Malay, put through a process of three hundred years of superstition in religion, dishonesty in dealing, disorder in habits of industry, and cruelty, caprice, and corruption in government. It is barely possible that 1,000 men in all the archipelago are capable of self-government in the Anglo-Saxon sense.

My own belief is that there are not 100 men among them who comprehend what Anglo-Saxon self-government even means, and there are over 5,000,000 people to be governed. . . . [Emilio] Aguinaldo is a clever, popular leader, able, brave, resourceful, cunning, ambitious, unscrupulous, and masterful. He is full of decision, initiative, and authority, and had the confidence of the masses. He is a natural dictator. His ideas of government are absolute orders, implicit obedience, or immediate death. He understands the character of his countrymen. He is . . . not a Filipino Washington. . . .

Abandonment Impossible

Here, then, Senators, is the situation. Two years ago there was no land in all the world which we could occupy for any purpose. Our commerce was daily turning toward the Orient, and geography and trade developments made necessary our commercial empire over the Pacific. And in that ocean we had no commercial, naval, or military base. To-day we have one of the three great ocean possessions of the globe, located at the most commanding commercial, naval, and military points in the eastern seas, within hail of India, shoulder to shoulder with China, richer in its own resources than any equal body of land on the entire globe, and peopled by a race which civilization demands shall be improved. Shall we abandon it? That man little knows the common people of the Republic, little understands the instincts of our race, who thinks we will not hold it fast and hold it forever, administering just government by simplest methods. We may trick up devices to shift our burden and lessen our opportunity; they will avail us nothing but delay. We may tangle conditions by applying academic arrangements of self-government to a crude situation; their failure will drive us to our duty in the end.

The military situation, past, present, and prospective, is no reason for abandonment. Our campaign has been as perfect as possible with the force at hand. We have been delayed, first, by a failure to comprehend the immensity of our acquisition; and, second, by insufficient force; and, third, by our efforts for peace. . . .

This war is like all other wars. It needs to be finished before it is stopped. I am prepared to vote either to make our work thorough or even now to abandon it. A lasting peace can be secured only by overwhelming forces in ceaseless action until universal and absolutely final defeat is inflicted on the enemy. To halt before every armed force, every guerrilla band, opposing us is dispersed or exterminated will prolong hostilities and leave alive the seeds of perpetual insurrection.

———— • ————

"We will not repudiate our duty in the archipelago. We will not abandon our opportunity in the Orient."

———— • ————

Even then we should not treat [negotiate]. To treat at all is to admit that we are wrong. And any quiet so secured will be delusive and fleeting. And a false peace will betray us; a sham truce will curse us. It is not to serve the purposes of the hour, it is not to salve a present situation, that peace should be established. It is for the tranquillity of the archipelago forever. It is for an orderly government for the Filipinos for all the future. It is to give this problem to posterity solved and settled; not vexed and involved. It is to establish the supremacy of the American Republic over the Pacific and throughout the East till the end of time.

It has been charged that our conduct of the war has been cruel. Senators, it has been the reverse. I have been in our hospitals and seen the Filipino wounded as carefully, tenderly cared for as our own. Within our lines they may plow and sow and reap and go about the affairs of peace with absolute liberty. And yet all this kindness was misunderstood, or rather not understood. Senators must remember that we are not dealing with Americans or Europeans. We are dealing with Orientals. We are dealing with Orientals who are Malays. We are dealing with Malays instructed in Spanish methods. They mistake kindness for weakness, forbearance for fear. It could not be otherwise unless you could erase hundreds of years of savagery, other hundreds of years of orientalism, and still other hundreds of years of Spanish character and custom.

Our mistake has not been cruelty; it has been kindness. . . .

The news that 60,000 American soldiers have crossed the Pacific; that, if necessary, the American Congress will make it 100,000 or 200,000 men; that, at any cost, we will establish peace and govern the islands, will do more to end the war than the soldiers themselves. But the report that we even discuss the withdrawal of a single soldier at the present time and that we even debate the possibility of not administering government throughout the archipelago ourselves will be misunderstood and misrepresented and will blow into a flame once more the fires our soldiers' blood has almost quenched.

War Opponents Betray Soldiers

Reluctantly and only from a sense of duty am I forced to say that American opposition to the war has been the chief factor in prolonging it. Had Aguinaldo not understood that in America, even in the American Congress, even here in the Senate, he and his cause were supported; had he not known that it was proclaimed on the stump and in the press of a faction in the United States that every shot his misguided followers fired into the breasts of American soldiers was like the volleys fired by Washington's men against the soldiers of King George his insurrection would have dissolved before it entirely crystallized.

The utterances of American opponents of the war are read to the ignorant soldiers of Aguinaldo and repeated in exaggerated form among the common people. Attempts have been made by wretches claiming American citizenship to ship arms and ammunition from Asiatic ports to the Filipinos, and these acts of infamy were coupled by the Malays with American assaults on our Government at home. The Filipinos do not understand free speech, and therefore our tolerance of American assaults on the American President and the American Government means to them that our President is in the minority or he would not permit what appears to them such treasonable criticism. It is believed and stated in Luzon, Panay, and Cebu that the Filipinos have only to fight, harass, retreat, break up into small parties, if necessary, as they are doing now, but by any means hold out until the next Presidential election, and our forces will be withdrawn.

All this has aided the enemy more than climate, arms, and battle. Senators, I have heard these reports myself; I have talked with the people; I have seen our mangled boys in the hospital and field; I have stood on the firing line and beheld our dead soldiers, their faces turned to the pitiless southern sky, and in sorrow rather than anger I say to those whose voices in America have cheered those misguided natives on to shoot our soldiers down, that the blood of those dead and wounded boys of ours is on their hands, and the flood of all the years can never wash that stain away. In sorrow rather than anger I say these words, for I earnestly believe that our brothers knew not what they did.

Filipinos and Self-Government

But, Senators, it would be better to abandon this combined garden and Gibraltar of the Pacific, and count our blood and treasure already spent a profitable loss, than to apply any academic arrangement of self-government to these children. They are not capable of self-government. How could they be? They are not of a self-governing race. They are Orientals, Malays, instructed by Spaniards in the latter's worst estate.

They know nothing of practical government except as they have witnessed the weak, corrupt, cruel, and capricious rule of Spain. What magic will anyone employ to dissolve in their minds and characters those impressions of governors and governed which three centuries of misrule has created? What alchemy will change the oriental quality of their blood and set the self-governing currents of the American pouring through their Malay veins? How shall they, in the twinkling of an eye, be exalted to the heights of self-governing peoples which required a thousand years for us to reach, Anglo-Saxon though we are?

Let men beware how they employ the term "self-government." It is a sacred term. It is the watchword at the door of the inner temple of liberty, for liberty does not always mean self-government. Self-government is a method of liberty—the highest, simplest, best—and it is acquired only after centuries of study and struggle and experiment and instruction and all the elements of the progress of man. Self-government is no base and common thing, to be bestowed on the merely audacious. It is the degree which crowns the graduate of liberty, not the name of liberty's infant class, who have not yet mastered the alphabet of freedom. Savage blood, oriental blood, Malay blood, Spanish example—are these the elements of self-government?

We must act on the situation as it exists, not as we would wish it. I have talked with hundreds of these people, getting their views as to the practical workings of self-government. The great majority simply do not understand any participation in any government whatever. The most enlightened among them declare that self-government will succeed because the employers of labor will compel their employees to vote as their employer wills and that this will insure intelligent voting. I was assured that we could depend upon good men always being in office because the officials who constitute the government will nominate their successors, choose those among the people who will do the voting, and determine how and where elections will be held.

The most ardent advocate of self-government that I met was anxious that I should know that such a government would be tranquil because, as he said, if anyone criticised it, the government would shoot the offender. A few of them have a sort of verbal understanding of the democratic theory, but the above are the examples of the ideas of the practical workings of self-government entertained by the aristocracy, the rich planters and traders, and heavy employers of labor, the men who would run the government.

An Indolent People

Example for decades will be necessary to instruct them in American ideas and methods of administration. Example, example; always example—this alone will teach them. As a race, their general ability is not excellent. Educators, both men and women, to whom I have talked in Cebu and Luzon, were unanimous in the opinion that in all solid and useful education they are, as a people, dull and stupid. In showy things, like carving and painting or embroidery or music, they have apparent aptitude, but even this is superficial and never thorough. They have facility of speech, too.

The three best educators on the island at different times made to me the same comparison, that the common people in their stupidity are like their caribou bulls. They are not even good agriculturists. Their waste of cane is inexcusable. Their destruction of hemp fiber is childish. They are incurably indolent. They have no continuity or thoroughness of industry. They will quit work without notice and amuse themselves until the money they have earned is spent. They are like children playing at men's work.

No one need fear their competition with our labor. No reward could beguile, no force compel, these children of indolence to leave their trifling lives for the fierce and fervid industry of high-wrought America. The very reverse is the fact. One great problem is the necessary labor to develop these islands—to build the roads, open the mines, clear the wilderness, drain the swamps, dredge the harbors. The natives will not supply it. A lingering prejudice against the Chinese may prevent us from letting them supply it. Ultimately, when the real truth of the climate and human conditions is known, it is barely possible that our labor will go there. Even now young men with the right moral fiber and a little capital can make fortunes there as planters. . . .

The Declaration of Independence

The Declaration of Independence does not forbid us to do our part in the regeneration of the world. If it did, the Declaration would be wrong, just as the Articles of Confederation, drafted by the very same men who signed the Declaration, was found to be wrong. The Declaration has no application to the present situation. It was written by self-governing men for self-governing men.

It was written by men who, for a century and a half, had been experimenting in self-government on this continent, and whose ancestors for hundreds of years before had been gradually developing toward that high and holy estate. The Declaration applies only to people capable of self-government. How dare any man prostitute this expression of the very elect of self-governing peoples to a race of Malay children of barbarism, schooled in Spanish methods and ideas? And you, who say the Declaration applies to all men, how dare you deny its application to the American Indian? And if you deny it to the Indian at home, how dare you grant it to the Malay abroad?

The Declaration does not contemplate that all government must have the consent of the governed. It announces that man's "inalienable rights are life, liberty, and the pursuit of happiness; that to secure these rights governments are established among men deriving their just powers from the consent of the governed; that when any form of government becomes destructive of those rights, it is the right of the people to alter or abolish it." "Life, liberty, and the pursuit of happiness" are the important things; "consent of the governed" is one of the means to those ends.

If "any form of government becomes destructive of those ends, it is the right of the people to alter or abolish it," says the Declaration. "Any form" includes all forms. Thus the Declaration itself recognizes other forms of government than those resting on the consent of the governed. The word "consent" itself recognizes other forms, for "consent" means the understanding of the thing to which the "consent" is given; and there are people in the world who do not understand any form of government. And the sense in which "consent" is used in the Declaration is broader than mere understanding; for "consent" in the Declaration means participation in the government "consented" to. And yet these people who are not capable of "consenting" to any form of government must be governed.

And so the Declaration contemplates all forms of government which secure the fundamental rights of life, liberty, and the pursuit of happiness. Self-government, when that will best secure these ends, as in the case of people capable of self-government; other appropriate forms when people are not capable of self-government. And so the authors of the Declaration themselves governed the Indian without his consent; the inhabitants of Louisiana without their consent; and ever since the sons of the makers of the Declaration have been governing not by theory, but by practice, after the fashion of our governing race, now by one form, now by another, but always for the purpose of securing the great eternal ends of life, liberty, and the pursuit of happiness, not in the savage, but in the civilized meaning of those terms—life according to orderly methods of civilized society; liberty regulated by law; pursuit of happiness limited by the pursuit of happiness by every other man. . . .

Expansion and the Constitution

Senators in opposition are estopped from denying our constitutional power to govern the Philippines as circumstances may demand, for such power is admitted in the case of Florida, Louisiana, Alaska. How, then, is it denied in the Philippines? Is there a geographical interpretation to the Constitution? Do degrees of longitude fix constitutional limitations? Does a thousand miles of ocean diminish constitutional power more than a thousand miles of land?

The ocean does not separate us from the field of our duty and endeavor—it joins us, an established highway needing no repair, and landing us at any point desired. The seas do not separate the Philippine Islands from us or from each other. The seas are highways through the archipelago, which would cost hundreds of millions of dollars to construct if they were land instead of water. Land may separate men from their desire, the ocean never. Russia has been centuries in crossing Siberian wastes; the Puritans cross the Atlantic in brief and flying weeks. . . .

No! No! The ocean unites us; steam unites us; electricity unites us; all the elements of nature unite us to the region where duty and interest call us. There is in the ocean no constitutional argument against the march of the flag, for the oceans, too, are ours. . . .

No; the oceans are not limitations of the power which the Constitution expressly gives Congress to govern all territory the nation may acquire. The Constitution declares that "Congress shall have power to dispose of and make all needful rules and regulations respecting the territory belonging to the United States." Not the Northwest Territory only; not Louisiana or Florida only; not territory on this continent only, but any territory anywhere belonging to the nation. The founders of the nation were not provincial. Theirs was the geography of the world. They were soldiers as well as landsmen, and they knew that where our ships should go our flag might follow. They had the logic of progress, and they knew that the Republic they were planting must, in obedience to the laws of our expanding race, necessarily develop into the greater Republic which the world beholds today, and into the still mightier Republic which the world will finally acknowledge as the arbiter, under God, of the destinies of mankind. And so our fathers wrote into the Constitution these words of growth, of expansion, of empire, if you will, unlimited by geography or climate or by anything but the vitality and possibilities of the American people: "Congress shall have power to dispose of and make all needful rules and regulations respecting the territory belonging to the United States."

The power to govern all territory the nation may acquire would have been in Congress if the language affirming that power had not been written in the Constitution. For not all powers of the National Government are expressed. Its principal powers are implied. The written Constitution is but the index of the living Constitution. Had this not been true, the Constitution would have failed. For the people in any event would have developed and progressed. And if the Constitution had not had the capacity for growth corresponding with the growth of the nation, the Constitution would and should have been abandoned as the Articles of Confederation were abandoned. For the Constitution is not immortal in itself, is not useful even in itself. The Constitution is immortal and even useful only as it serves the orderly development of the nation. The nation alone is immortal. The nation alone is sacred. The Army is its servant. The Navy is its servant. The President is its servant. This Senate is its servant. Our laws are its methods. Our Constitution is its instrument.

This is the golden rule of constitutional interpretation: The Constitution was made for the people, not the people for the Constitution. . . .

An Elemental Question

This question is deeper than any question of party politics; deeper than any question of the isolated policy of our county even; deeper even than any question of constitutional power. It is elemental. It is racial. God has not been preparing the English-speaking and Teutonic peoples for a thousand years for nothing but vain and idle self-contemplation and self-admiration. No! He has made us the master organizers of the world to establish system where chaos reigns. He has given us the spirit of progress to overwhelm the forces of reaction throughout the earth. He has made us adepts in government that we may administer government among savage and senile peoples. Were it not for such a force as this the world would relapse into barbarism and night. And of all our race He has marked the American people as His chosen nation to finally lead in the regeneration of the world. This is the divine mission of America, and it holds for us all the profit, all the glory, all the happiness possible to man. We are trustees of the world's progress, guardians of its righteous peace. The judgment of the Master is upon us: "Ye have been faithful over a few things; I will make you ruler over many things."

What shall history say of us? Shall it say that we renounced that holy trust, left the savage to his base condition, the wilderness to the reign of waste, deserted duty, abandoned glory, forgot our sordid profit even, because we feared our strength and read the charter of our powers with the doubter's eye and the quibbler's mind? Shall it say that, called by events to captain and command the proudest, ablest, purest race of history in history's noblest work, we declined that great commission? Our fathers would not have had it so. No! They founded no paralytic government, incapable of the simplest acts of administration. They planted no sluggard people, passive while the world's work calls them. They established no reactionary nation. They unfurled no retreating flag.

God's Hand in All

That flag has never paused in its onward march. Who dares halt it now—now, when history's largest events are carrying it forward; now, when we are at last one people, strong enough for any task, great enough for any glory destiny can bestow? How comes it that our first century closes with the process of consolidating the American people into a unit just accomplished, and quick upon the stroke of that great hour presses upon us our world opportunity, world duty, and world glory, which none but a people welded into an indivisible nation can achieve or perform?

Blind indeed is he who sees not the hand of God in events so vast, so harmonious, so benign. Reactionary indeed is the mind that perceives not that this vital people is the strongest of the saving forces of the world; that our place, therefore, is at the head of the constructing and redeeming nations of the earth; and that to stand aside while events march on is a surrender of our interests, a betrayal of our duty as blind as it is base. Craven indeed is the heart that fears to perform a work so golden and so noble; that dares not win a glory so immortal.

Do you tell me that it will cost us money? When did Americans ever measure duty by financial standards? Do you tell me of the tremendous toil required to overcome the vast difficulties of our task? What mighty work for the world, for humanity, even for ourselves, has ever been done with ease? Even our bread must we eat by the sweat of our faces. Why are we charged with power such as no people ever knew, if we are not to use it in a work such as no people ever wrought? Who will dispute the divine meaning of the [Biblical] fable of the talents?

Do you remind me of the precious blood that must be shed, the lives that must be given, the broken hearts of loved ones for their slain? And this is indeed a heavier price than all combined. And yet as a nation every historic duty we have done, every achievement we have accomplished, has been by the sacrifice of our noblest sons. Every holy memory that glorifies the flag is of those heroes who have died that its onward march might not be stayed. It is the nation's dearest lives yielded for the flag that makes it dear to us; it is the nation's most precious blood poured out for it that makes it precious to us. That flag is woven of heroism and grief, of the bravery of men and women's tears, of righteousness and battle, of sacrifice and anguish, of triumph and of glory. It is these which make our flag a holy thing. Who would tear from that sacred banner the glorious legends of a single battle where it has waved on land or sea? What son of a soldier of the flag whose father fell beneath it on any field would surrender that proud record for the heraldry of a king? In the cause of civilization, in the service of the Republic anywhere on earth, Americans consider wounds the noblest decorations man can win, and count the giving of their lives a glad and precious duty.

Pray God that spirit never fails. Pray God the time may never come when Mammon and the love of ease shall so debase our blood that we will fear to shed it for the flag and its imperial destiny. Pray God the time may never come when American heroism is but a legend like the story of the Cid, American faith in our mission and our might a dream dissolved, and the glory of our mighty race departed.

And that time will never come. We will renew our youth at the fountain of new and glorious deeds. We will exalt our reverence for the flag by carrying it to a noble future as well as by remembering its ineffable past. Its immortality will not pass, because everywhere and always we will acknowledge and discharge the solemn responsibilities our sacred flag, in its deepest meaning, puts upon us. And so, Senators, with reverent hearts, where dwells the fear of God, the American people move forward to the future of their hope and the doing of His work.

Senators, adopt the resolution offered, that peace may quickly come and that we may begin our saving, regenerating, and uplifting work. Adopt it, and this bloodshed will cease when these deluded children of our islands learn that this is the final word of the representatives of the American people in Congress assembled. Reject it, and the world, history, and the American people will know where to forever fix the awful responsibility for the consequences that will surely follow such failure to do our manifest duty. How dare we delay when our soldiers' blood is flowing?

VIEWPOINT 13B

America Should Not Rule the Philippines (1900)

Joseph Henry Crooker (1850–1931)

The American Anti-Imperialist League was founded in 1898 to protest the U.S. acquisition of Spanish colonies following the Spanish-American War. A central area of concern was the Philippines, a former Spanish colony ten thousand miles from California with a population of seven million people. In 1899 the newly annexed American colony became the site of a prolonged military struggle between American soldiers stationed there and nationalist rebels, which intensified the domestic controversy over American imperialism. The league pressed its case against colonizing the Philippines through meetings, speeches, and pamphlets. The following viewpoint is taken from a 1900 pamphlet written by league member Joseph Henry Crooker, a Unitarian clergyman and author of several books on religious issues.

What does Crooker see as most alarming about the American acquisition of the Philippines? How does he differentiate between continental and overseas expansion? Are Crooker's views of the Filipino people, as expressed in this viewpoint, more or less prejudiced than those of Albert J. Beveridge in viewpoint 13A?

A political doctrine is now preached in our midst that is the most alarming evidence of moral decay that ever appeared in American history. Its baleful significance consists, not simply in its moral hatefulness, but in the fact that its advo-

From Joseph Henry Crooker, *The Menace to America* (Chicago: American Anti-Imperialist League, 1900).

cates are so numerous and so prominent.

It is this: A powerful nation, representative of civilization, has the right, for the general good of humanity, to buy, conquer, subjugate, control, and govern feeble and backward races and peoples, without reference to their wishes or opinions.

This is preached from pulpits as the gospel of Christ. It is proclaimed in executive documents as American statesmanship. It is defended in legislative halls as the beginning of a more glorious chapter in human history. It is boastfully declaimed from the platform as the first great act in the regeneration of mankind. It is published in innumerable editorials, red with cries for blood and hot with lust for gold, as the call of God to the American people.

But how came these men to know so clearly the mind of the Almighty? Was the cant of piety ever more infamously used? Was selfishness ever more wantonly arrayed in the vestments of sanctity? Is this the modern chivalry of the strong to the weak? Then let us surrender all our fair ideals and admit that might alone makes right. Is this the duty of great nations to small peoples? Then morality is a fiction. Is this the gospel of Jesus? Then let us repudiate the Golden Rule. Is this the crowning lesson of America to the world? Then let us renounce our democracy.

A Hateful Doctrine

This doctrine is the maxim of bigotry, "The end justifies the means," reshaped by the ambition of reckless politicians and enforced by the greed of selfish speculators. It is infinitely worse than the policy of the old ecclesiastics, for they had in view the salvation of others, while the advocates of this seek the subjugation of others. The colonial motive, now stirring among us, is not love for others. The mask is too thin and too black to deceive even a savage Filipino.

A similar motive and policy piled the fagots [bundled sticks] about every burning martyr. It turned every thumbscrew that tortured heretics. It laid on the lash that drew blood from the back of every suffering slave. This teaching unbars the bottomless pit and lets loose upon the world every demon that ever vexed the human race. It unchains every wild passion that has lingered in man's blood since it flowed upward from the brute. It prepares the path by which the despot will reach his throne of tyranny and it arms him with instruments of oppression. . . .

To banish this theory of human affairs from the new world Washington suffered at Valley Forge and contended at Yorktown. To destroy the last vestige of this hateful policy, Grant conquered at Appomattox. This is not true Americanism, but the contradiction of every principle for which we have contended and in which we have gloried for over a century. This is not the upward way of civilization, but the backward descent to barbarism.

If this be Duty, let us recite no more the Master's [Jesus] creed of love. If this be Destiny, let us proclaim no more the rights of men. If this be Patriotism, let us sing no more "America." We must rewrite the "Star Spangled Banner," and make its theme the praise of conquest and colonization. We must erase the motto, "E Pluribus Unum," and inscribe instead: "One nation in authority over many people." We must tear up the Declaration of Independence and put in its place "A Summary of the Duties of Colonists to Their Master." But this is political atheism.

Something more than the welfare of distant peoples is at stake. We condemn this teaching and policy, not simply to secure justice for the brown man, but to insure justice and freedom for ourselves. The motive of our protest is more than friendship for him: it is devotion to principles of liberty that are the necessary conditions of universal human progress. The feelings of sympathy and justice ought to rule us in these relations. But every advocate of our present national policy outrages these sentiments whenever he makes his defense. His words ring false. And yet, the heart of the matter lies far deeper. The true glory of America is imperiled. The happiness of our descendants is assailed. The mission of America as the representative and guardian of Liberty is in question. The perpetuity of free institutions hangs in the balance.

Our National Shame

We cannot worship this golden calf and go unscourged. We cannot violate the principles of our government and enjoy the blessings of those principles. We cannot deny freedom across the ocean and maintain it at home. This Nation cannot endure with part of its people citizens and part colonists. The flag will lose all its glory if it floats at once over freemen and subjects. We cannot long rule other men and keep our own liberty. In the high and holy name of humanity, we are trampling upon the rights of men. But Nemesis will wake. The mask will fall; our joy will turn to bitterness; we shall find ourselves in chains.

Most of all, we lament the stain that has come to our flag, not from the soldier carrying it, but from the policy that has compelled him to carry it in an unjust cause. On executive hands falls, not only the blood of the hunted islander, but the blood of the American murdered by the ambition that sent him to invade distant lands. What we most deplore is the surrender that we as a nation have made of our leadership in the world's great work of human emancipation. What we most bitterly mourn is that we, by our selfish dreams of mere commercialism, have piled obstacles mountain high in the way of progress.

What is most surprising and most alarming is the fact that large numbers of our people still call this national ambition for conquest and dominion a form of exalted patriotism. But we are surely under the spell of a malign influence. A false Americanism has captivated our reason and corrupted our conscience. May this hypnotic lethargy, induced by the glittering but deceptive bauble of imperialism, speedily pass away; and may these fellow citizens become again true Americans, free to labor for the liberty of all men and intent on helping the lowly of all lands to independence.

———— • ————

"This Nation cannot endure with part of its people citizens and part colonists."

———— • ————

It is time that all American citizens should look more carefully into the conditions and tendencies which constitute what may well be called, "The Menace to America." Let me discuss briefly certain phases of what rises ominously before us as the Philippine problem. It is a problem of vast importance, and yet it has not been treated as fully as its great magnitude and inherent difficulties deserve. One of the alarming indications of the hour is the popular unwillingness to admit that these new policies present any serious problem. There seems to be no general recognition that anything strange or dangerous is happening. Those who raise a cry of warning are denounced as pessimists; those who enter criticism are branded as traitors. We are told in a jaunty manner to have faith in the American people. This blind trust in "destiny" makes the triumph of the demagogue easy. This indifference to political discussion is the symptom of the paralysis of true patriotism.

Slaughter and Destruction

The following is one phase of the popular argument in justification of our oriental aggressions: The obligations of humanity demanded that we take possession of the Philippine Islands in order to prevent the anarchy which would certainly have followed had we taken any other course than that which we did.

But would a little native-grown anarchy have been as bad as the slaughter and destruction which we have intruded? Let us remember that we ourselves have already killed and wounded thousands of the inhabitants. We have arrayed tribe against tribe; we have desolated homes and burned villages; agriculture and commerce have been prostrated; and finally, we have created hatred of ourselves in the breasts of millions of people to remain for years to plague us and them. It is not likely that if left to themselves anything half so serious would have occurred. It is perfectly clear that some other attitude towards those Islands besides that of domination, which this Nation most unfortunately took, would have prevented these results.

And we are not yet at the end. Recurring outbreaks against us as intruders, by people desirous of independence, will undoubtedly produce more distress and disorder in the next ten years (if our present policy is maintained) than would have resulted from native incapacity. Moreover, there are no facts in evidence that warrant the assertion that anarchy would have followed had we left them more to themselves. This is wholly an unfounded assumption. It would certainly have been well to have waited and given them a chance before interfering. That we did not wait, that we did not give them a chance, is proof positive that our national policy was not shaped by considerations of humanity or a reasonable desire to benefit them, but by a spirit of selfish aggrandizement. . . .

Whose Financial Gain?

It is pitiful that our people, and especially the common people, should be so carried away by wild and baseless dreams of the commercial advantage of these Islands. It is bad enough to sacrifice patriotism upon the altar of Mammon; but it is clear that in this case the sacrifice will be made without securing any benefit, even from Mammon.

The annual expense our Nation will incur by the military and naval establishment in the Philippines will be at least $100,000,000. This the taxpayer of America must pay. On the other hand the trade profits from these Islands—from the very nature of the case—will go directly into the pockets of millionaire monopolists, the few speculators who will get possession of the business interests there, in the line of hemp, sugar, tobacco and lumber.

The proposition is a plain one. These Islands will cost us, the common people, a hundred million dollars a year. The profits from them, possibly an equal sum, will go directly to a few very rich men. This is a very sleek speculative scheme for transferring vast sums of money from the people at large to the bank accounts of a few monopolists. Can any one see anything very helpful to the common taxpayer in such a policy? This is a serious problem for consideration, in addition to the competition of American labor with cheap Asiatic workmen—in itself sufficiently serious.

The question I press is this: Can such a policy work anything but financial harm to the average American citizen? For one, I do not care to pay this tribute money every time I draw a check or buy a bottle of medicine, tribute money that means oppression to those distant islanders, unnecessary burdens to our own people, and a still larger store for speculators to be used in corrupting American politics!

What Is "Expansion?"

A passionate demand for expansion has taken possession of the American imagination. It is contended, We must come out of our little corner and take our place on the worldstage of the nations.

But what has been the real expansion of our Nation for over a century? It has been two-fold. (1) The extension of our free institutions westward across the continent to the Pacific coast; (2) the powerful influence of our republican principles throughout the world. Our political ideals have modified the sentiments of great nations; our people have flowed over contiguous territories and planted there the same civic, social, religious and educational institutions that they possessed in their Eastern home. All this has been a normal and natural growth of true Americanism.

The policy that now popularly bears the name "expansion" is something radically different; and it is in no sense the expansion of America. Our people have been sadly deceived by something far worse than an optical illusion—a deceptive phrase has lured them into danger and toward despotism. To buy 10,000,000 distant islanders is the expansion of Jefferson Davis, not the expansion of Abraham Lincoln. To tax far-off colonists without their consent is the expansion of the policy of [British king] George III, not the expansion of the patriotism of George Washington. To rule without representation subject peoples is not the expansion of Americanism, but the triumph of imperialism.

The policy advocated is the suppression of American principles, the surrender of our sublime ideals, and the end of our beneficent ministry of liberty among the nations. Just because I want to see America expand I condemn the policy as unpatriotic. Let us not deceive ourselves; the expansion of military rule and sordid commercialism is not the expansion of our real strength or true glory. Let us not mistake the renunciation of American ideals for the expansion of American institutions.

Flag and Constitution

Wherever the flag goes, there the constitution must go. Wherever the flag waves, there the whole of the flag must be present. Wherever the constitution is extended, there the entire constitution must rule. If any one does not wish to accept these consequences, then let the flag be brought back to the spot where it can represent true Americanism, and Americanism in its entirety. What shall our banner be to the Filipino? A symbol of his own liberty or the hated emblem of a foreign oppressor? Shall it float over him in Manila as a mere subject and say to him when he lands in San Francisco that he is an alien? Then that flag will become the object of the world's derision!

If it does not symbolize American institutions in their fulness wherever it floats, then our starry banner becomes false to America and oppressive to those who may fear its authority, but do not share its freedom. Disgrace and harm will not come from taking the flag down, but rather from keeping it where it loses all that our statesmen, prophets and soldiers have put into it. The only way to keep "Old Glory" from becoming a falsehood is to give all under it the liberty that it represents. Nowhere must it remain simply to represent a power to be dreaded, but everywhere it must symbolize rights and privileges shared by all.

Among the many bad things bound up with this unfortunate business none is worse than the degradation of America, sure to follow in more ways than one, if we persist in the course that we are now following. No stronger or sadder proof of the unwise and harmful character of this policy is needed than the fact that its defenders are led so quickly to part company with sober argument and truthful statement and rush into virulent abuse and deceptive sophistries. Who would have believed two years ago that any sane man would have appealed to Washington in support of a policy so abhorrent to the Father of his Country? What ignoble unveracity in twisting his words into the approval of foreign conquest! Who would have thought it possible that scholars and statesmen would so soon become mere jugglers with words, pretending that our previous territorial expansion furnishes analogy and warrant for a colonial system far across the ocean, entered upon by warfare and maintained by Congress without constitutional safeguards! These facts show how virulent a poison is at work upon the national mind. We have here already a perversion of patriotism and a loss of political sagacity and veracity.

It is bad enough to hear men exclaim: "There is money in it and that is sufficient"—but a national venture that leads men to scoff at the Declaration of Independence, to ridicule the constitution as outgrown, to denounce the wisdom of the fathers as foolishness, and to declare that American glory dates from Manila bay: Is there not something ominous in such talk? If a brief experience in the expansion of America that scoffs at American principles produces such results, is it not time to sound the alarm? If the defense of a policy compels men to take such positions, there is something infinitely dangerous in that policy.

For Further Reading

John Braeman, *Albert J. Beveridge: American Nationalist*. Chicago: University of Chicago Press, 1971.

Henry F. Graff, ed., *American Imperialism and the Philippine Insurrection*. Boston: Little, Brown, 1969.

Richard H. Miller, *American Imperialism in 1898: The Quest for National Fulfillment*. New York: Wiley, 1970.

Stuart Creighton Miller, *"Benevolent Assimilation": The American Conquest of the Philippines, 1899–1903*. New Haven, CT: Yale University Press, 1982.

Thomas G. Paterson, ed., *American Imperialism and Anti-Imperialism*. New York: Crowell, 1973.

James C. Thomas Jr., Peter W. Stanley, and John Curtis Perry, *Sentimental Imperialists*. New York: Harper & Row, 1981.

Social Issues of the Progressive Era

VIEWPOINT 14A

American Women Should Have the Right to Vote (1909)
Julia Ward Howe (1819–1910)

Julia Ward Howe, a noted writer, lecturer, and social reformer, is perhaps best known as the author of "The Battle Hymn of the Republic," written during the Civil War. In 1869 she helped found the American Woman Suffrage Association, an organization that worked to gain the vote for women in individual states. She also was the first president of the New England Woman Suffrage Association. In the following viewpoint, taken from a 1909 article in *Outlook* magazine, she describes the positive results of woman suffrage in Colorado and other places, and argues for the right to vote for all American women.

Does Howe exhibit racial prejudice in her comments on black suffrage? What examples of the positive impact of woman suffrage on society does she stress? Does Howe argue that woman suffrage would cause radical changes in American society?

When the stripling David, having rashly undertaken to encounter the Philistine giant [Goliath], found himself obliged to choose a weapon for the unequal fight, he dismissed the costly armament offered him by the king, and went back to the simple stone and sling with which he was familiar. Even in like manner will I, pledged just now to make a plain statement of the claims of woman to suffrage, trust myself to state the case as it appeared to me when, after a delay of some years, I finally gave it my adhesion [assent].

Having a quick and rather preponderating sense of

From Julia Ward Howe, "The Case for Woman Suffrage," *Outlook*, April 3, 1909.

the ridiculous, I had easily apprehended the humorous associations which would at first attach themselves to any change in the political status of women. It had once appeared to me answer enough to the new demand to ask the mothers what they proposed to do with their babies, with their husbands, that they should find time for the exercise of these very superfluous functions.

Black Men Gain Suffrage

While I still so spake and so thought, behold, a race of men became enfranchised by the appeal to arms. The conquest of their rights demanded the power to defend those rights, and this power the logic of history had placed in the ballot, whose object it is to secure to every person of sane and sound mind the availing expression of his political faith and individual will.

I had by this time cast in my lot with those to whom the right of the negro to every human function and privilege appeared a point to be maintained at all hazards. It had been determined that the slave should become a free man, and, further than this, that, in order to maintain his freedom, he must perform the offices of a free citizen.

Two new thoughts now came to me in the shape of questions: Why was the vote so vital a condition of the freedom of an American citizen? And, if it was held to be so vital, why should every man possess it, and no woman? I did and do believe in equal civic rights for all human beings, without regard to race, subject only to such tests as may be applied impartially to all alike. But there seemed a special incongruity in putting this great mass of ignorant men into a position of political superiority to all women. The newly enfranchised men were generally illiterate and of rather low morality. Should they, simply on account of sex, be invested with a power and dignity withheld from women, who at that time were unquestionably better fitted to intervene in matters of government than men could be who for many generations past had been bought and sold like cattle, men who would have the whole gamut of civilization to learn by heart before they could have any availing knowledge of what a vote should really mean? Here were ignorance and low life commissioned to lord it over the august company of the mothers. Here were the natural guardians of childhood debarred from the highest office in its defense. I felt that this could not be right; and when the foremost friends of the negro showed themselves as the foremost champions of the political enfranchisement of women, I had no longer any hesitation in saying, This must be the keystone of the arch, whose absence leaves so sad and strange a gap in the construction of our political morality.

Since then the question of suffrage for women has passed out of the academic stage, and has become a matter of practical observation and experience in an ever-growing number of States and countries. Experience has shattered, like a house of cards, all the old predictions that it would destroy the home, subvert the foundations of society, and have a ruinous influence both on womanly delicacy and on public affairs. During many years the opponents of woman suffrage have been diligently gathering all the adverse testimony that they could find. So far as appears by their published literature, they have not found, in all our enfranchised States put together, a dozen respectable men, residents of those States, who assert over their own names and addresses that it has had any ill effects. A few say that it has done no good, and call it a failure on that ground. But the mass of testimony on the other side is overwhelming.

The fundamental argument for woman suffrage, of course, is its justice, and this would be enough were there no other. But a powerful argument can also be made for it from the standpoint of expediency. It has now been proved to demonstration, not only that woman suffrage has no bad results, but that it has certain definite good results.

1. It gives women a position of increased dignity and influence. On this point I will quote from . . . people whose word has weight in our own land and abroad.

Miss Margaret Long, daughter of the ex-Secretary of the Navy, who has resided for years in Denver, has written: "It seems impossible to me that any one can live in Colorado long enough to get into touch with the life here, and not realize that women count for more in all the affairs of this State than they do where they have not the power that the suffrage gives. More attention is paid to their wishes, and much greater weight given to their opinions and judgment."

Mrs. K.A. Sheppard, President of the New Zealand Council of Women, says: "Since women have become electors, their views have become important and command respect. Men listen to and are influenced by the opinions of women to a far greater degree than was the case formerly. There is no longer heard the contemptuous 'What do women know of such matters?' And so out of the greater civil liberty enjoyed by women has come a perceptible rise in the moral and humanitarian tone of the community. A young New Zealander in his teens no longer regards his mother as belonging to a sex that must be kept within a prescribed sphere. That the lads and young men of a democracy should have their whole conception of the rights of humanity broadened and measured by truer standards is in itself an incalculable benefit."

Improving the Position of Women

Mrs. A. Watson Lister, Secretary of the Woman's National Council of Australia, says: "One striking result of equal suffrage is that members of Parliament now consult us as to their bills, when these bear upon the interests of women. The author of the new divorce bill asked all the women's organizations to come together and hear him read it, and make criticisms and suggestions. I do not remember any such thing happening before, in all my years in Australia. When a naturalization bill was pending, one clause of which deprived Australian women of citizenship if they married aliens, a few women went privately to the Prime Minister and protested, and that clause was altered immediately. After we had worked for years with members of Parliament for various reforms, without avail, because we had no votes, you cannot imagine the difference it makes."

Ex-Premier Alfred Deakin, of the Commonwealth of Australia, says: "There is now a closer attention paid in Parliament to matters especially affecting the [feminine] sex or interesting them."

Improving the Laws

2. It leads to improvements in the laws. No one can speak more fitly of this than Judge Lindsey, of the Denver Juvenile Court. He writes: "We have in Colorado the most advanced laws of any State in the Union for the care and protection of the home and the children, the very foundation of the Republic. We owe this more to woman suffrage than to any one cause. It does not take any mother from her home duties to spend ten minutes in going to the polls, casting her vote, and returning to the bosom of her home; but during those ten minutes she wields a power which is doing more to protect that home, and all other homes, than any other power or influence in Colorado."

Mrs. Helen L. Grenfell, of Denver, served three terms as State Superintendent of Public Instruction for Colorado, and is highly esteemed by educators throughout the State. She introduced in Colorado the system of leasing instead of selling the lands set apart by the Government for the support of the public schools, thereby almost doubling the annual revenue available for education. Mrs. Grenfell was appointed by the Governor to represent Colorado at the Congress of the International Woman Suffrage Alliance at Amsterdam last summer. In her report to that Congress she enumerated a long list of improved laws obtained in Colorado since women were granted the ballot, and added: "Delegates of the Interparliamentary Union who visited different parts of the United States for the purpose of studying American institutions declared concerning our group of laws relating to child life in its various aspects of education, home, and labor, that 'they are the sanest, most humane, most progressive, most scientific laws relating to the child to be found on any statute-books in the world.'"

Wyoming, many years ago, passed a law that women teachers in the public schools should receive the same pay as men when the work done is the same. The news that Utah had granted full suffrage to women was quickly followed by the announcement of the passage of a bill providing that women teachers should have equal pay with men when they held certificates of the same grade. The State Superintendent of Public Instruction for Colorado says: "There is no difference made in teachers' salaries on account of sex."

Woman suffrage has also operated to take the schools out of politics. Mrs. Grenfell writes: "I have seen or heard of more party politics in school matters in one block in Albany, Buffalo, or Philadelphia than in the 103,928 square miles of Colorado soil."

Since women attained the ballot, all the four equal suffrage States have raised the age of protection for girls to eighteen. In Idaho and Wyoming the repeal of the laws that formerly licensed gambling is universally ascribed to the women. The Colorado statutes against cruelty to animals and against obscene literature are said to be models of their kind.

Within four years after equal suffrage was granted, the number of no-[saloon]-license towns in Colorado had more than quadrupled and it has increased much more largely since. The organ of the brewers of Denver says that Colorado made a great mistake in giving the ballot to women. So far as I am aware it is the only paper in Colorado which takes that ground.

Under the title "Fruits of Equal Suffrage," the National American Woman Suffrage Association has published a partial list of the improved laws passed in the four enfranchised States with the aid of women's votes, giving chapter and verse for each. It fills nearly eight pages.

Women's Influence

3. Women can bring their influence to bear on legislation more quickly and with less labor by the direct method than by the indirect. In Massachusetts the suffragists worked for fifty-five years before they succeeded in getting a law making mothers equal guardians of their minor children with the fathers. After half a century of effort by indirect influence, only twelve out of our forty-six States have taken similar action. In Colorado, when the women were enfranchised, the very next Legislature passed such a bill.

4. Equal suffrage often leads to the defeat of bad candidates. This is conceded even by Mr. A. Lawrence Lewis, whose article in *The Outlook* against woman suffrage in Colorado has been reprinted by the anti-

suffragists as a tract. He says:

"Since the extension of the franchise to women, political parties have learned the inadvisability of nominating for public offices drunkards, notorious libertines, gamblers, retail liquor dealers, and men who engage in similar discredited occupations, because the women almost always vote them down." During the fifteen years since equal suffrage was granted no saloon-keeper has been elected to the Board of Aldermen in Denver. Before that it was very common. I quote . . . from Governor Shafroth, of Colorado: "Women's presence in politics has introduced an independent element which compels better nominations."

Ex-Chief Justice Fisher, of Wyoming, says: "If the Republicans nominate a bad man and the Democrats a good one, the Republican women do not hesitate a moment to 'scratch' the bad and substitute the good. It is just so with the Democrats."

Ex-Governor Hunt, of Idaho: "The woman vote has compelled not only State conventions, but more particularly county conventions, of both parties to select the cleanest and best material for public office."

And quoting once more from Judge Lindsey, of Denver: "One of the greatest advantages from woman suffrage is the fear on the part of the machine politicians to nominate men of immoral character. While many bad men have been elected in spite of woman suffrage, they have not been elected because of woman suffrage. If the women alone had a vote, it would result in a class of men in public office whose character for morality, honesty, and courage would be of a much higher order."

The recent re-election of Judge Lindsey by the mothers of Denver, against the opposition of both the political machines, is only a striking instance of what has happened in a multitude of less conspicuous cases in the various enfranchised States.

"Experience has shattered, like a house of cards, all the old predictions that [suffrage] would destroy the home [and] subvert the foundations of society."

---

5. Equal suffrage broadens women's minds, and leads them to take a more intelligent interest in public affairs. President Slocum, of Colorado College, Enos A. Mills, the forestry expert, Mrs. Decker, and many others, bear witness to this. The Hon. W.E. Mullen, Attorney-General of Wyoming, who went there opposed to woman suffrage and has been converted, writes: "It stimulates interest and study, on the part of women, in public affairs. Questions of public interest are discussed in the home. As the mother, sister, or teacher of young boys, the influence of woman is very great. The more she knows about the obligations of citizenship, the more she is able to teach the boys." A leading bookseller of Denver says he sold more books on political economy in the first eight months after women were given the ballot than he had sold in fifteen years before.

6. It makes elections and political meetings more orderly. The Hon. John W. Kingman, of the Wyoming Supreme Court, says: "In caucus discussions the presence of a few ladies is worth a whole squad of police."

7. It makes it easier to secure liberal appropriations for educational and humanitarian purposes. In Colorado the schools are not scrimped for money, as they are in the older and richer States. So say Mrs. Grenfell, General Irving Hale, and others.

8. It opens to women important positions now closed to them because they are not electors. Throughout England, Scotland, Ireland, and a considerable part of Europe, a host of women are rendering admirable service to the community in offices from which women in America are still debarred.

9. It increases the number of women chosen to such offices as are already open to them. Thus, in Colorado women were eligible as county superintendents of schools before their enfranchisement; but when they obtained the ballot the number of women elected to those positions showed an immediate and large increase.

10. It raises the average of political honesty among the voters. Judge Lindsey says: "Ninety-nine per cent of our election frauds are committed by men."

11. It tends to modify a too exclusively commercial view of public affairs. G.W. Russell, Chairman of the Board of Governors of Canterbury College, New Zealand, writes: "Prior to women's franchise the distinctive feature of our politics was finance. Legislative proposals were regarded almost entirely from the point of view of (1) What would they cost? and (2) What would be their effect from a commercial standpoint? The woman's view is not pounds nor pence, but her home, her family. In order to win her vote, the politicians had to look at public matters from her point of view. Her ideal was not merely money, but happy homes and a fair chance in life for her husband, her intended husband, and her present or prospective family."

Suffrage and the Family

12. Last, but not least, it binds the family more closely together. I say this with emphasis, though it is in direct opposition to an argument much brought forward by the opponents of woman suffrage. Let us give ear to words that are written, like the last, from

a region where equal suffrage has been tried and proved.

The Hon. Hugh Lusk, ex-member of the New Zealand Parliament, says: "We find that equal suffrage is the greatest family bond and tie, the greatest strengthener of family life. It seemed odd at first to find half the benches at a political meeting occupied by ladies; but when men have got accustomed to it they do not like the other thing. When they found that they could take their wives and daughters to these meetings, and afterwards go home with them and talk it over, it was often the beginning of a new life for the family—a life of ideas and interests in common, and of a unison of thought."

It is related that the Japanese Government many years ago sent a commission to the United States to study the practical working of Christianity, with a view to introducing it into Japan as the State religion if the report of the commission proved favorable. The commission saw many evils rampant in America, and went home reporting that Christianity was a failure. The opponents of woman suffrage argue in the same way. They find evils in the enfranchised States, and straightway draw the conclusion that woman suffrage is a failure. But it may be said with truth of woman suffrage, as of Christianity, that these evils exist not because of it but in spite of it; and that it has effected a number of distinct improvements, and is on the way to effect yet more.

I have sat in the little chapel at Bethlehem in which tradition places the birth of the Saviour. It seemed fitting that it should be adorned with offerings of beautiful things. But while I mused there a voice seemed to say to me: "Look abroad! This divine child is a child no more. He has grown to be a man and a deliverer. Go out into the world! Find his footsteps and follow them. Work, as he did, for the redemption of mankind. Suffer as he did, if need be, derision and obloquy. Make your protest against tyranny, meanness, and injustice!"

The weapon of Christian warfare is the ballot, which represents the peaceable assertion of conviction and will. Society everywhere is becoming converted to its use. Adopt it, O you women, with clean hands and a pure heart! Verify the best word written by the apostle—"In Christ Jesus there is neither bond nor free, neither male nor female, but a new creature," the harbinger of a new creation!

VIEWPOINT 14B

American Women Should Not Have the Right to Vote (1909)

Emily P. Bissell (1861–1948)

Emily P. Bissell, an active opponent of woman suffrage, testified before Congress and lectured in various states on the issue. A 1909 pamphlet written by Bissell, from which this viewpoint is taken, was published and widely distributed by the New York State Association Opposed to Woman Suffrage.

In addition to working against suffrage, Bissell was heavily involved in public welfare activities. She organized the Delaware Chapter of the American Red Cross. As the first president of the Consumers' League of Delaware (1914), she helped secure passage of state laws regulating child labor and setting maximum hours for women working in industry. Bissell did not find such activities inconsistent with her anti-suffrage position, arguing that women had greater influence in promoting beneficial legislation precisely because of their position as non-voters, removed from the political process. "Let them [men] struggle with the vote," she wrote in a different pamphlet. "Let us aim at legislation. It takes less time, and gets greater results."

Why is suffrage different from reforms opening up higher education and work opportunities for women who desire them, according to Bissell? What opinions about the nature of the political process does she profess in this viewpoint? What distinctions does Bissell make between "good" women and "bad" women, and how important are these distinctions to her argument?

T here are three points of view from which woman today ought to consider herself—as an individual, as a member of a family, as a member of the state. Every woman stands in those three relations to American life. Every woman's duties and rights cluster along those three lines; and any change in woman's status that involves all of them needs to be very carefully considered by every thoughtful woman.

The proposal that women should vote affects each one of these three relations deeply. It is then a proposal that the American woman has been considering for sixty years, without accepting it. Other questions, which have been only individual, as the higher education for such individual women as desire it, or the opening of various trades and professions to such individual women as desire to enter them have not required any such thought or hesitation. They are individual, and individuals have decided on them and accepted them. But this great suffrage question, involving not only the individual, but the family and the state, has hung fire. There are grave objections to

From Emily P. Bissell, "A Talk to Women on the Suffrage Question," in *Selected Articles on Woman Suffrage*, 3rd rev. ed. (New York: H.W. Wilson, 1916).

woman suffrage on all these three counts. Sixty years of argument and of effort on the part of the suffragists have not in the least changed these arguments, because they rest on the great fundamental facts of human nature and of human government. The suffrage is "a reform against nature" and such reforms are worse than valueless.

Let us take these three points of view singly. Why, in the first place, is the vote a mistake for women as individuals? I will begin discussing that by another question. "How many of you have leisure to spare now, without the vote?" The claims upon a woman's time, in this twentieth century, are greater than ever before. Woman, in her progress, has taken up many important things to deal with, and has already overloaded herself beyond her strength. If she is a working-woman, her day is full—fuller than that of a workingman, since she has to attend, in many cases, to home duties or to sewing and mending for herself when her day's toil is over. If she is a wife and mother, she has her hands full with the house and the children. If she is a woman of affairs and charities, she has to keep a secretary or call in a stenographer to get through her letters and accounts. Most of the self-supporting women of my acquaintance do not want the ballot. They have no time to think about it. Most of the wives and mothers I know do not want to vote. They are too busy with other burdens. Most of the women of affairs I know do not want to vote. They are doing public work without it better than they could with it, and consider it a burden, not a benefit. The ballot is a duty, a responsibility; and most intelligent, active women to-day believe that it is man's duty and responsibility, and that they are not called to take it up in addition to their own share. The suffragists want the ballot individually. They have a perfect right to want it. They ask no leisure. And if it were only an individual question, then I should say heartily "Let them have it, as individuals, and let us refuse to take it, as individuals, and then the whole matter can be individually settled." But that is impossible, for there are two other aspects. The suffragists cannot get the vote without forcing it on all the rest of womankind in America; for America means unrestricted manhood suffrage, and an equal suffrage law would mean unrestricted womanhood suffrage, from the college girl to the immigrant woman who cannot read and the negro woman in the cotton-field, and from the leader of society down to the drunken woman in the police court. The individual aspect is only one of the three, and after all, the least important.

Duty to the Family

For no good woman lives to herself. She has always been part of a family as wife or sister or daughter from the time of Eve. . . . The American home is the foundation of American strength and progress. And in the American home woman has her own place and her own duty to the family.

It is an axiom in physics that two things cannot be in the same place at the same time. Woman, as an individual, apart from all home ties, can easily enough get into a man's place. There are thousands of women in New York to-day—business women, professional women, working girls, who are almost like men in their daily activity. But nearly all these women marry and leave the man's place for the woman's, after a few years of business life. It is this fact which makes their wages lower than men's, and keeps them from being a highly skilled class. They go back into the home, and take up a woman's duties in the family. If they are wise women, they give up their work; they do not try to be in a man's place and a woman's too. But when they do make this foolish resolve to keep on working the home suffers. There are no children; or the children go untrained; housekeeping is given up for boarding; there is no family atmosphere. The woman's place is vacant—and in a family, that is the most important place of all. The woman, who might be a woman, is half a man instead.

The family demands from a woman her very best. Her highest interests, and her unceasing care, must be in home life, if her home is to be what it ought to be. Here is where the vote for woman comes in as a disturbing factor. The vote is part of man's work. Ballot-box, cartridge box, jury box, sentry box, all go together in his part of life. Woman cannot step in and take the responsibilities and duties of voting without assuming his place very largely. The vote is a symbol of government, and leads at once into the atmosphere of politics; to make herself an intelligent voter (and no other kind is wanted) a woman must study up the subjects on which she is to vote and cast her ballot with a personal knowledge of current politics in every detail. She must take it all from her husband, which means that he is thus given two votes instead of one, not equal suffrage, but a double suffrage for the man.

A Man's Place

Home is meant to be a restful place, not agitated by the turmoil of outside struggles. It is man's place to support and defend the family, and so to administer the state that the family shall flourish in peace. He is the outside worker. Woman is the one whose place it is to bear and rear the children who shall later be the citizens of the state. As I have shown, she can, if she wishes, go into man's place in the world for a while. But man can never go into hers. (That proves she is superior, by the way.) He cannot create the home. He is too distracted by outside interests, too tired with his own duties, to create, an atmosphere of home. The woman who makes the mistake of trying to do his work and hers too, cannot create a home atmosphere, either. She cannot be in two places at once. I have known even one outside charity become so absorbing in its demands on a woman's time and thought that her children felt the difference, and knew and dreaded the day of the monthly meeting, and the incessant call of the telephone. There are certain times in a wife and mother's life, such as children's illnesses, the need of care for an over-worked husband, the crisis of some temptation or wrong tendency in a child's life, and so on, when all outside interests must abdicate before the family ones, and be shut out for a while. The vote, which means public life, does not fit into the ideal of family life. The woman who is busy training a family is doing her public service right in the home. She cannot be expected to be in two places at the same time, doing the work of the state as the man does.

Individualism and Family Life

The individualism of woman, in these modern days, is a threat to the family. There is one divorce in America nowadays to every dozen marriages. There are thousands of young women who crowd into factory or mill or office in preference to home duties. There is an impatience of ties and responsibilities, a restlessness, a fever for "living one's own life," that is unpleasantly noticeable. The desire for the vote is part of this restlessness, this grasping for power that shall have no responsibility except to drop a paper into a ballot box, this ignorant desire to do "the work of the world" instead of one's own appointed work. If women had conquered their own part of life perfectly, one might wish to see them thus leave it and go forth to set the world to rights. But on the contrary, never were domestic conditions so badly attended to. Until woman settles the servant question, how can she ask to run the government?

———— • ————

"The suffrage is 'a reform against nature' and such reforms are worse than valueless."

———— • ————

This brings us to the third point, which is, the effect on the state of a vote for women. Let us keep in mind, always, that in America we cannot argue about municipal suffrage, or taxpaying suffrage, or limited suffrage of any kind—"to one end they must all come," that of unrestricted woman suffrage, white and colored, illiterate and collegebred alike having the ballot. America recognizes no other way. Do not get the mistaken idea—which the suffragists cleverly present all the while—that the English system of municipal or restricted suffrage, or the Danish system, or any other system, is like ours. It is *not*. Other countries have restricted forms of suffrage by which individual women can be sorted out, so to speak. But America has equal manhood suffrage ingrained in her very state, in her very law. Once begin to give the suffrage to women, and there is but one end in this country. The question is always with us, "What effect will unrestricted female suffrage have on the state?" We must answer that question or beg the subject.

One thing sure—the women's vote would be an indifferent one. The majority of women do not want to vote—even the suffragists acknowledge that. Therefore, if given the vote, they would not be eager voters. There would be a number of highly enthusiastic suffrage voters—for a while. But when the coveted privilege became a commonplace, or even an irksome duty, the stay-at-home vote would grow larger and larger. The greatest trouble in politics to-day is the indifferent vote among men. Equal suffrage would add a larger indifferent vote among women.

A Corrupt Vote

Then there is the corrupt vote to-day. Among men it is bad enough. But among women it would be much worse. What, for example, would the Tenderloin [red-light district] woman's vote be in New York? for good measures and better city politics? In Denver, it has been found to work just as might be supposed, and in Denver the female ward politician appeared full-fledged in the Shafroth case, in the full swing of bribery and fraud. Unrestricted suffrage must reckon with all kinds of women, you see—and the unscrupulous woman will use her vote for what it is worth and for corrupt ends.

Today, without the vote, the women who are intelligent and interested in public affairs use their ability and influence for good measures. And the indifferent woman does not matter. The unscrupulous woman has no vote. We get the best, and bar out the rest. The state gets all the benefit of its best women, and none of the danger from its worst women. The situation is too beneficial to need any change in the name of progress. We have now two against one, a fine majority, the good men and the good women against the unscrupulous men. Equal suffrage would make it two to two—the good men and the good women against the unscrupulous men and the unscrupulous women—a tie vote between good and evil instead of a safe majority for good.

Then, beside the indifferent vote and the corrupt vote, there would be, in equal suffrage, a well-meaning, unorganized vote. But government is not run in America by unorganized votes—it is run by organized parties. To get results, one vote is absurd. An effectual vote means organization; and organization means primaries and conventions, and caucuses and office-holding, and work, and work, and more work. A ballot dropped in a box is not government, or power. This is what men are fighting out in politics, and we women ought to understand their problem. One reason that I, personally, do not want the ballot is that I have been brought up, in the middle of politics in a state that is full of them, and I know the labor they entail on public-spirited men. Politics, to me, does not mean unearned power, or the registering of one's opinion on public affairs—it means hard work, incessant organization and combination, continual perseverance against disappointment and betrayal, steadfast effort for small and hard-fought advance. I have seen too many friends and relatives in that battle to want to push any woman into it. And unless one goes into the battle the ballot is of no force. The suffragists do not expect to. They expect and urge that all that will be necessary will be for each woman to "register her opinion" and cast her ballot and go home.

Where would the state be then—with an indifferent vote, a corrupt vote, and a helpless, unorganized vote, loaded on to its present political difficulties? Where would the state be with a doubled negro vote in the Black Belt? Where would New York and Chicago be with a doubled immigrant vote? I have two friends, sisters, one of them living in Utah, the other in Colorado—both suffrage states. The one in Colorado belongs to the indifferent vote. She is too busy to vote, and doesn't believe in it anyhow. The one in Utah goes to the polls regularly, not because she wants to vote, but because as she says "The Mormons vote all their women solidly, and we Gentiles have to vote as a duty—and how we wish we were back again under manhood suffrage." Is the state benefited by an unwilling electorate such as that?

For Further Reading

Jane Jerome Camhi, *Women Against Women: American Anti-Suffragism, 1880–1920.* Brooklyn, NY: Carlson Publishing, 1994.

Mary H. Grant, *Private Woman, Public Person: An Account of the Life of Julia Ward Howe.* Brooklyn, NY: Carlson Publishing, 1994.

Florence Howe Hall, *Julia Ward Howe and the Woman Suffrage Movement.* New York: Arno Press, 1969.

Thomas J. Jablonsky, *The Home, Heaven, and Mother Party: Female Anti-Suffragists in the United States, 1868–1920.* Brooklyn, NY: Carlson Publishing, 1994.

Sheila M. Rothman, *Woman's Proper Place: A History of Changing Ideals and Practices, 1870 to the Present.* New York: Basic Books, 1978.

Anne Firor Scott and Andrew MacKay Scott, *One Half the People: The Fight for Woman Suffrage.* Philadelphia: Lippincott, 1975.

VIEWPOINT 15A

Hetch Hetchy Valley Should Be Preserved (1912)

John Muir (1838–1914)

John Muir was an explorer and naturalist who played a leading role in starting the conservation movement in the United States. The founder of the Sierra Club, a conservation and environmental organization, Muir's writings and campaigns led to the establishment in 1890 of Yosemite National Park (an area in California he had explored years earlier), and his contacts with President Theodore Roosevelt helped persuade the president to set aside millions of acres of other federal lands as parks and forest preserves.

The following viewpoint is taken from a chapter in Muir's 1912 book, *The Yosemite,* describing the Hetch Hetchy Valley. The valley became the subject of an intense national debate when the city of San Francisco in 1890 and again in 1907 proposed to dam it to create a water supply for the city. Muir was the leading advocate of the "preservationist" camp that argued for maintaining the valley and other wilderness areas in their natural states.

How does Muir characterize proponents of the dam? Are his views fundamentally opposed to the conservation beliefs of Gifford Pinchot, author of the opposing viewpoint? What does the national controversy over the project reveal about changing American values in the early twentieth century?

Yosemite [Valley] is so wonderful that we are apt to regard it as an exceptional creation, the only valley of its kind in the world; but Nature is not so poor as to have only one of anything. Several other yosemites have been discovered in the Sierra that occupy the same relative positions on the [Sierra Nevada] Range and were formed by the same forces in the same kind of granite. One of these, the Hetch Hetchy Valley, is in the Yosemite National Park about twenty miles from Yosemite and is easily accessible to all sorts of travelers by a road and trail that leaves the Big Oak Flat road at Bronson Meadows a few miles below Crane Flat, and to mountaineers by way of Yosemite Creek basin and the head of the middle fork of the Tuolumne [River].

It is said to have been discovered by Joseph Screech, a hunter, in 1850, a year before the discovery of the great Yosemite. After my first visit to it in the autumn of 1871, I have always called it the "Tuolumne Yosemite," for it is a wonderfully exact

From John Muir, *The Yosemite* (New York: Century, 1912).

counterpart of the [famous] Merced Yosemite, not only in its sublime rocks and waterfalls but in the gardens, groves and meadows of its flowery park-like floor. The floor of Yosemite is about 4000 feet above the sea; the Hetch Hetchy floor about 3700 feet. And as the Merced River flows through Yosemite, so does the Tuolumne through Hetch Hetchy. The walls of both are of gray granite, rise abruptly from the floor, are sculptured in the same style and in both every rock is a glacier monument.

Standing boldly out from the south wall is a strikingly picturesque rock called by the Indians, Kolana, the outermost of a group 2300 feet high, corresponding with the Cathedral Rocks of Yosemite both in relative position and form. On the opposite side of the Valley, facing Kolana, there is a counterpart of the El Capitan that rises sheer and plain to a height of 1800 feet, and over its massive brow flows a stream which makes the most graceful fall I have ever seen. From the edge of the cliff to the top of an earthquake talus it is perfectly free in the air for a thousand feet before it is broken into cascades among talus boulders. . . .

———— • ————

"Everybody needs beauty as well as bread, places to play in and pray in, where Nature may heal and cheer and give strength to body and soul alike."

———— • ————

The floor of the Valley is about three and a half miles long, and from a fourth to half a mile wide. The lower portion is mostly a level meadow about a mile long, with the trees restricted to the sides and the river banks, and partially separated from the main, upper, forested portion by a low bar of glacier-polished granite across which the river breaks in rapids.

The principal trees are the yellow and sugar pines, digger pine, incense cedar, Douglas spruce, silver fir, the California and golden-cup oaks, balsam cottonwood, Nuttall's flowering dogwood, alder, maple, laurel, tumion, etc. The most abundant and influential are the great yellow or silver pines like those of Yosemite, the tallest over two hundred feet in height, and the oaks assembled in magnificent groves with massive rugged trunks four to six feet in diameter, and broad, shady, wide-spreading heads. The shrubs forming conspicuous flowery clumps and tangles are manzanita, azalea, spiraea, brier-rose, several species of ceanothus, calycanthus, philadelphus, wild cherry, etc.; with abundance of showy and fragrant herbaceous plants growing about them or out in the open

in beds by themselves—lilies, Mariposa tulips, brodiaeas, orchids, iris, spraguea, draperia, collomia, collinsia, castilleja, nemophila, larkspur, columbine, goldenrods, sunflowers, mints of many species, honeysuckle, etc. Many fine ferns dwell here also, especially the beautiful and interesting rockferns—pellaea, and cheilanthes of several species—fringing and rosetting dry rock-piles and ledges; woodwardia and asplenium on damp spots with fronds six or seven feet high; the delicate maidenhair in mossy nooks by the falls, and the sturdy, broad-shouldered pteris covering nearly all the dry ground beneath the oaks and pines.

It appears, therefore, that Hetch Hetchy Valley, far from being a plain, common, rock-bound meadow, as many who have not seen it seem to suppose, is a grand landscape garden, one of Nature's rarest and most precious mountain temples. As in Yosemite, the sublime rocks of its walls seem to glow with life, whether leaning back in repose or standing erect in thoughtful attitudes, giving welcome to storms and calms alike, their brows in the sky, their feet set in the groves and gay flowery meadows, while birds, bees, and butterflies help the river and waterfalls to stir all the air into music—things frail and fleeting and types of permanence meeting here and blending, just as they do in Yosemite, to draw her lovers into close and confiding communion with her.

The Valley in Danger

Sad to say, this most precious and sublime feature of the Yosemite National Park, one of the greatest of all our natural resources for the uplifting joy and peace and health of the people, is in danger of being dammed and made into a reservoir to help supply San Francisco with water and light, thus flooding it from wall to wall and burying its gardens and groves one or two hundred feet deep. This grossly destructive commercial scheme has long been planned and urged (though water as pure and abundant can be got from sources outside of the people's park, in a dozen different places), because of the comparative cheapness of the dam and of the territory which it is sought to divert from the great uses to which it was dedicated in the Act of 1890 establishing the Yosemite National Park.

The making of gardens and parks goes on with civilization all over the world, and they increase both in size and number as their value is recognized. Everybody needs beauty as well as bread, places to play in and pray in, where Nature may heal and cheer and give strength to body and soul alike. This natural beauty-hunger is made manifest in the little window-sill gardens of the poor, though perhaps only a geranium slip in a broken cup, as well as in the carefully tended rose and lily gardens of the rich, the thousands of spacious city parks and botanical gardens, and in our magnificent National parks—the Yellowstone, Yosemite, Sequoia, etc.—Nature's sublime wonderlands, the admiration and joy of the world. Nevertheless, like anything else worth while, from the very beginning, however well guarded, they have always been subject to attack by despoiling gain-seekers and mischief-makers of every degree from Satan to Senators, eagerly trying to make everything immediately and selfishly commercial, with schemes disguised in smug-smiling philanthropy, industriously, sham-piously crying, "Conservation, conservation, panutilization," that man and beast may be fed and the dear Nation made great. Thus long ago a few enterprising merchants utilized the Jerusalem temple as a place of business instead of a place of prayer, changing money, buying and selling cattle and sheep and doves; and earlier still, the first forest reservation, including only one tree, was likewise despoiled. Ever since the establishment of the Yosemite National Park, strife has been going on around its borders and I suppose this will go on as part of the universal battle between right and wrong, however much its boundaries may be shorn, or its wild beauty destroyed.

The first application to the Government by the San Francisco Supervisors for the commercial use of Lake Eleanor and the Hetch Hetchy Valley was made in 1903, and on December 22nd of that year it was denied by the Secretary of the Interior, Mr. [Ethan A.] Hitchcock, who truthfully said:

> Presumably the Yosemite National Park was created such by law because of the natural objects of varying degrees of scenic importance located within its boundaries, inclusive alike of its beautiful small lakes, like Eleanor, and its majestic wonders, like Hetch Hetchy and Yosemite Valley. It is the aggregation of such natural scenic features that makes the Yosemite Park a wonderland which the Congress of the United States sought by law to reserve for all coming time as nearly as practicable in the condition fashioned by the hand of the Creator—a worthy object of National pride and a source of healthful pleasure and rest for the thousands of people who may annually sojourn there during the heated months.

In 1907 when Mr. [James R.] Garfield became Secretary of the Interior the application was renewed and granted; but under his successor, Mr. [Walter L.] Fisher, the matter has been referred to a Commission, which as this volume goes to press still has it under consideration. . . .

One of my later visits to the Valley was made in the autumn of 1907 with the late William Keith, the artist. The leaf-colors were then ripe, and the great godlike rocks in repose seemed to glow with life. The artist, under their spell, wandered day after day along the river and through the groves and gardens, studying the wonderful scenery; and, after making about forty sketches, declared with enthusiasm that although its walls were less sublime in height, in picturesque beauty and charm Hetch Hetchy surpassed even Yosemite.

Misleading Arguments

That any one would try to destroy such a place seems incredible; but sad experience shows that there are people good enough and bad enough for anything. The proponents of the dam scheme bring forward a lot of bad arguments to prove that the only righteous thing to do with the people's parks is to destroy them bit by bit as they are able. Their arguments are curiously like those of the devil, devised for the destruction of the first garden—so much of the very best Eden fruit going to waste; so much of the best Tuolumne water and Tuolumne scenery going to waste. Few of their statements are even partly true, and all are misleading.

Thus, Hetch Hetchy, they say, is a "low-lying meadow." On the contrary, it is a high-lying natural landscape garden. . . .

"It is a common minor feature, like thousands of others." On the contrary it is a very uncommon feature; after Yosemite, the rarest and in many ways the most important in the National Park.

"Damming and submerging it 175 feet deep would enhance its beauty by forming a crystal-clear lake." Landscape gardens, places of recreation and worship, are never made beautiful by destroying and burying them. The beautiful sham lake, forsooth, would be only an eyesore, a dismal blot on the landscape, like many others to be seen in the Sierra. For, instead of keeping it at the same level all the year, allowing Nature centuries of time to make new shores, it would, of course, be full only a month or two in the spring, when the snow is melting fast; then it would be gradually drained, exposing the slimy sides of the basin and shallower parts of the bottom, with the gathered drift and waste, death and decay of the upper basins, caught here instead of being swept on to decent natural burial along the banks of the river or in the sea. Thus the Hetch Hetchy dam-lake would be only a rough imitation of a natural lake for a few of the spring months, an open sepulcher for the others.

"Hetch Hetchy water is the purest of all to be found in the Sierra, unpolluted, and forever unpollutable." On the contrary, excepting that of the Merced below Yosemite, it is less pure than that of most of the other Sierra streams, because of the sewerage of camp grounds draining into it, especially of the Big Tuolumne Meadows camp ground, occupied by hundreds of tourists and mountaineers, with their animals, for months every summer, soon to be followed by thousands from all the world.

A Contempt for Nature

These temple destroyers, devotees of ravaging commercialism, seem to have a perfect contempt for Nature, and, instead of lifting their eyes to the God of the mountains, lift them to the Almighty Dollar.

Dam Hetch Hetchy! As well dam for water-tanks the people's cathedrals and churches, for no holier temple has ever been consecrated by the heart of man.

VIEWPOINT 15B

Hetch Hetchy Valley Should Be Dammed (1913)

Gifford Pinchot (1865–1946)

Gifford Pinchot was director of the U.S. Department of Agriculture's Division of Forestry from 1898 to 1910 (the division was reorganized and renamed the U.S. Forest Service in 1905). His position and his friendship with Theodore Roosevelt (U.S. president from 1901 to 1909) made Pinchot one of America's leading conservationists. Roosevelt and Pinchot placed millions of acres of forests off-limits to logging and private development. Pinchot advocated a multi-use approach to utilizing the nation's natural resources—a position that sometimes placed him at odds with "preservationists" such as Sierra Club founder John Muir who called for the setting aside of lands for the sole purpose of wilderness protection.

Pinchot's differences with preservationists were evident in the national debate over whether to dam the Hetch Hetchy Valley in Yosemite National Park to provide water for San Francisco—a development bitterly opposed by Muir and other environmentalists. In the following viewpoint, taken from testimony given before Congress in 1913, Pinchot defends his support of the dam as part of his general philosophy of favoring the utilization of America's natural resources for the greatest good of the people. Pinchot's testimony helped persuade Congress to pass a bill authorizing the Hetch Hetchy dam.

What does Pinchot stress as the fundamental goal of conservation? Judging from arguments presented in viewpoint 15A, how might John Muir respond to Pinchot's fundamental principle? How does Pinchot describe his differences with Muir?

W̲e come now face to face with the perfectly clean question of what is the best use to which this water that flows out of the Sier-

From Gifford Pinchot, testimony on the Hetch Hetchy Dam site, *Congressional Record*, 63rd Cong., 1st sess., June 25, 1913.

ras can be put. As we all know, there is no use of water that is higher than the domestic use. Then, if there is, as the engineers tell us, no other source of supply that is anything like so reasonably available as this one; if this is the best, and within reasonable limits of cost, the only means of supplying San Francisco with water, we come straight to the question of whether the advantage of leaving this valley in a state of nature is greater than the advantage of using it for the benefit of the city of San Francisco.

Now, the fundamental principle of the whole conservation policy is that of use, to take every part of the land and its resources and put it to that use in which it will best serve the most people, and I think there can be no question at all but that in this case we have an instance in which all weighty considerations demand the passage of the bill. There are, of course, a very large number of incidental changes that will arise after the passage of the bill. The construction of roads, trails, and telephone systems which will follow the passage of this bill will be a very important help in the park and forest reserves. The national forest telephone system and the roads and trails to which this bill will lead will form an important additional help in fighting fire in the forest reserves. . . . The presence of these additional means of communication will mean that the national forest and the national park will be visited by very large numbers of people who cannot visit them now. I think that the men who assert that it is better to leave a piece of natural scenery in its natural condition have rather the better of the argument, and I believe if we had nothing else to consider than the delight of the few men and women who would yearly go into the Hetch Hetchy Valley, then it should be left in its natural condition. But the considerations on the other side of the question to my mind are simply overwhelming, and so much so that I have never been able to see that there was any reasonable argument against the use of this water supply by the city of San Francisco. . . .

The Greatest Good

Mr. [John E.] Raker [U.S. Congressman from California]. Taking the scenic beauty of the park as it now stands, and the fact that the valley is sometimes swamped along in June and July, is it not a fact that if a beautiful dam is put there, as is contemplated, and as the picture is given by the engineers, with the roads contemplated around the reservoir and with other trails, it will be more beautiful than it is now, and give more opportunity for the use of the park?

Mr. Pinchot. Whether it will be more beautiful, I doubt, but the use of the park will be enormously increased. I think there is no doubt about that.

Mr. Raker. In other words, to put it a different way,

there will be more beauty accessible than there is now?

Mr. Pinchot. Much more beauty will be accessible than now.

Mr. Raker. And by putting in roads and trails the Government, as well as the citizens of the Government, will get more pleasure out of it than at the present time?

Mr. Pinchot. You might say from the standpoint of enjoyment of beauty and the greatest good to the greatest number, they will be conserved by the passage of this bill, and there will be a great deal more use of the beauty of the park than there is now.

•

"The fundamental principle of the whole conservation policy is that of use, to take every part of the land and its resources and put it to that use in which it will best serve the most people."

•

Mr. Raker. Have you seen Mr. John Muir's criticism of the bill? You know him?

Mr. Pinchot. Yes, sir; I know him very well. He is an old and very good friend of mine. I have never been able to agree with him in his attitude toward the Sierras for the reason that my point of view has never appealed to him at all. When I became Forester and denied the right to exclude sheep and cows from the Sierras, Mr. Muir thought I had made a great mistake, because I allowed the use by an acquired right of a large number of people to interfere with what would have been the utmost beauty of the forest. In this case I think he has unduly given away to beauty as against use.

For Further Reading

Michael P. Cohen, *The Pathless Way: John Muir and the American Wilderness.* Madison: University of Wisconsin Press, 1984.

Stephen R. Fox, *The American Conservation Movement: John Muir and His Legacy.* Madison: University of Wisconsin Press, 1985.

Samuel P. Hays, *Conservation and the Gospel of Efficiency: The Progressive Conservation Movement, 1890–1920.* New York: Atheneum, 1969.

M. Nelson McGeary, *Gifford Pinchot, Forester-Politician.* Princeton, NJ: Princeton University Press, 1960.

Roderick Nash, *Wilderness and the American Mind.* New Haven, CT: Yale University Press, 1973.

Bob Pepperman Taylor, *Our Limits Transgressed: Environmental Political Thought in America.* Lawrence: University Press of Kansas, 1992.

VIEWPOINT 16A

Immigrants Harm American Society (1914)

Edward Alsworth Ross (1866–1951)

Between 1880 and 1920 almost twenty-four million immigrants entered the United States. Many of them came from ethnic and religious backgrounds that put them at odds with America's white Protestant majority. Both the quantity and the ethnicity of the newcomers created much fear among Americans over immigration and its perceived threat to the American way of life. A good summary of the arguments made against immigration comes from the following viewpoint, excerpted from a book by Edward Alsworth Ross, a noted professor of sociology at the University of Wisconsin, Madison.

What does Ross believe to be the main problem immigrants bring to America? How do immigrants affect the American system of education, according to Ross? Do his arguments reveal racial, religious, or other prejudices? Use examples from the viewpoint to support your answer.

There is a certain anthracite town of 26,000 inhabitants in which are writ large the moral and social consequences of injecting 10,000 sixteenth-century people into a twentieth-century community. By their presence the foreigners necessarily lower the general plane of intelligence, self-restraint, refinement, orderliness, and efficiency. With them, of course, comes an increase of drink and of the crimes from drink. The great excess of men among them leads to sexual immorality and the diffusion of private diseases. A primitive midwifery is practised, and the ignorance of the poor mothers fills the cemetery with tiny graves. The women go about their homes barefoot, and their rooms and clothing reek with the odors of cooking and uncleanliness. The standards of modesty are Elizabethan. The miners bathe in the kitchen before the females and children of the household, and women soon to become mothers appear in public unconcerned. The foreigners attend church regularly, but their noisy amusements banish the quiet Sunday. The foreign men, three-eighths of whom are illiterate, pride themselves on their physical strength rather than on their skill, and are willing to take jobs requiring nothing but brawn.

Barriers of speech, education, and religious faith

From Edward Alsworth Ross, *The Old World in the New: The Significance of Past and Present Immigration to the American People* (New York: Century, 1914).

split the people into unsympathetic, even hostile camps. The worst element in the community makes use of the ignorance and venality of the foreign-born voters to exclude the better citizens from any share in the control of local affairs. In this babel no news-paper becomes strong enough to mold and lead pub-lic opinion. On account of the smallness of the Eng-lish-reading public,—the native-born men number slightly over two thousand and those of American parentage less than a thousand—the single English daily has so few subscribers that it cannot afford to offend any of them by exposing municipal rotten-ness. The chance to prey on the ignorant foreigner tempts to cupidity and corrupts the ethics of local business and professional men. The Slavic thirst, multiplying saloons up to one for every twenty-six families, is communicated to Americans, and results in an increase of liquor crimes among all classes. In like manner familiarity with the immodesties of the foreigners coarsens the native-born.

With the basest Americans and the lowest foreign-ers united by thirst and greed, while the decent Americans and the decent foreigners understand one another too little for team-work, it is not sur-prising that the municipal government is poor and that the taxpayers are robbed. Only a few of the main streets are paved; the rest are muddy and poorly gut-tered. Outside the central portion of the city one meets with open sewage, garbage, dung-heaps, and foul odors. Sidewalks are lacking or in bad repair. The police force, composed of four Lithuanians, two Poles, one German, and one Irishman, is so ineffi-cient that "pistol-toting" after nightfall is common among all classes. At times hold-ups have been so frequent that it was not considered safe for a well-dressed person to show himself in the foreign sec-tions after dark. In the words of a prominent local criminal lawyer: "We have a police force that can't speak English. Within the last few years there have been six unavenged murders in this town. Why, if there were anybody I wanted to get rid of, I'd entice him here, shoot him down in the street, and then go around and say good-by to the police."

Social Effects

Here in a nutshell are presented the social effects that naturally follow the introduction into an advanced people of great numbers of backward immigrants. One need not question the fundamental worth of the immigrants or their possibilities in order to argue that they must act as a drag on the social progress of the nation that incorporates them. . . .

While sister countries are fast nearing the goal of complete adult literacy, deteriorating immigration makes it very hard to lift the plane of popular intelli-gence in the United States. The foreign-born between twenty and thirty-four years of age, late-comers of course, show five times the illiteracy of native whites of the same age. But those above forty-five years of age, mostly earlier immigrants, have scarcely twice the illiteracy of native whites above forty-five. This shows how much wider is the gulf between the Amer-icans of to-day and the new immigrants than that between the Americans of a generation ago and the old immigrants.

Thanks to extraordinary educational efforts, the illiteracy of native white voters dropped a third dur-ing the last decade; that is, from 4.9 per cent. to 3.5 per cent. But the illiteracy of the foreign-born men rose to 12 per cent.; so that the proportion of white men in this country unable to read and write any lan-guage declined only 9 per cent. when, but for the influx of illiterates, it would have fallen 30 per cent.

In the despatches of August 16, 1912, is an account of a gathering of ten thousand afflicted peo-ple at a shrine at Carey, Ohio, reputed to possess a miraculous healing virtue. Special trains brought together multitudes of credulous, and at least one "miracle" was reported. As this country fills up with the densely ignorant, there will be more of this sort of thing. The characteristic features of the Middle Ages may be expected to appear among us to the degree that our population comes to be composed of persons at the medieval level of culture. . . .

In the South Side of Pittsburgh there are streets lined with the decent homes of German steelwork-ers. A glance down the paved passage leading to the rear of the house reveals absolute cleanliness, and four times out of five one glimpses a tree, a flower garden, an arbor, or a mass of vines. In Wood's Run, a few miles away, one finds the Slavic laborers of the Pressed Steel Car Company huddled in dilapidated rented dwellings so noisome and repulsive that one must visit the lower quarters of Canton to meet their like. One cause of the difference is that the Slavs are largely transients, who do nothing to house them-selves because they are saving in order to return to their native village.

The fact that a growing proportion of our immi-grants, having left families behind them, form no strong local attachments and have no desire to build homes here is one reason why of late the housing problem has become acute in American industrial centers.

Not least among the multiplying symptoms of social ill health in this country is the undue growth of cities. A million city-dwellers create ten times the amount of "problem" presented by a million on the farms. Now, as one traverses the gamut that leads from farms to towns, from towns to cities, and from little cities to big, the proportion of American stock steadily diminishes while the foreign stock increases its representation until in the great cities it constitutes nearly three-fourths of the population. In 1910 the percentage distribution of our white population was as follows:—

	Native White Stock	Foreign Stock	Foreign- Born
Rural districts	64.1	20.8	7.5
Cities 2,500-10,000	57.5	34.5	13.9
Cities 10,000-25,000	50.4	42.0	14.4
Cities 25,000-100,000	45.9	46.7	20.2
Cities 100,000-500,000	38.9	53.4	22.1
Cities 500,000 and over	25.6	70.8	33.6

It is not that the immigrants love streets and crowds. Two-thirds of them are farm bred, but they are dropped down in cities, and they find it easier to herd there with their fellows than to make their way into the open country. Our cities would be fewer and smaller had they fed on nothing but country-bred Americans. The later alien influx has rushed us into the thick of urban problems, and these are gravest where Americans are fewest. Congestion, misliving, segregation, corruption, and confusion are seen in motley groups like Pittsburgh, Jersey City, Paterson, and Fall River rather than in native centers like Indianapolis, Columbus, Nashville, and Los Angeles.

Pauperism

Ten years ago two-fifths of the paupers in our almshouses were foreign-born, but most of them had come over in the old careless days when we allowed European poorhouses to send us their inmates. Now that our authorities turn back such as appear likely to become a public charge, the obvious pauper is not entering this country. We know that virtually every Greek in America is self-supporting. The Syrians are said to be singularly independent. The Slavs and the Magyars are sturdy in spirit, and the numerous indigent Hebrews are for the most part cared for by their own race.

Nevertheless, dispensers of charity agree that many South Italians are landing with the most extravagant ideas of what is coming to them. They apply at once for relief with the air, "Here we are. Now what are you going to do for us?" They even insist on relief as a right. At home it had been noised about that in foolish America baskets of food are actually sent in to the needy, and some are coming over expressly to obtain such largess. Probably none are so infected with spiritual hookworm as the immigrants from Naples. It will be recalled that when Garibaldi and his thousand were fighting to break the Bourbon tyranny in the South [of Italy], the Neapolitans would hurrah for them, but would not even care for the wounded.

Says the Forty-seventh Annual Report of the New York Juvenile Asylum:

> It is remarkable that recently arrived immigrants who display small adaptability in American standards are by no means slow in learning about this and other institutions where they may safely leave their children to be fed, clothed, and cared for at the public expense. This is one of the inducements which led them to leave their native land.

Charity experts are very pessimistic as to what we shall see when those who come in their youth have passed their prime and met the cumulative effects of overwork, city life, drink, and vice. Still darker are their forebodings for a second generation, reared too often by ignorant, avaricious rustics lodging in damp cellars, sleeping with their windows shut, and living on the bad, cheap food of cities. Of the Italians in Boston Dr. Bushee writes:

> They show the beginnings of a degenerate class, such as has been fully developed among the Irish. . . . If allowed to continue in unwholesome conditions, we may be sure that the next generation will bring forth a large crop of dependents, delinquents and defectives to fill up our public institutions.

Says a charity superintendent working in a huge Polish quarter:

> It is the second generation that will give us trouble. The parents come with rugged peasant health, and many of them keep their strength even in the slum. But their children often start life weakened physically and mentally by the conditions under which they were reared. They have been raised in close, unsanitary quarters, in overlarge families, by parents who drunk up or saved too much, spent too little on the children, or worked them too soon. Their sole salvation is the open country, and they can't be pushed into the country. All of us are aghast at the weak fiber of the second generation. Every year I see the morass of helpless poverty getting bigger. The evil harvest of past mistakes is ripening, but it will take twenty years before we see the worst of it. If immigration were cut off short to-day, the burden from past neglect and exploitation would go on increasing for years.

In 1908 nine-tenths of the 2600 complaints of children going wrong made to the Juvenile Protective Association of Chicago related to the children of immigrants. It is said that four-fifths of the youths brought before the Juvenile Court of Chicago come from the homes of the foreign-born. In Pittsburgh the proportion is at least two-thirds. However startling these signs of moral breakdown in the families of the new immigrants, there is nothing mysterious about it. The lower the state from which the alien comes, the more of a grotesque he will appear in the shrewd eyes of his partly Americanized children. "Obedience to parents seems to be dying out among the Jews," says a Boston charity visitor. "The children feel it is n't necessary to obey a mother who wears a shawl or a father who wears a full beard." "Sometimes it is the young daughter who rules the Jewish family," observes a Pittsburgh settlement head, "because she alone knows what is 'American.' But see how this results in a great number of Jewish girls going astray. Since the mother continues to shave her head and wear a wig as she did in Poland, the daughter assumes that mother is equally old-fogyish when she insists that a nice girl does n't paint her face or run with boys in the evening."

———— • ————

"Those optimists who imagine that assimilation of the immigrant is proceeding unhindered are living in a fool's paradise."

———— • ————

Through their knowledge of our speech and ways, the children have a great advantage in their efforts to slip the parental leash. The bad boy tells his father that whipping "does n't go" in this country. Reversing the natural order, the child becomes the fount of knowledge, and the parents hang on the lips of their precocious offspring. If the policeman inquires about some escapade or the truant officer gives warning, it is the scamp himself who must interpret between parent and officer. The immigrant is braced by certain Old-World loyalties, but his child may grow up loyal to nothing whatever, a rank egoist and an incorrigible who will give us vast trouble before we are done with him.

Still, the child is not always to blame. "Often the homes are so crowded and dirty," says a probation officer, "that no boy can go right. The Slavs save so greedily that their children become disgusted with the wretched home conditions and sleep out." One hears of foreign-born with several boarders sending their children out to beg or to steal coal. In one city investigation showed that only a third of the Italian children taken from school on their fourteenth birthday were needed as bread-winners. Their parents thought only of the sixty cents a week. In another only one-fourteenth of the Italian school children are above the primary grades, and one-eleventh of the Slavic, as against two-fifths of the American school children in grammar grades or high school. Miss Addams tells of a young man from the south of Italy who was mourning the death of his little girl of twelve. In his grief he said quite simply: "She was my

oldest kid. In two years she would have supported me, and now I shall have to work five or six years longer until the next one can do it." He expected to retire permanently at the age of thirty-four.

Not only do the foreign-born appear to be more subject to insanity than the native-born, but when insane they are more likely to become a public charge. Of the asylum population they appear to constitute about a third. In New York during the year ending September 30, 1911, 4218 patients who were immigrants or of immigrant parents were admitted to the insane hospitals of the State. This is three-quarters of the melancholy intake for that year. Only one out of nine of the first admissions from New York City was of native stock. The New York State Hospital Commission declares that "the frequency of insanity in our foreign population is 2.19 times greater than in those of native birth." In New York City it "is 2.48 times that of the native-born."

Excessive insanity is probably a part of the price the foreign-born pay for the opportunities of a strange and stimulating environment, with greater strains than some of them are able to bear. America calls forth powerful reactions in these people. Here they feel themselves in the grasp of giant forces they can neither withstand nor comprehend. The passions and the exertions, the hopes and the fears, the exultations and the despairs America excites in the immigrant are likely to be intenser than anything he would have experienced in his natal village.

In view of the fact that every year New York cares for 15,000 foreign-born insane at a cost of $3,500,000 and that the State's sad harvest of demented immigrants during the single year 1911 will cost about $8,000,000 before they die or are discharged, there is some offset to be made to the profits drawn from the immigrants by the transporting companies, landlords, real-estate men, employers, contractors, brewers, and liquor-dealers of the State. Besides, there is the cost of the paupers and the law-breakers of foreign origin. All such burdens, however, since they fall upon the public at large, do not detract from or qualify that private or business-man's prosperity which it is the office of the true modern statesman to promote.

Immigration and the Separate School

In a polyglot mining town of Minnesota is a superintendent who has made the public school a bigger factor in Americanization than I have found it anywhere else. The law gives him the children until they are sixteen, and he holds them all. His school buildings are civic and social centers. Through the winter, in his high school auditorium, which seats 1200 persons, he gives a course of entertainment which is self-supporting, although his "talent" for a single evening will cost as much as $200. By means of the 400 foreigners in his night schools he has a grip on the voters which his foes have learned to dread. Under his lead the community has broken the mine-boss collar and won real self-government. The people trust him and bring him their troubles. He has jurisdiction over everything that can affect the children of the town, and his conception is wide. Wielding both legal and moral authority, he is, as it were, a corporation president and a medieval bishop rolled into one.

This man sets no limit to the transforming power of the public school. He insists that the right sort of schooling will not only alter the expression, but will even change the shape of the skull and the bony formation of the face. In his office is a beautiful tabouret made by a "wild boy" within a year after he had been brought in kicking and screaming. He scoffs at the fear of a lack of patriotism in the foreign-born or their children. He knows just how to create the sentiment. He has flag drills and special programs, and in the Fourth of July parade and the Decoration day procession the schools have always a fine float. He declares he can build human beings to order, and will not worry about immigration so long as the public school is given a chance at the second generation.

But is the public school to have this chance?

Multitudes of the new immigrants adhere to churches which do not believe in the public schools. "Their pupils," observed a priest to me, "are like wild children." Said a bishop: "No branches can be safely taught divorced from religion. We believe that geography, history, and even language ought to be presented from our point of view." Hence with great rapidity the children of Roman Catholics are being drawn apart into parochial schools. In Cleveland one-third of the population is supposed to be Catholic, and the 27,500 pupils in the parochial schools are nearly one-third of all school children. In Chicago there are 112,000 in the parish schools to 300,000 in the public schools. In New York the proportion is about one-sixth. In twenty-eight leading American cities the attendance of the parish schools increased 60 per cent. between 1897 and 1910, as against an increase of from 45 to 50 per cent. in the attendance of the public schools. The total number of children in the parochial schools is about 1,400,000. Separate education is a settled Catholic policy, and the bishops say they expect to enroll finally the children of all their people.

To bring this about, the public schools are denounced from the pulpit as "Godless" and "immoral," their product as mannerless and disobedient. "We think," says a Slovak leader, "that the parochial school pupils are more pious, more respectful toward parents and toward all persons in authority." The Polish, Lithuanian, or Slovak priest, less often the German or Bohemian, says bluntly: "If you send your children to the public school, they will go to hell." Sometimes the priest threatens to exclude from the confessional parents who send their children to the public school. An archbishop recently decreed that parents who without permission send their children to the public school after they have made their first communion "commit a grievous sin and cannot receive the sacraments of the church." Within the immigrant groups there is active opposition, but it appears to be futile. In the soft-coal mining communities of Pennsylvania 9 per cent. of the children of native white parentage attend the parochial schools, whereas 24 per cent. of the Polish children and 48 per cent. of the Slovak children are in these schools. In a certain district in Chicago where the public-school teachers had felt they could hold their own, the foreign mothers came at last to take away their children's school-books, weeping because they were forced to transfer their children to the parish school.

Now, the parish school tends to segregate the children of the foreign-born. Parishes are formed for groups of the same speech, so a parish school will embrace children of only one nationality—German, Polish, Bohemian, Lithuanian, Croatian, Slovak, Magyar, Portuguese, or French Canadian, as the case may be. Often priest and teachers have been imported, and only the mother-tongue is used. "English," says a school superintendent, "comes to be taught as a purely ornamental language, like French in the public high school." Hence American-born children are leaving school not only unable to read and write English, but scarcely able to speak it. The foreign-speech school, while it binds the young to their parents, to their people, and to the old country, cuts them off from America. Says a Chicago Lithuanian leader: "There are 3000 of our children in the parochial schools here. The teachers are ignorant, illiterate spinsters from Lithuania who have studied here two or three years. When at fourteen the pupils quit school, they are no more advanced than the public-school pupils of ten. This is why 50,000 Lithuanians here have only twenty children in the high school."

When, now, to the removal of the second generation from the public school there is added, as is often the case, the endeavor to keep them away from the social center, the small park field-house, the public playground, the social settlement, the secular American press and welfare work in the factories, it is plain that those optimists who imagine that assimilation of the immigrant is proceeding unhindered are living in a fool's paradise.

Social Decline

"Our descendants," a social worker remarked to me, "will look back on the nineteenth century as our

Golden Age, just as we look back on Greece." Thoughtful people whose work takes them into the slime at the bottom of our foreignized cities and industrial centers find decline actually upon us. A visiting nurse who has worked for seven years in the stock-yards district of Chicago reports that of late the drinking habit is taking hold of foreign women at an alarming rate. In the saloons there the dignified stein has given way to the beer pail. In the Range towns of Minnesota there are 356 saloons, of which eighty-one are run by native-born, the rest chiefly by recent immigrants. Into a Pennsylvania coal town of 1800 people, mostly foreign-born, are shipped each week a car-load of beer and a barrel of whisky. Where the new foreign-born are numerous, women and children frequent the saloons as freely as the men. In the cities family desertion is growing at a great rate among foreign-born husbands. Facts are justifying the forecast made ten years ago by H. G. Wells: "If things go on as they are going, the great mass of them will remain a very low lower class—will remain largely illiterate, industrialized peasants."

The continuance of depressive immigration will lead to nothing catastrophic. Riots and labor strife will oftener break out, but the country will certainly not weaken nor collapse. Of patriotism of the military type there will be no lack. Scientific and technical advance will go on the same. The spread of business organization and efficiency will continue. The only thing that will happen will be a mysterious slackening in social progress. The mass will give signs of sluggishness, and the social procession will be strung out.

We are engaged in a generous rivalry with the West Europeans and the Australians to see which can do the most to lift the plane of life of the masses. Presently we shall be dismayed by the sense of falling behind. We shall be amazed to find the Swiss or the Danes or the New Zealanders making strides we cannot match. Stung with mortification at losing our erstwhile lead in the advancement of the common people, we shall cast about for someone to blame. Ultimate causes, of course, will be overlooked; only proximate causes will be noticed. There will be loud outcry that mothers, or teachers, or clergymen, or editors, or social workers are not doing their duty. Our public schools, solely responsible as they obviously are for the intellectual and moral characteristics of the people, will be roundly denounced; and it will be argued that church schools must take their place. There will be trying of this and trying of that, together with much ingenious legislation. As peasantism spreads and inertia proves unconquerable, the opinion will grow that the old American faith in the capacity and desire of the common people for improvement was a delusion, and

that only the superior classes care for progress. Not until the twenty-first century will the philosophic historian be able to declare with scientific certitude that the cause of the mysterious decline that came upon the American people early in the twentieth century was the deterioration of popular intelligence by the admission of great numbers of backward immigrants.

VIEWPOINT 16B

Immigrants Do Not Harm American Society (1914)
A. Piatt Andrew (1873–1936)

The large influx of immigrants at the turn of the century prompted many calls for greater restrictions on immigration. A. Piatt Andrew, in a June 1914 North American Review *article excerpted here, takes issue with critics of immigration. Andrew, a professor of economics at Harvard University, argues that unwarranted fears of different racial and ethnic groups fuel criticism of immigrants. He defends the new immigrants against charges of inferior character and economic disruption.*

How consistent has been the American attitude toward immigrants, according to Andrew? Does he believe that immigrants should try to change and assimilate into American society? What does the debate over immigrants, as represented in these viewpoints, reveal about what Americans believed and felt about their country during the Progressive Era?

T he subject of immigration we have always with us in this country. It has been a topic of contentious interest and legislation almost continuously since the first Englishman set foot in the Western World. The Pilgrims and Puritans of Massachusetts Bay were scarcely settled in their log huts before they began planning a policy of exclusion, and already in 1637 they voted to keep out those who were not members of their own religious sect. So in the very earliest decades of the English settlement, immigration began to be restricted, and Quakers and Baptists, Episcopalians and Catholics, were banished and proscribed from the Commonwealth on the ground that American standards were apt to be impaired by their admission. From that day to this the older immigrants and their descendants have tried to keep this country for those already here and their kindred folk. They have looked upon them-

From A. Piatt Andrew, "The Crux of the Immigration Question," *North American Review*, June 1914.

selves as a kind of aristocracy, their supposed superiority being proportioned to the length of time that they and their ancestors have lived upon this continent, and each successive generation of immigrants newly arrived has tended with curious repetition to adopt the same viewpoint, to believe that the succeeding immigrants were inferior to the former in religion, habits, education, or what not, and ought to be kept out. Then for more than a hundred years a further motive for exclusion has found constant iteration. Each generation has been taught to believe that the country was rapidly filling to the brim, and that on that account also the doors of entry ought to be closed.

In the very first decade of our Federal Government, in 1797, when the first Alien Act was under consideration, we find passages in the records of Congress which sound much like the utterances of certain Congressmen in 1914:

> When the country, said Otis (in 1797), was new it may have been good policy to admit all. But it is so no longer. A bar should be placed against the admittance of those restless people who cannot be tranquil and happy at home. We do not want a vast horde of wild Irishmen let loose upon us. (McMasters' *History of the People of the United States*, Vol. II, page 332.)

Passage after passage of similar tenor could be cited from every subsequent decade, but I shall only quote one or two examples, beginning with a report made in 1819 by the Managers of the Society for the Prevention of Pauperism in the City of New York. In this report of nearly a hundred years ago the fear is expressed that through immigration

> pauperism threatens us with the most overwhelming consequences. . . . The present state of Europe contributes in a thousand ways to foster increasing immigration to the United States. . . . An almost innumerable population beyond the ocean is out of employment. . . . This country is the resort of vast numbers of these needy and wretched beings. . . . They are frequently found destitute in our streets: they seek employment at our doors: they are found in our almshouses and in our hospitals: they are found at the bar of our criminal tribunals, in our bridewell and our penitentiary and our State prison. (*Reports of the Industrial Commission*, Vol. XV, page 449.)

This was in 1819. Coming down another score of years, we find the next generation once more extolling the immigration up to its own time, but once more greatly perturbed by the supposedly inferior character of the immigrants then beginning to come. In a paper published in 1835, entitled "Imminent Dangers to the Institutions of the United States through Foreign Immigration," we read that formerly

our accessions of immigration were real accessions of strength from the ranks of the learned and the good, from enlightened mechanic and artisan and intelligent husbandmen. Now immigration is the accession of weakness, from the ignorant and vicious, or the priest-ridden slaves of Ireland and Germany, or the outcast tenants of the poorhouses and prisons of Europe. (*Hearings before the Committee on Immigration, Sixty-first Congress*, page 327.)

In the course of the twenty years that followed came the great increase of Irish immigrants during the famine in Ireland, and then again many Americans became panic-stricken at the thought of the possible consequences. A great secret order and a new political party, the so-called Know-Nothings, were organized to overcome the dire results that were apprehended. The abject squalor and wretchedness to which these Irish immigrants had for generations been accustomed, it was urged, could not but result in the degradation of American standards, and many seemed to fear that on account of their religion the immigrants would try to overthrow our democratic government and establish an ecclesiastic hierarchy in its stead. Feeling in some places was so bitter that the immigrants were mobbed in the streets, their churches were desecrated, and their children were persecuted in the public schools. One could spend hours reading passages from speeches and pamphlets of this period denouncing the Irish immigration.

Yet the American government still lives and, notwithstanding the abject condition of these Irish settlers and the fears and apprehensions which they aroused, we have absorbed and assimilated some four millions of them and no one has yet observed any deterioration of American standards and ideals in consequence. We and they have flourished and prospered, and we reckon their descendants among our best citizens. The names of many of them are daily on our lips and before our eyes in the headlines, for they are our political magnates, our aldermen and mayors and governors.

Germans and Scandinavians

Passing on to the next generation, during the later seventies and early eighties came a great migration of Germans and Scandinavians, and once more racial prejudice found a new objective. The previous immigrants had for the most part spoken our language, were akin, it was said, to our original stock and familiar with our traditions, but the new immigrants, ignorant of English and with different modes of thought and practice, were held to be unassimilable and to menace our standards and institutions. The apprehension was so great and the objection became so general as to induce in 1882 the first general immigration law. Nevertheless, we have absorbed over four million Germans and over two million Swedes and Norwegians, and to-day we count no more valuable factors in our national stock than their descendants.

The New Immigrants

But once again the racial currents shifted, and during the last fifteen years new vast streams have flowed to this country from Russia, Italy, and Austria-Hungary, and new smaller streams from Portugal and from Greece, Rumania, and other parts of Eastern Europe. During 1913 Russia, Italy, and Austria-Hungary offered each nearly a quarter of the year's total inflow. So once again the familiar clamor of alarm has been turned in another direction. It is now admitted that the millions of Irish and Germans and Scandinavians who have come into the country have been absorbed without any degradation of our standards, that they have rendered invaluable service in developing the country, and that the earlier fears have proven groundless. But it is said that the new immigrant is of a type radically less desirable than that of the earlier periods, and once more we hear the warning that the situation to-day is different in that the country is now thickly settled and land and opportunities are no longer available. As I recall the similar assertions and fears of earlier periods I must confess that I sympathize with the gentleman from Missouri who expressed a desire to have some evidence submitted. It looks as if in the eyes of some Americans the only good immigrants were the dead immigrants, and that the only opportunities for the country's development lay in the past. I want to know and you want to know in what sense the immigrants of to-day are thought to be inferior to those who preceded them, and on what grounds it is claimed that the country has reached the limit of profitable increase in population.

Important Questions

Are the new immigrants less sound of body and mind than those of earlier generations? Do they more frequently evince criminal proclivities? Are they more apt to become a charge upon the State? Is their standard of living lower? Are they less capable of becoming loyal, worthy American citizens? We may well inquire what the Immigration Commission, with their exhaustive investigations published in forty-one volumes, have to say in answer to these questions, and in this connection we may also turn to the volume upon *The Immigration Problem* prepared by Professors [Jeremiah W.] Jenks and [W. Jett] Lauck, the reputed authors of the Immigration Commission Report, which summarizes the data and conclusions of the Commission.

Are the new immigrants wanting in bodily vigor and health? The authors of the Immigration Com-

mission Report deny this.

Our later immigration laws have forbidden the entrance of those afflicted with any loathsome or contagious disease, or of those in such a condition of health as is likely to make them become a public charge. Under these laws, too, the steamship companies are held responsible and are compelled to return free of charge passengers rejected by our immigration officials, and in the case of the insane or diseased they are fined in addition one hundred dollars for each such passenger brought to this country. This legislation has brought about a very great change in the matter of inspection and exclusion, and the representatives of the Immigration Commission declare that

> the careful inspection abroad, sometimes by representatives of the United States Government, otherwise by inspectors of the steamship companies, and the final examination at the port of entry, have brought about the result that with very rare exceptions every immigrant admitted to this country is now in good health, and is not bringing with him the germs of any disease that might prove detrimental. (Jenks and Lauck, page 28.)

And they add that

> as far as one can judge from the records kept, the races of the recent immigration, those from Southern and Eastern Europe, are not so subject to diseases that seem to be allied with moral weaknesses as some of those of the older immigration races. (Jenks and Lauck, page 47.)

Are the new immigrants more addicted to crime? Again the authors of the Immigration Commission Report assert that there is no proof of this.

> No satisfactory evidence has yet been produced to show that immigration has resulted in an increase in crime disproportionate to the increase in the adult population. Such comparable statistics of crime and population as it has been possible to obtain indicate that immigrants are less prone to commit crime than are native Americans. (*Reports of the United States Immigration Commission*, Vol. XXXVI, page 1.)

Are the new immigrants more likely to become charges upon the community? The authors of the Immigration Commission Report declare the contrary.

> The Immigration Commission, with the assistance of the Associated Charities in forty-three cities, including practically all the large centers excepting New York, reached the conclusion that only a very small percentage of the immigrants now arriving apply for relief. (Jenks and Lauck, page 50.)

Is the standard of living of the new immigrants lower than that of the old? Any one who has read the contemporary descriptions of the living conditions of the Irish and German immigrants in the periods from 1840 to 1880 will hesitate to believe that the standard of living of the immigrants of our day is lower than the standard of living of the immigrants in the earlier period. Nothing could be more pitiful and depressing than the pictures of the poverty and wretchedness of the Irish settlers at the time of the great migration from Ireland. The majority of the Irish people for centuries had been forced to live in hovels with only the barest necessities in the way of furniture and clothing, and many of the thousands who came to this country were in serious danger of actual starvation if they remained at home. The authors of the Immigration Commission Report state that "practically none of our immigrants of the present day are in such a condition" (Jenks and Lauck, page 12).

The Melting Pot

In a very few years, with our free and compulsory schools, our free libraries, and the economic opportunities which this country has to offer, these people were transformed into ambitious, self-respecting, public-spirited citizens. And so it is with the Italians and Poles, the Russian Jews, and other poor immigrants of more recent times. They are often very poor in this world's goods when they enter our gates. One sees the mothers coming in with shawls in place of hats, often without shoes or stockings, and with all their worldly belongings in a rough box or tied in a single handkerchief. But it is one of the miraculous phases of our history how quickly we are able to transform, enrich, and absorb them. A few years later one sees the children of these same immigrants well dressed and ambitious, well educated, and literally undistinguishable in manners, morals, or appearance from the descendants of those who came over in the *Mayflower*. Such is the Aladdin-like power of the great American melting-pot.

It is easy to echo the cry of prejudice if you happen to be of Anglo-Saxon descent, and to assume an air of superiority and denounce the Italians, Greeks, Poles, Bohemians, and Russian Jews, as if they ranked somewhere between man and the beast, but were not yet wholly human. The same intolerant attitude of mind among the Anglo-Saxon Puritan settlers of early colonial days led to the whipping, imprisonment, banishment, and even hanging of Quakers and others of unlike religious beliefs. If you share these prejudices to-day, walk some Sunday afternoon through the galleries of the art-museums in our large cities and note who are the people most interested in their treasures; inquire at the public libraries who are their most appreciative patrons; visit the night schools and observe who constitute their most eager classes; study the lineage of the ranking students in our universities and you will find that our libraries, art-galleries, universities, and schools often find their best patrons among the off-spring of these despised races of Southern and Eastern Europe. Or if you seek your information in books, I would commend you to authorities who have studied the new immigrants at first-hand. If you will examine the volume on *The Italian in America*, by Messrs. [Eliot] Lord, Trenor, and Barrows, you will be reminded of what America owes to the Italians from Columbus down to our own day. And if you will read the study of *Our Slavic Fellow Citizens*, by Dr. [Emily] Balch, you will be reminded of what we owe to the Poles and Bohemians from the time of Pulaski and Kosciuszko down to our time. And if you will read the story of *The Promised Land* and *They Who Knock at Our Gates*, by Mary Antin, you will find descriptions of what we may expect from the Russian Jews. Incidentally you will also discover that the traditions and heroes of American history find their most ardent admirers to-day among these same people who but recently were aliens.

Immigrant Numbers

There is no evidence that the newer immigrants are inferior to the old. It is only the recurrence of a groundless prejudice which makes some people feel so. But even if the new immigration is not inferior in character to the old, we have still to ask whether there is not a menace in the very numbers of the immigrants now coming in. We hear a great deal these days about the alarming increase in immigration. We are told that more than a million foreign-born are coming into this country every year, that the number is increasing as never before, and that the country cannot absorb so great an influx. What are the facts in this regard?

———— • ————

"There is no evidence that the newer immigrants are inferior to the old."

———— • ————

As to the amount of recent immigration, the tide ebbs and flows with the alternating advances and recessions of business, and the tendency is for each successive wave to reach a higher level than its predecessors. In 1854 a record of 428,000 arrivals was established; then there was a great recession, and in 1873 a new high level of 460,000 was reached. The next wave culminated in 1882 with 789,000, and in 1907 the highest of all immigrant records was reached, 1,285,000. During the last ten years the average number of immigrants arriving in this country has not fallen much short of a million per year, and this figure considered by itself does look portentous. One must bear in mind, however, that it represents only one side of the ledger and is subject to very heavy deductions. If you are reckoning the extent to which your property has increased during a given period, it does not suffice merely to count up the income. You must also deduct the outgo. And if you are reckoning the actual addition to our population which results from immigration, if you would have in mind the actual number of immigrants that we have had to absorb, you must take account of both sides of the ledger, of the outgo as well as of the income. During the last six years the number of departing aliens has been carefully collated, and it appears that from 400,000 to 700,000 aliens depart from the United States every year. This leaves a net balance of arriving aliens of only about 550,000 per year, or only about one-half of the total that is commonly cited as representing the annual influx. Even this figure may look precarious, however, until we have considered it in its appropriate relations and comparisons.

America's Capacity

The capacity of the country to assimilate the incoming thousands without any serious modification of our institutions or standards depends in part upon two conditions: first, upon the proportion which the aliens bear to the resident population by which they are to be absorbed, and, second, upon whether the country is already approaching the saturation point as regards the density of its population. Now the proportion of foreign-born in our total population has not varied much in recent decades, and even in the record year of 1907 the percentage of immigrants to population was lower than it has been on several other occasions during the past sixty years. As compared with the population of the country the immigration of recent years has not bulked as large as the immigration of the early fifties, and if we consider only the net immigration, it makes to-day an addition to the total population of the country of only a little more than one-half of one per cent. per year.

Nor need one fear that we are reaching the point in this country where population presses upon the means of subsistence. The number of our people will have to be multiplied sixfold to equal the density of the population of France, to be multiplied tenfold to equal that of Germany or that of Italy, and to be multiplied eighteenfold to equal that of England. If the present population of the whole United States were located in the State of Texas alone, there would still not be two-thirds as many inhabitants per square mile in that State as there are to-day in England. One must, indeed, have little faith in the future of the United States who, in the face of such comparisons, believes that the population of this country as a whole is approaching the saturation point, or that from the standpoint of the country as a whole we need be terrified by the dimensions of present immigration. It amounts in annual net to little more than one-half of one per cent. of our present population, and that population will have to increase many hundred per cent. before we have reached a density remotely approaching that of any of the leading countries of Europe.

Timid Americans

There will, of course, always be timid Americans who will wonder how we can possibly hope to assimilate foreigners to the extent of as much as one-half of one per cent. of our population per year and who would prefer to see the country relatively weak and undeveloped than run the risk of continuing the experiment. When Jefferson proposed to purchase all of the great territory west of the Mississippi known as Louisiana, the citizens of Boston organized a public meeting to protest against the project. They thought it would destroy the relative influence of New England in the country's affairs, and they thought that the United States could not assimilate so vast a territory; and though their fears have been proven not only groundless but absurd by subsequent history, there are many still in Boston and elsewhere in the country who feel that our powers of assimilation have now reached their limit of capacity and ought not to be further taxed.

There will, of course, always be Americans absorbed in history and genealogy who will sigh for the good old days when America was only a sparsely settled fringe of seaboard States, and who will wish that the population of the country might still consist of the Sons and Daughters of the Revolution, the Colonial Dames, and the Sons of Colonial Wars. This might, indeed, have been a pleasant condition from certain points of view, but of one thing we may be certain: this country to-day would not be settled from coast to coast; our cities would not be a fifth of their present size; our powers as a nation and our prosperity as individuals would only have been a fraction of what they are had immigration been prevented.

For Further Reading

Edith Abbott, *Historical Aspects of the Immigration Problem: Select Documents.* Chicago: University of Chicago Press, 1926.

Roger Daniels, *Coming to America.* New York: HarperCollins, 1990.

Julius Weinberg, *Edward Alsworth Ross and the Sociology of Progressivism.* Madison: State Historical Society of Wisconsin, 1972.

Thomas C. Wheeler, ed., *The Immigrant Experience: The Anguish of Becoming American.* New York: Penguin, 1971.

New Nationalism vs. New Freedom

VIEWPOINT 17A

The Federal Government Should Regulate Trusts: Roosevelt's New Nationalism (1910)

Theodore Roosevelt (1858–1919)

Theodore Roosevelt served as president of the United States for seven-and-a-half years following the assassination of William McKinley in 1901. He instituted several Progressive reforms, including federal regulation of the food and drug industries, "trust busting," and expansion of the national park system. Roosevelt remained active in politics after leaving office in 1909. Disappointed in the relatively conservative policies of his hand-picked successor as president, William Howard Taft, he became increasingly convinced of the need for an activist federal government to intervene in the economic and social development of the nation.

In a famous speech to Civil War veterans at Osawatomie, Kansas, on August 31, 1910, Roosevelt spelled out his political philosophy, which he called the "New Nationalism." Roosevelt called for the establishment of government commissions to control (rather than break up) the business trusts (monopolies) that were playing a growing role in American life. The speech became the springboard for Roosevelt's political comeback, which ultimately split the Republican Party into conservative and progressive branches. Taft and Roosevelt both ran for president in 1912 (Roosevelt as candidate of the Progressive or "Bull Moose" Party), only to finish behind the Democratic candidate, Woodrow Wilson.

What does Roosevelt argue to be the proper functions of the national and state governments? What parts of the speech might be considered most objectionable to conservatives? Which elements differ most from the views of Woodrow Wilson, author of the opposing viewpoint? How would you concisely define the New Nationalism?

W e come here to-day to commemorate one of the epoch-making events of the long struggle for the rights of man—the long struggle for the uplift of humanity. Our country—this great Republic—means nothing unless it means

Excerpted from Theodore Roosevelt's campaign speech at Osawatomie, Kansas, August 31, 1910.

the triumph of a real democracy, the triumph of popular government, and, in the long run, of an economic system under which each man shall be guaranteed the opportunity to show the best that there is in him. That is why the history of America is now the central feature of the history of the world for the world has set its face hopefully toward our democracy; and, O my fellow citizens, each one of you carries on your shoulders not only the burden of doing well for the sake of your own country, but the burden of doing well and of seeing that this nation does well for the sake of mankind.

There have been two great crises in our country's history: first, when it was formed, and then, again, when it was perpetuated; and, in the second of these great crises—in the time of stress and strain which culminated in the Civil War, on the outcome of which depended the justification of what had been done earlier, you men of the Grand Army, you men who fought through the Civil War, not only did you justify your generation, not only did you render life worth living for our generation, but you justified the wisdom of Washington and Washington's colleagues. . . .

Equality of Opportunity

In every wise struggle for human betterment one of the main objects, and often the only object, has been to achieve in large measure equality of opportunity. In the struggle for this great end, nations rise from barbarism to civilization, and through it people press forward from one stage of enlightenment to the next. One of the chief factors in progress is the destruction of special privilege. The essence of any struggle for healthy liberty has always been, and must always be, to take from some one man or class of men the right to enjoy power, or wealth, or position, or immunity, which has not been earned by service to his or their fellows. That is what you fought for in the Civil War, and that is what we strive for now.

At many stages in the advance of humanity, this conflict between the men who possess more than they have earned and the men who have earned more than they possess is the central condition of progress. In our day it appears as the struggle of freemen to gain and hold the right of self-government as against the special interests, who twist the methods of free government into machinery for defeating the popular will. At every stage, and under all circumstances, the essence of the struggle is to equalize opportunity, destroy privilege, and give to the life and citizenship of every individual the highest possible value both to himself and to the commonwealth. That is nothing new. All I ask in civil life is what you fought for in the Civil War. I ask that civil life be carried on according to the spirit in which the army was carried on. You never get perfect justice, but the effort in handling the army was to bring to the front the men who could do the job. Nobody grudged promotion to Grant, or Sherman, . . . because they earned it. The only complaint was when a man got promotion which he did not earn.

Practical equality of opportunity for all citizens, when we achieve it, will have two great results. First, every man will have a fair chance to make of himself all that in him lies; to reach the highest point to which his capacities, unassisted by special privilege of his own and unhampered by the special privilege of others, can carry him, and to get for himself and his family substantially what he has earned. Second, equality of opportunity means that the commonwealth will get from every citizen the highest service of which he is capable. No man who carries the burden of the special privileges of another can give to the commonwealth that service to which it is fairly entitled.

The Square Deal

I stand for the square deal. But when I say that I am for the square deal, I mean not merely that I stand for fair play under the present rules of the game, but that I stand for having those rules change so as to work for a more substantial equality of opportunity and of reward for equally good service. One word of warning, which, I think, is hardly necessary in Kansas. When I say I want a square deal for the poor man, I do not mean that I want a square deal for the man who remains poor because he has not got the energy to work for himself. If a man who has had a chance will not make good, then he has got to quit. And you men of the Grand Army, you want justice for the brave man who fought, and punishment for the coward who shirked his work. Is not that so?

Now, this means that our government, National and State, must be freed from the sinister influence or control of special interests. Exactly as the special interests of cotton and slavery threatened our political integrity before the Civil War, so now the great special business interests too often control and corrupt the men and methods of government for their own profit. We must drive the special interests out of politics. That is one of our tasks to-day. Every special interest is entitled to justice—full, fair, and complete—and, now, mind you, if there were any attempt by mob-violence to plunder and work harm to the special interest, whatever it may be, that I most dislike, and the wealthy man, whomsoever he may be, for whom I have the greatest contempt, I would fight for him, and you would if you were worth your salt. He should have justice. For every special interest is entitled to justice, but not one is entitled to a vote in Congress, to a voice on the bench, or to representation in any public office. The Constitution

guarantees protection to property, and we must make that promise good. But it does not give the right of suffrage to any corporation.

The true friend of property, the true conservative, is he who insists that property shall be the servant and not the master of the commonwealth; who insists that the creature of man's making shall be the servant and not the master of the man who made it. The citizens of the United States must effectively control the mighty commercial forces which they have themselves called into being. There can be no effective control of corporations while their political activity remains. To put an end to it will be neither a short nor an easy task, but it can be done.

We must have complete and effective publicity of corporate affairs, so that the people may know beyond peradventure whether the corporations obey the law and whether their management entitles them to the confidence of the public. It is necessary that laws should be passed to prohibit the use of corporate funds directly or indirectly for political purposes; it is still more necessary that such laws should be thoroughly enforced. Corporate expenditures for political purposes, and especially such expenditures by public service corporations, have supplied one of the principal sources of corruption in our political affairs.

Government Supervision of Trusts

It has become entirely clear that we must have government supervision of the capitalization, not only of public-service corporations, including, particularly, railways, but of all corporations doing an interstate business. I do not wish to see the nation forced into the ownership of the railways if it can possibly be avoided, and the only alternative is thoroughgoing and effective regulation, which shall be based on a full knowledge of all the facts, including a physical valuation of property. This physical valuation is not needed, or, at least, is very rarely needed, for fixing rates; but it is needed as the basis of honest capitalization.

We have come to recognize that franchises should never be granted except for a limited time, and never without proper provision for compensation to the public. It is my personal belief that the same kind and degree of control and supervision which should be exercised over public-service corporations should be extended also to combinations which control necessaries of life, such as meat, oil, and coal, or which deal in them on an important scale. I have no doubt that the ordinary man who has control of them is much like ourselves. I have no doubt he would like to do well, but I want to have enough supervision to help him realize that desire to do well.

I believe that the officers, and, especially, the directors, of corporations should be held personally responsible when any corporation breaks the law.

Combinations in industry are the result of an imperative economic law which cannot be repealed by political legislation. The effort at prohibiting all combination has substantially failed. The way out lies, not in attempting to prevent such combinations, but in completely controlling them in the interest of the public welfare. For that purpose the Federal Bureau of Corporations is an agency of first importance. Its powers, and, therefore, its efficiency, as well as that of the Interstate Commerce Commission, should be largely increased. We have a right to expect from the Bureau of Corporations and from the Interstate Commerce Commission a very high grade of public service. We should be as sure of the proper conduct of the interstate railways and the proper management of interstate business as we are now sure of the conduct and management of the national banks, and we should have as effective supervision in one case as in the other. . . .

"Combinations in industry . . . cannot be repealed by political legislation. . . . The way out lies . . . in completely controlling them in the interest of the public welfare."

The absence of effective State, and, especially, national, restraint upon unfair money-getting has tended to create a small class of enormously wealthy and economically powerful men, whose chief object is to hold and increase their power. The prime need is to change the conditions which enable these men to accumulate power which it is not for the general welfare that they should hold or exercise. We grudge no man a fortune which represents his own power and sagacity, when exercised with entire regard to the welfare of his fellows. Again, comrades over there, take the lesson from your own experience. Not only did you not grudge, but you gloried in the promotion of the great generals who gained their promotion by leading the army to victory. So it is with us. We grudge no man a fortune in civil life if it is honorably obtained and well used. It is not even enough that it should have been gained without doing damage to the community. We should permit it to be gained only so long as the gaining represents benefit to the community. This, I know, implies a policy of a far more active governmental interference with social and economic conditions in this country than we have yet had, but I think we have got to face the fact that such an increase in governmental control is now necessary.

No man should receive a dollar unless that dollar has been fairly earned. Every dollar received should represent a dollar's worth of service rendered—not gambling in stocks, but service rendered. The really big fortune, the swollen fortune, by the mere fact of its size acquires qualities which differentiate it in kind as well as in degree from what is possessed by men of relatively small means. Therefore, I believe in a graduated income tax on big fortunes, and in another tax which is far more easily collected and far more effective—a graduated inheritance tax on big fortunes, properly safeguarded against evasion and increasing rapidly in amount with the size of the estate. . . .

Conservation

Of conservation I shall speak more at length elsewhere. Conservation means development as much as it does protection. I recognize the right and duty of this generation to develop and use the natural resources of our land; but I do not recognize the right to waste them, or to rob, by wasteful use, the generations that come after us. I ask nothing of the nation except that it so behave as each farmer here behaves with reference to his own children. That farmer is a poor creature who skins the land and leaves it worthless to his children. The farmer is a good farmer who, having enabled the land to support himself and to provide for the education of his children, leaves it to them a little better than he found it himself. I believe the same thing of a nation.

Moreover, I believe that the natural resources must be used for the benefit of all our people, and not monopolized for the benefit of the few, and here again is another case in which I am accused of taking a revolutionary attitude. People forget now that one hundred years ago there were public men of good character who advocated the nation selling its public lands in great quantities, so that the nation could get the most money out of it, and giving it to the men who could cultivate it for their own uses. We took the proper democratic ground that the land should be granted in small sections to the men who were actually to till it and live on it. Now, with the water-power, with the forests, with the mines, we are brought face to face with the fact that there are many people who will go with us in conserving the resources only if they are to be allowed to exploit them for their benefit. That is one of the fundamental reasons why the special interests should be driven out of politics. Of all the questions which can come before this nation, short of the actual preservation of its existence in a great war, there is none which compares in importance with the great central task of leaving this land even a better land for our descendants than it is for us, and training them into a better race to inhabit the land and pass it on. Conservation is a great moral issue, for it involves the patriotic duty of insuring the safety and continuance of the nation. Let me add that the health and vitality of our people are at least as well worth conserving as their forests, waters, lands, and minerals, and in this great work the national government must bear a most important part. . . .

Nothing is more true than that excess of every kind is followed by reaction; a fact which should be pondered by reformer and reactionary alike. We are face to face with new conceptions of the relations of property to human welfare, chiefly because certain advocates of the rights of property as against the rights of men have been pushing their claims too far. The man who wrongly holds that every human right is secondary to his profit must now give way to the advocate of human welfare, who rightly maintains that every man holds his property subject to the general right of the community to regulate its use to whatever degree the public welfare may require it.

But I think we may go still further. The right to regulate the use of wealth in the public interest is universally admitted. Let us admit also the right to regulate the terms and conditions of labor, which is the chief element of wealth, directly in the interest of the common good. The fundamental thing to do for every man is to give him a chance to reach a place in which he will make the greatest possible contribution to the public welfare. Understand what I say there. Give him a chance, not push him up if he will not be pushed. Help any man who stumbles; if he lies down, it is a poor job to try to carry him; but if he is a worthy man, try your best to see that he gets a chance to show the worth that is in him. No man can be a good citizen unless he has a wage more than sufficient to cover the bare cost of living, and hours of labor short enough so that after his day's work is done he will have time and energy to bear his share in the management of the community, to help in carrying the general load. We keep countless men from being good citizens by the conditions of life with which we surround them. We need comprehensive workmen's compensation acts, both State and national laws to regulate child labor and work for women, and, especially we need in our common schools not merely education in book-learning, but also practical training for daily life and work. We need to enforce better sanitary conditions for our workers and to extend the use of safety appliances for our workers in industry and commerce, both within and between the States. Also, friends, in the interest of the working man himself we need to set our faces like flint against mob-violence just as against corporate greed; against violence and injustice and lawlessness by wage-workers just as much as against lawless cunning and greed and selfish arrogance of employers. If I could

ask but one thing of my fellow countrymen, my request would be that, whenever they go in for reform, they remember the two sides, and that they always exact justice from one side as much as from the other. I have small use for the public servant who can always see and denounce the corruption of the capitalist, but who cannot persuade himself, especially before election, to say a word about lawless mob-violence. And I have equally small use for the man, be he a judge on the bench, or editor of a great paper, or wealthy and influential private citizen, who can see clearly enough and denounce the lawlessness of mob-violence, but whose eyes are closed so that he is blind when the question is one of corruption in business on a gigantic scale. Also remember what I said about excess in reformer and reactionary alike. If the reactionary man, who thinks of nothing but the rights of property, could have his way, he would bring about a revolution; and one of my chief fears in connection with progress comes because I do not want to see our people, for lack of proper leadership, compelled to follow men whose intentions are excellent, but whose eyes are a little too wild to make it really safe to trust them. Here in Kansas there is one paper which habitually denounces me as the tool of Wall Street, and at the same time frantically repudiates the statement that I am a Socialist on the ground that that is an unwarranted slander of the Socialists.

National Efficiency

National efficiency has many factors. It is a necessary result of the principle of conservation widely applied. In the end it will determine our failure or success as a nation. National efficiency has to do, not only with natural resources and with men, but it is equally concerned with institutions. The State must be made efficient for the work which concerns only the people of the State; and the nation for that which concerns all the people. There must remain no neutral ground to serve as a refuge for lawbreakers, and especially for lawbreakers of great wealth, who can hire the vulpine legal cunning which will teach them how to avoid both jurisdictions. It is a misfortune when the national legislature fails to do its duty in providing a national remedy, so that the only national activity is the purely negative activity of the judiciary in forbidding the State to exercise power in the premises.

I do not ask for overcentralization; but I do ask that we work in a spirit of broad and far-reaching nationalism when we work for what concerns our people as a whole. We are all Americans. Our common interests are as broad as the continent. I speak to you here in Kansas exactly as I would speak in New York or Georgia, for the most vital problems are those which affect us all alike. The National Government belongs to the whole American people, and where the whole American people are interested, that interest can be guarded effectively only by the National Government. The betterment which we seek must be accomplished, I believe, mainly through the National Government.

The American people are right in demanding that New Nationalism, without which we cannot hope to deal with new problems. The New Nationalism puts the national need before sectional or personal advantage. It is impatient of the utter confusion that results from local legislatures attempting to treat national issues as local issues. It is still more impatient of the impotence which springs from overdivision of governmental powers, the impotence which makes it possible for local selfishness or for legal cunning, hired by wealthy special interests, to bring national activities to a deadlock. This New Nationalism regards the executive power as the steward of the public welfare. It demands of the judiciary that it shall be interested primarily in human welfare rather than in property, just as it demands that the representative body shall represent all the people rather than any one class or section of the people.

I believe in shaping the ends of government to protect property as well as human welfare. Normally, and in the long run, the ends are the same; but whenever the alternative must be faced, I am for men and not for property, as you were in the Civil War. I am far from underestimating the importance of dividends; but I rank dividends below human character. Again, I do not have any sympathy with the reformer who says he does not care for dividends. Of course, economic welfare is necessary, for a man must pull his own weight and be able to support his family. I know well that the reformers must not bring upon the people economic ruin, or the reforms themselves will go down in the ruin. But we must be ready to face temporary disaster, whether or not brought on by those who will war against us to the knife. Those who oppose all reform will do well to remember that ruin in its worst form is inevitable if our national life brings us nothing better than swollen fortunes for the few and the triumph in both politics and business of a sordid and selfish materialism.

If our political institutions were perfect, they would absolutely prevent the political domination of money in any part of our affairs. We need to make our political representatives more quickly and sensitively responsive to the people whose servants they are. More direct action by the people in their own affairs under proper safeguards is vitally necessary. The direct primary is a step in this direction, if it is associated with a corrupt-practices act effective to prevent the advantage of the man willing recklessly

and unscrupulously to spend money over his more honest competitor. It is particularly important that all moneys received or expended for campaign purposes should be publicly accounted for, not only after election, but before election as well. Political action must be made simpler, easier, and freer from confusion for every citizen. I believe that the prompt removal of unfaithful or incompetent public servants should be made easy and sure in whatever way experience shall show to be most expedient in any given class of cases.

One of the fundamental necessities in a representative government such as ours is to make certain that the men to whom the people delegate their power shall serve the people by whom they are elected, and not the special interests. I believe that every national officer, elected or appointed, should be forbidden to perform any service or receive any compensation, directly or indirectly, from interstate corporations; and a similar provision could not fail to be useful within the States.

The People's Welfare

The object of government is the welfare of the people. The material progress and prosperity of a nation are desirable chiefly so far as they lead to the moral and material welfare of all good citizens. Just in proportion as the average man and woman are honest, capable of sound judgment and high ideals, active in public affairs—but, first of all, sound in their home life, and the father and mother of healthy children whom they bring up well—just so far, and no farther, we may count our civilization a success. We must have—I believe we have already—a genuine and permanent moral awakening, without which no wisdom of legislation or administration really means anything; and, on the other hand, we must try to secure the social and economic legislation without which any improvement due to purely moral agitation is necessarily evanescent. Let me again illustrate by a reference to the Grand Army. You could not have won simply as a disorderly and disorganized mob. You needed generals; you needed careful administration of the most advanced type; and a good commissary—the cracker line. You well remember that success was necessary in many different lines in order to bring about general success. You had to have the administration at Washington good, just as you had to have the administration in the field; and you had to have the work of the generals good. You could not have triumphed without that administration and leadership; but it would all have been worthless if the average soldier had not had the right stuff in him. He had to have the right stuff in him, or you could not get it out of him. In the last analysis, therefore, vitally necessary though it was to have the right kind of organization and the right kind of generalship, it was even more vitally necessary that the average soldier should have the fighting edge, the right character. So it is in our civil life. No matter how honest and decent we are in our private lives, if we do not have the right kind of law and the right kind of administration of the law, we cannot go forward as a nation. That is imperative; but it must be an addition to, and not a substitution for, the qualities that make us good citizens. In the last analysis, the most important elements in any man's career must be the sum of those qualities which, in the aggregate, we speak of as character. If he had not got it, then no law that the wit of man can devise, no administration of the law by the boldest and strongest executive, will avail to help him. We must have the right kind of character—character that makes a man, first of all, a good man in the home, a good father, a good husband—that makes a man a good neighbor. You must have that, and, then, in addition, you must have the kind of law and the kind of administration of the law which will give to those qualities in the private citizen the best possible chance for development. The prime problem of our nation is to get the right type of good citizenship, and, to get it, we must have progress, and our public men must be genuinely progressive.

VIEWPOINT 17B

The Federal Government Should Oppose Trusts: Wilson's New Freedom (1913)

Woodrow Wilson (1856–1924)

Woodrow Wilson was elected president of the United States in 1912 and served two terms. The former academic, college president, and New Jersey governor benefited from a split in the Republican Party between conservatives, who supported incumbent president William Howard Taft, and progressives, who backed former president Theodore Roosevelt. Wilson in his campaign speeches differentiated himself from his opponents by emphasizing his opposition to business trusts and monopolies. He argued that the national government should concentrate on eliminating social and economic privilege and restoring free business competition. Wilson's proposals became known as the "New Freedom" in contrast to Roosevelt's "New Nationalism," which emphasized government regulation, not dismantling, of large corporations and trusts. Wilson's speeches were collected and edited into book form by William

Excerpted from Woodrow Wilson, *The New Freedom* (New York: Double-day, Page, and Co., 1913).

B. Hale, and published in 1913 under the title *The New Freedom*. The following viewpoint consists of excerpts from that volume.

How does Wilson differentiate between big businesses and trusts? What are the main areas of disagreement between Wilson and Theodore Roosevelt, author of the opposing viewpoint? Are the differences between Roosevelt and Wilson, as expressed in this pair of viewpoints, fundamental?

Since I entered politics, I have chiefly had men's views confided to me privately. Some of the biggest men in the United States, in the field of commerce and manufacture, are afraid of somebody, are afraid of something. They know that there is a power somewhere so organized, so subtle, so watchful, so interlocked, so complete, so pervasive, that they had better not speak above their breath when they speak in condemnation of it.

They know that America is not a place of which it can be said, as it used to be, that a man may choose his own calling and pursue it just as far as his abilities enable him to pursue it; because to-day, if he enters certain fields, there are organizations which will use means against him that will prevent his building up a business which they do not want to have built up; organizations that will see to it that the ground is cut from under him and the markets shut against him. For if he begins to sell to certain retail dealers, to any retail dealers, the monopoly will refuse to sell to those dealers, and those dealers, afraid, will not buy the new man's wares.

No Longer a Land of Opportunity

And this is the country which has lifted to the admiration of the world its ideals of absolutely free opportunity, where no man is supposed to be under any limitation except the limitations of his character and of his mind; where there is supposed to be no distinction of class, no distinction of blood, no distinction of social status, but where men win or lose on their merits.

I lay it very close to my own conscience as a public man whether we can any longer stand at our doors and welcome all newcomers upon those terms. American industry is not free, as once it was free; American enterprise is not free; the man with only a little capital is finding it harder to get into the field, more and more impossible to compete with the big fellow. Why? Because the laws of this country do not prevent the strong from crushing the weak. That is the reason, and because the strong have crushed the weak the strong dominate the industry and the economic life of this country. No man can deny that the lines of endeavor have more and more narrowed and stiffened; no man who knows anything about the development of industry in this country can have failed to observe that the larger kinds of credit are more and more difficult to obtain, unless you obtain them upon the terms of uniting your efforts with those who already control the industries of the country; and nobody can fail to observe that any man who tries to set himself up in competition with any process of manufacture which has been taken under the control of large combinations of capital will presently find himself either squeezed out or obliged to sell and allow himself to be absorbed.

There is a great deal that needs reconstruction in the United States. I should like to take a census of the business men,—I mean the rank and file of the business men,—as to whether they think that business conditions in this country, or rather whether the organization of business in this country, is satisfactory or not. I know what they would say if they dared. If they could vote secretly they would vote overwhelmingly that the present organization of business was meant for the big fellows and was not meant for the little fellows; that it was meant for those who are at the top and was meant to exclude those who are at the bottom; that it was meant to shut out beginners, to prevent new entries in the race, to prevent the building up of competitive enterprises that would interfere with the monopolies which the great trusts have built up.

What this country needs above everything else is a body of laws which will look after the men who are on the make rather than the men who are already made. Because the men who are already made are not going to live indefinitely, and they are not always kind enough to leave sons as able and as honest as they are. . . .

Are Trusts Inevitable?

Gentlemen say, they have been saying for a long time, and, therefore, I assume that they believe, that trusts are inevitable. They don't say that big business is inevitable. They don't say merely that the elaboration of business upon a great co-operative scale is characteristic of our time and has come about by the natural operation of modern civilization. We would admit that. But they say that the particular kind of combinations that are now controlling our economic development came into existence naturally and were inevitable; and that, therefore, we have to accept them as unavoidable and administer our development through them. They take the analogy of the railways. The railways were clearly inevitable if we were to have transportation, but railways after they are once built stay put. You can't transfer a railroad at convenience; and you can't shut up one part of it and work another part. It is in the nature of what

economists, those tedious persons, call natural monopolies; simply because the whole circumstances of their use are so stiff that you can't alter them. Such are the analogies which these gentlemen choose when they discuss the modern trust.

I admit the popularity of the theory that the trusts have come about through the natural development of business conditions in the United States, and that it is a mistake to try to oppose the processes by which they have been built up, because those processes belong to the very nature of business in our time, and that therefore the only thing we can do, and the only thing we ought to attempt to do, is to accept them as inevitable arrangements and make the best out of it that we can by regulation.

I answer, nevertheless, that this attitude rests upon a confusion of thought. Big business is no doubt to a large extent necessary and natural. The development of business upon a great scale, upon a great scale of cooperation, is inevitable, and, let me add, is probably desirable. But that is a very different matter from the development of trusts, because the trusts have not grown. They have been artificially created; they have been put together, not by natural processes, but by the will, the deliberate planning will, of men who were more powerful than their neighbors in the business world, and who wished to make their power secure against competition.

The trusts do not belong to the period of infant industries. They are not the products of the time, that old laborious time, when the great continent we live on was undeveloped, the young nation struggling to find itself and get upon its feet amidst older and more experienced competitors. They belong to a very recent and very sophisticated age, when men knew what they wanted and knew how to get it by the favor of the government.

How Trusts Are Made

Did you ever look into the way a trust was made? It is very natural, in one sense, in the same sense in which human greed is natural. If I haven't efficiency enough to beat my rivals, then the thing I am inclined to do is to get together with my rivals and say: "Don't let's cut each other's throats; let's combine and determine prices for ourselves; determine the output, and thereby determine the prices: and dominate and control the market." That is very natural. That has been done ever since freebooting was established. That has been done ever since power was used to establish control. The reason that the masters of combination have sought to shut out competition is that the basis of control under competition is brains and efficiency. I admit that any large corporation built up by the legitimate processes of business, by economy, by efficiency, is natural; and I am not afraid of it, no matter how big it grows. It can stay big only by doing its work more thoroughly than anybody else. And there is a point of bigness,—as every business man in this country knows, though some of them will not admit it,—where you pass the limit of efficiency and get into the region of clumsiness and unwieldiness. You can make your combine so extensive that you can't digest it into a single system; you can get so many parts that you can't assemble them as you would an effective piece of machinery. The point of efficiency is overstepped in the natural process of development oftentimes, and it has been overstepped many times in the artificial and deliberate formation of trusts.

A trust is formed in this way: a few gentlemen "promote" it—that is to say, they get it up, being given enormous fees for their kindness, which fees are loaded on to the undertaking in the form of securities of one kind or another. The argument of the promoters is, not that every one who comes into the combination can carry on his business more efficiently than he did before; the argument is: we will assign to you as your share in the pool twice, three times, four times, or five times what you could have sold your business for to an individual competitor who would have to run it on an economic and competitive basis. We can afford to buy it at such a figure because we are shutting out competition. We can afford to make the stock of the combination half a dozen times what it naturally would be and pay dividends on it, because there will be nobody to dispute the prices we shall fix.

Talk of that as sound business? Talk of that as inevitable? It is based upon nothing except power. It is not based upon efficiency. It is no wonder that the big trusts are not prospering in proportion to such competitors as they still have in such parts of their business as competitors have access to; they are prospering freely only in those fields to which competition has no access. . . .

Unfair Competition

I take my stand absolutely, where every progressive ought to take his stand, on the proposition that private monopoly is indefensible and intolerable. And there I will fight my battle. And I know how to fight it. Everybody who has even read the newspapers knows the means by which these men built up their power and created these monopolies. Any decently equipped lawyer can suggest to you statutes by which the whole business can be stopped. What these gentlemen do not want is this: they do not want to be compelled to meet all comers on equal terms. I am perfectly willing that they should beat any competitor by fair means; but I know the foul means they have adopted, and I know that they can be stopped

by law. If they think that coming into the market upon the basis of mere efficiency, upon the mere basis of knowing how to manufacture goods better than anybody else and to sell them cheaper than anybody else, they can carry the immense amount of water that they have put into their enterprises in order to buy up rivals, then they are perfectly welcome to try it. But there must be no squeezing out of the beginner, no crippling his credit; no discrimination against retailers who buy from a rival; no threats against concerns who sell supplies to a rival; no holding back of raw material from him; no secret arrangements against him. All the fair competition you choose, but no unfair competition of any kind. And then when unfair competition is eliminated, let us see these gentlemen carry their tanks of water on their backs. All that I ask and all I shall fight for is that they shall come into the field against merit and brains everywhere. If they can beat other American brains, then they have got the best brains.

The People Have Become Outsiders

But if you want to know how far brains go, as things now are, suppose you try to match your better wares against these gentlemen, and see them undersell you before your market is any bigger than the locality and make it absolutely impossible for you to get a fast foothold. If you want to know how brains count, originate some invention which will improve the kind of machinery they are using, and then see if you can borrow enough money to manufacture it. You may be offered something for your patent by the corporation,—which will perhaps lock it up in a safe and go on using the old machinery; but you will not be allowed to manufacture. I know men who have tried it, and they could not get the money, because the great money lenders of this country are in the arrangement with the great manufacturers of this country, and they do not propose to see their control of the market interfered with by outsiders. And who are outsiders? Why, all the rest of the people of the United States are outsiders.

They are rapidly making us outsiders with respect even of the things that come from the bosom of the earth, and which belong to us in a peculiar sense. Certain monopolies in this country have gained almost complete control of the raw material, chiefly in the mines, out of which the great body of manufactures are carried on, and they now discriminate, when they will, in the sale of that raw material between those who are rivals of the monopoly and those who submit to the monopoly. We must soon come to the point where we shall say to the men who own these essentials of industry that they have got to part with these essentials by sale to all citizens of the United States with the same readiness and upon the same terms. Or else we shall tie up the resources of this country under private control in such fashion as will make our independent development absolutely impossible. . . .

I have been told by a great many men that the idea I have, that by restoring competition you can restore industrial freedom, is based upon a failure to observe the actual happenings of the last decades in this country; because, they say, it is just free competition that has made it possible for the big to crush the little. I reply, it is not free competition that has done that; it is illicit competition. It is competition of the kind that the law ought to stop, and can stop,—this crushing of the little man. . . .

Monopolies and Roosevelt

The doctrine that monopoly is inevitable and that the only course open to the people of the United States is to submit to and regulate it found a champion during the campaign of 1912 in the new party, or branch of the Republican party, founded under the leadership of Mr. [Theodore] Roosevelt. . . .

You know that Mr. Roosevelt long ago classified trusts for us as good and bad, and he said that he was afraid only of the bad ones. Now he does not desire that there should be any more bad ones, but proposes that they should all be made good by discipline, directly applied by a commission of executive appointment. All he explicitly complains of is lack of publicity and lack of fairness; not the exercise of power, for throughout that plank [of the new party platform] the power of the great corporations is accepted as the inevitable consequence of the modern organization of industry. All that it is proposed to do is to take them under control and regulation. The national administration having for sixteen years been virtually under the regulation of the trusts, it would be merely a family matter were the parts reversed and were the other members of the family to exercise the regulation. And the trusts, apparently, which might, in such circumstances, comfortably continue to administer our affairs under the mollifying influences of the federal government, would then, if you please, be the instrumentalities by which all the humanistic, benevolent program of the rest of that interesting platform would be carried out!

The third [Roosevelt's] party says that the present system of our industry and trade has come to stay. Mind you, these artificially built up things, these things that can't maintain themselves in the market without monopoly, have come to stay, and the only thing that the government can do, the only thing that the third party proposes should be done, is to set up a commission to regulate them. It accepts them. It says: "We will not undertake, it were futile to undertake, to prevent monopoly, but we will go into an arrangement by which we will make these monopolies kind to you. We will guarantee that they shall be pitiful. We will guarantee that they shall pay the right wages. We will guarantee that they shall do everything kind and public-spirited, which they have never heretofore shown the least inclination to do."

Don't you realize that that is a blind alley? You can't find your way to liberty that way. You can't find your way to social reform through the forces that have made social reform necessary. . . .

The Crucial Decision

Shall we try to get the grip of monopoly away from our lives, or shall we not? Shall we withhold our hand and say monopoly is inevitable, that all that we can do is to regulate it? Shall we say that all that we can do is to put government in competition with monopoly and try its strength against it? Shall we admit that the creature of our own hands is stronger than we are? We have been dreading all along the time when the combined power of high finance would be greater than the power of the government. Have we come to a time when the President of the United States or any man who wishes to be the President must doff his cap in the presence of this high finance, and say, "You are our inevitable master, but we will see how we can make the best of it"?

We are at the parting of the ways. We have, not one or two or three, but many, established and formidable monopolies in the United States. We have, not one or two, but many, fields of endeavor into which it is difficult, if not impossible, for the independent man to enter. We have restricted credit, we have restricted opportunity, we have controlled development, and we have come to be one of the worst ruled, one of the most completely controlled and dominated, governments in the civilized world— no longer a government by free opinion, no longer a government by conviction and the vote of the majority, but a government by the opinion and the duress of small groups of dominant men. . . .

———— • ————

"Our purpose is the restoration of freedom. We purpose to prevent private monopoly by law."

———— • ————

When you have thought the whole thing out, therefore, you will find that the program of the new party legalizes monopolies and systematically subordinates workingmen to them and to plans made by the government both with regard to employment and with regard to wages. Take the thing as a whole, and it looks strangely like economic mastery over the very lives and fortunes of those who do the daily work of the nation; and all this under the overwhelming power and sovereignty of the national government. What most of us are fighting for is to break up this very partnership between big business and the government. We call upon all intelligent men to bear witness that if this plan were consummated, the great employers and capitalists of the country would be under a more overpowering temptation than ever to take control of the government and keep it subservient to their purpose.

What a prize it would be to capture! How unassailable would be the majesty and the tyranny of monopoly if it could thus get sanction of law and the authority of government! By what means, except open revolt, could we ever break the crust of our life again and become free men, breathing an air of our own, living lives that we wrought out for ourselves?

You cannot use monopoly in order to serve a free people. You cannot use great combinations of capital to be pitiful and righteous when the consciences of great bodies of men are enlisted, not in the promotion of special privilege, but in the realization of human rights. When I read those beautiful portions of the program of the third party devoted to the uplift of mankind and see noble men and women attaching themselves to that party in the hope that regulated monopoly may realize these dreams of humanity, I wonder whether they have really studied the instruments through which they are going to do these things. The man who is leading the third party has not changed his point of view since he was President of the United States. . . .

Monopolies Cannot Change

I do not trust any promises of a change of temper on the part of monopoly. Monopoly never was conceived in the temper of tolerance Monopoly never was conceived with the purpose of general development. It was conceived with the purpose of special advantage. Has monopoly been very benevolent to its employees? Have the trusts had a soft heart for the working people of America? Have you found trusts that cared whether women were sapped of their vitality or not? Have you found trusts who are very scrupulous about using children in their tender years? Have you found trusts that were keen to protect the lungs and the health and the freedom of their employees? Have you found trusts that thought as much of their men as they did of their machinery? Then who is going to convert these men into the chief instruments of justice and benevolence? . . .

I do not want to see the special interests of the United States take care of the workingmen, women, and children. I want to see justice, righteousness, fairness and humanity displayed in all the laws of the United States, and I do not want any power to intervene between the people and their government. Justice is what we want, not patronage and condescension and pitiful helpfulness. The trusts are our masters now, but I for one do not care to live in a country called free even under kind masters. I prefer to live under no masters at all. . . .

The reason that America was set up was that she might be different from all the nations of the world in this: that the strong could not put the weak to the wall, that the strong could not prevent the weak from entering the race. America stands for opportunity. America stands for a free field and no favor. America stands for a government responsive to the interests of all. And until America recovers those ideals in practice, she will not have the right to hold her head high again amidst the nations as she used to hold it.

Restoring Freedom

It is like coming out of a stifling cellar into the open where we can breathe again and see the free spaces of the heavens to turn away from such a doleful program of submission and dependence toward the other plan, the confident purpose for which the people have given their mandate. Our purpose is the restoration of freedom. We purpose to prevent private monopoly by law, to see to it that the methods by which monopolies have been built up are legally made impossible. We design that the limitations on private enterprise shall be removed, so that the next generation of youngsters, as they come along, will not have to become protégés of benevolent trusts, but will be free to go about making their own lives what they will; so that we shall taste again the full cup, not of charity, but of liberty,—the only wine that ever refreshed and renewed the spirit of a people.

For Further Reading

John W. Chambers II, *The Tyranny of Change: America in the Progressive Era*. New York: St. Martin's Press, 1980.

John Milton Cooper, *The Warrior and the Priest: Woodrow Wilson and Theodore Roosevelt*. Cambridge, MA: Belknap Press, 1983.

Herbert Croly, *The Promise of American Life*. 1909. Reprint, New Brunswick: Transaction Publishers, 1993.

Arthur Alphonse Ekirch, *Progressivism in America: A Study of the Era from Theodore Roosevelt to Woodrow Wilson*. New York: New Viewpoints, 1974.

John A. Gable, *The Bull Moose Years: Theodore Roosevelt and the Progressive Party*. Port Washington, NY: Kennikat Press, 1978.

Arthur Link, *Woodrow Wilson and the Progressive Era*. New York: Harper & Row, 1963.

Edwin Charles Rozwenc, *Roosevelt, Wilson and the Trusts*. Boston: D.C. Heath, 1953.

World War I and the League of Nations

VIEWPOINT 18A

America Should Enter World War I (1917)

Woodrow Wilson (1856–1924)

When the countries of Europe plunged into war in 1914, Woodrow Wilson asked all Americans to "act and speak in the true spirit of neutrality." Wilson managed to maintain U.S. neutrality for the next thirty months and, running on the slogan "He kept us out of war," won reelection as president in 1916. On April 2, 1917, however, he appeared before a joint session of Congress to ask for a declaration of war against Germany.

Wilson's address, reprinted in large part below, tried to answer two major questions: (1) Why had America changed its stance from neutrality to hostility toward Germany? and (2) What did America hope to achieve by entering the war? Wilson emphasizes the problems caused by German submarine warfare in answering the first question. Through diplomatic pressure Wilson had managed to get Germany to restrict its use of submarines against American ships and those of other neutral nations. In January 1917, however, Germany resumed a policy of unrestricted submarine attacks, and American ships were being sunk without warning. In answering the second question Wilson established lofty and idealistic goals beyond the mere defeat of Germany: America was fighting to "end all wars" and make the world "safe for democracy."

Why is neutrality no longer feasible, according to Wilson? What does Wilson consider to be America's wartime objectives? What does he explicitly say are *not* America's objectives?

I have called the Congress into extraordinary session because there are serious, very serious, choices of policy to be made, and made immediately, which it was neither right nor constitutionally permissible that I should assume the responsibility of making.

On the 3rd of February last, I officially laid before you the extraordinary announcement of the Imperial German government that on and after the 1st day of February it was its purpose to put aside all restraints of law or of humanity and use its sub-

Excerpted from Woodrow Wilson's April 2, 1917, address to Congress, 65th Cong., 1st sess., Sen. Doc. 5.

marines to sink every vessel that sought to approach either the ports of Great Britain and Ireland or the western coasts of Europe or any of the ports controlled by the enemies of Germany within the Mediterranean.

That had seemed to be the object of the German submarine warfare earlier in the war, but since April of last year the Imperial government had somewhat restrained the commanders of its undersea craft in conformity with its promise then given to us that passenger boats should not be sunk and that due warning would be given to all other vessels which its submarines might seek to destroy, when no resistance was offered or escape attempted, and care taken that their crews were given at least a fair chance to save their lives in their open boats. The precautions taken were meager and haphazard enough, as was proved in distressing instance after instance in the progress of the cruel and unmanly business, but a certain degree of restraint was observed.

The new policy has swept every restriction aside. Vessels of every kind, whatever their flag, their character, their cargo, their destination, their errand, have been ruthlessly sent to the bottom without warning and without thought of help or mercy for those on board, the vessels of friendly neutrals along with those of belligerents. Even hospital ships and ships carrying relief to the sorely bereaved and stricken people of Belgium, though the latter were provided with safe conduct through the proscribed areas by the German government itself and were distinguished by unmistakable marks of identity, have been sunk with the same reckless lack of compassion or of principle.

I was for a little while unable to believe that such things would in fact be done by any government that had hitherto subscribed to the humane practices of civilized nations. International law had its origin in the attempt to set up some law which would be respected and observed upon the seas, where no nation had right of dominion and where lay the free highways of the world. By painful stage after stage has that law been built up, with meager enough results, . . . but always with a clear view, at least, of what the heart and conscience of mankind demanded.

This minimum of right the German government has swept aside under the plea of retaliation and necessity and because it had no weapons which it could use at sea except these which it is impossible to employ as it is employing them without throwing to the winds all scruples of humanity or of respect for the understandings that were supposed to underlie the intercourse of the world. I am not now thinking of the loss of property involved, immense and serious as that is, but only of the wanton and wholesale destruction of the lives of noncombatants, men, women, and children, engaged in pursuits which have always, even in the darkest periods of modern history, been deemed innocent and legitimate. Property can be paid for; the lives of peaceful and innocent people cannot be.

Not Just America's War

The present German submarine warfare against commerce is a warfare against mankind. It is a war against all nations. American ships have been sunk, American lives taken in ways which it has stirred us very deeply to learn of; but the ships and people of other neutral and friendly nations have been sunk and overwhelmed in the waters in the same way. There has been no discrimination. The challenge is to all mankind.

Each nation must decide for itself how it will meet it. The choice we make for ourselves must be made with a moderation of counsel and a temperateness of judgment befitting our character and our motives as a nation. We must put excited feeling away. Our motive will not be revenge or the victorious assertion of the physical might of the nation, but only the vindication of right, of human right, of which we are only a single champion.

When I addressed the Congress on the 26th of February last, I thought that it would suffice to assert our neutral rights with arms, our right to use the seas against unlawful interference, our right to keep our people safe against unlawful violence. But armed neutrality, it now appears, is impracticable. Because submarines are in effect outlaws when used as the German submarines have been used against merchant shipping, it is impossible to defend ships against their attacks as the law of nations has assumed that merchantmen would defend themselves against privateers or cruisers, visible craft giving chase upon the open sea. . . .

There is one choice we cannot make, we are incapable of making: we will not choose the path of submission and suffer the most sacred rights of our nation and our people to be ignored or violated. The wrongs against which we now array ourselves are no common wrongs; they cut to the very roots of human life.

With a profound sense of the solemn and even tragical character of the step I am taking and of the grave responsibilities which it involves, but in unhesitating obedience to what I deem my constitutional duty, I advise that the Congress declare the recent course of the Imperial German government to be in fact nothing less than war against the government and people of the United States; that it formally accept the status of belligerent which has thus been thrust upon it; and that it take immediate steps, not only to put the country in a more thorough state of defense but also to exert all its power and employ all its resources to bring the government of the German Empire to terms and end the war.

What this will involve is clear. It will involve the utmost practicable cooperation in counsel and action with the governments now at war with Germany and, as incident to that, the extension to those governments of the most liberal financial credits, in order that our resources may so far as possible be added to theirs. It will involve the organization and mobilization of all the material resources of the country to supply the materials of war and serve the incidental needs of the nation in the most abundant and yet the most economical and efficient way possible. It will involve the immediate full equipment of the Navy in all respects but particularly in supplying it with the best means of dealing with the enemy's submarines. It will involve the immediate addition to the armed forces of the United States already provided for by law in case of war at least 500,000 men, who should, in my opinion, be chosen upon the principle of universal liability to service, and also the authorization of subsequent additional increments of equal force so soon as they may be needed and can be handled in training.

It will involve also, of course, the granting of adequate credits to the government, sustained, I hope, so far as they can equitably be sustained by the present generation, by well-conceived taxation. . . .

Our object now, as then, is to vindicate the principles of peace and justice in the life of the world as against selfish and autocratic power and to set up among the really free and self-governed peoples of the world such a concert of purpose and of action as will henceforth ensure the observance of those principles. Neutrality is no longer feasible or desirable where the peace of the world is involved and the freedom of its peoples, and the menace to that peace and freedom lies in the existence of autocratic governments backed by organized force which is controlled wholly by their will, not by the will of their people. We have seen the last of neutrality in such circumstances. We are at the beginning of an age in which it will be insisted that the same standards of conduct and of responsibility for wrong done shall be observed among nations and their governments that are observed among the individual citizens of civilized states.

We have no quarrel with the German people. We have no feeling toward them but one of sympathy and friendship. It was not upon their impulse that their government acted in entering this war. It was not with their previous knowledge or approval. It was a war determined upon as wars used to be determined upon in the old, unhappy days when peoples were nowhere consulted by their rulers and wars were provoked and waged in the interest of dynasties or of little groups of ambitious men who were accustomed to use their fellowmen as pawns and tools.

Self-governed nations do not fill their neighbor states with spies or set the course of intrigue to bring about some critical posture of affairs which will give them an opportunity to strike and make conquest. Such designs can be successfully worked out only under cover and where no one has the right to ask questions. Cunningly contrived plans of deception or aggression, carried, it may be, from generation to generation, can be worked out and kept from the light only within the privacy of courts or behind the carefully guarded confidences of a narrow and privileged class. They are happily impossible where public opinion commands and insists upon full information concerning all the nation's affairs.

A steadfast concert for peace can never be maintained except by a partnership of democratic nations. No autocratic government could be trusted to keep faith within it or observe its covenants. It must be a league of honor, a partnership of opinion. Intrigue would eat its vitals away; the plottings of inner circles who could plan what they would and render account to no one would be a corruption seated at its very heart. Only free peoples can hold their purpose and their honor steady to a common end and prefer the interests of mankind to any narrow interest of their own.

Does not every American feel that assurance has been added to our hope for the future peace of the world by the wonderful and heartening things that have been happening within the last few weeks in Russia? Russia was known by those who knew it best to have been always in fact democratic at heart, in all the vital habits of her thought, in all the intimate relationships of her people that spoke their natural instinct, their habitual attitude toward life. The autocracy that crowned the summit of her political structure, long as it had stood and terrible as was the reality of its power, was not in fact Russian in origin, character, or purpose; and now it has been shaken off and the great, generous Russian people have been added in all their naive majesty and might to the forces that are fighting for freedom in the world, for justice, and for peace. Here is a fit partner for a League of Honor.

One of the things that has served to convince us that the Prussian autocracy was not and could never be our friend is that from the very outset of the present war it has filled our unsuspecting communities and even our offices of government with spies and set criminal intrigues everywhere afoot against our national unity of counsel, our peace within and without, our industries and our commerce. Indeed, it is now evident that its spies were here even before the war began; and it is unhappily not a matter of conjecture but a fact proved in our courts of justice that the intrigues which

have more than once come perilously near to disturbing the peace and dislocating the industries of the country have been carried on at the instigation, with the support, and even under the personal direction of official agents of the Imperial government accredited to the government of the United States.

Even in checking these things and trying to extirpate them, we have sought to put the most generous interpretation possible upon them because we knew that their source lay, not in any hostile feeling or purpose of the German people toward us (who were no doubt as ignorant of them as we ourselves were) but only in the selfish designs of a government that did what it pleased and told its people nothing. But they have played their part in serving to convince us at last that that government entertains no real friendship for us and means to act against our peace and security at its convenience. That it means to stir up enemies against us at our very doors the intercepted note to the German minister at Mexico City is eloquent evidence.

———— • ————

"The day has come when America is privileged to spend her blood and her might for the principles that gave her birth and happiness."

———— • ————

We are accepting this challenge of hostile purpose because we know that in such a government, following such methods, we can never have a friend; and that in the presence of its organized power, always lying in wait to accomplish we know not what purpose, there can be no assured security for the democratic governments of the world. We are now about to accept gage of battle with this natural foe to liberty and shall, if necessary, spend the whole force of the nation to check and nullify its pretensions and its power. We are glad, now that we see the facts with no veil of false pretense about them, to fight thus for the ultimate peace of the world and for the liberation of its peoples, the German peoples included: for the rights of nations great and small and the privilege of men everywhere to choose their way of life and of obedience.

The world must be made safe for democracy. Its peace must be planted upon the tested foundations of political liberty. We have no selfish ends to serve. We desire no conquest, no dominion. We seek no indemnities for ourselves, no material compensation for the sacrifices we shall freely make. We are but one of the champions of the rights of mankind. We shall be satisfied when those rights have been made as secure as the faith and the freedom of nations can make them.

Just because we fight without rancor and without selfish object, seeking nothing for ourselves but what we shall wish to share with all free peoples, we shall, I feel confident, conduct our operations as belligerents without passion and ourselves observe with proud punctilio the principles of right and of fair play we profess to be fighting for. . . .

It will be all the easier for us to conduct ourselves as belligerents in a high spirit of right and fairness because we act without animus, not in enmity toward a people or with the desire to bring any injury or disadvantage upon them, but only in armed opposition to an irresponsible government which has thrown aside all considerations of humanity and of right and is running amuck. We are, let me say again, the sincere friends of the German people, and shall desire nothing so much as the early reestablishment of intimate relations of mutual advantage between us—however hard it may be for them, for the time being, to believe that this is spoken from our hearts.

We have borne with their present government through all these bitter months because of that friendship—exercising a patience and forbearance which would otherwise have been impossible. We shall, happily, still have an opportunity to prove that friendship in our daily attitude and actions toward the millions of men and women of German birth and native sympathy who live among us and share our life, and we shall be proud to prove it toward all who are in fact loyal to their neighbors and to the government in the hour of test. They are, most of them, as true and loyal Americans as if they had never known any other fealty or allegiance. They will be prompt to stand with us in rebuking and restraining the few who may be of a different mind and purpose. If there should be disloyalty, it will be dealt with with a firm hand of stern repression; but, if it lifts its head at all, it will lift it only here and there and without countenance except from a lawless and malignant few.

It is a distressing and oppressive duty, gentlemen of the Congress, which I have performed in thus addressing you. There are, it may be, many months of fiery trial and sacrifice ahead of us. It is a fearful thing to lead this great peaceful people into war, into the most terrible and disastrous of all wars, civilization itself seeming to be in the balance. But the right is more precious than peace, and we shall fight for the things which we have always carried nearest our hearts—for democracy, for the right of those who submit to authority to have a voice in their own governments, for the rights and liberties of small nations, for a universal dominion of right by such a concert of free peoples as shall bring peace and safety to all nations and make the world itself at last free.

To such a task we can dedicate our lives and our fortunes, everything that we are and everything that we have, with the pride of those who know that the day has come when America is privileged to spend her blood and her might for the principles that gave her birth and happiness and the peace which she has treasured. God helping her, she can do no other.

VIEWPOINT 18B

America Should Not Enter World War I (1917)

George W. Norris (1861–1944)

President Woodrow Wilson's call in 1917 for a declaration of war against Germany was opposed in Congress by fifty representatives and six senators. One of the six senators was George W. Norris of Nebraska, a Progressive Republican who at that time had served for thirteen years in the House of Representatives and in the Senate. In a speech before the Senate on April 4, 1917, Norris questions America's prior commitment to neutrality (arguing that U.S. policy actually was tilted toward Germany's enemy Great Britain), and contends that the main supporters and beneficiaries of war would be the Wall Street financiers, industrialists, and wealthy Americans in general.

Why is Great Britain as blameworthy as Germany for violating American neutral rights, according to Norris? How does Norris describe the state of public opinion concerning war and peace? What are America's objectives in entering the war, according to Norris? How do they differ from those offered by Woodrow Wilson in the opposing viewpoint?

T he resolution now before the Senate is a declaration of war. Before taking this momentous step, and while standing on the brink of this terrible vortex, we ought to pause and calmly and judiciously consider the terrible consequences of the step we are about to take. We ought to consider likewise the route we have recently traveled and ascertain whether we have reached our present position in a way that is compatible with the neutral position which we claimed to occupy at the beginning and through the various stages of this unholy and unrighteous war.

No close student of recent history will deny that both Great Britain and Germany have, on numerous occasions since the beginning of the war, flagrantly violated in the most serious manner the rights of

From George W. Norris, *Congressional Record*, 65th Cong., 1st sess. (April 4, 1917), pp. 212–14.

neutral vessels and neutral nations under existing international law as recognized up to the beginning of this war by the civilized world.

The reason given by the President in asking Congress to declare war against Germany is that the German Government has declared certain war zones, within which, by the use of submarines, she sinks, without notice, American ships and destroys American lives.

Let us trace briefly the origin and history of these so-called war zones. The first war zone was declared by Great Britain. She gave us and the world notice of it on the 4th day of November, 1914. The zone became effective November 5, 1914, the next day after the notice was given. This zone so declared by Great Britain covered the whole of the North Sea. The order establishing it sought to close the north of Scotland route around the British Isles to Denmark, Holland, Norway, Sweden, and the Baltic Sea. The decree of establishment drew an arbitrary line from the Hebrides Islands along the Scottish coast to Iceland, and warned neutral shipping that it would cross those lines at its peril, and ordered that ships might go to Holland and other neutral nations by taking the English Channel route through the Strait of Dover.

The first German war zone was declared on the 4th day of February, 1915, just three months after the British war zone was declared. Germany gave 15 days' notice of the establishment of her zone, which became effective on the 18th day of February, 1915. The German war zone covered the English Channel and the high sea waters around the British Isles. It sought to close the English Channel route around the British Isles to Holland, Norway, Sweden, Denmark, and the Baltic Sea. The German war zone decreed that neutral vessels would be exposed to danger in the English Channel route, but that the route around the north of Scotland and in the eastern part of the North Sea, in a strip 30 miles wide along the Dutch coast, would be free from danger.

It will thus be seen that the British Government declared the north of Scotland route into the Baltic Sea as dangerous and the English Channel route into the Baltic Sea as safe.

The German Government in its order did exactly the reverse. It declared the north of Scotland route into the Baltic Sea as safe and the English Channel route into the Baltic Sea as dangerous. . . .

Thus we have the two declarations of the two Governments, each declaring a military zone and warning neutral shipping from going into the prohibited area. England sought to make her order effective by the use of submerged mines. Germany sought to make her order effective by the use of submarines. Both of these orders were illegal and contrary to all international law as well as the principles of human-

ity. Under international law no belligerent Government has the right to place submerged mines in the high seas. Neither has it any right to take human life without notice by the use of submarines. If there is any difference on the ground of humanity between these two instrumentalities, it is certainly in favor of the submarines. The submarine can exercise some degree of discretion and judgment. The submerged mine always destroys without notice, friend and foe alike, guilty and innocent the same. In carrying out these two policies, both Great Britain and Germany have sunk American ships and destroyed American lives without provocation and without notice. There have been more ships sunk and more American lives lost from the action of submarines than from English mines in the North Sea: for the simple reason that we finally acquiesced in the British war zone and kept our ships out of it, while in the German war zone we have refused to recognize its legality and have not kept either our ships or our citizens out of its area. If American ships had gone into the British war zone in defiance of Great Britain's order, as they have gone into the German war zone in defiance of the German Government's order, there would have been many more American lives lost and many more American ships sunk by the instrumentality of the mines than the instrumentality of the submarines.

A Neutral America?

We have in the main complied with the demands made by Great Britain. Our ships have followed the instructions of the British Government in going not only to England but to the neutral nations of the world, and in thus complying with the British order American ships going to Holland, Denmark, Norway, and Sweden have been taken by British officials into British ports, and their cargoes inspected and examined. All the mails we have carried even to neutral countries have been opened and censored, and oftentimes the entire cargo confiscated by the Government. Nothing has been permitted to pass to even the most neutral nations except after examination and with the permission of the officials of the British Government.

I have outlined the beginning of the controversy. I have given in substance the orders of both of these great Governments that constituted the beginning of our controversy with each. . . .

The only difference is that in the case of Germany we have persisted in our protest, while in the case of England we have submitted. What was our duty as a Government and what were our rights when we were confronted with these extraordinary orders declaring these military zones? First, we could have defied both of them and could have gone to war against both of these nations for this violation of international law and interference with our neutral rights. Second, we had the technical right to defy one and to acquiesce in the other. Third, we could, while denouncing them both as illegal, have acquiesced in them both and thus remained neutral with both sides, although not agreeing with either as to the righteousness of their respective orders. We could have said to American shipowners that, while these orders are both contrary to international law and are both unjust, we do not believe that the provocation is sufficient to cause us to go to war for the defense of our rights as a neutral nation, and, therefore, American ships and American citizens will go into these zones at their own peril and risk. Fourth, we might have declared an embargo against the shipping from American ports of any merchandise to either one of these Governments that persisted in maintaining its military zone. We might have refused to permit the sailing of any ship from any American port to either of these military zones. In my judgment, if we had pursued this course, the zones would have been of short duration. England would have been compelled to take her mines out of the North Sea in order to get any supplies from our country. When her mines were taken out of the North Sea then the German ports upon the North Sea would have been accessible to American shipping and Germany would have been compelled to cease her submarine warfare in order to get any supplies from our Nation into German North Sea ports.

There are a great many American citizens who feel that we owe it as a duty to humanity to take part in this war. Many instances of cruelty and inhumanity can be found on both sides. Men are often biased in their judgment on account of their sympathy and their interests. To my mind, what we ought to have maintained from the beginning was the strictest neutrality. If we had done this I do not believe we would have been on the verge of war at the present time. We had a right as a nation, if we desired, to cease at any time to be neutral. We had a technical right to respect the English war zone and to disregard the German war zone, but we could not do that and be neutral. I have no quarrel to find with the man who does not desire our country to remain neutral. While many such people are moved by selfish motives and hopes of gain, I have no doubt but that in a great many instances, through what I believe to be a misunderstanding of the real condition, there are many honest, patriotic citizens who think we ought to engage in this war and who are behind the President in his demand that we should declare war against Germany. I think such people err in judgment and to a great extent have been misled as to the real history and the true facts by the almost unanimous demand of the great combination of wealth that has a direct financial interest in our participation in the war. We have loaned many hundreds of millions of dollars to the allies in this controversy. While such action was legal and countenanced by international law, there is no doubt in my mind but the enormous amount of money loaned to the allies in this country has been instrumental in bringing about a public sentiment in favor of our country taking a course that would make every bond worth a hundred cents on the dollar and making the payment of every debt certain and sure. Through this instrumentality and also through the instrumentality of others who have not only made millions out of the war in the manufacture of munitions, etc., and who would expect to make millions more if our country can be drawn into the catastrophe, a large number of the great newspapers and news agencies of the country have been controlled and enlisted in the greatest propaganda that the world has ever known, to manufacture sentiment in favor of war. It is now demanded that the American citizens shall be used as insurance policies to guarantee the safe delivery of munitions of war to belligerent nations. The enormous profits of munition manufacturers, stockbrokers, and bond dealers must be still further increased by our entrance into the war. This has brought us to the present moment, when Congress, urged by the President and backed by the artificial sentiment, is about to declare war and engulf our country in the greatest holocaust that the world has ever known. . . .

———— • ————

"The troubles of Europe ought to be settled by Europe, and . . . we ought to . . . permit them to settle their questions without our interference."

———— • ————

To whom does war bring prosperity? Not to the soldier who for the munificent compensation of $16 per month shoulders his musket and goes into the trench, there to shed his blood and to die if necessary; not to the broken-hearted widow who waits for the return of the mangled body of her husband; not to the mother who weeps at the death of her brave boy; not to the little children who shiver with cold; not to the babe who suffers from hunger; nor to the millions of mothers and daughters who carry broken hearts to their graves. War brings no prosperity to the great mass of common and patriotic citizens. It increases the cost of living of those who toil and those who already must strain every effort to keep soul and body together. War brings prosperity to the stock gambler on Wall Street—to those who are already in possession of more wealth than can be realized or enjoyed. . . .

Their object in having war and in preparing for war is to make money. Human suffering and the sacrifice of human life are necessary, but Wall Street considers only the dollars and the cents. The men who do the fighting, the people who make the sacrifices, are the ones who will not be counted in the measure of this great prosperity. . . . The stock brokers would not, of course, go to war, because the very object they have in bringing on the war is profit, and therefore they must remain in their Wall Street offices in order to share in that great prosperity which they say war will bring. The volunteer officer, even the drafting officer, will not find them. They will be concealed in their palatial offices on Wall Street, sitting behind mahogany desks, covered up with clipped coupons—coupons soiled with the sweat of honest toil, coupons stained with mothers' tears, coupons dyed in the lifeblood of their fellow men.

We are taking a step to-day that is fraught with untold danger. We are going into war upon the command of gold. We are going to run the risk of sacrificing millions of our countrymen's lives in order that other countrymen may coin their lifeblood into money. And even if we do not cross the Atlantic and go into the trenches, we are going to pile up a debt that the toiling masses that shall come many generations after us will have to pay. Unborn millions will bend their backs in toil in order to pay for the terrible step we are now about to take. We are about to do the bidding of wealth's terrible mandate. By our act we will make millions of our countrymen suffer, and the consequences of it may well be that millions of our brethren must shed their lifeblood, millions of broken-hearted women must weep, millions of children must suffer with cold, and millions of babes must die from hunger, and all because we want to preserve the commercial right of American citizens to deliver munitions of war to belligerent nations. . . .

A Dollar Sign on the Flag

I know that I am powerless to stop it. I know that this war madness has taken possession of the financial and political powers of our country. I know that nothing I can say will stay the blow that is soon to fall. I feel that we are committing a sin against humanity and against our countrymen. I would like to say to this war god, You shall not coin into gold the lifeblood of my brethren. I would like to prevent this terrible catastrophe from falling upon my people. I would be willing to surrender my own life if I could cause this awful cup to pass. I charge no man here with a wrong motive, but it seems to me that this war craze has robbed us of our judgment. I wish we might delay our action until reason could again be enthroned in the brain of man. I feel that we are about to put the dollar sign upon the American flag.

I have no sympathy with the military spirit that dominates the Kaiser and his advisers. I do not believe that they represent the heart of the great German people. I have no more sympathy with the submarine policy of Germany than I have with the mine-laying policy of England. I have heard with rejoicing of the overthrow of the Czar of Russia and the movement in that great country toward the establishment of a government where the common people will have their rights, liberty, and freedom respected. I hope and pray that a similar revolution may take place in Germany, that the Kaiser may be overthrown, and that on the ruins of his military despotism may be established a German republic, where the great German people may work out their world destiny. The working out of that problem is not an American burden. We ought to remember the advice of the Father of our Country and keep out of entangling alliances. Let Europe solve her problems as we have solved ours. Let Europe bear her burdens as we have borne ours. In the greatest war of our history and at the time it occurred, the greatest war in the world's history, we were engaged in solving an American problem. We settled the question of human slavery and washed our flag clean by the sacrifice of human blood. It was a great problem and a great burden, but we solved it ourselves. Never once did we think of asking Europe to take part in its solution. Never once did any European nation undertake to settle the great question. We solved it, and history has rendered a unanimous verdict that we solved it right. The troubles of Europe ought to be settled by Europe, and wherever our sympathies may lie, disagreeing as we do, we ought to remain absolutely neutral and permit them to settle their questions without our interference. We are now the greatest neutral nation. Upon the passage of this resolution we will have joined Europe in the great catastrophe and taken America into entanglements that will not end with this war, but will live and bring their evil influences upon many generations yet unborn.

For Further Reading

N. Gordon Levin Jr., *Woodrow Wilson and World Politics.* New York: Oxford University Press, 1968.

Seward W. Livermore, *Politics Is Adjourned: Woodrow Wilson and the War Congress, 1916–1918.* Middletown, CT: Wesleyan University Press, 1966.

Earnest R. May, *The World War and American Isolation, 1914–1917.* Cambridge: Harvard University Press, 1959.

H.C. Peterson and Gilbert C. Fite, *Opponents of War, 1917–1918.* Madison: University of Wisconsin Press, 1957.

Norman L. Zucker, *George W. Norris; Gentle Knight of American Democracy.* Urbana: University of Illinois Press, 1966.

VIEWPOINT 19A

World War I Protesters Should Be Guaranteed Freedom of Speech (1919)

Oliver Wendell Holmes (1841–1935)

Following America's entry into World War I in 1917, Congress passed the Espionage Act of 1917 and the Sedition Act of 1918. Both laws made it a crime to help the enemy and/or hinder America's war effort. The two laws, especially the 1918 statute, defined such help and hindrance so broadly as to include in the latter "disloyal" speech, making them the first national laws limiting free speech since the short-lived Alien and Sedition Acts of 1798. Anarchists, pacifists, members of the Socialist Party, and other left-wing dissenters were arrested, tried, and convicted under these laws for making speeches and distributing pamphlets urging Americans to work against the war. Several of those convicted appealed up to the Supreme Court. In *Schenck v. United States* and *Debs v. United States*, the Court ruled unanimously against the defendants. In *Abrams v. United States*, however, associate justices Oliver Wendell Holmes and Louis Brandeis dissented, arguing that in this case applications of these laws had violated free speech. Excerpts of Holmes's path-breaking dissent appear below. Holmes, a member of an aristocratic Boston family, a Civil War veteran, and a noted legal philosopher, served on the Supreme Court from 1902 to 1932.

What were the contents of the inflammatory pamphlets in question, as summarized by Holmes? What situation justifies limiting free speech, according to Holmes? Why, in his view, do the pamphlets in question fail to fall within such a situation?

This indictment is founded wholly upon the publication of two leaflets which I shall describe in a moment. The first count charges a conspiracy pending the war with Germany to publish abusive language about the form of government of the United States, laying the preparation and publishing of the first leaflet as overt acts. The second count charges a conspiracy pending the war to publish language intended to bring the form of government into contempt, laying the preparation and publishing of the two leaflets as overt acts. The third count alleges a conspiracy to encourage resistance to the United States in the same war and to attempt to effec-

Excerpted from Oliver Wendell Holmes, dissenting opinion in *Abrams v. United States*, 250 U.S. 616 (1919).

tuate the purpose by publishing the same leaflets. The fourth count lays a conspiracy to incite curtailment of production of things necessary to the prosecution of the war and to attempt to accomplish it by publishing the second leaflet to which I have referred.

The Pamphlets in Question

The first of these leaflets says that the President's cowardly silence about the intervention in Russia reveals the hypocrisy of the plutocratic gang in Washington. It intimates that "German militarism combined with Allied capitalism to crush the Russian revolution," goes on that the tyrants of the world fight each other until they see a common enemy—working-class enlightenment— when they combine to crush it; and that now militarism and capitalism combined, though not openly, to crush the Russian revolution. It says that there is only one enemy of the workers of the world and that is capitalism; that it is a crime for workers of America, &c., to fight the workers' republic of Russia, and ends "Awake! Awake, you workers of the world!" Signed "Revolutionists." A note adds, "It is absurd to call us pro-German. We hate and despise German militarism more than do you hypocritical tyrants. We have more reasons for denouncing German militarism than has the coward of the White House."

The other leaflet, headed "Workers—Wake Up," with abusive language says that America together with the Allies will march for Russia to help the Czecho-Slovaks in their struggle against the Bolsheviki, and that this time the hypocrites shall not fool the Russian emigrants and friends of Russia in America. It tells the Russian emigrants that they now must spit in the face of false military propaganda by which their sympathy and help to the prosecution of the war have been called forth and says that with the money they have lent or are going to lend "they will make bullets not only for the Germans but also for the Workers' Soviets of Russia," and further, "Workers in the ammunition factories, you are producing bullets, bayonets, cannon, to murder not only the Germans but also your dearest, best, who are in Russia fighting for freedom." It then appeals to the same Russian emigrants at some length not to consent to the "inquisitionary expedition to Russia," and says that the destruction of the Russian revolution is "the politics of the march on Russia." The leaflet winds up by saying "Workers, our reply to this barbaric intervention has to be a general strike!" and after a few words on the spirit of revolution, exhortations not to be afraid, and some usual tall talk, ends "Woe unto those who will be in the way of progress. Let solidarity live! The Rebels."

No argument seems to me necessary to show that these pronunciamentos in no way attack the form of government of the United States, or that they do not support either of the first two counts. What little I have to say about the third count may be postponed until 1 have considered the fourth. With regard to that it seems too plain to be denied that the suggestion to workers in ammunition factories that they are producing bullets to murder their dearest, and the further advocacy of a general strike, both in the second leaflet, do urge curtailment of production of things necessary to the prosecution of the war within the meaning of the [Sedition] Act of May 16, 1918 . . . amending § [[Section] 3 of the earlier [Espionage] Act of 1917. But to make the conduct criminal that statute requires that it should be "with intent by such curtailment to cripple or hinder the United States in the prosecution of the war." It seems to me that no such intent is proved.

———— • ————

"It is only the present danger of immediate evil . . . that warrants Congress in setting a limit to the expression of opinion. . . . Congress certainly cannot forbid all effort to change the mind of the country."

———— • ————

I am aware of course that the word intent as vaguely used in ordinary legal discussion means no more than knowledge at the time of the act that the consequences said to be intended will ensue. Even less than that will satisfy the general principle of civil and criminal liability. A man may have to pay damages, may be sent to prison, at common law might be hanged, if at the time of his act he knew facts from which common experience showed that the consequences would follow, whether he individually could foresee them or not. But, when words are used exactly, a deed is not done with intent to produce a consequence unless that consequence is the aim of the deed. It may be obvious, and obvious to the actor, that the consequence will follow, and he may be liable for it even if he forgets it, but he does not do the act with intent to produce it unless the aim to produce it is the proximate motive of the specific act, although there may be some deeper motive behind.

It seems to me that this statute must be taken to use its words in a strict and accurate sense. They would be absurd in any other. A patriot might think that we were wasting money on aeroplanes, or making more cannon of a certain kind than we needed, and might advocate curtailment with success, yet even if it turned out that the curtailment hindered and was thought by other minds to have been obvi-

ously likely to hinder the United States in the prosecution of the war, no one would hold such conduct a crime. I admit that my illustration does not answer all that might be said but it is enough to show what I think and to let me pass to a more important aspect of the case. I refer to the First Amendment to the Constitution that Congress shall make no law abridging the freedom of speech.

First Amendment Concerns

I never have seen any reason to doubt that the questions of law that alone were before this Court in the cases of *Schenck*, *Frohwerk* and *Debs*, were rightly decided. I do not doubt for a moment that by the same reasoning that would justify punishing persuasion to murder, the United States constitutionally may punish speech that produces or is intended to produce a clear and imminent danger that it will bring about forthwith certain substantive evils that the United States constitutionally may seek to prevent. The power undoubtedly is greater in time of war than in time of peace because war opens dangers that do not exist at other times.

But as against dangers peculiar to war, as against others, the principle of the right to free speech is always the same. It is only the present danger of immediate evil or an intent to bring it about that warrants Congress in setting a limit to the expression of opinion where private rights are not concerned. Congress certainly cannot forbid all effort to change the mind of the country. Now nobody can suppose that the surreptitious publishing of a silly leaflet by an unknown man, without more, would present any immediate danger that its opinions would hinder the success of the Government arms or have any appreciable tendency to do so. Publishing these opinions for the very purpose of obstructing, however, might indicate a greater danger and at any rate would have the quality of an attempt. So I assume that the second leaflet, if published for the purpose alleged in the fourth count, might be punishable. But it seems pretty clear to me that nothing less than that would bring these papers within the scope of this law.

An actual intent in the sense that I have explained is necessary to constitute an attempt, where a further act of the same individual is required to complete the substantive crime, for reasons given in *Swift & Co. v. United States*, 196 U. S. 375, 396. It is necessary where the success of the attempt depends upon others, because if that intent is not present the actor's aim may be accomplished without bringing about the evils sought to be checked. An intent to prevent interference with the revolution in Russia might have been satisfied without any hindrance to carrying on the war in which we were engaged.

I do not see how anyone can find the intent

required by the statute in any of the defendants' words. The second leaflet is the only one that affords even a foundation for the charge, and there, without invoking the hatred of German militarism expressed in the former one, it is evident from the beginning to the end that the only object of the paper is to help Russia and stop American intervention there against the popular government—not to impede the United States in the war that it was carrying on. To say that two phrases taken literally might import a suggestion of conduct that would have interference with the war as an indirect and probably undesired effect seems to me by no means enough to show an attempt to produce that effect.

I return for a moment to the third count. That charges an intent to provoke resistance to the United States in its war with Germany. Taking the clause in the statute that deals with that in connection with the other elaborate provisions of the Act, I think that resistance to the United States means some forcible act of opposition to some proceeding of the United States in pursuance of the war. I think the intent must be the specific intent that I have described and for the reasons that I have given. I think that no such intent was proved or existed in fact. I also think that there is no hint at resistance to the United States as I construe the phrase.

In this case sentences of twenty years' imprisonment have been imposed for the publishing of two leaflets that I believe the defendants had as much right to publish as the Government has to publish the Constitution of the United States now vainly invoked by them. Even if I am technically wrong and enough can be squeezed from these poor and puny anonymities to turn the color of legal litmus paper— I will add, even if what I think the necessary intent were shown—the most nominal punishment seems to me all that possibly could be inflicted, unless the defendants are to be made to suffer not for what the indictment alleges but for the creed that they avow—a creed that I believe to be the creed of ignorance and immaturity when honestly held, as I see no reason to believe that it was held here, but which, although made the subject of examination at the trial, no one has a right even to consider in dealing with the charges before the Court.

Persecution for the expression of opinions seems to me perfectly logical. If you have no doubt of your premises or your power and want a certain result with all your heart you naturally express your wishes in law and sweep away all opposition. To allow opposition by speech seems to indicate that you think speech impotent, as when a man says that he has squared the circle, or that you do not care wholeheartedly for the result, or that you doubt either your power or your premises.

Free Trade in Ideas

But when men have realized that time has upset many fighting faiths, they may come to believe even more than they believe the very foundations of their own conduct that the ultimate good desired is better reached by free trade in ideas—that the best test of truth is the power of the thought to get itself accepted in the competition of the market, and that truth is the only ground upon which their wishes safely can be carried out. That, at any rate, is the theory of our Constitution. It is an experiment, as all life is an experiment. Every year if not every day we have to wager our salvation upon some prophecy based upon imperfect knowledge. While that experiment is part of our system I think that we should be eternally vigilant against attempts to check the expression of opinions that we loathe and believe to be fraught with death, unless they so imminently threaten immediate interference with the lawful and pressing purposes of the law that an immediate check is required to save the country.

I wholly disagree with the argument of the Government that the First Amendment left the common law as to seditious libel in force. History seems to me against the notion. I had conceived that the United States through many years had shown its repentance for the Sedition Act of 1798 by repaying fines that it imposed. Only the emergency that makes it immediately dangerous to leave the correction of evil counsels to time warrants making any exception to the sweeping command, "Congress shall make no law . . . abridging the freedom of speech." Of course I am speaking only of expressions of opinion and exhortations, which were all that were uttered here, but I regret that I cannot put into more impressive words my belief that in their conviction upon this indictment the defendants were deprived of their rights under the Constitution of the United States.

VIEWPOINT 19B

World War I Protesters Should Not Be Guaranteed Freedom of Speech (1920)

John H. Wigmore (1864–1943)

John H. Wigmore served as dean of Northwestern Law School from 1902 to 1929, and was one of America's most distinguished legal scholars and writers. The following viewpoint is excerpted from an article by Wigmore first published in the *Illinois Law*

Excerpted from John H. Wigmore, "*Abrams v. U.S.*: Freedom of Speech and Freedom of Thuggery in War-Time and Peace-Time," *Illinois Law Review*, vol. 14, no. 8, March 1920.

Review in 1920. Wigmore severely criticizes the dissenting opinion written by Supreme Court justice Oliver Wendell Holmes in the 1919 case *Abrams v. United States* (see viewpoint 19A). Holmes had contended that Jacob Abrams's rights of free speech were violated when he was arrested and convicted of distributing antiwar pamphlets during World War I. Wigmore defends the wartime laws under which Abrams was convicted, and argues that construing the Bill of Rights to protect the advocacy of violent acts against the government is a dangerous misuse of America's Constitution.

What fundamental assumption by Holmes (author of the opposing viewpoint) is erroneous, according to Wigmore? Does he acknowledge any limitation on what the government can do to restrict free speech in times of war? What was the general state of free speech in the United States at the time of this writing, according to Wigmore?

T he Minority Opinion in *Abrams v. United States*, decided on November 10, 1919 (40 Sup. 21), represents poor law and poor policy; and I wish to point out its dangerous implications. . . .

The individuals who combined in printing and distributing the circulars involved in *Abrams v. United States* had lived in this country for from five to ten years, without applying for naturalization. Four took the witness stand voluntarily, of whom three avowed that they were "rebels," "revolutionists," "anarchists"— did not believe in government in any form, and had no interest whatever in the government of the United States. . . .

What did these circulars say? . . .

The specific and concrete actions here urged are reducible to these: (1) A concerted general strike, or cessation of work; (2) particularly by workers in war-munitions factories; (3) with such armed violence that the American troops remaining in the United States would be kept at home to oppose this violence and to preserve civic order.

These three things stare out in plain words. Only the wilfully blind could refuse to see them.

What provisions of law would be violated by the action thus urged?

Under the Espionage Act of 1917, it is a crime (1) to "incite, provoke, and encourage resistance to the United States in said war"; (2) to "urge, incite and advocate curtailment of production of things and products, to-wit, ordnance and ammunition necessary and essential to the prosecution of the war." It is also a crime to utter "scurrilous and abusive language about the form of government of the United States, or to bring that form of government into contempt, scorn, contumely, and disrepute." But no stress was

laid on this offense in the majority opinion of the Supreme Court.

That the first two unlawful acts were specifically and exactly committed by the publication of these circulars is obvious.

The Supreme Court

What was the attitude of the Supreme Court?

The majority of seven of the Supreme Court held that there was "competent and substantial evidence before the jury, fairly tending to sustain the verdict of guilty in the third and fourth counts" (representing the first and second offenses above described). There is here nothing further to say as to the majority opinion.

The minority of two held that there was no proof of intent to commit such offenses. We are here concerned with the minority opinion.

It is shocking in its obtuse indifference to the vital issues at stake in August, 1918, and it is ominous in its portent of like indifference to pending and coming issues. That is why it is worth analysis now.

(1) As to the intent to provoke *resistance to the United States in the war*, the Minority Opinion says that "there is no such hint at resistance to the United States," because that statutory resistance must be "some forcible act of opposition to some proceeding of the United States in pursuance of the war," and none such is evident.

(2) As to the intent to *curtail production of munitions*, the Minority Opinion admits that "it seems too plain to be denied," but that to make the conduct criminal the statute elsewhere requires an intent to "cripple or hinder the United States in the prosecution of the war," and that this additional intent was not proved.

And, as to both the foregoing, the minority (in a passage which is, however, so unclear that its exact point is difficult to gather) further say that a restriction of free speech is warranted only by "the present danger of immediate evil, or an intent to bring it about"; and that "the surreptitious publishing of a silly leaflet by an unknown man, without more," could not involve any "present danger" to the "success of the government armies.". . .

What we are here concerned with is that state of mind. In a period when the fate of the civilized world hung in the balance, how could the Minority Opinion interpret law and conduct in such a way as to let loose men who were doing their hardest to paralyze the supreme war efforts of our country?

But this attitude of mind, operating subconsciously, must, in consciously and openly justifying itself, invoke some distinct legal principle of universally acknowledged soundness. That is the natural process, deep in human nature, for all of us.

What was this saving principle? The constitutional right of Freedom of Speech.

We are reminded in the Minority Opinion that, after all, Truth is the great desideratum, and that Truth can only be expected to emerge through the unpleasant processes of Freedom of Speech. "Free trade in ideas" is recommended as the panacea. Our anxious overstrained patriotism is soothingly pointed away from the disagreeable war situation (there was no "present danger"!); and our minds are recommended to dwell upon the civic blessings of Truth—that ultimate Truth which will some day emerge through the leisurely comparison of what now may only be the obvious seeming truths. "Men may come to believe, even more than they believe the very foundations of their conduct, that the *ultimate good* desired is better reached by free trade in ideas—that the best test of Truth is the *power of the thought to get itself accepted* in the competition of the market.". . .

———— • ————

"It will not do to let freedom of speech obscure for us the demands of other elements of liberty and safety."

———— • ————

This disquisition on Truth seems sadly out of place. To weigh in juxtaposition the dastardly sentiments of these circulars and the great theme of world-justice for which our armies were sacrificing themselves, and then to assume the sacred cause of Truth as equally involved in both, is to misuse high ideals. This Opinion, if it had made the law as a majority opinion, would have ended by our letting soldiers die helpless in France, through our anxiety to protect the distribution of a leaflet whose sole purpose was to cut off the soldiers' munitions and supplies. How would this have advanced the cause of Truth?

However, the Minority Opinion does go through the forms of reasoning, though in elliptical fashion, and without definite formulation of rule for the principle of freedom of speech; and we must meet this issue raised by the invocation of freedom of speech.

Out of its indefiniteness, the following two points of issue seem tangible:

(a) If restriction of speech is lawful at all (the Minority Opinion implies), it is only when in wartime there is "the present danger of immediate evil, or an intent to bring it about," and no such danger here existed. Here, of course, we come back to the Minority Opinion's blindness to the danger. To argue about seeing that danger is useless; the dangerous thing to the country is that there are responsible persons who did not and do not see the danger.

(b) But (apart from this danger question) the fundamental assumption of the Minority Opinion is that the principle of freedom of speech does apply to protect these particular circulars, because "expressions of opinion and exhortations were *all that were uttered here.*" It is this fundamental assumption that is thoroughly erroneous. And as thousands of well-meaning persons are obsessed by it, an attempt to clear it up is worth while.

The dilemma, or conflict of principles, is this: The United States may (admits the Minority Opinion) constitutionally "punish persuasion to murder," yet it may not punish a mere "expression of opinion or exhortation" concerning an unlawful or deleterious act, as here. This contrast between persuasion to lethal deed and persuasion to mere change of opinions, is inherent in the situation. We have to face it if any workable rule is ever to be formulated.

"Free trade in ideas," says the Minority Opinion, is vital—"the best test of truth is the power of the thought to get itself accepted in the competition of the market." Very well; but does "free trade in ideas" mean that those who desire to gather and set in action a band of thugs and murderers may freely go about publicly circularizing and orating upon the attractions of loot, proposing a plan of action for organized thuggery, and enlisting their converts, yet not be constitutionally interfered with until the gathered band of thugs actually sets the torch and lifts the rifle? Certainly not, they concede. Then where is the dead-line to be drawn at which Freedom of Speech does not become identical with Freedom of Thuggery?

That is where the champions of freedom of speech give us no solution.

What is that solution?

We must distinguish here the abnormal and the normal situations.

The *abnormal* situation is presented in time of a foreign war.

Where a nation has definitely committed itself to a foreign war, all principles of normal internal order may be suspended. As property may be taken and corporal service may be conscripted, so liberty of speech may be limited or suppressed, so far as deemed needful for the successful conduct of the war. The normal rights to life, liberty and property are certainly no less important civically than the normal right to expression of opinion; and all rights of the individual, and all internal civic interests, become subordinated to the national right in the struggle for national life. . . .

Furthermore, any other solution, in a national war by a democracy, stultifies itself. The modern war—our latest, and let us hope, our last war—is fought by the nation itself; and a general consensus of citizen-views against the war must mean a failure in the war itself. Whether the forces be filled by enlistment or by conscription, an unwilling citizenry will soon deplete the forces. I was personally near enough to the center of man-power recruitment to realize keenly that the raising of the nearly 5,000,000 men, whose battle-array ultimately gave Germany its quietus, was due to the popular conviction favoring the prosecution of the war. Had the popular conviction disfavored it, the last 3,000,000 or so would never have been got into uniform, and America's part in the war would have ended ignominiously. The conclusion is that when a nation has once decided upon war, it must stop any further hesitation, or it will fail in the very purpose of the decision. This is sound psychology for the individual, and it is equally sound for the nation.

Hence, the *moral right of the majority to enter upon the war imports the moral right to secure success by suppressing public agitation against the completion of the struggle.* If a company of soldiers in war-time on their way to the front were halted for rest in the public highway, and a disaffected citizen, going among them, were to begin thus to harangue: "Boys! this is a bad war! We ought not to be in it! And you ought not to be in it—" the state would have a moral right to step promptly up to that man and smite him on the mouth. So would any well-meaning citizen, for that matter. And that moral right is the basis of the Espionage Act, in its application to these circulars. . . .

So, on all these grounds, when war is once nationally decided upon, public speech against the rightness of the war may justly be limited or suppressed. And it *must* be limited or suppressed in a war like that one which has just brought victorious relief to the civilized world.

Times of Peace

The *normal* situation, in time of peace, is different. Here the "free trade in ideas" may be left to signify unlicensed ventilation of the most extreme views, sane or insane, on any subject whatsoever. The only problem is (as above noted) to draw the dead-line between "persuasion to murder" (in the phrase of the Minority Opinion), and discussion of the theoretic right and wrong of murder.

Where is the line to be drawn?

The Minority Opinion, and its congeners, seem to go upon the assumption that when in any utterance there is an "expression of opinion" as such, that expression of opinion should include and condone and immune an "exhortation" to illegal acts with which the expression of opinion may culminate. For example, in this view, if I circularize my associates thus: "I want and urge you to go to Washington and kill any two of the Supreme Justices," that utterance

may constitutionally be made punishable, in spite of "freedom of speech." But if I precede that incitement by a preambular form of reasoning, thus: "The Government of the United States is capitalistic; it was founded on force; it embedded in the Constitution the foul grip of the property holders of 1789, who have never since let go; it provided a Supreme Court which will nullify any statute that attempts to free the people from that tyrannous clutch; those justices have ratified the verdicts of juries (packed by those same capitalists) which sent to jail such heroes as [Eugene] Debs and [Emma] Goldman, and have upheld the statute which deported our sainted leader, [Alexander] Berkman, and hundreds of other innocent persons; there is no hope of freeing the Nation from the incubus of this constitution until these pusillanimous judges are terrorized and shown what the future portends for them; and the hope of happiness for the down-trodden multitudes of this doomed country can never revive unless these judges are made to feel that the safety of their lives depends upon right decisions; as the only way to give effect to these views, therefore, *I urge you to go to Washington and kill any two of the Supreme Court Justices.*"

If this preamble of opinion and reasoning be employed, it saves and immunes the murderous incitement in which it culminates— an incitement which would by itself have been punishable.

Such seems to be the underlying notion of the Minority Opinion.

If it is not, let some one who supports that Minority Opinion come forward and provide us with some concrete illustration of what it does mean. Judged by the *Abrams* case, it goes the above length and no less. If such horrific and absurd consequences are not meant, it is time that its defenders clarify its meaning with some canon which the friends of law and order can accept. . . .

The problem as a whole includes always two persons and three or four stages of conduct; (a) A's expression of opinion on a subject, (b) ending in A's exhortation or incitement of (c) B to do an act (d) having consequences deemed deleterious. Suppose a law is passed forbidding A to exhort or incite B to a certain act. If this act is per se illegal, there is virtually no difficulty; a statute may concededly forbid exhortation to do an illegal act. But the act may not in itself be illegal; it may merely have deleterious consequences. For example, the munition workers' cessation of work might be in itself legal; it was the consequences that were deleterious, by curtailment in war-time of indispensable war material. The Legislature must be permitted to take measures to prevent such consequences. The problem is how to define the scope of statute which may thus aim to prevent these consequences while leaving sufficient play for the constitutional sanction of freedom of discussion.

The following would do it:

A statute does not abridge constitutional freedom of speech if it *forbids A's exhortation of B to do a specific act which would have consequences deemed by the legislature to be deleterious to the commonwealth.* But a statute does abridge such freedom which forbids A's expression of opinion to B that a specific act and its consequences ought not to be prevented by law, or forbids A's *exhortation to B to join in removing that legal obstacle by the usual legislative methods.* . . .

For example, take the prohibition measures. It is yet lawful for A to drink intoxicating liquor from his domestic stock, and for B to drink from it at A's invitation. Suppose that a statute should forbid A to invite B to his house for the purpose of so drinking; and suppose that an indignant A circularizes his friends arguing for the folly of such a restriction and urging them to come to his house for the purpose. Could this circular be protected by constitutional freedom of speech? Certainly not. It defies the practical enforcement of the law, and invites to action having precisely the disapproved consequences. Let A, however, if he pleases, argue with his friends that the restriction is excessive, and let him persuade them to appeal to the legislature for a repeal of the statute. But, so long as it remains law, let him not be licensed to undermine its operation on the pretext of freedom of speech. The pretext is needless, for he is still at liberty to discuss the wisdom of the law and to seek to change it by usual methods of changing the public opinion to sounder judgment. And that is all that the right of freedom of speech exists for, in the last analysis.

Americans Have True Freedom of Speech

After all, is not this tenderness for the right of freedom of speech an over-anxiety? Is not this sensitive dread of its infringement an anachronism? Has not the struggle for the establishment of that freedom been won, and won permanently, a century ago? Do we not really possess, in the fullest permanent safety, a freedom and a license for the *discussion* of the pros and cons of every subject under the sun? Simply as a matter of "free trade in ideas," is there not in Anglo-America today an irrevocably established free trade in every blasphemous, scurrilous, shocking, iconoclastic, or lunatic idea that any fanatical or unbalanced brain can conceive? And is there any axiom of law, constitution, morals, religion, or decency which you and I cannot today publicly dispute with legal immunity?

I firmly believe that in these days the tender champions of free speech are, like Don Quixote, fighting giants and ogres who have long since been laid in the dust. John Huss, in his day, five centuries ago, was genuinely in need of a freedom-of-speech right. Galileo suffered for lack of it. Through the long centuries its evolution was landmarked by other champions or victims—Martin Luther, Algernon Sidney, Hugh Latimer, Michael Servetus, William Prynne, John Milton, Jeremy Taylor, Voltaire, John Wilkes, Thomas Paine, Thomas Erskine, Charles James Fox, William Hone—some demagogues, some divines; some scholars, some statesmen; and all of them shatterers of orthodoxy. But when the nineteenth century dawned, the struggle had been won. The principle was established. And, in Anglo-America, at least, there never has been a time since the 1820's when it was really in danger. . . .

Time does settle some things. The emotional conditions of religious and political intolerance and persecution out of which emerged a perception of the need for "free trade in ideas" have long since quieted down. It is an anachronism to imagine that they continue, and to argue as though we were still living in the days of Huss and Galileo and Latimer.

And so the danger now is rather that this misplaced reverence for freedom of speech should lead us to minimize or ignore other fundamentals which in today's conditions are far more in need of reverence and protection. Let us show some sense of proportion in weighing the several fundamentals. No single political principle can override all the others. It will not do to let freedom of speech obscure for us the demands of other elements of liberty and safety. . . .

The truth is that the constitutional guarantee of freedom of speech is being invoked more and more in misuse. It represents the unfair protection much desired by impatient and fanatical minorities—fanatically committed to some new revolutionary belief, and impatient of the usual process of rationally converting the majority. The period is one of changing views in multifarious fields. Institutional reconstruction on a wide scale is due in the coming generation—reconstruction on a wider scale than at any time since three generations ago. Certain leaders of thought—some idealists, some materialists—see only red when their own particular doctrines are balked of immediate general acceptance. Impatient of that "free trade in ideas" which the Minority Opinion assures us will exhibit ultimately the "power of the thought to get itself accepted," these fanatical leaders invoke club-law. They call for "direct action" (this cowardly euphemism for brutal mob-violence must now be familiar to all readers of recent periodical literature). And when their urgent propaganda of club-law meets lawful interference, they invoke the sacred constitutional guarantee of "freedom of speech." It is simply a profanation of that term. . . .

The reason that we should view the Minority Opinion with apprehension is that it is symptomatic. Hundreds of well-meaning citizens—"parlor bolsheviks" and "pink racials," as the phrase goes—are showing a similar complaisant or good-natured tolerance to this licensing of the violence-propaganda. If such treacherous thuggery as these circulars, designed to hamstring our boys in France, and issued amidst the anxieties and agonies of wartime, could be calmly condoned by those who sit on high, what may we expect in peace-time, now that the easy moments have returned, and the forces of impatient fanaticism are let loose upon our constitutional government?

For Further Reading

Liva Baker, *The Justice from Beacon Hill.* New York: Harper-Collins, 1991.

Frederick C. Giffin, *Six Who Protested: Radical Opposition to the First World War.* Port Washington, NY: Kenikat Press, 1977.

Paul L. Murphy, *World War I and the Origin of Civil Liberties in the United States.* New York: Norton, 1979.

William R. Roalfe, *John Henry Wigmore: Scholar and Reformer.* Evanston, IL: Northwestern University Press, 1977.

VIEWPOINT 20A

The United States Should Join the League of Nations (1919)

James D. Phelan (1861–1930)

A crucial decision facing America following World War I was whether to join the League of Nations. The league was largely the creation of President Woodrow Wilson. As early as January 8, 1918, Wilson was calling for "a general association of nations" to preserve the territorial integrity of countries and to prevent war. In 1919 he strove to make this global vision a reality as head of the U.S. peace delegation in Versailles, France, by insisting that the Treaty of Versailles agreed to by the nations of World War I include the creation of such an international organization. The League of Nations, as formulated by Wilson, was to consist of an Assembly to represent all member nations, a Council controlled by leading powers including the United States, and a Permanent Court of International Justice to arbitrate disputes between nations.

Wilson's vision of a new world order faced a serious obstacle in the U.S. Senate, where the Treaty of Versailles, like all U.S. treaties, had to be ratified by a two-thirds majority. Many opponents cited what they viewed as America's historic tradition, dating back to George Washington's 1796 Farewell Address, of

James D. Phelan, *Congressional Record*, 66th Cong., 1st sess. (March 3, 1919), pp. 4870–71.

avoiding "foreign entanglements." Those arguments and others are addressed in the following viewpoint, taken from a speech by one of the League of Nation's supporters, Democratic senator James D. Phelan of California. The former San Francisco mayor served in the U.S. Senate from 1915 to 1921. The February 20, 1919, address reprinted here was originally given before a group of internationalist Republicans led by former president William Howard Taft.

How does Phelan respond to anti-league arguments based on George Washington's Farewell Address? Why is public opinion more important than ever in influencing U.S. government policy decisions, according to Phelan? What analogy does he make between the League of Nations and civil society?

Now, I should think that all men of good will would support the principle of the league of nations. We may differ as to the details of the power which might be granted to the league. But as to the essential principle, to organize to avert the horrors of war, if possible, in this world, there can be no question. . . .

There is no partisanship involved in this. As President Taft said the other day, "In matters international, Woodrow Wilson and myself stand together." [Applause.] And the gentlemen who are so fond these days of quoting George Washington must have forgotten that in the Farewell Address there is a condemnation of partisan spirit. It was one of the things against which he warned his countrymen. And now they are suffering the partisan spirit to influence their sober judgment.

Woodrow Wilson declared long ago that the object of this war—and, I remember, he declared it at the tomb of Washington at Mount Vernon—was to establish "a reign of law with the consent of the governed and sustained by the organized opinion of mankind." [Applause.] The organized opinion of mankind means nothing less than a league of nations, because it is only through the nations, unless you are ready to destroy all international barriers, that the opinion of mankind can be organized. And he has been busy ever since in making good his word.

But those Senators—and you see I am not in accord with their utterances, and they represent, I am glad to assure the league, a very small minority, I believe, of that body [applause]—are fond of quoting Washington, who warned us also against international entanglements. That sounds very good. But Washington also said in a letter to one of his contemporaries that we can not participate in European affairs for at least 20 years, because we have not the power to treat with them on terms of equality, and we might endanger our hard-won independence. But 120 years have passed, and the United States is the most powerful Nation in the world. [Applause.] So what Washington said at that time, modified by his own words in private correspondence, certainly does not apply to the United States today. And, as the object of this war was to give democracy to the small nations, and to the large ones as well, and to destroy autocracy and tyranny, George Washington, undoubtedly, if consulted, would say, "Those are the very purposes to which I have dedicated my word and my sword," and he would speed us on that road.

If we were acting contrary to the principles of Washington and the Fathers, it might be well to call a halt and say that we are traveling upon forbidden ground. But we have gone to Europe, and our boys have given the decisive blow to autocracy [applause], and this is merely a question in the organization of a league, of something to sustain them in their work. And I feel that there should be as much enthusiasm in this cause as there was in that other cause when we believed that our national rights at home and abroad, aye, our national existence, perhaps was involved in the issue of the conflict; because we can not sit down now and serenely regard Europe. On the contrary, the situation is full of misgivings. I will not enlarge upon the argument, which has been so elaborately set forth by our worthy President. But he has told you again and again that a large number of small countries have been set up and given democracy, and if they be abandoned to their fate we will have, within a very short time, the most horrible war in history in its ferocity, outclassing and distancing the conflict through which we have just passed. Because racial animosities would be aroused, and the old order, often sleeping but never dying, in clashes like this will reassert itself, and the little countries will make a futile resistance and be again amalgamated in the great nations over which tyrants will rule.

A Plea for the League

So, unless this league is established, there is absolutely no hope for democratic Europe; there will be no hope for the men, women, and children; there will be no hope for the workers, because their protection is in the establishment and in the maintenance of democracy, in which their voices are so tremendously potent. They are rudely expressing themselves in some of the countries today. But looking back upon history, we must not be alarmed, because it is only through revolution that order comes. That is the world's history. That must not discourage us. But when they return to reason and know that in this world there must be responsible government, without which there will be neither labor nor wages, then and in that event they will, I

am convinced, yield to the arguments which have been advanced in their interests.

It has been said that a league of nations is impossible. When the American Engineers went to Europe, and when we shipped over two millions of men, with all the accessories of war, and built railroads and built great warehouses and provided the food not only for our own men but for the men of other lands, it was an achievement of great magnitude. And somebody said, and I believe it has clung as a sentiment to the American Engineers, "It can not be done, but here it is!" A league can not be formed, but here it is. [Applause.] The President is on the ocean bearing the first draft, adopted unanimously, under pressure which I believe he exerted, as the one thing that he desired of all others to bring back to his countrymen as the reward of the war—not captives, not lands and territory, but peace for all the world. What greater ideal could there be? What greater achievement could he have won? And that is a thing accomplished by unanimous vote. The nations in conference having approved of the idea of the league, and their committee has drafted this measure, which will very soon, probably, be presented in an authoritative way by the President himself to the American people. And then he will go back, having consulted public sentiment—and, by the way, that is the work we are doing here, creating a public sentiment, without which there can be no government, and without which the President unsustained would be a mere pawn upon the European chessboard. He must have it, and he knows it, because his democracy is pure. He knows that without the people he can not succeed, and he always appeals over the heads of Senators and editors, even, to the great body of the people. [Applause.]

"We are disloyal to our ideals if we refuse to let our country enlist in this cause."

And I think, Mr. President, that it is more important for the audiences which you address throughout the land to respond to this call than it is for individual Senators, because the Senators, I must say in their defense, feel that after all they are representatives of the people. It is not the body that it was in the olden time—now your Senators come from the people, elected by popular vote, and not puppets set up by legislatures to serve private interests. They are amenable to your demands. They respond to your call. And I am glad to see here an audience so great tonight, because every man and woman of you must feel that you are rendering a substantial aid in the settlement of this question. If you show apathy, your representatives will show apathy. If you show interest, they will show interest. If you are for it, they are for it. [Applause.]

Individuals and Nations

One word more, Mr. President. I suppose the argument has often been made; but it seems to me that in its simplest form a league of nations bears a close analogy to civil society. Democracy is a league of men, banded together for mutual protection. And they yield certain of their natural rights for the purpose of establishing this democracy as ordered government. In a league of nations the nations must necessarily yield some of the exclusive rights which they now hold for the same purpose—their mutual protection. Is there anything wrong with that? Is the right of the individual more sacred than the right of the nation? But grant for the moment that it is. It is yielded willingly in the interest of organized government, organized democracies, where all have a voice and where all thrive; it is their self-determination, freely given, and all abide by the result of the expression of that voice, and the minorities are given protection. They are not destroyed, as in the old days of the Crusaders. And you may recall in this connection the story of the Crusader, who was told on his deathbed that he had to repent and forgive his enemies, and he naïvely responded, "Why, I have no enemies; I have killed them all." But a democracy respects the minority which does not quite agree with the majority government, and that is a little sacrifice they must make in order to preserve the peace of society.

Now, the United States, going into a compact of this kind will, let us concede to the objecting Senators, yield a part of what they regard as their exclusive rights about which they are very tender. But is not the prize worth the game? Is not the peace of the world worth the sacrifice? [Applause.] Is there anything more terrible than unleashed human beings destroying each other under circumstances of greatest cruelty? War, we are told, burdens a people with debt to go down from one generation to another, like the curse of original sin. It wipes the people from the earth as though Heaven had repented the making of man. Its evils can not be written, even in human blood. And our campaign is against war. And in that campaign every man is enlisted as a patriot, just as much as every man was enlisted in our recent campaign, where his loyalty was never questioned, to carry the Stars and Stripes, standing for equal rights and justice throughout the benighted countries of Europe and bringing hope and succor to those who for centuries have been the victims of oppression.

But we are disloyal to our ideals if we refuse to let our country enlist in this cause. We are all, by sacrifice and concession, working for a perfect State at home. The league is working for a more perfect world. And, my friends, just as the organization of society has abolished violence in the settlement of disputes and set up legislatures and courts, so this league of nations, if it carries its purpose through to the finish by creating international tribunals, will abolish war, which is only violence on a broader scale. Let us not dismiss this question by saying it belongs only to the sentimental. Sentiment is the best thing in the world, and the difficulty is in living up to it. Human nature is the meanest thing about us, and we are always trying to keep it down. That is the function of society; it is as well the function of the league.

VIEWPOINT 20B

The United States Should Not Join the League of Nations (1919)

Lawrence Sherman (1858–1939)

The League of Nations was the centerpiece of President Woodrow Wilson's vision of reshaping the world order and America's place in it. Wilson succeeded in incorporating the league's creation within the Treaty of Versailles, negotiated in 1919 by the nations that had fought World War I. But Wilson faced significant opposition in the U.S. Senate, which had to ratify the treaty. Entry into the League of Nations would represent a major break from isolationism—America's traditional foreign policy of self-protective neutrality and avoidance of foreign entanglements. A faction of senators, dubbed the "irreconcilables," was steadfastly opposed on philosophical grounds to involvement in European or world affairs, and would have no part of the League of Nations on any terms. One of these senators was Lawrence Sherman, a Republican from Illinois who served in the Senate from 1913 to 1921. In the following viewpoint, excerpted from his remarks before the Senate on March 13, 1919, Sherman stakes out a position of classic American isolationism and emphasizes the danger of burdening the new nation of America with the conflicts of the old nations of Europe.

What contrasts does Sherman draw between the United States and the nations of Europe? How does his view of George Washington's Farewell Address differ from that of James D. Phelan, author of the opposing viewpoint? What concerns does Sherman

From Lawrence Sherman, *Congressional Record*, 66th Cong., 1st sess. (March 3, 1919), pp. 4865–67.

express about the Bolshevik Revolution in Russia? What distinctions does he make between the decision to enter World War I and the decision to enter the League of Nations?

———

Mr. President, the President and his appointees on the peace conference have no instructions from the American people to bind them in a perpetual alliance with the several nations of the earth. The Senate has no popular mandate to ratify such a proposed treaty. Neither the President nor the Senate nor both jointly has power to abrogate the Constitution that created them or transfer the sovereignty of the United States nor any of its essential attributes to any other human authority exercising or attempting to exercise that sovereignty over our Government or our citizens.

The qualified voters of this country and the indestructible States are the source of sovereignty. From them sprang the Federal Government, dual in nature and national in character. This mechanism so framed operates by the power transmitted through frequent elections and regulated by constitutional grants and limitations. Nowhere is the Government, its Congress, its Executive, or its courts given authority to surrender or transfer its powers to any alien creation. . . .

This peace conference will be a body of men from many nations, languages, customs, standards of conduct, races, habits, and religions. Their hopes, purposes, and national ideals develop under widely varying impulses. They may or may not excel ours and surpass us in the several fields of human achievement.

That is not the issue. What must be steadily seen is committing our country and our lives and our posterity irrevocably to an invisible and unknown power. If we cut the cables of constitutional government here we are caught in the irresistible tides that sweep us into the maelstrom of the Old World's bloody currents flowing from every shore. The feuds and spoliations of a thousand years become our daily chart of action. It is not do they threaten or menace us. All we can know is a few men in some hidden chamber, known as the executive council [of the League of Nations], wield over us powers of life and death.

An oligarchy is the worst possible form of government. The executive council is the worst possible form of an oligarchy. It orders Congress today to send half a million of our young men into central Asia to be hacked to pieces on the plateau of Tibet. Tomorrow Egypt is assailed by desert hordes and more levies are sent to slaughter in a struggle that does not remotely concern our peace.

We are not colonizers. We have not sought to sound our morning drumbeats around the world. From the day the first settler landed on the James River in the Old Dominion [Virginia] and the Pilgrim's prayer rose in the primeval forest of the old Bay State [Massachusetts] we have been content to cultivate and develop this our portion of the continent, and point the way for the industrious God-fearing immigrant to make a new home from across the sea. The great labor-saving machines, the communication of thought, the secrets of nature's processes seized and adapted to human use, the greatest of world discoveries have been our contribution to mankind.

The Old World

While nations fought for supremacy and territory around the globe, we labored with what we had to make the most of our blessings. They desolated the earth for glory and for gold. We tilled the earth and sailed the seas in peace. In turn the Dane, the Spaniard, the Briton, the Frank, and the Hun has stripped the confines of every land of its gold. The American has dug it from the mine and washed it from the sands. We created it from our fertile soil and inexhaustible resources. From commerce the calm pulse of nations showed no poison of ignoble conquest in our veins, no stains to sully an honorable ambition for bloodless gain.

While Europe, Asia, and Africa robbed and murdered, we farmed and manufactured, built railroads, and annexed nobody's territory. The Old World simply harvested the destruction she sowed. Her heritage has been war and ours peace. We are asked to abandon our own and adopt another's.

Now, having helped put the German where he belongs, and being willing in like circumstances to help do so again, we are asked to lend our lives and treasures to every feud that blazes out in three continents, whether it concerns or menaces our interests or safety or not. We are invited to become the knight-errant of the world. A nation's first duty is to its own people. Its government is for them.

Nearly four months ago the belligerent nations signed the armistice that saved Germany from a destructive atonement for her crimes. In that time the responsible agents of the United States of America have not occupied themselves in ending the war and writing terms of peace upon which Germany shall pay the penalty of acknowledged defeat in her attempts against civilized mankind. They have busied themselves with an effort to create a superstate above the governments and peoples of nations to exercise supersovereignty over both nations and their individual citizens and subjects.

Advantage is taken of a wish for universal and permanent peace to present this device as a certain instrumentality to that desired end. . . .

[But] the constitution of the league of nations

must be submitted to that scrutiny which will assay its service as a charter prescribing a rule of conduct among nations and whether obedience can be secured. It must be tested by the peoples grouped under sovereign governments to ascertain how it will affect them and what burdens are likely to be assumed; what measure of relief is practicable. Does this document give it, or if not, what can be written reasonably calculated to accomplish that measure of relief? These are inquiries which merit the highest effort of which this Senate and the American Nation are capable. Such a momentous issue seldom challenges free people for decision.

The nations now occupying the earth came from a remote past. Whatever others may think of history, I am compelled at times to have recourse to the history of the various governments and nations that have occupied the earth in order to obtain light on the present. Their governments descended from ancient thrones, sprang from revolution, or are the heritage of development and accumulated experience. Their customs, usages, and laws vary. They comprise many religions and ethics and standards of morals. Their ethnology embraces the entire human family with their several languages. History is the philosophic chain that binds the past with the living present and its deep, pulsating currents of action.

———— • ————

"The league of nations is a Pandora's box of evil to empty upon the American people the aggregated calamities of the world."

———— • ————

All nations with organic government sufficient to be dealt with as responsible powers can be assembled by their voluntary act under a code of international law. Twenty-six nations so obligated themselves in 1899 in the first Hague convention. Forty-four nations were signatory in 1907 to the second Hague convention. When the armistice was signed November 11, 1918, all the warring nations were contracting parties agreeing in 1907 to arbitrate differences as a substitute for war. Every outrage perpetrated by Germany she had bound herself not to commit. Her deliberate policy of frightfulness she had solemnly covenanted should never be pursued. The indispensable end to be sought, therefore, is not to multiply international agreements, but to discover means of compelling or persuading nations to keep them when made.

I am skeptical on moral suasion as a coercive agency on some governments. It is idle to appeal to the people ruled by such governments for an improved or higher sense of right or wrong. Independent nations having their own governments generally have as good ones as they are capable of operating. Not as good as they desire often, but as good as they can get and keep in the long run. It is a considerable journey from despotism to free government. It is a ceaseless task to prevent free government from degenerating into a dissolution of just restraints. At one extreme is arbitrary power to a king; at the other, arbitrary power in a class or multitude, and there is no difference in the intrinsic evils of either.

What Germany or Russia may develop lies in the realm of conjecture. What their established relations may be with the rest of the world is uncharted diplomacy. Who knows whether they will emerge from their civil chaos and bloody tumults with a sense of national honor and obligation that will make them keep their faith when pledged or be merely predatory freebooters, to be restrained only by armies and navies?

Conflicts in Europe

Europe contains many independent sovereign nations. Some submerged nationalities, overwhelmed by wars reaching back some centuries, will undoubtedly rise to reassumed sovereignty. With the latter we may be concerned. They might be converted into warlike forces against us if subject to a dominant government, our enemy. Much European bloodshed has had its origin in commercial rivalry resulting in territorial aggression. It may be repeated. Most wars of modern times have begun in Europe. Kings have fought to gain thrones for their kin and subordinates. Ancient feuds of reigning families have sent armies into many a disastrous field. Ambitious men have risen to shake continents with their struggles for power.

That is all to end, however, because we now hear that kings are no more and the people will administer all future governments. We fervently pray it may be so. Yet some of the people we are asked by this league to invest with sovereign power over us may well engage our concern.

Russia is the fountainhead of bloody chaos and the attempted dissolution of every civil and domestic tie dear to the Anglo-Saxon race. Germany may be passing from despotic rule to class government founded on Marxian socialism.

The restless elements of Europe, inured to violence and disliking the monotony of private industry, are always explosive material. Erecting them into states does not insure tranquillity. To all such people, if they have not wisdom and virtue, self-restraint and justice to the minority, liberty is the greatest of all possible evils, not only to them but to the world.

If we ratify this league in its present form, we invest such people with equal power over us. Their vices and misfortunes react upon us. Their follies and crimes become in turn a menace, because we have given them an equal vote in the league with our own country. It may become not a means of removing a menace but of creating one beyond our power either to abate or to remove.

The constitution of the league of nations is a Pandora's box of evil to empty upon the American people the aggregated calamities of the world, and only time is the infallible test even of our own institutions.

What is our internal strength, and what burdens can we safely carry from the Old World? Are we the governmental Ajax upon whose shoulders rest the calamities and the burdens of the earth? This document assumes it. It was this wholesome solicitude that woke the wise counsels of those who hewed with sturdy stroke and laid deep and strong the great foundation stones of civil liberty and self-government.

Not doctrinaires nor dreamers floating serenely in the cloud-lands of speculative philosophy were the men who wrote our charters and forged the mighty instruments of freedom in the Western Hemisphere. They were not novices. They had fought battles. They had felt the depression of defeat. Victory had not relaxed their unceasing vigilance. With peace they returned to their homes and families and the cares of private life. They assumed the task of framing a Government to save in peace what they had gained in war. We are asked to ratify and create something that will lose in peace what we won in war. . . .

Our forefathers warred . . . with their lives and fortunes at stake. They left us the heritage of their sacrifices and their solemn admonitions summed up in the Farewell Address [of George Washington] read annually in this Chamber. Against their wisdom and experience now rise the dreamer and the bookman, the Socialist, and the mere haberdasher in phrases which intoxicate and mislead; sincere men some whose zeal for the millenium made by human hands blinds them to mere human faults and limitations. . . .

The founders of this Government had a working knowledge of the great headlands of civil liberty. They had known the elemental struggles to safeguard human rights, to curb the great and raise the low. They knew Europe, its quicksands, its bloody pitfalls in which their ancestors had died for a thousand years. They hated its kings, its nobles, its mobs, its revolutions, its heartless caste, its cruelty, and its crimes. They left their solemn warning to posterity to let Europe settle her own quarrels. . . .

World War I

When the United States by joint resolution of Congress entered the war April 6, 1917, we signed no pact with the Governments arrayed against the central powers. The American felt in his heart Germany was a menace to the free governments of the world. There was an instinctive horror at Germany's methods of making war and her avowed policy of frightfulness. It was known she aimed at world dominion. Those in authority at this Capitol knew we must fight the danger alone or jointly with the allies.

We chose to make common cause against a common danger. To do so we abdicated no sovereign power. We bound ourselves in no perpetual alliance to draw the sword whenever and so long as a majority of European governments voted it upon us. Our practical expression in this crisis was to reserve for ourselves the power to decide when and how long a controversy between two or more nations in some quarter of the globe was of such magnitude as to warrant our interference even to the extremity of war.

A working status was in fact established between our Government and the allies. Under it the war was fought successfully to the armistice of November 11, 1918. No nation surrendered its sovereignty. They voluntarily combined their strength against the common peril. It was a union of equals, and each was in an equally common self-defense bound to give all it had if the struggle demanded it. This is the key to any league of nations that will survive the ephemeral theories and impossible yearnings of the alleged friends of humanity who are more fertile in phrase making than successful in the practical affairs of men. . . .

The actual working alliance between our Government and Germany's European enemies . . . implies no loss of sovereignty and no violence to national sentiment. It is a cooperative expression of the law of self-defense, an American doctrine on which every patriot can join his fellow man. It impairs no constitutional power of Congress. It invades no executive domain, and it leaves our Government the responsible instrumentality to direct the will of our people. We escape the perils of surrendering our country to the mandates of a majority of the Governments of the Old World by this course.

The same public opinion in a free government that would unite our people under the proposed league would lead to concerted action under a treaty whose obligation rests in good faith. If public opinion does not support the league, it can not send armies into the field. America will not sacrifice her lives and her treasure unless her heart is in the war. No mere language written on parchment can in practice make any compact between sovereign nations more binding than a treaty unless some supersovereign force be contemplated as a coercive agent upon the American Government and its people. Force converts such a league into a tyranny and international oppressor. Such a compact becomes the source of universal war, not the means of permanent peace. . . .

Article 10

In article 10 [of the Covenant (constitution) of the League of Nations] the members of the league bind themselves to preserve each other, and the executive council is required to advise upon the means by which all the league members shall be protected against external aggression which will impair their territorial integrity and political independence. If this article avails anything it binds our Government, its Army, its Navy, its people, and its Treasury to defend Great Britain's colonial dependencies any place in the world. A like obligation attends us for France, Italy, and every other league member. England's territorial possessions are in every part of the globe. Russia is a vast area with 180,000,000 people, and Germany with 70,000,000. The United Kingdom of Great Britain has in Europe fewer than 50,000,000 population. More than 300,000,000 souls acknowledge the supremacy of England's flag in Asia. Great Britain feels, as seldom before, the need of help to maintain her territorial integrity. . . .

I decline to vote to bind the American people to maintain the boundary lines and political independence of every nation that may be a league member. It ought to be done only when the question menaces our peace and safety. It must be a treaty uniting our associated nations in the mutual and common bonds of self-defense. It becomes, then a league of sovereigns acting with the common purpose of self-preservation. The law of nations is like the law of individuals. Self-defense is the first law and is justified before every tribunal known to civilized man. . . .

This league, Mr. President, sends the angel of death to every American home. In every voice to ratify it we can hear the beating of his wing. There will be none to help; no decrees from omniscience will direct us to sprinkle with blood the lintel of every American home. If this supersovereignty be created, conscription will take from all, and we will bear the white man's burden in every quarter of the world.

On this issue I challenge the President and his administration and the sympathizers with this constitution to appeal to the great jury of the American people. I will be content with no less, whatever the Senate may do. I am willing to take that responsibility. I invite the President to remove the limitations upon a censored press and censored free speech that we may combat with him in an open forum and on equal terms. If he is not a political and governmental coward, he will give us that right. An honorable antagonist would do no less.

For Further Reading

Robert Ferrell, *Woodrow Wilson and World War I, 1917–1921.* New York: Harper & Row, 1985.

Robert E. Hennings, *James D. Phelan and the Wilson Progressives of California.* New York: Garland Publications, 1985.

Arthur S. Link, *Wilson the Diplomatist.* Baltimore: The Johns Hopkins University Press, 1957.

Ralph A. Stone, *The Irreconcilables.* Lexington: University of Kentucky Press, 1970.

Ralph A. Stone, ed., *Wilson and the League of Nations.* New York: Holt, Rinehart and Winston, 1967.

PART III:
PROSPERITY, DEPRESSION, AND WAR, 1920–1945

❦

**Social and Cultural
Issues of the Twenties**

**The Great Depression
and the New Deal**

World War II

1920

January 1   Government agents in several cities arrest thousands of suspected communist and anarchist immigrants in "Palmer raids"

January 16   Eighteenth Amendment (alcohol prohibition) goes into effect

March 19   U.S. Senate rejects Treaty of Versailles and the League of Nations

May 5   Anarchists Nicola Sacco and Bartolomeo Vanzetti arrested for murder

May 31   U.S. government ends price guarantees on wheat, triggering a downward spiral for all crop prices

August 26   Nineteenth Amendment, granting women the right to vote, is ratified

November 2   Warren G. Harding elected president

1921

May 9   Emergency Quota Act restricts the number of immigrants allowed into the country

November 2   Margaret Sanger founds American Birth Control League (later called Planned Parenthood)

1928

August 27   The Kellogg-Briand Pact outlawing war is signed by the U.S. and other nations

November 6   Herbert Hoover elected president

December 17   Clark Memorandum; U.S. repudiates 1904 Roosevelt Corollary to Monroe Doctrine and pledges to stop intervening in Latin America

1926

March   Robert Goddard test-flies world's first liquid-fueled rocket

1929

October   The stock market crashes, triggering the Great Depression

1930

June 17   Smoot-Hawley Tariff Act drastically raises duties on numerous industrial and agricultural products

1932

January   The Stimson Doctrine: U.S. refuses to recognize the 1931 Japanese conquest of Manchuria

January 22   Reconstruction Finance Corporation established by President Hoover

November 8   Franklin D. Roosevelt elected president

1920   **1925**   **1930**

1923

March 3   Henry Luce publishes the first issue of *Time* magazine

August 2   President Harding dies; Vice President Calvin Coolidge succeeds to the presidency

December   Equal Rights Amendment to Constitution introduced in Congress

1924

Act of Congress makes American Indians full U.S. citizens

November 4   Calvin Coolidge elected president; two women elected as state governors: Nellie Tayloe Ross in Wyoming and Miriam ("Ma") Ferguson in Texas

1927

February 23   Congress creates the Federal Radio Commission to regulate radio broadcasters

April 7   First successful demonstration of television

May 20–21   Charles Lindbergh's solo flight across the Atlantic Ocean

August 23   Sacco and Vanzetti are executed

October   Premiere of *The Jazz Singer* ushers in era of sound movies

1925

July 10–21   The Scopes evolution trial is held in Dayton, Tennessee

August 8   40,000 Ku Klux Klan members march in Washington, D.C.

1933

February 6   Twentieth Amendment to Constitution ratified, moving future presidential inauguration dates from March 4 to January 20

March 4   Frances Perkins, appointed secretary of labor, becomes first woman to hold cabinet-level post

March 5   Roosevelt declares a national bank holiday

March 9–June 16   "First Hundred Days" of New Deal: special session of Congress results in creation of Federal Deposit Insurance Corporation, National Recovery Administration, the Federal Emergency Relief Administration, and other programs

April 19   U.S. abandons gold standard

November 16   Roosevelt extends formal diplomatic recognition to the Soviet Union

December 5   Prohibition ends when Eighteenth Amendment is repealed

1934

May   Dust storm destroys topsoil in Texas, Oklahoma, and other states

May 29   1901 Platt Amendment superseded by new U.S.-Cuba treaty that ends Cuba's status as U.S. protectorate

June 18   Congress enacts the Indian Reorganization Act to help preserve Indian tribal culture; reverses Dawes Act of 1887

1935

May 27   The Supreme Court strikes down several New Deal measures as unconstitutional

July 5   President Roosevelt signs the National Labor Relations Act

August   Congress passes the first in a series of neutrality acts designed to prevent American entry into another European war

August 14   The Social Security Act is signed by Roosevelt

1940

June   Germany conquers France; controls most of Europe

September   America First Committee is organized to oppose U.S. involvement in war in Europe

September 3   U.S. exchanges 50 destroyers to Great Britain for leases on naval and air bases

September 16   Congress passes first peacetime draft in American history

September 27   Germany, Italy, and Japan sign military alliance

November 5   President Roosevelt wins an unprecedented third term

1941

March   Lend-lease aid to Great Britain and other nations authorized by Congress

June 22   Nazi Germany invades the Soviet Union

June 25   Roosevelt establishes Fair Employment Practices Board and bans racial discrimination by defense contractors

August 1   U.S. bans exports of aviation oil to Japan

August 9   Roosevelt and Churchill meet off Newfoundland and formulate the Atlantic Charter

September 11   Roosevelt orders navy to shoot German submarines "on sight"

December 7–11   Japanese attack on Pearl Harbor; Congress declares war against Japan; Germany and Italy declare war on the U.S.

1943

June 4   White soldiers invade Mexican-American communities in "zoot-suit" riots of Los Angeles

June 20–22   Race riot in Detroit

November 28–December 1   Teheran Conference: Roosevelt, British prime minister Winston Churchill, and Soviet leader Joseph Stalin meet together for first time

---

1935   **1940**   **1945**

1936

November 3   Roosevelt reelected president

December   United Automobile Workers stage a successful sit-down strike against General Motors in Detroit

1937

February 5   President Roosevelt proposes his plan (rejected by Congress) to expand size of Supreme Court

April 12   The Supreme Court upholds the constitutionality of the National Labor Relations Act

May 6   *Hindenburg* airship disaster

1939

February 27   Supreme Court outlaws sit-down strikes

August 22   Germany and Soviet Union sign nonaggression pact

September 3   France and Great Britain declare war on Germany following German invasion of Poland

1942

February 20   Roosevelt authorizes the military internment and relocation of Japanese-Americans

June 3–6   Battle of Midway: turning point in U.S. war against Japan

1944

June 6   D Day: Allied forces cross English Channel and land in Normandy, France

November 7   Roosevelt reelected to a fourth term

1945

February   Yalta Conference between Roosevelt, Churchill, and Stalin

April 12   President Roosevelt dies; Vice President Harry S. Truman succeeds to the presidency

May 8   Victory in Europe Day

June 26   United Nations Charter signed by U.S. and 50 other nations in San Francisco

July 16   United States successfully explodes first atomic bomb in New Mexico

July 17–August 2   Truman meets Stalin and Churchill at Potsdam Conference in suburb of Berlin

August 6   Atomic bomb dropped on Hiroshima

August 8   The Soviet Union declares war on Japan

August 9   Atomic bomb dropped on Nagasaki

August 14   The Japanese government announces its intention to surrender

September 2   Victory over Japan Day; World War II ends

PART III:
PROSPERITY, DEPRESSION,
AND WAR, 1920–1945

The quarter century following World War I was one of the most eventful periods of American history. These years featured new heights in economic prosperity and technological development, the most severe financial crash in all of American history and a corresponding economic depression, revolutionary developments in the role of the national government in American life, and another cataclysmic world conflict. Americans often profoundly disagreed on how to meet the challenges created by these events.

Uneven Economic Prosperity

Following World War I, and especially from 1923 to 1929, America enjoyed significant economic growth. Experts believed that a "permanent plateau" of prosperity had been reached. Innovative methods of manufacturing, such as the use of the assembly line and the replacement of steam power with electricity, greatly improved productivity. These and other technologies led to the development of new consumer goods—including the radio, the vacuum cleaner, and the refrigerator—and the creation of entire industries, including that of the automobile.

The automobile was perhaps the single key factor behind America's economic growth in the 1920s. Due to the manufacturing innovations of Henry Ford, the automobile was transformed from an expensive plaything for an elite few into an affordable necessity for the middle class. Passenger-car registrations rose from 8 million in 1920 to 23 million in 1930. The automobile industry employed thousands of workers and spurred the development of many secondary industries, including rubber and oil.

The development of the auto industry helped fuel a growing economy and rising standard of living for many Americans. During the 1920s, per capita income rose 20 percent, unemployment averaged 3.7 percent, and inflation was virtually nonexistent at less than 1 percent. Low inflation and steady economic growth meant higher standards of living; by the mid-1920s the typical middle-class family owned a car, a radio, a phonograph, a telephone, and other consumer goods. These goods were often purchased on installment plans from national chain stores—two other important economic developments of the 1920s.

Not all Americans shared in the economic good times. Older industries, such as the railroads and coal mines, struggled in the face of new competition. Due in part to a reduction of union membership, workers received a declining share of business profits. Farmers were hit hard by falling crop prices; net farm income dropped from $9.5 billion in 1920 to $5.3 billion in 1928.

However, despite the economic hardships of some, the majority of Americans continued to have confidence in the economy and in the pro-business Republican leadership in Washington, as evidenced by the Republican presidential election victories of 1920, 1924, and 1928 (despite significant political scandals during the Harding administration in the early 1920s). In many respects, the Democrats followed the Republicans' lead and offered few alternative economic proposals. Although in the country at large there were debates over taxes, the Federal Reserve System, and the stock market, these issues were not of fundamental concern to most Americans.

Culture Clash

The most burning controversies of the 1920s were not economic or political, but rather cultural. The decade was marked by numerous national disagreements on various social and cultural issues, ranging from the teaching of Darwinian evolution in public schools to the impact of immigrants on American society. To some degree the cultural debates of the 1920s reveal a clash between the traditional values of small-town America and the new values emerging in the modernizing American cities.

One of the defining controversies of the era was the national debate over the prohibition of alcohol, instituted by the Eighteenth Amendment to the Constitution in 1919 and eventually repealed by the Twenty-First Amendment in 1933. Prohibition was enthusiastically supported by many white Protestant residents of America's rural areas and small towns, especially in the South and the Midwest. It was generally opposed by several distinct groups of Americans—urban Catholic immigrants, the wealthy and cosmopolitan elite, intellectuals, and social liberals—whom many of Prohibition's supporters viewed with profound suspicion. In many respects, the debate for and against Prohibition reflected the underlying cultural divide in America at this time.

The most extreme reactionary movement of the 1920s was the revival of the Ku Klux Klan. Its members preached American racial, ethnic, and moral purity against the presumed threats posed by blacks, immigrants, Catholics, and others. At its height, membership in the Ku Klux Klan reached five million and attained significant political power in several states far beyond the boundaries of the Old South, the territory of the original Klan of the post–Civil War period. But financial and sexual scandals caused the membership and power of the new Klan to greatly decline after 1925.

The Great Depression and the New Deal

Debate on cultural issues was overshadowed by concern about the state of the economy following the stock market crash of October 1929 and the onset of the worst and longest economic collapse in America's history. The human suffering of the Great Depression can be only dimly perceived by looking at economic statistics, but a few numbers can provide a glimpse. Between 1929 and 1932, unemployment rose from 3 percent to nearly 25 percent. America's gross national product (GNP) plunged from $104 billion in 1929 to $59 billion in 1932. More than five thousand banks closed, wiping out the savings of millions of Americans. Farm and home foreclosures skyrocketed. All these economic calamities came at a time when there was little or no safety net of government relief, welfare programs, or unemployment compensation. Care of the unemployed was primarily a responsibility of private charities, which often found themselves stretched beyond their capabilities during the depression.

The initial response of government at all levels to this economic disaster was limited. At the federal level President Herbert Hoover strongly believed that government intrusion into the private sphere would undermine American individualism and contribute to the creation of an oppressive bureaucracy at best or full-blown socialism at worst. Elected president in 1928 with the promise of continued prosperity, Hoover saw his role as that of an "influential adviser and well-placed cheerleader." As such he exhorted business leaders to maintain high levels of employment while cutting back on production (since he believed that the country's economic dilemma resulted from an excess of goods in circulation). He also urged banking leaders to cooperate among themselves to prevent weak banks from failing. And he encouraged American workers and consumers to spend with the confidence that recovery was just around the corner. Hoover's approach proved unsuccessful at alleviating the Great Depression. He was defeated for reelection in 1932 by a wide margin.

Hoover's vanquisher was Franklin D. Roosevelt, a New York governor and Democratic politician who would go on to win an unprecedented four consecutive presidential elections and dominate American political life until his death in 1945. Roosevelt led the country both in its fight against the Great Depression and in its fight against Germany and Japan in World War II.

Pledging a "New Deal" to the American people, in his first term Roosevelt launched a flurry of federal programs aimed at bringing relief to beleaguered people and recovery and reform to the economy. These programs included public works projects to create jobs, government regulation and reform of the nation's financial institutions, a social security system for the elderly and retired, natural resource preservation, and collective bargaining guarantees for the American worker. Conservatives on the right argued that the New Deal was drifting dangerously into socialism; radicals on the left argued that the New Deal was too concerned with preserving an obsolete and disgraced capitalism. But such criticisms did not prevent Roosevelt's reelection by large margins to three subsequent terms in 1936, 1940, and 1944. Historians and economists still argue over the benefits of Roosevelt's New Deal and how much it helped America end its Great Depression (most conclude that the nation's involvement in World War II had a greater role). However, the New Deal did, for better or worse, greatly expand the size, reach, and responsibilities of the federal government in managing America's economy and providing for the people's welfare.

The End of Isolationism

Even as Franklin D. Roosevelt and his political opponents were arguing over various aspects of the New Deal, events in Europe and Asia were beginning to turn the country's attention to world affairs. Within a few years America would have to make the crucial decision over whether or not to intervene in yet another world war.

Following the rejection of American membership in the League of Nations, the new international organization championed by President Woodrow Wilson after World War I, most Americans shared an isolationist outlook. The Senate repeatedly rebuffed presidential efforts to sanction American membership on the World Court (an arm of the League of Nations). Congress passed immigration laws in the early 1920s that sharply limited the number of immigrants allowed into the country—another reflection of the isolationist spirit of the times.

In addition, many historians, writers, and some congressional committees severely criticized America's 1917 decision to intervene in World War I, blaming that choice on the conspirings of British diplomats, international bankers, and arms manufacturers. So persuasive were their arguments that isolationism returned in full force after World War I, reaching a peak in the mid-1930s when Congress passed a series of neutrality laws designed to prohibit Americans from lending money and selling arms to warring nations. These laws were an attempt to prevent repetition of what were viewed as the mistakes of 1917.

Meanwhile, international tensions were building around the world. The League of Nations, bereft of American support, was unable to prevent wars or protect nations from attack. Japan invaded the northern Chinese province of Manchuria in 1931. In Europe the countries of Italy and Germany had adopted fascist regimes and had become increasingly aggressive toward their neighbors. In 1937 Roosevelt suggested that such aggressor nations be "quarantined" by the collective action of peace-loving nations. But he quickly backed away from concrete action to carry out such a quarantine in the face of strong isolationist sentiment from members of Congress and the media.

Thus, when war broke out in Europe in 1939, Roosevelt had almost no choice but to proclaim American neutrality (although he did not follow Woodrow Wilson's 1914 lead by asking Americans to be neutral in their "hearts and minds" as well). For the next two years Roosevelt prodded Congress to modify the neutrality laws to permit American trade and aid to Great Britain, France (conquered by Germany in June 1940), and the Soviet Union (invaded by Germany in June 1941). He also presided over an American military buildup, pressed for the country's first peacetime draft, negotiated a controversial agreement to trade American destroyers for rights to British naval bases, and deployed the U.S. Navy to patrol the Atlantic Ocean against German submarines. All of these actions were opposed by a vociferous isolationist movement that abated only after Japan's surprise attack on Pearl Harbor on December 7, 1941.

World War II

The United States was far more heavily involved in World War II than it had been in World War I. Fifteen million men and 338,000 women served in America's armed forces. The United States suffered one million casualties during the war, including 292,000 battlefield deaths. The war affected most Americans at home as well. Income taxes increased significantly. The government rationed food and goods, including beef and gasoline, and housing shortages were a critical problem in many areas. However, by 1943 unemployment had almost vanished as millions of men and women went to work in defense plants manufacturing war materials. Most historians have credited the war and its massive military spending (the United States spent an estimated total of $350 billion during the war) for finally bringing the country out of the Great Depression.

World War II brought new challenges and opportunities for women and minorities. Between 1941 and 1945 six million women entered the labor force. Many worked in manufacturing jobs previously dominated by men. The war also opened up new roles and opportunities for blacks. Some fought in World War II in segregated units; others found employment in American factories. In response to pressure from A. Philip Randolph and other black leaders, President Roosevelt in June 1941 issued an executive order banning discriminatory employment practices in federal agencies and companies doing defense-related work. However, fearing sabotage and disloyalty, the U.S. government interned 112,000 members of another minority—Japanese-Americans—in detention camps during the war. Many of those detained lost their homes, businesses, and farms as a result of their internment.

The war in Europe ended in the spring of 1945 with the surrender of Germany. The war in Asia ended in August 1945 following the dropping of atomic bombs on the Japanese cities of Hiroshima and Nagasaki in early August 1945. The decision to use this new weapon, developed by a massive research effort during World War II, contributed to Japan's surrender, but it also engendered great controversy around the world.

With the war's end America faced the challenge of attempting to return its economy to peacetime conditions and reintegrate its soldiers into civilian life. There also came an American resolve not to repeat the retreat to isolationism that followed World War I. In 1945 America's political leadership was willing to assume a significant role in world politics. Not all Americans shared this determination, however. The years after World War II brought renewed debate on both the government's role in American life and America's role in the world.

Social and Cultural Issues of the Twenties

VIEWPOINT 21A

The Department of Justice Is Defending America from Communist Subversion (1920)

A. Mitchell Palmer (1872–1936)

A. Mitchell Palmer, appointed attorney general of the United States by President Woodrow Wilson in 1919, was one of the leading figures of America's first "Red Scare." The successful Bolshevik (communist) revolution in Russia in 1917 seemed to some Americans poised to spread to other nations following World War I. The fear (and, for some, the hope) of communist revolution in America grew in 1919 with the formation of two communist parties in the United States and the establishment of the Comintern (Communist International) in Russia to promote world revolution. That was also a year of social unrest in America. The war had left the American economy with high rates of inflation and unemployment. Workers launched thousands of strikes in 1919, including a general strike in the city of Seattle—strikes blamed by many on revolutionaries, who were also blamed for a wave of bomb scares and explosions.

In January 1920 Palmer, who harbored ambitions of running for president, organized and launched a nationwide crackdown against "suspicious" foreigners. Some were charged with breaking laws originally passed to limit opposition to World War I; many

Excerpted from A. Mitchell Palmer, "The Case Against the 'Reds,'" *Forum*, February 1920.

were held for months with no specific charges made against them at all. These government actions, which were widely criticized as disregarding civil liberties, became known as "Palmer raids." In the following viewpoint, taken from a February 1920 article written for the *Forum* magazine, Palmer justifies his actions as necessary to defend America from subversion from within.

What complaint does Palmer make about Congress? On what grounds does he refuse to make "nice distinctions" between violations of criminal laws and the ideals of radicals? How does he respond to charges that his deportations of suspicious immigrants were unjust?

I n this brief review of the work which the Department of Justice has undertaken, to tear out the radical seeds that have entangled American ideas in their poisonous theories, I desire not merely to explain what the real menace of communism is, but also to tell how we have been compelled to clean up the country almost unaided by any virile legislation. Though I have not been embarrassed by political opposition, I have been materially delayed because the present sweeping processes of arrests and deportation of seditious aliens should have been vigorously pushed by Congress last spring. The failure of this is a matter of record in the Congressional files.

The anxiety of that period in our responsibility when Congress, ignoring the seriousness of these vast organizations that were plotting to overthrow the Government, failed to act, has passed. The time came when it was obviously hopeless to expect the hearty co-operation of Congress, in the only way to stamp out these seditious societies in their open defiance of law by various forms of propaganda.

Like a prairie-fire, the blaze of revolution was sweeping over every American institution of law and order a year ago. It was eating its way into the homes of the American workman, its sharp tongues of revolutionary heat were licking the altars of the churches, leaping into the belfry of the school bell, crawling into the sacred corners of American homes, seeking to replace marriage vows with libertine laws, burning up the foundations of society.

Robbery, not war, is the ideal of communism. This has been demonstrated in Russia, Germany, and in America. As a foe, the anarchist is fearless of his own life, for his creed is a fanaticism that admits no respect of any other creed. Obviously it is the creed of any criminal mind, which reasons always from motives impossible to clean thought. Crime is the degenerate factor in society.

Upon these two basic certainties, first that the "Reds" were criminal aliens, and secondly that the American Government must prevent crime, it was decided that there could be no nice distinctions drawn between the theoretical ideals of the radicals and their actual violations of our national laws. An assassin may have brilliant intellectuality, he may be able to excuse his murder or robbery with fine oratory, but any theory which excuses crime is not wanted in America. This is no place for the criminal to flourish, nor will he do so, so long as the rights of common citizenship can be exerted to prevent him.

Our Government in Jeopardy

It has always been plain to me that when American citizens unite upon any national issue, they are generally right, but it is sometimes difficult to make the issue clear to them. If the Department of Justice could succeed in attracting the attention of our optimistic citizens to the issue of internal revolution in this country, we felt sure there would be no revolution. The Government was in jeopardy. My private information of what was being done by the organization known as the Communist Party of America, with headquarters in Chicago, of what was being done by the Communist Internationale under their manifesto planned at Moscow last March [1919] by Trotzky [Leon Trotsky], Lenine [Vladimir Lenin] and others, addressed "To the Proletariats of All Countries," of what strides the Communist Labor Party was making, removed all doubt. In this conclusion we did not ignore the definite standards of personal liberty, of free speech, which is the very temperament and heart of the people. The evidence was examined with the utmost care, with a personal leaning toward freedom of thought and word on all questions.

The whole mass of evidence, accumulated from all parts of the country, was scrupulously scanned, not merely for the written or spoken differences of view-

point as to the Government of the United States, but, in spite of these things, to see if the hostile declarations might not be sincere in their announced motive to improve our social order. There was no hope of such a thing.

By stealing, murder and lies, Bolshevism has looted Russia not only of its material strength, but of its moral force. A small clique of outcasts from the East Side of New York has attempted this, with what success we all know [several of the leaders of the Bolshevik revolution had resided in exile in New York City]. Because a disreputable alien—Leon Bronstein, the man who now calls himself Trotzky—can inaugurate a reign of terror from his throne room in the Kremlin; because this lowest of all types known to New York can sleep in the Czar's bed, while hundreds of thousands in Russia are without food or shelter, should Americans be swayed by such doctrines?

———— • ————

"No alien, advocating the overthrow of existing law and order in this country, shall escape arrest and prompt deportation."

———— • ————

Such a question, it would seem, should receive but one answer from America.

My information showed that communism in this country was an organization of thousands of aliens, who were direct allies of Trotzky. Aliens of the same misshapen caste of mind and indecencies of character, and it showed that they were making the same glittering promises of lawlessness, of criminal autocracy to Americans, that they had made to the Russian peasants. How the Department of Justice discovered upwards of 60,000 of these organized agitators of the Trotzky doctrine in the United States, is the confidential information upon which the Government is now sweeping the nation clean of such alien filth. Merely as a part of this review, to make it complete, it must be shown how the Department of Justice proceeds to cause deportations today. For the moment we must go back to my report to the Senate of the United States, on November 4th, 1919, in response to the Senate Resolution of October 14, 1919, which is as follows:

> Resolved, that the Attorney-General of the United States is requested to advise and inform the Senate whether or not the Department of Justice has taken the legal proceedings, and if not, why not, and if so, to what extent, for the arrest and punishment of the various persons within the United States, who, during recent days and weeks, and for a considerable

time, continuously previous thereto, it is alleged, have attempted to bring about the forcible overthrow of the Government of the United States; who, it is alleged have preached anarchy and perdition, and who it is alleged have advised the defiance of law and authority, both by the printing and circulation of printed newspapers, books, pamphlets, circulars, stickers, and dodgers, and also by spoken word; and who, in like manner it is alleged, have advised and openly advocated the unlawful obstruction of industry and the unlawful and violent destruction of property, in the pursuance of a deliberate plan and purpose to destroy existing property rights and to impede and obstruct the conduct of business essential to the prosperity and life of the community.

Also the Attorney-General is requested to advise and inform the Senate whether or not the Department of Justice has taken legal proceedings for the arrest and deportation of aliens, who, it is alleged, have, within the United States, permitted the acts aforesaid, and if not, why not, and if so, to what extent.

In replying to this request, I found it necessary to divide the subject under three headings as follows:

(1) The Conditions of Our Legislation; (2) The Deportation of Aliens; (3) General Activities of the Bureau of Investigation of the Department of Justice.

Briefly, in this article, the entire surface of the work of the Department of Justice will be surveyed.

Sedition Reached by Espionage Act

It was shown in my report to the Senate that the Espionage Act, approved June 15, 1917, and amended May 16, 1918, was invoked to be used against seditious utterances and acts, although I felt that it was limited to acts and utterances only which tended to weaken the waging of actual hostilities. . . . Nevertheless, I caused to be brought several test prosecutions in order to obtain a court ruling on the Espionage Law and its application to seditions committed since the cessation of the armed activity of our forces.

I did this because our general statutes as to treason and rebellion do not apply to the present radical activities, with the exception of Section 6 of the Federal Penal Code of 1910, which says:

If two or more persons in any State or Territory or in any place subject to the jurisdiction of the United States conspire to overthrow, put down or to destroy by force, the Government of the United States, or to levy war against them, or to oppose by force the authority thereof, or by force to prevent, hinder or delay, the execution of any law of the United States, or by force to seize, take or possess any property of the United States, contrary to the authority thereof, they shall each be fined, not more than $5,000 or imprisonment not more than six years, or both.

Although this Act by no means covered individual activities, under this law I prosecuted the El Arieto

Society, an anarchistic organization in operation in Buffalo, N.Y., indicting three of its members for circulating a manifesto which was an appeal to the proletariat to arise and destroy the Government of the United States by force, and substitute Bolshevism or anarchy in place thereof. It was printed in Spanish. Phrases such as, "the proletariat of all countries to invite to participate the revolution," "for all others who suffer the evils of servitude must join in the conflict," "to attach the State directly and assail it without hesitation or compunction," were uncompromisingly seditious advice. In threatening the officers of the Government, the manifesto went on to say, presumably addressing the officers themselves:

Cannibals, your hour of reckoning has arrived. You have fattened before having your throats cut like hogs. You haven't lived and consequently cannot die decently like men. You are at your wits ends and at the prospects of millions of human beings everywhere rising and not only asking, but demanding and executing vengeance for the promotion of your usurpt interests. Yes, they will overwhelm you. We are convinced that rebellion is the noble vindication of slaves, that from generation to generation the shameful reproach of slavery has now come. Make way for Bolshevism, for the Department of Labor, Mines, Railroads, fields, factories, and shops. Let the Soviet be organized promptly. The ideal is not converted into facts until it has come to consciousness after having been acquired by the sacrifice of innumerable voluntary victims.

On motion to dismiss the indictment this case came before Judge Hazel of the Western District Court of New York, July 24, 1919, who, after hearing counsel, dismissed the case and discharged the defendants. In his opinion the Court, after citing Section 6, said:

I do not believe that the acts and deeds set forth in the indictment and the evidence given in support of it establish an offense such as this Section which I have just read contemplates.

However, the language of this Spanish document was so violent and desperate in its declarations of defiance to the existing Government of the United States, that I, at once, placed the entire record of this case before the Commissioner of Immigration, with a recommendation that the defendants involved be deported as undesirable aliens.

All deportation activities conducted since by the Department of Justice against the "Reds" have been with the co-operation of the Department of Labor, which issued the warrants of arrest and deportation recommended by evidence that meets the conditions of the Federal Penal Code of 1910. I pointed out to the Senate certain classes of radical activities that might come under certain sections of this Penal Code:

1. Those who have "attempted to bring about the forcible overthrow of the Government of the United States have committed no crime unless their acts amount to treason, rebellion or seditious conspiracy." This is defined in Section 1, 4 and 6 of the Criminal Code above quoted.

There were other activities of the Reds, however, for which there was no legislation. These were:

2. The preaching of anarchy and sedition is not a crime under the general criminal statutes of the United States.

3. Advising the defiance of law is not a crime under the general criminal laws whether the same be done by printing and circulating literature or by the spoken word.

4. Nor is the advising and openly advocating the unlawful obstruction of industry and the unlawful and violent destruction of property a crime under the United States general statutes.

These conclusions were reached after wide consultation with the best criminal lawyers in the country. In my testimony before the sub-committee of the Judiciary Committee of the Senate on July 14, 1919, at its request, I had fully outlined the conditions threatening internal revolution in the nation that confronted us. Legislation which I then recommended to meet this great menace has not been enacted. This is not my fault, for I knew that Congress was fully aware of the "Reds'" activities in this country.

Many States passed certain acts which embodied the basis of my request to Congress for national legislation bearing upon radicalism. California, Indiana, Michigan, New York, Ohio, Pennsylvania, Washington and West Virginia have passed State laws governing the rebellious acts of the "Reds" in their separate territories. These States have infinitely greater legal force at their command against the revolutionary element than the United States Government, for detecting and punishing seditious acts. In their equipment of men to carry out their laws, they far surpass the facilities of the Department of Justice. New York City alone has 12,000 policemen charged with the duty of investigation, and the District Attorney of New York County has a force of over fifty prosecuting attorneys.

Under the appropriations granted by Congress to the Department of Justice, the maximum number of men engaged in the preparation of the violation of all United States laws is limited to about 500 for the entire country. Startling as this fact may seem to the reader who discovers it for the first time, it is the highest testimony to the services of these men, that the Department of Justice of the United States, is today, a human net that no outlaw can escape. It has been netted together in spite of Congressional indif-ference, intensified by the individual patriotism of its personnel aroused to the menace of revolution, inspired to superlative action above and beyond private interests.

One of the chief incentives for the present activity of the Department of Justice against the "Reds" has been the hope that American citizens will, themselves, become voluntary agents for us, in a vast organization for mutual defense against the sinister agitation of men and women aliens, who appear to be either in the pay or under the criminal spell of Trotzky and Lenine.

Deportations Under Immigration Laws

Temporary failure to seize the alien criminals in this country who are directly responsible for spreading the unclean doctrines of Bolshevism here, only increased the determination to get rid of them. Obviously, their offenses were related to our immigration laws, and it was finally decided to act upon that principle. Those sections of the Immigration Law applicable to the deportation of aliens committing acts enumerated in the Senate Resolution of October 14, 1919, above quoted, were found in the Act of Congress, approved October 16, 1918, amending the immigration laws of the United States.

By the administration of this law deportations have been made, the law being as follows:

Be it enacted by the Senate and House of Representatives of the United States of America in Congress assembled:

Sec. 1. That aliens who are anarchists; aliens who believe in or advocate the overthrow by force or violence of the Government of the United States or of all forms of law; aliens who disbelieve in or who are opposed to all organized government; aliens who advocate or teach the assassination of public officials; aliens who advocate or teach the unlawful destruction of property; aliens who are members of or affiliated with any organization that entertains a belief in, teaches, or advocates the overthrow by force or by violence of the Government of the United States or of all forms of law, or that entertains or teaches disbelief in or opposition to all organized Government, or that advocates the duty, necessity or propriety of the unlawful assaulting or killing of any officer or officers, either of specific individuals or of officers generally, of the Government of the United States, or of any other organized Government, because of his or their official character, or that advocates or teaches the unlawful destruction of property, shall be excluded from admission into the United States.

Sec. 2. That any alien who, at any time, after entering the United States, is found to have been at the time of entry, or to become thereafter, a member of any one of the classes of aliens enumerated in Sec.

1 of this Act, shall upon the warrant of the Secretary of Labor, be taken into custody and deported in the manner provided in the Immigration Act of Feb. 5, 1917. The provisions of this Section shall be applicable to the classes of aliens mentioned in this Act irrespective of the time of their entry into the United States.

Although this law is entirely under the jurisdiction of the Department of Labor, it seemed to be the only means at my disposal of attacking the radical movement. To further this plan, as Congress had seen fit to refuse appropriations to the Department of Labor which might have enabled it to act vigorously against the "Reds," I offered to co-operate with the immigration officials to the fullest extent. My appropriation became available July 19, 1919. I then organized what is known as the Radical Division.

Briefly this is a circumstantial statement of the present activities of the Department of Justice, co-operating with the Department of Labor, against the "Reds." They require no defense, nor can I accept as true the counter claims of the "Reds" themselves, who, apparently indifferent to their disgrace, violent in their threats against the United States Government, until they are out of sight and sound of it, betray the characterless ideas and purposes that Trotzky has impressed upon the criminal classes which constitute communism.

Will Deportations Check Bolshevism?

Behind, and underneath, my own determination to drive from our midst the agents of Bolshevism with increasing vigor and with greater speed, until there are no more of them left among us, so long as I have the responsible duty of that task, I have discovered the hysterical methods of these revolutionary humans with increasing amazement and suspicion. In the confused information that sometimes reaches the people, they are compelled to ask questions which involve the reasons for my acts against the "Reds." I have been asked, for instance, to what extent deportation will check radicalism in this country. Why not ask what will become of the United States Government if these alien radicals are permitted to carry out the principles of the Communist Party as embodied in its so-called laws, aims and regulations?

There wouldn't be any such thing left. In place of the United States Government we should have the horror and terrorism of bolsheviki tyranny such as is destroying Russia now. Every scrap of radical literature demands the overthrow of our existing government. All of it demands obedience to the instincts of criminal minds, that is, to the lower appetites, material and moral. The whole purpose of communism appears to be a mass formation of the criminals of the world to overthrow the decencies of private life, to usurp property that they have not earned, to disrupt the present order of life regardless of health, sex or religious rights. By a literature that promises the wildest dreams of such low aspirations, that can occur to only the criminal minds, communism distorts our social law.

The chief appeal communism makes is to "The Worker." If they can lure the wage-earner to join their own gang of thieves, if they can show him that he will be rich if he steals, so far they have succeeded in betraying him to their own criminal course.

Read this manifesto issued in Chicago:

THE COMMUNIST PARTY MANIFESTO

The world is on the verge of a new era. Europe is in revolt. The masses of Asia are stirring uneasily. Capitalism is in collapse. The workers of the world are seeing a new light and securing new courage. Out of the night of war is coming a new day.

The spectre of communism haunts the world of capitalism. Communism, the hope of the workers to end misery and oppression.

The workers of Russia smashed the front of international Capitalism and Imperialism. They broke the chains of the terrible war; and in the midst of agony, starvation and the attacks of the Capitalists of the world, they are creating a new social order.

The class war rages fiercely in all nations. Everywhere the workers are in a desperate struggle against their capitalist masters. The call to action has come. The workers must answer the call!

The Communist Party of America is the party of the working class. The Communist Party proposes to end Capitalism and organize a workers' industrial republic. The workers must control industry and dispose of the product of industry. The Communist Party is a party realizing the limitation of all existing workers' organizations and proposes to develop the revolutionary movement necessary to free the workers from the oppression of Capitalism. The Communist Party insists that the problems of the American worker are identical with the problems of the workers of the world.

These are the revolutionary tenets of Trotzky and the Communist Internationale. Their manifesto further embraces the various organizations in this country of men and women obsessed with discontent, having disorganized relations to American society. These include the I.W.W.'s [International Workers of the World], the most radical socialists, the misguided anarchists, the agitators who oppose the limitations of unionism, the moral perverts and the hysterical neurasthenic women who abound in communism. The phraseology of their manifesto is practically the same wording as was used by the Bolsheviks for their

International Communist Congress. . . .

There is no legislation at present which can reach an American citizen who is discontented with our system of American Government, nor is it necessary. The dangerous fact to us is that the Communist Party of America is actually affiliated and adheres to the teaching program and tactics of the 3d Internationale. Consider what this means. The first congress of the Communist Nationale held March 6, 1919, in Moscow, subscribed to by Trotzky and Lenine, adopted the following:

> This makes necessary the disarming of the bourgeoisie at the proper time, the arming of the laborer, and the formation of a communist army as the protectors of the rules of the proletariat and the inviolability of the social structure.

When we realize that each member of the Communist Party of America pledges himself to the principles above set forth, deportation of men and women bound to such a theory is a very mild reformatory sentence. . . .

It has been inferred by the "Reds" that the United States Government, by arresting and deporting them, is returning to the autocracy of Czardom, adopting the system that created the severity of Siberian banishment. My reply to such charges is, that in our determination to maintain our government we are treating our alien enemies with extreme consideration. To deny them the privilege of remaining in a country which they have openly deplored as an unenlightened community, unfit for those who prefer the privileges of Bolshevism, should be no hardship. It strikes me as an odd form of reasoning that these Russian Bolsheviks who extol the Bolshevik rule, should be so unwilling to return to Russia. The nationality of most of the alien "Reds" is Russian and German. There is almost no other nationality represented among them.

It has been impossible in so short a space to review the entire menace of the internal revolution in this country as I know it, but this may serve to arouse the American citizen to its reality, its danger, and the great need of united effort to stamp it out, under our feet, if needs be. It is being done. The Department of Justice will pursue the attack of these "Reds" upon the Government of the United States with vigilance, and no alien, advocating the overthrow of existing law and order in this country, shall escape arrest and prompt deportation.

It is my belief that while they have stirred discontent in our midst, while they have caused irritating strikes, and while they have infected our social ideas with the disease of their own minds and their unclean morals, we can get rid of them! and not until we have done so shall we have removed the menace of Bolshevism for good.

VIEWPOINT 21B

The Department of Justice Is Violating Constitutional Freedoms (1920)

National Popular Government League

In January 1920 the U.S. Department of Justice, under the leadership of Attorney General A. Mitchell Palmer and his assistant J. Edgar Hoover, launched surprise raids on meetings of suspected communist and anarchist agitators. Most of the 6,000 people arrested were foreign immigrants who faced the possibility of deportation. Many were detained for months.

Many Americans questioned the tactics of the "Palmer raids." Among them were members of the National Popular Government League (NPGL), a group of prominent liberal lawyers and others including Felix Frankfurter (a future Supreme Court justice), Zechariah Chafee Jr. (Harvard law professor and author), and Roscoe Pound (dean of Harvard Law School). The league investigated the Department of Justice actions against radicals and immigrants, and in 1920 released a stinging report accusing the U.S. government of wholesale violations of civil liberties. The following viewpoint consists of the conclusions of the NPGL report and selected excerpts from the testimony of people arrested by the government, appended to the report as documentary evidence.

Do the members of the National Popular Government League take a stand here on the merits of radicalism? What do they find most disturbing about the government's actions? What allegations of violations of the Constitution can you find in the testimony of those arrested?

TO THE AMERICAN PEOPLE:
For more than six months we, the undersigned lawyers, whose sworn duty it is to uphold the Constitution and Laws of the United States, have seen with growing apprehension the continued violation of that Constitution and breaking of those Laws by the Department of Justice of the United States government.

Under the guise of a campaign for the suppression of radical activities, the office of the Attorney General, acting by its local agents throughout the country, and giving express instructions from Washington,

From the National Popular Government League, *Report upon the Illegal Practices of the United States Department of Justice*. Washington, DC: National Popular Government League, 1920.

has committed continual illegal acts. Wholesale arrests both of aliens and citizens have been made without warrant or any process of law; men and women have been jailed and held *incommunicado* without access of friends or counsel; homes have been entered without search-warrant and property seized and removed; other property has been wantonly destroyed; workingmen and workingwomen suspected of radical views have been shamefully abused and maltreated. Agents of the Department of Justice have been introduced into radical organizations for the purpose of informing upon their members or inciting them to activities; these agents have even been instructed from Washington to arrange meetings upon certain dates for the express object of facilitating wholesale raids and arrests. In support of these illegal acts, and to create sentiment in its favor, the Department of Justice has also constituted itself a propaganda bureau, and has sent to newspapers and magazines of this country quantities of material designed to excite public opinion against radicals, all at the expense of the government and outside the scope of the Attorney General's duties.

Illegal Acts

We make no argument in favor of any radical doctrine as such, whether Socialist, Communist or Anarchist. No one of us belongs to any of these schools of thought. Nor do we now raise any question as to the Constitutional protection of free speech and a free press. We are concerned solely with bringing to the attention of the American people the utterly illegal acts which have been committed by those charged with the highest duty of enforcing the laws—acts which have caused widespread suffering and unrest, have struck at the foundation of American free institutions, and have brought the name of our country into disrepute.

These acts may be grouped under the following heads:

(1) Cruel and Unusual Punishments:

The Eighth Amendment to the United States Constitution provides:

> Excessive bail shall not be required nor excessive fines imposed, nor cruel and unusual punishments inflicted.

Punishments of the utmost cruelty, and heretofore unthinkable in America, have become usual. Great numbers of persons arrested, both aliens and citizens, have been threatened, beaten with blackjacks, struck with fists, jailed under abominable conditions, or actually tortured. . . .

(2) Arrests without Warrant:

The Fourth Amendment to the Constitution provides:

> The right of the people to be secure in their persons, houses, papers, and effects, against unreasonable searches and seizures, shall not be violated, and no Warrants shall issue, but upon probable cause, supported by Oath or affirmation, and particularly describing the place to be searched, and the persons or things to be seized.

Many hundreds of citizens and aliens alike have been arrested in wholesale raids, without warrants or pretense of warrants. They have then either been released, or have been detained in police stations or jails for indefinite lengths of time while warrants were being applied for. This practice of making mass raids and mass arrests without warrant has resulted directly from the instructions, both written and oral, issued by the Department of Justice at Washington. . . .

(3) Unreasonable Searches and Seizures:

The Fourth Amendment has been quoted above.

In countless cases agents of the Department of Justice have entered the homes, offices, or gathering places of persons suspected of radical affiliations, and, without pretense of any search warrant, have seized and removed property belonging to them for use by the Department of Justice. In many of these raids property which could not be removed or was not useful to the Department, was intentionally smashed and destroyed. . . .

(4) Provocative Agents:

We do not question the right of the Department of Justice to use its agents in the Bureau of Investigation to ascertain when the law is being violated. But the American people has never tolerated the use of undercover provocative agents or "agents provocateurs," such as have been familiar in old Russia or Spain. Such agents have been introduced by the Department of Justice into the radical movements, have reached positions of influence therein, have occupied themselves with informing upon or instigating acts which might be declared criminal, and at the express direction of Washington have brought about meetings of radicals in order to make possible wholesale arrests at such meetings. . . .

(5) Compelling Persons to be Witnesses against Themselves:

The Fifth Amendment provides as follows:

> No person . . . shall be compelled in any criminal case to be a witness against himself, nor be deprived of life, liberty, or property, without due process of law.

It has been the practice of the Department of Justice and its agents, after making illegal arrests without warrant, to question the accused person and to force admissions from him by terrorism, which admissions were subsequently to be used against him in deportation proceedings. . . .

(6) Propaganda by the Department of Justice:

The legal functions of the Attorney General are: to advise the Government on questions of law, and to prosecute persons who have violated federal statutes. For the Attorney General to go into the field of propaganda against radicals is a deliberate misuse of his office and a deliberate squandering of funds entrusted to him by Congress. . . .

Evidence Presented

The Exhibits attached are only a small part of the evidence which may be presented of the continued violation of law by the Attorney General's Department. These Exhibits are, to the best of our knowledge and belief (based upon careful investigation) truthful both in substance and detail. Drawn mainly from the four centers of New York City, Boston, Mass., Detroit, Mich., and Hartford, Conn., we know them to be typical of conditions which have prevailed in many parts of the country.

Since these illegal acts have been committed by the highest legal powers in the United States, there is no final appeal from them except to the conscience and condemnation of the American people. American institutions have not in fact been protected by the Attorney General's ruthless suppression. On the contrary those institutions have been seriously undermined, and revolutionary unrest has been vastly intensified. No organizations of radicals acting through propaganda over the last six months could have created as much revolutionary sentiment in America as has been created by the acts of the Department of Justice itself.

Even were one to admit that there existed any serious "Red menace" before the Attorney General started his "unflinching war" against it, his campaign has been singularly fruitless. Out of the many thousands suspected by the Attorney General (he had already listed 60,000 by name and history on Nov. 14, 1919, aliens and citizens), what do the figures show as net results? Prior to January 1, 1920, there were actually deported 263 persons. Since January 1 there have been actually deported 18 persons. Since January 1 there have been ordered deported an additional 529 persons, and warrants for 1,547 have been cancelled (after full hearings and consideration of the evidence) by Assistant Secretary of Labor Louis F. Post, to whose courageous reëstablishment of American Constitutional Law in deportation proceedings are due the attacks that have been made upon him. The Attorney General has consequently got rid of 810 alien suspects, which, on his own

showing, leaves him at least 59,160 persons (aliens and citizens) still to cope with.

A Government of Laws

It has always been the proud boast of America that this is a government of laws and not of men. Our Constitution and laws have been based on the simple elements of human nature. Free men cannot be driven and repressed; they must be led. Free men respect justice and follow truth, but arbitrary power they will oppose until the end of time. There is no danger of revolution so great as that created by suppression, by ruthlessness, and by deliberate violation of the simple rules of American law and American decency.

It is a fallacy to suppose that, any more than in the past, any servant of the people can safely arrogate to himself unlimited authority. To proceed upon such a supposition is to deny the fundamental American theory of the consent of the governed. Here is no question of a vague and threatened menace, but a present assault upon the most sacred principles of our Constitutional liberty. . . .

EXHIBIT 1.

HARTFORD JAIL SITUATION.

In Bridgeport, Conn., on November 8, 1919, various workingmen had come together to discuss ways and means for buying an automobile to be employed for instruction purposes. The meeting was raided and 63 men arrested without warrants by agents of the Department of Justice and taken to the police station. A day or two later, 16 of these were released. The remaining 47, after being held three days in the police station, where they slept on iron bunks without cover or mattress, and where they were fed little or nothing, were transferred by the Department of Justice to the Hartford jail. Other persons who were arrested in this way or who had applied at the Hartford jail for permission to see their friends, were also taken up and confined in the jail. There were finally 97 men held for deportation. Most of them were questioned by Department of Justice agents; some were beaten or threatened with hanging or suffocation in order to obtain answers from them. Warrants of arrest for these men were requested and obtained from the Department of Labor by the Department of Justice. Most of the 97 prisoners remained in practically solitary confinement until the end of April—five months. When the facts finally came to the attention of Mr. Louis F. Post, Assistant Secretary of Labor, he ordered the men all transferred to the Immigrant Station at Deer Island, Boston.

During these five months the prisoners were allowed no reading matter; were kept alone in their cells except for occasional visits from Department of

Justice agents or hearings before Department of Labor Inspectors; were refused, in some cases, knowledge of the charges against them; were refused, in some cases, knowledge of the amount of bail under which they were held; were allowed only 2 to 5 minutes a day to wash their face and hands at a sink outside their cells, and 5 minutes once a month to wash their bodies in a tub, were given practically no exercise, and were fed with foul and insufficient food.

In the Hartford jail there exist four punishment rooms, all alike, unventilated and utterly dark, size 4 feet 3 inches by 8 feet 10 inches, with solid concrete floors, no furniture of any kind, and placed over the pump room of the boiler so that the temperature in them becomes unbearably high. A number of the supposed anarchist or Communist prisoners, probably ten to fifteen, were confined in these rooms for periods of 36 to 60 hours. During their imprisonment in the suffocating heat without air, they were given one glass of water and one slice of bread every 12 hours. Some of them on being released had to be revived before they could be carried to their cells; one man who was in only 36 hours was able to get to his cell unaided.

These Hartford prisoners were practically buried alive for five months, being even denied the privilege of seeing their relatives or friends, who made constant attempts to communicate with them. Only after a lawyer had finally succeeded in gaining access to the jail, were the conditions at all ameliorated and the men ultimately moved to Deer Island. That there were no substantial charges against at least ten of them is shown by the fact that after being held in $10,000 bail for two months and a half, those ten were released without bail on January 24th. It seems probable that at least a majority had no political views of any special nature, but were simply workingmen of Russian nationality speaking little or no English.

The foregoing statement, with many details, is evidenced by the statements of Isaac Shorr of the New York bar, who represented these men, of an impartial expert investigator who was sent to the jail, and personal interviews with some of the men. Affidavits by some of them follow:

EXHIBIT 1a.

State of Connecticut,
  City of Bridgeport, ss [sworn statement]:

SEMEON NAKHWAT, being duly sworn, deposes and says:

I was born in Grodno, Russia, and am thirty-three years old and unmarried.

In the autumn of 1919 I was a member of the Union of Russian Workers. I am not an anarchist, Socialist or Bolshevik and do not take much interest in political theories. I joined the Russian Workers because I was a workman speaking Russian and wanted to associate with other Russians and have the benefit of the social intercourse and instruction in mechanics which the society gave. By trade I am a machinist.

On November 8, 1919, I was at a meeting of Russians in Bridgeport, who had come together to discuss ways and means for buying an automobile to be used for instruction purposes. At that time I was employed by the American Brass Co. in Ansonia as a machinist, working a ten hour day at 46½ cents an hour. At the meeting I speak of, I was arrested with all the other men at the meeting, 63 in number. The arrest was made by Edward J. Hickey, a special agent of the Department of Justice, who had helping him about fourteen Bridgeport policemen in uniform and about nine Department of Justice agents in plain clothes. No warrant of arrest was shown me then or at any other time, nor did I see any warrant shown to anyone else who was arrested.

———— • ————

"Under the guise of a campaign for the suppression of radical activities, the office of the Attorney General . . . has committed continual illegal acts."

———— • ————

I was taken with the other men to the police station on Fairfield Avenue and held there three days, being in a cell with two other men. During these three days no one gave me any hearing or asked me any questions. I was then taken to Hartford, Conn., with about forty-eight of the men, being informed that the rest of those arrested had been released.

I was held in the Hartford Jail for six weeks without any hearing. In the seventh week I had one hearing before the Labor Department, which hearing was held in the Post Office Building and was then returned to jail.

In the thirteenth week of my confinement Edward J. Hickey came into my cell and asked me to give him the address of a man called Boyko in Greenpoint, Brooklyn. I did not know this man and told Hickey that I did not. Hickey thereupon struck me twice with his fist, once in the forehead and once in the jaw, whereupon I fell. He then kicked me and I became unconscious. Hickey is a big man, weighing two hundred pounds. For three weeks after this I suffered severe pain where I was kicked in the back.

In the last part of January or early in February, my finger was severely infected. I asked the guards to let me have a doctor to treat my finger. They refused, and I asked again, whereupon they said to come with them. They took me to a room in the basement of the jail with a cement floor, cement walls and an iron door. The room was pitch dark, and the only means for lighting or ventilating it that I could see was a small hole in the door. The floor of this room was hot and the walls were very warm to the touch. I stayed in this room for thirty-six hours, from 8:30 one morning to 8:30 the following evening. At times the room was so hot that I was forced to remove all my clothing except my underwear; at other times I found it necessary to resume my clothing. The evening of the first day I was given one glass of water and one slice of bread, and the morning of the second day I was given the same. I received no other food or water during the thirty-six hours. There was no furniture in the room, and no sanitary facilities except an iron pail. On my release from this room I was barely able to move. No medical attention was provided for my infected finger which did not heal entirely until some time after my release from jail in April. . . .

EXHIBIT 1b.

STATE OF CONNECTICUT,
  City of Bridgeport, ss:

PETER MUSEK, being duly sworn, says:
I reside at No. 437 Helen Street, Bridgeport, Conn. I am 33 years of age and am working as a tailor in Bridgeport. On the 24th day of December, 1919, I left Bridgeport for Hartford and applied for a pass to see a friend, Mike Lozuk, who was arrested on the 8th day of November, 1919, at a meeting place of Russians in Bridgeport. I heard that Lozuk was confined in the Hartford Jail and wanted to see me. As soon as I appeared in the U.S. Post Office Building at Hartford, Conn., where I asked for a pass to see Lozuk, I was searched and immediately put under arrest and questioned by an agent of the Department of Justice. Six men, I presume agents of the Department of Justice, questioned me and threatened to hang me if I do not tell them the truth. In one instance, an agent of the Department of Justice, whose name I do not know, brought a rope and tied it around my neck, stating that he will hang me immediately if I do not tell him who conducts the meetings and who are the main workers in an organization called the Union of Russian Workers. This inquisition lasted fully three hours, after which I was again threatened to be put into a gas-room and suffocated unless I gave more particulars about other men in the Union of Russian Workers. This was all done in the U.S. Post Office Building in the presence of six agents of the Department of Justice.
From the Post Office Building I was taken to a police station in Hartford, where I was placed in a cell and released about eleven o'clock A.M. on the 26th day of December and taken to the U.S. Post Office Building, where I was again questioned by about five agents of the Department of Justice up to five o'clock in the afternoon. A statement was prepared by these agents in English, which I was ordered to sign. After this I was taken to jail, where I was kept for fully two weeks without any hearings. No visitors were allowed to see me. I was not permitted to write any letters. At the end of about two weeks I was chained to another man and led through the streets of Hartford from the jail to the Department of Justice, where I was questioned by an immigration inspector. At the end of the hearing I was informed that if I wish to be released I will have to put up $10,000 bail. Then I was taken back to the jail, where I remained continually up to and including the 18th day of March, 1920, when I was released on bail.

During my confinement I was given an opportunity to write two letters, was not permitted to have any reading matter and was not given any writing paper, so that I remained in the cell all this time without an opportunity to even see a newspaper or see a friend, with the exception of three visits granted to my sister, who made numerous attempts to see me. My cell was always locked with the exception of two or three minutes a day, when I was permitted to run to a sink and wash my face. I was not even permitted to speak to my neighbor in the next cell, even though I could not see him because of an intervening wall. I was hungry during all the time of my confinement, for it was impossible to eat the food that was supplied by the jail, and I was not permitted to buy anything with my own money. On four or five occasions my sister brought some food, which was delivered to the office and then delivered to me by the jailer. This food assisted materially, and if not for that I would probably have starved. . . .

EXHIBIT 2.

RAID ON RUSSIAN PEOPLE'S HOUSE.

On November 7, 1919, the most violent of six raids, by agents of the Department of Justice and the New York Bomb Squad, was made upon the Russian People's House, 133 East 15th Street, New York City, in search of supposed anarchists and anarchistic literature.

The executive committee of the Federated Unions of Russian Workers occupied an office in the building, which was confined to one room. The other rooms were used principally as educational classrooms, except a small restaurant or cafeteria.

At the time of the raid the Department agents had a few warrants for the arrest of supposed offenders.

They went through the building and broke up and destroyed most of the furniture in the place, including desks and typewriting machines. They "beat up" the persons in the place, amounting to several hundred, with blackjacks and stair rails; broke up all the classes then in session and herded the students to the stairways, beating them as they went, shoving them from the landing on to the stairway so that many fell and rolled down the stairs and were trampled upon by those who were shoved after them.

After this raid several hundred prisoners were taken to the office of the Department of Justice at 13 Park Row and there put through the third degree of inquisition. Less than one-fifth of them were held for deportation charges and all the remainder were released to go about their business as being innocent of any wrongdoing.

Many of the persons assaulted suffered serious wounds, and one man who was taken to Ellis Island was in a terrible condition. The manner in which these acts were committed caused a mass meeting of protest to be held the following evening (November 8) at Madison Square Garden. . . .

EXHIBIT 2b.

CITY OF NEW YORK,
  County of New York,
    State of New York, ss:

MITCHEL LAVROWSKY, being duly sworn deposes and says: I am fifty years old; am married and have two children; I reside at #999 Southern Boulevard Borough of Bronx, City of New York, I am a professional teacher and was Principal and teacher in a Russian High School known as Iglitsky High School for fifteen years in the City of Odessa, Russia; I declared my intention to become a citizen of the United States.

On the 7th day of November, 1919, I conducted a class in Russian at 133 East 15th Street, in the Borough of Manhattan, City of New York. At about 8:00 o'clock in the evening, while I was teaching algebra and Russian, an agent of the Department of Justice opened the door of the school, walked in with a revolver in his hands and ordered everybody in the school to step aside; then ordered me to step towards him. I wear eye-glasses and the agent of the Department of Justice ordered me to take them off. Then without any provocation, [he] struck me on the head and simultaneously two others struck and beat me brutally. After I was beaten and without strength to stand on my feet, I was thrown down stairs and while I rolled down, other men, I presume also agents of the Department of Justice, beat me with pieces of wood which I later found out were obtained by breaking the banisters. I sustained a fracture of my

head, left shoulder, left foot, and right side. Then I was ordered to wash myself and was taken, as I now understand, to 13 Park Row [offices of the Department of Justice], Borough of Manhattan, City of New York, where I was examined by various people and released about 12:00 midnight. . . .

EXHIBIT 2c.

CITY OF NEW YORK,
  County of New York,
    State of New York, ss:

NICAOLI MELIKOFF being duly sworn, says: I reside at 342 East 13th Street, in the Borough of Manhattan, City of New York; I was one of the students in a class-room at 133 East 15th Street, on the second floor. While the class was in session, a few detectives came in and ordered everybody to get up and keep quiet, which everybody obeyed. They then searched everyone in the class-room including me. I had Twenty ($20) Dollars in my pocket, in addition to other papers. These $20 including the other papers were taken from me and I never received the money back. We were then ordered to go out of the room. Outside of the class-room there were two detectives standing and everyone that passed out of the room was beaten. I was struck on my head, and being the last one to go out, was attacked by one detective, who knocked me down again, sat on my back, pressing me down to the floor with his knee and bending my body back until blood flowed out of my mouth and nose. I was then taken to a sink where I was ordered to drink some water and was also ordered to wash my face. After this, I was thrown down stairs where I fell with my head down to the ground floor, after which I was arrested and taken to 13 Park Row, where I was questioned and released. . . .

EXHIBIT 5.

JAILING RADICALS IN DETROIT.
By Frederick R. Barkley.
(*The Nation*, N.Y., Jan. 31, 1920, and April 10, 1920.)

On January 2 Arthur L. Barkey, chief agent of the Department of Justice in Detroit, received an order from Attorney General Palmer instructing Mr. Barkey, according to his own statement, to raid the headquarters of a group of interdicted organizations, principally the Communist party "as long as they continue to meet," in a "supreme effort to break the back of radicalism" in Detroit. As a result, eight hundred men were imprisoned for from three to six days in a dark, windowless, narrow corridor running around the big central areaway of the city's antiquated Federal Building; they slept on the bare stone floor at night. . . . They were compelled to stand in long lines for access to the solitary drinking fountain and the one toilet; they were denied all food for twenty hours, and after that were fed on what their families brought in; and they were refused all communication with relatives or with attorneys. These eight hundred men, so closely packed that they had to step over one another's bodies to move about at all, included in their number citizens and aliens, college graduates and laborers, skilled mechanics making $15 a day and boys not yet out of short trousers. They were seized without warrant while attending dances and classes in physical geography and similar subjects. . . .

[On] January 19, the 300 men left of the 800 seized are housed in an old army fort here. In addition, about 140 are out on bond. Warrants for holding these 440 arrived from Washington on January 12, ten days after the raids.

Three months after their arrest in mass raids conducted by the Department of Justice, 150 Detroit aliens are still held in an old army fort in this city, with no information available from Immigration Bureau officials, who are in charge of them, concerning when or whether they will be deported or freed. . . .

In the meantime the dependents of many are in a state of apprehension and uncertainty, cared for by a charitable agency which came to their aid only when a committee of prominent Detroit clubwomen had brought their plight to public attention, six weeks after their supporters had been arrested. . . .

EXHIBIT 5a.

STATE OF MICHIGAN,
  County of Wayne, ss:

ALEXANDER BUKOWETSKY, being duly sworn according to law, deposes and says:

On November 8, 1919, I was arrested while attending a concert given by the Union of Russian Workers at the Social Turner Hall, and with thirteen other men was taken to Hunt Street Station. . . .

When I came to America I came with the thought that I was coming to a free country,—a place of freedom and happiness, and I was anxious to come,—to get away from the Czaristic form of Government. As much as I was anxious to come here to America I am a hundred times more anxious to run away from Americanism to return to Soviet Russia, where I will at least be able to live.

For six months I have been confined in jail, the Government refusing to either deport or release me together with my wife and children. They have been left, during this time, without means of support. Had it not been for the kindness of the poor, who are our friends, our women and children would have perished.

The Government has decided that we are to be deported. We ask only that this sentence be carried out that we with our families be deported to Soviet

Russia, and that this cruel and inhuman policy of keeping men for six months in jail under sentence of deportation, refusing to either deport or release us, and leaving our families to starve, be ended. We ask only of you that you carry out the sentence which you yourself have decreed,—that we be deported immediately with our families to Soviet, Russia.

I ask this in the name of Justice.

For Further Reading

Stanley Coben, *A. Mitchell Palmer, Politician.* New York: Columbia University Press, 1963.

Theodore Draper, *American Communism and Soviet Russia: The Formative Period.* New York: Vintage Books, 1986.

Edwin Palmer Hoyt, *The Palmer Raids, 1919–1920.* New York: Seabury Press, 1969.

Robert K. Murray, *Red Scare: A Study in National Hysteria, 1919–1920.* Minneapolis: University of Minnesota Press, 1955.

VIEWPOINT 22A

H.L. Mencken
Critiques America (1922)

H.L. Mencken (1880–1956)

H.L. Mencken was a noted journalist, writer, and satirist. He was a columnist for the *Baltimore Sun* from 1906 to 1948, and the founder and editor of the magazine *American Mercury.* Mencken became celebrated during the 1920s for his caustic commentaries on the "traditional" American values of rural and small-town America, in which he criticized in colorful prose the American "booboisie" for their provincialism and narrow-mindedness. His social and literary criticism greatly influenced a generation of intellectuals, many of whom became part of the "Lost Generation" that moved to Europe in the 1920s while decrying the limits of American culture. The following viewpoint presents a sampling of Mencken's writing on American society. It is excerpted from *Prejudices: Third Series,* a collection of his newspaper and magazine essays published in book form in 1922.

On what points does Mencken agree with the intellectuals leaving America? What attitude or bias does he reveal toward Germany and World War I? Which portions of this viewpoint would you rate most controversial? Why?

A pparently there are those who begin to find it disagreeable—nay, impossible. Their anguish fills the Liberal weeklies and every ship that

Excerpted from "On Being an American" by H.L. Mencken, in *Prejudices: Third Series* (New York: Knopf, 1922).

puts out from New York carries a groaning cargo of them, bound for Paris, London, Munich, Rome and way points—anywhere to escape the great curses and atrocities that make life intolerable for them at home. Let me say at once that I find little to cavil at in their basic complaints. In more than one direction, indeed, I probably go a great deal further than even the Young Intellectuals. It is, for example, one of my firmest and most sacred beliefs, reached after an inquiry extending over a score of years and supported by incessant prayer and meditation, that the government of the United States, in both its legislative arm and its executive arm, is ignorant, incompetent, corrupt, and disgusting—and from this judgment I except no more than twenty living lawmakers and no more than twenty executioners of their laws. It is a belief no less piously cherished that the administration of justice in the Republic is stupid, dishonest, and against all reason and equity—and from this judgment I except no more than thirty judges, including two upon the bench of the Supreme Court of the United States. It is another that the foreign policy of the United States—its habitual manner of dealing with other nations, whether friend or foe—is hypocritical, disingenuous, knavish, and dishonorable—and from this judgment I consent to no exceptions whatever, either recent or long past. And it is my fourth (and, to avoid too depressing a bill, final) conviction that the American people, taking one with another, constitute the most timorous, sniveling, poltroonish, ignominious mob of serfs and goosesteppers ever gathered under one flag in Christendom since the end of the Middle Ages, and that they grow more timorous, more sniveling, more poltroonish, more ignominious every day.

So far I go with the fugitive Young Intellectuals—and into the Bad Lands beyond. Such, in brief, are the cardinal articles of my political faith, held passionately since my admission to citizenship and now growing stronger and stronger as I gradually disintegrate into my component carbon, oxygen, hydrogen, phosphorus, calcium, sodium, nitrogen and iron. This is what I believe and preach, *in nomine Domini*, Amen. Yet I remain on the dock, wrapped in the flag, when the Young Intellectuals set sail. Yet here I stand, unshaken and undespairing, a loyal and devoted Americano, even a chauvinist, paying taxes without complaint, obeying all laws that are physiologically obeyable, accepting all the searching duties and responsibilities of citizenship unprotestingly, investing the sparse usufructs of my miserable toil in the obligations of the nation, avoiding all commerce with men sworn to overthrow the government, contributing my mite toward the glory of the national arts and sciences, enriching and embellishing the native language, spurning all lures (and even all invitations) to

get out and stay out—here am I, a bachelor of easy means, forty-two years old, unhampered by debts or issue, able to go wherever I please and to stay as long as I please—here am I, contentedly and even smugly basking beneath the Stars and Stripes, a better citizen, I daresay, and certainly a less murmurous and exigent one, than thousands who put the Hon. Warren Gamaliel Harding beside Friedrich Barbarossa and Charlemagne, and hold the Supreme Court to be directly inspired by the Holy Spirit, and belong ardently to every Rotary Club, Ku Klux Klan, and Anti-Saloon League, and choke with emotion when the band plays "The Star-Spangled Banner," and believe with the faith of little children that one of Our Boys, taken at random, could dispose in a fair fight of ten Englishmen, twenty Germans, thirty Frogs, forty Wops, fifty Japs, or a hundred Bolsheviki.

Why I Stay

Well, then, why am I still here? Why am I so complacent (perhaps even to the point of offensiveness), so free from bile, so little fretting and indignant, so curiously happy? Why did I answer only with a few academic "Hear, Hears" when Henry James, Ezra Pound, Harold Stearns and the *émigrés* of Greenwich Village issued their successive calls to the cornfed *intelligentsia* to flee the shambles, escape to fairer lands, throw off the curse forever? The answer, of course, is to be sought in the nature of happiness, which tempts to metaphysics. But let me keep upon the ground. To me, at least (and I can only follow my own nose), happiness presents itself in an aspect that is tripartite. To be happy (reducing the thing to its elementals) I must be:

a. Well-fed, unhounded by sordid cares, at ease in Zion.

b. Full of a comfortable feeling of superiority to the masses of my fellow-men.

c. Delicately and unceasingly amused according to my taste.

It is my contention that, if this definition be accepted, there is no country on the face of the earth wherein a man roughly constituted as I am—a man of my general weaknesses, vanities, appetites, prejudices, and aversions—can be so happy, or even one-half so happy, as he can be in these free and independent states. Going further, I lay down the proposition that it is a sheer physical impossibility for such a man to live in These States and *not* be happy—that it is as impossible to him as it would be to a schoolboy to weep over the burning down of his schoolhouse. If he says that he isn't happy here, then he either lies or is insane. Here the business of getting a living, particularly since the war brought the loot of all Europe to the national strong-box, is enormously easier than it is in any other Christian land—so easy, in fact, that an educated and forehanded man who fails at it must actually make deliberate efforts to that end. Here the general average of intelligence, of knowledge, of competence, of integrity, of self-respect, of honor is so low that any man who knows his trade, does not fear ghosts, has read fifty good books, and practices the common decencies stands out as brilliantly as a wart on a bald head, and is thrown willy-nilly into a meager and exclusive aristocracy. And here, more than anywhere else that I know of or have heard of, the daily panorama of human existence, of private and communal folly—the unending procession of governmental extortions and chicaneries, of commercial brigandages and throat-slittings, of theological buffooneries, of aesthetic ribaldries, of legal swindles and harlotries, of miscellaneous rogueries, villainies, imbecilities, grotesqueries, and extravagances—is so inordinately gross and preposterous, so perfectly brought up to the highest conceivable amperage, so steadily enriched with an almost fabulous daring and originality, that only the man who was born with a petrified diaphragm can fail to laugh himself to sleep every night, and to awake every morning with all the eager, unflagging expectation of a Sunday-school superintendent touring the Paris peep-shows. . . .

A Third-Rate Country

The United States is essentially a commonwealth of third-rate men—that distinction is easy here because the general level of culture, of information, of taste and judgment, of ordinary competence is so low. No sane man, employing an American plumber to repair a leaky drain, would expect him to do it at the first trial, and in precisely the same way no sane man, observing an American Secretary of State in negotiation with Englishmen and Japs, would expect him to come off better than second best. Third-rate men, of course, exist in all countries, but it is only here that they are in full control of the state, and with it of all the national standards. The land was peopled, not by the hardy adventurers of legend, but simply by incompetents who could not get on at home, and the lavishness of nature that they found here, the vast ease with which they could get livings, confirmed and augmented their native incompetence. . . .

The average American is a prude and a Methodist under his skin, and the fact is never more evident than when he is trying to disprove it. His vices are not those of a healthy boy, but those of an ancient paralytic escaped from the *Greisenheim* [nursing home]. If you would penetrate to the causes thereof, simply go down to Ellis Island and look at the next shipload of immigrants. You will not find the spring of youth in their step; you will find the shuffling of exhausted men. From such exhausted men the

American stock has sprung. It was easier for them to survive here than it was where they came from, but that ease, though it made them feel stronger, did not actually strengthen them. It left them what they were when they came: weary peasants, eager only for the comfortable security of a pig in a sty. Out of that eagerness has issued many of the noblest manifestations of American *Kultur:* the national hatred of war, the pervasive suspicion of the aims and intents of all other nations, the short way with heretics and disturbers of the peace, the unshakable belief in devils, the implacable hostility to every novel idea and point of view.

All these ways of thinking are the marks of the peasant—more, of the peasant long ground into the mud of his wallow, and determined at last to stay there—the peasant who has definitely renounced any lewd desire he may have ever had to gape at the stars. The habits of mind of this dull, sempiternal *fellah*—the oldest man in Christendom—are, with a few modifications, the habits of mind of the American people. The peasant has a great practical cunning, but he is unable to see any further than the next farm. He likes money and knows how to amass property, but his cultural development is but little above that of the domestic animals. He is intensely and cocksurely moral, but his morality and his self-interest are crudely identical. He is emotional and easy to scare, but his imagination cannot grasp an abstraction. He is a violent nationalist and patriot, but he admires rogues in office and always beats the tax-collector if he can. He has immovable opinions about all the great affairs of state, but nine-tenths of them are sheer imbecilities. He is violently jealous of what he conceives to be his rights, but brutally disregardful of the other fellow's. He is religious, but his religion is wholly devoid of beauty and dignity. This man, whether city or country bred, is the normal Americano—the 100 per cent Methodist, Odd Fellow, Ku Kluxer, and Know-Nothing. He exists in all countries, but here alone he rules—here alone his anthropoid fears and rages are accepted gravely as logical ideas, and dissent from them is punished as a sort of public offense. Around every one of his principal delusions—of the sacredness of democracy, of the feasibility of sumptuary law, of the incurable sinfulness of all other peoples, of the menace of ideas, of the corruption lying in all the arts—there is thrown a barrier of taboos, and woe to the anarchist who seeks to break it down! . . .

America and World War I

Coming down to the time of the world war, one finds precious few signs that the American people, facing an antagonist of equal strength and with both hands free, could be relied upon to give a creditable account of themselves. The American share in that great struggle, in fact, was marked by poltroonery almost as conspicuously as it was marked by knavery. Let us consider briefly what the nation did. For a few months it viewed the struggle idly and unintelligently, as a yokel might stare at a sword-swallower at a county fair. Then, seeing a chance to profit, it undertook with sudden alacrity the ghoulish office of *Kriegslieferant* [war supplier]. One of the contestants being debarred, by the chances of war, from buying, it devoted its whole energies, for two years, to purveying to the other. Meanwhile, it made every effort to aid its customer by lending him the cloak of its neutrality—that is, by demanding all the privileges of a neutral and yet carrying on a stupendous wholesale effort to promote the war. On the official side, this neutrality was fraudulent from the start . . . ; popularly it became more and more fraudulent as the debts of the customer contestant piled up, and it became more and more apparent—a fact diligently made known by his partisans—that they would be worthless if he failed to win. Then, in the end, covert aid was transformed into overt aid. And under what gallant conditions! In brief, there stood a nation of 65,000,000 people, which, without effective allies, had just closed two and a half years of homeric conflict by completely defeating an enemy state of 135,000,000 and two lesser ones of more than 10,000,000 together, and now stood at bay before a combination of at least 140,000,000. Upon this battle-scarred and war-weary foe the Republic of 100,000,000 freemen now flung itself, so lifting the odds to 4 to 1. And after a year and a half more of struggle it emerged triumphant—a knightly victor surely!

"The American people . . . grow more timorous, more sniveling, more poltroonish, more ignominious every day."

There is no need to rehearse the astounding and unprecedented swinishness that accompanied this glorious business—the colossal waste of public money, the savage persecution of all opponents and critics of the war, the open bribery of labor, the half-insane reviling of the enemy, the manufacture of false news, the knavish robbery of enemy civilians, the incessant spy hunts, the floating of public loans by a process of blackmail, the degradation of the Red Cross to partisan uses, the complete abandonment of all decency, decorum and self-respect. The facts must be remembered with shame by every civilized American; lest they be forgotten by the generations of the future I am even now engaged with collaborators upon an exhaustive record of them, in twenty volumes folio. More important to the present purpose are two things that are apt to be overlooked, the first of which is the capital fact that the war was "sold" to the American people, as the phrase has it, not by appealing to their courage, but by appealing to their cowardice—in brief, by adopting the assumption that they were not warlike at all, and certainly not gallant and chivalrous, but merely craven and fearful. The first selling point of the proponents of American participation was the contention that the Germans, with gigantic wars still raging on both fronts, were preparing to invade the United States, burn down all the towns, murder all the men, and carry off all the women—that their victory would bring staggering and irresistible reprisals for the American violation of the duties of a neutral. The second selling point was that the entrance of the United States would end the war almost instantly—that the Germans would be so overwhelmingly outnumbered, in men and guns, that it would be impossible for them to make any effective defense—above all, that it would be impossible for them to inflict any serious damage upon their new foes. Neither argument, it must be plain, showed the slightest belief in the warlike skill and courage of the American people. Both were grounded upon the frank theory that the only way to make the mob fight was to scare it half to death, and then show it a way to fight without risk, to stab a helpless antagonist in the back. And both were mellowed and reenforced by the hint that such a noble assault, beside being safe, would also be extremely profitable—that it would convert very dubious debts into very good debts, and dispose forever of a diligent and dangerous competitor for trade, especially in Latin America. All the idealist nonsense emitted by Dr. [Woodrow] Wilson and company was simply icing on the cake. Most of it was abandoned as soon as the bullets began to fly, and the rest consisted simply of meaningless words—the idiotic babbling of a Presbyterian evangelist turned prophet and seer. . . .

The Greatest Show on Earth

All the while I have been forgetting the third of my reasons for remaining so faithful a citizen of the Federation, despite all the lascivious inducements from expatriates to follow them beyond the seas, and all the surly suggestions from patriots that I succumb. It is the reason which grows out of my medieval but unashamed taste for the bizarre and indelicate, my congenital weakness for comedy of the grosser varieties. The United States, to my eye, is incomparably the greatest show on earth. It is a show which avoids diligently all the kinds of clowning which tire me most quickly—for example, royal ceremonials, the tedious hocus-pocus of *haute politique*, the taking of politics seriously—and lays chief stress upon the kinds which delight me unceasingly—for example, the ribald combats of demagogues, the exquisitely ingenious operations of master rogues, the pursuit of witches and heretics, the desperate struggles of inferior men to claw their way into Heaven. We have clowns in constant practice among us who are as far above the clowns of any great state as a Jack Dempsey is above a paralytic—and not a few dozen or score of them, but whole droves and herds. Human enterprises which, in all other Christian countries, are resigned despairingly to an incurable dullness—things that seem devoid of exhilarating amusement by their very nature—are here lifted to such vast heights of buffoonery that contemplating them strains the midriff almost to breaking. I cite an example: the worship of God. Everywhere else on earth it is carried on in a solemn and dispiriting manner; in England, of course, the bishops are obscene, but the average man seldom gets a fair chance to laugh at them and enjoy them. Now come home. Here we not only have bishops who are enormously more obscene than even the most gifted of the English bishops; we have also a huge force of lesser specialists in ecclesiastical mountebankery—tin-horn Loyolas, Savonarolas and Xaviers of a hundred fantastic rites, each performing untiringly and each full of a grotesque and illimitable whimsicality. Every American town, however small, has one of its own: a holy clerk with so fine a talent for introducing the arts of jazz into the salvation of the damned that his performance takes on all the gaudiness of a four-ring circus, and the bald announcement that he will raid Hell on such and such a night is enough to empty all the town blind-pigs and bordellos and pack his sanctuary to the doors. And to aid him and inspire him there are traveling experts to whom he stands in the relation of a wart to the Matterhorn—stupendous masters of theological imbecility, contrivers of doctrines utterly preposterous, heirs to the Joseph Smith, Mother Eddy and John Alexander Dowie tradition—[William J.] Bryan, [Billy] Sunday, and their like. These are the eminences of the American Sacred College. I delight in them. Their proceedings make me a happier American.

Turn, now, to politics. Consider, for example, a campaign for the Presidency. Would it be possible to imagine anything more uproariously idiotic—a deafening, nerve-wracking battle to the death between Tweedledum and Tweedledee, Harlequin and Sganarelle, Gobbo and Dr. Cook—the unspeakable, with fearful snorts, gradually swallowing the inconceivable? I defy any one to match it elsewhere on this earth. In other lands, at worst, there are at least

intelligible issues, coherent ideas, salient personalities. Somebody says something, and somebody replies. But what did [Warren G.] Harding say in 1920, and what did [James] Cox reply? Who was Harding, anyhow, and who was Cox? Here, having perfected democracy, we lift the whole combat to symbolism, to transcendentalism, to metaphysics. Here we load a pair of palpably tin cannon with blank cartridges charged with talcum powder, and so let fly. Here one may howl over the show without any uneasy reminder that it is serious, and that some one may be hurt. I hold that this elevation of politics to the plane of undiluted comedy is peculiarly American, that nowhere else on this disreputable ball has the art of the sham-battle been developed to such fineness. . . .

Mirth is necessary to wisdom, to comfort, above all, to happiness. Well, here is the land of mirth, as Germany is the land of metaphysics and France is the land of fornication. Here the buffoonery never stops. What could be more delightful than the endless struggle of the Puritan to make the joy of the minority unlawful and impossible? The effort is itself a greater joy to one standing on the sidelines than any or all of the carnal joys that it combats. . . . One man prefers the Republic because it pays better wages than Bulgaria. Another because it has laws to keep him sober and his daughter chaste. Another because the Woolworth Building is higher than the cathedral at Chartres. Another because, living here, he can read the New York *Evening Journal.* Another because there is a warrant out for him somewhere else. Me, I like it because it amuses me to my taste. I never get tired of the show. It is worth every cent it costs.

VIEWPOINT 22B

A Critique of H.L. Mencken (1928)

Catherine Beach Ely (dates unknown)

Catherine Beach Ely was a writer on art criticism and social issues. In the following viewpoint, taken from an article published in the *North American Review* in January 1928, she takes aim at H.L. Mencken, perhaps America's most prominent cultural critic of the 1920s. Her criticism of Mencken is also a defense of the American society Mencken made a point of satirizing, with its optimism, religious faith, and patriotism.

How does Ely describe Mencken? Does her description of Mencken accurately describe the tone of the opposing viewpoint? Do you think she pre-

Catherine Beach Ely, "The Sorrows of Mencken," *North American Review*, vol. 225, no. 1 (January 1928).

sents an adequate response to Mencken's arguments? Why or why not?

The exile of Henry Mencken among us ignorant, naïve Americans is a tragedy of modern letters. Self-condemned to this unhappy existence by his own decision, and not by our insistence, he continues to afford us the unparalleled spectacle of his supreme condescension. He endures our stupidities and crudenesses with pained disgust. With what one would call a missionary's zeal, were not the concept missionary so foreign to his taste, he labors to convert us to the sophisticate's viewpoint. He abandons the civilizations of other lands, presumably more in harmony with his fastidious predilections, in order that we Americans may feel the contrast between his lofty intelligence and our inane futilities.

What desperate isolation, that of this apostle of pessimism stranded on the shores of cheerful, constructive America! Constructive—the very word makes the indignant Mencken shudder at the rawness of a nation bent on erecting its own destiny and well being, though undoubtedly this egregiously prosperous country of ours offers a convenient financial environment to the mental alien.

Mencken laments the blundering ineptitude of America's history. With consummate disregard for the fitness of things, we left an enlightened Old World in the Seventeenth Century and embarked in crude boats, landed upon crude shores, and began our crude career. Gathering momentum, our foolishness launched us into the international disagreement of 1917. Not content with the bourgeois obsession for engineering our own destiny, we must needs meddle in the affairs of Europe at a moment when our intrusion was most embarrassing to the theories of the defeatists and to the schedule of the Teutons—our absurd chivalry of 1917 was the bitterest dreg in Mencken's sorrow-cup. Since then he castigates us with the whip-lash of his exasperation. Increasingly we provoke his diatribes concerning our inferiority to a sophisticated Europe which he voluntarily abandons to dwell among us "boobs," as he airily designates us.

America's Exasperating Qualities

Our idiotic cheerfulness aggravates Mencken. Destitute of the acrimony which marks the superiority of the alien *literati*, we pursue our inferior bourgeois objectives with hopeful vigor, with candid and unseemly optimism. The world has been revolving on its axis since 1492, and America has not yet learned the proper attitude of cynical acquiescence to fate and of jesting unconcern for human responsibility. She insists on being useful and altruistic in

spite of the oral and written precepts of our conspicuous intellectual, Mencken the Mentor. Full many a time he pushes us Yankees beneath the dark waters of pessimism, but unfailingly we bob up again on the life-preserver of our buoyant instinct for overcoming difficulties and dangers. In America apparently we cannot realize that conquering obstacles is obsolete.

Mencken deplores our antiquated regard for the sacredness of home, church, and history. We are so slow to learn that there is no such word as tradition in the lexicon of modern thought. Tradition implies affection for the past, whereas the Mencken school would have us understand that we have no past and no future worth cherishing, only the present for donning harlequin's attire and proclaiming the farcical futility of human endeavor.

•

"[America] insists on being useful and altruistic in spite of the oral and written precepts of our conspicuous intellectual, Mencken the Mentor."

•

Hero worship exasperates the cynics as the most foolish phase of tradition. To make a hero of an American is to imply that there is something fine in human nature and, worst of all, in American human nature. Acknowledging gratitude for a salient personality in public life runs counter to the sophisticate's assumption that gratitude is a weakness and that there is no greatness of character. Yet, in spite of Mencken's tutoring, incorrigibly stupid America continues to cherish her sacred memories and hopes. She persists in erecting monuments to her heroes, and in teaching her school-children to believe in Country and Flag—foolish America! disgruntled Mencken!

Patriotism heads Mencken's list of bourgeois offences. To be a patriot is to stir the risibles of advanced thinkers. How arrogant of America to value her experiences as a Nation, how tasteless her self-reminders of her evolution as a Republic! Columbus might better have remained comfortably in Italy; as for the Puritans, if they had foundered in the deep sea, we should have been spared the record of their austere follies. England was well rid of us, yet we are none the better for our independence. This dollar-chasing America presumes to prate of patriotism, to sing the glories of her birth, and to seek divine guidance. Mencken sorrows over all these childish tendencies, sorrows because our Nation will not cast aside her preoccupation with reminiscent emotions. Patriotism implies team-work, the submersion of the Ego, the upward look, the strong right arm, the romance of history, whereas Menckenism puts the individual in a vacuum and tells him to exist without the atmosphere of enthusiasm expressed in national service and devotion.

America is incurably religious, although Mencken points inexorably to the signposts of modern intellectualism. She persists in putting faith and will power above barren mental cerebration. Underneath her crust of materialism she cherishes spiritual ideals. America's spiritual energy angers Mencken, because he makes himself believe that the religion of America is synonymous with hypocrisy, superstition and wrong-headedness. What right have we Americans to the consolations and inspirations of piety—we least of all peoples!

For the Mencken school faith is demoded, aspiration a weak delusion. Yet America refuses to repudiate religion. She makes it the foundation of her institutions, the motive-power of her charities, the keynote of her progress. Mencken sorrows over America's narrow conformities, so contrary to the self-sufficiency of intellectualism. The American bourgeois blunders onward and upward instead of reclining at full length in the dry lands of Rationalism.

Mencken's Imitators

As an alleviation for the crass stupidities of the American "booboisie", Mencken has founded a school of congenial spirits. A select inner circle of Americans choose him as their guide and pattern. Our Menckenites form an esoteric band of superior minds, whose special function it is to deride all things American. They reflect his prejudices and imitate his cawings and croakings at our absurdities. Chief among them in stereotyped implicit obedience is Sinclair Lewis. Self-acknowledged star pupil of Menckenism, Lewis incorporates his master's theories into novels which put the dunce cap on America and condemn her to the dark corner as the world's most imbecile race.

Mencken's band of imitators—the bad boys of literature—console him for his grievance at sentimental America. He has imparted to them his swagger, his bravado. They jeer at the plain person, who in the grapple with life turns to sentiments which brighten the bleakness of an unkind environment by revealing a goal worth a struggle. Like street arabs pelting strangers in comely garments, they throw derisive epithets at the kindly virtues and gracious deeds which brighten sombre places.

They have the brawler's delight in destruction—the instinct to break the bright wings of idealism, to silence the song of hope, the flutter of expectation. They love to tease, to worry, to injure the purposeful citizen pursuing the round of homely existence.

"What's the use!" they sneer; "your work is futile, your faith nonsensical, your courage childish—you poor dupe, you preposterous bourgeois!" Thumbing the nose, they scoff at the harmless effusions of life. Parades, both literal and figurative, with the old fellows in uniform, the young ones beating the drum and playing the fife, the applause and enthusiasms of the crowd as an outlet for human ardor, offend the superiority complex of the Mencken coterie.

Mencken, critic *in perpetuum*, assuages his vexation at our perverse Americanisms with the cup of malice which he prepares for himself. His caustic middle age will pass into tart old age spent in the America he disdains but refuses to desert. For, were he absent from foolish America, his occupation would cease. With no America to berate, his career would vanish, his mentality atrophy. Having stored up for himself no gentle thoughts, no mellow traditions, no mild benignant pleasures of the mind, how could he live in a land he did not despise? How could he endure a congenial environment after the bracing air of antagonism to all things American? On his peak of scorn he noisily bewails America; but he enjoys his sorrows.

For Further Reading

Lorin Baritz, ed., *The Culture of the Twenties.* Indianapolis: Bobbs-Merrill, 1970.

Stanley Coben, *Rebellion Against Victorianism.* New York: Oxford University Press, 1991.

George H. Douglas, *H.L. Mencken: Critic of American Life.* Hamden, CT: Archon Books, 1978.

Edward A. Martin, *H.L. Mencken and the Debunkers.* Athens: University of Georgia Press, 1984.

VIEWPOINT 23A

Prohibition Is a Success (1924)
John Gordon Cooper (1872–1955)

A significant issue during the 1920s was Prohibition. The Eighteenth Amendment to the Constitution, which was ratified in 1919 and which took effect in 1920, prohibited the manufacture, transportation, and sale of "intoxicating liquors" in the United States. Congress passed the Volstead Act in 1919 to enforce the amendment (defining "intoxicating liquors" to mean any beverage that was more than .5 percent alcohol), and consumption of alcohol at first declined. However, federal and state enforcement efforts failed to stop the smuggling and selling of alcohol, much of it produced and sold by organized crime syndicates. Within a few years there was discussion on modifying the Volstead Act, to allow

John Gordon Cooper, "The Benefits of Prohibition," *Forum*, June 1924.

the sale of beer and wine or to turn over its enforcement to the states. Some people began calling for the repeal of the Eighteenth Amendment altogether. The following viewpoint, a defense of Prohibition, is taken from a 1924 magazine article by John Gordon Cooper. Cooper, a former railroad worker and engineer, was a Republican congressman from Ohio from 1915 to 1937.

What importance does Cooper attach to the fact that Prohibition is not just a federal law, but part of the U.S. Constitution? How effective has Prohibition been, according to Cooper? What benefits of the ban on alcohol does he list? What arguments does he make about the opponents of Prohibition?

That prohibition should be strictly enforced as long as it is a part of the Constitution of the United States, and that as part of the Constitution it is deserving of the respect and support of the citizens of the United States, is not a debatable question. Our whole system of government, our greatness as a nation, and the unequaled benefits, opportunities, and privileges which we enjoy as individual Americans are all based on the Constitution. A blow at the Constitution is a blow at all that is near and dear to us. The Eighteenth Amendment prohibiting the traffic in intoxicating liquor as a beverage is an integral part of the Constitution and as such is as much entitled to respect and obedience as any other part of the fundamental law of the land. Disregard of the Eighteenth Amendment is just as serious as disregard of the guarantee that life, liberty, and property may not be taken from a citizen without due process of law. Disobedience of one law inevitably breeds disobedience of other laws and leads to anarchy. We may change the Constitution but we can not nullify it.

Even the most active enemies of prohibition do not openly advocate disobedience to the Constitution. They propose instead that the sale of beer and wine be legalized on the claim that such beverages are not intoxicating. It is not within the scope of this article to go at length into this phase of the subject, but experience has amply proved that the liquor traffic cannot be regulated, that when it is granted an inch it will take a mile, that the only way to meet the evil is to place it outside the law and then enforce the law. To legalize the sale and traffic in wine and beer would enormously increase illicit traffic in "hard" liquor.

The Effectiveness of Prohibition

The extent to which prohibition is effective today depends on the point of view. To contend that it is entirely effective in parts of some of our great cities where the entire population is of foreign extraction

and where the law officers wink at violations is, of course, useless. But it is just as far from the fact to argue, as do some liquor advocates, that prohibition has increased drinking and intemperance throughout the country. Relatively, prohibition is effective and it will advance toward complete effectiveness just as rapidly as citizens come to a full realization that it is a vital part of the fundamental law of the land, and to the degree that enforcement officers are selected because of fitness and determination to do their duty instead of because of political influence and "pull". Of course it will become more effective as a new generation which never knew the open saloon takes the place of those who cannot forget their appetites for strong drink.

The effectiveness of prohibition has been a varying quantity. When war-time prohibition went into effect July 1, 1919, it was obeyed even by the hardened bootleggers and moonshiners to a remarkable degree because the people were still living under the influence of the discipline and unselfish zeal of war days. Our police statistics mirror this condition. Then came the reaction from the strain of the war, such reaction as has always followed war. There was a moral let down. Violations of the prohibition law were the result, not the cause, of this moral reaction and a turn toward the pursuit of selfish pleasures and desires.

The liquor interests soon saw what they believed to be a chance to resurrect their outlawed business. They began their smuggling operations and encouraged moonshining in order to secure supplies of intoxicating beverages for the thoughtless and the indifferent. They revived their slimy tactics of graft and bribery so that they might secure permits to withdraw bonded liquor and secure the protection of officers sworn to enforce the law. They formed alliances with corrupt politicians, and the whole country has been subjected to an unceasing propaganda aimed at law and order and a sober and decent America. Unfortunately this propaganda was aided by the leniency of the courts. Petty fines practically licensed the bootleg trade and the law's delay made conviction impossible in many cases.

Americans Want Enforcement of the Laws

But the American people have again demonstrated their essential soundness and the truth of Lincoln's wise adage that the people cannot be fooled. Each Congress that has been elected has a larger dry majority, and popular elections in many States have resulted in increased votes for law enforcement. The Christian people of America, the legal profession, the newly enfranchised women, and many other elements have joined together to urge more sincerity of purpose in law enforcement.

Handicaps placed upon enforcement agencies

have been removed. The rum smuggler has been removed from the protection of the Union Jack by the recent treaty with Great Britain, and similar treaties with other powers will soon outlaw this twentieth century pirate. The Coast Guard has been granted means to protect the shores of the United States. Civil Service regulations will soon replace the spoils system in selecting honest and competent enforcement agents beyond the influence of wet politicians.

Despite all obstacles and handicaps the social, economic, and industrial reforms accomplished by prohibition are so numerous that it is impossible even to catalogue them within the limited scope of this statement. No longer are there 177,790 open, legalized saloons inviting patronage and serving as centers of evil, vice, corruption, and death. The country has never been so rich and the people so sober. But for prohibition, readjustment from the war could not have gone forward so rapidly and successfully.

Benefits of Prohibition

The death rate in the United States has fallen amazingly. In the first four years under prohibition the decrease was equivalent to saving 873,000 lives. Crime has lessened. More people may be arrested,—but for traffic law violations, breaches of some automobile, food, or sanitary regulation and not for drunkenness. The federal census shows a decrease of 5.8 per 100,000 in our criminal population from 1917 to 1922. Hundreds of penal institutions have been closed since prohibition. Judge William M. Gemmill, of Chicago, a foremost criminal authority, says that the drop in the number of arrests for drunkenness is equivalent to 500,000 a year. The licensed liquor traffic was the most fertile source of crime, and much of the existing criminality is traceable to the now outlawed liquor traffic which is encouraged by the advocates of nullification of the Constitution.

America's prosperity is the wonder of the whole world. We have five-sixths of the world's motor vehicles. Mr. R.T. Hodgkins, Vice-President of the Rollin Motors Company, asserts that at least seven million motor cars have been bought with money that formerly went to the saloon. [Business statistician] Roger Babson says that prohibition turned what would normally have been a downward trend into an upward one and thus accounts for much of our recent and present prosperity. Two or three billion dollars yearly were turned from the destructive channels of drink to the constructive channels of legitimate business.

Last year alone the savings deposits of the country increased a billion dollars. Insurance holdings gained eleven billion dollars and vast sums were expended for the radio, moving pictures, and other entertainments. Stock in the nation's great enterprises has been acquired by a much larger number of people. The growth of the Labor Banks is another indication that the workers are saving their money more than ever before.

---•---

"Despite all obstacles and handicaps the social, economic, and industrial reforms accomplished by prohibition are . . . numerous."

---•---

That drunkenness has dropped to a minimum under prohibition is proved by the fact that in most cities a drunkard is a rare sight on the streets, and the homes for alcoholics have decreased from 238 in the time of the licensed saloon to 38 last year. There are few communities in America where it is not almost as easy to enter the lodge of a secret society without a password as it is for any one to buy a drink of intoxicating liquor without being sponsored by an acquaintance of the dealer.

The average man is the greatest gainer from prohibition. In the past ten years the per capita wealth of America has increased from $968 to $2,918, most of the gain coming after the adoption of prohibition. It is not the men and women who work for a living and are busily engaged in producing the wealth and prosperity of the nation who are agitating against prohibition. Such agitation finds far more willing supporters among the wealthy idle who want liquor to stimulate their jaded appetites in their pursuit of pleasure. It is among these people far more than among those who work with their hands that the advocates of beer and wine find aid and comfort and sympathy.

Statement of Locomotive Engineers

I am proud to be a member of Division No. 565, Brotherhood of Locomotive Engineers, which organization through its officers recently sent a stinging rebuke to the propagandists who have been seeking the support of labor for legislation attacking prohibition.

"It is somewhat of a mystery to us men engaged in the dangerous business of railroading why any wage-earner would want a return to the misery of the evils of pre-Volstead days," said this organization in a reply to a request for support from the wets. "To say that the Eighteenth Amendment has been a total failure, that the drink habit is as bad or worse than before, we know is simply propaganda of those interested in the return of a business that has done more to retard civilization and human progress than any one thing in the world's history.

"We men in the railroad game know that the Eighteenth Amendment has been the greatest blessing we ever received; we know that we are better off morally, financially, intellectually, and in every other way by the outlawing of the booze business."

Prohibition Is a Failure (1926)

William H. Stayton (1861–1942)

The enactment of the Eighteenth Amendment to the Constitution and the Volstead Act prohibiting the manufacture and sale of "intoxicating liquors" did not end the consumption of alcohol in the United States or the debates over the wisdom of Prohibition. Throughout the 1920s there was a growing political divide between "wets" who wanted the Volstead Act relaxed or the amendment repealed entirely, and "drys" who supported Prohibition and its strict enforcement. This political faultline reflected in some respects a deeper social division between America's urban and rural areas.

In 1926 the U.S. Senate held hearings on the effectiveness of Prohibition. Among those testifying was William H. Stayton, the founder and head of the Association Against the Prohibition Amendment. The AAPA, begun in 1922, consisted of wealthy industrialists who supported "wet" candidates for political office and campaigned for the repeal of the Eighteenth Amendment. Stayton in his testimony summarized what he considered to be the harmful effects of Prohibition on American society.

What has been the effect of Prohibition on the nation's drinking habits, according to Stayton? How has Prohibition changed the role of the federal government, in his opinion? How does Stayton respond to arguments that Prohibition has contributed to American economic prosperity?

The evidence presented in the hearings before the subcommittee of the Senate Judiciary Committee, uncontroverted and unchallenged, shows:

That authenticated statistics compiled and reported by the police departments of practically all of the larger cities of the United States, and many smaller ones, reveal a progressive and continuous increase in arrests for drunkenness from 1920, the first year of constitutional prohibition, to 1925, inclusive, thereby proving that prohibition is not now effectively

William H. Stayton, *Congressional Digest*, vol. 5, no. 6 (June 1926).

enforced anywhere in the United States.

That arrests for drunkenness began to decline in practically all cities of the United States in 1917 and continued to drop rapidly during 1918 and 1919, and that during the period of this decline in arrests for public intoxication, milder beverages, such as beer and wine, were the principal drinks readily available for public consumption.

That by 1924 the arrests for drunkenness in the principal cities of the United States were practically as great in number as in 1916 and 1917 when they reached the high peak, and that available reports show that in 1925 they had gone higher than the pre-prohibition peak, thus proving that prohibition as a remedy for intemperance is a total failure.

Failure of Enforcement

That attempted prohibition enforcement, for the first time in the history of the Republic, has introduced into important departments of the Federal Government, corruption on a colossal scale, and scandals of such magnitude as to bring discredit upon the agencies of the Government and shake the faith of the people in the integrity of the government they set up for their protection.

The testimony of Assistant Secretary of the Treasury, General Andrews, revealed that 875 prohibition agents have been dismissed for corruption. These figures represent only the discovered corruption, and there are none so sanguine as to believe that they represent more than a small proportion of the actual corruption that has existed in the prohibition unit from the day it was originated.

That after six years of national prohibition, and the expenditure of vast sums of money to enforce the law, the manufacture of alcoholic beverages by illicit distillation and diversion and conversion of denatured industrial alcohol, has become a great and growing industry. The money value of the output of these products was estimated by accredited agents of the Federal Government, charged with the duty of enforcing the prohibition law, as several times as great as the combined expenditures for whisky, wine, beer, and other alcoholic beverages before the ratification of the Eighteenth Amendment.

Federal District Attorney Buckner of New York estimated the money value of alcoholic liquor fabricated from redistilled denatured alcohol in the States of New York and Pennsylvania alone, to be more than $3,600,000,000 a year, and Federal Prohibition Administrator Frederick C. Baird of the Pittsburgh district, estimated the value of the moonshine products of the stills he had captured in his district, in an eight-months period, to be in excess of $2,000,000,000 a year.

These facts show the value of the unlawful output

of alcoholic liquor in a very small territory of the United States, not including any smuggled liquors, to be approximately $5,600,000,000 a year—about four times the value of all alcoholic liquors consumed in the United States before prohibition. In these calculations no account is taken of moonshining, unlawful distilling, diversion and conversion of industrial alcohol, outside of the States of New York and Pennsylvania, nor has consideration been given to the facts that moonshining is a much more general practice at points removed from the seaboard, and in so-called dry territory, than in the Eastern part of the United States where there has been an almost uninterrupted supply of smuggled liquors.

———————— • ————————

"Prohibition has created a vast army of rum-runners, moonshiners, bootleggers, and corrupt public officials."

———————— • ————————

Furthermore, these estimates do not touch the value of the quantity of liquors—whisky, gin, wine, cider, beer, applejack, and other alcoholic concoctions now generally made in the homes throughout the length and breadth of the country—in the cities, in the suburbs, and on the farms.

That the manufacture of moonshine whisky is an almost universal practice, as illustrated by the fact that 172,000 stills or parts of stills were captured in 1925, and that the number captured year after year, has increased rather than diminished, and that the Federal Administrator of Prohibition admitted that not one still in ten in actual operation is captured by the agents of the Government.

That the stills and parts of stills were captured in vastly greater numbers in so-called dry States than in wet States, proving conclusively that where it is more difficult to obtain smuggled or diverted whisky, the demand is supplied by local manufacture.

That the enforcement of the prohibition law in centers where the sentiment of the people is strongly arrayed against it—which condition prevails in most of the populous centers of the United States and in many of the smaller cities—has become such a difficult, corrupting and crime breeding problem, that the time and effort of public officials is so largely occupied in attempted suppression of its evils that they are compelled to neglect other vastly more important public duties.

Increased Drinking

That prohibition has led to increased drinking of intoxicating liquor on the part of women and chil-

dren; that it has popularized the hip pocket flask; that it has made the serving of liquors in the homes a social custom; that it has contributed directly to a condition of immorality graphically and tragically illustrated in an alarming increase in social diseases, especially among the youth of the land.

That prohibition has created a vast army of rum-runners, moonshiners, bootleggers, and corrupt public officials, thereby directly breeding a condition of lawlessness unequaled in the history of the Republic, and that this era of lawlessness has been disastrous to the moral standards of government and individual citizenship, and that its evil outcroppings have been evidenced by the preponderance of desperate and violent crime now being perpetrated by the very young.

That the cost of even moderately effective control of the commercialized traffic would mount to prohibitive sums, it being estimated by United States District Attorney Buckner of New York that it would require an appropriation of at least $75,000,000 a year to restrain the commercialized industry in the State of New York.

That in addition to its complete failure as a temperance measure, as shown by the fact that public drunkenness is now as great as in any period before prohibition, it has visited upon the country a train of evils of far reaching and deadening effect upon the public morals and public conscience; that it has been a prolific breeder of crime; that it has demoralized the youth of the land, and that altogether it has been the greatest curse that ever came upon the country disguised as a blessing.

Prohibition in Chicago

Judge Dever, the Mayor of Chicago, appeared before the committee and described with much detail how the entire police force of Chicago had been employed for three years in a continuous effort to suppress the commercialized traffic in alcoholic liquors, and how the time and effort of public officials were drawn from other vastly more important duties to enforce prohibition. The Federal District Attorney and the Mayor of Chicago were in substantial agreement that the commercialized traffic in Chicago was fairly under suppression, although the cost had been very great. Now, let us see just what enforcement means, even as effective as can be attained by combined and coordinated effort of Federal and municipal authorities.

Judge Dever explained that public drunkenness is not a violation of the law in Illinois. To get one's self arrested for being drunk it is necessary to become drunk and disorderly. So arrests for drunkenness are merged with disorderly conduct. Our information, which we believe to be correct, is that all but 10 per cent of the combined arrests for drunkenness and disorderly conduct in Chicago are for plain drunkenness.

The enforcement program in Chicago began in 1923. We turn back to 1922 and find that there were 64,853 arrests for drunkenness and disorderly conduct in that year. In 1923, under the enforcement program, the arrests increased to 75,800. In 1924, after two years of enforcement, the arrests jumped up to 86,072, and in 1925, after three years of the most effective enforcement attainable by combined Federal, State and municipal action, the arrests for drunkenness and disorderly conduct mounted up to the astonishing total of 92,888.

Philadelphia also had two years of police enforcement of prohibition under General Smedley D. Butler. In 1923, the year before General Butler embarked upon his spectacular career as enforcement officer extraordinary, Philadelphia staggered along under a burden of only 45,226 arrests for drunkenness, but in 1924, after General Butler got into action, the arrests climbed up to 55,766 and in 1925, after he had been slashing away at enforcement for two years, the arrests for drunkenness reached the peak of 58,617.

The foregoing facts are conclusive proof that the trend toward national sobriety under sane restrictions which enabled citizens to supply their requirements for beer and wine of low alcoholic content, which was progressing so favorably between 1917 and 1919, was completely overthrown by national prohibition, and that drunkenness today, under the Volstead Act, and State prohibition acts in all but a few of the States, is as uncontrolled as it was when the saloons were running wide open and there were no restrictions or limitations upon alcoholic liquors.

Prohibition and Business

It has been the boast of the drys that prohibition is good for business. We beg to remind you that prohibition was put forward as being good for public morals, and that it has been shown that it has been disastrous to public morals. The only defense that can now be made of it is that it is a good economic measure. Prohibitionists have quoted glibly many captains of industry as being favorable to prohibition, but they did not bring any industrial leaders here to so testify. They fall back upon the testimony of Professor [Irving] Fisher of Yale University that it has saved the country $6,000,000,000 a year.

The defect in Professor Fisher's testimony is that he did not take into consideration the desperate financial plight of American farmers, who, according to Senator Capper of Kansas, have sustained a loss of $20,000,000,000 in farm values during the past five years [due to a decrease in demand for crops previously used in alcoholic beverages]; and who are now pressing before this Congress numerous bills designed to relieve them from an almost bankrupt condition.

Neither did Professor Fisher take into account the fact that men who are actually engaged in banking and business admit freely that much of present day prosperity is due to unparalleled buying on installments, with 75 to 85 per cent of all automobiles, furniture, jewelry and numerous other commodities being bought on time payments. The estimates of bankers who have studied the problem, and who have actual knowledge of the question through handling the installment paper, is that in 1925 this installment buying aggregated more than five billion dollars. It is admitted by bankers and real economists actually engaged in business that the present flourishing volume of business in the automobile industry—of which we have heard so much—is due entirely to the installment buying of motor cars. It is not, in any sense, due to prohibition, because the evidence in this case shows that vastly greater amount of money is now being spent for some kind of alcoholic liquors than before prohibition.

For Further Reading

Norman H. Clark, *Deliver Us from Evil: An Interpretation of American Prohibition.* New York: Norton, 1976.

Thomas M. Coffey, *The Long Thirst: Prohibition in America, 1920–1933.* New York: Norton, 1975.

David Leigh Colvin, *Prohibition in the United States.* New York: George H. Doran, 1926.

Charles Merz, *The Dry Decade.* New York: Doubleday, 1931.

Andrew Sinclair, *The Era of Excess: A Social History of the Prohibition Movement.* New York: Harper & Row, 1964.

The Great Depression and the New Deal

VIEWPOINT 24A

Self-Help Is the Best Response to Unemployment (1932)

Henry Ford (1863–1947)

Henry Ford, pioneering automaker and founder of the Ford Motor Company, was perhaps the most famous American businessman of his time. A self-made man with little formal schooling, he occasionally wrote newspaper and magazine articles expounding his views on American social problems. The following viewpoint is taken from two such editorials inserted by Ford Motor Company into the magazine *Literary Digest* in 1932, during the Great Depression. Ford advocates encouraging the unemployed to

Henry Ford, "On Unemployment," *Literary Digest,* June 11 & 18, 1932.

help themselves rather than to depend on charity or government relief as the best approach to coping with America's economic difficulties. He also reveals his idealization of rural life, encouraging people to live off the land. In June 1932, when these articles first appeared, approximately 13 million people—about one-quarter of America's labor force—were unemployed in the United States.

What objections does Ford have to "routine" charity? What steps has the Ford Motor Company taken to reduce unemployment and to help the poor, according to the author? What specific steps should the unemployed take to help themselves, according to Ford?

I have always had to work, whether any one hired me or not. For the first forty years of my life, I was an employe. When not employed by others, I employed myself. I found very early that being out of hire was not necessarily being out of work. The first means that your employer has not found something for you to do; the second means that you are waiting until he does.

We nowadays think of work as something that others find for us to do, call us to do, and pay us to do. No doubt our industrial growth is largely responsible for that. We have accustomed men to think of work that way.

In my own case, I was able to find work for others as well as myself. Outside my family life, nothing has given me more satisfaction than to see jobs increase in number and in profit to the men who handle them. And beyond question, the jobs of the world today are more numerous and profitable in wages than they were even eighteen years ago.

The Problem of Unemployment

But something entirely outside the workshops of the nation has affected this hired employment very seriously. The word "unemployment" has become one of the most dreadful words in the language. The condition itself has become the concern of every person in the country.

When this condition arrived, there were just three things to be done. The first, of course, was to maintain employment at the maximum by every means known to management. Employment—hire—was what the people were accustomed to; they preferred it; it was the immediate solution of the difficulty. In our plants we used every expedient to spread as much employment over as many employes as was possible. I don't believe in "make work"—the public pays for all unnecessary work—but there are times when the plight of others compels us to do the human thing even though it be but a makeshift; and

I am obliged to admit that, like most manufacturers, we avoided layoffs by continuing work that good business judgment would have halted. All of our non-profit work was continued in full force and much of the shop work. There were always tens of thousands employed—the lowest point at Dearborn [Michigan] was 40,000—but there were always thousands unemployed or so meagerly employed, that the situation was far from desirable.

When all possible devices for providing employment have been used and fall short, there remains no alternative but self-help or charity.

I do not believe in routine charity. I think it a shameful thing that any man should have to stoop to take it, or give it. I do not include human helpfulness under the name of charity. My quarrel with charity is that it is neither helpful nor human. The charity of our cities is the most barbarous thing in our system, with the possible exception of our prisons. What we call charity is a modern substitute for being personally kind, personally concerned and personally involved in the work of helping others in difficulty. True charity is a much more costly effort than money-giving. Our donations too often purchase exemption from giving the only form of help that will drive the need for charity out of the land.

"Great numbers of people have made the stimulating discovery that they need not depend on employers to find work for them—they can find work for themselves."

Our own theory of helping people has been in operation for some years. We used to discuss it years ago—when no one could be persuaded to listen. Those who asked public attention to these matters were ridiculed by the very people who now call most loudly for some one to do something.

Our own work involves the usual emergency relief, hospitalization, adjustment of debt, with this addition—we help people to alter their affairs in common-sense accordance with changed conditions, and we have an understanding that all help received should be repaid in reasonable amounts in better times. Many families were not so badly off as they thought; they needed guidance in the management of their resources and opportunities. Human nature, of course, presented the usual problems. Relying on human sympathy many develop a spirit of professional indigence. But where co-operation is given, honest and self-respecting persons and families can usually be assisted to a condition which is much less distressing than they feared.

One of our responsibilities, voluntarily assumed—not because it was ours, but because there seemed to be no one else to assume it—was the care of a village of several hundred families whose condition was pretty low. Ordinarily a large welfare fund would have been needed to accomplish anything for these people. In this instance, we set the people at work cleaning up their homes and backyards, and then cleaning up the roads of their town, and then plowing up about 500 acres of vacant land around their houses. We abolished everything that savored of "handout" charity, opening instead a modern commissary where personal IOU's were accepted and a garment-making school, and setting the cobblers and tailors of the community to work for their neighbors. We found the people heavily burdened with debt, and we acted informally as their agents in apportioning their income to straighten their affairs. Many families are now out of debt for the first time in years. There has appeared in this village not only a new spirit of confidence in life, but also a new sense of economic values, and an appreciation of economic independence which we feel will not soon be lost. None of these things could have been accomplished by paying out welfare funds after the orthodox manner. The only true charity for these people was somehow to get under their burdens with them and lend them the value of our experience to show them what can be done by people in their circumstances.

Our visiting staff in city work has personally handled thousands of cases in the manner above described. And while no one institution can shoulder all the burden, we feel that merely to mitigate present distress is not enough—we feel that thousands of families have been prepared for a better way of life when the wheels of activity begin turning again.

Self-Help

But there is still another way, a third way, so much better than the very best charitable endeavor that it simply forbids us to be satisfied with anything less. That is the way of Self-Help. . . .

If it is right and proper to help people to become wise managers of their own affairs in good times, it cannot be wrong to pursue the same object in dull times. Independence through self-dependence is a method which must commend itself when understood.

Methods of self-help are numerous and great numbers of people have made the stimulating discovery that they need not depend on employers to find work for them—they can find work for themselves. I have more definitely in mind those who have not yet made that discovery, and I should like to express certain convictions I have tested.

The land! That is where our roots are. There is the basis of our physical life. The farther we get away from the land, the greater our insecurity. From the land comes everything that supports life, everything we use for the service of physical life. The land has not collapsed or shrunk in either extent or productivity. It is there waiting to honor all the labor we are willing to invest in it, and able to tide us across any dislocation of economic conditions.

No unemployment insurance can be compared to an alliance between a man and a plot of land. With one foot in industry and another foot in the land, human society is firmly balanced against most economic uncertainties. With a job to supply him with cash, and a plot of land to guarantee him support, the individual is doubly secure. Stocks may fail, but seedtime and harvest do not fail.

I am not speaking of stop-gaps or temporary expedients. Let every man and every family at this season of the year cultivate a plot of land and raise a sufficient supply for themselves or others. Every city and village has vacant space whose use would be permitted. Groups of men could rent farms for small sums and operate them on the co-operative plan. Employed men, in groups of ten, twenty or fifty, could rent farms and operate them with several unemployed families. Or, they could engage a farmer with his farm to be their farmer this year, either as employe or on shares. There are farmers who would be glad to give a decent indigent family a corner of a field on which to live and provide against next winter. Industrial concerns everywhere would gladly make it possible for their men, employed and unemployed, to find and work the land. Public-spirited citizens and institutions would most willingly assist in these efforts at self-help.

I do not urge this solely or primarily on the ground of need. It is a definite step to the restoration of normal business activity. Families who adopt self-help have that amount of free money to use in the channels of trade. That in turn means a flow of goods, an increase in employment, a general benefit.

No One Is Hurt

When I suggested this last year and enabled our own people to make the experiment, the critics said that it would mean competition with the farmer. If that were true it would constitute a serious defect in the plan. My interest in the success and prosperity of the farmer is attested by my whole business career. The farmer is carrying in the form of heavy taxes the burden of families who cannot afford to buy his produce. Enabling them to raise their own food would not be taking a customer away from the farmer, but would be actually lifting a family off the tax-payer's back. It is argued that farm products are so cheap that it is better to buy than to grow them. This would be impressive if every one had money to spend. Farm products are cheap because purchasing power is low. And the farmer paying taxes helps to pay the difference. The course I suggest is not competition with the farmer; it deprives him of no customer; it does not affect the big market crops. Gardens never hurt the farmer. Partnerships between groups of city men and individual farmers certainly help the farmer. When a family lifts itself off the welfare lists or increases its free cash by raising its food, it actually helps the farmer as it does every one else, including itself. In fact, it is fundamental that *no one is hurt by self-help*. In the relief of tax burdens and the revival of industry the farmer would share the benefit.

VIEWPOINT 24B

Self-Help Is Not Enough (1932)
Charles R. Walker (1893–1974)

Unemployment during the Great Depression was high, eventually peaking at about 25 percent of America's labor force. In the following viewpoint, Charles R. Walker examines the fate of one laborer who was laid off from the Ford Motor Company. He goes on to examine the effects of unemployment on workers in Detroit and surrounding areas in Michigan, suggesting in his depiction of these workers the limits of self-help as advocated by Henry Ford (see viewpoint 24A). Walker, a former steelworker, was a writer whose works, fictional and nonfictional, examined the effects of industrial technology on the American worker.

How does John Boris, the Ford worker Walker profiles, respond to unemployment? Why is Boris relatively lucky, in Walker's view? Does Boris's situation provide an example of the efficacy as well as the limits of self-help? Why or why not?

I n 1914 an extraordinary thing occurred in America. An automobile manufacturer in Detroit announced that he was raising wages for common labor to five dollars a day. Newspaper headlines in Detroit went a little crazy; the streets of the city and of the [nearby] little town of Dearborn were packed with workmen fighting for a chance to work at the new wage. And automobile manufacturers of Detroit and elsewhere raged and gave out desperate interviews prophesying doom. Detectives came to Detroit to investigate Henry Ford. But above all, workmen from all over the United States bought rail-

Excerpted from Charles R. Walker, "Down and Out in Detroit," in *America Faces the Future*, edited by Charles A. Beard (Boston: Houghton Mifflin, 1932).

road tickets and boarded trains for Detroit. Among the latter was John (once Anton) Boris, American citizen of Slav descent, father of a family, who had ambitions to be a 'millerwright' and needed cash for an expanding family. He had been a logger in a Michigan lumber camp, then a worker in an Ohio steel mill where he earned from two to three dollars a day. With thousands of others, he now came to Detroit.

Working at Ford

'In dose days work was hard all right at Ford's, but dey treat us like mens.' One day the straw boss fired a workman in anger. The employment manager stood between the boss and the workman. 'You can't discharge a man out of spite,' he said. 'I am putting you back to work—both of you—in different shops.' Boris remembered the episode a long time. Another day a boy in his department suggested over their noon sandwiches that they should have a union at Ford's. The boy was a skilled worker with a good record. The next week he did not appear in the millwrights' gang. When Boris asked where he was, his companions raised their shoulders. Boris remembered this, too. He decided not to listen to men talking about unions even though they were 'good millerwrights.' He decided not to talk about unions himself.

John Boris's wages at Ford's rose steadily as the years passed, till he was making eight dollars a day. His young wife, whom he had found it a delight to cherish as he had promised the priest, had borne him eight children, five of whom were living and going to Michigan schools. One day a letter arrived from a friend in a Texas oil field, saying to come out there for a good job. 'I think I go all right,' he told me, 'can get twenty dollar a day.' But his wife expressed other ideas. 'You stay wid Ford; here steady job—better dan big money for you; las' all de years what you live.' Boris stayed at Ford's.

'The American way,' said the automobile manufacturers in 1927, 'is to pay wages sufficient to guarantee the workingman not only subsistence, but the comforts and some of the luxuries of life. Let him buy a car, a radio, and an American home!' The children wanted a radio, so John got one; but he resisted his foreman's appeal to buy a car, even though American salesmanship did what it could against his Slavic conservatism. Public advice to 'buy a home,' however, appealed to an instinct. The real estate agent made out his contract. There was a five hundred dollars down payment and fifty dollars a month. He started payments and moved in. The house seemed in a sense to be rounding out his millwright's career for him; and better, he thought, than a car—even though the neighbors boasted of both.

It was in this house, under the shaded light of the 'parlor lamp,' that Boris the other day gave me in his own words the final chapter of this history. The house was subject to foreclosure in default of payment, but the furniture was still intact. The radio stood at the left of the chair where Boris sat; a double door led into a pleasant dining-room.

'Fourteen year,' said Boris, leaning forward, 'I work for Henry Ford. All kin' jobs . . . millerwright, danger jobs; I put in all my young days Henry Ford. Las' July, what you know, he lay me off. When I go out of factory that day I don' believe; I don' believe he do such ting to me. I tink trouble wid man in de office who don' un'erstan'.' His voice ceased and he took a deep breath which was expended in the earnest emphasis of his next words: 'I tink,' he said, 'I go Henry Ford *pers'nally!* But what you know!' He looked like a boy whom a drunken father had whipped into physical submission. His voice was angry, but with a deep hurt at the core of it. 'I can' get close to him,' he cried, 'I can' get clos' even employment man. De guard say, "We got your name in dere all right, we let you know when we wan' you." Nine mont',' he concluded, 'I go no work.'

Coping with Unemployment

Figures show that 14.2 per cent of Detroit's normally employed are out of jobs. Other cities follow close, with Cleveland at 13.8 per cent and Chicago at 13.3. The distinction of Detroit, however, is not that she has been hardest hit in the depression, but that she has done something to buck it. Municipal and community leadership—not the manufacturers—are doing what they can.

During the first of his workless periods, Boris was able to support his family and to continue regular payments on his home. Against public pressure he had exercised thrift, and had in reserve a few hundred dollars. But misfortunes did not attack him singly. His wife fell ill and an operation for tumor was demanded. Boris met the emergency and hired the best doctor he could find. A kidney operation on the woman followed the first, running up medical charges for hospital and doctor to eight hundred dollars. Somewhere during this epoch the son of John Boris, who had gone to an American school and could put matters clearly in written English, composed a letter to the welfare department of the Ford Motor Company.

An 'investigator' arrived promptly, and took the chair, Boris informed me, in which I was sitting. 'Investigator say, "Boris, employment have no right do that to you. You get job back right away. Seven o'clock tomorrow morning you go employment; he put you back on job; tak' this slip."'

Going back the next morning through the high mill gate, with the slip tightly held in his fingers, Boris found delightedly that he was admitted to the office. 'We cannot give you your old job,' they told him, 'at eight dollars a day, but we will give you a new one at six dollars for three days a week.' 'Yes, all right,' said Boris. Lay-off and rehire with a dock of a dollar or two a day is common in the automobile industry. It enables the manufacturer to give the appearance of 'maintaining wages' while effecting the needed economies in his payroll. The same work is performed on 'the new job.' Boris was glad. 'Hard times for everybody,' he explained, 'sure, I take.' The employment manager continued courteously: 'After you work sixty days, you will receive seven dollars a day.'. . .

On the sixty-first day, Boris received the promised seven dollars. On the sixty-third his foreman fired him. 'You're finished, Boris,' he said. To Boris it seemed clear that he had been dropped because he was 'making too much money.' And because there were thousands waiting to take his job at minimum pay. But he repressed this resentment and went to the office. 'Anything wrong wid my work for comp'ny?' he asked earnestly. No, the employment man assured him; his work was satisfactory. 'Wid my records for comp'ny?' he persisted, knowing that in hard times a man's record is his friend. 'No,' said the employment man, 'you have a good record with the company. But there is no longer any work for you.' The office then stated that this was not a lay-off, but, as Boris had expressed it, 'finish.' Boris then exploded. In reminiscence of what he had said, his voice came somewhere from the middle of his chest; it was compacted of fourteen years of exploded loyalty.

'I haf' no money now,' he cried, 'lose my home quick, what I do chil'ren, what I do doctor? Fourteen years!' he returned to his original cry, 'I work Henry Ford!'

The employment man looked at him. 'That is a long time; you should have saved money, Boris, to take care of you in your old age.'

Boris trembled. 'You say dat to me!' he cried, struggling for possession of himself. 'I give up my strength to you; I put in all my young days work good for Henry Ford—you can' do dis to me now!'

'Why did you spend all your money?' asked the employment man.

'For why? I tell you. I spen' money for house,' replied John Boris, 'to raise fam'ly, to sen' my chil'ren school, to buy foods, *dat's how I spen' money——*'

'Your children are your own business,' said the other, 'not Henry Ford's.'

Betrayed Loyalty

Even in recollection of this episode which terminated his career and hastened the break-up of his family, I was struck by the special character of Boris's resentment. It seemed clear that he was torn as terribly by the blasting of his workman's loyalty as by the enormity of his personal loss.

'I go out from mill,' he continued. 'I try tink what I do help mysel'. Who I go to? I use tink,' he cried, 'if something come like dis, go to Henry Ford yoursel'. But I tell you no workman beeg enough see Henry Ford! Well, I go lawyer—I happen to know him once—who knows ting like dis more what I do. I say: "What can I do now?" He say: "Nutting, John, ain' nutting you can do!"'

John Boris refused to accept the dictum of the lawyer that there was nothing he could do. In accordance with the formula that 'there is plenty of work in the world if a man be willing to take it,' he buried the pride of a skilled maturity, and found a few hours' work in a cushion factory, accepting a wage twenty-seven and one half cents an hour less than Ford's minimum rate in 1914. But long before he managed this, his daughters had taken jobs in the same factory to which he came ultimately. They carried and are still carrying the bulk of the family load.

These latter items make the story of John Boris a relatively lucky one. The family enjoys a small income from wages; John Boris is not, and except only for a few weeks between the time of 'finish' at Ford's and the cushion factory job, has not been rated as one of the unemployed. And he is lucky enough to have escaped charity.

As I was sitting in the Boris parlor, the two girls came in from work. It was nine o'clock. He introduced his daughters to me; they excused themselves and went to the kitchen. John Boris explained: 'Only when they work late, comp'ny give time for supper.' Work begins at seven-thirty; lunch at twelve. 'How late do you work?' I asked the younger girl, when she reappeared. 'Sometimes till nine o'clock,' she answered, 'sometimes till ten. One night last week we worked till eleven-thirty.' I checked up on this and found that in the smaller concerns which have sprung up in the wake of depression, no regularity prevails: the workmen are expected to finish the work available, which sometimes takes five hours, sometimes ten.

'Alice, Louie's girl,' said one of the girls, 'said she felt faint tonight'—it seemed to me that Miss Boris thought Alice a little silly for it—'so I sent her upstairs to my coat where I keep cookies.'

John Boris had been silent a long time. He moved his shoulders restlessly and looked down at the thick fingers of his hands. 'Las' July,' he said, 'I was good man.' He raised his eyes slowly. 'I ain't man now,' he said.

One of the Lucky Ones

With some effort I looked into the work of the Ford employment office and of the welfare department of the Ford Motor Company. A comprehensive stagger system I found had been organized to spread work among the largest possible number. Further than this, a sincere effort was being made everywhere to give jobs to the neediest. Boris was dismissed, I am ready to believe, not through carelessness—but because relatively worse cases needed his job more. In fact the wealth of data put before me by the mayor's unemployment committee of the city of Detroit confirms me in the belief that his particular case, in which job, savings, and home were wiped out, was one of the lucky ones.

•

"[The unemployed] were caught in the lay-off which everyone from their employers to the President of the United States assured them was a temporary dip in the cycle of prosperity."

•

In addition to Mr. Boris's case, there are 227,000 men totally unemployed. Let us consider some of these. Out of the number, fifteen thousand are reported homeless. Boris as yet is not of this class and will probably escape it by living with relatives. These men are now housed in the 'emergency lodges,' better known as 'flop houses,' which are maintained at the city's expense. What are they like? Take the 'Fisher East Side Lodge.' It is a huge unused factory building lent to the city by Fisher Brothers and housing, when I visited it, sixteen hundred men. Here I found bank tellers with twenty to thirty years' experience, traveling salesmen, expert toolmakers, a vice-president or two, and workmen of every variety.

The mayor's committee estimates that of the 'homeless men' on their records, about ten per cent are chronic vagrants who would be looking for handouts in fat times as well as lean. The rest are *bona-fide* unemployment cases with a large white-collar sprinkling. Fifteen thousand homeless is considered large for the size of the city and is generally attributed by manufacturers I talked with to the army of unmarried men attracted to Detroit by the high wages and short hours of the automobile factories. But I discovered that over ten per cent of the homeless group are married men. These are perhaps the least fortunate cases, as contrasted with the relatively fortunate who, like Boris, still command resources of a sort. What is their history? What, for example, becomes of the wife, and what happens to the kids? The story of the married homeless averages as follows. (I am omitting the cases of suicide and actual starvation.)

A majority of the men are automobile workers; the average age is thirty-eight. Fifteen years ago they came to Detroit attracted by the good wages. A considerable number are college men; as skilled workers, tool designers, and engineers, they made from ten to fifteen dollars a day. They laughed at their white-collar classmates making forty per—and obliged to 'keep up appearances.' The ordinary workers among them were making five dollars a day, or six dollars, or seven dollars, with steady jobs. They married, bought a car, and ultimately started payments on a 'home of their own.'

About six years ago the 'inventory period' of the manufacturers began to stretch. From two weeks' 'vacation' in summer—without pay—it edged up to a month. 'Changing tools' for the new model, repair periods, 'reorganization,' sliced another week or two from the winter months. As a rule the single man didn't care; for him it *was* a vacation. But his married brother got fidgety. He hadn't rigged his budget for a ten-month year. Then among Ford men came the five months' shutdown in 1927. This wiped out a good many surpluses. The surpluses were not large. Why? Most of the men had bought a car, had taken out insurance, and begun payments on the 'home.' By 1929, the family men were worried. Not in a panic, but thinking hard. They still had their homes, they still had the car, but their savings were gone. The expanding vacations gave them an increasing sense of insecurity.

The Depression Hits

Then descended the first months of the depression a year and a half ago. They were caught in the lay-off which everyone from their employers to the President of the United States assured them was a temporary dip in the cycle of prosperity. The first act of the conservative householder was to sell his car—the purchase of which a year before had been all but compelled by company salesmanship. 'It is your duty,' the married man had been told; 'it will guarantee your job.' Two months passed. Just as the newspapers agreed that the 'worst was over,' the married man borrowed four hundred dollars on his furniture. This to keep his end up, to continue payment on his home, pay his insurance premiums, buy food, and keep the boy at school. At this point he had adopted his employers' optimism. 'Things *must* pick up. In another month I'll be back at work.' But the month passes, and the furniture goes to meet the loan. However, there is the hundred dollars which Alice hasn't told him about. With it he manages one more payment on the house, hoping that the rumor about a 'pick-up' at Fisher's will come true. It doesn't.

In a Michigan 'land contract' the owner holds the deed; in case of the tenant's default, payments go to the deed-holder. At this point his contract is foreclosed, and with the house passes forever the three thousand dollars paid to date toward ownership. The children, who have been denied milk for a couple of months, are now sent to grandmother's, or parked around among relatives. The married man and his wife move into two rooms in the suburbs she had always scorned. With the change there passes into discard the emotions which cling to a united family, and to the home as a physical possession, somehow defensible.

The married man, however, at this point is really just beginning to fight. He tells his wife this in as many words. With the burden of the kids off his mind, and with no payments to make on the lost home, he is ready for any kind of work at any pay. It is the mood endorsed by so many well-wishers who themselves are in more fortunate positions. And he gets the work. Any number of young men found a month's neighborhood work, repairing the front steps, trimming hedges, mowing the lawn, or cleaning out the furnace—at a dollar a day, or two.

But this permits a physical subsistence only; it doesn't constitute what the married man hopes for and desires passionately—the beginnings of rehabilitation. After a couple of months the odd-job market is exhausted, and he has learned either to pity or to despise himself. The mental attitude of his new employers is, I find, almost without exception a compound of self-interest and charity. They demand two things of the ex-tool-maker who has asked the privilege of tending furnace for them: first, that he take a rate lower than they would pay an ordinary workman at the job; second, that he show himself abundantly grateful.

At some point during this odd-job epoch, the wife goes back upstate to live with her mother. She suggests he come too. But in the group I am considering, when the man's nerve is still strong, the husband answers: 'No. You go ahead, but I'll stick it in Detroit. This has been our home since 1918, and I certainly can find something. Before you know it I'll be sending for you.' He tries another six months, paying five dollars (a month) for his room. Finally pawns his overcoat, his watch; applies at last to the Welfare for an old pair of shoes.

You and I can call on him today at the Fisher Lodge, where at the moment the city will be able, if tax receipts hold up, to expend twenty-two and a half cents a day on him. Out of this comes a clean cot, clean laundry, and two meals a day. And he—with most of his fellows with whom I talked—is still looking for that job, working a week or two without pay for the city to pay for the winter's board.

For Further Reading

Irving Bernstein, *The Lean Years.* Boston: Houghton Mifflin, 1960.

Sean Dennis Cashman, *America in the Twenties and Thirties.* New York: New York University Press, 1989.

Edward Keller, *Mister Ford—What Have You Done?: Henry Ford's Views on Economics.* Qubin, MO: Keaton Keller, 1993.

John B. Rae, ed., *Henry Ford.* Englewood Cliffs, NJ: Prentice-Hall, 1969.

Studs Terkel, *Hard Times: An Oral History of the Great Depression.* New York: Pantheon Books, 1986.

VIEWPOINT 25A

America Needs a New Deal (1932)

Franklin D. Roosevelt (1882–1945)

In July 1932, with the nation still in the depths of the Great Depression, the Democratic Party nominated Franklin D. Roosevelt to run for president against the increasingly unpopular Republican incumbent, Herbert Hoover. Roosevelt was then governor of New York, where he had presided over the expansion of state government programs designed to deal with unemployment and other problems of the Great Depression. In accepting the presidential nomination, he broke with tradition by personally addressing the Democratic National Convention. In his speech, excerpted here, Roosevelt describes what he holds as fundamental differences between the nation's two main political parties concerning government and the people's welfare, and proposes new actions by the federal government to help farmers, the unemployed, and others hurt by the Great Depression. It was in this speech that he introduced the term "New Deal" to the American public.

How does Roosevelt describe the differences between the Republican and Democratic parties? How does he describe the causes and results of the Great Depression? What "simple moral principle" does Roosevelt state is the basis for his program?

T he great social phenomenon of this depression, unlike others before it, is that it has produced but a few of the disorderly manifestations that too often attend upon such times.

Wild radicalism has made few converts, and the greatest tribute that I can pay to my countrymen is that in these days of crushing want there persists an orderly and hopeful spirit on the part of the millions

Franklin D. Roosevelt, from his address to the Democratic National Convention, July 2, 1932. Reprinted in *Nothing to Fear: The Selected Addresses of Franklin Delano Roosevelt, 1932–1945*, edited by B.C. Zevin (Boston: Houghton Mifflin, 1946).

of our people who have suffered so much. To fail to offer them a new chance is not only to betray their hopes but to misunderstand their patience.

To meet by reaction that danger of radicalism is to invite disaster. Reaction is no barrier to the radical. It is a challenge, a provocation. The way to meet that danger is to offer a workable program of reconstruction, and the party to offer it is the party with clean hands.

This, and this only, is a proper protection against blind reaction on the one hand and an improvised, hit-or-miss, irresponsible opportunism on the other.

Two Views of Government

There are two ways of viewing the Government's duty in matters affecting economic and social life. The first sees to it that a favored few are helped and hopes that some of their prosperity will leak through, sift through, to labor, to the farmer, to the small business man. That theory belongs to the party of Toryism, and I had hoped that most of the Tories left this country in 1776.

But it is not and never will be the theory of the Democratic Party. This is no time for fear, for reaction or for timidity. Here and now I invite those nominal Republicans who find that their conscience cannot be squared with the groping and the failure of their party leaders to join hands with us; here and now, in equal measure, I warn those nominal Democrats who squint at the future with their faces turned toward the past, and who feel no responsibility to the demands of the new time, that they are out of step with their Party.

Yes, the people of this country want a genuine choice this year, not a choice between two names for the same reactionary doctrine. Ours must be a party of liberal thought, of planned action, of enlightened international outlook, and of the greatest good to the greatest number of our citizens.

Now it is inevitable—and the choice is that of the times—it is inevitable that the main issue of this campaign should revolve about the clear fact of our economic condition, a depression so deep that it is without precedent in modern history. It will not do merely to state, as do Republican leaders to explain their broken promises of continued inaction, that the depression is worldwide. That was not their explanation of the apparent prosperity of 1928. The people will not forget the claim made by them then that prosperity was only a domestic product manufactured by a Republican President and a Republican Congress. If they claim paternity for the one they cannot deny paternity for the other.

I cannot take up all the problems today. I want to touch on a few that are vital. Let us look a little at the recent history and the simple economics, the kind of economics that you and I and the average man and woman talk.

In the years before 1929 we know that this country had completed a vast cycle of building and inflation; for ten years we expanded on the theory of repairing the wastes of the War, but actually expanding far beyond that, and also beyond our natural and normal growth. Now it is worth remembering, and the cold figures of finance prove it, that during that time there was little or no drop in the prices that the consumer had to pay, although those same figures proved that the cost of production fell very greatly; corporate profit resulting from this period was enormous; at the same time little of that profit was devoted to the reduction of prices. The consumer was forgotten. Very little of it went into increased wages; the worker was forgotten, and by no means an adequate proportion was even paid out in dividends—the stockholder was forgotten.

And, incidentally, very little of it was taken by taxation to the beneficent Government of those years.

What was the result? Enormous corporate surpluses piled up—the most stupendous in history. Where, under the spell of delirious speculation, did those surpluses go? Let us talk economics that the figures prove and that we can understand. Why, they went chiefly in two directions: first, into new and unnecessary plants which now stand stark and idle; and second, into the call-money market [options to buy stock based on the belief the price will rise] of Wall Street, either directly by the corporations, or indirectly through the banks. Those are the facts. Why blink at them?

The Stock Market Crash

Then came the crash. You know the story. Surpluses invested in unnecessary plants became idle. Men lost their jobs; purchasing power dried up; banks became frightened and started calling loans. Those who had money were afraid to part with it. Credit contracted. Industry stopped. Commerce declined, and unemployment mounted.

And there we are today.

Translate that into human terms. See how the events of the past three years have come home to specific groups of people: first, the group dependent on industry; second, the group dependent on agriculture; third, and made up in large part of members of the first two groups, the people who are called "small investors and depositors." In fact, the strongest possible tie between the first two groups, agriculture and industry, is the fact that the savings and to a degree the security of both are tied together in that third group—the credit structure of the Nation.

Never in history have the interests of all the people been so united in a single economic problem.

Picture to yourself, for instance, the great groups of property owned by millions of our citizens, represented by credits issued in the form of bonds and mortgages—Government bonds of all kinds, Federal, State, county, municipal; bonds of industrial companies, of utility companies; mortgages on real estate in farms and cities, and finally the vast investments of the Nation in the railroads. What is the measure of the security of each of those groups? We know well that in our complicated, interrelated credit structure if any one of these credit groups collapses they may all collapse. Danger to one is danger to all.

How, I ask, has the present Administration in Washington treated the interrelationship of these credit groups? The answer is clear: It has not recognized that interrelationship existed at all. Why, the Nation asks, has Washington failed to understand that all of these groups, each and every one, the top of the pyramid and the bottom of the pyramid, must be considered together, that each and every one of them is dependent on every other; each and every one of them affecting the whole financial fabric?

Statesmanship and vision, my friends, require relief to all at the same time.

Taxes and Spending

Just one word or two on taxes, the taxes that all of us pay toward the cost of Government of all kinds.

I know something of taxes. For three long years I have been going up and down this country preaching that Government—Federal and State and local—costs too much. I shall not stop that preaching. As an immediate program of action we must abolish useless offices. We must eliminate unnecessary functions of Government—functions, in fact, that are not definitely essential to the continuance of Government. We must merge, we must consolidate subdivisions of Government, and, like the private citizen, give up luxuries which we can no longer afford.

By our example at Washington itself, we shall have the opportunity of pointing the way of economy to local government, for let us remember well that out of every tax dollar in the average State in this Nation, forty cents enter the treasury in Washington, D.C., ten or twelve cents only go to the State capitals, and forty-eight cents are consumed by the costs of local government in counties and cities and towns.

I propose to you, my friends, and through you, that Government of all kinds, big and little, be made solvent and that the example be set by the President of the United States and his Cabinet. . . .

Unemployment

And now one word about unemployment, and incidentally about agriculture. I have favored the use of certain types of public works as a further emergency means of stimulating employment and the issuance of bonds to pay for such public works, but I have pointed out that no economic end is served if we merely build without building for a necessary purpose. Such works, of course, should insofar as possible be self-sustaining if they are to be financed by the issuing of bonds. So as to spread the points of all kinds as widely as possible, we must take definite steps to shorten the working day and the working week.

———— • ————

"Republican leaders not only have failed in material things, they have failed in national vision. . . . I pledge myself to a new deal for the American people."

———— • ————

Let us use common sense and business sense. Just as one example, we know that a very hopeful and immediate means of relief, both for the unemployed and for agriculture, will come from a wide plan of the converting of many millions of acres of marginal and unused land into timberland through reforestation. There are tens of millions of acres east of the Mississippi River alone in abandoned farms, in cut-over land, now growing up in worthless brush. Why, every European Nation has a definite land policy, and has had one for generations. We have none. Having none, we face a future of soil erosion and timber famine. It is clear that economic foresight and immediate employment march hand in hand in the call for the reforestation of these vast areas. In so doing, employment can be given to a million men. That is the kind of public work that is self-sustaining, and therefore capable of being financed by the issuance of bonds which are made secure by the fact that the growth of tremendous crops will provide adequate security for the investment.

Yes, I have a very definite program for providing employment by that means. I have done it, and I am doing it today in the State of New York. I know that the Democratic Party can do it successfully in the Nation. That will put men to work, and that is an example of the action that we are going to have.

Aid to Agriculture

Now as a further aid to agriculture, we know perfectly well—but have we come out and said so clearly and distinctly?—we should repeal immediately those provisions of law that compel the Federal Government to go into the market to purchase, to sell, to speculate in farm products in a futile attempt to reduce farm surpluses. And they are the people who are talking of keeping Government out of business.

The practical way to help the farmer is by an arrangement that will, in addition to lightening some of the impoverishing burdens from his back, do something toward the reduction of the surpluses of staple commodities that hang on the market. It should be our aim to add to the world prices of staple products the amount of a reasonable tariff protection, to give agriculture the same protection that industry has today.

And in exchange for this immediately increased return I am sure that the farmers of this Nation would agree ultimately to such planning of their production as would reduce the surpluses and make it unnecessary in later years to depend on dumping those surpluses abroad in order to support domestic prices. That result has been accomplished in other Nations; why not in America, too? . . .

Rediscounting of farm mortgages under salutary restrictions must be expanded and should, in the future, be conditioned on the reduction of interest rates. Amortization payments, maturities should likewise in this crisis be extended before rediscount is permitted where the mortgagor is sorely pressed. That, my friends, is another example of practical, immediate relief: Action.

I aim to do the same thing, and it can be done, for the small home-owner in our cities and villages. We can lighten his burden and develop his purchasing power. Take away, my friends, that spectre of too high an interest rate. Take away that spectre of the due date just a short time away. Save homes; save homes for thousands of self-respecting families, and drive out that spectre of insecurity from our midst.

The Harms of Tariffs

Out of all the tons of printed paper, out of all the hours of oratory, the recriminations, the defenses, the happy-thought plans in Washington and in every State, there emerges one great, simple, crystal-pure fact that during the past ten years a Nation of one hundred twenty million people has been led by the Republican leaders to erect an impregnable barbed wire entanglement around its borders through the instrumentality of tariffs which have isolated us from all the other human beings in all the rest of the round world. I accept th[e] admirable tariff statement in the platform of this convention. It would protect American business and American labor. By our acts of the past we have invited and received the retaliation of other nations. I propose an invitation to them to forget the past, to sit at the table with us, as friends, and to plan with us for the restoration of the trade of the world.

Go into the home of the business man. He knows what the tariff has done for him. Go into the home of the factory worker. He knows why goods do not move. Go into the home of the farmer. He knows how the tariff has helped to ruin him.

At last our eyes are open. At last the American people are ready to acknowledge that Republican leadership was wrong and that the Democracy is right.

Work and Security

My program, of which I can only touch on these points, is based upon this simple moral principle: the welfare and the soundness of a nation depend first upon what the great mass of the people wish and need; and second, whether or not they are getting it.

What do the people of America want more than anything else? To my mind, they want two things: work, with all the moral and spiritual values that go with it; and with work, a reasonable measure of security—security for themselves and for their wives and children. Work and security—these are more than words. They are more than facts. They are the spiritual values, the true goal toward which our efforts of reconstruction should lead. These are the values that this program is intended to gain; these are the values we have failed to achieve by the leadership we now have.

Our Republican leaders tell us economic laws—sacred, inviolable, unchangeable—cause panics which no one could prevent. But while they prate of economic laws, men and women are starving. We must lay hold of the fact that economic laws are not made by nature. They are made by human beings.

Yes, when—not if—when we get the chance, the Federal Government will assume bold leadership in distress relief. For years Washington has alternated between putting its head in the sand and saying there is no large number of destitute people in our midst who need food and clothing, and then saying the State should take care of them, if there are. Instead of planning two and a half years ago to do what they are now trying to do, they kept putting it off from day to day, week to week, and month to month, until the conscience of America demanded action.

I say that while primary responsibility for relief rests with localities now, as ever, yet the Federal Government has always had and still has a continuing responsibility for the broader public welfare. It will soon fulfill that responsibility. . . .

One word more: Out of every crisis, every tribulation, every disaster, mankind rises with some share of greater knowledge, of higher decency, of purer purpose. Today we shall have come through a period of loose thinking, descending morals, an era of selfishness, among individual men and women and among nations. Blame not Governments alone for this. Blame ourselves in equal share. Let us be frank in acknowledgment of the truth that many amongst us have made obeisance to Mammon, that the profits of speculation, the easy road without toil, have lured us from the old barricades. To return to higher standards we must abandon the false prophets and seek new leaders of our own choosing.

A New Deal

Never before in modern history have the essential differences between the two major American parties stood out in such striking contrast as they do today. Republican leaders not only have failed in material things, they have failed in national vision, because in disaster they have held out no hope, they have pointed out no path for the people below to climb back to places of security and of safety in our American life.

Throughout the Nation men and women, forgotten in the political philosophy of the Government of the last years, look to us here for guidance and for more equitable opportunity to share in the distribution of national wealth.

On the farms, in the large metropolitan areas, in the smaller cities and in the villages, millions of our citizens cherish the hope that their old standards of living and of thought have not gone forever. Those millions cannot and shall not hope in vain.

I pledge you, I pledge myself, to a new deal for the American people. Let us all here assembled constitute ourselves prophets of a new order of competence and of courage. This is more than a political campaign; it is a call to arms. Give me your help, not to win votes alone, but to win in this crusade to restore America to its own people.

VIEWPOINT 25B

Roosevelt's New Deal Would Destroy America (1932)

Herbert Hoover (1874–1964)

Elected in 1928, Herbert Hoover was president of the United States during the first years of the Great Depression. His popularity suffered sharply as economic conditions worsened in the early 1930s. Nonetheless, he was renominated for the presidency by the Republican Party in 1932. During the campaign he both defended his presidency and attacked his Democratic opponent, Franklin D. Roosevelt. In the following viewpoint, excerpted from a campaign address given at New York City's Madison Square Garden on October 31, 1932, Hoover defends his record and what he calls the "American system" of individual freedom and limited government.

Herbert Hoover, from a campaign speech delivered at Madison Square Garden, New York City, October 31, 1932. Reprinted in *The State Papers and Other Public Writings of Herbert Hoover*, vol. 2, edited by William Starr Myers (New York: Doubleday, Dorian & Co., 1934).

What does Hoover see as the proper role for the federal government in managing the nation's economy? What aspects of the "American system" are most threatened by a Roosevelt presidency, according to Hoover? What hope does Hoover offer the nation of the Great Depression's ending?

This campaign is more than a contest between two men. It is more than a contest between two parties. It is a contest between two philosophies of government.

We are told by the opposition that we must have a change, that we must have a new deal. It is not the change that comes from normal development of national life to which I object, but the proposal to alter the whole foundations of our national life which have been builded through generations of testing and struggle, and of the principles upon which we have builded the Nation. The expressions our opponents use must refer to important changes in our economic and social system and our system of Government, otherwise they are nothing but vacuous words. And I realize that in this time of distress many of our people are asking whether our social and economic system is incapable of that great primary function of providing security and comfort of life to all of the firesides of our 25,000,000 homes in America, whether our social system provides for the fundamental development and progress of our people, whether our form of government is capable of originating and sustaining that security and progress.

This question is the basis upon which our opponents are appealing to the people in their fears and distress. They are proposing changes and so-called new deals which would destroy the very foundations of our American system. . . .

The American System

Let us pause for a moment and examine the American system of government, of social and economic life, which it is now proposed that we should alter. Our system is the product of our race and of our experience in building a nation to heights unparalleled in the whole history of the world. It is a system peculiar to the American people. It differs essentially from all others in the world. It is an American system.

It is founded on the conception that only through ordered liberty, through freedom to the individual, and equal opportunity to the individual will his initiative and enterprise be summoned to spur the march of progress.

It is by the maintenance of equality of opportunity and therefore of a society absolutely fluid in freedom of the movement of its human particles that our individualism departs from the individualism of Europe. We resent class distinction because there can be no rise for the individual through the frozen strata of classes, and no stratification of classes can take place in a mass livened by the free rise of its particles. Thus in our ideals the able and ambitious are able to rise constantly from the bottom to leadership in the community.

This freedom of the individual creates of itself the necessity and the cheerful willingness of men to act cooperatively in a thousand ways and for every purpose as occasion arises; and it permits such voluntary cooperations to be dissolved as soon as they have served their purpose, to be replaced by new voluntary associations for new purposes.

"Our opponents . . . are proposing changes and so-called new deals which would destroy the very foundations of our American system."

There has thus grown within us, to gigantic importance, a new conception. That is, this voluntary cooperation within the community. Cooperation to perfect the social organization; cooperation for the care of those in distress; cooperation for the advancement of knowledge, of scientific research, of education; for cooperative action in the advancement of many phases of economic life. This is self-government by the people outside of Government; it is the most powerful development of individual freedom and equal opportunity that has taken place in the century and a half since our fundamental institutions were founded.

It is in the further development of this cooperation and a sense of its responsibility that we should find solution for many of our complex problems, and not by the extension of government into our economic and social life. The greatest function of government is to build up that cooperation, and its most resolute action should be to deny the extension of bureaucracy. We have developed great agencies of cooperation by the assistance of the Government which promote and protect the interests of individuals and the smaller units of business. The Federal Reserve System, in its strengthening and support of the smaller banks; the Farm Board, in its strengthening and support of the farm cooperatives; the Home Loan Banks, in the mobilizing of building and loan associations and savings banks; the Federal Land Banks, in giving independence and strength to land mortgage associations; the great mobilization of relief to distress, the mobilization of business and industry in measures of recovery, and a score of other activities are not socialism—they are the essence of protection to the development of free men.

The primary conception of this whole American system is not the regimentation of men but the cooperation of free men. It is founded upon the conception of responsibility of the individual to the community, of the responsibility of local government to the state, of the state to the National Government.

It is founded on a peculiar conception of self-government designed to maintain this equal opportunity to the individual, and through decentralization it brings about and maintains these responsibilities. The centralization of government will undermine responsibilities and will destroy the system. . . .

Democratic Proposals

A proposal of our opponents which would break down the American system is the expansion of Government expenditure by yielding to sectional and group raids on the Public Treasury. The extension of Government expenditures beyond the minimum limit necessary to conduct the proper functions of the Government enslaves men to work for the Government. If we combine the whole governmental expenditures—National, state, and municipal—we will find that before the World War each citizen worked, theoretically, 25 days out of each year for the Government. In 1924 he worked 46 days a year for the Government. Today he works for the support of all forms of government 61 days out of the year.

No nation can conscript its citizens for this proportion of men's time without national impoverishment and destruction of their liberties. Our Nation cannot do it without destruction to our whole conception of the American system. The Federal Government has been forced in this emergency to unusual expenditures but in partial alleviation of these extraordinary and unusual expenditures, the Republican Administration has made a successful effort to reduce the ordinary running expenses of the Government. Our opponents have persistently interfered with such policies. I only need recall to you that the Democratic House of Representatives passed bills in the last session that would have increased our expenditures by $3,500,000,000, or 87 per cent. Expressed in day's labor, this would have meant the conscription of 16 days' additional work from every citizen for the Government. This I stopped. . . . But the major point I wish to make— the disheartening part of these proposals of our opponents—is that they represent successful pressures of minorities. They would appeal to sectional and group political support, and thereby impose terrific burdens upon every home in the country. These things can and must be resisted. But they can only be resisted if there shall be live and virile public support to the Administration, in opposition to political log-rolling and the sectional and group raids on the Treasury for distribution of public money, which is cardinal in the congeries of elements which make up the Democratic party.

These expenditures proposed by the Democratic House of Representatives for the benefit of special groups and special sections of our country directly undermine the American system. Those who pay are, in the last analysis, the man who works at the bench, the desk, and on the farm. They take away his comfort, stifle his leisure, and destroy his equal opportunity. . . .

The Growth of Government

No man who has not occupied my position in Washington can fully realize the constant battle which must be carried on against incompetence, corruption, tyranny of government expanded into business activities. If we first examine the effect on our form of government of such a program, we come at once to the effect of the most gigantic increase in expenditure ever known in history. That alone would break down the savings, the wages, the equality of opportunity among our people. These measures would transfer vast responsibilities to the Federal Government from the states, the local governments, and the individuals. But that is not all; they would break down our form of government. Our legislative bodies can not delegate their authority to any dictator, but without such delegation every member of these bodies is impelled in representation of the interest of his constituents constantly to seek privilege and demand service in the use of such agencies. Every time the Federal Government extends its arm, 531 Senators and Congressmen become actual boards of directors of that business.

Capable men can not be chosen by politics for all the various talents required. Even if they were supermen, if there were no politics in the selection of the Congress, if there were no constant pressure for this and for that, so large a number would be incapable as a board of directors of any institution. At once when these extensions take place by the Federal Government, the authority and responsibility of state governments and institutions are undermined. Every enterprise of private business is at once halted to know what Federal action is going to be. It destroys initiative and courage. . . .

The Cost of Freedom

Even if the Government conduct of business could give us the maximum of efficiency instead of least efficiency, it would be purchased at the cost of freedom. It would increase rather than decrease abuse and corruption, stifle initiative and invention, undermine development of leadership, cripple mental and spiritual energies of our people, extinguish equality of opportunity, and dry up the spirit of liberty and progress. Men who are going about this country announcing that they are liberals because of their promises to extend the Government in business are not liberals, they are reactionaries of the United States. . . .

Ending Poverty

I am not setting up the contention that our American system is perfect. No human ideal has ever been perfectly attained, since humanity itself is not perfect. But the wisdom of our forefathers and the wisdom of the 30 men who have preceded me in this office hold to the conception that progress can only be attained as the sum of accomplishments of free individuals, and they have held unalterably to these principles.

In the ebb and flow of economic life our people in times of prosperity and ease naturally tend to neglect the vigilance over their rights. Moreover, wrongdoing is obscured by apparent success in enterprise. Then insidious diseases and wrongdoings grow apace. But we have in the past seen in times of distress and difficulty that wrongdoing and weakness come to the surface and our people, in their endeavors to correct these wrongs, are tempted to extremes which may destroy rather than build.

It is men who do wrong, not our institutions. It is men who violate the laws and public rights. It is men, not institutions, which must be punished.

In my acceptance speech four years ago at Palo Alto I stated that—

> One of the oldest aspirations of the human race was the abolition of poverty. By poverty I mean the grinding by under-nourishment, cold, ignorance, fear of old age to those who have the will to work.

I stated that—

> In America today we are nearer a final triumph over poverty than in any land. The poorhouse has vanished from amongst us; we have not reached that goal, but given a chance to go forward, we shall, with the help of God, be in sight of the day when poverty will be banished from this Nation.

Our Democratic friends have quoted this passage many times in this campaign. I do not withdraw a word of it. When I look about the world even in these times of trouble and distress I find it more true in this land than anywhere else under the traveling sun. I am not ashamed of it, because I am not ashamed of holding ideals and purposes for the progress of the American people. Are my Democratic opponents prepared to state that they do not stand for this ideal or this hope? For my part, I propose to continue to strive for it, and I hope to live to see it accomplished. . . .

America's Choice

My countrymen, the proposals of our opponents represent a profound change in American life—less in concrete proposal, bad as that may be, than by implication and by evasion. Dominantly in their spirit they represent a radical departure from the foundations of 150 years which have made this the greatest nation in the world. This election is not a mere shift from the ins to the outs. It means deciding the direction our Nation will take over a century to come.

For Further Reading

Frank Freidel, *FDR: Rendezvous with Destiny.* Boston: Little, Brown, 1990.

Elliot A. Rosen, *Hoover, Roosevelt, and the Brains Trust.* New York: Columbia University Press, 1977.

Harris Gaylord Warren, *Herbert Hoover and the Great Depression.* New York: Oxford University Press, 1959.

Joan Hoff Wilson, *Herbert Hoover, Forgotten Progressive.* Boston: Little, Brown, 1975.

VIEWPOINT 26A

The New Deal Is a Momentous Achievement (1933)

Allan Nevins (1890–1971)

Franklin D. Roosevelt was elected president in 1932 promising a "New Deal" for the American people. He called Congress into special session shortly after his inauguration in March 1933 to carry out his promise. Over the next hundred days, Roosevelt and Congress passed numerous laws and programs designed to reduce unemployment and promote economic activity. Among the federal agencies and programs created were the National Recovery Administration (NRA), the Agricultural Adjustment Administration (AAA), the Federal Emergency Relief Administration (FERA), the Securities and Exchange Commission (SEC), and the Federal Deposit Insurance Corporation (FDIC).

The following viewpoint is taken from a December 31, 1933, article in the *New York Times Magazine*, in which well-known historian Allan Nevins attempts to summarize the historical events of that year and to evaluate Roosevelt's New Deal. Nevins compares the actions of the United States with those of other countries facing economic depression and argues that the New Deal is an impressive showing of America's ability to adapt to new conditions. Nevins taught American history at Columbia University in New York and held editorial posts at the *New York*

From "1933–34: Two Momentous Years" by Allan Nevins, *The New York Times Magazine*, December 31, 1933.

World and *New York Sun.*

Have the ideas of government undergone a radical change in the United States, according to Nevins? What comments does he make about President Roosevelt's leadership abilities and the American constitutional system? What assertions does Nevins make about the economic prosperity of the 1920s?

The year that now draws to a close has been marked by extraordinary fluctuations and changes. It has been on the whole a year of storm, with nations struggling in the waves left by the World War. Many countries had been half-submerged ever since that conflict. The United States, which for a time had ridden on the top of the surge, fell at the beginning of the year deeper into the trough than any other. In its extremity it turned, like Europe, to new experiments. Certainly in no other year since 1919 has the world seen so many radically new ideas and principles broached.

There has been what seemed to many a great change in ideas of government. Fascism has been striding onward; the United States has entrusted unprecedented peacetime authority to Mr. Roosevelt. There has been a radical revision of men's ideas upon international relationships. World organization has suffered heavily, and theories of "autarchy" or self-containment have made many converts.

In the field of economics also there has been a momentous shifting of ideas—in the United States in particular, which has turned to reduction of production, to restriction of competition and to government intervention for the raising of commodity prices. Bold new financial theories are accepted in high places; most of the world is off the gold standard; the validity of that standard in its old form is being questioned, and in the two most powerful nations [Great Britain and the United States] attempts are being made to manage the currency.

Ideas Born of Crisis

These new ideas, however varied, have one common quality. They are fundamentally the products of a time of unexampled crisis. A number of them bear plain evidence of exaggeration or distortion and one or two even of hysteria. During great tempests there are moments when the earth itself seems to heave and tremble. After they have passed men realize that this was a delusion, that through all the rush and shock of wind and wave the earth stood solid as ever—its quivers were imagined.

Of late, Americans have had a tendency to pass from one exaggeration to another. Six years ago they talked of a new economic era of unprecedented possibilities, of prosperity that nothing could check and

stocks that "will go to a thousand" [as measured by the Dow Jones Industrial Average Index]. Bank presidents said that we had but started on our way, and economists of repute wrote that the soaring stock prices registered a permanent revolution in national well-being. It is possible that at the nadir of the depression many ideas are as warped as were those expressed at the crest of the wave. When we get back to a fairly calm sea we may perceive that both were askew, and that "If hopes [1928] were dupes, fears [in 1933] may be liars."

At any rate, the year 1934 is certain to offer a severe test for many of the ideas and principles propounded in 1933. There is evidence that it will be a year of slowly returning prosperity. The best reason for thinking this is that the recent upward tendency seems to be world-wide. It is the same in England, America, Scandinavia and Australia, which are off the gold basis, and in France, Belgium and Switzerland, which are still on it; the same in nations with managed currencies and in nations without them; the same in high-tariff countries and in moderate-tariff countries. A general trend, whose origins economists trace back to midsummer of 1932, seems to be at work.

---•---

"What actually happened in this nation in 1933 was . . . a magnificent vindication of democracy."

---•---

Theories formed to fit a depression will soon, we may hope, be working in a period of growing normality. Laws and governmental agencies devised for populations badly frightened, and hence ductile and obedient, will have to be applied to populations which are resuming their individualistic habits. And there are other factors as well. Men's whole attitude toward great public questions may change rapidly, as our recent dramatic verdict [repeal] upon Prohibition has just indicated. Altogether, the next twelve-month will undoubtedly sift much which the last year has produced.

Without violating Lowell's wise maxim, "Don't prophesy onless ye know," it is possible to make one flat statement: The recent assertions that ideas of government have undergone a radical change will not be sustained by future events. These assertions rest upon a misreading of the facts. The assumption in certain quarters that in the United States something has befallen democracy, that the concentration of power in the President's hands has meant a "revolution," already begins to appear absurd. No country, for evident reasons, is less inclined to revolution than the United States. What actually happened in this nation in 1933 was just the opposite, a magnificent vindication of democracy. We proved anew the flexibility of our government, its capacity for meeting unexpected tensions.

The sudden expansion of Presidential authority to overcome a great emergency conformed entirely with the intent of the founders of the Republic. They meant that in war, in periods of internal strife and in great economic crises the President should be endowed with sufficient power to conquer all difficulties. Again and again Presidents have assumed such power. Jefferson did so when he stretched the Constitution till it cracked, Jackson when he met nullification, Lincoln during the Civil War, Wilson during the World War. When the present crisis subsides, Mr. Roosevelt's powers will subside also.

In fact, it is in times like the present and under such bold and resourceful leaders as Mr. Roosevelt that our democratic institutions are at their best. There is some reason to feel discouraged about them when weak Presidents fail to exercise their authority in due degree—and we do not need to go back to Pierce and Buchanan to name such Presidents. There is no reason to feel anything but optimism when we see Congress and President cooperating as they did last spring, the Chief Executive showing sustained leadership and the people responding loyally to the demands of the government. This is representative government as [John] Locke and Montesquieu outlined it two centuries ago and as James Bryce and Woodrow Wilson expounded it more recently.

We have plenty of balance in reserve. The legislative branch will be playing its usual rôle in a few days, and the judiciary is still to be heard from. But the best defenders of democracy have always contended that balance has to give way at times to stern executive leadership. . . .

A New Economic Philosophy

In the economic sphere there is much that is still confused and bewildering. In many respects the American people are still at a half-way point. Yet, again a few statements may be ventured without treading on the dangerous ground of prophecy. For one, the year 1933 seemed to show that the United States is at last accepting a long-contested principle: the principle that no prosperity is a true prosperity unless it embraces substantially the entire population.

This may sound axiomatic. Yet we can now see that during the decade of the Twenties it was disregarded by most Easterners and by a number of those in the highest governmental places. The prosperity which we boasted from 1921 to 1929, and which many

recklessly misused, left large sections of the country untouched. The great mass of the American farmers, the great majority of bituminous [coal] miners, a large part of our textile workers, to name only three groups, were shut out in the cold.

The first of these groups was all-important. Mr. [George] Peek said a few pungent words in Chicago the other day about the folly of trying to make a profit system work while depriving 6,000,000 farmers, who are at the foundation of our whole national life, of any hope of profits. It has been generally acknowledged during 1933 that if the administrations which scolded the farmer so vigorously for demanding just such aid as had been granted to industry in the postwar tariffs had spent a little more energy in devising rational assistance to agriculture, we might have been far better off today. A dollar spent six or eight years ago . . . would have saved many dollars this last year. Instead, the farmer was rebuffed with a lecture on political economy—the lecturers themselves forgetting some of the most elementary tenets of national economy in the larger sense.

Of all the new ideas put into effect by the Roosevelt administration, the idea that the prosperity of the farmers is worth just as much governmental thought and effort as that of the industrialists ought to be surest of continued approval. The administration has turned to a series of frankly experimental devices to help agriculture.

The policy that men should be paid not to grow wheat, cotton, corn and hogs would have astounded an earlier generation. It may not win indefinite acceptance; the coming year may bring it under heavy fire. The farmer himself, still a stanch individualist, who would far rather grow all he could for a large foreign market than grow half of what he could for a restricted domestic market, may insist on changes. Some of them have already been hinted at by Secretary [of Agriculture] Henry Wallace in his utterances on foreign trade as it affects the farmer. But the general principle that the country can never again afford to let the prairies and the plantations drop lower and lower in poverty and discouragement just because its factories and brokerage houses are still flourishing may be taken as fairly established for 1934 and all future years.

Industrial Reform

The fate during the coming year of the various ideas bound up in the NRA [National Recovery Administration] will likewise be interesting to watch. That system of government advisership and assistance to industry, as Mr. Roosevelt calls it—repudiating the word "control"—has hitherto been under the guidance and surveillance of the Executive alone. It will now pass under that of Congress as well, while the legislation creating it remains to be tested in the highest court.

Unquestionably, if and as the economic crisis passes, the tendency to regard this as purely emergency legislation will gain strength. With much of it certain to lapse, the really interesting question is what permanent residuum will remain. That it will at least leave some permanent benefits of a social nature in higher minimum-wage standards, in shorter hours and in the reduction of child labor may be devoutly hoped.

Some of these benefits will have to be embodied in entirely new legislation. To make sure of the one last named, the abolition of child labor, another constitutional amendment will be required, and already there is evidence that Mr. Roosevelt's bold measures have given impetus to the movement in the States for ratifying it. We may hope that 1934 will prove that much in the NRA standards which has been hailed by social meliorists most jubilantly will remain as a permanent legacy.

Doubtless the fundamental question in the economic sphere, however, is whether the country will long support the new principle that prosperity may be attained and kept by cutting down production, restricting competition and thus raising price levels. This principle, if carried to its logical conclusion, really comes near being "revolutionary" in a minor sense of the word. It is certainly in direct conflict with some of the convictions most deeply ingrained in the American breast.

Most plain citizens of this country still regard the anti-trust laws and all other legislation against collusion, combination, interlocking directorates and the like with the deepest jealousy. Many people have a keen remembrance of some of the evils of monopoly in the days when trusts were most lawless; many have an unshakable faith in the value of competition. The West in particular looks upon this legislation as one of the bulwarks of economic and political liberty.

In general, again, most Americans, however illogically, hold that there is a direct connection between unfettered production and a rising standard of comfort. Various writers, like Walter Lippmann, have lately pointed out that the outcry against overproduction is always raised when depressions occur, that we have often heard it in the past when production was but a fraction of what it now is, and that it has always been forgotten when good times recur.

As for prices, the American public is capable of coming very quickly and sharply to the conclusion that prices and living costs are too high. In this whole field it is clear that the Roosevelt administration has raised many questions which are far from settled. The coming year must go a long way toward providing the answers.

The Gold Standard

Questions of finance may well be left to the experts who are now quarreling so acrimoniously upon the subject. Obviously this debate has as yet come nowhere near its conclusion. Its vehemence has so far perhaps succeeded in impressing upon the general public just one truth. There is no fiat from Heaven which has ordained that the gold dollar of 23.22 grains shall be immutably indispensable to American well-being.

That dollar was fixed, not by supernatural decree, but by act of Congress in 1834. This legislation superseded an earlier law of Congress, which in 1792 fixed a decidedly different gold content (to wit, 24.75 grains) for the dollar. It is possible to conceive of the government fixing a third gold content in 1934 without bringing the nation to utter ruin. The most important characteristic that money can have is stability, and gold has been far from stable.

When, once before, in the years preceding 1896, declining prices called the gold standard into sharp question, the problem was solved by a greatly enlarged production of gold. William Jennings Bryan was able to remark, with complete justice, that the Republicans wanted the gold standard and got it, and that the Democrats wanted more money and got it. Today the solution may have to be very different. It is clearly evident that it will have to be a compromise solution and that it will have to take into account the arguments for higher commodity prices and for a scaling down of debts.

Moreover, most people are now convinced that we need not expect an ideal solution, for in the very nature of the question that is impossible. We did not have an ideal currency before the crash and we should not expect or demand to have it afterward.

The World Situation

As we look back over the year 1933, viewing the world as a whole, it is impossible to avoid the conclusion that the most disturbing development has been the weakening of international ties. So far as the hope of world cooperation and unity goes, the past twelve-month has recorded several heavy defeats. The World Economic Conference in London, while not completely fruitless, did in general prove empty and abortive. The Disarmament Conference came to nothing. Moreover, Germany's rupture with it led to a still more deplorable event. The League of Nations has now been weakened by the withdrawal of the Reich, following hard on that of Japan. Of the world's seven greatest powers, four—United States, Germany, Russia and Japan—are left on New Year's Day of 1934 outside its portals. . . .

The largest single source of the world's present ills,

economic as well as political, is to be found in nationalistic conflicts and barriers. The world depression has descended directly from the World War, its effects accentuated by nationalistic jealousies and disputes over reparations, debts and tariffs. If the coming year is to bring us a permanent hope of better times it must do something to reverse these unfortunate tendencies of 1933—to strengthen the League, to reduce the burden of armaments, to lessen the constant danger of an explosion in Europe, to lower trade barriers and to bring the nations of the world into closer relations and greater friendliness.

VIEWPOINT 26B

The New Deal Is a Limited Achievement (1933)

Suzanne La Follette (1894–1983)

Feminist and journalist Suzanne La Follette was a contributing author and editor for several magazines, including the *Nation* and *American Mercury*. In the following viewpoint, taken from an October 1933 article in *Current History*, La Follette argues that people expecting a radical revolution in government from Franklin D. Roosevelt's New Deal have been or will be disappointed. The New Deal merely attempts to patch up America's capitalist system, she asserts, while leaving broader problems of economic exploitation unsolved.

How do La Follette's views on how radically Roosevelt has changed America differ from those of Allan Nevins (author of the opposing viewpoint)? How will the New Deal affect ordinary workers, according to La Follette? What past sources of employment and opportunity for the unemployed no longer exist, in her view?

There is a strange air of unreality about the New Deal somewhat suggestive of adventure on a rocking-horse. President Roosevelt and his subordinates are attacking real problems—no doubt of that—energetically, enthusiastically, and with wonderful devotion to their tasks. But they appear to be no more aware of the economic implications of those problems than the public whose fears and desperate hopes they unquestionably represent. Their program thus lacks the coherence that understanding would give it, and the contradictions involved make the United States of America in 1933 seem like the world of Lewis Carroll, where anything

From "The Roosevelt 'Revolution'" by Suzanne La Follette, *Current History*, October 1933.

is possible and nothing is real.

As one considers this appearance of unreality, one realizes that it is not strange at all. It is the distinguishing and perennial characteristic of liberal thought and action. Self-deception is the primary requisite of the liberal mind. The liberal does not dare see the reality of the economic injustice whose effects make him so indignant. If he did, he would be obliged to admit that economic injustice should be abolished, not tinkered with; and for a complex of reasons ranging from self-interest to the chance that God may have made him a tinker by temperament, he does not want it abolished. He wants it "regulated in the public interest." His labor is accordingly out of all proportion to his results, and these are likely to be not at all what he expected. He is like a gallant St. George, trying not to kill the dragon but to pull a few of his teeth without hurting him. It is much more difficult, and the results are unpredictable.

Roosevelt's Radicalism

President Roosevelt has been described as "the most radical man in Washington." From the radical point of view this is such faint praise that it does not do him justice. He is a radical in the American tradition of radicalism—that is, a radical by temperament and instinct. He is for the underdog and against the powerful interests that exploit the underdog. He is genuinely concerned for the fifteen million unemployed; he is genuinely concerned for the debt-burdened farmer victimized by low prices for his own product and high prices for the things he must buy. He is quite in the Jeffersonian tradition of radicalism in that he is instinctively on the side of the producing interest in society and against the speculating interest. But like Jefferson's, his championship of the producing interest is only instinctive. It is a far cry from instinctive radicalism to the radicalism which is inspired by an understanding of what economics and politics are really about. To put it concretely, there is a vast difference between having Wall Street investigated and setting out to abolish the economic system which makes Wall Street possible.

Mr. Roosevelt is far from wishing to abolish the economic system which involves the injustice against which he is tilting. Otherwise he would not be in the White House. The will to change in the American people, which he represents and which is the source of his extraordinary influence, is by no means a will to radical change. There is no widespread discontent with the existing economic system; there is only discontent with its inevitable working-out in hardship for the vast majority and enormous wealth for the few. Psychologically we are still under the spell of the freedom of opportunity offered by a vanished frontier. The nineteenth century took this freedom to inhere in our political and economic institutions, and the twentieth has not yet discovered its error. Thanks to the influence of this self-deception, nine out of ten Americans still believe that the system is divinely ordained and has only somehow fallen into bad hands from which some of its spoils must be rescued for the masses.

———— • ————

"It seems questionable whether the Forgotten Man is likely to share very handsomely in the New Deal."

———— • ————

Let us not minimize the revolutionary feeling which unquestionably existed during the last years of the Hoover regime. One has only to remember the general satisfaction with the political and economic reaction of the post-war period to realize what an extraordinary change the depression brought about in the national temper, which may possibly have momentous consequences, unless renewed prosperity shall change it once more into complacence. But when the American public becomes revolutionary in feeling it cannot, so long as its peculiar attitude toward existing political and economic institutions remains unchanged, translate that feeling into any kind of fundamentally revolutionary action. This perhaps explains the paradox of Mr. Roosevelt. He is a liberal meliorist acting in a revolutionary situation which allows of nothing more fundamental than liberal meliorism. . . .

One cannot foresee, of course, to what lengths or in what direction events may drive the public and the government, but at present it is quite just to say that the New Deal is another attempt to secure everybody's right to life, liberty and the pursuit of happiness by obviating the more onerous effects of the monopolistic system of ownership which denies that right. Mr. Roosevelt clearly expresses its purpose in his book, *Looking Forward:*

> I believe that the government, without becoming a prying bureaucracy, can act as a check or counterbalance of this oligarchy [the "few hundred corporations" and "fewer than three dozen banks" which control our economic life] so as to secure initiative, life, a chance to work, and the safety of savings to men and women, rather than the safety of exploitation to the exploiter, safety of manipulation to the manipulator, safety of unlicensed power to those who would speculate to the bitter end with the welfare and property of other people.

The method by which the President hopes to attain this highly desirable purpose, the method

which has already been embodied in the Securities Act, the Banking Act, the National Industrial Recovery Act, is not revolutionary at all. . . . Mr. Roosevelt's method is the old familiar one of government supervision and regulation, valiantly fought for from the day of this country's birth by a long line of liberals whose Pyrrhic victories strew the pages of its history. In the very nature of the situation it could never be anything else.

Why, then, is everyone so hopeful? Because Americans are very slow to learn that it is economic relationships that govern political actions, and not political actions that govern economic relationships. This is another way of saying that those who own rule, and they rule because they own. In a political democracy they may appear to be beaten for a while, but in the end the victory is theirs because the economic power is theirs. They furnish the big campaign contributions; they can use their control of wealth to corrupt public officers; they can even use the people's money to corrupt the people's mind to their purposes, and they are welded into a united front against mercurial popular movements by "the cohesive power of public plunder." At present the owning oligarchy appears to be on the run. The collapse of the philanthropic pretensions with which it masked its unbridled theft, the amazing discovery that not a few of its revered leaders were little better than morons—these developments have served to discredit it in the public mind. But discredited as it is, it still owns—a fact worth bearing in mind as one watches the government's attempts to "regulate it in the public interest."

It is a tremendous economic power which Mr. Roosevelt is trying to "check and counterbalance," for it is concentrated in very few hands. There is, moreover, the curious spectacle of his trying to preserve it in order to check and counterbalance it, for he is continuing Mr. Hoover's policy of propping up with government credit the capital structure through which the American people are exploited. Let us not impugn his motive. As he sees it, the life of the country depends on the capital structure—the jobs of the workers, the savings of all the citizens, the profits of the industrialists and bankers and shopkeepers, the livelihood of the farmers, the incomes of landowners and bondholders. And it is quite true that the capitalist way of life depends upon the preservation of the capitalist system. The vast majority of Mr. Roosevelt's fellow-citizens see the thing as he does. They cannot envisage any other way of life. As Trotsky says, "society actually takes the institutions that depend upon it as given once for all."

The Forgotten Man

But with the structure preserved unaltered, with its liens on production unrevised, it seems questionable whether the Forgotten Man is likely to share very handsomely in the New Deal. He will still be obliged to carry the heavy load of unearned income—on capitalized franchises, capitalized earning power, bonds issued to enrich underwriters, mortgages held at usurious rates of interest, overcapitalized land values. In addition, he must bear a tax burden which has mounted fantastically since the beginning of the century and has increased rather than lessened during the depression. Contrary to popular belief, all income, unearned as well as earned, and all taxes come out of the labor of the producing classes; there is no other source for them to come from.

A Cursory Glance

Thus, at a cursory glance the New Deal looks like a plan to employ more workers at higher wages so that they can pay higher prices so that interest can be paid on inflated bond-issues, dividends on watered stock, and rents on inflated land values. This is certainly not what Mr. Roosevelt has been promising. Yet might not a stranger, watching the New Deal as it gets under way and not knowing its author's expressed intention to abolish exploitation, be likely to assume that its primary purpose was to rationalize unearned income, which is to say, to stabilize the right of exploitation?

This may be challenged on the ground of the "peaceful revolution" supposedly proceeding under the National Industrial Recovery Act. One should be reluctant to attack this attempt to restore workers to employment if for no other reason than that it is meeting with resistance at the moment from some of the most ruthless of the exploiting interests, such as the steel trust and the coal operators. Moreover, it seems to be eliminating child labor, and we are emotionally stirred by that prospect even though intellectually we should realize that employers can well afford this apparently humanitarian gesture when adult labor can be had at wages as low as those provided in some of the codes submitted or already adopted under the act—codes which indicate that neither the employers nor the government officials have forgotten the sacred right of exploitation that inheres in ownership.

Here the obvious retort may be anticipated by remarking that the administration cannot demand higher minimum conditions than the employers will accept. If you are compromising with an exploiting system you have to respect the right to exploit.

Exploitation of Workers

We say to ourselves, "What must the exploitation of men and women have been during this depression if these minimums mean an improvement in their condition!" We know something of it, for official

agencies have enlightened us from time to time. Women in Pennsylvania sweatshops have been reported as receiving less than $2 for two weeks' work. In the South the textile workers have lived in a state of virtual peonage for so long that a $12 minimum wage and a 40-hour week must seem like wealth and leisure to them. But while the government is raising minimum wages it is also trying to raise prices, and even holding inflation in reserve as a means to that end. Suppose the purchasing power of the dollar should drop once more to 50 cents—which seems not at all improbable—what then will be the condition of the worker who is now sure of a minimum wage ranging from $10 to $15 a week? One is reminded of the minimum-wage laws for women that liberal reformers have pounded through State Legislatures only to see them rendered valueless by a rise in the cost of living.

To be sure, the National Industrial Recovery Act gives the President dictatorial powers. It authorizes him not only to approve but to prescribe "maximum hours of labor, minimum rates of pay, and other conditions of employment." Theoretically he could use these powers to abolish the exploitation of labor; practically he could and would do no such thing. In order to do so he would have to prescribe wages and conditions of labor which would eliminate unearned income from production, and that would be to destroy the credit structure which the government is maintaining at the taxpayers' expense. Therefore he would not eliminate exploitation. . . .

Viewed objectively, then, the administration's program looks like an attempt to rationalize and stabilize exploitation on a nationalist basis. Through subsidizing a reduction of acreage the government proposes to relieve the farmer from dependence on the export market; at the same time it is trying to raise the domestic price of agricultural staples through the processing tax. Thus the agricultural community is to be enabled to bear its annual rent burden of $700,000,000, meet the interest on its $8,500,000,000 of mortgages and pay monopoly prices for farm machinery. And the domestic market for agricultural products at higher prices, and for industrial products, too, is to be enlarged through the National Industrial Recovery Act, which by shortening hours of labor will bring about extensive re-employment—if production continues to improve—and by setting minimum wages for the workers re-employed will increase their buying power—if higher prices do not cancel the value of higher wages. . . .

No New Frontier

The attempt to increase employment by shortening the hours of labor is extremely interesting and significant. It is the only new thing, indeed, about the

New Deal, with the significant exception of the spirit which animates it. Depressions can be lifted only through the opening up of new economic opportunities for the workers who have been squeezed out of their livelihood by licensed greed. In the past these opportunities have been furnished by free land or the rise of new industries. But for the past forty years this country has had no frontier; the industrial worker can no longer avail himself of the free opportunity to "labor the earth" for himself; nor has any industry arisen during this depression, as the automobile and radio industries have in the past, on a scale so large as to absorb enough jobless workers to start the whole productive mechanism anew.

The National Industrial Recovery Act is an attempt to provide a substitute for this means of renewing economic activity. It seems to be regarded by its advocates as a means of restoring equality of opportunity. If the New Deal is successful, it may work in that direction, though only, for reasons already adduced, toward equality of opportunity to be exploited. The fact that even this should at the moment seem like a tremendous social improvement is a terrible indictment of our economic system.

Should Not Expect Miracles

Significant as it is that we have in Washington an administration trying to fight the battle of the suffering masses against their exploiters, it is nevertheless unfortunate that more should be expected of its plan of campaign than is warranted by the plan itself and by the essential liberal meliorism of the American public and the administration. If the New Deal, in spite of the spirit animating it, has here been rather mercilessly analyzed, it is because it seems important that we cease to expect miracles of it. If we do not delude ourselves with extravagant hopes, what is going on in Washington will be of great educational value in showing up the nature and workings of economic forces in this country. If we regard the New Deal as at best a first halting step in the general direction of revolutionary improvement, instead of the revolution sprung full-panoplied from the brow of Mr. Roosevelt, we may save ourselves some disagreeable surprises.

For Further Reading

Paul Conkin, *The New Deal.* New York: Thomas Crowell, 1967.

Kenneth Davis, *FDR: The New Deal Years.* New York: Random House, 1986.

Carl N. Degler, ed., *The New Deal.* Chicago: Quadrangle Books, 1970.

William E. Leuchtenburg, *The New Deal: A Documentary History.* New York: Harper & Row, 1968.

Raymond Moley, *After Seven Years.* Lincoln: University of Nebraska Press, 1971.

VIEWPOINT 27A

Social Security Will Harm America (1935)

John C. Gall (1901–1957)

One of the most significant and lasting New Deal measures was the passage of the Social Security Act in 1935. Prior to this time the United States, unlike many countries in Europe and elsewhere, did not have a national system of old-age pensions, unemployment insurance, or public relief. The Great Depression led to growing demand for such programs, including a national movement for old-age pensions led by Francis Townsend, a California physician. Partly in response to public pressure, the Roosevelt administration presented to Congress the Social Security Act, a series of programs that included a partial retirement pension funded by payroll taxes as well as three joint federal-state systems of unemployment insurance, disability insurance, and welfare for mothers with dependent children.

Congress debated Roosevelt's social security bill in the summer of 1935. Among the opponents of the measure was John C. Gall, a labor lawyer and former Treasury official who worked for many years for the National Association of Manufacturers, a business lobbying organization. In the following viewpoint Gall criticizes the proposed Social Security Act and its payroll taxes as impractical and costly to business. The viewpoint is taken from a radio address by Gall on June 6, 1935.

What distinctions does Gall draw between the fundamental objectives of the Social Security Act and the results he predicts of the act itself? What concerns about compulsory insurance does Gall express? Why might the Social Security Act increase unemployment, according to Gall?

I approach a discussion of the subject of Social Security with full realization that the position of the manufacturer with respect to social legislation is easily misunderstood and as readily misinterpreted. Objection to the form of legislation, or to its timeliness, or to any of its details, is translated by many into opposition to its objective. But that is not the attitude of those for whom I am privileged to speak.

We agree at once that society must, as a matter of self-defense, care for all those persons who for one reason or another have become unwilling victims of

John C. Gall, "Will the Administration's Social Security Bill Promote Recovery?" a radio speech broadcast June 6, 1935. Reprinted in *Vital Speeches of the Day*, vol. 1, pp. 610–13 (1935).

any of the great hazards of life and who have no means of livelihood save that provided by society itself. We make no distinction in this respect between old age destitution and that arising from accident, ill health, or unemployment.

Debating the Means

But the means by which this objective is to be accomplished, the political and social organizations which have the responsibility for providing the necessary assistance, and the extent of the assistance to be given are fundamental matters upon which we believe there not only can be, but is, great disagreement among people who, like ourselves, are sympathetic with the objective.

Will the Administration's Social Security Bill promote recovery? If I wished to indulge in the kind of wisecracking to which employers have been constantly subjected during the past two years, I should comment that *if this* bill will promote recovery it is the single exception which proves the rule. . . .

The Proposed Plan

For the purpose of our discussion, we shall have to assume that, broadly speaking, the Administration's proposal is for a measure embodying two groups of provisions, the one of a permanent character, the other temporary. The permanent features are a system of so-called unemployment insurance, more accurately described as "unemployment benefits"; a Federal contributory old-age pension provision; and provision for permanent entry of the Federal Government into the field of insurance through sale of old-age annuities. The features presumably intended to be temporary contemplate outright Federal appropriations to the several States to supplement State appropriations for relief of old-age dependency, aids to dependent children, maternal and child welfare, vocational rehabilitation, and public health services. The permanent features, except for the voluntary annuities to be sold, are to be supported by a special tax levy upon employers and employees. The annual appropriations by the Federal Government itself, for operation of the temporary provisions, will be approximately one hundred millions of dollars in the first year, and not less than two hundred millions per year in succeeding years until the permanent system becomes effective. These amounts take no account whatever of the additional State and local taxes and appropriations necessary to meet the minimum requirements for receipt of Federal appropriations.

The permanent old-age pension feature is to be supported through taxes on employers and employees subject to the Act. The unemployment benefit provisions do not represent a Federal system, but

through the levy of a heavy payroll tax against employers, passage of State laws would be compelled in order that the employer's Federal tax might be remitted in proportion to his liability under State laws. The Federal Act does not require any levy whatever against employees who are ultimately supposed to benefit by the Act. The burdens levied under these permanent features begin almost at once, but no benefits are payable for several years to come.

------- • -------

"How can real recovery . . . be promoted by discouraging employers from expanding employment and increasing payrolls?"

------- • -------

That, briefly, is a broad outline of the so-called Social Security scheme. We are now asked whether it will promote recovery. The answer would seem too obvious to argue: How can recovery be promoted by additional expenditures from a Federal treasury already far in the red? How can recovery be promoted by the levy of new and additional taxes on employers and employees, when the effect is to withdraw from the channels of trade and commerce a substantial portion of the income normally spent for goods and services? How can real recovery, which means restoration of normal employment and payrolls, be promoted by discouraging employers from expanding employment and increasing payrolls? How can recovery be promoted by payroll taxes which directly induce the substitution of machinery for men? Let us not forget that employers pay men, not machines.

But let us see what some of the advocates of this bill have said of it as a recovery measure. The Secretary of Labor [Frances Perkins] herself said, last November [1934]:

> Unemployment insurance alone is not a cure-all. It will not put men back to work and it does not eliminate the necessity for relief. Obviously, we need more than unemployment insurance. We need work programs and well conceived plans for economic rehabilitation. We need to revive the construction and other durable goods industries and to stimulate increased production by private industry.

Senator Pat Harrison, of Mississippi, in charge of the bill in the Senate, said on May 30th:

> At the outset I wish to impress upon you that it is not the purpose of unemployment compensation to meet the extraordinary situation with which we are now faced, for this emergency is being largely met by the public works program. The social security

bill, on the other hand, looks to the future and seeks to provide ways and means for permanently dealing with the problem of unemployment in the years to come. . . .

These remarks related primarily to the unemployment compensation features of the measure. I presume no one will contend that the permanent old-age pension plan will promote recovery, since no benefits are to be paid under it until approximately 1942. Where, then, are the "recovery" features of the bill? In the mere appropriation of funds to the States under the temporary provisions of the Act? If so, and if that is a sound method of promoting recovery, why stop at one hundred million dollars, or even two hundred, per annum? Why not adopt the Townsend plan [a proposed $200 monthly national old-age pension] and purchase recovery even more quickly? Any argument that the mere distribution of public money promotes recovery is based on the fallacious proposition that consumer purchasing power can be produced and maintained by legislative fiat. The Secretary of Labor in April 1934 said that unemployment insurance "would have the important advantage of giving purchasing power to a small but steady market for the products of all our businesses and all our great industrial institutions. It would put a bottom to the fall of depression and unemployment as it has done in England."

England's Example

Well, let us see whether the English agree with her about that. The Royal Commission on Unemployment Insurance, appointed in 1930 after the British Unemployment Insurance system had completely broken down, reported after careful investigation, as follows:

> The effect of an insurance or a relief scheme upon the community's purchasing power varies. It is sometimes represented as an infallible remedy for unemployment, maintaining purchasing power under all circumstances and so providing a demand for unemployed labour. If the unemployment relieved is due to any causes . . . except general trade depression, there is no ground for this view. It overlooks the fact that the payment of unemployment benefit is merely a transfer of purchasing power to the beneficiaries from contributors and taxpayers who supply the Fund, and others who lend to the Government when the Fund is in debt. To the extent that it enables the unemployed to maintain their purchasing power without contributing currently to society's income, it reduces the resources and purchases of these others. The aggregate of purchases made, and therefore, it may be assumed, of employment given, is the same, the only difference is in the distribution of these purchases. . . .

What about foreign experience with compulsory unemployment insurance? It is obvious that Russia, Germany and Italy, operating under dictatorships, and with complete state control of industry and labor, offer no precedent unless the advocates of compulsory insurance wish to concede an analogy of political and economic conditions. There is much that we can learn from England, but even there the record is one of a complete breakdown of the insurance fund, and a resort to the public treasury. Their Act has been amended 25 times in the 24 years of its existence and is even now undergoing revision.

The Secretary of Labor in a radio address of February 25, 1935, said:

> It is not amiss to note here that social legislation in European countries, begun some 25 years ago, is still in a developmental state and has been subjected to numerous changes as experience and changing conditions dictated.

The question before us is not whether there is enough merit in compulsory social insurance to warrant our experimenting with it at the proper time. The question is whether we are warranted in experimenting in a time like this, when there is still widespread unemployment. Remember that no responsible advocate of unemployment insurance claims it will put a single unemployed man to work. On the other hand, official reports of the British Government show that certain types of unemployment are made chronic as a result of social insurance. All of you may not agree with Henry Ford but there is much common sense in his observation, made since the depression began, that:

> To regard present conditions as permanent and then to legislate as if they were, is a serious mistake. It is the surest way to keep these wrong things with us. I would not insure unemployment; to me that looks like the surest way of establishing unemployment as a permanent evil. . . . In every case where it exists, unemployment insurance is simply taken out of industry's pay envelope in advance. The men can do that for themselves if they want to, as well as any government can do it. . . . Somebody has to earn everything that is paid. No amount of juggling can change that fact. There is no exempt class. Establish unemployment insurance and you simply remove the pressure toward abolishing unemployment. The people then accept unemployment as a not too serious fact. But it is useless to discuss that, because if you insure unemployment it is only a matter of time before the insurance collapses under the load of unemployment it creates.

In my opinion, the temporary provisions of the Social Security Bill should be segregated from the permanent features. Congress has already appropriated some five billions of dollars to be used by the President for relief of economic distress. Let the necessary amount be allocated from that fund to meet the requirements of destitution and dependency in the several States.

No Need for Haste

As to the permanent system contemplated by the bill enough has been said to indicate that it has no relation to recovery except, as many believe, to defer and retard it. As to those portions, there is no necessity for unseemly haste. The year 1936, after all, is not necessarily the millennium. Let us therefore proceed after mature study and consideration. Many problems have scarcely been touched by the studies so far made. It took the British two years to study a proposed revision after 20 years of experience.

These observations are, I believe, adequate to demonstrate the necessity for making haste slowly. This is particularly true in a country like ours where unemployment on a wide scale has been the exception and not the rule throughout our history; where natural resources abound; where new industries employing hundreds of thousands of people have developed and will continue to develop from year to year; and where many of our most serious social, political, and economic problems arise out of failure to balance the interests of industry and agriculture. It must be borne in mind that the agricultural population of Great Britain constitutes only about 8 per cent of the total. In this country our agricultural population is ¼ of our total. What will be the effect on them if they are left out of any system which may be adopted and yet are called upon to contribute to its support, both directly through taxation and indirectly through increased costs of the goods and services they must buy?

Must we institute a system, change it twenty-five times in the next twenty-five years as England has done, and at the end of that time find it necessary to constitute a commission to salvage the essentials of the system and restore the fund to solvency? Or shall we determine in advance what plan, if any, is best suited to our own people and our own standards?

Constitutional Questions

I regret that time does not permit me to discuss the serious constitutional questions involved in the Social Security Bill. The Associated Press informs us that the Secretary of Labor, upon leaving the White House on Tuesday, declared:

> The Social Security measure is not based on the interstate commerce clause, but rather on the Federal Government's taxing clause. We have consulted eminent lawyers on this legislation.

It would be interesting to know whether this legal advice was received from the same source that advised the Administration that the National Industrial Recovery Act was constitutional; that the Rail-

way Pension Act was constitutional; that the Frazier-Lemke Act was constitutional; and that the removal of a member of the Federal Trade Commission was authorized by law,—as to all of which the Supreme Court held there was no constitutional warrant.

What a tragedy it would be for the Administration again to hold the promise to the ear and break it to the heart by forcing enactment of another law of doubtful constitutionality! That would promote, not social security, but a fresh wave of social insecurity. . . .

May I conclude with the admonition of that great friend of young America, Edmund Burke:

> Better to be despised for too anxious apprehensions than ruined by too confident security.

VIEWPOINT 27B

Social Security Will Benefit America (1935)

Frances Perkins (1880–1965)

A central figure in President Franklin D. Roosevelt's New Deal, and especially the enactment of the Social Security Act of 1935, was Frances Perkins. The first woman to serve in the cabinet of a U.S. president, she was secretary of labor from 1933 to 1945. Perkins, whose earlier career included teaching, social work, and service as New York state industrial commissioner, chaired a special committee appointed by Roosevelt to draft social welfare legislation. The committee drafted the Social Security Act, which was introduced to Congress in June and passed and signed into law on August 14, 1935. The following viewpoint is taken from a radio speech Perkins gave on September 2, 1935, to describe the benefits of the newly passed law to the American people.

Who will be the main beneficiaries of the Social Security Act, according to Perkins? In her view, how will the act help prevent future depressions?

People who work for a living in the United States of America can join with all other good citizens on this forty-eighth anniversary of Labor Day in satisfaction that the Congress has passed the Social Security Act. This Act establishes unemployment insurance as a substitute for haphazard methods of assistance in periods when men and women willing and able to work are without jobs. It provides for old age pensions which mark great progress over the measures upon which we have hitherto depended in caring for those who have been

From Frances Perkins, "The Social Security Act," a radio speech broadcast September 2, 1935. Reprinted in *Vital Speeches of the Day*, vol. 1, pp. 792–94 (1935).

unable to provide for the years when they no longer can work. It also provides security for dependent and crippled children, mothers, the indigent disabled and the blind.

Old people who are in need, unemployables, children, mothers and the sightless, will find systematic regular provisions for needs. The Act limits the Federal aid to not more than $15 per month for the individual, provided the State in which he resides appropriates a like amount. There is nothing to prevent a State from contributing more than $15 per month in special cases and there is no requirement to allow as much as $15 from either State or Federal funds when a particular case has some personal provision and needs less than the total allowed.

Following essentially the same procedure, the Act as passed provides for Federal assistance to the States in caring for the blind, a contribution by the State of up to $15 a month to be matched in turn by a like contribution by the Federal Government. The Act also contains provision for assistance to the States in providing payments to dependent children under sixteen years of age. There also is provision in the Act for cooperation with medical and health organizations charged with rehabilitation of physically handicapped children. The necessity for adequate service in the fields of public and maternal health and child welfare calls for the extension of these services to meet individual community needs.

Old-Age Benefits

Consider for a moment those portions of the Act which, while they will not be effective this present year, yet will exert a profound and far-reaching effect upon millions of citizens. I refer to the provision for a system of old-age benefits supported by the contributions of employer and employees, and to the section which sets up the initial machinery for unemployment insurance.

Old-age benefits in the form of monthly payments are to be paid to individuals who have worked and contributed to the insurance fund in direct proportion to the total wages earned by such individuals in the course of their employment subsequent to 1936. The minimum monthly payment is to be $10, the maximum $85. These payments will begin in the year 1942 and will be to those who have worked and contributed.

Because of difficulty of administration not all employments are covered in this plan at this time so that the law is not entirely complete in coverage, but it is sufficiently broad to cover all normally employed industrial workers.

As an example of the practical operation of the old-age benefit system, consider for a moment a typical young man of thirty-five years of age, and let us compute the benefits which will accrue to him. Assuming that his income will average $100 per month over the period of thirty years until he reaches the age of sixty-five, the benefit payments due him from the insurance fund will provide him with $42.50 per month for the remainder of his life. If he has been fortunate enough to have an income of $200 per month, his income will subsequently be $61.25 per month. In the event that death occurs prior to the age of sixty-five, 3½% of the total wages earned by him subsequent to 1936 will be returned to his dependents. If death occurs after the age of sixty-five, his dependents receive the same amount, less any benefits paid to him during his lifetime.

This vast system of old-age benefits requires contributions both by employer and employee, each to contribute 3% of the total wage paid to the employee. This tax, collected by the Bureau of Internal Revenue, will be graduated, ranging from 1% in 1937 to the maximum 3% in 1939 and thereafter. That is, on this man's average income of $100 a month he will pay to the usual fund $3 a month and his employer will also pay the same amount over his working years.

Unemployment Insurance

In conjunction with the system of old-age benefits, the Act recognizes that unemployment insurance is an integral part of any plan for the economic security of millions of gainfully employed workers. It provides for a plan of cooperative Federal-State action by which a State may enact an insurance system, compatible with Federal requirements and best suited to its individual needs.

The Federal Government attempts to promote and effectuate these State systems, by levying a uniform Federal pay-roll tax of 3% on employers employing eight or more workers, with the proviso that an employer who contributes to a State unemployment compensation system will receive a credit of 90% of this Federal tax. After 1937, additional credit is also allowable to any employer who, because of favorable employment experience or adequate reserves, is permitted by the State to reduce his payments.

In addition, the Act provides that after the current fiscal year the Federal Government allocate annually to the States $49,000,000 solely for the administration of their respective insurance systems, thus assuring that all money paid for State unemployment compensation will be reserved for the purpose of compensation to the worker. It has been necessary, at the present time, to eliminate essentially the same groups from participation under the unemployment insurance plan as in the old-age benefit plan, though it is possible that at some future time a more complete coverage will be formulated.

The State of New York, at the present time, has a

system of unemployment compensation which might well illustrate the salient factors desired in such a plan; in the event of unemployment, the worker is paid 50% of his wages weekly for a period not exceeding 16 weeks in any 52 weeks. This payment begins within three weeks after the advent of actual unemployment. California, Washington, Utah and New Hampshire have passed unemployment insurance laws in recent months and Wisconsin's law is already in effect. Thirty-five States have old-age pension statutes and mothers' pension acts are in force in all but three States.

With the States rests now the responsibility of devising and enacting measures which will result in the maximum benefits to the American workman in the field of unemployment compensation. I am confident that impending State action will not fail to take cognizance of this responsibility. The people of the different States favor the program designed to bring them greater security in the future and their legislatures will speedily pass appropriate laws so that all may help to promote the general welfare.

Federal legislation was framed in the thought that the attack upon the problems of insecurity should be a cooperative venture participated in by both the Federal and State Governments, preserving the benefits of local administration and national leadership. It was thought unwise to have the Federal Government decide all questions of policy and dictate completely what the States should do. Only very necessary minimum standards are included in the Federal measure leaving wide latitude to the States.

———— • ————

"Our social security program will be a vital force working against the recurrence of severe depressions in the future."

———— • ————

While the different State laws on unemployment insurance must make all contributions compulsory, the States, in addition to deciding how these contributions shall be levied, have freedom in determining their own waiting periods, benefit rates, maximum benefit periods and the like. Care should be taken that these laws do not contain benefit provisions in excess of collections. While unemployment varies greatly in different States, there is no certainty that States which have had less normal unemployment heretofore will in the future have a more favorable experience than the average for the country.

It is obvious that in the best interests of the worker, industry and society, there must be a certain uniformity of standards. It is obvious, too, that we must prevent the penalizing of competitive industry in any State which plans the early adoption of a sound system of unemployment insurance, and provide effective guarantees against the possibility of industry in one State having an advantage over that of another. This the uniform Federal tax does, as it costs the employer the same whether he pays the levy to the Federal Government or makes a contribution to a State unemployment insurance fund. The amount of the tax itself is a relative assurance that benefits will be standardized in all States, since under the law the entire collection must be spent on benefits to unemployed.

A Sound and Reasonable Plan

The social security measure looks primarily to the future and is only a part of the administration's plan to promote sound and stable economic life. We cannot think of it as disassociated from the Government's program to save the homes, the farms, the businesses and banks of the Nation, and especially must we consider it a companion measure to the Works Relief Act which does undertake to provide immediate increase in employment and corresponding stimulation to private industry by purchase of supplies.

While it is not anticipated as a complete remedy for the abnormal conditions confronting us at the present time, it is designed to afford protection for the individual against future major economic vicissitudes. It is a sound and reasonable plan and framed with due regard for the present state of economic recovery. It does not represent a complete solution of the problems of economic security, but it does represent a substantial, necessary beginning. It has been developed after careful and intelligent consideration of all the facts and all of the programs that have been suggested or applied anywhere.

Few legislative proposals have had as careful study, as thorough and conscientious deliberation, as that which went into the preparation of the social security programs. It is embodied in perhaps the most useful and fundamental single piece of Federal legislation in the interest of wage earners in the United States. As President Roosevelt said when he signed the measure: "If the Senate and House of Representatives in their long and arduous session had done nothing more than pass this bill, the session would be regarded as historic for all time."

This is truly legislation in the interest of the national welfare. We must recognize that if we are to maintain a healthy economy and thriving production, we need to maintain the standard of living of the lower income groups of our population who constitute ninety per cent of our purchasing power. The President's Committee on Economic Security, of which I had the honor to be chairman, in drawing up the plan, was convinced that its enactment into law would not only carry us a long way toward the goal of economic security for the individual, but also a long way toward the promotion and stabilization of mass purchasing power without which the present economic system cannot endure.

That this intimate connection between the maintenance of mass purchasing power through a system of protection of the individual against major economic hazards is not theoretical is evidenced by the fact that England has been able to withstand the effects of the world-wide depression, even though her prosperity depends so largely upon foreign trade. English economists agree with employers and workers that this ability to weather adverse conditions has been due in no small part to social insurance benefits and regular payments which have served to maintain necessary purchasing power.

Our social security program will be a vital force working against the recurrence of severe depressions in the future. We can, as the principle of sustained purchasing power in hard times makes itself felt in every shop, store and mill, grow old without being haunted by the spectre of a poverty-ridden old age or of being a burden on our children.

The costs of unemployment compensation and old-age insurance are not actually additional costs. In some degree they have long been borne by the people, but irregularly, the burden falling much more heavily on some than on others, and none of such provisions offering an orderly or systematic assurance to those in need. The years of depression have brought home to all of us that unemployment entails huge costs to government, industry and the public alike.

Unemployment insurance will within a short time considerably lighten the public burden of caring for those unemployed. It will materially reduce relief costs in future years. In essence, it is a method by which reserves are built up during periods of employment from which compensation is paid to the unemployed in periods when work is lacking.

The passage of this act with so few dissenting votes and with so much intelligent public support is deeply significant of the progress which the American people have made in thought in the social field and awareness of methods of using cooperation through government to overcome social hazards against which the individual alone is inadequate.

During the fifteen years I have been advocating such legislation as this I have learned that the American people want such security as the law provides. It will make this great Republic a better and a happier place in which to live—for us, our children and our children's children. It is a profound and sacred satisfaction to have had some part in securing this great boon to the people of our country.

For Further Reading

Arthur Joseph Altmeyer, *The Formative Years of Social Security.* Madison: University of Wisconsin Press, 1966.

George Whitney Martin, *Madam Secretary, Frances Perkins.* Boston: Houghton Mifflin, 1976.

Frances Perkins, *The Roosevelt I Knew.* New York: The Viking Press, 1946.

George Wolfskill, *Revolt of the Conservatives.* Boston: Houghton Mifflin, 1962.

World War II

VIEWPOINT 28A

The United States Should Give Lend-Lease Aid to Great Britain (1940)

Franklin D. Roosevelt (1882–1945)

The outbreak of war in Europe in 1939, much like the outbreak of war in 1914, forced the United States to face a series of decisions on how to respond. Some Americans, believing that the United States should not repeat its 1917 decision to send troops to Europe, urged that the United States remain strictly neutral. This stance was consistent with a series of Neutrality Acts passed by Congress in the 1930s that prevented the United States from providing arms or monetary loans to warring nations or in other ways becoming embroiled in foreign wars. President Franklin D. Roosevelt, in the early months of World War II, successfully pressed Congress to relax the arms embargo and to sell arms to the Allies (Great Britain and France) on a limited "cash and carry" basis. Controversy remained as to whether such limited aid would be enough for the Allies, and if not, whether America should do more.

The following viewpoint is taken from one of the most significant of President Roosevelt's "fireside chats"—his radio speeches to the American public discussing important problems and decisions of his presidency. Roosevelt made this particular address on December 29, 1940, at the close of an eventful year that saw the fall of France, Denmark, Norway, Belgium, and Holland to Nazi Germany; the passage of the first peacetime military draft in U.S. history; and Roosevelt's own reelection to an unprecedented third term as president. Great Britain, the sole remaining European democracy, had informed the United States it was running out of money to pay for needed arms, planes, tanks, and other supplies. Roo-

Excerpted from Franklin D. Roosevelt's "fireside chat" radio broadcast of December 29, 1940.

sevelt responded by proposing what became known as the Lend-Lease Act, under which the United States would provide military supplies to Great Britain with repayment decisions deferred to the end of the war. Lend-lease aid needed congressional approval; this speech was part of Roosevelt's campaign to gather public support for the idea, and to defend such aid against charges that it would inevitably lead America into war. Roosevelt emphasizes the dangers posed to the United States by the nations of Germany, Italy, and Japan, which had signed a mutual defense pact aimed at the United States in September 1940.

What would happen to the United States if Great Britain fell to Germany, according to Roosevelt? How does he characterize those who oppose aiding the Allies? What does Roosevelt assert concerning the possibility of lend-lease aid's leading to direct U.S. involvement in the war?

M y friends, this is not a Fireside Chat on war. It is a talk on national security; because the nub of the whole purpose of your president is to keep you now, and your children later, and your grandchildren much later, out of a last-ditch war for the preservation of American independence and all of the things that American independence means to you and to me and to ours.

Tonight, in the presence of a world crisis, my mind goes back eight years to a night in the midst of a domestic crisis. It was a time when the wheels of American industry were grinding to a full stop, when the whole banking system of our country had ceased to function.

I well remember that while I sat in my study in the White House, preparing to talk with the people of the United States, I had before my eyes the picture of all those Americans with whom I was talking. I saw the workmen in the mills, the mines, the factories; the girl behind the counter; the small shopkeeper; the farmer doing his spring plowing; the widows and the old men wondering about their life's savings. I tried to convey to the great mass of American people what the banking crisis meant to them in their daily lives.

Tonight, I want to do the same thing, with the same people, in this new crisis which faces America.

We met the issue of 1933 with courage and realism.

We face this new crisis—this new threat to the security of our nation—with the same courage and realism.

A New Crisis

Never before since Jamestown and Plymouth Rock has our American civilization been in such danger as now.

For on September 27, 1940, this year, by an agreement signed in Berlin, three powerful nations, two in Europe and one in Asia, joined themselves together in the threat that if the United States of America interfered with or blocked the expansion program of these three nations—a program aimed at world control—they would unite in ultimate action against the United States.

The Nazi masters of Germany have made it clear that they intend not only to dominate all life and thought in their own country, but also to enslave the whole of Europe, and then to use the resources of Europe to dominate the rest of the world.

It was only three weeks ago that their leader stated this: "There are two worlds that stand opposed to each other." And then in defiant reply to his opponents, he said this: "Others are correct when they say: With this world we cannot ever reconcile ourselves . . . I can beat any other power in the world." So said the leader of the Nazis.

In other words, the Axis not merely admits, but the Axis *proclaims*, that there can be no ultimate peace between their philosophy, their philosophy of government, and our philosophy of government.

In view of the nature of this undeniable threat, it can be asserted, properly and categorically, that the United States has no right or reason to encourage talk of peace, until the day shall come when there is a clear intention on the part of the aggressor nations to abandon all thought of dominating or conquering the world.

"We must be the great arsenal of democracy."

At this moment, the forces of the states that are leagued against all peoples who live in freedom are being held away from our shores. The Germans and the Italians are being blocked on the other side of the Atlantic by the British, and by the Greeks, and by thousands of soldiers and sailors who were able to escape from subjugated countries. In Asia, the Japanese are being engaged by the Chinese nation in another great defense.

In the Pacific Ocean is our fleet.

Some of our people like to believe that wars in Europe and in Asia are of no concern to us. But it is a matter of most vital concern to us that European and Asiatic war-makers should not gain control of the oceans which lead to this hemisphere.

One hundred and seventeen years ago the Monroe Doctrine [which stated that the United States opposed further European colonization of or intervention in the Western Hemisphere] was conceived by our government as a measure of defense in the face of a threat against this hemisphere by an alliance in continental Europe. Thereafter, we stood guard in the Atlantic, with the British as neighbors. There was no treaty. There was no "unwritten agreement."

And yet, there was the feeling, proven correct by history, that we as neighbors could settle any disputes in peaceful fashion. And the fact is that during the whole of this time the Western Hemisphere has remained free from aggression from Europe or from Asia.

Does anyone seriously believe that we need to fear attack anywhere in the Americas while a free Britain remains our most powerful naval neighbor in the Atlantic? And does anyone seriously believe, on the other hand, that we could rest easy if the Axis powers were our neighbors there?

If Great Britain goes down, the Axis powers will control the continents of Europe, Asia, Africa, Australasia, and the high seas—and they will be in a position to bring enormous military and naval resources against this hemisphere. It is no exaggeration to say that all of us, in all the Americas, would be living at the point of a gun—a gun loaded with explosive bullets, economic as well as military.

We should enter upon a new and terrible era in which the whole world, our hemisphere included, would be run by threats of brute force. And to survive in such a world, we would have to convert ourselves permanently into a militaristic power on the basis of war economy.

The Oceans Are No Protection

Some of us like to believe that even if Britain falls, we are still safe, because of the broad expanse of the Atlantic and of the Pacific.

But the width of those oceans is not what it was in the days of clipper ships. At one point between Africa and Brazil the distance is less than it is from Washington to Denver, Colorado—five hours for the latest type of bomber. And at the North end of the Pacific Ocean, America and Asia almost touch each other.

Why even today we have planes that could fly from the British Isles to New England and back again without refueling. And remember that the range of the modern bomber is ever being increased.

During the past week many people in all parts of the nation have told me what they wanted me to say tonight. Almost all of them expressed a courageous desire to hear the plain truth about the gravity of the situation. One telegram, however, expressed the attitude of the small minority who want to see no evil and hear no evil, even though they know in their hearts that evil exists. That telegram begged me not to tell again of the ease with which our American cities could be bombed by any hostile power which had gained bases in this Western Hemisphere. The gist of that telegram was, "Please, Mr. President, don't frighten us by telling us the facts."

Frankly and definitely there is danger ahead—danger against which we must prepare. But we well know that we cannot escape danger, or the fear of danger, by crawling into bed and pulling the covers over our heads.

Some nations of Europe were bound by solemn nonintervention pacts with Germany. Other nations were assured by Germany that they need *never* fear invasion. Nonintervention pact or not, the fact remains that they *were* attacked, overrun, thrown into modern slavery at an hour's notice, or even without any notice at all. As an exiled leader of one of these nations said to me the other day—"The notice was a minus quantity. It was given to my government two hours after German troops had poured into my country in a hundred places."

The fate of these nations tells us what it means to live at the point of a Nazi gun.

The Nazi Threat

The Nazis have justified such actions by various pious frauds. One of these frauds is the claim that they are occupying a nation for the purpose of "restoring order." Another is that they are occupying or controlling a nation on the excuse that they are "protecting it" against the aggression of somebody else.

For example, Germany has said that she was occupying Belgium to save the Belgians from the British. Would she then hesitate to say to any South American country, "We are occupying you to protect you from aggression by the United States"?

Belgium today is being used as an invasion base against Britain, now fighting for its life. And any South American country, in Nazi hands, would always constitute a jumping-off place for German attack on any one of the other republics of this hemisphere.

Analyze for yourselves the future of two other places even nearer to Germany if the Nazis won. Could Ireland hold out? Would Irish freedom be permitted as an amazing pet exception in an unfree world? Or the Islands of the Azores, which still fly the flag of Portugal after five centuries? You and I think of Hawaii as an outpost of defense in the Pacific. And yet, the Azores are closer to our shores in the Atlantic than Hawaii is on the other side.

There are those who say that the Axis powers would never have any desire to attack the Western Hemisphere. That is the same dangerous form of wishful thinking which has destroyed the powers of resistance of so many conquered peoples. The plain facts are that the Nazis have proclaimed, time and again, that all other races are their inferiors and therefore subject to their orders. And most important of all, the vast resources and wealth of this American hemisphere constitute the most tempting loot in all of the round world.

Let us no longer blind ourselves to the undeniable fact that the evil forces which have crushed and undermined and corrupted so many others are already within our own gates. Your government knows much about them and every day is ferreting them out.

Their secret emissaries are active in our own and in neighboring countries. They seek to stir up suspicion and dissension to cause internal strife. They try to turn capital against labor, and vice versa. They try to reawaken long-slumbering racial and religious enmities which should have no place in this country. They are active in every group that promotes intolerance. They exploit for their own ends our own natural abhorrence of war. These trouble-breeders have but one purpose. It is to divide our people, to divide them into hostile groups and to destroy our unity and shatter our will to defend ourselves.

American Appeasers

There are also American citizens, many of them in high places, who, unwittingly in most cases, are aiding and abetting the work of these agents. I do not charge these American citizens with being foreign agents. But I do charge them with doing exactly the kind of work that the dictators want done in the United States.

These people not only believe that we can save our own skins by shutting our eyes to the fate of other nations. Some of them go much further than that. They say that we can and should become the friends and even the partners of the Axis powers. Some of them even suggest that we should imitate the methods of the dictatorships. But Americans never can and never will do that.

The experience of the past two years has proven beyond doubt that no nation can appease the Nazis. No man can tame a tiger into a kitten by stroking it. There can be no appeasement with ruthlessness. There can be no reasoning with an incendiary bomb. We know now that a nation can have peace with the Nazis only at the price of total surrender.

Even the people of Italy have been forced to become accomplices of the Nazis; but at this moment they do not know how soon they will be embraced to death by their allies.

The American appeasers ignore the warning to be found in the fate of Austria, Czechoslovakia, Poland, Norway, Belgium, the Netherlands, Denmark, and France. They tell you that the Axis powers are going to win anyway; that all of this bloodshed in the world could be saved; that the United States might just as well throw its influence into the scale of a dictated peace, and get the best out of it that we can.

They call it a "negotiated peace." Nonsense! Is it a negotiated peace if a gang of outlaws surrounds your community and on threat of extermination makes you pay tribute to save your own skins?

For such a dictated peace would be no peace at all. It would be only another armistice, leading to the most gigantic armament race and the most devastating trade wars in all history. And in these contests the Americas would offer the only real resistance to the Axis powers.

With all their vaunted efficiency, with all their parade of pious purpose in this war, there are still in their background the concentration camp and the servants of God in chains.

The history of recent years proves that the shootings and the chains and the concentration camps are not simply the transient tools but the very altars of modern dictatorships. They may talk of a "new order" in the world, but what they have in mind is only a revival of the oldest and the worst tyranny. In that there is no liberty, no religion, no hope.

The proposed "new order" is the very opposite of a United States of Europe or a United States of Asia. It is not a government based upon the consent of the governed. It is not a union of ordinary, self-respecting men and women to protect themselves and their freedom and their dignity from oppression. It is an unholy alliance of power and pelf to dominate and to enslave the human race.

The British people and their allies today are conducting an active war against this unholy alliance. Our own future security is greatly dependent on the outcome of that fight. Our ability to keep out of war is going to be affected by that outcome.

Keeping America Out of War

Thinking in terms of today and tomorrow, I make the direct statement to the American people that there is far less chance of the United States getting into war if we do all we can now to support the nations defending themselves against attack by the Axis than if we acquiesce in their defeat, submit tamely to an Axis victory, and wait our turn to be the object of attack in another war later on.

If we are to be completely honest with ourselves, we must admit that there is risk in any course we may take. But I deeply believe that the great majority of our people agree that the course that I advocate involves the least risk now and the greatest hope for world peace in the future.

The people of Europe who are defending themselves do not ask us to do their fighting. They ask us for the implements of war, the planes, the tanks, the guns, the freighters which will enable them to fight for their liberty and for our security. Emphatically we must get these weapons to them, get them to them in sufficient volume and quickly enough, so that we and our children will be saved the agony and suffering of war which others have had to endure.

Let not the defeatists tell us that it is too late. It will never be earlier. Tomorrow will be later than today.

Certain facts are self-evident.

In a military sense Great Britain and the British Empire are today the spearhead of resistance to world conquest. And they are putting up a fight which will live forever in the story of human gallantry.

There is no demand for sending an American Expeditionary Force outside our own borders. There is no intention by any member of your government to send such a force. You can, therefore, nail, nail any talk about sending armies to Europe as deliberate untruth.

Our national policy is not directed toward war. Its sole purpose is to keep war away from our country and away from our people.

Democracy's fight against world conquest is being greatly aided, and must be more greatly aided, by the rearmament of the United States and by sending every ounce and every ton of munitions and supplies that we can possibly spare to help the defenders who are in the front lines. And it is no more unneutral for us to do that than it is for Sweden, Russia, and other nations near Germany, to send steel and ore and oil and other war materials into Germany every day in the week.

We are planning our own defense with the utmost urgency and in its vast scale we must integrate the war needs of Britain and the other free nations which are resisting aggression.

This is not a matter of sentiment or of controversial personal opinion. It is a matter of realistic, practical military policy, based on the advice of our military experts who are in close touch with existing warfare. These military and naval experts and the members of the Congress and the administration have a single-minded purpose—the defense of the United States.

This nation is making a great effort to produce everything that is necessary in this emergency—and with all possible speed. And this great effort requires great sacrifice. . . .

The Arsenal of Democracy

We must be the great arsenal of democracy. For us this is an emergency as serious as war itself. We must apply ourselves to our task with the same resolution, the same sense of urgency, the same spirit of patriotism and sacrifice as we would show were we at war.

We have furnished the British great material support and we will furnish far more in the future.

There will be no bottlenecks in our determination to aid Great Britain. No dictator, no combination of dictators, will weaken that determination by threats of how they will construe that determination.

The British have received invaluable military support from the heroic Greek army, and from the forces of all the governments in exile. Their strength is growing. It is the strength of men and women who value their freedom more highly than they value their lives.

I believe that the Axis powers are not going to win this war. I base that belief on the latest and best of information.

We have no excuse for defeatism. We have every good reason for hope—hope for peace, yes, and hope for the defense of our civilization and for the building of a better civilization in the future.

I have the profound conviction that the American people are now determined to put forth a mightier effort than they have ever yet made to increase our production of all the implements of defense to meet the threat to our democratic faith.

As president of the United States I call for that national effort. I call for it in the name of this nation which we love and honor and which we are privileged and proud to serve. I call upon our people with absolute confidence that our common cause will greatly succeed.

VIEWPOINT 28B

Lend-Lease Aid Will Drag the United States into War (1941)

James F. O'Connor (1878–1945)

In January 1941 Congress began debate on H.R. 1776, later known as the Lend-Lease Act. Prompted by British pleas to President Franklin D. Roosevelt for aid against Germany, the bill gave sweeping new powers to the president to provide assistance to any nation he designated as vital for America's defense, and appropriated $7 billion for that purpose. The bill provoked bitter debate in Congress, where it was strenuously opposed by isolationists who feared American involvement in yet another European war. Among the opponents of lend-lease aid were James F. O'Connor, a Democratic representative from Montana, whose January 21, 1941, remarks on the floor of Congress are reprinted in part here.

O'Connor, a former rancher, banker, and judge, served in Congress from 1937 to 1945. In his speech

James F. O'Connor, *Congressional Record*, 77th Cong., 1st sess., January 21, 1941, pp. 211–13.

he argues that the passage of the bill would represent a direct step toward further intervention in Europe and would eventually cause the United States "to plunge headlong into war." He states that while he shares with others a desire for a British victory over Germany, such a goal is not worth risking American lives in a foreign conflict. Despite the efforts of O'Connor and others, the Lend-Lease Act passed in March 1941 by wide margins in both houses of Congress. Eventually the United States sent $50 billion in lend-lease aid to Great Britain and other countries during World War II.

What does the "average American" want, according to O'Connor? Is Franklin D. Roosevelt's proposal (see viewpoint 28A) consistent with this? Why or why not? What arguments does O'Connor make about the proper duties and powers of Congress and the president? How important to his position is his opinion concerning the possibility of a German invasion of the United States?

On its face, H.R. 1776 is a bill "to promote the defense of the United States."

If the 435 Members of this House believed that this really is a bill "to promote the defense of the United States" then this bill would be passed in a few minutes' time without a single vote being cast against it, because every one of us here believes in defending the United States.

I speak to you today, my colleagues, as one of many who feels that this legislation would not do what it proposes to accomplish, namely: "To promote the defense of the United States."

The decision this Congress makes in passing on this bill will affect the lives of millions of people throughout the world. I want that decision to be in favor of the American people.

I do not propose, myself, and I do not think that you intend, to support this, or any other measure that is not in the best interests of the American people.

There is not a question in my mind as to where the sympathies of our people lie in regard to the wars raging across the oceans. By thought, word, deed, and prayer Americans have indicated plainly they prefer that the victors of these wars shall be the democracies of Great Britain, China, and Greece.

The average American, in my opinion, is thinking something like this: "Let us give them anything we have in the way of materials that will help them win the war so long as it does not jeopardize the safety and security of the United States."

But the American people do not want this country to plunge headlong into war.

Help Britain? Help China? Help Greece? Emphatically "Yes."

But to the extent of sending troops their answer, a thousand times more emphatic, is "No."

This Nation has been committed to a policy, so far as the democracies are concerned, of "all aid short of war."

The people, at least up to now, have taken those words at their literal meaning.

Perhaps, now, they finally have come to realize that "short of war" is vague and may be misleading.

This bill, H.R. 1776, is an act to carry out the "short of war" policy.

Lend-Lease Will Lead to War

Under this bill, in its present form, it would be possible, without any doubt whatsoever, for circumstances to arise which most certainly would involve the United States in war.

Let me illustrate just one such circumstance.

Suppose we were to send our warships into danger zones or use them to convoy supply ships to Great Britain or Ireland. Is there any doubt whatever that Britain's foes would attempt to sink our vessels? Is there any doubt that such an attack on our ships would not plunge the United States into war?

And this is but one of similar situations that could arise.

And let me ask you this question, colleagues:

Would any of us whom the American people honored by election to public office last November be here today if, prior to election day, we had stood before the American voters and openly proclaimed:

"I am in favor of the United States entering war."

Or if we had proclaimed:

"I will support legislation that may involve the United States in war."

Of course we would not be here if we had made any such campaign statement. No Member here, I am confident, will dispute me on this point.

If, then, I gave my pledge to Montana voters to do my best to "promote the defense of the United States," and keep us out of war, how can I be expected to support a bill that my conscience tells me exposes the United States to the gravest danger of being forced into war?

As it now reads, this bill, in my opinion, would do just that. . . .

What condition exists now that did not exist last fall when I gave my pledge to Montana voters—except the emotional hysteria that has been manufactured by the press, the radio, and the motion-picture theaters? . . .

Congress passed the Neutrality Act for the precise purpose of keeping America out of war. Then, at the President's insistence, we amended that act to strengthen our position as a neutral.

Now, after election is over, we have before us a bill

that many of us feel would serve to get us into—not keep us out of—war.

Giving the President Too Much Power

In the first place, passage of this bill would amount to a complete abdication of the legislative branch of the Government. Congress already has surrendered so much of its authority as to be virtually incapable of discharging its duty as the law-making representatives of the electorate.

By the unprecedented powers this bill gives to the Office of the Chief Executive, powers that easily could lead to involvement of the Nation in war, Congress would give up the authority vested in it, exclusively, under the Constitution, to decide when the United States shall go to war.

Let us, my friends, keep faith with our people. Let us take no affirmative action that seems to me, without a doubt, will cause our naval and military forces to go into this war in Europe. . . .

Already, out of the Constitution and the interpretations by our Supreme Court, the President has plenary power in our external affairs. He is the sole agency and representative of our policy with foreign nations. Pass this bill, as it stands, and it would give him the same total power over our domestic defense powers.

While I am 100 percent for the purpose of the bill—to promote the defense of the United States—I cannot support this bill in its present form.

Please understand that I do not contend that any course, in these days, is bulletproof against involvement of this Nation in war. The only thing Congress can do is keep its pledge to the people to try to keep them out of war. We cannot keep that pledge by supporting bills that permit aggressive and unneutral acts that are sure to get us into war.

Perhaps the course I suggest is wrong. I do not know. Only the future holds the answer. No human being has it.

Let us consider what are Britain's aims and what are our aims in this crisis.

Are not the words, "Hitlerism must be crushed" familiar to you? Do you not recall 25 years ago almost the same sort of excuse for war? Only then it was "Kaiserism."

What happened to the Kaiser after his army was defeated? He was placed in a little place of his own, which, according to good information, afforded him luxurious living. Of course, the cost to the German people was $70,000,000.

What is going to happen when "Hitlerism" is crushed? How much further will Britain want to go? Has Britain said she wants to restore the status quo in Europe as it existed as of August 31, 1939? Has she said that France, Poland, Austria, Belgium, Hol-land, Poland, Rumania, and the other countries are to be restored? Would Britain need troops to accomplish this? Would we be asked to supply them?

A Dark Future

If so, the future looks dark for the flower of American manhood.

If we are to attempt to right the wrongs of Europe, 3,000 miles away, God help America.

Let us think a little further.

Suppose Germany is licked. That will not mean she is conquered. Great nations never are conquered, unless they are exterminated, which is impossible.

France is prostrated today, but not conquered. The spirit of France will rise. On the ruins perhaps a greater nation than ever before will be born. France may profit by her mistakes.

If Germany should defeat Great Britain, would the English people be conquered? Oh, no; they are not made of faulty fiber. The fight would have just begun.

The seed for disorder in the world is planted by selfish, greedy, war-minded men who find themselves adrift from Christianity.

Europe is dark today because most of Europe has forsaken Christian principles.

As I see it, the duty of this Congress is not to take any step that might involve this Nation in war, but rather to assume a statesmanlike leadership toward the goal of peace.

Involving this Nation, the most powerful on earth, in war certainly is not a step toward peace. You cannot quench a fire by adding a huge amount of new fuel to it.

Peace is an active and positive thing. Peace is not merely a cessation of war through some peace treaty. History is filled with the fragments of broken pledges for peace. . . .

The First World War

Do you wonder, my friends, that I shudder at the prospects of America becoming embroiled in Europe's wars? At the prospect of having to pledge not only the lives of American young men but the homes of the people who have worked and saved a lifetime to own—in fact, their all—to prosecute a war in Europe?

The first World War, you will recall, was fought to "save democracy."

Today the same nations are taking part in another great conflict, eyed in the same purpose, only with added fury, cruelty, barbarity, hatred, and viciousness. What is it about? The same things that caused the first World War.

The picture is repainted, of course, by adding a touch here and there—but the face of the war monster is still vivid. The mask does not hide the horrid expression of greed, desire for power, trade, gold, land, hatred of fellow man, and the hideous gaunt jaws and empty eye sockets.

The President, in recent eloquent speeches, visualized a world of religious freedom, freedom of speech, freedom from want, freedom from fear.

What a great and happy world that would be. Christ visualized such a world. As I heard the President's words, I pondered the picture he painted.

But we are not living today in that God-like world. This is a world of chaos created by man's greed.

Can we wipe out want in Europe when we have not wiped out want here?

I can take you into any town, city, village, or county in this country and show you want.

A Military Blood Bank

Dare we set America up and commit her as the financial and military blood bank of the rest of the world when the proportion of want in this country is still so great that by doing this our country would become a victim of financial and military pernicious anemia? . . .

Should we not appreciate the fact that we cannot right every wrong in this man-made world? We cannot police this world. To do so would require many millions of soldiers and billions more dollars of armaments.

The forgotten man, to my way of thinking, was the American soldier of World War No. 1. When he came home he found his job gone. He had to abandon gradually the ideals he thought he had fought for. He saw his hope of material prosperity dwindle. He took any job he could get.

If he were so unfortunate as to be injured in body or in mind, he found himself, perhaps, in a hospital or confined in his own home. The help his Government extended was not too much.

If America gets into this world war we will have 10 times as many of these "forgotten men" when the conflict is concluded. Go back to the cause of the Russian revolution and see if that could not have been avoided had the powers that be not forgot to remember.

And we will have a bankrupt Nation—of that there can be no doubt.

To finance this war we already have seen what the cost would be. America would be economically annihilated.

Of course, I want to defend America. But I do not want to be a party to putting my country into such a position that if England sinks, or any other nation sinks the United States will go down with her.

I do not believe it is possible for any outside enemy to invade America successfully.

Is America Vulnerable?

Germany could not invade the United States, with any hope of victory, without enormous numbers of troops. How could she get them actually onto our shores—with our naval and military and aerial might to fend her off?

Could Germany—if she is victorious in the war in Europe—hold many more millions of people than there are Germans under her heel while she is attempting to conquer America? Would all the other nations abroad stand idle, totally helpless, if Germany were so foolish as to move her military machine off the European Continent to undertake a conquest of another continent?

No; my friends, I think military invasion of America by any outside enemy is fantastically impossible.

I fully realize that national defense in its broader sense means more than keeping hostile forces from this continent. It means, insofar as we can, protecting ourselves from other threats to our security. There is not a single doubt but what our interests— financial and economic—are tied in with Britain's victory, but I am not one of those who believes that we are tied in to such an extent that such a victory is essential to our economic existence and to the continuation of our way of life. Regardless of the outcome of this war, a new order is in the making with reference to our domestic economy and our trade with foreign nations. Our whole internal set-up is going to have to be revamped and revised to meet the change in world conditions. . . .

———•———

"Under this bill, . . . it would be possible, without any doubt whatsoever, for circumstances to arise which most certainly would involve the United States in war."

———•———

Unless peace can be brought about it is imperative, until we get in better shape to defend ourselves, that we do everything for the democracies that we possibly can within the framework of the Constitution and our laws to enable them to carry on, but I am not prepared to surrender the power of Congress under the Constitution and to jeopardize the future of my country to the point where we are going to populate the cemeteries of Europe again.

No, my friends, to me the role for us is clear. It is the role of peace seeker, not war seeker.

A warring world is a sick world. Peace is to the world body politic what health is to an individual.

Individuals rejoice when health is restored—not when they start a sickness.

Nations rejoice when peace is declared—not when they begin a war.

We must study the mistakes that have caused wars, if we are to prevent the spread of war and our involvement. No one nation ever has a monopoly on mistakes. Every nation lives in a glass house. At some time or other every nation has played the role of traitor to Christianity and the cause of peace. . . .

In conclusion I believe that we should proceed cautiously. . . .

I would feel that I would be untrue to myself, the laws of my country, and my country, were I to support this bill as written.

For Further Reading

Wayne S. Cole, *Roosevelt and the Isolationists, 1932–1945.* Lincoln: University of Nebraska Press, 1983.

Robert Dallek, *Franklin D. Roosevelt and American Foreign Policy.* New York: Oxford University Press, 1979.

Warren F. Kimball, *The Most Unsordid Act: Lend-Lease, 1939–1941.* Baltimore: Johns Hopkins University Press, 1969.

Bruce Russett, *No Clear and Present Danger.* New York: Harper & Row, 1972.

John E. Wiltz, *From Isolation to War, 1931–1941.* New York: Crowell, 1968.

VIEWPOINT 29A

The Internment of Japanese-Americans Was Justified (1944)

Hugo Black (1886–1971)

Following the Japanese attack on Pearl Harbor, Hawaii, the United States declared war on Japan on December 8, 1941. At that time approximately 110,000 Japanese-Americans, two-thirds of them American citizens, resided on the West Coast of the United States. They quickly became objects of fear and suspicion. Officials and other citizens worried that they would sabotage America's military effort and assist a possible Japanese invasion. In 1942, under authority of an executive order by President Franklin D. Roosevelt, the U.S. military declared the entire West Coast a vital military area and forcibly evacuated all Japanese-American residents from their homes. They detained these people in barbed wire–enclosed "relocation centers" constructed in California, Montana, and other states, holding them for the duration of the war.

The relocation program received several legal challenges during World War II that reached the

From the majority opinion of the U.S. Supreme Court in *Korematsu v. United States,* 319 U.S. 624 (1944).

Supreme Court. One such case involved Fred Korematsu, a shipyard worker who was arrested and convicted for refusing to obey an evacuation order to leave his home in San Leandro, California. He appealed his conviction, eventually reaching the Supreme Court, which in a 6–3 vote ruled against him in 1944. Writing for the majority was Hugo Black, an associate justice from 1937 to 1971, who is remembered today as a staunch defender of the Bill of Rights. Citing a 1943 case, *Hirabayashi v. United States*, in which the Supreme Court upheld a curfew regulation on Japanese-Americans as a necessary war measure, Black defends the evacuation program of the U.S. government. While declaring that civil rights restrictions on the basis of race were "immediately suspect," he ultimately upholds the military evacuation measures as justifiable because of national security concerns.

How does war affect civil liberties, according to Black? How does he defend the actions taken against Japanese-Americans against the charge of racism?

The petitioner, an American citizen of Japanese descent, was convicted in a federal district court for remaining in San Leandro, California, a "Military Area," contrary to Civilian Exclusion Order No. 34 of the Commanding General of the Western Command, U.S. Army, which directed that after May 9, 1942, all persons of Japanese ancestry should be excluded from that area. No question was raised as to petitioner's loyalty to the United States. The Circuit Court of Appeals affirmed, and the importance of the constitutional question involved caused us to grant certiorari.

It should be noted, to begin with, that all legal restrictions which curtail the civil rights of a single racial group are immediately suspect. That is not to say that all such restrictions are unconstitutional. It is to say that courts must subject them to the most rigid scrutiny. Pressing public necessity may sometimes justify the existence of such restrictions; racial antagonism never can. . . .

War Powers

The 1942 Act was attacked in the *Hirabayashi* case as an unconstitutional delegation of power; it was contended that the curfew order and other orders on which it rested were beyond the war powers of the Congress, the military authorities and of the President, as Commander in Chief of the Army; and finally that to apply the curfew order against none but citizens of Japanese ancestry amounted to a constitutionally prohibited discrimination solely on account of race. To these questions, we gave the serious consideration which their importance justified. We upheld the curfew order as an exercise of the power of the government to take steps necessary to prevent espionage and sabotage in an area threatened by Japanese attack.

In the light of the principles we announced in the *Hirabayashi* case, we are unable to conclude that it was beyond the war power of Congress and the Executive to exclude those of Japanese ancestry from the West Coast war area at the time they did. True, exclusion from the area in which one's home is located is a far greater deprivation than constant confinement to the home from 8 p.m. to 6 a.m. Nothing short of apprehension by the proper military authorities of the gravest imminent danger to the public safety can constitutionally justify either. But exclusion from a threatened area, no less than curfew, has a definite and close relationship to the prevention of espionage and sabotage. The military authorities, charged with the primary responsibility of defending our shores, concluded that curfew provided inadequate protection and ordered exclusion. They did so, as pointed out in our *Hirabayashi* opinion, in accordance with Congressional authority to the military to say who should, and who should not, remain in the threatened areas.

In this case the petitioner challenges the assumptions upon which we rested our conclusions in the *Hirabayashi* case. He also urges that by May 1942, when Order No. 34 was promulgated, all danger of Japanese invasion of the West Coast had disappeared. After careful consideration of these contentions we are compelled to reject them.

———— • ————

"When under conditions of modern warfare our shores are threatened by hostile forces, the power to protect must be commensurate with the threatened danger."

———— • ————

Here, as in the *Hirabayashi* case, *supra*, p. 99, ". . . we cannot reject as unfounded the judgment of the military authorities and of Congress that there were disloyal members of that population, whose number and strength could not be precisely and quickly ascertained. We cannot say that the war-making branches of the Government did not have ground for believing that in a critical hour such persons could not readily be isolated and separately dealt with, and constituted a menace to the national defense and safety, which demanded that prompt and adequate measures be taken to guard against it."

Like curfew, exclusion of those of Japanese origin was deemed necessary because of the presence of an unascertained number of disloyal members of the group, most of whom we have no doubt were loyal to this country. It was because we could not reject the finding of the military authorities that it was impossible to bring about an immediate segregation of the disloyal from the loyal that we sustained the validity of the curfew order as applying to the whole group. In the instant case, temporary exclusion of the entire group was rested by the military on the same ground. The judgment that exclusion of the whole group was for the same reason a military imperative answers the contention that the exclusion was in the nature of group punishment based on antagonism to those of Japanese origin. That there were members of the group who retained loyalties to Japan has been confirmed by investigations made subsequent to the exclusion. Approximately five thousand American citizens of Japanese ancestry refused to swear unqualified allegiance to the United States and to renounce allegiance to the Japanese Emperor, and several thousand evacuees requested repatriation to Japan.

The Burdens of Citizenship

We uphold the exclusion order as of the time it was made and when the petitioner violated it. . . . In doing so, we are not unmindful of the hardships imposed by it upon a large group of American citizens. . . . But hardships are part of war and war is an aggregation of hardships. All citizens alike, both in and out of uniform, feel the impact of war in greater or lesser measure. Citizenship has its responsibilities as well as its privileges, and in time of war the burden is always heavier. Compulsory exclusion of large groups of citizens from their homes, except under circumstances of direst emergency and peril, is inconsistent with our basic governmental institutions. But when under conditions of modern warfare our shores are threatened by hostile forces, the power to protect must be commensurate with the threatened danger. . . .

Racial Prejudice Not an Issue

It is said that we are dealing here with the case of imprisonment of a citizen in a concentration camp solely because of his ancestry, without evidence or inquiry concerning his loyalty and good disposition towards the United States. Our task would be simple, our duty clear, were this a case involving the imprisonment of a loyal citizen in a concentration camp because of racial prejudice. Regardless of the true nature of the assembly and relocation centers—and we deem it unjustifiable to call them concentration camps with all the ugly connotations that term implies—we are dealing specifically with nothing but an exclusion order. To cast this case into outlines of racial prejudice, without reference to the real military dangers which were presented, merely confuses the issue. Korematsu was not excluded from the Military Area because of hostility to him or his race. He *was* excluded because we are at war with the Japanese Empire, because the properly constituted military authorities feared an invasion of our West Coast and felt constrained to take proper security measures, because they decided that the military urgency of the situation demanded that all citizens of Japanese ancestry be segregated from the West Coast temporarily, and finally, because Congress, reposing its confidence in this time of war in our military leaders—as inevitably it must—determined that they should have the power to do just this. There was evidence of disloyalty on the part of some, the military authorities considered that the need for action was great, and time was short. We cannot—by availing ourselves of the calm perspective of hindsight—now say that at that time these actions were unjustified.

VIEWPOINT 29B

The Internment of Japanese-Americans Was Not Justified (1944)

Frank Murphy (1890–1949)

During World War II the United States forcibly moved thousands of Japanese-Americans from their homes on the West Coast and detained them in barbed wire–enclosed detention centers. The evacuations provoked sharp debate as to whether such curtailment of civil liberties that are normally protected under the Bill of Rights was justified in time of war. The following viewpoint is taken from a dissenting opinion in the 1944 Supreme Court case *Korematsu v. United States*, in which shipyard worker Fred Korematsu challenged his evacuation from his California home. The majority of the Supreme Court voted to uphold the evacuation as a legitimate war measure. One of the dissenters was Frank Murphy, an associate justice of the Supreme Court from 1940 to 1949. As a Michigan governor, a U.S. attorney general who established the first civil liberties unit in the Justice Department, and a Supreme Court justice, Murphy gained a reputation as a strong advocate and defender of civil liberties.

What deference should be shown to the judgment of military authorities, according to Murphy? Which constitutional rights does he say were being violated in the internment program? What arguments does he make in implicating racism as the reason behind the detentions?

From the dissenting opinion in *Korematsu v. United States*, 319 U.S. 624 (1944).

This exclusion of "all persons of Japanese ancestry, both alien and non-alien," from the Pacific Coast area on a plea of military necessity in the absence of martial law ought not to be approved. Such exclusion goes over "the very brink of constitutional power" and falls into the ugly abyss of racism.

In dealing with matters relating to the prosecution and progress of a war, we must accord great respect and consideration to the judgments of the military authorities who are on the scene and who have full knowledge of the military facts. The scope of their discretion must, as a matter of necessity and common sense, be wide. And their judgments ought not to be overruled lightly by those whose training and duties ill-equip them to deal intelligently with matters so vital to the physical security of the nation.

At the same time, however, it is essential that there be definite limits to military discretion, especially where martial law has not been declared. Individuals must not be left impoverished of their constitutional rights on a plea of military necessity that has neither substance nor support. Thus, like other claims conflicting with the asserted constitutional rights of the individual, the military claim must subject itself to the judicial process of having its reasonableness determined and its conflicts with other interests reconciled. "What are the allowable limits of military discretion, and whether or not they have been overstepped in a particular case, are judicial questions."

Violating Constitutional Rights

The judicial test of whether the Government, on a plea of military necessity, can validly deprive an individual of any of his constitutional rights is whether the deprivation is reasonably related to a public danger that is so "immediate, imminent, and impending" as not to admit of delay and not to permit the intervention of ordinary constitutional processes to alleviate the danger. . . . Civilian Exclusion Order No. 34, banishing from a prescribed area of the Pacific Coast "all persons of Japanese ancestry, both alien and non-alien," clearly does not meet that test. Being an obvious racial discrimination, the order deprives all those within its scope of the equal protection of the laws as guaranteed by the Fifth Amendment. It further deprives these individuals of their constitutional rights to live and work where they will, to establish a home where they choose and to move about freely. In excommunicating them without benefit of hearings, this order also deprives them of all their constitutional rights to procedural due process. Yet no reasonable relation to an "immediate, imminent, and impending" public danger is evident to support this racial restriction which is one of the most sweeping and complete deprivations of constitutional rights in the history of this nation in the absence of martial law.

It must be conceded that the military and naval situation in the spring of 1942 was such as to generate a very real fear of invasion of the Pacific Coast, accompanied by fears of sabotage and espionage in that area. The military command was therefore justified in adopting all reasonable means necessary to combat these dangers. In adjudging the military action taken in light of the then apparent dangers, we must not erect too high or too meticulous standards; it is necessary only that the action have some reasonable relation to the removal of the dangers of invasion, sabotage and espionage. But the exclusion, either temporarily or permanently, of all persons with Japanese blood in their veins has no such reasonable relation. And that relation is lacking because the exclusion order necessarily must rely for its reasonableness upon the assumption that all persons of Japanese ancestry may have a dangerous tendency to commit sabotage and espionage and to aid our Japanese enemy in other ways. It is difficult to believe that reason, logic or experience could be marshalled in support of such an assumption.

That this forced exclusion was the result in good measure of this erroneous assumption of racial guilt rather than bona fide military necessity is evidenced by the Commanding General's Final Report on the evacuation from the Pacific Coast area. In it he refers to all individuals of Japanese descent as "subversive," as belonging to "an enemy race" whose "racial strains are undiluted," and as constituting "over 112,000 potential enemies . . . at large today" along the Pacific Coast. In support of this blanket condemnation of all persons of Japanese descent, however, no reliable evidence is cited to show that such individuals were generally disloyal, or had generally so conducted themselves in this area as to constitute a special menace to defense installations or war industries, or had otherwise by their behavior furnished reasonable ground for their exclusion as a group.

Racial Prejudice

Justification for the exclusion is sought, instead, mainly upon questionable racial and sociological grounds not ordinarily within the realm of expert military judgment, supplemented by certain semi-military conclusions drawn from an unwarranted use of circumstantial evidence. Individuals of Japanese ancestry are condemned because they are said to be "a large, unassimilated, tightly knit racial group, bound to an enemy nation by strong ties of race, culture, custom and religion." They are claimed to be given to "emperor worshipping ceremonies" and to "dual citizenship." Japanese language schools and allegedly pro-Japanese organizations are cited as evidence of possible group disloyalty, together with facts as to certain persons being educated and residing at length in Japan. It is intimated that many of these individuals deliberately resided "adjacent to strategic points," thus enabling them "to carry into execution a tremendous program of sabotage on a mass scale should any considerable number of them have been inclined to do so." . . . Finally, it is intimated, though not directly charged or proved, that persons of Japanese ancestry were responsible for three minor isolated shellings and bombings of the Pacific Coast area, as well as for unidentified radio transmissions and night signalling.

The main reasons relied upon by those responsible for the forced evacuation, therefore, do not prove a reasonable relation between the group characteristics of Japanese Americans and the dangers of invasion, sabotage and espionage. The reasons appear, instead, to be largely an accumulation of much of the misinformation, half-truths and insinuations that for years have been directed against Japanese Americans by people with racial and economic prejudices—the same people who have been among the foremost advocates of the evacuation. A military judgment based upon such racial and sociological considerations is not entitled to the great weight ordinarily given the judgments based upon strictly military considerations. Especially is this so when every charge relative to race, religion, culture, geographical location, and legal and economic status has been substantially discredited by independent studies made by experts in these matters.

———— • ————

"This racial restriction . . . is one of the most sweeping and complete deprivations of constitutional rights in the history of this nation in the absence of martial law."

———— • ————

The military necessity which is essential to the validity of the evacuation order thus resolves itself into a few intimations that certain individuals actively aided the enemy, from which it is inferred that the entire group of Japanese Americans could not be trusted to be or remain loyal to the United States. No one denies, of course, that there were some disloyal persons of Japanese descent on the Pacific Coast who did all in their power to aid their ancestral land. Similar disloyal activities have been engaged in by many persons of German, Italian and even more pioneer stock in our country. But to infer that examples of individual disloyalty prove group disloyalty and justify discriminatory action against the entire group is to deny that under our system of law individual guilt is the sole basis for deprivation of rights. Moreover, this inference, which is at the very heart of the evacuation orders, has been used in support of the abhorrent and despicable treatment of minority groups by the dictatorial tyrannies which this nation is now pledged to destroy. To give constitutional sanction to that inference in this case, however well-intentioned may have been the military command on the Pacific Coast, is to adopt one of the cruelest of the rationales used by our enemies to destroy the dignity of the individual and to encourage and open the door to discriminatory actions against other minority groups in the passions of tomorrow.

No adequate reason is given for the failure to treat these Japanese Americans on an individual basis by holding investigations and hearings to separate the loyal from the disloyal, as was done in the case of persons of German and Italian ancestry. . . . It is asserted merely that the loyalties of this group "were unknown and time was of the essence." Yet nearly four months elapsed after Pearl Harbor before the first exclusion order was issued; nearly eight months went by until the last order was issued; and the last of these "subversive" persons was not actually removed until almost eleven months had elapsed. Leisure and deliberation seem to have been more of the essence than speed. And the fact that conditions were not such as to warrant a declaration of martial law adds strength to the belief that the factors of time and military necessity were not as urgent as they have been represented to be.

Moreover, there was no adequate proof that the Federal Bureau of Investigation and the military and naval intelligence services did not have the espionage and sabotage situation well in hand during this long period. Nor is there any denial of the fact that not one person of Japanese ancestry was accused or convicted of espionage or sabotage after Pearl Harbor while they were still free, a fact which is some evidence of the loyalty of the vast majority of these individuals and of the effectiveness of the established methods of combatting these evils. It seems incredible that under these circumstances it would have been impossible to hold loyalty hearings for the mere 112,000 persons involved—or at least for the 70,000 American citizens—especially when a large part of this number represented children and elderly men and women. Any inconvenience that may have accompanied an attempt to conform to procedural due process cannot be said to justify violations of constitutional rights of individuals.

All Americans Have Equal Rights

I dissent, therefore, from this legalization of racism. Racial discrimination in any form and in any degree has no justifiable part whatever in our democratic way of life. It is unattractive in any setting but it is utterly revolting among a free people who have embraced the principles set forth in the Constitution of the United States. All residents of this nation are kin in some way by blood or culture to a foreign land. Yet they are primarily and necessarily a part of the new and distinct civilization of the United States. They must accordingly be treated at all times as the heirs of the American experiment and as entitled to all the rights and freedoms guaranteed by the Constitution.

For Further Reading

John W. Dower, *War Without Mercy: Race and Power in the Pacific War.* New York: Pantheon Books, 1986.

Sidney Fine, *Frank Murphy.* Ann Arbor: University of Michigan Press, 1984.

Peter Irons, *Justice at War.* New York: Oxford University Press, 1983.

John Tateishi, *And Justice for All: An Oral History of the Japanese-American Detention Camps.* New York: Random House, 1984.

Michi Weglyn, *The Untold Story of America's Concentration Camps.* New York: Morrow, 1976.

Tinsley E. Yarborough, *Mister Justice Black and His Critics.* Durham, NC: Duke University Press, 1988.

VIEWPOINT 30A

The United States Should Not Drop the Atomic Bomb on Japan (1945)

The Franck Committee

In 1942 the United States undertook a secret research effort—the Manhattan Project—to develop a new kind of weapon powered by the splitting of the atom. The original impetus for the Manhattan Project was the fear of Germany's developing such a weapon. Following Germany's surrender in May 1945, however, discussion within the U.S. government and military focused on using the bomb against America's other main World War II enemy, Japan.

Many of the scientists who were part of the massive effort to invent the atom bomb were troubled about the ethical and political questions regarding the bomb's use. In 1944 and early 1945, Manhattan Project scientists based at the Metallurgical Laboratory (Met Lab) at the University of Chicago held seminars, circulated petitions, and in general raised concerns about the future implications of their research. One of these scientists was James Franck (1882–1964), an eminent German physicist who had been forced to leave Germany in 1933, and who had

Excerpted from *The Franck Report,* June 11, 1945.

agreed to join the Manhattan Project in 1942 on the condition that he could express his views on how the bomb, if successfully developed, should be used.

The physicist who recruited Franck for the Manhattan Project, Arthur H. Compton, was a member of the scientific panel of the special Interim Committee appointed by Secretary of War Henry L. Stimson to advise President Harry S. Truman on the atomic bomb (see viewpoint 30B). At the Interim Committee's meeting on May 31 in Washington, Compton urged that the concerns of Franck and the other Chicago scientists be considered. On June 2, in Chicago, Compton met with the scientist, who subsequently formed several committees to write reports and recommendations concerning the future use of atomic bombs and energy. Franck chaired a committee of seven Met Lab scientists to discuss and report on the political and social implications of the new weapon. The Franck Committee's report, excerpted here, stresses the importance of international control of atomic weapons, and provides arguments against a surprise bomb attack on Japan.

Franck traveled to Washington on June 12, 1945, to join Compton in presenting the report to Stimson, but the secretary of war was out of town. The report was left in Stimson's office; it is uncertain whether and how closely he or other government officials read it. America dropped an atomic bomb on Hiroshima less than two months later.

What predictions does the committee make concerning future U.S./Soviet Union relations? Are the committee's objections to using the atomic bomb against Japan primarily moral or practical? What uses of the atomic bomb do they recommend?

I. PREAMBLE

The only reason to treat nuclear power differently from all the other developments in the field of physics is the possibility of its use as a means of political pressure in peace and sudden destruction in war. All present plans for the organization of research, scientific and industrial development, and publication in the field of nucleonics [the science of nuclear phenomena such as fission and fusion] are conditioned by the political and military climate in which one expects those plans to be carried out. Therefore, in making suggestions for the postwar organization of nucleonics, a discussion of political problems cannot be avoided. The scientists on this Project do not presume to speak authoritatively on problems of national and international policy. However, we found ourselves, by the force of events during the last five years, in the position of a small group of citizens cognizant of a grave danger for the safety of this country as well as for the future of all the other nations, of which the rest of mankind is unaware. We therefore feel it our duty to urge that the political problems, arising from the mastering of nuclear power, be recognized in all their gravity, and that appropriate steps be taken for their study and the preparation of necessary decisions. We hope that the creation of the Committee by the Secretary of War to deal with all aspects of nucleonics, indicates that these implications have been recognized by the government. We believe that our acquaintance with the scientific elements of the situation and prolonged preoccupation with its world-wide political implications, imposes on us the obligation to offer to the Committee some suggestions as to the possible solution of these grave problems.

Scientists have often before been accused of providing new weapons for the mutual destruction of nations, instead of improving their well-being. It is undoubtedly true that the discovery of flying, for example, has so far brought much more misery than enjoyment and profit to humanity. However, in the past, scientists could disclaim direct responsibility for the use to which mankind had put their disinterested discoveries. We feel compelled to take a more active stand now because the success which we have achieved in the development of nuclear power is fraught with infinitely greater dangers than were all the inventions of the past. All of us, familiar with the present state of nucleonics, live with the vision before our eyes of sudden destruction visited on our own country, of a Pearl Harbor disaster repeated in thousand-fold magnification in every one of our major cities.

In the past, science has often been able to provide also new methods of protection against new weapons of aggression it made possible, but it cannot promise such efficient protection against the destructive use of nuclear power. This protection can come only from the political organization of the world. Among all the arguments calling for an efficient international organization for peace, the existence of nuclear weapons is the most compelling one. *In the absence of an international authority which would make all resort to force in international conflicts impossible, nations could still be diverted from a path which must lead to total mutual destruction, by a specific international agreement barring a nuclear armaments race.*

II. PROSPECTS OF ARMAMENTS RACE

It could be suggested that the danger of destruction by nuclear weapons can be avoided—at least as far as this country is concerned—either by keeping our discoveries secret for an indefinite time, or else by developing our nucleonic armaments at such a pace that no other nations would think of attacking us from fear of overwhelming retaliation.

The answer to the first suggestion is that although we undoubtedly are at present ahead of the rest of the world in this field, the fundamental facts of nuclear power are a subject of common knowledge. British scientists know as much as we do about the basic wartime progress of nucleonics—if not of the specific processes used in our engineering developments—and the role which French nuclear physicists have played in the pre-war development of this field, plus their occasional contact with our Projects, will enable them to catch up rapidly, at least as far as basic scientific discoveries are concerned. German scientists, in whose discoveries the whole development of this field originated, apparently did not develop it during the war to the same extent to which this has been done in America; but to the last day of the European war, we were living in constant apprehension as to their possible achievements. The certainty that German scientists are working on this weapon and that their government would certainly have no scruples against using it when available, was the main motivation of the initiative which American scientists took in urging the development of nuclear power for military purposes on a large scale in this country. In Russia, too, the basic facts and implications of nuclear power were well understood in 1940, and the experience of Russian scientists in nuclear research is entirely sufficient to enable them to retrace our steps within a few years, even if we should make every attempt to conceal them. Furthermore, we should not expect too much success from attempts to keep basic information secret in peacetime, when scientists acquainted with the work on this and associated Projects will be scattered to many colleges and research institutions and many of them will continue to work on problems closely related to those on which our developments are based. In other words, even if we can retain our leadership in basic knowledge of nucleonics for a certain time by maintaining secrecy as to all results achieved on this and associated Projects, it would be foolish to hope that this can protect us for more than a few years.

It may be asked whether we cannot prevent the development of military nucleonics in other countries by a monopoly on the raw materials of nuclear power. The answer is that even though the largest now known deposits of uranium ores are under the control of powers which belong to the "western" group (Canada, Belgium, and British India), the old deposits in Czechoslovakia are outside this sphere. Russia is known to be mining radium on its own territory; and even if we do not know the size of the deposits discovered so far in the USSR, the probability that no large reserves of uranium will be found in a country which covers ⅙ of the land area of the earth (and whose sphere of influence takes in additional territory), is too small to serve as a basis for security. *Thus, we cannot hope to avoid a nuclear armament race either by keeping secret from the competing nations the basic scientific facts of nuclear power or by cornering the raw materials required for such a race.*

———— • ————

"If the United States were to be the first to release this new means of indiscriminate destruction upon mankind, she would sacrifice public support throughout the world [and] precipitate the race for armaments."

———— • ————

We now consider the second of the two suggestions made at the beginning of this section, and ask whether we could not feel ourselves safe in a race of nuclear armaments by virtue of our greater industrial potential, including greater diffusion of scientific and technical knowledge, greater volume and efficiency of our skilled labor corps, and greater experience of our management—all the factors whose importance has been so strikingly demonstrated in the conversion of this country into an arsenal of the Allied Nations in the present war. The answer is that all that these advantages can give us is the accumulation of a large number of bigger and better atomic bombs—and this only if we produce these bombs at the maximum of our capacity in peace time, and do not rely on conversion of a peace-time nucleonics industry to military production after the beginning of hostilities.

However, such a quantitative advantage in reserves of bottled destructive power will not make us safe from sudden attack. Just because a potential enemy will be afraid of being "outnumbered and outgunned," the temptation for him may be overwhelming to attempt a sudden unprovoked blow—particularly if he should suspect us of harboring aggressive intentions against his security or his sphere of influence. In no other type of warfare does the advantage lie so heavily with the aggressor. He can place his "infernal machines" in advance in all our major cities and explode them simultaneously, thus destroying a major part of our industry and a large part of our population, aggregated in densely populated metropolitan districts. Our possibilities of retaliation— even if retaliation should be considered adequate compensation for the loss of millions of lives and destruction of our largest cities—will be greatly handicapped because we must rely on aerial transportation of the bombs, and also because we may have to deal with an enemy whose industry and population are dispersed over a large territory.

In fact, if the race for nuclear armaments is allowed to develop, the only apparent way in which our country can be protected from the paralyzing effects of a sudden attack is by dispersal of those industries which are essential for our war effort and dispersal of the populations of our major metropolitan cities. As long as nuclear bombs remain scarce (i.e., as long as uranium and thorium remain the only basic materials for their fabrication), efficient dispersal of our industry and the scattering of our metropolitan population will considerably decrease the temptation to attack us by nuclear weapons. . . .

We are fully aware of the staggering difficulties involved in such a radical change in the social and economic structure of our nation. We felt, however, that the dilemma had to be stated, to show what kind of alternative methods of protection will have to be considered if no successful international agreement is reached. It must be pointed out that in this field we are in a less favorable position than nations which are either now more diffusely populated and whose industries are more scattered, or whose governments have unlimited power over the movement of population and the location of industrial plants.

If no efficient international agreement is achieved, the race for nuclear armaments will be on in earnest not later than the morning after our first demonstration of the existence of nuclear weapons. After this, it might take other nations three or four years to overcome our present head start, and eight or ten years to draw even with us if we continue to do intensive work in this field. This might be all the time we would have to bring about the regroupment of our population and industry. Obviously, no time should be lost in inaugurating a study of this problem by experts.

III. PROSPECTS OF AGREEMENT

The consequences of nuclear warfare, and the type of measures which would have to be taken to protect a country from total destruction by nuclear bombing, must be as abhorrent to other nations as to the United States. England, France, and the smaller nations of the European continent, with their congeries of people and industries, would be in a particularly desperate situation in the face of such a threat. Russia and China are the only great nations at present which could survive a nuclear attack. However, even though these countries may value human life less than the peoples of Western Europe and America, and even though Russia, in particular, has an immense space over which its vital industries could

be dispersed and a government which can order this dispersion the day it is convinced that such a measure is necessary—there is no doubt that Russia will shudder at the possibility of a sudden disintegration of Moscow and Leningrad and of its new industrial cities in the Urals and Siberia. Therefore, only lack of mutual *trust*, and not lack of *desire* for agreement, can stand in the path of an efficient agreement for the prevention of nuclear warfare. The achievement of such an agreement will thus essentially depend on the integrity of intentions and readiness to sacrifice the necessary fraction of one's own sovereignty, by all the parties to the agreement.

Revealing Nuclear Weapons to the World

From this point of view, the way in which the nuclear weapons now being secretly developed in this country are first revealed to the world appears to be of great, perhaps fateful importance.

One possible way—which may particularly appeal to those who consider nuclear bombs primarily as a secret weapon developed to help win the present war—is to use them without warning on an appropriately selected object in Japan. It is doubtful whether the first available bombs, of comparatively low efficiency and small size, will be sufficient to break the will or ability of Japan to resist, especially given the fact that the major cities like Tokyo, Nagoya, Osaka and Kobe already will largely have been reduced to ashes by the slower process of ordinary aerial bombing. Although important tactical results undoubtedly can be achieved by a sudden introduction of nuclear weapons, we nevertheless think that the question of the use of the very first available atomic bombs in the Japanese war should be weighed very carefully, not only by military authorities, but by the highest political leadership of this country. If we consider international agreement on total prevention of nuclear warfare as the paramount objective, and believe that it can be achieved, this kind of introduction of atomic weapons to the world may easily destroy all our chances of success. Russia, and even allied countries which bear less mistrust of our ways and intentions, as well as neutral countries may be deeply shocked. It may be very difficult to persuade the world that a nation which was capable of secretly preparing and suddenly releasing a weapon as indiscriminate as the rocket bomb and a million times more destructive, is to be trusted in its proclaimed desire of having such weapons abolished by international agreement. We have large accumulations of poison gas, but do not use them, and recent polls have shown that public opinion in this country would disapprove of such a use even if it would accelerate the winning of the Far Eastern war. It is true that some irrational element in mass psychology makes gas poisoning more revolting than blasting by explosives, even though gas warfare is in no way more "inhuman" than the war of bombs and bullets. Nevertheless, it is not at all certain that American public opinion, if it could be enlightened as to the effect of atomic explosives, would approve of our own country being the first to introduce such an indiscriminate method of wholesale destruction of civilian life.

Thus, from the "optimistic" point of view—looking forward to an international agreement on the prevention of nuclear warfare—the military advantages and the saving of American lives achieved by the sudden use of atomic bombs against Japan may be outweighed by the ensuing loss of confidence and by a wave of horror and repulsion sweeping over the rest of the world and perhaps even dividing public opinion at home.

From this point of view, a demonstration of the new weapon might best be made, before the eyes of representatives of all the United Nations, on the desert or a barren island. The best possible atmosphere for the achievement of an international agreement could be achieved if America could say to the world, "You see what sort of a weapon we had but did not use. We are ready to renounce its use in the future if other nations join us in this renunciation and agree to the establishment of an efficient international control."

After such a demonstration the weapon might perhaps be used against Japan if the sanction of the United Nations (and of public opinion at home) were obtained, perhaps after a preliminary ultimatum to Japan to surrender or at least to evacuate certain regions as an alternative to their total destruction. This may sound fantastic, but in nuclear weapons we have something entirely new in order of magnitude of destructive power, and if we want to capitalize fully on the advantage their possession gives us, we must use new and imaginative methods.

Starting an Arms Race

It must be stressed that if one takes the pessimistic point of view and discounts the possibility of an effective international control over nuclear weapons at the present time, then the advisability of an early use of nuclear bombs against Japan becomes even more doubtful—quite independently of any humanitarian considerations. If an international agreement is not concluded immediately after the first demonstration, this will mean a flying start toward an unlimited armaments race. If this race is inevitable, we have every reason to delay its beginning as long as possible in order to increase our head start still further. . . . The benefit to the nation, and the saving of American lives in the future, achieved by renouncing

an early demonstration of nuclear bombs and letting the other nations come into the race only reluctantly, on the basis of guesswork and without definite knowledge that the "thing does work," may far outweigh the advantages to be gained by the immediate use of the first and comparatively inefficient bombs in the war against Japan. On the other hand, it may be argued that without an early demonstration it may prove difficult to obtain adequate support for further intensive development of nucleonics in this country and that thus the time gained by the postponement of an open armaments race will not be properly used. Furthermore one may suggest that other nations are now, or will soon be, not entirely unaware of our present achievements, and that consequently the postponement of a demonstration may serve no useful purpose as far as the avoidance of an armaments race is concerned, and may only create additional mistrust, thus worsening rather than improving the chances of an ultimate accord on the international control of nuclear explosives.

Thus, if the prospects of an agreement will be considered poor in the immediate future, the pros and cons of an early revelation of our possession of nuclear weapons to the world—not only by their actual use against Japan, but also by a prearranged demonstration—must be carefully weighed by the supreme political and military leadership of the country, and the decision should not be left to military tacticians alone.

One may point out that scientists themselves have initiated the development of this "secret weapon" and it is therefore strange that they should be reluctant to try it out on the enemy as soon as it is available. The answer to this question was given above—the compelling reason for creating this weapon with such speed was our fear that Germany had the technical skill necessary to develop such a weapon, and that the German government had no moral restraints regarding its use.

Another argument which could be quoted in favor of using atomic bombs as soon as they are available is that so much taxpayers' money has been invested in these Projects that the Congress and the American public will demand a return for their money. The attitude of American public opinion, mentioned earlier, in the matter of the use of poison gas against Japan, shows that one can expect the American public to understand that it is sometimes desirable to keep a weapon in readiness for use only in extreme emergency; and as soon as the potentialities of nuclear weapons are revealed to the American people, one can be sure that they will support all attempts to make the use of such weapons impossible.

Once this is achieved, the large installations and the accumulation of explosive material at present earmarked for potential military use will become available for important peace-time developments, including power production, large engineering undertakings, and mass production of radioactive materials. In this way, the money spent on wartime development of nucleonics may become a boon for the peacetime development of national economy. . . .

SUMMARY

The development of nuclear power not only constitutes an important addition to the technological and military power of the United States, but also creates grave political and economic problems for the future of this country.

Nuclear bombs cannot possibly remain a "secret weapon" at the exclusive disposal of this country for more than a few years. The scientific facts on which their construction is based are well known to scientists of other countries. Unless an effective international control of nuclear explosives is instituted, a race for nuclear armaments is certain to ensue following the first revelation of our possession of nuclear weapons to the world. Within ten years other countries may have nuclear bombs, each of which, weighing less than a ton, could destroy an urban area of more than ten square miles. In the war to which such an armaments race is likely to lead, the United States, with its agglomeration of population and industry in comparatively few metropolitan districts, will be at a disadvantage compared to nations whose population and industry are scattered over large areas.

We believe that these considerations make the use of nuclear bombs for an early unannounced attack against Japan inadvisable. If the United States were to be the first to release this new means of indiscriminate destruction upon mankind, she would sacrifice public support throughout the world, precipitate the race for armaments, and prejudice the possibility of reaching an international agreement on the future control of such weapons.

Much more favorable conditions for the eventual achievement of such an agreement could be created if nuclear bombs were first revealed to the world by a demonstration in an appropriately selected uninhabited area.

In case chances for the establishment of an effective international control of nuclear weapons should have to be considered slight at the present time, then not only the use of these weapons against Japan, but even their early demonstration, may be contrary to the interests of this country. A postponement of such a demonstration will have in this case the advantage of delaying the beginning of the nuclear armaments race as long as possible. If, during the time gained, ample support can be made available for further development of the field in this country, the postponement

will substantially increase the lead which we have established during the present war, and our position in an armament race or in any later attempt at international agreement would thus be strengthened.

On the other hand, if no adequate public support for the development of nucleonics will be available without a demonstration, the postponement of the latter may be deemed inadvisable, because enough information might leak out to cause other nations to start the armament race, in which we would then be at a disadvantage. There is also the possibility that the distrust of other nations may be aroused if they know that we are conducting a development under cover of secrecy, and that this will make it more difficult eventually to reach an agreement with them.

If the government should decide in favor of an early demonstration of nuclear weapons, it will then have the possibility of taking into account the public opinion of this country and of the other nations before deciding whether these weapons should be used in the war against Japan. In this way, other nations may assume a share of responsibility for such a fateful decision.

To sum up, we urge that the use of nuclear bombs in this war be considered as a problem of long-range national policy rather than of military expediency, and that this policy be directed primarily to the achievement of an agreement permitting an effective international control of the means of nuclear warfare.

The vital importance of such a control for our country is obvious from the fact that the only effective alternative method of protecting this country appears to be a dispersal of our major cities and essential industries.

J. FRANCK, CHAIRMAN
D.J. HUGHES
J.J. NICKSON
E. RABINOWITCH
G.T. SEABORG
J.C. STEARNS
L. SZILARD

VIEWPOINT 30B

The Decision to Drop the Atomic Bomb on Japan Was Justified (1947)

Henry L. Stimson (1867–1950)

The United States dropped an atomic bomb on the Japanese city of Hiroshima on August 6, 1945, and a second bomb on Nagasaki three days later. The two detonations reduced most of both cities to rubble and killed, both instantly and by subsequent radiation poisoning, tens of thousands of Japanese (estimates range from 80,000 to 200,000). Within a few days Japan surrendered and World War II was over. For some Americans victory was clouded by the revelation of the atomic bomb's destructive power and America's decision to use it. An editorial in the journal *Christian Century* held that "use of the atomic bomb has placed our nation in an indefensible moral position." Partly to counter this and other criticisms, Henry L. Stimson, secretary of war during World War II, wrote an article, published in *Harper's Magazine* in February 1947, that subsequently became well known. In the article, excerpted here, Stimson defends the decision to drop two atomic bombs on Japan and describes the process behind the decision.

Stimson, a secretary of state under President Herbert Hoover in the 1930s, was appointed secretary of war by President Franklin D. Roosevelt in 1940. After Roosevelt's death on April 12, 1945, Stimson continued to serve as secretary of war under the new president, Harry S. Truman, until September 1945. Stimson was the chief adviser to Roosevelt and Truman on atomic policy and was in charge of the effort to produce an atomic bomb. On May 31, 1945, shortly after Roosevelt's death, he chaired a special Interim Committee meeting of leading government and military officials as well as a scientific panel of four nuclear physicists from the Manhattan Project. Following this and other meetings, he and the committee recommended to Truman that the atomic bomb be used against Japan.

What were the primary reasons for using the atomic bomb, according to Stimson? How important, according to his account, were reservations such as those expressed in viewpoint 30A by the Franck Committee? What response does he offer to these concerns? What reasons does Stimson provide for rejecting the idea of a noncombat demonstration of the bomb?

I n recent months there has been much comment about the decision to use atomic bombs in attacks on the Japanese cities of Hiroshima and Nagasaki. This decision was one of the gravest made by our government in recent years, and it is entirely proper that it should be widely discussed. I have therefore decided to record for all who may be interested my understanding of the events which led up to the attack on Hiroshima on August 6, 1945, on Nagasaki on August 9, and the Japanese decision to surrender, on August 10. No single individual can hope to know exactly what took place in the minds of all of those who had a share in these events, but what

follows is an exact description of our thoughts and actions as I find them in the records and in my clear recollection.

Plans and Preparations

It was in the fall of 1941 that the question of atomic energy was first brought directly to my attention. At that time President Roosevelt appointed a committee consisting of Vice President [Henry] Wallace, General [George C.] Marshall, Dr. Vannevar Bush, Dr. James B. Conant, and myself. The function of this committee was to advise the President on questions of policy relating to the study of nuclear fission which was then proceeding both in this country and in Great Britain. For nearly four years thereafter I was directly connected with all major decisions of policy on the development and use of atomic energy, and from May 1, 1943, until my resignation as Secretary of War on September 21, 1945, I was directly responsible to the President for the administration of the entire undertaking; my chief advisers in this period were General Marshall, Dr. Bush, Dr. Conant, and Major General Leslie R. Groves, the officer in charge of the project. At the same time I was the President's senior adviser on the military employment of atomic energy.

A Simple Policy

The policy adopted and steadily pursued by President Roosevelt and his advisers was a simple one. It was to spare no effort in securing the earliest possible successful development of an atomic weapon. The reasons for this policy were equally simple. The original experimental achievement of atomic fission had occurred in Germany in 1938, and it was known that the Germans had continued their experiments. In 1941 and 1942 they were believed to be ahead of us, and it was vital that they should not be the first to bring atomic weapons into the field of battle. Furthermore, if we should be the first to develop the weapon, we should have a great new instrument for shortening the war and minimizing destruction. At no time, from 1941 to 1945, did I ever hear it suggested by the President, or by any other responsible member of the government, that atomic energy should not be used in the war. All of us of course understood the terrible responsibility involved in our attempt to unlock the doors to such a devastating weapon; President Roosevelt particularly spoke to me many times of his own awareness of the catastrophic potentialities of our work. But we were at war, and the work must be done. I therefore emphasize that it was our common objective, throughout the war, to be the first to produce an atomic weapon and use it. The possible atomic weapon was considered to be a new and tremendously powerful explosive, as legitimate as any other of the deadly explosive weapons of modern war. The entire purpose was the production of a military weapon; on no other ground could the wartime expenditure of so much time and money have been justified. The exact circumstances in which that weapon might be used were unknown to any of us until the middle of 1945, and when that time came, as we shall presently see, the military use of atomic energy was connected with larger questions of national policy.

———— • ————

"This deliberate, premeditated destruction was our least abhorrent choice. The destruction of Hiroshima and Nagasaki put an end to the Japanese war."

———— • ————

The extraordinary story of the successful development of the atomic bomb has been well told elsewhere. As time went on it became clear that the weapon would not be available in time for use in the European Theater, and the war against Germany was successfully ended by the use of what are now called conventional means. But in the spring of 1945 it became evident that the climax of our prolonged atomic effort was at hand. By the nature of atomic chain reactions, it was impossible to state with certainty that we had succeeded until a bomb had actually exploded in a fullscale experiment; nevertheless it was considered exceedingly probable that we should by midsummer have successfully detonated the first atomic bomb. This was to be done at the Alamogordo Reservation in New Mexico. It was thus time for detailed consideration of our future plans. What had begun as a well-founded hope was now developing into a reality.

On March 15, 1945, I had my last talk with President Roosevelt. . . .

This conversation covered the three aspects of the question which were then uppermost in our minds. First, it was always necessary to suppress a lingering doubt that any such titanic undertaking could be successful. Second, we must consider the implications of success in terms of its long-range postwar effect. Third, we must face the problem that would be presented at the time of our first use of the weapon, for with that first use there must be some public statement.

Briefing Harry S. Truman

I did not see Franklin Roosevelt again. The next time I went to the White House to discuss atomic energy was April 25, 1945, and I went to explain the

nature of the problem to a man whose only previous knowledge of our activities was that of a Senator who had loyally accepted our assurance that the matter must be kept a secret from him. Now he was President and Commander-in-Chief, and the final responsibility in this as in so many other matters must be his. President Truman accepted this responsibility with the same fine spirit that Senator Truman had shown before in accepting our refusal to inform him.

I discussed with him the whole history of the project. We had with us General Groves, who explained in detail the progress which had been made and the probable future course of the work. I also discussed with President Truman the broader aspects of the subject, and the memorandum which I used in this discussion is again a fair sample of the state of our thinking at the time.

Memorandum Discussed with President Truman, April 25, 1945

1. Within four months we shall in all probability have completed the most terrible weapon ever known in human history, one bomb of which could destroy a whole city.

2. Although we have shared its development with the U.K., physically the U.S. is at present in the position of controlling the resources with which to construct and use it and no other nation could reach this position for some years.

3. Nevertheless it is practically certain that we could not remain in this position indefinitely.

a. Various segments of its discovery and production are widely known among many scientists in many countries, although few scientists are now acquainted with the whole process which we have developed.

b. Although its construction under present methods requires great scientific and industrial effort and raw materials, which are temporarily mainly within the possession and knowledge of U.S. and U.K., it is extremely probable that much easier and cheaper methods of production will be discovered by scientists in the future, together with the use of materials of much wider distribution. As a result, it is extremely probable that the future will make it possible for atomic bombs to be constructed by smaller nations or even groups, or at least by a larger nation in a much shorter time.

4. As a result, it is indicated that the future may see a time when such a weapon may be constructed in secret and used suddenly and effectively with devastating power by a wilful nation or group against an unsuspecting nation or group of much greater size and material power. With its aid even a very powerful unsuspecting nation might be conquered within a very few days by a very much smaller one. . . .

5. The world in its present state of moral advancement compared with its technical development would be eventually at the mercy of such a weapon. In other words, modern civilization might be completely destroyed.

6. To approach any world peace organization of any pattern now likely to be considered, without an appreciation by the leaders of our country of the power of this new weapon, would seem to be unrealistic. No system of control heretofore considered would be adequate to control

this menace. Both inside any particular country and between the nations of the world, the control of this weapon will undoubtedly be a matter of the greatest difficulty and would involve such thoroughgoing rights of inspection and internal controls as we have never heretofore contemplated.

7. Furthermore, in the light of our present position with reference to this weapon, the question of sharing it with other nations and, if so shared, upon what terms, becomes a primary question of our foreign relations. Also our leadership in the war and in the development of this weapon has placed a certain moral responsibility upon us which we cannot shirk without very serious responsibility for any disaster to civilization which it would further.

8. On the other hand, if the problem of the proper use of this weapon can be solved, we would have the opportunity to bring the world into a pattern in which the peace of the world and our civilization can be saved.

9. As stated in General Groves' report, steps are under way looking towards the establishment of a select committee of particular qualifications for recommending action to the executive and legislative branches of our government when secrecy is no longer in full effect. The committee would also recommend the actions to be taken by the War Department prior to that time in anticipation of the postwar problems. All recommendations would of course be first submitted to the President.

The next step in our preparations was the appointment of the committee referred to in paragraph (9) above. This committee, which was known as the Interim Committee, was charged with the function of advising the President on the various questions raised by our apparently imminent success in developing an atomic weapon. I was its chairman, but the principal labor of guiding its extended deliberations fell to George L. Harrison, who acted as chairman in my absence. It will be useful to consider the work of the committee in some detail. Its members were the following, in addition to Mr. Harrison and myself:

James F. Byrnes (then a private citizen) as personal representative of the President [later appointed Truman's secretary of state].

Ralph A. Bard, Under Secretary of the Navy.

William L. Clayton, Assistant Secretary of State.

Dr. Vannevar Bush, Director, Office of Scientific Research and Development, and president of the Carnegie Institution of Washington.

Dr. Karl T. Compton, Chief of the Office of Field Service in the Office of Scientific Research and Development, and president of the Massachusetts Institute of Technology.

Dr. James B. Conant, Chairman of the National Defense Research Committee, and president of Harvard University.

Broad Discussions

The discussions of the committee ranged over the whole field of atomic energy, in its political, military,

and scientific aspects. That part of its work which particularly concerns us here relates to its recommendations for the use of atomic energy against Japan, but it should be borne in mind that these recommendations were not made in a vacuum. The committee's work included the drafting of the statements which were published immediately after the first bombs were dropped, the drafting of a bill for the domestic control of atomic energy, and recommendations looking toward the international control of atomic energy. The Interim Committee was assisted in its work by a Scientific Panel whose members were the following: Dr. A. H. Compton, Dr. Enrico Fermi, Dr. E. O. Lawrence, and Dr. J. R. Oppenheimer. All four were nuclear physicists of the first rank; all four had held positions of great importance in the atomic project from its inception. At a meeting with the Interim Committee and the Scientific Panel on May 31, 1945, I urged all those present to feel free to express themselves on any phase of the subject, scientific or political. Both General Marshall and I at this meeting expressed the view that atomic energy could not be considered simply in terms of military weapons but must also be considered in terms of a new relationship of man to the universe.

Recommendations of the Committee

On June 1, after its discussions with the Scientific Panel, the Interim Committee unanimously adopted the following recommendations:

(1) The bomb should be used against Japan as soon as possible.

(2) It should be used on a dual target—that is, a military installation or war plant surrounded by or adjacent to houses and other buildings most susceptible to damage, and

(3) It should be used without prior warning [of the nature of the weapon]. One member of the committee, Mr. Bard, later changed his view and dissented from recommendation (3).

In reaching these conclusions the Interim Committee carefully considered such alternatives as a detailed advance warning or a demonstration in some uninhabited area. Both of these suggestions were discarded as impractical. They were not regarded as likely to be effective in compelling a surrender of Japan, and both of them involved serious risks. Even the New Mexico test would not give final proof that any given bomb was certain to explode when dropped from an airplane. Quite apart from the generally unfamiliar nature of atomic explosives, there was the whole problem of exploding a bomb at a predetermined height in the air by a complicated mechanism which could not be tested in the static test of New Mexico. Nothing would have been more damaging to our effort to obtain surrender than a warning or a demonstration followed by a dud—and this was a real possibility. Furthermore, we had no bombs to waste. It was vital that a sufficient effect be quickly obtained with the few we had.

Views of Other Scientists

The Interim Committee and the Scientific Panel also served as a channel through which suggestions from other scientists working on the atomic project were forwarded to me and to the President. Among the suggestions thus forwarded was one memorandum which questioned using the bomb at all against the enemy. On June 16, 1945, after consideration of that memorandum, the Scientific Panel made a report, from which I quote the following paragraphs:

> The opinions of our scientific colleagues on the initial use of these weapons are not unanimous: they range from the proposal of a purely technical demonstration to that of the military application best designed to induce surrender. Those who advocate a purely technical demonstration would wish to outlaw the use of atomic weapons, and have feared that if we use the weapons now our position in future negotiations will be prejudiced. Others emphasize the opportunity of saving American lives by immediate military use, and believe that such use will improve the international prospects, in that they are more concerned with the prevention of war than with the elimination of this special weapon. We find ourselves closer to these latter views; *we can propose no technical demonstration likely to bring an end to the war; we see no acceptable alternative to direct military use.* [Italics mine]

> With regard to these general aspects of the use of atomic energy, it is clear that we, as scientific men, have no proprietary rights. It is true that we are among the few citizens who have had occasion to give thoughtful consideration to these problems during the past few years. We have, however, no claim to special competence in solving the political, social, and military problems which are presented by the advent of atomic power.

The foregoing discussion presents the reasoning of the Interim Committee and its advisers. I have discussed the work of these gentlemen at length in order to make it clear that we sought the best advice that we could find. The committee's function was, of course, entirely advisory. The ultimate responsibility for the recommendation to the President rested upon me, and I have no desire to veil it. The conclusions of the committee were similar to my own, although I reached mine independently. I felt that to extract a genuine surrender from the Emperor and his military advisers, they must be administered a tremendous shock which would carry convincing proof of our power to destroy the Empire. Such an effective shock would save many times the number of lives, both American and Japanese, that it would cost. . . .

Memorandum on Japan

I wrote a memorandum for the President, on July 2, which I believe fairly represents the thinking of the American government as it finally took shape in action. This memorandum was prepared after discussion and general agreement with Joseph C. Grew, Acting Secretary of State, and Secretary of the Navy [James] Forrestal, and when I discussed it with the President, he expressed his general approval.

Memorandum for the President, Proposed Program for Japan, July 2, 1945

1. The plans of operation up to and including the first landing have been authorized and the preparations for the operation are now actually going on. This situation was accepted by all members of your conference on Monday, June 18.

2. There is reason to believe that the operation for the occupation of Japan following the landing may be a very long, costly, and arduous struggle on our part. The terrain, much of which I have visited several times, has left the impression on my memory of being one which would be susceptible to a last ditch defense such as has been made on Iwo Jima and Okinawa and which of course is very much larger than either of those two areas. According to my recollection it will be much more unfavorable with regard to tank maneuvering than either the Philippines or Germany.

3. If we once land on one of the main islands and begin a forceful occupation of Japan, we shall probably have cast the die of last ditch resistance. The Japanese are highly patriotic and certainly susceptible to calls for fanatical resistance to repel an invasion. Once started in actual invasion, we shall in my opinion have to go through with an even more bitter finish fight than in Germany. We shall incur the losses incident to such a war and we shall have to leave the Japanese islands even more thoroughly destroyed than was the case with Germany. This would be due both to the difference in the Japanese and German personal character and the differences in the size and character of the terrain through which the operations will take place.

4. A question then comes: Is there any alternative to such a forceful occupation of Japan which will secure for us the equivalent of an unconditional surrender of her forces and a permanent destruction of her power again to strike an aggressive blow at the "peace of the Pacific"? I am inclined to think that there is enough such chance to make it well worthwhile our giving them a warning of what is to come and a definite opportunity to capitulate. As above suggested, it should be tried before the actual forceful occupation of the homeland islands is begun and furthermore the warning should be given in ample time to permit a national reaction to set in.

We have the following enormously favorable factors on our side—factors much weightier than those we had against Germany:

Japan has no allies.

Her navy is nearly destroyed and she is vulnerable to a surface and underwater blockade which can deprive her of sufficient food and supplies for her population.

She is terribly vulnerable to our concentrated air attack upon her crowded cities, industrial and food resources.

She has against her not only the Anglo-American forces but the rising forces of China and the ominous threat of Russia.

We have inexhaustible and untouched industrial resources to bring to bear against her diminishing potential.

We have great moral superiority through being the victim of her first sneak attack.

The problem is to translate these advantages into prompt and economical achievement of our objectives. I believe Japan *is* susceptible to reason in such a crisis to a much greater extent than is indicated by our current press and other current comment. Japan is not a nation composed wholly of mad fanatics of an entirely different mentality from ours. On the contrary, she has within the past century shown herself to possess extremely intelligent people, capable in an unprecedentedly short time of adopting not only the complicated technique of Occidental civilization but to a substantial extent their culture and their political and social ideas. Her advance in all these respects during the short period of sixty or seventy years has been one of the most astounding feats of national progress in history— a leap from the isolated feudalism of centuries into the position of one of the six or seven great powers of the world. She has not only built up powerful armies and navies. She has maintained an honest and effective national finance and respected position in many of the sciences in which we pride ourselves. Prior to the forcible seizure of power over her government by the fanatical military group in 1931, she had for ten years lived a reasonably responsible and respectable international life.

My own opinion is in her favor on the two points involved in this question:

a. I think the Japanese nation has the mental intelligence and versatile capacity in such a crisis to recognize the folly of a fight to the finish and to accept the proffer of what will amount to an unconditional surrender; and

b. I think she has within her population enough liberal leaders (although now submerged by the terrorists) to be depended upon for her reconstruction as a responsible member of the family of nations. I think she is better in this last respect than Germany was. Her liberals yielded only at the point of the pistol and, so far as I am aware, their liberal attitude has not been personally subverted in the way which was so general in Germany.

On the other hand, I think that the attempt to exterminate her armies and her population by gunfire or other means will tend to produce a fusion of race solidity and antipathy which has no analogy in the case of Germany. We have a national interest in creating, if possible, a condition wherein the Japanese nation may live as a peaceful and useful member of the future Pacific community.

5. It is therefore my conclusion that a carefully timed warning be given to Japan by the chief representatives of the United States, Great Britain, China, and, if then a belligerent, Russia by calling upon Japan to surrender and permit the occupation of her country in order to insure its complete demilitarization for the sake of the future peace. This warning should contain the following elements:

The varied and overwhelming character of the force we are about to bring to bear on the islands.

The inevitability and completeness of the destruction which the full application of this force will entail.

The determination of the Allies to destroy permanently all authority and influence of those who have deceived and misled the country into embarking on world conquest.

The determination of the Allies to limit Japanese sovereignty to her main islands and to render them powerless to mount and support another war.

The disavowal of any attempt to extirpate the Japanese as a race or to destroy them as a nation.

A statement of our readiness, once her economy is purged of its militaristic influence, to permit the Japanese to maintain such industries, particularly of a light consumer character, as offer no threat of aggression against their neighbors, but which can produce a sustaining economy, and provide a reasonable standard of living. The statement should indicate our willingness, for this purpose, to give Japan trade access to external raw materials, but no longer any control over the sources of supply outside her main islands. It should also indicate our willingness, in accordance with our now established foreign trade policy, in due course to enter into mutually advantageous trade relations with her.

The withdrawal from their country as soon as the above objectives of the Allies are accomplished, and as soon as there has been established a peacefully inclined government, of a character representative of the masses of the Japanese people. I personally think that if in saying this we should add that we do not exclude a constitutional monarchy under her present dynasty, it would substantially add to the chances of acceptance.

6. Success of course will depend on the potency of the warning which we give her. She has an extremely sensitive national pride and, as we are now seeing every day, when actually locked with the enemy will fight to the very death. For that reason the warning must be tendered before the actual invasion has occurred and while the impending destruction, though clear beyond peradventure, has not yet reduced her to fanatical despair. If Russia is a part of the threat, the Russian attack, if actual, must not have progressed too far. Our own bombing should be confined to military objectives as far as possible.

It is important to emphasize the double character of the suggested warning. It was designed to promise destruction if Japan resisted, and hope, if she surrendered.

It will be noted that the atomic bomb is not mentioned in this memorandum. On grounds of secrecy the bomb was never mentioned except when absolutely necessary, and furthermore, it had not yet been tested. It was of course well forward in our minds, as the memorandum was written and discussed, that the bomb would be the best possible sanction if our warning were rejected.

The Use of the Bomb

The adoption of the policy outlined in the memorandum of July 2 was a decision of high politics; once it was accepted by the President, the position of the atomic bomb in our planning became quite clear. I find that I stated in my diary, as early as June 19, that "the last chance warning . . . must be given before an actual landing of the ground forces in Japan, and fortunately the plans provide for enough time to bring in the sanctions to our warning in the shape of heavy ordinary bombing attack and an attack of S-1." S-1 was a code name for the atomic bomb.

There was much discussion in Washington about the timing of the warning to Japan. The controlling factor in the end was the date already set for the Potsdam meeting of the Big Three. It was President Truman's decision that such a warning should be solemnly issued by the U.S. and the U.K. from this meeting, with the concurrence of the head of the Chinese government, so that it would be plain that *all* of Japan's principal enemies were in entire unity. This was done, in the Potsdam ultimatum of July 26, which very closely followed the above memorandum of July 2, with the exception that it made no mention of the Japanese Emperor.

On July 28 the Premier of Japan, [Kantaro] Suzuki, rejected the Potsdam ultimatum by announcing that it was "unworthy of public notice." In the face of this rejection we could only proceed to demonstrate that the ultimatum had meant exactly what it said when it stated that if the Japanese continued the war, "the full application of our military power, backed by our resolve, will mean the inevitable and complete destruction of the Japanese armed forces and just as inevitably the utter devastation of the Japanese homeland."

A Suitable Weapon

For such a purpose the atomic bomb was an eminently suitable weapon. The New Mexico test occurred while we were at Potsdam, on July 16. It was immediately clear that the power of the bomb measured up to our highest estimates. We had developed a weapon of such a revolutionary character that its use against the enemy might well be expected to produce exactly the kind of shock on the Japanese ruling oligarchy which we desired, strengthening the position of those who wished peace, and weakening that of the military party. . . .

Hiroshima was bombed on August 6, and Nagasaki on August 9. These two cities were active working parts of the Japanese war effort. One was an army center; the other was naval and industrial. Hiroshima was the headquarters of the Japanese Army defending southern Japan and was a major military storage and assembly point. Nagasaki was a a major seaport and it contained several large industrial plants of great wartime importance. We believed that our attacks had struck cities which must certainly be

important to the Japanese military leaders, both Army and Navy, and we waited for a result. We waited one day.

Many accounts have been written about the Japanese surrender. After a prolonged Japanese cabinet session in which the deadlock was broken by the Emperor himself, the offer to surrender was made on August 10. It was based on the Potsdam terms, with a reservation concerning the sovereignty of the Emperor. While the Allied reply made no promises other than those already given, it implicitly recognized the Emperor's position by prescribing that his power must be subject to the orders of the Allied Supreme Commander. These terms were accepted on August 14 by the Japanese, and the instrument of surrender was formally signed on September 2 in Tokyo Bay. Our great objective was thus achieved, and all the evidence I have seen indicates that the controlling factor in the final Japanese decision to accept our terms of surrender was the atomic bomb. . . .

A Personal Summary

In the foregoing pages I have tried to give an accurate account of my own personal observations of the circumstances which led up to the use of the atomic bomb and the reasons which underlay our use of it. To me they have always seemed compelling and clear, and I cannot see how any person vested with such responsibilities as mine could have taken any other course or given any other advice to his chiefs. . . .

As I read over what I have written, I am aware that much of it, in this year of peace, may have a harsh and unfeeling sound. It would perhaps be possible to say the same things and say them more gently. But I do not think it would be wise. As I look back over the five years of my service as Secretary of War, I see too many stern and heartrending decisions to be willing to pretend that war is anything else than what it is. The face of war is the face of death; death is an inevitable part of every order that a wartime leader gives. The decision to use the atomic bomb was a decision that brought death to over a hundred thousand Japanese. No explanation can change that fact and I do not wish to gloss it over. But this deliberate, premeditated destruction was our least abhorrent choice. The destruction of Hiroshima and Nagasaki put an end to the Japanese war. It stopped the fire raids and the strangling blockade; it ended the ghastly specter of a clash of great land armies.

In this last great action of the Second World War we were given final proof that war is death. War in the twentieth century has grown steadily more barbarous, more destructive, more debased in all its aspects. Now, with the release of atomic energy, man's ability to destroy himself is very nearly complete. The bombs dropped on Hiroshima and Nagasaki ended a war. They also made it wholly clear that we must never have another war. This is the lesson men and leaders everywhere must learn, and I believe that when they learn it they will find a way to lasting peace. There is no other choice.

For Further Reading

Barton J. Bernstein, ed., *The Atomic Bomb: The Critical Issues.* Boston: Little, Brown, 1976.

Herbert Feis, *The Atomic Bomb and the End of World War II.* Princeton, NJ: Princeton University Press, 1966.

Martin Sherman, *A World Destroyed: Hiroshima and the Origins of the Arms Race.* New York: Vintage Books, 1987.

Alice Kimball Smith, *A Peril and a Hope.* Cambridge, MA: MIT Press, 1971.

Henry L. Stimson and McGeorge Bundy, *On Active Service in Peace and War.* New York: Harper & Row, 1948.

PART IV:
THE COLD WAR ABROAD AND AT HOME, 1945–1992

⟨⟩

The Beginnings
of the Cold War

The Eisenhower Years

The Turbulent Sixties

From Nixon to Reagan

The End of the Cold War

1945

April   Vice President Harry S. Truman becomes president after death of Franklin D. Roosevelt

September 2   World War II ends

1948

November 2 Truman wins 1948 presidential election

1947

March 12 Truman Doctrine: U.S. pledges aid to countries threatened by communist aggression

April   Major league baseball desegregated with the debut of Jackie Robinson

1949

September 23   Truman announces that the Soviet Union has tested an atomic bomb

1953

July 27   Armistice ends fighting in the Korean War, with North and South Korea still divided

August 12   Soviet Union successfully detonates a hydrogen bomb

1952

November 1 U.S. explodes hydrogen bomb

November 4 Dwight D. Eisenhower elected president

1950

February 9 Senator Joseph R. McCarthy begins accusations of widespread communist subversion

June 25 North Korea invades South Korea

1954

May 17 Supreme Court, in *Brown v. Board of Education*, declares segregated schools unconstitutional

1960

September 26 John Kennedy and Richard Nixon engage in the first televised presidential election debate

November 8 Kennedy elected president

1957

September 24 Eisenhower sends in federal troops to enforce desegregation of Central High School in Little Rock, Arkansas

October 4 The Soviet Union launches *Sputnik I*, the world's first space satellite

1959

January 1 Fidel Castro comes to power in Cuba

January 3 Alaska becomes 49th state

August 21 Hawaii becomes 50th state

1956

November 6 Eisenhower reelected president

1955

April 12   The Salk vaccine against polio is declared safe and effective

December   Martin Luther King Jr. and others lead a boycott of bus service in Montgomery, Alabama

1963

August 28   March on Washington for civil rights

October 7   Kennedy signs limited nuclear test ban treaty

November 22   President Kennedy assassinated in Dallas; Vice President Lyndon Johnson becomes president

1962

October 22–November 2   The Cuban missile crisis

1961

May 5 Alan Shepard becomes the first American in space

August Berlin Wall constructed

1964

January 11   U.S. surgeon general Luther Terry issues report on health dangers of smoking

August   Tonkin Gulf Resolution authorizes military action against North Vietnam

November 3 Lyndon Johnson elected president

1969

June 27   Stonewall riots signal start of gay rights movement

July 20   Neil Armstrong becomes first man on the moon

1965

August 11–16 Riots in Watts, Los Angeles, leave 35 dead

September Creation of Medicare and Medicaid

October 3 National origins quotas for immigrants are abolished by Immigration Reform Act

1967

July 23   Race riot in Detroit kills 43

October 2 Thurgood Marshall sworn in as nation's first black Supreme Court justice

1968

January 31   The Tet Offensive shakes American confidence in Vietnam

April 4   Martin Luther King assassinated

June 5   Robert Kennedy assassinated

November 5   Richard Nixon elected president

1945	1950	1955	1960	1965

1970

April 20   The first Earth Day observations signal growing environmental movement

May 4   National Guard troops kill 4 students at Kent State University

June 24   U.S. Senate votes to terminate 1964 Tonkin Gulf Resolution

1972

February/May   Nixon visits China and the Soviet Union

June 17   The Watergate break-in occurs

November 7   Nixon reelected president

1974

July 27   The House Judiciary Committee passes the first of three articles of impeachment against President Nixon

August 9   Nixon becomes the first president to resign from office; Vice President Gerald Ford becomes president

1978

April   The U.S. Senate ratifies a treaty turning over the Panama Canal to Panama in 2000

1979

March 28   Nuclear accident narrowly averted at Three Mile Island, Pennsylvania

November 4   The U.S. embassy is stormed in Teheran, Iran: 66 Americans are taken hostage

1982

October 23   Terrorist truck bomb explosion kills 241 U.S. Marines in Beirut, Lebanon

October 24   U.S. invades Grenada

1987

October 19   The stock market plunges a record 500 points

December   Reagan and Gorbachev sign INF Treaty

1988

November George Bush elected president

1989

November Opening of Berlin Wall signals end of the Cold War

December U.S. invades Panama to extradite its leader, Manuel Noriega, wanted on drug smuggling charges

1970	1975	1980	1985	1990

1975

April   South Vietnam falls to North Vietnam

November 20   A Senate committee investigation reports FBI and CIA abuses against U.S. citizens and foreign governments

1976

November 2 Jimmy Carter elected president

1980

November 4 Ronald Reagan elected president

1984

November 6 Reagan reelected president

1991

January   Persian Gulf War: U.S. leads multinational force to rout Iraqi army and liberate Kuwait

December   Gorbachev resigns; Soviet Union dissolves

1973

January 22   U.S. agrees to withdraw all its troops from Vietnam; Supreme Court, in *Roe v. Wade*, legalizes abortion during the first trimester of pregnancy

July 16   The Senate committee investigating Watergate learns of the taping system in the Nixon White House

October 10   Vice President Spiro Agnew pleads no contest to tax evasion and resigns

October 18   Arab oil embargo begins

December 6   Gerald Ford sworn in as nation's first nonelected vice president

1981

January 20 The American hostages in Iran are released

June   First published reports of AIDS cases in the U.S.

September 25 Sandra Day O'Connor sworn in as first woman Supreme Court justice

1985

November   First of four summits between President Reagan and new reformist Soviet leader Mikhail Gorbachev

1992

November Bill Clinton elected president

Part IV:
The Cold War Abroad
and at Home, 1945–1992

The Cold War provides one of the main unifying themes for post–World War II American history. For more than four decades the conflict between the United States and the Soviet Union (which never escalated into direct military engagement) dominated U.S. foreign policy and overshadowed much of American life. In large part because of the Cold War, the United States reversed its pre–World War II policy of isolationism, entered into several military alliances, sent its soldiers to fight in Korea and Vietnam, and went to great lengths to promote a spirit of patriotism and sense of conformity at home.

Cold War Origins

The basis of the Cold War as it began in the late 1940s had both strategic and ideological dimensions. Actions taken by each nation immediately following World War II were considered threatening by the other. The United States objected to the Soviet Union's establishment of Soviet-controlled communist regimes in Eastern Europe. The Soviet government viewed Eastern Europe as a necessary defensive buffer and perceived U.S. demands for democratic elections in the region as an attempt to surround the Soviet Union with hostile neighbors. The line between Eastern and Western Europe, which ran through Germany itself, thus became the first and central dividing line of the Cold War. Relations between the United States and the Soviet Union were further complicated by the ideological divide between the two nations' respective political and economic systems: capitalist democracy in the United States and communism in the Soviet Union. Both sides believed in the superiority of their respective systems and feared the other. For many Americans the Cold War was as much a struggle against the idea of communism as it was against the Soviet Union and its allies.

Responding to Soviet expansion into Europe and to fears of worldwide communist agitation and revolution, some leading U.S. foreign policy experts, led by George Kennan, formulated the doctrine of containment. America should not risk open war to force the Soviet Union to relinquish its hold on Eastern Europe or change its system of government, they argued, but all further expansion of Soviet influence on other countries should be prevented. The central goal of U.S. Cold War policy, they believed, should be to contain the spread of Soviet control and of communism (which many viewed as one and the same). Because of the broad goals of containment, which guided U.S. policy for four decades, the United States viewed almost all areas of the world as potentially vital national interests.

Repercussions of the Cold War

For more than forty years the two superpowers competed against each other in several different areas. They struggled over the fate of Germany and control of Europe. They sought the allegiances of nations in Asia, Africa, and Central and South America. They raced to develop space vehicles and to be the first to send a person to the moon.

Perhaps most ominously, the two countries competed in a nuclear arms race. By 1949 the Soviet Union had produced its own atomic weapons. Both nations shortly thereafter developed the more powerful hydrogen bomb. The development of rocket missile technology meant that nuclear weapons, once launched, could reach targets thousands of miles away in a matter of minutes instead of hours. Eventually both nations targeted thousands of intercontinental missiles with multiple nuclear warheads at each other's cities and military bases. By doing so, both the United States and the Soviet Union sought to deter the other side from military attack by convincing each other that such an attack would result in massive nuclear retaliation and widespread nuclear destruction. The deterrent factor of nuclear weapons was, in the opinion of some, the main reason full-scale war never erupted between the Cold War adversaries (perhaps the closest brush with nuclear war was in 1962 when the two nations confronted each other over the installation of Soviet missiles in Cuba).

Americans differed over the use of nuclear weapons and the nuclear arms race during the Cold War. Some saw nuclear weapons as useful tools for influencing the Soviet Union's behavior and for possibly waging limited nuclear war. Others were haunted by fears of a "nuclear holocaust" and sought to place nuclear weapons under international control.

The Cold War strongly colored American domestic issues as well as foreign policy. One direct result of the conflict was the fear held by many Americans of communist subversion and betrayal. Beginning in the 1940s government agencies, congressional committees, and private groups investigated thousands of American citizens for suspected communist affiliations and beliefs—investigations that some people criticized as witch-hunts. Another consequence of the Cold War was the creation of a large military and foreign policy apparatus— what President Dwight D. Eisenhower in 1961 called the "military-industrial complex." Some Americans viewed this development as a Cold War necessity, but others feared the potential of a professional standing army to influence America's government.

Many of the ongoing debates over American society and government were framed by the Cold War. In their arguments, both critics and defenders of America's social, economic, and political beliefs and institutions compared and contrasted America with the Soviet Union. Supporters of America's freedom of speech and political dissent pointed out that such freedoms were largely absent in the Soviet Union's totalitarian society. Defenders of America's free-market economic system, and its attendant potential to generate wealth, argued that the Soviets' state-controlled system was inefficient and oppressive. On the other hand, critics of American capitalism maintained that the Soviet system was more egalitarian than the U.S. system because it guaranteed jobs, pensions, and other government assistance to Soviet citizens.

A Quarter Century of Economic Growth

When World War II ended in 1945 many Americans were afraid that the U.S. economy would slip back into depression. Such fears proved unfounded as the country instead entered the greatest period of sustained economic growth in its history. National income almost doubled in the 1950s and again in the 1960s. Spurred by technology and education, workers' productivity rose steadily, doubling between 1950 and 1970. Such growth brought America's standard of living to new heights. Builders created an unprecedented number of new homes, many in suburban sites away from city centers. By 1960 approximately 60 percent of American families owned their own homes, 75 percent possessed cars (a suburban necessity), and 87 percent had a television set. Comprising only 6 percent of the world's population, Americans consumed about 40 percent of the world's resources.

America's prosperity and dominance in the world economy was founded on several factors. One was the fact that the United States, unlike much of the industrialized world, escaped most of the physical destruction of World War II. Another was the military spending that accompanied the Cold War. Defense spending accounted for nearly 10 percent of America's gross national product (GNP) during the 1950s. Supporters of the military buildup argued that besides stimulating the economy and spurring employment, defense spending also financed a great deal of scientific research and development that helped establish new high-technology industries, especially in aerospace and electronics. Critics accused the United States of creating a "permanent war economy" that was dependent on defense dollars to keep it strong. A third important factor in America's economic growth was cheap energy, aided by American control of the international oil business. A fourth factor was the "baby boom"—the sharp rise in births between 1946 and 1964—that helped fuel economic growth and in other ways greatly shaped American society.

Civil Rights and the Great Society

In the early 1950s national debates over social change were relatively limited, as many Americans believed that economic growth and rising incomes could solve most individual and societal needs. Beginning with the black civil rights movement, however, a growing number of Americans began to debate and demonstrate for political change and social reform—a development that peaked in the 1960s.

In 1954 the Supreme Court issued its historic *Brown v. Board of Education* decision declaring racially segregated schools unconstitutional. The decision struck down the judicial foundations of the Jim Crow legal structure, which had instituted racial segregation in the South since the 1890s. Actual school desegregation, however, proved slow in coming, as whites in southern states resisted court orders to integrate their schools. Black civil rights leaders such as Martin Luther King Jr. led marches, boycotts, and other actions of nonviolent resistance against discriminatory laws in the South. Some critics of the civil rights movement tried to discredit King and his followers by linking them to communism; more extreme opponents resorted to violence, intimidation, and even murder of civil rights activists. Despite such opposition, the civil rights movement raised the nation's awareness about racial inequality and helped pave the way for historic national civil rights legislation in 1964 and 1965.

The federal government, both through Supreme Court decisions and congressional legislation, played a key role in effecting progress on civil rights. Partly as a result, an increasing number of Americans began to advocate utilizing the federal government to address problems of poverty, crime, and health. Lyndon B. Johnson, who became president in 1963 following the assassination of John F. Kennedy, sought to expand the welfare functions of the federal government with his calls for a "war on poverty," medical care for the elderly, and numerous social programs aimed at creating what Johnson termed a "Great Society." Johnson's proposals stimulated much debate and controversy within the nation on how best to deal with social problems.

Sixties Movements

The Civil Rights Acts of 1964 and 1965 all but ended state-supported segregation and helped ensure the right to vote for African-Americans, some of whom also benefited from Johnson's Great Society programs. Many blacks, however, still faced significant poverty, prejudice, and discrimination in employment and housing, not only in the South but throughout the nation. King led demonstrations in Chicago and other northern cities to protest residential segregation, but these proved less successful in effecting change than his protests against legal segregation in the South. Some black activists, such as Stokely Carmichael and Malcolm X, questioned King's principle of nonviolence and the goal of racial integration. They called for black separatism and more militant assertions of "black power." Optimism over the progress of civil rights and racial equality faded in the last half of the 1960s, which were marked by urban riots in Los Angeles, Detroit, and other major cities, and the 1968 assassinations of King and Robert Kennedy, brother of the late president.

Despite its internal divisions, the civil rights movement helped to inspire other groups of people to demonstrate and work for social change. The 1960s saw a revival of feminism as women's groups organized against workplace discrimination and restrictions on abortion. In *The Feminine Mystique*, which came to be regarded as the manifesto of the feminist movement, Betty Friedan criticized American society for limiting women to the roles of wives and mothers. To different degrees, Hispanics, American Indians, and gays and lesbians also organized and pressed for equality and redresses for past injustices. A highly visible minority of America's baby boomers became part of a counterculture that explored alternatives to mainstream American society, including communal living arrangements, Eastern religions, and experimentation with drugs. By the late 1960s, however, the dominant political question in American life was not civil rights, poverty, or youth culture, but the Vietnam War.

The Cold War and Vietnam

The Vietnam War was a product of America's Cold War strategy, first voiced by President Harry S. Truman in 1947, to aid all nations threatened by communist takeover. Truman administration policymakers took credit for successfully containing communism in Western Europe through economic aid (the Marshall Plan) and a treaty alliance (the North Atlantic Treaty Organization, or NATO), but were bitterly attacked by some critics for "losing" China in 1949, when the American-supported regime of Jiang Jieshi (Chiang Kai-shek) fell after a long war to communist revolutionaries led by Mao Zedong (Mao Tse-tung). In 1950 the United States sent soldiers to fight in Korea to prevent that divided country from being united under North Korean communist rule. During the administration of President Dwight D. Eisenhower (1953–1961), the United States made defense treaties in the Middle East and Southeast Asia and sponsored Central Intelligence Agency (CIA) operations that helped topple left-wing regimes in Guatemala and Iran.

It was in this Cold War context that a series of U.S. presidents gradually committed American military power to Vietnam. The former French colony in Southeast Asia was divided between communist North Vietnam and noncommunist South Vietnam after France's withdrawal in 1954. The American-supported regime in South Vietnam was threatened by communist rebels within its territory and eventually by forces from North Vietnam itself. In the

1950s President Eisenhower sent several hundred civilian and military advisers to South Vietnam. John F. Kennedy, president from 1961 to 1963, increased the number of advisers to 16,000, including members of the Green Berets, a special counterinsurgency force. Lyndon B. Johnson, president from 1963 to 1969, began to commit regular combat troops to South Vietnam and to initiate massive bombing raids on North Vietnam in 1965. By 1969 the number of U.S. soldiers in Vietnam stood at 543,000.

The Vietnam War drained funds from Johnson's Great Society domestic programs and played a large part in Johnson's 1968 decision not to run for reelection. Richard M. Nixon, elected president that year after promising to carry out a "secret plan" to end the war, pursued the gradual withdrawal of American soldiers from South Vietnam, an increase in bombing raids, and controversial air and ground incursions into neighboring Cambodia and Laos. Nixon also sought improved relations with China and the Soviet Union, in part to encourage those nations to pressure North Vietnam to agree to a peace settlement. The United States and North Vietnam finally signed a peace agreement in January 1973 providing for the removal of American forces. By 1975 South Vietnam had fallen and Vietnam was unified under communist rule.

The Vietnam War was one of the most controversial wars in American history. The nation was bitterly torn in the 1960s between "hawks" who wanted increased military action and immediate victory in Vietnam (a few advocated the use of nuclear weapons) and "doves" who opposed the war and demanded an immediate military withdrawal (even if it meant American defeat). The war shattered the general Cold War consensus that had guided foreign policy of both Republicans and Democrats since World War II.

Those who opposed the war staged numerous antiwar marches and demonstrations. Two of the most notable protests were a march in Washington, D.C., in October 1967, in which 50,000 people participated, and a demonstration on the campus of Kent State University in Ohio on May 4, 1970, in which National Guardsmen fired into a crowd and killed four students. Many Americans were shocked by the Kent State incident. Some U.S. citizens, however, directed their anger at the antiwar demonstrators for what they believed to be a lack of patriotism and proper support of the government.

An Era of Limits

If the 1960s could be generalized as an era of protests, the 1970s could be called an era of limits. Much of the optimism for the possibilities of social change in America faded. Social problems such as poverty and crime persisted despite government programs. The Vietnam experience seemed to many to demonstrate the limits of American military power. Even technology itself—which many people celebrated for enabling America to land a man on the moon in 1969—was under attack by a growing environmental movement that questioned the ecological costs of America's industrialization.

In many respects the early 1970s marked the end of an economic era for the United States. Two important factors that had helped sustain the nation's phenomenal economic growth and world economic leadership since the end of World War II were gone: cheap, unlimited energy (especially oil) and the lack of foreign competition in the manufacture and trade of goods and services. In 1971 the United States ran its first trade deficit since 1890, as countries such as Germany and Japan threatened American dominance in automobile manufacturing and other key industries. Under three successive presidents, the

United States struggled against "stagflation"—the combination of high inflation, high unemployment, and sluggish productivity growth that plagued the United States for much of the 1970s. By the end of the decade income growth had slowed significantly and increasing numbers of American families were depending on two incomes to maintain their standard of living.

The decade also was one in which numerous Americans questioned their faith in their own government. The Vietnam War caused many citizens to doubt America's effectiveness as a world power and led others to question the morality of their government's actions. This distrust was heightened by the Watergate affair, a series of political scandals that forced the 1974 resignation of Richard Nixon (the first such departure by a U.S. president). Investigations in 1973 and 1974 by journalists, Congress, and special federal prosecutors had revealed to the nation that members of Nixon's staff had tried to sabotage the president's Democratic challengers in the 1972 presidential election and that Nixon had actively impeded investigations into their activities and had lied to the American people about his own knowledge of the events. Vice President Gerald Ford became president after Nixon's resignation; one month later Ford pardoned Nixon from all crimes Nixon committed or might have committed while in office, an act criticized by many Americans disillusioned by Watergate.

Carter and Reagan

Democrat Jimmy Carter, a relative unknown running on a platform of restoring trust in government, defeated Ford in the 1976 presidential election. Carter impressed many Americans with his personal honesty and his strong commitment to human rights, but much of the public came to question his ability to lead America out of its economic difficulties and to preserve American influence abroad. Inflation, spurred by oil price hikes, soared during his term. The Iranian hostage crisis, in which the Islamic government of Iran seized and held fifty-two Americans from November 1979 to January 1981, was for many Americans (especially after a failed April 1980 military rescue mission) a powerful symbol of American impotence and even humiliation. Carter was defeated for reelection by Ronald Reagan in 1980.

A former motion picture actor and conservative governor of California, Ronald Reagan entered the Oval Office pledging to cut taxes, decrease government spending and regulation, reduce inflation, restore America's international prestige, and improve the nation's moral climate. After a severe recession in 1981 and 1982, the U.S. economy did improve, with years of steady growth and little inflation. Reagan became the first president to be reelected and serve two full terms since Eisenhower. However, federal budget deficits during Reagan's presidency added nearly $2 trillion to the national debt, leaving the long-term economic legacy of the "Reagan revolution" an uncertain one. Reagan's budgetary and rhetorical attacks on social programs were a sharp repudiation of Johnson's Great Society, and many believed that cutbacks in social welfare promoted by Reagan unfairly hurt the poor. Americans remained divided on whether such programs should be supported or eliminated.

Revival and End of the Cold War

Reagan entered office pledging an intensification of the Cold War against the Soviet Union. Under Presidents Nixon, Ford, and Carter, the United States had sought to ease Cold War tensions by pursuing a policy of diplomatic cooperation, negotiating the SALT I and SALT II nuclear arms accords, and establishing trade agreements. Reagan and other conservatives argued that such an approach had placed the United States in a weak position and had enabled the Soviet Union to expand its influence into Central America, West Africa, and the Middle East. Reagan's Cold War initiatives were in some respects foreshadowed by events in the last year of Carter's presidency following the Soviet invasion of Afghanistan in December 1979. Carter responded to the invasion by dropping the SALT II nuclear arms treaty, canceling trade agreements with the Soviet Union, increasing military spending, and calling for the placement of intermediate-range nuclear missiles in Europe. Reagan continued and greatly expanded Carter's Cold War policies, especially in the area of defense spending, which increased from $171 billion in 1981 to $360 billion in 1986. He sent military aid to anticommunist forces in Nicaragua and to Afghans fighting Soviet occupation of their country. In 1983 he proposed a "strategic defense initiative" (SDI), or space-based antimissile defense system of orbiting satellites that would detect and intercept incoming Soviet missiles.

Reagan's foreign policy was not without its critics. Many Americans questioned the technical feasibility of SDI; others argued that it was a waste of money and a dangerous escalation of the nuclear arms race. Some called for a "nuclear freeze" on the development and deployment of any new nuclear weapons systems. And while there was relatively little opposition to Reagan's Afghanistan policy, there was much controversy over what critics labeled a U.S.-sponsored covert war in Nicaragua.

During Reagan's second term, the Cold War took a striking new turn. A new Soviet leader, Mikhail Gorbachev, promised major concessions on nuclear arms control, Afghanistan, and other issues and sought to lessen Cold War tensions between the United States and Soviet Union. Gorbachev also implemented major internal social and economic reforms that seemed to some Americans to narrow the ideological divide between the two nations. Reagan and Gorbachev met four times in four years, and in 1988 they signed a treaty calling for the destruction of all intermediate-range nuclear missiles in Europe.

During the presidency of George Bush (1989–1993) the Cold War came to an end. In 1989 the people in several nations in Eastern Europe rose up against communist rule; unlike previous instances, the Soviet Union did not militarily intervene to crush such developments. The Berlin Wall, a symbol of Cold War division since its construction in 1961, was dismantled, and East and West Germany were reunited. The Cold War's end was marked by the dissolution of the Soviet Union itself. By the end of 1991 an attempted coup by hardline Soviet communists had failed, Gorbachev had resigned, the Soviet Communist Party (which had ruled the Soviet Union since 1917) had lost power, and the Soviet Union's republics had become independent nations under noncommunist rule.

The United States experienced no such dramatic internal developments at the end of the Cold War. What it did face was the loss of a constant enemy that had helped define America's place in the world and provide a focus for its energies at home. While many Americans celebrated the Cold War's end as a great triumph for the United States, others questioned the relevance of the Soviet Union's collapse to the well-being of most Americans as they continued to grapple with domestic economic and social problems.

The Beginnings of the Cold War

VIEWPOINT 31A

America Should Seek Peace with the Soviet Union (1946)

Henry A. Wallace (1888–1960)

Relations between the United States and the Soviet Union, World War II allies who had emerged from the conflict as the world's dominant powers, deteriorated in the months after the war. Despite pledges made by the two superpowers (and Great Britain) at the Yalta and Potsdam conferences during World War II to support postwar democratic elections in Germany and the rest of Europe, after the war the Soviet Union established communist regimes in the areas under its military control. Faltering negotiations made the prospect of a permanently divided Germany seem increasingly likely. On March 6, 1946, former British prime minister Winston Churchill captured the attention of Americans when, in a speech in Fulton, Missouri, he accused the Soviet Union of creating an "iron curtain" around Eastern Europe. Disputes between the Soviet Union and the United States briefly threatened to erupt into a military confrontation over oil concessions in Iran, and conflict between the two nations derailed a proposed American plan for the international control of nuclear weapons under the new United Nations.

Many historians have wondered how the United States might have responded to such situations had Henry A. Wallace been president. Wallace was vice president of the United States under Franklin D. Roosevelt from 1941 to 1945, having previously been Roosevelt's secretary of agriculture. Replaced as vice president by Harry S. Truman for Roosevelt's fourth election in 1944, Wallace became secretary of commerce shortly before Roosevelt's death and Truman's assumption of the presidency in April 1945. Wallace differed with many in the Truman administration over what he saw as confrontational policies toward the Soviet Union. On September 12, 1946, in a speech at Madison Square Garden in New York City, Wallace called for a higher priority on improving relations with the Soviet Union. (Wallace refers in his speech to Russia, by far the largest and most dominant member of the Union of Soviet Socialist Republics, or Soviet Union. During much of the Soviet Union's existence from 1922 to 1991 it was

Henry A. Wallace, a speech delivered at Madison Square Garden in New York City, September 12, 1946. Reprinted in *Vital Speeches of the Day*, October 1, 1946.

common to treat the "Soviet Union" and "Russia" as synonymous terms). In his speech, excerpted here, Wallace asserts that the United States should not interfere too much within the Soviet Union's "sphere of influence," which he defines to include Eastern Europe. Wallace's address angered many within the Truman administration and led to his resignation from Truman's cabinet. He ran unsuccessfully for president against Truman in 1948 on a platform calling for disarmament and the end of the Cold War.

What aspects of the Russians' past must be understood in order to reach a peaceful understanding with them, according to Wallace? Why, in his view, should the United States have limited involvement in determining the future of Eastern Europe? What future role does Wallace see for the United Nations?

Tonight I want to talk about peace—and how to get peace. Never have the common people of all lands so longed for peace. Yet, never in a time of comparative peace have they feared war so much.

Up till now peace has been negative and unexciting. War has been positive and exciting. Far too often, hatred and fear, intolerance and deceit have had the upper hand over love and confidence, trust and joy. Far too often, the law of nations has been the law of the jungle; and the constructive spiritual forces of the Lord have bowed to the destructive forces of Satan.

Another War Would Be Disastrous

During the past year or so, the significance of peace has been increased immeasurably by the atom bomb, guided missiles and airplanes which soon will travel as fast as sound. Make no mistake about it—another war would hurt the United States many times as much as the last war. We cannot rest in the assurance that we invented the atom bomb—and therefore that this agent of destruction will work best for us. He who trusts in the atom bomb will sooner or later perish by the atom bomb—or something worse.

I say this as one who steadfastly backed preparedness throughout the Thirties. We have no use for namby-pamby pacifism. But we must realize that modern inventions have now made peace the most exciting thing in the world—and we should be willing to pay a just price for peace. If modern war can cost us $400 billion, we should be willing and happy to pay much more for peace. But certainly, the cost of peace is to be measured not in dollars but in the hearts and minds of men. . . .

I plead for an America vigorously dedicated to peace—just as I plead for opportunities for the next generation throughout the world to enjoy the abundance which now, more than ever before, is the birthright of man.

The Russian Character

To achieve lasting peace, we must study in detail just how the Russian character was formed—by invasions of Tartars, Mongols, Germans, Poles, Swedes, and French; by the czarist rule based on ignorance, fear and force; by the intervention of the British, French and Americans in Russian affairs from 1919 to 1921; by the geography of the huge Russian land mass situated strategically between Europe and Asia; and by the vitality derived from the rich Russian soil and the strenuous Russian climate. Add to all this the tremendous emotional powers which Marxism and Leninism give to the Russian leaders—and then we can realize that we are reckoning with a force which cannot be handled successfully by a "Get tough with Russia" policy. "Getting tough" never bought anything real and lasting—whether for schoolyard bullies or businessmen or world powers. The tougher we get, the tougher the Russians will get.

Throughout the world there are numerous reactionary elements which had hoped for Axis victory—and now profess great friendship for the United States. Yet these enemies of yesterday and false friends of today continually try to provoke war between the United States and Russia. They have no real love of the United States. They only long for the day when the United States and Russia will destroy each other.

We must not let our Russian policy be guided or influenced by those inside or outside the United States who want war with Russia. This does not mean appeasement.

Peace with Russia

We must earnestly want peace with Russia—but we want to be met half way. We want cooperation. And I believe that we can get cooperation once Russia understands that our primary objective is neither saving the British Empire nor purchasing oil in the Near East with the lives of American soldiers. We cannot allow national oil rivalries to force us into war. All of the nations producing oil, whether inside or outside of their own boundaries, must fulfill the provisions of the United Nations Charter and encourage the development of world petroleum reserves so as to make the maximum amount of oil available to all nations of the world on an equitable peaceful basis—and not on the basis of fighting the next war.

For her part, Russia can retain our respect by cooperating with the United Nations in a spirit of openminded and flexible give-and-take.

The real peace treaty we now need is between the United States and Russia. On our part, we should recognize that we have no more business in the *political* affairs of Eastern Europe than Russia has in the *political* affairs of Latin America, Western Europe and the United States. We may not like what Russia does in Eastern Europe. Her type of land reform, industrial expropriation, and suppression of basic liberties offends the great majority of the people of the United States. But whether we like it or not the Russians will try to socialize their sphere of influence just as we try to democratize our sphere of influence. This applies also to Germany and Japan. We are striving to democratize Japan and our area of control in Germany, while Russia strives to socialize eastern Germany.

———— • ————

"The real peace treaty we now need is between the United States and Russia."

———— • ————

As for Germany, we all must recognize that an equitable settlement, based on a unified German nation, is absolutely essential to any lasting European settlement. This means that Russia must be assured that never again can German industry be converted into military might to be used against her—and Britain, Western Europe and the United States must be certain that Russia's German policy will not become a tool of Russian design against Western Europe.

The Russians have no more business in stirring up native communists to political activity in Western Europe, Latin America and the United States than we have in interfering in the politics of Eastern Europe and Russia. We know what Russia is up to in Eastern Europe, for example, and Russia knows what we are up to. We cannot permit the door to be closed against our trade in Eastern Europe any more than we can in China. But at the same time we have to recognize that the Balkans are closer to Russia than to us—and that Russia cannot permit either England or the United States to dominate the politics of that area.

The Case of China

China is a special case and although she holds the longest frontier in the world with Russia, the interests of world peace demand that China remain free from any sphere of influence, either politically or economically. We insist that the door to trade and economic development opportunities be left wide open in China as in all the world. However, the open door to trade and opportunities for economic development in China are meaningless unless there is a unified and peaceful China—built on the cooperation of the various groups in that country and based on a hands-off policy of the outside powers.

We are still arming to the hilt. Our excessive expenses for military purposes are the chief cause for our unbalanced budget. If taxes are to be lightened we must have the basis of a real peace with Russia— a peace that cannot be broken by extremist propagandists. We do not want our course determined for us by master minds operating out of London, Moscow or Nanking.

A Friendly Cooperation

Russian ideas of social-economic justice are going to govern nearly a third of the world. Our ideas of free enterprise democracy will govern much of the rest. The two ideas will endeavor to prove which can deliver the most satisfaction to the common man in their respective areas of political dominance. But by mutual agreement, this competition should be put on a friendly basis and the Russians should stop conniving against us in certain areas of the world just as we should stop scheming against them in other parts of the world. Let the results of the two systems speak for themselves.

Meanwhile, the Russians should stop teaching that their form of communism must, by force if necessary, ultimately triumph over democratic capitalism—while we should close our ears to those among us who would have us believe that Russian communism and our free enterprise system cannot live, one with another, in a profitable and productive peace.

Under friendly peaceful competition the Russian world and the American world will gradually become more alike. The Russians will be forced to grant more and more of the personal freedoms; and we shall become more and more absorbed with the problems of social-economic justice.

Russia must be convinced that we are not planning for war against her and we must be certain that Russia is not carrying on territorial expansion or world domination through native communists faithfully following every twist and turn in the Moscow party line. But in this competition, we must insist on an open door for trade throughout the world. There will always be an ideological conflict—but that is no reason why diplomats cannot work out a basis for both systems to live safely in the world side by side.

The United Nations

Once the fears of Russia and the United States Senate have been allayed by practical regional political reservations, I am sure that concern over the veto power would be greatly diminished. Then the United Nations would have a really great power in those areas which are truly international and not regional.

In the world-wide, as distinguished from the regional field, the armed might of the United Nations should be so great as to make opposition useless. Only the United Nations should have atomic bombs and its military establishment should give special emphasis to air power. It should have control of the strategically located air bases with which the United States and Britain have encircled the world. And not only should individual nations be prohibited from manufacturing atomic bombs, guided missiles and military aircraft for bombing purposes, but no nation should be allowed to spend on its military establishment more than perhaps 15 per cent of its budget. . . .

In brief, as I see it today, the World Order is bankrupt—and the United States, Russia and England are the receivers. These are the hard facts of power politics on which we have to build a functioning, powerful United Nations and a body of international law. And as we build, we must develop fully the doctrine of the rights of small peoples as contained in the United Nations Charter. This law should ideally apply as much to Indonesians and Greeks as to Bulgarians and Poles—but practically, the application may be delayed until both British and Russians discover the futility of their methods.

In the full development of the rights of small nations, the British and Russians can learn a lesson from the Good Neighbor policy of Franklin Roosevelt. For under Roosevelt, we in the Western Hemisphere built a workable system of regional internationalism that fully protected the sovereign rights of every nation—a system of multilateral action that immeasurably strengthened the whole of world order.

Organizing for Peace

In the United States an informed public opinion will be all-powerful. Our people are peace-minded. But they often express themselves too late—for events today move much faster than public opinion. The people here, as everywhere in the world, must be convinced that another war is not inevitable. And through mass meetings such as this, and through persistent pamphleteering, the people can be organized for peace—even though a large segment of our press is propagandizing our people for war in the hope of scaring Russia. And we who look on this war-with-Russia talk as criminal foolishness must carry our message direct to the people—even though we may be called communists because we dare to speak out.

I believe that peace—the kind of peace I have outlined tonight—is the basic issue, both in the Congressional campaign this fall and right on through the Presidential election in 1948. How we meet this issue will determine whether we live not in "one world" or "two worlds"—but whether we live at all.

VIEWPOINT 31B

America Should Contain the Soviet Union (1947)

George F. Kennan (b. 1904)

In July 1947 an article attributed only to "X," entitled "The Sources of Soviet Conflict," appeared in *Foreign Affairs*, a quarterly journal of world politics. Published at a time of growing tensions between the United States and the Soviet Union, the article became one of the most widely discussed and reprinted articles on foreign affairs ever published. Its arguments for containment of the Soviet Union formed a basis for U.S. foreign policy for the next forty years.

"X" was eventually revealed to be George F. Kennan, the director of the Policy Planning Staff at the U.S. State Department in Washington. Kennan had recently returned from the Soviet Union, where he had worked at the U.S. embassy in Moscow and was one of the first U.S. diplomats to express pessimism about continuing the cooperation with the Soviet Union that had begun during World War II. Kennan later became the U.S. ambassador to the Soviet Union, and, following his retirement from government, he became a noted author, scholar, and teacher on the Soviet Union and on U.S. foreign policy.

In his *Foreign Affairs* article, excerpted here, Kennan argues that the ideology and dictatorial positions of the leaders of the Soviet Union compel them to seek increasing international domination and to take an adversarial stance toward the United States. To counter these threats, Kennan advocates a policy of containment—of preventing Soviet power and communist ideology from spreading to additional countries. He argues that the United States should not risk open war by forcing the Soviet Union to withdraw from Eastern Europe or by otherwise directly challenging them, but it should take steps, he says, to ensure that the Soviet Union does not expand its military influence to other areas of the world. Kennan's prescriptions were influential in the formation of the "Truman Doctrine," in which President Harry S. Truman pledged American support to regimes in Greece and Turkey as part of a worldwide struggle against communism.

What important ideological factors motivate the behavior of the Kremlin (the Soviet communist leadership), according to Kennan? What predictions does he make concerning the future of the Soviet Union? What positive benefits to the United States does Kennan foresee from the Cold War?

George F. Kennan, "The Sources of Soviet Conduct," *Foreign Affairs*, Spring 1987, p. 51. Reprinted by permission of *Foreign Affairs*.

The political personality of Soviet power as we know it today is the product of ideology and circumstances: ideology inherited by the present Soviet leaders from the movement in which they had their political origin, and circumstances of the power which they now have exercised for nearly three decades in Russia. There can be few tasks of psychological analysis more difficult than to try to trace the interaction of these two forces and the relative rôle of each in the determination of official Soviet conduct. Yet the attempt must be made if that conduct is to be understood and effectively countered.

Soviet Ideology

It is difficult to summarize the set of ideological concepts with which the Soviet leaders came into power. Marxian ideology, in its Russian-Communist projection, has always been in process of subtle evolution. The materials on which it bases itself are extensive and complex. But the outstanding features of Communist thought as it existed in 1916 may perhaps be summarized as follows: (a) that the central factor in the life of man, the factor which determines the character of public life and the "physiognomy of society," is the system by which material goods are produced and exchanged; (b) that the capitalist system of production is a nefarious one which inevitably leads to the exploitation of the working class by the capital-owning class and is incapable of developing adequately the economic resources of society or of distributing fairly the material goods produced by human labor; (c) that capitalism contains the seeds of its own destruction and must, in view of the inability of the capital-owning class to adjust itself to economic change, result eventually and inescapably in a revolutionary transfer of power to the working class; and (d) that imperialism, the final phase of capitalism, leads directly to war and revolution. . . .

The circumstances of the immediate post-revolution period—the existence in Russia of civil war and foreign intervention, together with the obvious fact that the Communists represented only a tiny minority of the Russian people—made the establishment of dictatorial power a necessity. . . .

Now the outstanding circumstance concerning the Soviet régime is that down to the present day . . . the men in the Kremlin have continued to be predominantly absorbed with the struggle to secure and make absolute the power which they seized in November 1917. They have endeavored to secure it primarily against forces at home, within Soviet society itself. But they have also endeavored to secure it against the outside world. . . .

As long as remnants of capitalism were officially recognized as existing in Russia, it was possible to place on them, as an internal element, part of the blame for the maintenance of a dictatorial form of society. But as these remnants were liquidated, little by little, this justification fell away; and when it was indicated officially that they had been finally destroyed, it disappeared altogether. And this fact created one of the most basic of the compulsions which came to act upon the Soviet régime: since capitalism no longer existed in Russia and since it could not be admitted that there could be serious or widespread opposition to the Kremlin springing spontaneously from the liberated masses under its authority, it became necessary to justify the retention of the dictatorship by stressing the menace of capitalism abroad. . . .

By the same token, tremendous emphasis has been placed on the original Communist thesis of a basic antagonism between the capitalist and Socialist worlds. It is clear, from many indications, that this emphasis is not founded in reality. The real facts concerning it have been confused by the existence abroad of genuine resentment provoked by Soviet philosophy and tactics and occasionally by the existence of great centers of military power, notably the Nazi régime in Germany and the Japanese Government of the late 1930's, which did indeed have aggressive designs against the Soviet Union. But there is ample evidence that the stress laid in Moscow on the menace confronting Soviet society from the world outside its borders is founded not in the realities of foreign antagonism but in the necessity of explaining away the maintenance of dictatorial authority at home. . . .

Soviet Policy

So much for the historical background. What does it spell in terms of the political personality of Soviet power as we know it today?

Of the original ideology, nothing has been officially junked. Belief is maintained in the basic badness of capitalism, in the inevitability of its destruction, in the obligation of the proletariat to assist in that destruction and to take power into its own hands. But stress has come to be laid primarily on those concepts which relate most specifically to the Soviet régime itself: to its position as the sole truly Socialist régime in a dark and misguided world, and to the relationships of power within it.

The first of these concepts is that of the innate antagonism between capitalism and Socialism. We have seen how deeply that concept has become imbedded in foundations of Soviet power. It has profound implications for Russia's conduct as a member of international society. It means that there can never be on Moscow's side any sincere assumption of a community of aims between the Soviet Union and powers which are regarded as capitalist. It must

invariably be assumed in Moscow that the aims of the capitalist world are antagonistic to the Soviet régime, and therefore to the interests of the peoples it controls. If the Soviet Government occasionally sets its signature to documents which would indicate the contrary, this is to be regarded as a tactical manœuvre permissible in dealing with the enemy (who is without honor) and should be taken in the spirit of *caveat emptor*. Basically, the antagonism remains. It is postulated. And from it flow many of the phenomena which we find disturbing in the Kremlin's conduct of foreign policy: the secretiveness, the lack of frankness, the duplicity, the wary suspiciousness, and the basic unfriendliness of purpose. These phenomena are there to stay, for the foreseeable future. There can be variations of degree and of emphasis. When there is something the Russians want from us, one or the other of these features of their policy may be thrust temporarily into the background; and when that happens there will always be Americans who will leap forward with gleeful announcements that "the Russians have changed," and some who will even try to take credit for having brought about such "changes." But we should not be misled by tactical manœuvres. These characteristics of Soviet policy, like the postulate from which they flow, are basic to the internal nature of Soviet power, and will be with us, whether in the foreground or the background, until the internal nature of Soviet power is changed.

———— • ————

"The main element of any United States policy toward the Soviet Union must be that of a long-term, patient but firm and vigilant containment of Russian expansive tendencies."

———— • ————

This means that we are going to continue for a long time to find the Russians difficult to deal with. It does not mean that they should be considered as embarked upon a do-or-die program to overthrow our society by a given date. The theory of the inevitability of the eventual fall of capitalism has the fortunate connotation that there is no hurry about it. The forces of progress can take their time in preparing the final *coup de grâce*. Meanwhile, what is vital is that the "Socialist fatherland"—that oasis of power which has been already won for Socialism in the person of the Soviet Union—should be cherished and defended by all good Communists at home and abroad, its fortunes promoted, its enemies badgered and confounded. The promotion of premature, "adventuristic" revolutionary projects abroad which might embarrass Soviet power in any way would be an inexcusable, even a counter-revolutionary act. The cause of Socialism is the support and promotion of Soviet power, as defined in Moscow.

Kremlin Authority

This brings us to the second of the concepts important to contemporary Soviet outlook. That is the infallibility of the Kremlin. The Soviet concept of power, which permits no focal points of organization outside the Party itself, requires that the Party leadership remain in theory the sole repository of truth. For if truth were to be found elsewhere, there would be justification for its expression in organized activity. But it is precisely that which the Kremlin cannot and will not permit. . . .

But we have seen that the Kremlin is under no ideological compulsion to accomplish its purposes in a hurry. Like the Church, it is dealing in ideological concepts which are of long-term validity, and it can afford to be patient. It has no right to risk the existing achievements of the revolution for the sake of vain baubles of the future. The very teachings of Lenin himself require great caution and flexibility in the pursuit of Communist purposes.

Again, these precepts are fortified by the lessons of Russian history: of centuries of obscure battles between nomadic forces over the stretches of a vast unfortified plain. Here caution, circumspection, flexibility and deception are the valuable qualities; and their value finds natural appreciation in the Russian or the oriental mind. Thus the Kremlin has no compunction about retreating in the face of superior force. And being under the compulsion of no timetable, it does not get panicky under the necessity for such retreat. Its political action is a fluid stream which moves constantly, wherever it is permitted to move, toward a given goal. Its main concern is to make sure that it has filled every nook and cranny available to it in the basin of world power. But if it finds unassailable barriers in its path, it accepts these philosophically and accommodates itself to them. The main thing is that there should always be pressure, unceasing constant pressure, toward the desired goal. There is no trace of any feeling in Soviet psychology that that goal must be reached at any given time.

Soviet Diplomacy

These considerations make Soviet diplomacy at once easier and more difficult to deal with than the diplomacy of individual aggressive leaders like Napoleon and Hitler. On the one hand it is more sensitive to contrary force, more ready to yield on individual sectors of the diplomatic front when that force is felt to be too strong, and thus more rational in the logic and rhetoric of power. On the other hand it cannot be easily defeated or discouraged by a single victory on the part of its opponents. And the patient persistence by which it is animated means that it can be effectively countered not by sporadic acts which represent the momentary whims of democratic opinion but only by intelligent long-range policies on the part of Russia's adversaries— policies no less steady in their purpose, and no less variegated and resourceful in their application, than those of the Soviet Union itself.

In these circumstances it is clear that the main element of any United States policy toward the Soviet Union must be that of a long-term, patient but firm and vigilant containment of Russian expansive tendencies. It is important to note, however, that such a policy has nothing to do with outward histrionics: with threats or blustering or superfluous gestures of outward "toughness." While the Kremlin is basically flexible in its reaction to political realities, it is by no means unamenable to considerations of prestige. Like almost any other government, it can be placed by tactless and threatening gestures in a position where it cannot afford to yield even though this might be dictated by its sense of realism. The Russian leaders are keen judges of human psychology, and as such they are highly conscious that loss of temper and of self-control is never a source of strength in political affairs. They are quick to exploit such evidences of weakness. For these reasons, it is a *sine qua non* of successful dealing with Russia that the foreign government in question should remain at all times cool and collected and that its demands on Russian policy should be put forward in such a manner as to leave the way open for a compliance not too detrimental to Russian prestige.

In the light of the above, it will be clearly seen that the Soviet pressure against the free institutions of the western world is something that can be contained by the adroit and vigilant application of counter-force at a series of constantly shifting geographical and political points, corresponding to the shifts and manœuvres of Soviet policy, but which cannot be charmed or talked out of existence. The Russians look forward to a duel of infinite duration, and they see that already they have scored great successes. It must be borne in mind that there was a time when the Communist Party represented far more of a minority in the sphere of Russian national life than Soviet power today represents in the world community.

But if ideology convinces the rulers of Russia that truth is on their side and that they can therefore afford to wait, those of us on whom that ideology has no claim are free to examine objectively the validity of that premise. The Soviet thesis not only implies complete lack of control by the west over its own economic destiny, it likewise assumes Russian unity, discipline and patience over an infinite period. Let us bring this apocalyptic vision down to earth, and suppose that the western world finds the strength and resourcefulness to contain Soviet power over a period of ten to fifteen years. What does that spell for Russia itself?

Predicting the Soviet Future

The Soviet leaders, taking advantage of the contributions of modern technique to the arts of despotism, have solved the question of obedience within the confines of their power. Few challenge their authority; and even those who do are unable to make that challenge valid as against the organs of suppression of the state.

The Kremlin has also proved able to accomplish its purpose of building up in Russia, regardless of the interests of the inhabitants, an industrial foundation of heavy metallurgy, which is, to be sure, not yet complete but which is nevertheless continuing to grow and is approaching those of the other major industrial countries. All of this, however, both the maintenance of internal political security and the building of heavy industry, has been carried out at a terrible cost in human life and in human hopes and energies. It has necessitated the use of forced labor on a scale unprecedented in modern times under conditions of peace. It has involved the neglect or abuse of other phases of Soviet economic life, particularly agriculture, consumers' goods production, housing and transportation.

To all that, the war has added its tremendous toll of destruction, death and human exhaustion. In consequence of this, we have in Russia today a population which is physically and spiritually tired. The mass of the people are disillusioned, skeptical and no longer as accessible as they once were to the magical attraction which Soviet power still radiates to its followers abroad. The avidity with which people seized upon the slight respite accorded to the Church for tactical reasons during the war was eloquent testimony to the fact that their capacity for faith and devotion found little expression in the purposes of the régime.

In these circumstances, there are limits to the physical and nervous strength of people themselves. These limits are absolute ones, and are binding even for the cruelest dictatorship, because beyond them people cannot be driven. The forced labor camps and the other agencies of constraint provide temporary means of compelling people to work longer hours than their own volition or mere economic

pressure would dictate; but if people survive them at all they become old before their time and must be considered as human casualties to the demands of dictatorship. In either case their best powers are no longer available to society and can no longer be enlisted in the service of the state. . . .

Meanwhile, a great uncertainty hangs over the political life of the Soviet Union. That is the uncertainty involved in the transfer of power from one individual or group of individuals to others. . . .

Thus the future of Soviet power may not be by any means as secure as Russian capacity for self-delusion would make it appear to the men in the Kremlin. That they can keep power themselves, they have demonstrated. That they can quietly and easily turn it over to others remains to be proved. Meanwhile, the hardships of their rule and the vicissitudes of international life have taken a heavy toll of the strength and hopes of the great people on whom their power rests. It is curious to note that the ideological power of Soviet authority is strongest today in areas beyond the frontiers of Russia, beyond the reach of its police power. This phenomenon brings to mind a comparison used by Thomas Mann in his great novel *Buddenbrooks*. Observing that human institutions often show the greatest outward brilliance at a moment when inner decay is in reality farthest advanced, he compared the Buddenbrook family, in the days of its greatest glamour, to one of those stars whose light shines most brightly on this world when in reality it has long since ceased to exist. And who can say with assurance that the strong light still cast by the Kremlin on the dissatisfied peoples of the western world is not the powerful afterglow of a constellation which is in actuality on the wane? This cannot be proved. And it cannot be disproved. But the possibility remains (and in the opinion of this writer it is a strong one) that Soviet power, like the capitalist world of its conception, bears within it the seeds of its own decay, and that the sprouting of these seeds is well advanced.

A Rival, Not a Partner

It is clear that the United States cannot expect in the foreseeable future to enjoy political intimacy with the Soviet régime. It must continue to regard the Soviet Union as a rival, not a partner, in the political arena. It must continue to expect that Soviet policies will reflect no abstract love of peace and stability, no real faith in the possibility of a permanent happy coexistence of the Socialist and capitalist worlds, but rather a cautious, persistent pressure toward the disruption and weakening of all rival influence and rival power.

Balanced against this are the facts that Russia, as opposed to the western world in general, is still by far the weaker party, that Soviet policy is highly flex-ible, and that Soviet society may well contain defi-ciencies which will eventually weaken its own total potential. This would of itself warrant the United States entering with reasonable confidence upon a policy of firm containment, designed to confront the Russians with unalterable counter-force at every point where they show signs of encroaching upon the interests of a peaceful and stable world.

But in actuality the possibilities for American poli-cy are by no means limited to holding the line and hoping for the best. It is entirely possible for the United States to influence by its actions the internal developments, both within Russia and throughout the international Communist movement, by which Russian policy is largely determined. This is not only a question of the modest measure of informational activity which this government can conduct in the Soviet Union and elsewhere, although that, too, is important. It is rather a question of the degree to which the United States can create among the peo-ples of the world generally the impression of a coun-try which knows what it wants, which is coping suc-cessfully with the problems of its internal life and with the responsibilities of a World Power, and which has a spiritual vitality capable of holding its own among the major ideological currents of the time. To the extent that such an impression can be created and maintained, the aims of Russian Communism must appear sterile and quixotic, the hopes and enthusi-asm of Moscow's supporters must wane, and added strain must be imposed on the Kremlin's foreign poli-cies. For the palsied decrepitude of the capitalist world is the keystone of Communist philosophy. Even the failure of the United States to experience the early economic depression which the ravens of the Red Square have been predicting with such com-placent confidence since hostilities ceased would have deep and important repercussions throughout the Communist world. . . .

It would be an exaggeration to say that American behavior unassisted and alone could exercise a power of life and death over the Communist move-ment and bring about the early fall of Soviet power in Russia. But the United States has it in its power to increase enormously the strains under which Soviet policy must operate, to force upon the Kremlin a far greater degree of moderation and circumspection than it has had to observe in recent years, and in this way to promote tendencies which must eventually find their outlet in either the break-up or the grad-ual mellowing of Soviet power. For no mystical, Mes-sianic movement—and particularly not that of the Kremlin—can face frustration indefinitely without eventually adjusting itself in one way or another to the logic of that state of affairs.

Thus the decision will really fall in large measure in this country itself. The issue of Soviet-American relations is in essence a test of the over-all worth of the United States as a nation among nations. To avoid destruction the United States need only mea-sure up to its own best traditions and prove itself worthy of preservation as a great nation.

Surely, there was never a fairer test of national quality than this. In the light of these circumstances, the thoughtful observer of Russian-American rela-tions will find no cause for complaint in the Krem-lin's challenge to American society. He will rather experience a certain gratitude to a Providence which, by providing the American people with this implacable challenge, has made their entire security as a nation dependent on their pulling themselves together and accepting the responsibilities of moral and political leadership that history plainly intended them to bear.

For Further Reading

George F. Kennan, *Memoirs, 1925–1950*. Boston: Little, Brown, 1967.

Deborah Larson, *Origins of Containment: A Psychological Expla-nation*. Princeton, NJ: Princeton University Press, 1985.

Melvyn P. Leffler, *A Preponderance of Power: National Security, the Truman Administration, and the Cold War*. Stanford, CA: Stanford University Press, 1992.

David Mayers, *George Kennan and the Dilemma of U.S. Foreign Policy*. New York: Oxford University Press, 1988.

Henry A. Wallace, *Toward World Peace*. New York: Reynal & Hitchcock, 1948.

Daniel Yergin, *Shattered Peace: The Origins of the Cold War and the National Security State*. Boston: Houghton Mifflin, 1977.

VIEWPOINT 32A

Communist Subversives Threaten America (1950)

Joseph R. McCarthy (1908–1957)

The Cold War had profound effects on America's domestic situation as well as its foreign policy. One of the most spectacular episodes of the early Cold War period was the rise and fall of Joseph R. McCarthy, a Republican senator from Wisconsin who gained notoriety for his obsessive hunts for communists within the U.S. government. McCarthy was little known before gaining national attention with a speech in Wheeling, West Virginia, on February 9, 1950. The following viewpoint is excerpted from the text of that speech as entered by McCarthy into the *Congressional Record* several days later (which was

Joseph R. McCarthy, *Congressional Record*, 81st Cong., 2nd sess., 1950, pp. 1952–57.

probably modified by the senator). McCarthy argues that the United States was denied the fruits of victory from World War II by treasonous subversives in the U.S. State Department. McCarthy's source of information was never identified, and no communists were ever found as a direct result of his accusations; but despite lack of proof, McCarthy gained widespread media attention and public support.

Several events probably contributed to public acceptance of McCarthy's charges. China had undergone a communist revolution in 1949, prompting an intense debate over how America "lost" China. The Soviet Union exploded its own atomic bomb the same year, depriving the United States of its nuclear monopoly and raising fears of Soviet espionage. Alger Hiss, a ranking American diplomat who had assisted Franklin D. Roosevelt at the 1945 Yalta summit, was charged with and found guilty of subversion and espionage in 1949, convincing many Americans of the possibility of treason in high places.

How is the United States faring in the Cold War, according to McCarthy? How does McCarthy characterize those he accuses of treason? Why is the case of Alger Hiss important, in his view?

Five years after a world war has been won, men's hearts should anticipate a long peace, and men's minds should be free from the heavy weight that comes with war. But this is not such a period—for this is not a period of peace. This is a time of the "cold war." This is a time when all the world is split into two vast, increasingly hostile armed camps—a time of a great armaments race. . . .

Ladies and gentlemen, can there be anyone here tonight who is so blind as to say that the war is not on? Can there be anyone who fails to realize that the Communist world has said, "The time is now"—that this is the time for the show-down between the democratic Christian world and the Communist atheistic world?

Unless we face this fact, we shall pay the price that must be paid by those who wait too long.

Communist Gains

Six years ago, at the time of the first conference to map out the peace—Dumbarton Oaks—there was within the Soviet orbit 180,000,000 people. Lined up on the antitotalitarian side there were in the world at that time roughly 1,625,000,000 people. Today, only 6 years later, there are 800,000,000 people under the absolute domination of Soviet Russia—an increase of over 400 percent. On our side, the figure has shrunk to around 500,000,000. In other words, in less than 6 years the odds have changed from 9 to 1 in our favor to 8 to 5 against us. This indicates the

swiftness of the tempo of Communist victories and American defeats in the cold war. As one of our outstanding historical figures once said, "When a great democracy is destroyed, it will not be because of enemies from without, but rather because of enemies from within."

The truth of this statement is becoming terrifyingly clear as we see this country each day losing on every front.

At war's end we were physically the strongest nation on earth and, at least potentially, the most powerful intellectually and morally. Ours could have been the honor of being a beacon in the desert of destruction, a shining living proof that civilization was not yet ready to destroy itself. Unfortunately, we have failed miserably and tragically to arise to the opportunity.

The reason why we find ourselves in a position of impotency is not because our only powerful potential enemy has sent men to invade our shores, but rather because of the traitorous actions of those who have been treated so well by this Nation. It has not been the less fortunate or members of minority groups who have been selling this Nation out, but rather those who have had all the benefits that the wealthiest nation on earth has had to offer—the finest homes, the finest college education, and the finest jobs in Government we can give.

This is glaringly true in the State Department. There the bright young men who are born with silver spoons in their mouths are the ones who have been worst. . . .

In my opinion the State Department, which is one of the most important government departments, is thoroughly infested with Communists.

I have in my hand 57 cases of individuals who would appear to be either card carrying members or certainly loyal to the Communist Party, but who nevertheless are still helping to shape our foreign policy.

One thing to remember in discussing the Communists, in our Government is that we are not dealing with spies who get 30 pieces of silver to steal the blueprints of a new weapon. We are dealing with a far more sinister type of activity because it permits the enemy to guide and shape our policy. . . .

Alger Hiss

This brings us down to the case of one Alger Hiss who is important not as an individual any more, but rather because he is so representative of a group in the State Department. It is unnecessary to go over the sordid events showing how he sold out the Nation which had given him so much. Those are rather fresh in all of our minds.

However, it should be remembered that the facts in regard to his connection with this international

Communist spy ring were made known to the then Under Secretary of State [Adolf] Berle 3 days after Hitler and Stalin signed the Russo-German alliance pact. At that time one Whittaker Chambers—who was also part of the spy ring—apparently decided that with Russia on Hitler's side, he could no longer betray our Nation to Russia. He gave Under Secretary of State Berle—and this is all a matter of record—practically all, if not more, of the facts upon which Hiss' conviction was based.

"In my opinion the State Department, which is one of the most important government departments, is thoroughly infested with Communists."

Under Secretary Berle promptly contacted Dean Acheson [then an assistant secretary of state] and received word in return that Acheson (and I quote) "could vouch for Hiss absolutely"—at which time the matter was dropped. And this, you understand, was at a time when Russia was an ally of Germany. This condition existed while Russia and Germany were invading and dismembering Poland, and while the Communist groups here were screaming "warmonger" at the United States for their support of the allied nations.

Again in 1943, the FBI had occasion to investigate the facts surrounding Hiss' contacts with the Russian spy ring. But even after that FBI report was submitted, nothing was done.

Then late in 1948—on August 5—when the Un-American Activities Committee called Alger Hiss to give an accounting, President Truman at once issued a Presidential directive ordering all Government agencies to refuse to turn over any information whatsoever in regard to the Communist activities of any Government employee to a congressional committee.

Incidentally, even after Hiss was convicted—it is interesting to note that the President still labeled the exposé of Hiss as a "red herring.". . .

As you hear this story of high treason, I know that you are saying to yourself, "Well, why doesn't the Congress do something about it?" Actually, ladies and gentlemen, one of the important reasons for the graft, the corruption, the dishonesty, the disloyalty, the treason in high Government positions—one of the most important reasons why this continues is a lack of moral uprising on the part of the 140,000,000 American people. In the light of history, however, this is not hard to explain.

It is the result of an emotional hang-over and a temporary moral lapse which follows every war. It is the apathy to evil which people who have been subjected to the tremendous evils of war feel. As the people of the world see mass murder, the destruction of defenseless and innocent people, and all of the crime and lack of morals which go with war, they become numb and apathetic. It has always been thus after war.

However, the morals of our people have not been destroyed. They still exist. This cloak of numbness and apathy has only needed a spark to rekindle them. Happily, this spark has finally been supplied.

Attacking Dean Acheson

As you know, very recently the Secretary of State proclaimed his loyalty to a man guilty of what has always been considered as the most abominable of all crimes—of being a traitor to the people who gave him a position of great trust. The Secretary of State in attempting to justify his continued devotion to the man who sold out the Christian world to the atheistic world, referred to Christ's Sermon on the Mount as a justification and reason therefor, and the reaction of the American people to this would have made the heart of Abraham Lincoln happy.

When this pompous diplomat in striped pants, with a phony British accent, proclaimed to the American people that Christ on the Mount endorsed communism, high treason, and betrayal of a sacred trust, the blasphemy was so great that it awakened the dormant indignation of the American people.

He has lighted the spark which is resulting in a moral uprising and will end only when the whole sorry mess of twisted, warped thinkers are swept from the national scene so that we may have a new birth of national honesty and decency in Government.

VIEWPOINT 32B

McCarthyism Threatens America (1950)

The Tydings Committee

Senator Joseph R. McCarthy's charges of communist subversion in the U.S. State Department caused a national uproar. On March 8, 1950, a subcommittee of the Senate Foreign Relations Committee, headed by Maryland senator Millard Tydings, a Democrat, was established to investigate McCarthy's accusations. After testimony by McCarthy and those he had accused proved inconclusive (none of the nine people McCarthy specifically named were communists), the committee decided to compare McCarthy's

Senate Committee on Foreign Relations, *State Department Employee Loyalty Investigation*, 81st Cong., 2nd sess., July 20, 1950, S. Rept. 2108.

charges with internal State Department loyalty files.

These files had been kept since President Harry S. Truman issued an executive order in 1947 requiring loyalty and background investigations of all government employees. The Federal Bureau of Investigation investigated thousands of people, not only for acts of espionage, but for any association with organizations or people considered "disloyal" or "subversive." Truman at first resisted the Tydings committee's request to release the files, but eventually relented. McCarthy argued that the files, which failed to substantiate his charges, had been "raped" to remove derogatory material. The Tydings committee disagreed, and in its concluding report, excerpted here, sharply criticizes McCarthy for making false accusations and leading the country into hysteria.

McCarthy continued making news with his accusations of communist subversion until December 1954, when he was officially censured by the U.S. Senate. He died in relative obscurity in 1957. "McCarthyism" became a term describing personal attacks in the form of indiscriminate allegations unsupported by evidence.

Did the Tydings committee uncover the presence of communists in the State Department? What tactics of McCarthy does the Tydings committee criticize?

Of the 81 alleged State Department employees, only 40 were found to be employed by the State Department at the time of the review. Seven of the so-called 81 were never employed by the State Department and the remaining 33 are no longer in the Department, having been separated either through resignation, termination, or reduction in force. Specifically, of the 33 former employees, 3 were separated in 1949; 16, in 1948; 12, in 1947; and 2, in 1946. . . .

We have carefully and conscientiously reviewed each and every one of the loyalty files relative to the individuals charged by Senator McCarthy. In no instance was any one of them now employed in the State Department found to be a "card-carrying Communist," a member of the Communist Party, or "loyal to the Communist Party." Furthermore, in no instance have we found in our considered judgment that the decision to grant loyalty and security clearance has been erroneously or improperly made in the light of existing loyalty standards. Otherwise stated, we do not find basis in any instance for reversing the judgment of the State Department officials charged with responsibility for employee loyalty; or concluding that they have not conscientiously discharged their duties. . . .

What the State Department knows concerning an employee's loyalty is to be found in its loyalty and

security files. These files contain all information bearing on loyalty, obtained from any and all sources, including, of course, the reports of full field investigations by the FBI. Interestingly, in this regard, no sooner had the President indicated that the files would be available for review by the subcommittee than Senator McCarthy charged they were being "raped," altered, or otherwise subjected to a "housecleaning." This charge was found to be utterly without foundation in fact. The files were reviewed by representatives of the Department of Justice, and the Department has certified that all information bearing on the employee's loyalty as developed by the FBI appears in the files which were reviewed by the subcommittee. . . .

The Facts Behind the Charge of "Whitewash"

Seldom, if ever, in the history of congressional investigations has a committee been subjected to an organized campaign of vilification and abuse comparable to that with which we have been confronted throughout this inquiry. This campaign has been so acute and so obviously designed to confuse and confound the American people that an analysis of the factors responsible therefor is indicated.

The first of these factors was the necessity of creating the impression that our inquiry was not thorough and sincere in order to camouflage the fact that the charges made by Senator McCarthy were groundless and that the Senate and the American people had been deceived. No sooner were hearings started than the cry of "whitewash" was raised along with the chant "investigate the charges and not McCarthy." This chant we have heard morning, noon, and night for almost 4 months from certain quarters for readily perceptible motives. Interestingly, had we elected to investigate Senator McCarthy, there would have been ample basis therefor, since we have been reliably informed that at the time he made the charges initially he had no information whatever to support them, and, furthermore, it early appeared that in securing Senate Resolution 231 [passed in February 1950, authorizing a "full and complete study and investigation as to whether persons who are disloyal to the United States are, or have been, employed by the Department of State"] a fraud had been perpetrated upon the Senate of the United States.

From the very outset of our inquiry, Senator McCarthy has sought to leave the impression that the subcommittee has been investigating him and not "disloyalty in the State Department." The reason for the Senator's concern is now apparent. He had no facts to support his wild and baseless charges, and lived in mortal fear that this situation would be exposed.

Few people, cognizant of the truth in even an elementary way, have, in the absence of political partisanship, placed any credence in the hit-and-run tactics of Senator McCarthy. He has stooped to a new low in his cavalier disregard of the facts.

———— • ————

"It is . . . clearly apparent that the charges of Communist infiltration of and influence upon the State Department are false."

———— • ————

The simple truth is that in making his speech at Wheeling, Senator McCarthy was talking of a subject and circumstances about which he knew nothing. His extreme and irresponsible statements called for emergency measures. As Senator [Kenneth S.] Wherry told Emmanuel S. Larsen, "Oh, Mac has gone out on a limb and kind of made a fool of himself and we have to back him up now." Starting with nothing, Senator McCarthy plunged headlong forward, desperately seeking to develop some information, which colored with distortion and fanned by a blaze of bias, would forestall a day of reckoning.

Certain elements rallied to his support, particularly those who ostensibly fight communism by adopting the vile methods of the Communists themselves and in so doing actually hinder the fight of all right-minded people who detest and abhor communism in all its manifestations. We cannot, however, destroy one evil by the adoption of another. Senator McCarthy and McCarthyism have been exposed for what they are—and the sight is not a pretty one. . . .

The Big Lie

In concluding our report, we are constrained to make observations which we regard as fundamental.

It is, of course, clearly apparent that the charges of Communist infiltration of and influence upon the State Department are false. This knowledge is reassuring to all Americans whose faith has been temporarily shaken in the security of their Government by perhaps the most nefarious campaign of untruth in the history of our Republic.

We believe, however, that this knowledge and assurance, while important, will prove ultimately of secondary significance in contemplating the salutary aspects of our investigation. For, we believe that, inherent in the charges that have been made and the sinister campaign to give them ostensible verity, are lessons from which the American people will find inspiration for a rededication to the principles and ideals that have made this Nation great.

We have seen the technique of the "Big Lie," else-where employed by the totalitarian dictator with devastating success, utilized here for the first time on a sustained basis in our history. We have seen how, through repetition and shifting untruths, it is possible to delude great numbers of people.

We have seen the character of private citizens and of Government employees virtually destroyed by public condemnation on the basis of gossip, distortion, hearsay, and deliberate untruths. By the mere fact of their associations with a few persons of alleged questionable proclivities an effort has been made to place the stigma of disloyalty upon individuals, some of whom are little people whose only asset is their character and devotion to duty and country. This has been done without the slightest vestige of respect for even the most elementary rules of evidence or fair play or, indeed, common decency. Indeed, we have seen an effort not merely to establish guilt by association but guilt by accusation alone. The spectacle is one we would expect in a totalitarian nation where the rights of the individual are crushed beneath the juggernaut of statism and oppression; it has no place in America where government exists to serve our people, not to destroy them.

Creating Hysteria

We have seen an effort to inflame the American people with a wave of hysteria and fear on an unbelievable scale in this free Nation. Were this campaign founded in truth it would be questionable enough; where it is fraught with falsehood from beginning to end, its reprehensible and contemptible character defies adequate condemnation.

We sincerely believe that charges of the character which have been made in this case seriously impair the efforts of our agencies of Government to combat the problem of subversion. Furthermore, extravagant allegations, which cannot be proved and are not subject to proof, have the inevitable effect of dulling the awareness of all Americans to the true menace of communism. . . .

At a time when American blood is again being shed to preserve our dream of freedom, we are constrained fearlessly and frankly to call the charges, and the methods employed to give them ostensible validity, what they truly are: A fraud and a hoax perpetrated on the Senate of the United States and the American people. They represent perhaps the most nefarious campaign of half-truths and untruths in the history of this Republic. For the first time in our history, we have seen the totalitarian technique of the "big lie" employed on a sustained basis. The result has been to confuse and divide the American people, at a time when they should be strong in their unity, to a degree far beyond the hopes of the Communists themselves whose stock in trade is confusion and division. In such a disillusioning setting, we appreciate as never before our Bill of Rights, a free press, and the heritage of freedom that has made this Nation great.

For Further Reading

William F. Buckley Jr. and L. Brent Bozell, *McCarthy and His Enemies.* Chicago: H. Regnery Co., 1954.

Richard Freeland, *The Truman Doctrine and the Origins of McCarthyism.* New York: Knopf, 1972.

Richard M. Fried, *Nightmare in Red: The McCarthy Era in Perspective.* New York: Oxford University Press, 1990.

Joseph R. McCarthy, *McCarthyism: The Fight for America.* New York: Devin-Adair Co., 1952.

David M. Oshinsky, *A Conspiracy So Immense: The World of Joe McCarthy.* New York: Free Press, 1983.

Thomas Reeves, *The Life and Times of Joe McCarthy.* New York: Stein and Day, 1982.

The Eisenhower Years

VIEWPOINT 33A

Racial Segregation in Public Schools Is Unconstitutional (1954)

Earl Warren (1891–1974)

Earl Warren, a moderate Republican governor of California and presidential contender in 1948 and 1952, was appointed Supreme Court chief justice in 1953 by President Dwight D. Eisenhower. Warren went on to become one of the most influential chief justices in the nation's history, presiding over many landmark decisions on social and civil rights issues. Perhaps the most important of these rulings was the first: the 1954 unanimous decision in *Brown v. Board of Education* declaring that racially segregated public schools were unconstitutional. The ruling reversed the "separate but equal" doctrine affirmed by the 1896 Supreme Court decision in *Plessy v. Ferguson* (see viewpoint 12A). Warren wrote the opinion of the Court in *Brown*, reprinted below, making significant use of the arguments advanced by Thurgood Marshall of the National Association for the Advancement of Colored People (NAACP), the organization that represented the black plaintiffs challenging racial segregation.

What are the limitations of examining the history of the Fourteenth Amendment for the purposes of deciding this case, according to Warren? How has segregation harmed black children, in Warren's opinion?

From the Supreme Court's unanimous decision in *Brown v. Board of Education*, 347 U.S. 483 (1954).

These cases come to us from the States of Kansas, South Carolina, Virginia, and Delaware. They are premised on different facts and different local conditions, but a common legal question justifies their consideration together in this consolidated opinion.

In each of the cases, minors of the Negro race, through their legal representatives, seek the aid of the courts in obtaining admission to the public schools of their community on a nonsegregated basis. In each instance, they had been denied admission to schools attended by white children under laws requiring or permitting segregation according to race. This segregation was alleged to deprive the plaintiffs of the equal protection of the laws under the Fourteenth Amendment. In each of the cases other than the Delaware case, a three-judge federal district court denied relief to the plaintiffs on the so-called "separate but equal" doctrine announced by this Court in *Plessy v. Ferguson....* Under that doctrine, equality of treatment is accorded when the races are provided substantially equal facilities, even though these facilities be separate. In the Delaware case, the Supreme Court of Delaware adhered to that doctrine, but ordered that the plaintiffs be admitted to the white schools because of their superiority to the Negro schools.

The plaintiffs contend that segregated public schools are not "equal" and cannot be made "equal," and that hence they are deprived of the equal protection of the laws. Because of the obvious importance of the question presented, the Court took jurisdiction. Argument was heard in the 1952 Term, and reargument was heard this Term on certain questions propounded by the Court.

The Fourteenth Amendment

Reargument was largely devoted to the circumstances surrounding the adoption of the Fourteenth Amendment in 1868. It covered exhaustively consideration of the Amendment in Congress, ratification by the states, then existing practices in racial segregation, and the views of proponents and opponents of the Amendment. This discussion and our own investigation convince us that, although these sources cast some light, it is not enough to resolve the problem with which we are faced. At best, they are inconclusive. The most avid proponents of the post-War Amendments undoubtedly intended them to remove all legal distinctions among "all persons born or naturalized in the United States." Their opponents, just as certainly, were antagonistic to both the letter and the spirit of the Amendments and wished them to have the most limited effect. What others in Congress and the state legislatures had in mind cannot be determined with any degree of certainty.

An additional reason for the inconclusive nature of the Amendment's history, with respect to segregated schools, is the status of public education at that time. In the South, the movement toward free common schools, supported by general taxation, had not yet taken hold. Education of white children was largely in the hands of private groups. Education of Negroes was almost nonexistent, and practically all of the race were illiterate. In fact, any education of Negroes was forbidden by law in some states. Today, in contrast, many Negroes have achieved outstanding success in the arts and sciences as well as in the business and professional world. It is true that public school education at the time of the Amendment had advanced further in the North, but the effect of the Amendment on Northern States was generally ignored in the congressional debates. Even in the North, the conditions of public education did not approximate those existing today. The curriculum was usually rudimentary; ungraded schools were common in rural areas; the school term was but three months a year in many states; and compulsory school attendance was virtually unknown. As a consequence, it is not surprising that there should be so little in the history of the Fourteenth Amendment relating to its intended effect on public education.

———— • ————

"We conclude that in the field of public education the doctrine of 'separate but equal' has no place."

———— • ————

In the first cases in this Court construing the Fourteenth Amendment, decided shortly after its adoption, the Court interpreted it as proscribing all state-imposed discriminations against the Negro race. The doctrine of "separate but equal" did not make its appearance in this Court until 1896 in the case of *Plessy v. Ferguson*, . . . involving not education but transportation. American courts have since labored with the doctrines for over half a century. In this Court, there have been six cases involving the "separate but equal" doctrine in the field of public education. In *Cumming v. County Board of Education* . . . and *Gong Lum v. Rice*, . . . the validity of the doctrine itself was not challenged. In more recent cases, all on the graduate school level, inequality was found in that specific benefits enjoyed by white students were denied to Negro students of the same educational qualifications. . . . In none of these cases was it necessary to re-examine the doctrine to grant relief to the Negro plaintiff. And in *Sweatt v. Painter*, . . .

the Court expressly reserved decision on the question whether *Plessy v. Ferguson* should be held inapplicable to public education.

In the instant cases, that question is directly presented. Here, unlike *Sweatt v. Painter*, there are findings below that the Negro and white schools involved have been equalized, or are being equalized, with respect to buildings, curricula, qualifications and salaries of teachers, and other "tangible" factors. Our decision, therefore, cannot turn on merely a comparison of these tangible factors in the Negro and white schools involved in each of the cases. We must look instead to the effect of segregation itself on public education.

Segregation and Education

In approaching this problem, we cannot turn the clock back to 1868 when the Amendment was adopted, or even to 1896 when *Plessy v. Ferguson* was written. We must consider public education in the light of its full development and its present place in American life throughout the Nation. Only in this way can it be determined if segregation in public schools deprives these plaintiffs of the equal protection of the laws.

Today, education is perhaps the most important function of state and local governments. Compulsory school attendance laws and the great expenditures for education both demonstrate our recognition of the importance of education to our democratic society. It is required in the performance of our most basic public responsibilities, even service in the armed forces. It is the very foundation of good citizenship. Today it is a principal instrument in awakening the child to cultural values, in preparing him for later professional training, and in helping him to adjust normally to his environment. In these days, it is doubtful that any child may reasonably be expected to succeed in life if he is denied the opportunity of an education. Such an opportunity, where the state has undertaken to provide it, is a right which must be made available to all on equal terms.

We come then to the question presented: Does segregation of children in public schools solely on the basis of race, even though the physical facilities and other "tangible" factors may be equal, deprive the children of the minority group of equal educational opportunities? We believe that it does.

In *Sweatt v. Painter*, . . . in finding that a segregated law school for Negroes could not provide them equal educational opportunities, this Court relied in large part on "those qualities which are incapable of objective measurement but which make for greatness in a law school." In *McLaurin v. Oklahoma State Regents*, . . . the Court, in requiring that a Negro admitted to a white graduate school be treated like all other students, again resorted to intangible considerations: ". . . his ability to study, to engage in discussions and exchange views with other students, and, in general, to learn his profession." Such considerations apply with added force to children in grade and high schools. To separate them from others of similar age and qualifications solely because of their race generates a feeling of inferiority as to their status in the community that may affect their hearts and minds in a way unlikely ever to be undone. The effect of this separation on their educational opportunities was well stated by a finding in the Kansas case by a court which nevertheless felt compelled to rule against the Negro plaintiffs:

> Segregation of white and colored children in public schools has a detrimental effect upon the colored children. The impact is greater when it has the sanction of the law; for the policy of separating the races is usually interpreted as denoting the inferiority of the negro group. A sense of inferiority affects the motivation of a child to learn. Segregation with the sanction of law, therefore, has a tendency to [retard] the education and mental development of negro children and to deprive them of some of the benefits they would receive in a racial[ly] integrated school system.

Whatever may have been the extent of psychological knowledge at the time of *Plessy v. Ferguson*, this finding is amply supported by modern authority. Any language in *Plessy v. Ferguson* contrary to this finding is rejected.

Separate and Unequal

We conclude that in the field of public education the doctrine of "separate but equal" has no place. Separate educational facilities are inherently unequal. Therefore, we hold that the plaintiffs and others similarly situated for whom the actions have been brought are, by reason of the segregation complained of, deprived of the equal protection of the laws guaranteed by the Fourteenth Amendment. This disposition makes unnecessary any discussion whether such segregation also violates the Due Process Clause of the Fourteenth Amendment.

Because these are class actions, because of the wide applicability of this decision, and because of the great variety of local conditions, the formulation of decrees in these cases presents problems of considerable complexity. On reargument, the consideration of appropriate relief was necessarily subordinated to the primary question—the constitutionality of segregation on public education. We have now announced that such segregation is a denial of the equal protection of the laws. In order that we may have the full assistance of the parties in formulating decrees, the cases will be restored to the docket, and the parties

are requested to present further argument on Questions 4 and 5 previously propounded by the Court for the reargument this Term. The Attorney General of the United States is again invited to participate. The Attorneys General of the states requiring or permitting segregation in public education will also be permitted to appear as *Amici Curiae* upon request, to do so by September 15, 1954, and submission of briefs by October 1, 1954.

VIEWPOINT 33B

The Supreme Court Should Not Interfere in Southern Racial Practices (1956)

The Southern Manifesto

The U.S. Supreme Court in the landmark case *Brown v. Board of Education* ruled that racially segregated public schools were unconstitutional. The Court made no direct statement on how this ruling was to be implemented; one year later the Court issued an "Enforcement Decree" calling for states to desegregate their schools "with all deliberate speed." Despite these pronouncements, many southern states actively resisted school desegregation. In 1956 one hundred senators and congressional representatives from eleven southern states signed a declaration of opposition to *Brown*, entitled the "Southern Manifesto." Most of the writing of the Southern Manifesto was the work of North Carolina senator Sam J. Ervin Jr. Among its signers were Senators Strom Thurmond, J. William Fullbright, and Richard B. Russell. The declaration, reprinted here, argues that the Supreme Court went beyond its proper authority in its ruling. The signing members of Congress go on to support all efforts to "resist forced integration by any lawful means."

What evidence is presented to demonstrate that the Constitution and the Fourteenth Amendment do not support racial integration? How has the *Brown* ruling affected race relations in the South, according to the Manifesto?

The unwarranted decision of the Supreme Court in the public school cases is now bearing the fruit always produced when men substitute naked power for established law.

The Founding Fathers gave us a Constitution of checks and balances because they realized the inescapable lesson of history that no man or group of

"The Southern Manifesto: Declaration of Constitutional Principles," *Congressional Record*, 84th Cong., 2nd sess., March 12, 1956.

men can be safely entrusted with unlimited power. They framed this Constitution with its provisions for change by amendment in order to secure the fundamentals of government against the dangers of temporary popular passion or the personal predilections of public office-holders.

An Abuse of Power

We regard the decision of the Supreme Court in the school cases as a clear abuse of judicial power. It climaxes a trend in the Federal Judiciary undertaking to legislate, in derogation of the authority of Congress, and to encroach upon the reserved rights of the States and the people.

The original Constitution does not mention education. Neither does the 14th amendment nor any other amendment. The debates preceding the submission of the 14th amendment clearly show that there was no intent that it should affect the system of education maintained by the States.

The very Congress which proposed the amendment subsequently provided for segregated schools in the District of Columbia.

When the amendment was adopted in 1868, there were 37 States of the Union. Every one of the 26 States that had any substantial racial differences among its people, either approved the operation of segregated schools already in existence or subsequently established such schools by action of the same law-making body which considered the 14th amendment.

———— • ————

"This unwarranted exercise of power by the Court, contrary to the Constitution, is creating chaos and confusion in the States principally affected."

———— • ————

As admitted by the Supreme Court in the public school case (*Brown* v. *Board of Education*), the doctrine of separate but equal schools "apparently originated in *Roberts* v. *City of Boston* (1849), upholding school segregation against attack as being violative of a State constitutional guarantee of equality." This constitutional doctrine began in the North, not in the South, and it was followed not only in Massachusetts, but in Connecticut, New York, Illinois, Indiana, Michigan, Minnesota, New Jersey, Ohio, Pennsylvania and other northern States until they, exercising their rights as States through the constitutional processes of local self-government, changed their school systems.

In the case of *Plessy* v. *Ferguson* in 1896 the Supreme Court expressly declared that under the 14th amendment no person was denied any of his rights if the States provided separate but equal public facilities. This decision has been followed in many other cases. It is notable that the Supreme Court, speaking through Chief Justice [William H.] Taft, a former President of the United States, unanimously declared in 1927 in *Lum* v. *Rice* that the "separate but equal" principle is "within the discretion of the State in regulating its public schools and does not conflict with the 14th amendment."

This interpretation, restated time and again, became a part of the life of the people of many of the States and confirmed their habits, customs, traditions, and way of life. It is founded on elemental humanity and commonsense, for parents should not be deprived by Government of the right to direct the lives and education of their own children.

Though there has been no constitutional amendment or act of Congress changing this established legal principle almost a century old, the Supreme Court of the United States, with no legal basis for such action, undertook to exercise their naked judicial power and substituted their personal political and social ideas for the established law of the land.

This unwarranted exercise of power by the Court, contrary to the Constitution, is creating chaos and confusion in the States principally affected. It is destroying the amicable relations between the white and Negro races that have been created through 90 years of patient effort by the good people of both races. It has planted hatred and suspicion where there has been heretofore friendship and understanding.

Without regard to the consent of the governed, outside agitators are threatening immediate and revolutionary changes in our public-school systems. If done, this is certain to destroy the system of public education in some of the States.

Responding to Outside Meddlers

With the gravest concern for the explosive and dangerous condition created by this decision and inflamed by outside meddlers:

We reaffirm our reliance on the Constitution as the fundamental law of the land.

We decry the Supreme Court's encroachments on rights reserved to the States and to the people, contrary to established law, and to the Constitution.

We commend the motives of those States which have declared the intention to resist forced integration by any lawful means.

We appeal to the States and people who are not directly affected by these decisions to consider the constitutional principles involved against the time when they too, on issues vital to them, may be the victims of judicial encroachment.

Even though we constitute a minority in the present Congress, we have full faith that a majority of the American people believe in the dual system of government which has enabled us to achieve our greatness and will in time demand that the reserved rights of the States and of the people be made secure against judicial usurpation.

We pledge ourselves to use all lawful means to bring about a reversal of this decision which is contrary to the Constitution and to prevent the use of force in its implementation.

In this trying period, as we all seek to right this wrong, we appeal to our people not to be provoked by the agitators and trouble-makers invading our States and to scrupulously refrain from disorder and lawless acts.

For Further Reading

Numan V. Bartley, *The Rise of Massive Resistance: Race & Politics in the South During the 1950s.* Baton Rouge: Louisiana State University Press, 1969.

Richard Kluger, *Simple Justice: The History of Brown v. Board of Education and Black America's Struggle for Equality.* New York: Knopf, 1976.

G. Edward White, *Earl Warren, A Public Life.* New York: Oxford University Press, 1982.

Mark Whitman, ed., *Removing the Badge of Slavery: The Record of Brown v. Board of Education.* Princeton, NJ: Markus Wiener, 1993.

Raymond Wolters, *The Burden of Brown.* Knoxville: University of Tennessee Press, 1984.

VIEWPOINT 34A

The Suburbs:
The New American Dream
(1953)

Harry Henderson (b. 1914)

Between 1945 and 1960, 40 million Americans migrated from the cities to the suburbs. Spurred by government programs designed to encourage home ownership, developers created whole new communities. Many developments, such as those by builder William Levitt, consisted of row upon row of nearly identical mass-produced homes. In the following viewpoint, journalist Harry Henderson examines the lives of people living in these "Levittowns" and other suburban areas. The article, first published in *Harper's Magazine* in November 1953, offers a mixed but generally positive portrayal of American suburbia.

What attractions do the new suburbs have for the people living in them, according to Henderson? What generalizations does he make about the economic and social situation of these suburban residents? What does he find most appealing about this form of suburban life?

Since World War II, whole new towns and small cities, consisting of acres of near-identical Cape Cod and ranch-type houses, have been bulldozed into existence on the outskirts of America's major cities. Begun as "veterans' housing," and still commonly called "projects," these new communities differ radically from the older urban areas whose slow, cumulative growth depended on rivers and railroads, raw materials or markets, industries and available labor. They also differ from the older suburbs which were built around existing villages. These new communities are of necessity built on open farmland—to house people quickly, cheaply, and profitably. They reflect not only the increased number of young American families, but an enormous expansion of the middle class via the easy credit extended to veterans.

The best known of these communities, Levittown, Long Island [New York], is also the largest; its population is now estimated at 70,000. Lakewood, near Long Beach in the Los Angeles area, is a close second. Park Forest, some thirty miles south of Chicago—which has significant qualitative differences from the others, in that its social character was as conscientiously planned as its physical layout—now has 20,000 people and will have 30,000 when completed. No one knows exactly how many of these postwar communities exist in all. The Federal Home and Housing Authority, which insured mortgages for nearly all the houses, has no records in terms of communities or even large developments. However, one can safely assume that their combined population totals several million people.

These communities have none of the long-festering social problems of older towns, such as slums, crowded streets, vacant lots that are both neighborhood dumps and playgrounds, or sagging, neon-fronted business districts that sprawl in all directions. Instead everything is new. Dangerous traffic intersections are almost unknown. Grassy play areas abound. Shops are centrally located and under one roof, at least theoretically, with adjacent off-street parking.

Socially, these communities have neither history, tradition, nor established structure—no inherited customs, institutions, "socially important" families, or "big houses." Everybody lives in a "good neighborhood"; there is, to use that classic American euphemism, no "wrong side of the tracks." Outwardly, there are neither rich nor poor, and initially there were no older people, teen-agers, in-laws, family doctors, "big shots," churches, organizations, schools, or local governments. Since the builder required a large cheap site, the mass-produced suburbs are usually located at the extreme edge of the commuting radius. This means they are economically dependent on the big city, without local industry to provide employment and share tax burdens.

Studying the Suburbs

Three years ago I began a series of extensive visits to these new communities to learn what effect this kind of housing and social organization has on people. I was particularly interested in what customs developed, what groups became important, what attitudes and ways of handling problems were created. I wanted to know, for instance, how people made friends, how you became a "big shot," and how life in these towns differed from that of our older towns.

The notes below are an attempt to describe what I found out, a reporter's report on a new generation's version of the "American way." They are based on interviews and my own observations in six such communities, including Levittown and Park Forest. While each community is different, certain common patterns exist, although their strength varies in accordance with two factors: screening and size.

Screening—or the selection of people by fixed criteria—obviously affects the economic, social, and cultural life. Where screening is based on something more than the ability to make a down payment, the population tends to become a narrow, specialized, upper stratum of the middle class. Size affects the community in another way. The construction of fifty or a hundred new homes on a common plot immediately beside a suburb of 5,000 merely results in their becoming part of that community, adopting its social structure. But when the number of new homes is many times larger than the old, both problems, and new ways of living emerge with greater force. (However, even in small projects some new patterns are present.)

These notes are, of course, subjective and as such liable to personal distortion. Valid statistical data—because of the short time people stay put in these towns, plus a host of other factors—are simply beyond the reach of one man. But, for whatever they are worth, here they are.

Companionship

At first glance, regardless of variations in trim, color, and position of the houses, they seem monotonous; nothing rises above two stories, there are no full-grown trees, and the horizon is an endless picket fence of telephone poles and television aerials.

(The mass builder seeks flat land because it cuts his construction costs.)

However one may feel about it aesthetically, this puts the emphasis on people and their activities. One rarely hears complaints about the identical character of the houses. "You don't feel it when you live here," most people say. One mother, a Midwestern college graduate with two children, told me: "We're not peas in a pod. I thought it would be like that, especially because incomes are nearly the same. But it's amazing how different and varied people are, likes and dislikes, attitude and wants. I never really knew what people were like until I came here."

Since no one can acquire prestige through an imposing house, or inherited position, activity—the participation in community or group affairs—becomes the basis of prestige. In addition, it is the quickest way to meet people and make friends. In communities of strangers, where everybody realizes his need for companionship, the first year is apt to witness almost frantic participation in all kinds of activities. Later, as friends are made, this tapers off somewhat.

———— • ————

The standardized house also creates an emphasis on interior decorating. Most people try hard to achieve "something different." In hundreds of houses I never saw two interiors that matched—and I saw my first tiger-striped wallpaper. (The only item that is endlessly repeated is a brass skillet hung on a red brick wall.) Yet two styles predominate: Early American and Modern. What is rarely seen, except in homes of older-than-average people, is a family heirloom.

Taste levels are high. My interviews with wives revealed that their models and ideas came primarily from pictures of rooms in national magazines. Nobody copies an entire room, but they take different items from different pictures. At first most women said, "Well, moving into a new house, you want everything new." Later some altered this explanation, saying, "Nearly everybody is new. . . . I mean, they are newly married and new to the community. They don't feel too certain about things, especially moving into a place where everyone is a stranger. If you've seen something in a magazine—well, people will nearly always like it." So many times were remarks of this character repeated that I concluded that what many sought in their furniture was a kind of "approval insurance."

———— • ————

Asked whom they missed most, women usually replied, "My mother." Men's answers were scattered, apt to be old friends, neighbors, relatives. Many women said; "I wish there was some place close by to walk to, like the candy store in the city. Just some place to take the kids to buy a cone or newspaper in the afternoon. It helps break up the monotony of the day." They considered the centrally located shopping centers too distant for such outings.

———— • ————

Because these communities were built from scratch, they afforded a degree of planning impossible in our older cities, and—depending on the builder's foresight and awareness of social problems—advantage was taken of this. Planners solved complex problems in traffic flow, space arrangement, play areas, heating problems, site locations to provide sunlight, and kitchen traffic. But nobody thought about dogs.

Dogs in Suburbia

The people in these communities have generally escaped from crowded city apartments. Their 50 x 100–foot plot seems to them to be the size of a ranch. One of their first acts is to buy a dog, on the theory that "it's good for the children," an old idea in American family folklore, and to turn the dog loose. Usually the people know nothing about dogs or their training. Theoretically, the dog is the children's responsibility; generally they are too young to handle it.

The result is that the dogs form great packs which race through the area, knocking down small boys and girls, wrecking gardens and flower beds, and raising general hell. Then people try tying them up; the dogs howl and bark until no one can stand it. Locked up inside the house, they are a constant worry, and charge out to bite the mailmen and deliverymen. In one community thirteen mailmen were bitten in one summer.

Dogs, along with children, are the greatest cause of tension within a block. In Park Forest, outside Chicago, dogs were finally voted out of the 3,000 unit rental area in the bitterest, hottest, meanest, most tearful fight in that community's history. But they are permitted in the private-home area because our conception of private property includes the right to own a dog even though he may be the damnedest nuisance in the world. One can hardly describe the emotions aroused by dogs in these communities. One man told me he had bought his dog simply "because I am damn sick and tired of my neighbor's dog yapping all night. I just want to give them a taste of what it's like."

Suburban Populations

The populations differ strikingly from those of the older towns. The men's ages average 31 years; the women's about 26. Incomes fall somewhere between $4,000 and $7,000 yearly, although incomes in excess of this can be found everywhere. Their homes cost between $7,000 and $12,000. Roughly 90 per cent of the men are veterans. Their major occupational clas-

sifications are managers, professionals, salesmen, skilled workers, and small business men. Most communities also have sizable numbers of transient army families.

Buying or renting a home in one of these communities is, of course, a form of economic and personal screening. As a result, there are no poor, no Negroes; and, as communities, these contain the best educated people in America. In Park Forest, where the screening was intensive, more than 50 per cent of the men and 25 per cent of the women are college graduates; the local movie theater survives by showing Westerns for the kids in the afternoon and foreign "art films" for the adults in the evening.

———— • ————

Initially, city-bred women, accustomed to the constant sights and sounds of other people, suffer greatly from loneliness, especially if their children are as yet unborn. One woman expressed it this way: "Your husband gets up and goes off in the morning—and you're left with the day to spend. The housework is a matter of minutes. I used to think that I had been brought to the end of the earth and deserted." Another said, "I used to sit by the window . . . just wishing someone would go by."

Generally this disappears as friends are made and children appear. Today most communities have "older" (by several years) residents who make real effort to help newcomers overcome their "newness."

———— • ————

Hardware stores report their biggest selling item year-round is floor wax. "Honest to God," said one store manager, "I think they eat the stuff."

———— • ————

The daily pattern of household life is governed by the husband's commuting schedule. It is entirely a woman's day because virtually every male commutes. Usually the men must leave between 7:00 and 8:00 A.M.; therefore they rise between 6:00 and 7:00 A.M. In most cases the wife rises with her husband, makes his breakfast while he shaves, and has a cup of coffee with him. Then she often returns to bed until the children get up. The husband is not likely to be back before 7:00 or 7:30 P.M.

Domestic Life

This leaves the woman alone all day to cope with the needs of the children, her housekeeping, and shopping. (Servants, needless to say, are unknown.) When the husband returns, he is generally tired, both from his work and his traveling. (Three hours a day is not uncommon; perhaps the most widespread dream of the men is a job nearer to the community, and they often make earnest efforts to find it.) Often by the time the husband returns the children are ready for bed. The husband helps put them to bed; as they grow older, they are allowed to stay up later. Then he and his wife eat their supper and wash the dishes. By 10:00 P.M. most lights are out.

For the women this is a long, monotonous daily proposition. Generally the men, once home, do not want to leave. They want to "relax" or "improve the property"—putter around the lawn or shrubbery. However, the women want a "change." Thus, groups of women often go to the movies together.

Usually both husband and wife are involved in some group activity and have meetings to go to. A frequent complaint is: "We never get time to see each other"; or, "We merely pass coming and going." On the one occasion when I was refused an interview, the husband said, "Gee, I'd like to help, but I so seldom get a chance to see my wife for a whole evening. . . . I'd rather not have the interruption."

Many couples credit television, which simultaneously eased baby-sitting, entertainment, and financial problems, with having brought them closer. Their favorites are comedy shows, especially those about young couples, such as *I Love Lucy*. Though often contemptuous of many programs, they speak of TV gratefully as "something we can share," as "bringing the romance back." Some even credit it with having "saved our marriage." One wife said: "Until we got that TV set, I thought my husband had forgotten how to neck."

These are the first towns in America where the impact of TV is so concentrated that it literally affects everyone's life. Organizations dare not hold meetings at hours when popular shows are on. In addition, it tends to bind people together, giving the whole community a common experience.

———— • ————

The Coffee Klatsch is an institution everywhere. A kind of floating, day-long talkfest, shifting from house to house, it has developed among young women to help fill their need for adult conversation and companionship. The conversation is strictly chit-chat. One woman described is as "Just small talk . . . about what's new . . . about whose kid is sick . . . and then about who is apt to get sick." Yet many women complain there is "too much talk," and some are very critical of the gregariousness.

New Lifestyles

When people moved into these communities, they shed many of their parents' and their home-town customs. For instance, slacks or shorts are standard wear for both men and women at all times, including trips to the shopping center. Visiting grandparents invariably are shocked and whisper: "Why, nobody dresses around here!". . .

Gone also are most rituals and ceremonies. If you want to know someone, you introduce yourself; there is no waiting for the "right people." You "drop in" without phoning. If you have an idea that will solve some problem, you immediately call up everybody concerned. One result is that, generally speaking, there is less lag than elsewhere between an idea and "getting something done," which may be anything from organizing a dance to getting a stop sign for your corner.

———— • ————

The attitude toward pregnancy is unusually casual. Because it is so common, pregnancy is regarded more objectively and referred to in terms that would seem outlandish in older communities. It is often called "our major industry"; or someone will say, "That's the Levittown Look," or "It must be the water; you don't see any men around.". . .

———— • ————

A marked feeling of transience pervades everything from shopping to friendships. This feeling reflects both optimism and uncertainty, and it encourages a tendency to seek expedient solutions. For instance, the question of whether or not one plans to spend his life there is shunted aside—optimistically. This has serious effects on school and town government problems.

The uncertainty stems, as one young salesman expressed it, from the fact that "you just don't know—whether you'll make the grade, whether the company will transfer you, whether you'll be getting along with your wife five years from now, whether the neighbors will move out and monsters will move in. So you hesitate to sink deep roots." In general, optimism prevails over uncertainty. Many—a majority, I would say—consider this merely their "first" house. They insist that they are young, and they confidently look forward to owning a $15,000 to $20,000 house some day.

Interestingly, while most look upon their present house as a "temporary deal," because "under the GI-Bill owning is cheaper than renting," the most orthodox and conservative views prevail concerning property and home ownership. There is more talk about property values than you would hear in older towns and much effort is put into "making the place look like something." This may mean the addition of fences, garage, patio, etc. A standard proud comment is: "We could walk out of this place with $1,000 profit tomorrow."

———— • ————

Actual transience is high. Business transfers and

increased incomes are its major causes. As a result, there is a flourishing business in the resale of houses. In one community where I interviewed twelve families in one block three years ago, all but four have since moved. From the remaining families I learned that the removals had nearly all been due to increased incomes which permitted more expensive homes. Others had moved to cut commuting time or because of company transfers. Unfortunately, no over-all statistics on transience exist.

———— • ————

"The people who live in these communities are for the most part enthusiastic about them."

———— • ————

The replacements for departed families are often older, 45 to 50 being the average age of the men. Their goal is the $7,000 to $12,000 house. More certain of what they can and will do, they are less anxious about "success," and financially not so hard pressed. Having resided in older towns, they like these new communities because of their friendliness and optimism. "The older towns are dead," said one small business man who is typical of this group.

Usually these "second generation" people have teen-age children and, in interviews, they emphasized the absence of "bad neighborhoods" and ample play areas as reasons for moving. Many also liked the idea that economically everyone is in the same class. One father, a skilled aviation worker, said, "Where we used to live we had both rich and very poor. Our girls were caught in the middle because the rich kids dressed better and hung out together, and the poor kids dressed poorer and hung out together. They were nobody's friend, while here they are everybody's friend. I'd say they are happier than they ever were."

———— • ————

Except for Park Forest, none of the communities I visited has a local police force. Yet crime can hardly be said to exist—probably the most spectacular aspect of these new towns. In one community with 15,000 people the crime record amounted, in two years to 6 burglary cases, 35 larceny cases, 13 assault cases (husband-wife rows), and 6 disorderly conduct cases. Typically, the communities are patrolled by existing county and township police, who report their only major problems are traffic and lost children.

Crime in Suburbia

Even Levittown, with 70,000 people not far from New York's turbulent, scheming underworld, has vir-

tually no crime. According to the Nassau County police, who studied one year's record, it had no murders, robberies, or auto thefts during that period; an average city of that size during the same period would have had 4 murders, 3 robberies, and 149 auto thefts.

Levittown had 3 assault cases, 16 burglaries, and 200 larceny cases while comparable cities averaged 73 assault cases, 362 burglaries, and 942 larcenies. Larceny in Levittown was mainly bicycle stealing. (Since these statistics were gathered, the FBI has caught a Levittowner who planned a payroll robbery and a young mother, later adjudged insane, has asphyxiated her two small children.)

Police attribute this lack of crime to the fact that nearly all the men were honorably discharged from the armed services and subjected to a credit screening. This, they say, "eliminated the criminal element and riff-raff." Some police officials included the absence of slums and disreputable hang-outs as causes. Personally, I felt many more factors were involved, including the absence of real poverty; the strong ties of family, religious, and organizational activities; steady employment; and the absence of a restrictive, frustrating social structure.

Family Economics

Every family operates, or tries to operate, under a budget plan. Most families report their living standards have been raised by moving into the community. There is almost constant self-scolding because living costs outrun the budget. The shining goal: economic security. The word "success" is on everyone's lips and "successful people" are those who advance economically.

———— • ————

Most families report it costs a minimum of between $100 and $150 a month to live in these communities. While the rent or mortgage payment may come to only $65 or $75 monthly, other expenses—commuting, garbage, water, utilities—push the total much higher. In addition, distances to the shopping center and commuting stations virtually require a car and all its expenses.

If the axiom, "a week's pay for a month's rent," is applied, it is obvious that many families are barely making ends meet and some are having real difficulty. Typical comments on their economic situation: "We're just like everyone else here—broke," or, "We're all in the same boat, economically. Just getting by, I'd say." I estimated the average man's income from his regular job to be under $100 a week.

Where screening was based only on ability to make the down payment rather than ability to pay, you often find a sizable number of men seeking supplementary work: weekend clerking in stores; finishing attics; door-to-door selling. In one community a man who acts as a clearing house for jobs told me: "I'd say that 50 per cent of these people are running on their nerve. One winter of sickness would knock them out." A great number of women whose children have reached school age seek work, but it is hard to find and pays less than they were used to earning in the city. I talked to a night taxi-driver in one community whose job stemmed from his children's illnesses. This supplementary work left him only six hours between jobs. It was rough, he admitted, ". . . but I figure it's worth it to have the kids here. I couldn't stand taking them back to the city. I'll get these bills cleaned up yet."

In addition, the economic pinch is relieved in some families by subsidies from parents. "There are a fair percentage of them who are still leaning on Mama and Papa," one store proprietor said. "I know because I cash their checks." In other cases the pressure is relieved by "doubling up." This seldom means two young families in one house; usually the "doubling up" is with in-laws, who share expenses. Technically this produces substandard housing; the people involved regard this as nonsense. No stigma is attached to the practice and many women expressed the wish to have their parents live with them, mainly because they wanted companionship and guidance on child-raising. . . .

Optimism

Both the individual and the community face these economic stresses with a powerful, deep-seated optimism based on the conviction that they are just starting their careers. The men sometimes say with a grim: "After all, this is only the first wife, first car, first house, first kids—wait till we get going." Though, in the long run, they measure success in economic terms, people are frank about "being broke" and there is no stigma attached to it by anyone, including families with larger incomes. "Money just doesn't cut any ice around here," said one young engineer whose earnings put him in the $8,000-a-year class. "We've all been broke at one time or another. The important thing is, nobody expects to stay broke.". . .

———————— • ————————

Socially, the outstanding characteristic of these people is their friendliness, warmth, and lack of pretentious snobbery. Outgoing and buoyant, they are quick to recognize common problems and the need for co-operation, one does not find the indifference, coldness, and "closed doors" of a long-established community. There is much casual "dropping in" and visiting from house to house which results in the sharing of many problems and pleasures. Often the discussion of a few women over supper plans will end up with four or five families eating together. This may then lead to "fun," which may be anything from cards to "just talk" or "everybody trying to roller-skate, acting like a bunch of kids." Nobody goes "out" often. Many report that, as a result of this pattern of living, they "drink more often but get high less" than they used to. Drinking, it seemed to me, had become much more of a social amenity and less of an emotional safety valve than it is elsewhere.

Suburban Friendliness

This generalized, informal friendliness assumes so many forms that it is a very real part of everyone's life, replacing the thousand-skeined social structure of older American towns. It explains why the people who live in these communities are for the most part enthusiastic about them. "Here, for the first time in my life," one salesman said, "I don't have to worry about my family when on the road. Here at least a dozen families are constantly in touch with them and ready to help if anything goes wrong, whether it's the car, the oil heater, or one of the kids getting sick. In Pittsburgh I had to rely on scattered relatives who weren't in touch with my family more than once a week."

This is the big cushion which, while making life more enjoyable, protects the inhabitants of the new suburbs and solves their minor problems. It absorbs innumerable small transportation needs, puts up TV aerials, repairs cars, finishes attics, and carries the load of sudden emergencies. Nothing in these communities, to me, is more impressive than this uniform pattern of casual but warm friendliness and co-operation.

VIEWPOINT 34B

The Suburbs: The New American Nightmare (1956)

John C. Keats (b. 1920)

Eighty-five percent of the 13 million homes built in the United States during the 1950s were in the suburbs—the areas just outside established towns and cities. These fast-growing regions were the subject of much analysis—and criticism—by sociologists and others studying American ways of life. The following viewpoint, excerpted from the 1956 book *The Crack in the Picture Window* by writer and social critic John C. Keats, provides a sharply satirical look at suburban life in the 1950s. A former newspaper reporter, Keats has also written biographies of Howard Hughes and Dorothy Parker, and has contributed articles to various magazines, including *Esquire*.

How important have federal government programs been to the growth of the suburbs, according to Keats? Why are suburbs continuing to be built, in his view? How do the opinions of both Keats and of sociologist Harold Mendelsohn (quoted in this viewpoint) concerning suburban neighborliness differ from the views expressed by Harry Henderson, author of the opposing viewpoint?

For literally nothing down—other than a simple two per cent and a promise to pay, and pay, and pay until the end of your life—you too . . . can find a box of your own in one of the fresh-air slums we're building around the edges of America's cities. There's room for all in any price range, for even while you read this, whole square miles of identical boxes are spreading like gangrene throughout New England, across the Denver prairie, around Los Angeles, Chicago, Washington, New York, Miami— everywhere. In any one of these new neighborhoods, be it in Hartford or Philadelphia, you can be certain all other houses will be precisely like yours, inhabited by people whose age, income, number of children, problems, habits, conversation, dress, possessions and perhaps even blood type are also precisely like yours. In any one of these neighborhoods it is possible to make enemies of the folks next door with unbelievable speed. If you buy a small house, you are assured your children will leave you perhaps even sooner than they should, for at once they will learn never to associate home with pleasure. In short, ladies and gentlemen, we offer here for your inspection facts relative to today's housing developments— developments conceived in error, nurtured by greed, corroding everything they touch. They destroy established cities and trade patterns, pose dangerous problems for the areas they invade, and actually drive mad myriads of housewives shut up in them.

These facts are well known to responsible economists, sociologists, psychiatrists, city managers and bankers, and certainly must be suspected by the people who live in the suburban developments, yet there's no end in sight to the construction. Indeed, Washington's planners exult whenever a contractor vomits up five thousand new houses on a rural tract that might better have remained in hay, for they see in this little besides thousands of new sales of labor, goods and services. Jobs open for an army of bulldozer operators, carpenters, plasterers, plumbers, electricians, well-diggers, bricklayers, truck drivers, foremen and day laborers. Then come the new householders, followed by their needs. A shopping center and supermarket are hurriedly built, and into this pours another army of clerical and sales personnel, butchers, bakers, janitors, auto dealers, restaurateurs, waitresses, door-to-door salesmen, mail carriers, rookie cops, firemen, schoolteachers, medicine men of various degrees—the whole ruck and stew of civilization's auxiliaries. Thus with every new development, jobs are born, money is earned, money is spent, and pretty soon everyone can afford a new television set, and Washington calls this prosperity.

That such prosperity is entirely material, possibly temporary and perhaps even illusory, causes little concern at present. . . .

The GI Bill

Let's step back in time to consider the history of today's housing developments:

The first good intentions which pave our modern Via Dolorosa were laid at war's end. Conscious of the fact that some 13,000,000 young men risked disfigurement, dismemberment and death in circumstances not of their choosing, a grateful nation decided to show its appreciation to the survivors. The GI Bill of Rights was enacted, and one of the articles provided an incentive for bankers to assume low-interest mortgages on houses purchased by veterans. The deal was, the bankers could recover a certain guaranteed sum from the government in event of the veteran's default. The real-estate boys read the Bill, looked at one another in happy amazement, and the dry, rasping noise they made rubbing their hands together could have been heard as far away as Tawi Tawi. Immediately, thanks to modern advertising, movable type, radio, television and other marvels, the absurdity was spread—and is still spread—that the veteran should own his home.

There was never the slightest justification for this nonsense. Never in the last 180 years of United States history was there an indication that a young man entering civil life from childhood or war should thereupon buy a house.

Young People Should Be Mobile

It is and has always been the nature of young people to be mobile. Rare indeed is the man whose life is a straight arrow's-flight from the classroom to the job he'll hold until he dies. Many a retiring corporate officer put in his early years driving a bread truck, then had a fling at a little unsuccessful business of his own, then wandered into the door-to-door sale of cemetery lots before catching on at the buttonworks he was one day to direct. Owning property implies a certain permanence—precisely that quality a bright young man should, and does, lack. A young man should be mobile until he finds his proper path. A man with a house is nailed to its floor.

The housing article in the GI Bill, however, opened vast vistas. Not only was there a government guarantee to be had, but there was also land to be sold, and since the veteran had been led both by private and government propaganda to believe he should own his home, the remaining consideration in the hard, practical minds of the real-estate men was how much house could be offered for how little money. Or, to put it in the more usual way, how little house could be offered for how much money. Cost became the sole criterion of the first postwar house, and the first economy was in space.

Tiny Homes

The typical postwar development operator was a man who figured how many houses he could possibly cram onto a piece of land and have the local zoning board hold still for it. Then he whistled up the bulldozers to knock down all the trees, bat the lumps off the terrain, and level the ensuing desolation. Then up went the houses, one after another, all alike, and none of those built immediately after the war had any more floor space than a moderately-priced, two-bedroom apartment. The dining room, the porch, the basement, and in many cases the attic, were dispensed with and disappeared from the American scene. The result was a little box on a cold concrete slab containing two bedrooms, bath, and an eating space the size of a broom closet tucked between the living room and the tiny kitchen. A nine-by-twelve rug spread across the largest room wall to wall, and there was a sheet of plate glass in the living-room wall. That, the builder said, was the picture window. The picture it framed was of the box across the treeless street. The young Americans who moved into these cubicles were not, and are not, to know the gracious dignity of living that their parents knew in the big two- and three-story family houses set well back on grassy lawns off the shady streets of, say, Watertown, New York. For them and their children, there would be only the box on its slab. The Cape Cod Rambler had arrived.

It was inevitable that the development house was looked upon as an expedient by the young purchasers. It was most certainly not the house of their dreams, nor was the ready-made neighborhood a thing to make the soul sing. It was, simply, the only thing available. They had no choice—they couldn't afford to build their house, nor were they given a choice of architecture. Instead, they were offered a choice between a house they didn't much want and the fantastic rents that bobbed to the surface as soon as the real-estate lobby torpedoed rent control. The development house was the only living space on the market priced just within the means of the young veterans.

It is still a maxim with responsible land agents that you should never purchase a home in which you do not intend to dwell for at least ten years. Moreover,

they'll say, a house in which you have no equity cannot be considered an investment. Despite these truths, houses were bought on the assumption they would serve only as brief campsites on life's wilderness trail, and incredibly enough, the government in the past two years has given encouragement to this singular point of view. With government blessing, purchasers are now being advised that buying a new house is like buying a new car. Old one too small for the growing family? Trade your old home in and buy a new one, the government suggests, meanwhile helping the developers to continue their dirty work in order that prosperity's bubble doesn't burst.

The first veterans' developments set a pattern for the builders. They sold the first houses like hotcakes, so they've been making hotcakes ever since. Today's new houses differ from those of 1947 only insofar as the materials are better and the workmen have now mastered their jobs. The basic living problems are unchanged—they're built right in. These problems will remain unchanged unless the whole construction pattern changes; until a housing development becomes something more than just a lot of houses.

Problems of Housing Developments

First of all, a housing development cannot be called a community, for that word implies a balanced society of men, women and children wherein work and pleasure are found and the needs of all the society's members are served. Housing developments offer no employment and as a general rule lack recreational areas, churches, schools, or other cohesive influences.

A second present and future national danger lies in the fact that developments are creating stratified societies of singular monotony in a nation whose triumph to date has depended on its lack of a stratified society, on the diversity of its individuals. Yet today it is possible to drive through the various developments that surround one of our cities and tell at a glance the differing social strata.

Here is the $10,000 development—two bedrooms, low-priced cars, average income $75 a week after taxes, three children, average food budget $25 weekly; jobs vary from bus driver to house painter. Here is the $13,950 house—three bedrooms, available to foremen and successful newspapermen, medium-priced cars, two and a half children per average home; men's shoes cost $12 to $20 at this level. Next is the $17,450 split level, especially designed for split personalities, upper-medium cars; liquor bill is $25 weekly; inmates take fly-now-pay-later air rides to Europe.

The appearance of several square miles of new housing units in a once rural area adjacent to a city normally brings about a violent clash of interests.

The young new householders, conscious only of their unmet needs, are intolerant of the political milieu they've invaded. Indeed, if there was any cohesive force acting on typical development householders, it would be that of hatred. Well might they form a sort of mutual loathing society where the first target of their wrath is the builder, the second, the community around them.

For its part, the invaded community eyes the newcomers with something less than wild enthusiasm. The administrative problems handed a county government by the sudden appearance of several thousand new families are enough to make a strong man blench. And, when the guts of a city are deserted by a middle class that flocks to the suburbs, the tax problems created for the city fathers are even more frightening. . . .

A Lack of True Community

The first and most important fact to realize about housing development neighbors is that they are not really friends. They can never be friends; the best relationship they can achieve with one another is a superficial acquaintance based on service needs. Harold Mendelsohn, American University sociologist, put it thus:

"In housing developments patterns emerge which make for superficial cohesiveness. It is entirely artificial, based on providing mutual conveniences, rather than on a basis of friendship, or on a basis of fundamental needs. A wants a hammer. He borrows one from B. If he is feuding with B, it makes no difference, he'll borrow one from C. D and E get into a mutual baby-sitting agreement. There is a car pool. All these are conveniences, just service needs. A man in a development has no need to socialize with the other men; his socializing takes place in the city where he works. Therefore, development men are apt to nod to one another, or borrow things from one another, and their relationships in borrowing hammers, say, are no deeper than the relationships you have with the man who comes to fix the plumbing in a city apartment. The development women socialize because they can't escape one another—they're always out on the lawns with their children and the children play together and therefore the mothers meet. But most of *their* acquaintance is based on service needs—the borrowed cup of sugar; the spoonful of cornstarch for baby's sore bottom. They merely supply services to one another—the same services a city would normally supply through its stores and delivery services.

"Moreover," Mr. Mendelsohn said, "these people lack a basis of deep friendships with one another. They are too much alike in age, jobs, number of children, and so on. Normally, you make friends where you live, or where you work. If you live in a community of people very much like yourselves, the pressure for making friends is great. But in an homogenous community, no one has anything to offer anyone else. What ideas are expressed? What values formed? What do you give to your neighbor? What can he give you?

"Development people," Mr. Mendelsohn answered himself, "have nothing to gain from one another. There is a great deal of neighboring among the women, but no real friendships emerge, for too-much-alike people have nothing to communicate to each other; no fundamentally different ideas are exchanged.". . .

Suburbs and Children

"In a normal community," Mr. Mendelsohn said nostalgically, "there would be YMCA and church facilities for dances, sports and social life; there would be public libraries—even corner stores. In the modern development the houses are too small for young families. Today's families can't entertain at home now, and when today's children are teen-age, where do you suppose they will hold *their* parties and normal social life? They certainly won't be able to conduct it anywhere in a development that is simply a lot of houses.

---•---

"Today's housing developments . . . destroy established cities and trade patterns, pose dangerous problems for the areas they invade, and actually drive mad myriads of housewives shut up in them."

---•---

"To a sociologist," Mr. Mendelsohn said, "a community is a cohesive entity that supplies essential needs and services to all the people who live in it. In developments, we have already seen that churches are nonexistent or too few; that parks and recreational areas are most often missing. These developments are just bedrooms on the edge of town. What do you suppose will happen when the preschool children in all these places are ten years older? Where will they go, and what will they do? You know perfectly well they will find all their pleasures outside the development.

"Since even the movies are often miles away in the shopping center at the other end of the development, you know the only thing for tomorrow's children will be to borrow the family car. In other words, *all* their recreation will be away from home. There will be no chance for them to associate home with fun. To them, fun will always mean something that happens away from home—away from any sort of parental supervision.

"Not all the features of a development are bad," Mr. Mendelsohn said judiciously. "For one thing, there is no question that the development is a far healthier place to live than the tenement or row house on a dingy, traffic-choked industrial street. Crime rates in the development areas are insignificant at present. Of course, what the crime rate will be ten years from now when the children grow up with no place to meet or play under adult supervision is something else again."

For Further Reading

Scott Donaldson, *The Suburban Myth.* New York: Columbia University Press, 1969.

Robert Fishman, *Bourgeois Utopias: The Rise and Fall of Suburbia.* New York: Basic Books, 1987.

Betty Friedan, *The Feminine Mystique.* New York: Norton, 1963.

Kenneth Jackson, *Crabgrass Frontier: The Suburbanization of the United States.* New York: Oxford University Press, 1985.

J. Ronald Oakley, *God's Country: America in the Fifties.* New York: Dembner Books, 1986.

The Turbulent Sixties

VIEWPOINT 35A

America Should Send a Man to the Moon (1961)

John F. Kennedy (1917–1963)

On October 4, 1957, the Soviet Union launched *Sputnik I,* the world's first artificial satellite. The event stunned the American people, who had been largely confident in U.S. technological supremacy over their Cold War rival. Over the next decade and beyond, for reasons both of military strategy and international prestige, the superpowers engaged in a "space race." They competed in developing rocket technology and sending satellites and people into outer space—a competition in which the Soviet Union at first maintained its early lead. On April 12, 1961, Soviet Yuri A. Gagarin became the first man in space. Alan B. Shepard became the first American in space a few weeks later on May 5.

Perhaps the element of the space race that most completely captured the imaginations of Americans was the race to send a person to the moon. The start

Excerpted from John F. Kennedy's speech to the 87th Congress, 2nd sess., May 25, 1961. The complete speech can be found in the June 15, 1961, *Vital Speeches of the Day.*

of America's effort toward this goal can be traced back in part to a speech by President John F. Kennedy to a joint session of Congress on May 25, 1961, excerpts of which appear here. Speaking a few weeks after Shepard's space flight, Kennedy proposes that America commit itself to a manned lunar expedition. Kennedy placed the idea in the context of a deadly serious competition with the "adversaries of freedom" (the Soviet Union and other communist nations) for world power and influence. Kennedy succeeded in getting congressional approval for the lunar project; eight years and $24 billion later, American astronaut Neil Armstrong became the first man to set foot on the moon.

How does Kennedy characterize the enemies of America? Why is space exploration so important for the lives of Americans, according to Kennedy?

Mr. Speaker, Mr. Vice President, my copartners in Government, and ladies and gentlemen: The Constitution imposes upon me the obligation to from time to time give to the Congress information on the state of the Union. While this has traditionally been interpreted as an annual affair, this tradition has been broken in extraordinary times.

These are extraordinary times. We face an extraordinary challenge. But our strength as well as our convictions have imposed upon this Nation the role of leader in freedom's cause. We face opportunities and adversaries that do not wait for annual addresses or fiscal years. This Nation is engaged in a long and exacting test for the future of freedom—a test which may well continue for decades to come. Our strength as well as our convictions have imposed upon this Nation the role of leader in freedom's cause.

We Stand for Freedom

No role in history could be more difficult or more important. It is not a negative or defensive role—it is a great positive adventure. We stand for freedom. That is our conviction for ourselves, that is our only commitment to others. No friend, no neutral, and no adversary should think otherwise. We are not against any man, or any nation, or any system, except as it is hostile to freedom. Nor am I here to present a new military doctrine bearing any one name or aimed at any one area. I am here to promote the freedom doctrine.

The great battleground for the defense and expansion of freedom today is the whole southern half of the globe—Asia, Latin America, Africa, and the Middle East—the lands of rising peoples. Their revolution, the greatest in human history, is one of peace and hope for freedom and equality, for order and independence. They seek an end, they seek a beginning. And theirs is a revolution which we would support regardless of the cold war, and regardless of which political or economic route they choose to freedom.

Adversaries of Freedom

For the adversaries of freedom did not create this revolution; nor did they create the conditions which compel it. But they are seeking to ride the crest of its wave, to capture it for themselves.

Yet their aggression is more often concealed than open. They have fired no missiles; and their troops are seldom seen. They send arms, agitators, aid, technicians and propaganda to every troubled area. But where the fighting is required, it is usually done by others, by guerrillas striking at night, by assassins striking alone, assassins who have taken the lives of 4,000 civil officers in the last 12 months in Vietnam, by subversives and saboteurs and insurrectionists, who in some cases control whole areas inside of independent nations.

They possess a powerful intercontinental striking force, large forces for conventional war, a well-trained underground in nearly every country, the power to conscript talent and manpower for any purpose, the capacity for quick decisions, a closed society without dissent or free information, and long experience in the techniques of violence and subversion. They make the most of their scientific successes, their economic progress and their pose as a foe of colonialism and friend of popular revolution. They prey on unstable or unpopular governments, unsealed or unknown boundaries, unfilled hopes, convulsive change, massive poverty, illiteracy, unrest and frustration.

---•---

"I believe that this Nation should commit itself to achieving the goal, before this decade is out, of landing a man on the moon and returning him safely to earth."

---•---

With these formidable weapons, the adversaries of freedom plan to consolidate their territory, to exploit, to control, and finally to destroy the hopes of the world's newest nations, and they have ambition to do it before the end of this decade. It is a contest of will and purpose as well as force and violence, a battle for minds and souls as well as lives and territory. In that contest we cannot stand aside. . . .

There is no single simple policy with which to meet this challenge. Experience has taught us that no one nation has the power or the wisdom to solve all the problems of the world or manage all its revolutionary tides; that extending our commitments does not always increase our security; that any initiative carries with it the risk of temporary defeat; that nuclear weapons cannot prevent subversion; that no free peoples can be kept free without will and energy of their own; and that no two nations or situations are exactly alike.

Yet there is much we can do and must do. The proposals I bring before you today are numerous and varied. They arise from the host of special opportunities and dangers which have become increasingly clear in recent months. Taken together, I believe that they mark another step forward in our effort as a people. Taken together they will help advance our own progress, encourage our friends, and strengthen the opportunities for freedom and peace. I am here to ask the help of this Congress for freedom and peace. I am here to ask the help of this Congress and the Nation in approving these necessary measures. . . .

The Importance of Space

If we are to win the battle that is going on around the world between freedom and tyranny, if we are to win the battle for men's minds, the dramatic achievements in space which occurred in recent weeks should have made clear to us all, as did the sputnik in 1957, the impact of this adventure on the minds of men everywhere who are attempting to make a determination of which road they should take. Since early in my term our efforts in space have been under review. With the advice of the Vice President, who is Chairman of the National Space Council, we have examined where we are strong and where we are not, where we may succeed and where we may not. Now it is time to take longer strides—time for a great new American enterprise—time for this Nation to take a clearly leading role in space achievement which in many ways may hold the key to our future on earth.

I believe we possess all the resources and all the talents necessary. But the facts of the matter are that we have never made the national decisions or marshaled the national resources required for such leadership. We have never specified long-range goals on an urgent time schedule, or managed our resources and our time so as to insure their fulfillment.

Recognizing the head start obtained by the Soviets with their large rocket engines, which gives them many months of leadtime, and recognizing the likelihood that they will exploit this lead for some time to come in still more impressive successes, we nevertheless are required to make new efforts on our own. For while we cannot guarantee that we shall one day be first, we can guarantee that any failure to make this effort will find us last. We take an additional risk by making it in full view of the world—but as shown by the feat of Astronaut [Alan B.] Shepard, this very risk enhances our stature when we are successful. But this is not merely a race. Space is open to us now; and our eagerness to share its meaning is not governed by the efforts of others. We go into space because whatever mankind must undertake, freemen must fully share.

National Goals

I therefore ask the Congress, above and beyond the increases I have earlier requested for space activities, to provide the funds which are needed to meet the following national goals:

First, I believe that this Nation should commit itself to achieving the goal, before this decade is out, of landing a man on the moon and returning him safely to earth. No single space project in this period will be more exciting, or more impressive to mankind, or more important for the long-range exploration of space; and none will be so difficult or expensive to accomplish. Including necessary supporting research, this objective will require an additional $531 million this year and still higher sums in the future. We propose to accelerate development of the appropriate lunar spacecraft. We propose to develop alternate liquid and solid fuel boosters much larger than any now being developed, until certain which is superior. We propose additional funds for other engine development and for unmanned explorations—explorations which are particularly important for one purpose which this Nation will never overlook; the survival of the man who first makes this daring flight. But in a very real sense, it will not be one man going to the moon—we make this judgment affirmatively—it will be an entire nation. For all of us must work to put him there.

Other Space Goals

Second, an additional $23 million, together with $7 million already available, will accelerate development of the ROVER nuclear rocket. This is a technological enterprise in which we are well on the way to striking progress, and which gives promise of some day providing a means for even more exciting and ambitious exploration of space, perhaps beyond the moon, perhaps to the very ends of the solar system itself.

Third, an additional $50 million will make the most of our present leadership by accelerating the use of space satellites for worldwide communications. When we have put into space a system that will enable people in remote areas of the earth to exchange messages, hold conversations, and eventually see television programs, we will have achieved a success as beneficial as it will be striking.

Fourth, an additional $75 million—of which $53 million is for the Weather Bureau—will help give us at the earliest possible time a satellite system for worldwide weather observation. Such a system will be of inestimable commercial and scientific value; and the information it provides will be made freely available to all the nations of the world.

Let it be clear—and this is a judgment which the Members of the Congress must finally make—let it be clear that I am asking the Congress and the country to accept a firm commitment to a new course of action—a course which will last for many years and carry very heavy costs, $531 million in the fiscal year 1962 and an estimated $7–9 billion additional over the next five years. If we are to go only halfway, or reduce our sights in the face of difficulty, in my judgment it would be better not to go at all. This is a choice which this country must make, and I am confident that under the leadership of the Space committees of the Congress and the appropriations committees you will consider the matter carefully. It is a most important decision that we make as a nation; but all of you have lived though the last 4 years and have seen the significance of space and the adventures in space, and no one can predict with certainty what the ultimate meaning will be of the mastery of space. I believe we should go to the moon. But I think every citizen of this country as well as the Members of the Congress should consider the matter carefully in their judgment, to which we have given attention over many weeks and months, as it is a heavy burden; and there is no sense in agreeing, or desiring, that the United States take an affirmative position in outer space unless we are prepared to do the work and bear the burdens to make it successful. If we are not, we should decide today.

A National Commitment

Let me stress also that more money alone will not do the job. This decision demands a major national commitment of scientific and technical manpower, material and facilities, and the possibility of their diversion from other important activities where they are already thinly spread. It means a degree of dedication, organization, and discipline which have not always characterized our research and development efforts. It means we cannot afford undue work stoppages, inflated costs of material or talent, wasteful interagency rivalries, or a high turnover of key personnel.

New objectives and new money cannot solve these problems. They could, in fact, aggravate them further—unless every scientist, every engineer, every serviceman, every technician, contractor, and civil servant involved gives his personal pledge that this Nation will move forward, with the full speed of freedom, in the exciting adventure of space.

VIEWPOINT 35B

America's Race to the Moon Is Misguided (1962)

Carl Dreher (1896–1976)

Following John F. Kennedy's 1961 proposal that America send a man to the moon within the decade, the National Aeronautics and Space Administration (NASA) began plans for a manned lunar expedition. Annual government appropriations for space exploration rose to $5 billion during the Kennedy administration. Many scientists and others questioned the wisdom of devoting so many national resources to the "space race" with the Soviet Union to land a man on the moon. Several concerns are expressed in the following viewpoint, taken from an article by Carl Dreher, science editor of the *Nation* magazine from 1961 to 1975. In the article, written for the *Nation* in 1962, Dreher notes such objections to a manned lunar expedition as excessive costs, the risks to astronauts, and the disadvantages of pursuing Cold War competition instead of international cooperation in the exploration of space.

Why is Dreher skeptical of the "cries of anguish" made over the Soviet Union's lead in space? How much does he estimate the cost of a moon landing to be? In what areas does Dreher believe international space cooperation is most likely to develop?

Before the [Soviet] Vostok III and IV flights, some prominent scientists and politicians were expressing misgivings about the cost of American participation in the race to the moon. The rising volume of protest was drowned out by the cries of anguish over the manifest Soviet lead. Most of this clamor was quite baldly inspired by partisan and commercial considerations, and since the earlier criticism had and still has a solid technological basis, no doubt it will be voiced anew. Those who say what they think, rather than what the Pentagon and the aerospace industry would like them to say, will be helping to safeguard the lives of our astronauts, which are endangered by energetic space promoters like Vice President Lyndon Johnson, who incessantly warns us that "our future as a nation is at stake," and that "we dare not lose."

In the first place, we may lose even if we commit everything we have: neither men nor money will necessarily overcome a late start. In the second place, why don't we dare? The moon race has little to

Carl Dreher, ""Wrong Way to the Moon," *The Nation*, September 15, 1962. Reprinted with permission of *The Nation* magazine, ©The Nation Company, L.P.

do with military power at the present time and, the Air Force and its Congressional reserve generals to the contrary, may never assume decisive military importance. A space war is much more likely to be fought in earth orbit. We cannot, then, be overwhelmed by a Soviet victory in the lunar sweepstakes. Nor has the breakneck effort now in the whooping-up stage anything to do with our industrial and agricultural capacity and our ability to aid other nations; rather, it detracts from these assets. And they are assets in that older race against hunger and disease; the sick and hungry are not interested in the moon, but in food and medicine. As for the things of the spirit, if our national self-respect is on such a shaky basis that it cannot survive one more Russian triumph in space, we are in a bad way indeed. The Russians launched the first satellite and we felt somewhat humiliated, yet here we are, five years later, still grappling with them and causing them as many worries as they cause us.

Aside from the extravagant and juvenile character of these alarums, their authors ignore the fact that a premature moon landing, followed by the death of the astronauts on the moon or subsequently in space, would not enhance national prestige. This is a risk for the Soviets as well as for us. The more sanguine contestant may fail; the more wary one may wait, learn from the other's disasters and succeed. That is, indeed, a likely denouement, for the lunar problem is one of enormous difficulty. Hans Thirring, the noted Austrian physicist, has likened it to the leveling of the Rocky Mountains. If the first attempts succeed, it will be little short of a miracle.

On the side of moderation there are some impressive names and arguments. Already in December, 1960, when plans and budgets were still relatively modest (and they will seem minuscule in another year), Dr. James R. Killian, chairman of the M.I.T. Corporation and President Eisenhower's first scientific adviser in the post-sputnik era, said, "Will several billion dollars a year additional for enhancing the quality of education not do more for the future of the United States and its position in the world than several billions a year additional for man in space?" More recently, General Eisenhower has inveighed against what he called "a mad effort to win a stunt race," which it is, and "a great boondoggle," which is rather an oversimplification. More conversant with the technological realities, Dr. Lee DuBridge, whose California Institute of Technology manages the Jet Propulsion Laboratory for the National Aeronautics and Space Administration [NASA], has referred to "space idiots" and shown that the arguments for a military crash program in space are fallacious. Dr. George B. Kistiakowsky, another scientific adviser to President Eisenhower, Dr. James Van Allen, Dr.

Edward U. Condon and Senator William Proxmire have reasoned to much the same effect.

None of these critics can be brushed off, but perhaps the most cogent evaluation has been provided by Dr. Warren Weaver, former president of the American Association for the Advancement of Science and one of the most highly respected of scientists, in the *Saturday Review* of August 4 [1962]. Assuming that it would cost the United States $30 billion to put a man on the moon, Dr. Weaver pointed out that this would give a 10 per cent raise in salary to every teacher in the country over a ten-year period, give $10 million each to 200 of the best small colleges, finance seven-year scholarships (freshman through Ph.D.) for 50,000 new scientists and engineers, contribute $200 million each toward the creation of ten new medical schools, build and largely endow complete universities for all fifty-three of the nations added to the United Nations since its founding, create three more Rockefeller Foundations and still have $100 million left over to popularize science, which bestrides us like a colossus and of whose spirit, principles and procedures probably not one American in a hundred has the faintest conception.

Costs of the Space Race

We have got so used to throwing around billions that we no longer comprehend what a billion means in human terms, but even these comparisons fall far short of the actuality. There is no assurance that the moon operation will come in at $30 billion; all such forecasts have turned out to be low, and this one is little more than a guess. Before the House Appropriations Subcommittee, NASA Deputy Administrator Robert C. Seamans, Jr., estimated the agency would require $50–60 billion over the next ten years. The June [1962] *Fortune* put the cost of the space effort at about $20 billion *annually* by 1970 and calculated that by that time the United States will have spent $75–100 billion on space activities, while missiles will have accounted for another $50 billion. No downtrend in NASA's spending is expected after the moon has been conquered; races to Mars and Venus are planned next. And of course any slackening in the missile and nuclear bomb races would be over the dead bodies of thousands of admirals, generals, veterans, munition manufacturers, labor leaders and other dedicated patriots, aided by [Soviet] Marshal Rodion Y. Malinovsky who, after Major [Andrian G.] Nikolayev and Lieut. Col. [Pavel P.] Popovich landed [on earth following successful orbital flights], rubbed it in with the admonition: "Let our enemies know what techniques and what soldiers our Soviet power disposes of."

The monetary argument does carry some weight and should continue to be pressed, but it does not follow that because the money could be put to good use here below there will be a popular revulsion against shooting it off into space. The moon race, as Dr. Condon has pointed out, is a kind of lunar Olympic game, exciting to both Russians and Americans and providing a much-needed effervescence for millions of drab lives. The astronauts have largely supplanted movie stars and ordinary athletes as popular heroes.

Endangering Lives

Instead of talking only about money, therefore, we should be talking of ways to spare as many of these attractive young men as possible, rather than offering them as a human sacrifice on the altar of nationalistic passions. There will be fatalities in any event, but we cannot condemn the moon project on that account. There is nothing particularly admirable about dying in bed. The appeal, if it is to be effective, must be based on the fact that astronauts will die unnecessarily and, by accelerating the moon race, we shall be accessories to a crime.

Of this there can be no doubt in the mind of anyone who is willing to make an honest appraisal. The moon program is in a state of flux bordering on confusion. Up to a few months ago NASA seemed committed to the method of direct ascent. A single heavy vehicle would be put into a moon trajectory by an enormous rocket, on arrival would decelerate itself by proportionately powerful retro-rocket action, land, stay a while, then take off with another massive spurt of rocket power for the trip home. When it was realized that a booster large enough for this brute-force method could not be built until the 1970s, if then, the planners turned to earth orbit rendezvous and coupling—sending the astronauts and the moon vehicle, or the fuel, into earth orbit in separate packages and connecting them at an absolute speed of some 18,000 miles per hour and a differential speed of about a foot per second.

Although rendezvous and coupling is an untried procedure, a mishap in earth orbit would not necessarily be fatal. The man-carrying vehicle might be able to re-enter, or other vehicles might be orbited rapidly for rescue operations. But then, from earth-orbit planning, NASA switched to lunar rendezvous and coupling. This involves sending a duplex vehicle from the earth into moon orbit and dropping a part of the assembly with two men to the moon, while one man stays with the main vehicle. The ferry, or "bug," returns to lunar orbit for rendezvous with the mother ship, couples to it, the two lunar explorers go back into the main cabin, the bug is jettisoned, and the three astronauts return to earth in the remaining unit.

All the modes of getting to the moon (and getting back) must give the experienced engineer the shivers, but the lunar rendezvous technique seems the most perilous of all. The juncture must be accomplished hundreds of thousands of miles from earth, with very little chance of survival if something should go wrong. The rapid transition from direct ascent to earth orbit to lunar orbit also raises a question. Does it represent technological progress, or are the planners merely jumping from one tour de force to another?

Some of the NASA engineers contend that lunar rendezvous and coupling is not only the fastest and cheapest method, but the one most likely to succeed. It is true that takeoff from the moon will be in a relatively light vehicle, in an environment where gravity is only one-sixth that of the earth, and the "bug" may approach the mother ship at a relatively low speed—only about one mile per second. But there will still be the risk of takeoff from a probably unfavorable surface and topography and the subsequent problems of coupling will be extremely critical.

Just when these matters are being debated in NASA's conference rooms, the Department of Defense has adopted a policy of restrictions on information based on the "need to know" principle. Tight secrecy is likely to spread to NASA, if it has not already done so. This would be a disservice to all concerned. Scientists and engineers inside and outside the government should be able to obtain the facts on which to base an opinion, and to criticize the conclusions reached by the insiders if they wish. Above all, safety, not speed, should be the overriding consideration. James E. Webb, Lyndon Johnson's choice as NASA administrator, may deny that there is a lunar race, but of course there is one and this fact alone may influence the judgment of the teams inside the agency whose members are making crucial decisions that will affect not only their own careers, but decide the fate of the astronauts. The more publicity there is, the better the latter's chances. The scientists who have spoken out against the general aspects of the project as it is being conducted might well have something to say on the technical decisions as well.

Another direction in which the risks of the lunar venture can be reduced is through cooperation between the contestants. Since, no matter what experiments precede the initial attempts to land on and escape from the moon, the odds will be against the early explorers, one would think that the two sides would at least exchange views on rescue techniques and perhaps work out a plan for common utilization of rescue facilities. They could still compete, but must it be a competition to the death? After the Nikolayev-Popovich flights the director of Britain's radio-astronomy and satellite-tracking station at Jodrell Bank, Sir Bernard Lovell, remarked, "More than ever one is appalled by the foolishness of these two countries attempting the moon problem in competition. After all, the common problem is the exploration of space and the manned conquest of the solar system." The common problem, unhappily, is subordinate to the separate problem of the superpowers, which is to do each other in by whatever means come to hand. Space may be infinite, but in the minds of the diplomats and militarists it is compressed into just one more counter in the war game. They brush off advice of the sort offered by Sir Bernard, just as they frustrate the attempts of the neutrals to get them to stop nuclear testing. They are perfectly ready to sacrifice the astronauts, their own lionized fellow countrymen, to national ambition, and in the fullness of their masculinity and patriotism the astronauts are willing and eager to take their chances.

———————— • ————————

"If our national self-respect is on such a shaky basis that it cannot survive one more Russian triumph in space, we are in a bad way indeed."

———————— • ————————

This perhaps paints the situation darker than it actually is—but not much, I am afraid. To some extent the governments do realize what is at stake and that if the moon voyagers do not return the governments themselves will not go unscathed. Last March, in a letter to [Soviet] Premier [Nikita] Khrushchev, President Kennedy made a number of cautious proposals for cooperation in space. One called for a satellite weather observation system with the two countries sending their respective satellites into complementary orbits. Also, radio tracking stations might be established in each other's territory, manned by indigenous personnel. Information on developments in space medicine would be exchanged, etc.

Mr. Kennedy's letter was forwarded two days after Mr. Khrushchev sent a congratulatory message on Colonel [John] Glenn's flight [the first orbital flight by an American]. At the same time the twenty-eight-nation U.N. Committee on the Peaceful Uses of Outer Space was meeting in New York and U.S. delegate Francis T. P. Plimpton told the opening session that "there are hopeful prospects of collaboration between my country and the Soviet Union in outer space projects," and Soviet delegate Platon D. Morozov replied in kind.

Mr. Khrushchev, replying to Mr. Kennedy, suggested that space cooperation was linked "in some degree" with the solution of the disarmament problem which, of course, was not, and is not, being solved with notable celerity. Nevertheless, in June,

Dr. Hugh L. Dryden, deputy director of NASA, its top technical administrator from the beginning, and a very solid citizen, met in Geneva with Prof. Anatoly Blagonravov of the Soviet Academy of Science, and the State Department reported that the talks had been "businesslike and useful." Another meeting was to be held, perhaps in Moscow.

Public Oblivious to Dangers

Progress will be at best slow and whenever cold-war tensions are exacerbated will come to a standstill or retrogress. It may be that only after they have broken the necks of a goodly band of their respective heroes, who look so much alike that it is impossible to distinguish them except by their uniforms, the chastened governments will lay aside their lethal antagonisms. Clearly, that time is not yet. But it may come. The sports-minded public has no conception of the difficulties of lunar exploration, and even the heads of governments, with access to expert information but no expertise of their own, tend to be oblivious to the obstacles and disasters that lie ahead. But this will not avert the troubles.

For the present, the prospects of limited cooperation among voluntary bodies, with the sufferance of the governments, are considerably better than for cooperation between the governments themselves. Enlightened scientists and engineers on both sides, as well as their counterparts in the allied and neutral camps, know that the existing status of space research is grossly improvident, that it risks human lives unnecessarily, and that it tends to retard rather than promote progress. Celestial mechanics is the same for Russians and Americans and for all races and nationalities. The two sides are simply duplicating each other's research and in the end arrive at the same techniques and vehicles. Along the way sometimes one will be ahead, sometimes the other, in some particular sector. Just now the Soviets are ahead in boosters and life-support systems, while the United States is ahead in the number and versatility of its unmanned satellites. But, as the race continues, the technological and industrial resources of both will be taxed to the utmost. The moon flight alone threatens to swallow up a significant proportion of the superpowers' resources and to keep the Soviet people, in particular, in a state of permanent poverty. The military technicians of each look jealously on the funding of quasipeaceful space activity and struggle for a better position at the public trough. To the extent that the superpowers find it possible to cooperate, these dangers and burdens may be mitigated. The scientists see this more clearly than any other group and it is the obligation of the big names among them to call attention to it at opportune times.

An International Space Effort

The ultimate, sensible answer would be an international consortium of the industrialized powers in which, it should be noted, the Germans would have to be given a prominent place. Before and during World War II they were the leaders not only in military rocketry but in many phases of theoretical space research. But the prerequisite to anything like this is an end to the cold war.

The scientists, in the meantime, are steering a course between nationalism and the traditional internationalism of their fraternity. As this is written, preparations are under way for the 13th International Astronautical Congress, to be held September 23–29 under the auspices of the International Astronautical Federation. The federation is a nongovernmental, professional organization of astronautical societies in nearly forty nations. It was founded "to encourage international cooperation in this field and specifically for facilitating the exchange of technical information on an international scale in the many disciplines of the astronautics field." The U.S. voting member society is the American Rocket Society, which will probably merge in the next year or two with the Institute of Aerospace Sciences, to form an organization of 40,000 professional members.

The advance program lists technical papers to be delivered by forty-five Americans, nine Russians, five Rumanians, four Bulgarians, three Japanese, three Belgians, two Poles, two Englishmen, and one apiece from Sweden, France, Ireland, South Africa and Israel. In this company the United States is certainly not hiding its light under a bushel. An even more international group will discuss the law of outer space under the auspices of the International Institute of Space Law.

The Congress is being held at Varna, Bulgaria. In all this there is some modest ground for encouragement. The world is not altogether sane, but it is not altogether crazy either. There is room for a continuance of efforts to slow down the moon race and eventually to establish it on a civilized basis.

For Further Reading

William B. Breuer, *Race to the Moon: America's Duel with the Soviets.* Westport, CT: Praeger, 1993.

Amitai Etzioni, *The Moon-Doggle: Domestic and International Implications of the Space Race.* Garden City, NY: Doubleday, 1964.

James N. Giglio, *The Presidency of John F. Kennedy.* Lawrence: University Press of Kansas, 1991.

Walter McDougal, *The Heavens and the Earth: A Political History of the Space Age.* New York: Basic Books, 1985.

Charles A. Murray and Catherine Bly Cox, *Apollo.* New York: Simon and Schuster, 1989.

VIEWPOINT 36A

U.S. Actions in Vietnam Are Justified (1965)

Lyndon B. Johnson (1908–1973)

When Vice President Lyndon B. Johnson became president of the United States upon the assassination of John F. Kennedy in 1963, he inherited the conflict in Vietnam, which remained a dominant issue throughout the five years and two months of his presidency.

Vietnam was an Asian nation that had been under French colonial rule. In 1954 Vietnamese rebel forces led by Ho Chi Minh, a longtime nationalist leader, defeated the French and established a communist government in what became North Vietnam. Determined not to let all of Vietnam become communist, the United States under President Dwight Eisenhower supported a noncommunist regime in what became South Vietnam. Eisenhower pledged to support and defend South Vietnam and sent several hundred military advisers and millions of dollars in economic aid to that country. John F. Kennedy increased the number of U.S. troops in Vietnam to sixteen thousand during his brief presidency. Under Johnson the United States began extensive bombing campaigns against North Vietnam in early 1965 and increased the number of U.S. troops deployed there to 267,000 by 1966, and eventually to a peak of 543,000 in 1969.

As U.S. involvement escalated, the war became an increasingly divisive issue within the nation. In the following viewpoint, taken from an April 7, 1965, speech delivered at Johns Hopkins University, Johnson defends his actions, arguing that communists in Vietnam are being supported by the communist regime in China, and that American involvement is necessary to fight communism in that area of the world.

What American goals and ideals are at stake, according to Johnson? What objectives of U.S. involvement in the Vietnam War does he state? What policies other than war does he propose to help the Vietnamese people?

Tonight Americans and Asians are dying for a world where each people may choose its own path to change.

This is the principle for which our ancestors fought in the valleys of Pennsylvania. It is the principle for which our sons fight tonight in the jungles of

Reprinted from *Public Papers of the Presidents: Lyndon B. Johnson, 1965* (Washington, DC: Government Printing Office, 1966).

Viet-Nam.

Viet-Nam is far away from this quiet campus. We have no territory there, nor do we seek any. The war is dirty and brutal and difficult. And some 400 young men, born into an America that is bursting with opportunity and promise, have ended their lives on Viet-Nam's steaming soil.

Why must we take this painful road?

Why must this Nation hazard its ease, and its interest, and its power for the sake of a people so far away?

Why We Fight

We fight because we must fight if we are to live in a world where every country can shape its own destiny. And only in such a world will our own freedom be finally secure.

This kind of world will never be built by bombs or bullets. Yet the infirmities of man are such that force must often precede reason, and the waste of war, the works of peace.

We wish that this were not so. But we must deal with the world as it is, if it is ever to be as we wish.

The world as it is in Asia is not a serene or peaceful place.

The first reality is that North Viet-Nam has attacked the independent nation of South Viet-Nam. Its object is total conquest.

Of course, some of the people of South Viet-Nam are participating in attack on their own government. But trained men and supplies, orders and arms, flow in a constant stream from north to south. This support is the heartbeat of the war.

And it is a war of unparalleled brutality. Simple farmers are the targets of assassination and kidnapping. Women and children are strangled in the night because their men are loyal to their government. And helpless villages are ravaged by sneak attacks. Large-scale raids are conducted on towns, and terror strikes in the heart of cities.

The confused nature of this conflict cannot mask the fact that it is the new face of an old enemy.

The Threat of China

Over this war—and all Asia—is another reality: the deepening shadow of Communist China. The rulers in Hanoi [the capital of North Vietnam] are urged on by Peking [Beijing, the capital of China]. This is a regime which has destroyed freedom in Tibet, which has attacked India, and has been condemned by the United Nations for aggression in Korea. It is a nation which is helping the forces of violence in almost every continent. The contest in Viet-Nam is part of a wider pattern of aggressive purposes.

Why are these realities our concern? Why are we in South Viet-Nam?

We are there because we have a promise to keep. Since 1954 every American President has offered support to the people of South Viet-Nam. We have helped to build, and we have helped to defend. Thus, over many years, we have made a national pledge to help South Viet-Nam defend its independence.

And I intend to keep that promise.

To dishonor that pledge, to abandon this small and brave nation to its enemies, and to the terror that must follow, would be an unforgivable wrong.

We're also there to strengthen world order. Around the globe, from Berlin to Thailand, are people whose well-being rests, in part, on the belief that they can count on us if they are attacked. To leave Viet-Nam to its fate would shake the confidence of all these people in the value of an American commitment and in the value of America's word. The result would be increased unrest and instability, and even wider war.

Important Stakes

We are also there because there are great stakes in the balance. Let no one think for a moment that retreat from Viet-Nam would bring an end to conflict. The battle would be renewed in one country and then another. The central lesson of our time is that the appetite of aggression is never satisfied. To withdraw from one battlefield means only to prepare for the next. We must say in southeast Asia—as we did in Europe—in the words of the Bible: "Hitherto shalt thou come, but no further."

There are those who say that all our effort there will be futile—that China's power is such that it is bound to dominate all southeast Asia. But there is no end to that argument until all of the nations of Asia are swallowed up.

There are those who wonder why we have a responsibility there. Well, we have it there for the same reason that we have a responsibility for the defense of Europe. World War II was fought in both Europe and Asia, and when it ended we found ourselves with continued responsibility for the defense of freedom.

Our objective is the independence of South Viet-Nam, and its freedom from attack. We want nothing for ourselves—only that the people of South Viet-Nam be allowed to guide their own country in their own way.

We will do everything necessary to reach that objective. And we will do only what is absolutely necessary.

In recent months attacks on South Viet-Nam were stepped up. Thus, it became necessary for us to increase our response and to make attacks by air. This is not a change of purpose. It is a change in what we believe that purpose requires.

We do this in order to slow down an aggression.

We do this to increase the confidence of the brave people of South Viet-Nam who have bravely borne this brutal battle for so many years with so many casualties.

We Will Not Lose

And we do this to convince the leaders of North Viet-Nam—and all who seek to share their conquest—of a very simple fact:

We will not be defeated.

We will not grow tired.

We will not withdraw, either openly or under the cloak of a meaningless agreement.

We know that air attacks alone will not accomplish all of these purposes. But it is our best and prayerful judgment that they are a necessary part of the surest road to peace. . . .

Because we fight for values and we fight for principles, rather than territory or colonies, our patience and our determination are unending.

Once this is clear, then it should also be clear that the only path for reasonable men is the path of peaceful settlement.

Such peace demands an independent South Viet-Nam—securely guaranteed and able to shape its own relationships to all others—free from outside interference—tied to no alliance—a military base for no other country.

These are the essentials of any final settlement.

We will never be second in the search for such a peaceful settlement in Viet-Nam.

There may be many ways to this kind of peace: in discussion or negotiation with the governments concerned; in large groups or in small ones; in the reaffirmation of old agreements or the strengthening with new ones.

———— • ————

"Over this war—and all Asia—is another reality: the deepening shadow of Communist China. . . . The contest in Viet-Nam is part of a wider pattern of aggressive purposes."

———— • ————

We have stated this position over and over again, fifty times and more, to friend and foe alike. And we remain ready, with this purpose, for unconditional discussions. . . .

These countries of southeast Asia are homes for millions of impoverished people. Each day these people rise at dawn and struggle through until the night to wrestle existence from the soil. They are often wracked by disease, plagued by hunger, and death comes at the early age of 40.

Stability and peace do not come easily in such a land. Neither independence nor human dignity will ever be won, though, by arms alone. It also requires the work of peace. The American people have helped generously in times past in these works. Now there must be a much more massive effort to improve the life of man in that conflict-torn corner of our world.

Economic Development

The first step is for the countries of southeast Asia to associate themselves in a greatly expanded cooperative effort for development. We would hope that North Viet-Nam would take its place in the common effort just as soon as peaceful cooperation is possible.

The United Nations is already actively engaged in development in this area. As far back as 1961 I conferred with our authorities in Viet-Nam in connection with their work there. And I would hope tonight that the Secretary General of the United Nations could use the prestige of his great office, and his deep knowledge of Asia, to initiate, as soon as possible, with the countries of that area, a plan for cooperation in increased development.

For our part I will ask the Congress to join in a billion-dollar American investment in this effort as soon as it is under way.

And I would hope that all other industrialized countries, including the Soviet Union, will join in this effort to replace despair with hope, and terror with progress. . . .

I also intend to expand and speed up a program to make available our farm surpluses to assist in feeding and clothing the needy in Asia. We should not allow people to go hungry and wear rags while our own warehouses overflow with an abundance of wheat and corn, rice and cotton.

So I will very shortly name a special team of outstanding, patriotic, distinguished Americans to inaugurate our participation in these programs. This team will be headed by Mr. Eugene Black, the very able former President of the World Bank.

In areas that are still ripped by conflict, of course, development will not be easy. Peace will be necessary for final success. But we cannot and must not wait for peace to begin this job. . . .

We often say how impressive power is. But I do not find it impressive at all. The guns and the bombs, the rockets and the warships, are all symbols of human failure. They are necessary symbols. They protect what we cherish. But they are witness to human folly.

A dam built across a great river is impressive.

In the countryside where I was born, and where I live, I have seen the night illuminated, and the kitchens warmed, and the homes heated, where once the cheerless night and the ceaseless cold held sway. And all this happened because electricity came to our area along the humming wires of the REA Electrification of the countryside—yes, that, too, is impressive. . . .

Every night before I turn out the lights to sleep I ask myself this question: Have I done everything that I can do to unite this country? Have I done everything I can to help unite the world, to try to bring peace and hope to all the peoples of the world? Have I done enough?

Ask yourselves that question in your homes—and in this hall tonight. Have we, each of us, all done all we could? Have we done enough?

We Must Choose

We may well be living in the time foretold many years ago when it was said: "I call heaven and earth to record this day against you, that I have set before you life and death, blessing and cursing: therefore choose life, that both thou and thy seed may live."

This generation of the world must choose: destroy or build, kill or aid, hate or understand.

We can do all these things on a scale never dreamed of before.

Well, we will choose life. In so doing we will prevail over the enemies within man, and over the natural enemies of all mankind.

VIEWPOINT 36B

U.S. Actions in Vietnam Are Not Justified (1968)
Young Hum Kim (b. 1920)

Between 1950 and 1975 the conflict in Vietnam cost the United States more than 58,000 lives and $150 billion. As military intervention sharply escalated in the 1960s, peace demonstrations and debates swept the United States. The Vietnam War, like the Korean War of the 1950s, was fought as part of America's Cold War containment policy of opposing the spread of communism (and the influence of communist China and the Soviet Union) throughout the world. Defenders of the Vietnam War justified sending U.S. forces to help prevent South Vietnam from becoming communist, arguing that if such a development were to happen other nations in the

Young Hum Kim, "Toward a Rational View of China: The Vietnam War," in *Struggle Against History*, edited by Neil D. Houghton (New York: Washington Square Press, 1968); ©1968 by Washington Square Press. Reprinted with permission.

area would become communist as well.

Many opponents of the Vietnam conflict began to question this reasoning and other basic assumptions and goals of the Cold War. In the following analysis, Young Hum Kim argues that the reasoning behind U.S. involvement in Vietnam is seriously flawed. Kim states that communism is not a monolithic force that threatens to occupy all of Asia. He further asserts that the North Vietnamese and Vietcong that the American soldiers were fighting were motivated not so much by communism as by nationalistic desires to drive foreigners from their land. Kim advocates that the United States withdraw from Vietnam and open up diplomatic channels with China. Kim is a professor of history and international relations at United States International University in San Diego, California, and the author of several books, including *Twenty Years of Crises: The Cold War Era* and *The War of No Return*.

How does Young Hum Kim's image of China differ from that of President Lyndon B. Johnson (see viewpoint 36A)? What five fallacies lie behind U.S. involvement in Vietnam, according to Kim? What limits does he see for the policy of containment?

I n recent decades the American image of China has changed to one of a monstrous society of human insects, destined to take over the world under the banner of Communism. The American obsessive and groundless fear that the Chinese will devastate the earth with their nuclear bombs and that the surviving Chinese will emerge from atomic ashes like the phoenix to inherit this troubled world is driving the United States to the brink of war with the Chinese through escalation of the war in Vietnam. . . .

Is the United States really on a collision course with the People's Republic of China? If so, how can the United States avoid it? What course of action or policy should the United States take or formulate to rectify the present unhealthy state of affairs?

Some of the guidelines, if not answers, to these crucial questions may be found in the pages of history. A realistic and sober reexamination and reevaluation of some of the fundamental issues and attitudes in United States–Chinese relations in the past two decades may provide helpful clues and insights into the immediate problems confronting the two countries. In formulating a foreign policy, a nation should look back upon the road it has trodden in order to chart a new route for the future.

America and the World After World War II

The end of World War II left the United States in a position to assume unilaterally a stance of "free world leadership." In Europe, Britain, France and

Italy were exhausted. Russia was no longer in that "free world." And Germany, having been put through the wringer of "unconditional surrender," was again supposed not to "come back" within the predictable future. And however that might turn out, Germany was partly under the "joint occupation" of non–"free world" Russia.

So, Washington underwrote the economic and political recovery of Western Europe through the Marshall Plan. Designed to be a military bulwark to contain an imaginary threat of Soviet expansion, the formation of the North Atlantic Treaty Organization followed the Marshall Plan. The extension of power and influence of the United States in Europe was only blocked by the power of the USSR at the direct line of contact.

In the Near East, effectuation of the Truman Doctrine is said to have thwarted Communist subversion and infiltration. In the Middle East, Soviet occupation of part of Iran was abandoned through a combination of factors.

In the Far East, the United States did not encounter much difficulty in filling the military power vacuum left by the fall of the Japanese Empire. The only major obstacle lay in China—a huge land mass of Asia larger in area than the United States with a population of over 600 million, more than three times that of the United States.

Unfortunately, China was torn by a titanic civil war between the Nationalists and the Communists, a situation which presented the United States with four possible alternatives: (1) complete withdrawal from China; (2) military intervention on a major scale to aid the Nationalists to destroy the Communists; (3) efforts to avoid a [continuing] civil war by working for a compromise between the two sides; and (4) wholehearted acceptance of the new Communist China. . . .

At first the United States understandably attempted to influence the course of events in favor of the Nationalists. Later, as the fortunes of war were turning in the Communists' favor, Washington endeavored to establish a Nationalist-Communist coalition government. Failing in this, the United States' dream of a friendly and unified capitalistic China as the basis for Far Eastern stability—and a place for profitable private corporate operations—was shattered.

By the summer of 1949, the Chinese Communists had swept the country and achieved victory. Americans were astounded; it was a frustrating reality for them to admit defeat. Critics called the United States' China policy "a tragic failure" and a "crime.". . .

Vietnam

In Vietnam the United States again faced the problem of making a fateful choice from available alternatives. The domestic situation in South Vietnam in the 1960s was somewhat comparable to that of China in the years immediately following World War II. The [Ngo Dinh] Diem regime, like Chiang Kai-shek's, was autocratic, undemocratic, and oppressive. It did not have a foundation of popular support and had been unable to destroy or check the rising influence and prestige of the Vietcong [communists rebels in South Vietnam].

After the fall of the Diem government, the successive military coups further destroyed all vestiges of political stability in South Vietnam. On the other hand, like the Chinese Communists, the Vietcong steadily increased their power and ultimately controlled two-thirds of the area. They were inspired to the point of fanaticism by the revolutionary zeal of national independence and of liberation from colonial rule. To them, the presence of foreign troops, friendly or otherwise, on their soil symbolized the return of imperialism in the form of "neo colonialism." Against this background the United States determined to pursue the second alternative course—*military intervention on a major scale to assist the Saigon* [capital of South Vietnam] *government and to destroy the Vietcong and their supporters.*

The United States' choice of this alternative seems to have been based upon five possible fallacies which should be carefully scrutinized.

The first was the misapplication of the containment policy to Southeast Asia. The United States had made the halting of Communist expansion, regardless of time, place, character, methods, and tactics, the supreme goal of its foreign policy. In the words of Secretary of State Dean Rusk:

> What we are seeking to achieve in South Vietnam is part of a process that has continued for a long time—a process of preventing the expansion and extension of Communist domination by the use of force against the weaker nations on the perimeter of Communist power.

With sweeping generalizations the United States extended the policy of so-called containment, erroneously considered successful in Europe, to Southeast Asia where Communist influence has direct appeal in these underdeveloped societies. To be sure, with the inauguration of the Southeast Asia Treaty Organization [SEATO] in 1954 as a military countermeasure to balance political settlements at Geneva, and the formation of the Baghdad Pact (which later became the Central Treaty Organization), the United States had created a superficial wall of containment of Communism, stretching from the Atlantic to the Pacific through Western Europe and the Middle East. But, it was destined to be ineffective.

The second fallacy was the underestimation of Vietcong and North Vietnamese strength, on several accounts: namely, their military capability to carry on the protracted war, their sense of dedication to what they believe to be a sacred cause, the potent force of their nationalism, their pride and stamina, and the cohesive strength of national unity. Believing that its industrial, technological, and military power was insurmountable, the United States naively expected the Communists to fall to their knees as soon as its power was introduced in the struggle. . . .

America's Crusade Against Communism

The third oversight was the failure to recognize the changing character of Communism. As the cold war crystallized in the wake of World War II, both the United States and the Soviet Union abandoned the spirit of cooperation and mutual understanding and sought to promote their respective interests, while assuming that a gain by one was ipso facto a loss to the other.

With the outbreak of the Korean War and through the subsequent years, United States leadership hardened in its conviction that Communism, as a monolithic and invincible force spearheaded in Asia by Communist China, was bent on a conquest of the entire world. A number of Americans failed to exercise reason and came to look upon any settlement, compromise, or ordinary diplomatic dealings with Communist nations as "evil" and "immoral."

The United States poured money, manpower, and military hardware into the poor and unstable countries of the world so long as they professed to be anti-Communist. It justified alignment with any dictatorial, totalitarian, antidemocratic—even corrupt—regime of dubious color so long as it was not Red. Taking the attitude that "if you are not with us, you are against us," the United States neither tolerated neutralism nor recognized nationalistic anticolonialism, thus alienating many Jeffersonian nationalists in Asia and Africa. It talked so much of great crusades against Communism that it mesmerized itself into recklessly undertaking what were considered to be "messianic missions."

The United States should recognize that Communism comes in many shades and colors. There is no monolithic Communist world any more than there is a unified "free world." Yugoslavia, Albania, and Rumania are definitely defiant of the Soviet Union; North Korea has taken a neutral stance; Poland, Hungary, and Czechoslovakia have gained greater freedom of action than most Central American republics. The Sino-Soviet rift is so obvious and well known that it requires no elaboration. . . .

The Reliability Gap

The fourth error was the attempt to bridge what may be called the "reliability gap." One of the principal arguments of the United States in justifying its presence in Vietnam is the contention that if Washington fails to honor its commitments, most Asian allies will lose confidence in the United States and will give second thoughts to their alignment with it. The truth is that, throughout the cold war period, the United States has created an immense "reliability gap" in its relations with those nations which have been placed under its protective assistance treaties. In the course of remaking these nations in its own image, and with anxiety and impatience, the United States has unilaterally assumed a leadership which was paternalistic and meddlesome as well as indifferent to the initiative of indigenous leaders and to the needs of the people. The United States has demanded their absolute loyalty and mistaken their self-assertion for anti-American posture. It fostered a sense of doubt and suspicion instead of one of trust and confidence in the minds of the leaders. To them, the American attitude has been frequently arrogant and domineering, but they dare not express their feelings overtly lest they incur American displeasure and anger.

The Pattern of U.S. Diplomacy

When the Korean War broke out, the United States took up arms to repel the alleged aggressors. This action was based on the assumption that if the open aggression was unchecked and if South Korea's pleas for help went unanswered, the United States would demonstrate to the world that it was indeed a "paper tiger" unconcerned with the safety of its allies. Thus the United States returned to rescue the country which it had recently left unprotected. The pattern of United States diplomacy in its worst aspect may therefore be categorized as follows: (1) empty promises and slogans; (2) indecision and vacillation; and (3) impulsive reaction to the positive action taken by its adversaries.

———— • ————

"The United States . . . should realize that the independence and security of a nation do not always require Washington's protection or intervention."

———— • ————

The "reliability gap" was further widened after America's alliance partners witnessed the performance, or sometimes the nonperformance, of the United States with respect to such crucial issues as the East European uprisings in 1953, the Geneva Accords of 1954, the Anglo-French-Israeli invasion of Egypt, the Hungarian Revolution of 1956, the Laotian conflict of 1960, the Congo crisis, the handling of the U-2 incident, the Bay of Pigs, and the Dominican intervention, to name a few. From the standpoint of many Afro-Asian peoples, the "reliability gap" is so great that a single stroke of military operation in Vietnam will not be able to bridge it. On the contrary, it may have an adverse effect because they believe that rather than righting the wrongs committed in the 1950s, the American military campaign in Vietnam serves only to double the wrong. The United States must not entertain the illusion that military power is a panacea for all the political, social, and economic ills of a nation. Power demonstrated without humility is arrogance; power used without prudence is affront; and power mobilized without discretion is aggression. . . .

Pitfalls of Hostility Toward China

Fifth, and finally, the concept of Communist China as the ultimate enemy has certain pitfalls. In clarifying the purpose of America's involvement in Vietnam, Secretary of Defense Robert McNamara stated: "The choice is not simply whether to continue our efforts to keep South Vietnam free and independent, but rather, whether to continue our struggle to halt Communist expansion in Asia." He did not say that we *will* have a war with Communist China, but the implication is clear that the United States is determined to carry on the struggle, so long as Communism exists in Asia. . . .

No sane leader would contemplate sending millions of American troops to fight on the mainland of China. President Eisenhower expressed his conviction that there could be "no greater tragedy than for the United States to become involved in an all-out war in Indochina," let alone in China. General MacArthur advised President Kennedy not to send American soldiers to the Asian mainland to combat the Chinese. China has proved to be Asia's "quicksand" for foreign invaders, for no nation or people has ever really conquered China. . . .

Should the United States get itself entangled in hostilities with China, which is no longer a "paper tiger," but a "baby dragon with thermonuclear teeth," the tragic consequences are too horrendous to contemplate.

In view of these analyses, the United States' China policy should be reformulated on the basis of certain immediate essentials, including (1) de-escalation of the war in Vietnam, and (2) a normalization of Sino-American relations.

Peace in Vietnam

The first recommendation to be considered is de-escalation. As pointed out, since one of the most important features of escalation in the Vietnam war has been the process of eliminating the proxies, the first step toward de-escalation lies in reversing that process. Through a positive and imaginative diplomacy, means can be found to disengage the United States and North Vietnam forces from combat. A cessation of United States bombing of North Vietnam may be a beginning toward that goal, followed by gradual reduction or withdrawal of both forces from South Vietnam. The parties involved must come to believe that what they have failed to achieve on the battlefield can be achieved at the conference table. . . .

The Virtues of Flexibility

The United States should cast off the old habits of thought and rhetoric, and should introduce the virtues of flexibility and sophistication into the conduct of its foreign policy, especially with respect to the Communist world. It should realize that the independence and security of a nation do not always require Washington's protection or intervention. . . .

The United States must come to the realization that competitive coexistence with China is no more difficult than with the Soviet Union. Recognizing China's great power status, the United States should allow China to participate in major international parleys, and at the opportune moment, extend to it de jure recognition, admit its representatives to United Nations organs and processes, lift its embargo, and institute an exchange of personnel.

Practicing the Blessings of Liberty

In conclusion, in this age of multirevolutions, the United States—"a nation conceived in liberty and dedicated to the proposition that all men are created equal"—should preach *and practice* the blessings of that liberty at home and abroad, and should respect and honor the principle of "sovereign equality," that all nations are equal.

For Further Reading

Doris Kearns Goodwin, *Lyndon Johnson and the American Dream.* New York: Harper & Row, 1976.

George C. Herring, *America's Longest War.* New York: Knopf, 1986.

Stanley Karnow, *Vietnam: A History.* New York: Viking, 1991.

David Levy, *The Debate over Vietnam.* Baltimore: Johns Hopkins University Press, 1991.

Norman Podhoretz, *Why We Were in Vietnam.* New York: Simon and Schuster, 1982.

Herbert Schandler. *The Unmaking of a President: Lyndon Johnson and Vietnam.* Princeton, NJ: Princeton University Press, 1977.

Nancy Zaroulis and Gerald Sullivan, *Who Spoke Up: American Protest Against the War in Vietnam, 1963–1975.* Garden City, NY: Doubleday, 1984.

VIEWPOINT 37A

America's Youth Must Lead a New Revolution (1962, 1968)

Students for a Democratic Society (SDS)

During the 1960s the activities of America's youth attracted much public and media attention. This was in part due to baby-boom demographics; by 1970 people under the age of thirty constituted more than half the U.S. population. But in addition to sheer numbers, many (not all) young Americans drew attention by reexamining and rebelling against the values and institutions of mainstream American society. Young people engaged in activities ranging from psychedelic drug experimentation to civil rights and peace demonstrations, some of which escalated into violent clashes with the police. Some youth focused on political issues such as the Vietnam War. Others rebelled against traditional American beliefs on sex, work, and family.

For much of the decade a vocal segment of college students was at the forefront of both political and cultural radicalism. One leading radical political organization of the 1960s was Students for a Democratic Society (SDS). The following viewpoint consists of two SDS documents from different points in the organization's history. Part I is the introduction to a political platform drafted at an early SDS meeting in Port Huron, Michigan. The 1962 document was written primarily by Tom Hayden (b. 1939), a University of Michigan student who was later elected president of SDS, and who in the 1980s became a California state legislator. The "Port Huron Statement," calling on college students to organize against racism, nuclear war, and other perceived injustices of American society, was widely distributed on college campuses. SDS organized various projects in subsequent years in pursuit of its goal of "participatory democracy." Due in part to increased student unrest over the escalation of the Vietnam War and the end of automatic student deferments from the military draft, by the end of 1967 SDS claimed about three hundred campus chapters.

Part II consists of a resolution passed by SDS in its December 1968 National Council meeting. The document reflects the tumultuous events of that year, during which SDS members organized numerous demonstrations protesting the Vietnam War and university ties to the military, including an uprising at

"Port Huron Statement" of the Students for a Democratic Society, 1962. Reprinted in *Anatomy of a Student Movement* of the U.S. House of Representatives Committee on Internal Security, 91st Cong., 2nd sess., October 6, 1970. "Toward a Revolutionary Youth Movement," a 1968 resolution of the Students for a Democratic Society. Reprinted by permission of the Radical Education Project.

Columbia University in New York that shut down the university's operations. Members of SDS had also been among the crowd involved in a violent confrontation with Chicago riot police during the Democratic National Convention. The resolution argues for the need for a "revolutionary youth movement" that would help transform society. Shortly after the December meeting, SDS split into various factions, some of which became involved in riots, bombings, and other violent activities; it never regained its former prominence.

What faults does SDS see in American society? What events during this particular generation's coming of age account for feelings of discontentment with America, according to SDS? What differences in tone and content do you see between the 1962 and 1968 statements?

I

We are people of this generation, bred in at least modest comfort, housed now in universities, looking uncomfortably to the world we inherit.

When we were kids the United States was the wealthiest and strongest country in the world; the only one with the atom bomb, the least scarred by modern war, an initiator of the United Nations that we thought would distribute Western influence throughout the world. Freedom and equality for each individual, government of, by, and for the people—these American values we found good, principles by which we could live as men. Many of us began maturing in complacency.

As we grew, however, our comfort was penetrated by events too troubling to dismiss. First, the permeating and victimizing fact of human degradation, symbolized by the Southern struggle against racial bigotry, compelled most of us from silence to activism. Second, the enclosing fact of the Cold War, symbolized by the presence of the Bomb, brought awareness that we ourselves, and our friends, and millions of abstract "others" we knew more directly because of our common peril, might die at any time. We might deliberately ignore, or avoid, or fail to feel all other human problems, but not these two, for these were too immediate and crushing in their impact, too challenging in the demand that we as individuals take the responsibility for encounter and resolution.

Paradoxes of America

While these and other problems either directly oppressed us or rankled our consciences and became our own subjective concerns, we began to see complicated and disturbing paradoxes in our surrounding

America. The declaration "all men are created equal . . ." rang hollow before the facts of Negro life in the South and the big cities of the North. The proclaimed peaceful intentions of the United States contradicted its economic and military investments in the Cold War status quo.

We witnessed, and continue to witness, other paradoxes. With nuclear energy whole cities can easily be powered, yet the dominant nation-states seem more likely to unleash destruction greater than that incurred in all wars of human history. Although our own technology is destroying old and creating new forms of social organization, men still tolerate meaningless work and idleness. While two-thirds of mankind suffers undernourishment, our own upper classes revel amidst superfluous abundance. Although world population is expected to double in forty years, the nations still tolerate anarchy as a major principle of international conduct and uncontrolled exploitation governs the sapping of the earth's physical resources. Although mankind desperately needs revolutionary leadership, America rests in national stalemate, its goals ambiguous and tradition-bound instead of informed and clear, its democratic system apathetic and manipulated rather than "of, by, and for the people."

———— • ————

"Youth around the world have the potential to become a critical force. A youth movement raises the issues about a society in which it will be forced to live."

———— • ————

Not only did tarnish appear on our image of American virtue, not only did disillusion occur when the hypocrisy of American ideals was discovered, but we began to sense that what we had originally seen as the American Golden Age was actually the decline of an era. The worldwide outbreak of revolution against colonialism and imperialism, the entrenchment of totalitarian states, the menace of war, overpopulation, international disorder, supertechnology—these trends were testing the tenacity of our own commitment to democracy and freedom and our abilities to visualize their application to a world in upheaval.

Our work is guided by the sense that we may be the last generation in the experiment with living. But we are a minority—the vast majority of our people regard the temporary equilibriums of our society and world as eternally-functional parts. In this is perhaps the outstanding paradox: we ourselves are imbued with urgency, yet the message of our society is that there is no viable alternative to the present. Beneath the reassuring tones of the politicians, beneath the common opinion that America will "muddle through," beneath the stagnation of those who have closed their minds to the future, is the pervading feeling that there simply are no alternatives, that our times have witnessed the exhaustion not only of Utopias, but of any new departures as well. Feeling the press of complexity upon the emptiness of life, people are fearful of the thought that at any moment things might thrust out of control. They fear change itself, since change might smash whatever invisible framework seems to hold back chaos for them now. For most Americans, all crusades are suspect, threatening. The fact that each individual sees apathy in his fellows perpetuates the common reluctance to organize for change. The dominant institutions are complex enough to blunt the minds of their potential critics, and entrenched enough to swiftly dissipate or entirely repel the energies of protest and reform, thus limiting human expectancies. Then, too, we are a materially improved society, and by our own improvements we seem to have weakened the case for further change.

Some would have us believe that Americans feel contentment amidst prosperity—but might it not better be called a glaze above deeply-felt anxieties about their role in the new world? And if these anxieties produce a developed indifference to human affairs, do they not as well produce a yearning to believe there *is* an alternative to the present, that something *can* be done to change circumstances in the school, the workplaces, the bureaucracies, the government? It is to this latter yearning, at once the spark and engine of change, that we direct our present appeal. The search for truly democratic alternatives to the present, and a commitment to social experimentation with them, is a worthy and fulfilling human enterprise, one which moves us and, we hope, others today. On such a basis do we offer this document of our convictions and analysis: as an effort in understanding and changing the conditions of humanity in the late twentieth century, an effort rooted in the ancient, still unfulfilled conception of man attaining determining influence over his circumstances of life.

II

At this point in history, SDS is faced with its most crucial ideological decision, that of determining its direction with regards to the working class. At this time there must be a realization on the part of many in our movement that students alone cannot and will not be able to bring about the downfall of capitalism, the system which is at the root of man's oppression. Many of us are going to have to go through important changes, personally. As students, we have been indoctrinated with many racist and anti-working-class notions that in turn have produced racism and

class-chauvinism in SDS and were responsible largely for the student-power focus which our movement has had for many years. Student power at this stage of our movement has to be seen as economism: that is, organizing people around a narrow definition of self-interest as opposed to class-interest. We are moving beyond this now, but that movement must be planned carefully and understood by all.

The fact that we saw ourselves as students as well as radicals, and accepted that classification of ourselves and many of the false privileges that went along with it (2-S deferment [the draft deferment for students], promise of the "good life" upon graduation, etc.) was primarily responsible for the reactionary tendencies in SDS.

Main Task

The main task now is to begin moving beyond the limitations of struggle placed upon a student movement. We must realize our potential to reach out to new constituencies both on and off campus and build SDS into a youth movement that is revolutionary.

The notion that we must remain simply "an anti-imperialist student organization" is no longer viable. The nature of our struggle is such that it necessitates an organization that is made up of youth and not just students, and that these youth become class-conscious. This means that our struggles must be integrated into the struggles of working people.

One thing should be clear. This perspective doesn't see youth as a class or say that youth will make the revolution by itself. Neither does it say that youth are necessarily more oppressed than older people, simply that they are oppressed in different ways. There are contradictions that touch youth specifically. To understand why there is a need for a youth movement, first we must come to see how youth are oppressed.

Oppression of Youth

Youth around the world have the potential to become a critical force. A youth movement raises the issues about a society in which it will be forced to live. It takes issues to the working class. They do this because, in America, there exists an enormous contradiction around the integration of youth into the system. The period of pre-employment has been greatly extended due to the affluence of this highly industrialized society and the lack of jobs.

Institutions like the schools, the military, the courts and the police all act to oppress youth in specific ways, as does the work place. The propaganda and socialization processes focused at youth act to channel young people into desired areas of the labor market as well as to socialize them to accept without rebellion the miserable quality of life in America both on and off the job.

The ruling class recognizes the critical potential of young people. This is why they developed so many organizational forms to contain them. Many young people have rejected the integration process that the schools are supposed to serve and have broken with and begun to struggle against the "establishment." This phenomenon has taken many forms, ranging from youth dropping out as a response to a dying capitalist culture, to young workers being forced out by industry that no longer has any room for the untrained, unskilled, and unorganized. Both the dropout and the forced-out youth face the repressive nature of America's police, courts, and military, which act to physically and materially oppress them. The response from various strata of youth has been rebellion, from the buildings at Columbia to the movement in the streets of Chicago to Haight-Ashbury [a famous San Francisco "hippie" area] to the Watts uprising [a 1965 Los Angeles riot].

Revolutionary Youth

We must also understand what role a youth movement would have in the context of building a revolution. An organized class-conscious youth movement would serve basically four functions in building revolutionary struggle:

1. An organized revolutionary youth movement is itself a powerful force for revolutionary struggle. In other words, our struggle is the class struggle, as is the Vietnamese and the black liberation struggle. To call youth or even the student movement a section of the bourgeoisie which must simply support any struggle fought by working people is economism. The struggle of youth is as much a part of the class struggle as a union strike. We ally with workers by waging struggle against a common enemy, not by subjugating our movement patronizingly to every trade union battle. We also ally with the liberation struggle of those fighting against imperialism, recognizing that this is the true expression of the working class at its most conscious level.

2. Youth is a critical force which—through struggle—can expose war, racism, the exploitation of labor and the oppression of youth. We do this by putting forth our class analysis of capitalist institutions via propaganda and sharp actions. Exemplary actions of the youth movement lead to higher consciousness and struggle among other people.

3. Because we can organize—as a student movement—around those contradictions which affect youth specifically, we can organize young working people into our class-conscious anti-capitalist movement. These young workers will (a) strengthen the anti-capitalist movement among the work force, (b) provide an organic link between the student movement and the movement of working people, and (c)

add to the effect that we will have as a critical force on older working people today.

4. The expansion of the base of the youth movement to include young working people changes the character of our movement importantly: because it fights the tendency of our student movement to define itself in terms of "student interest" rather than class interest.

Because we see a revolutionary youth movement as an important part of building a full revolutionary working-class movement we must shape our own strategy self-consciously now with a view to that youth movement. This means that, in addition to expanding our base to include more young working people, we must insure the class-consciousness of our movement now, and we must attack the class nature of the schools we are organizing against.

Racism

Building a class-conscious youth movement means fighting racism. SDS must see this fight as a primary task. Racism is a central contradiction in American society, since racism is an inherent part of capitalism and a primary tool used to exploit all working people. In order to fight racism, we must recognize that there is a struggle being fought right now for black liberation in America with which we must ally. This fight for black liberation is at once an anti-colonial struggle against racism and the racist imperialist power structure, as well as being part of the class struggle because black workers are among the most oppressed. It is through racism and its development into colonial oppression that black people are maintained as the most oppressed sector of the working class. Racism (white supremacy) ties white people to the state by splitting them from the most aggressive class struggle.

We must also fight racism within our own movement and among youth in general and make our loyalty to the black liberation struggle more solid. While recognizing that "black capitalism" is not a solution to the problem of racism, we must be careful not to dismiss the anti-colonial nature of the black liberation struggle by simply calling it bourgeois nationalism.

Implementation

The implementation part of this proposal should not be seen as a national program of action but rather as some suggested actions as well as some necessary actions to be taken if such a youth movement is to be built.

1. BUILD CLASS-CONSCIOUSNESS IN THE STUDENT MOVEMENT IN THE DEVELOPMENT TOWARD A REVOLUTIONARY YOUTH MOVEMENT.

a. SDS organizers should direct the focus of their

energies to organizing on campuses of working-class colleges, community schools, trade schools and technical schools as well as high schools and junior colleges.

b. Attacks should also focus on the *university as an arm of the corporations* that exploit and oppress workers. Corporations that exploit workers should be fought on campus. (Aside from producing napalm [an incendiary substance used in U.S. bombs in the Vietnam War], Dow Chemical Co. has plants in 27 countries of the Third World and is among the largest international corporations.)

c. SDS should move toward the building of alliances with nonacademic employees on the campus based on struggle against the common enemy, the university. SDS should view the university as a corporation that directly oppresses the working class.

d. SDS should move to "destudentize" other students by attacking the false privileges of the university—e.g. the 2-S deferment should be attacked on that basis.

e. Some of us should move into factories and shops as well as into working-class communities, to better understand the material oppression of industrial workers, as well as to eradicate prejudices against workers.

f. We should move into the liberation struggle now being fought inside the armed forces and take an active part. Up until now, we have paid only lip service to that struggle of mostly working-class youth.

g. Youth should be made to see their own struggle and the struggle of the Vietnamese against imperialism as the same struggle. The war must continue to be an important focus for SDS organizing.

h. We must join the fight against the class and racist nature of the public school system.

i. Dropout and forced-out youth both should be encouraged to join our movement.

2. ATTACK ON INSTITUTIONAL RACISM. We must view the university as a racist and imperialist institution which acts to oppress the working class and is the brain center of repression against the liberation struggles at home and around the world. Programs should be developed which aggressively attack it as such and attempt to stop it from functioning in that manner. Targets should include:

a. Police institutes on the campus.

b. The real estate establishment.

c. Centers for counterinsurgency (both domestic and foreign) including research and planning centers and sociology and education schools which teach people racism so that they can help defeat the struggles of the blacks.

d. Racism in the classroom, especially in high schools where students are forced by law to sit and listen to racist and class-prejudiced distortions of history.

e. A fight should be waged for the admission of black students and brown students to help wage the fight against racism on the campus. Blacks are carrying on the most militant fights both on and off the campus, and more black admissions means a more militant campus movement. We must also expose the racist and class nature of admissions systems and the high school track system and demand that the schools be opened up to the community so that they too can struggle to stop its oppression.

VIEWPOINT 37B

Student Rebellion Leaders Are a Disgrace (1969)

K. Ross Toole (1920–1981)

Campus unrest and student demonstrations attracted national attention in the 1960s. In the spring of 1968 at least forty thousand students on one hundred campuses took part in demonstrations against war and racism—protests that sometimes turned violent. University buildings were seized, American flags and draft cards were burned, and universities were closed. Similar demonstrations continued in 1969, when the article reprinted here was first published. The writer was K. Ross Toole, a history professor at the University of Montana. The essay, critical of the direction student movements were taking, was widely reprinted in newspapers and magazines across the country.

How does Toole defend his own generation? How do his views on American society differ from those expressed in the opposing viewpoint? How should the police and college authorities respond to student radicals, according to Toole?

I am forty-nine years old. It took me years of considerable anguish to get where I am, which isn't much of any place except exurbia. I was nurtured in the Depression; I lost four years to war; I have had one coronary; I am a "liberal," a square and a professor of history.

As such, I am supposed to have "liaison" with the young. But the fact is that I am fed up with hippies, Yippies, militants and nonsense.

I am also the father of seven children, ranging in age from seven to twenty-three. And I am beginning to wonder what the hell I am incubating as a "permissive" parent. Maybe, indeed, *I* am the fellow who

From K. Ross Toole, *An Angry Man Talks Up to Youth* (New York: Award Books, 1970); ©1969 by K. Ross Toole. Reprinted with permission.

is producing the "campus rebel," whose bearded visage, dirty hair, body odor and "tactics" are childish but brutal, naive but dangerous, and the essence of arrogant tyranny—the tyranny of spoiled brats. Maybe all of this begins with me and my kind.

Wherever and however it begins, it is time to call a halt, time to live in an adult world where we belong and time to put these "children" in their places. We have come by what we have and become what we are through work, sweat, anguish and time. We owe the "younger generation" what all "older generations" have owed younger generations— love, protection to a point and respect when they deserve it. We do not owe them our souls, our privacy, our whole lives; and, above all, we do not owe them immunity from our mistakes or their own.

Every generation makes mistakes, always has and always will. We have made our share. But my generation has made America the most affluent country on earth; it has tackled, head-on, a racial problem which no nation on earth in the history of mankind had dared to do. It has publicly declared war on poverty and it has gone to the moon; it has desegregated schools and abolished polio; it has presided over the beginning of what is probably the greatest social and economic revolution in man's history. It has *begun* these things, not finished them. It has declared itself and committed itself and taxed itself and damn near run itself into the ground in the cause of social justice and reform.

Its mistakes are fewer than my father's generation, or his father's, or his father's. Its greatest mistake is *not* Viet Nam; it is the abdication of its first responsibility, its pusillanimous capitulation to its youth and its sick preoccupation with the problems, the minds, and the psyches, the *raison d'être* of the young.

Since when have children ruled this country? By virtue of what right or what accomplishment should thousands of teenagers, wet behind the ears and utterly without the benefit of having lived long enough to have either judgment or wisdom, become the sages of our time?

Well, say the psychologists, the educators and preachers, the young are rebelling against our archaic mores and morals, our materialistic approach to life, our failures in diplomacy, our terrible ineptitude in racial matters, our narrowness as parents, our blindness to the root ills of society. Balderdash!

Society hangs together by the stitching of many threads. No eighteen-year-old is simply the product of his eighteen years; he is the product of three thousand years of the development of mankind. And throughout those years, injustice has existed and has been fought; rules have grown outmoded and been changed; doom has hung over the heads of men and been avoided; unjust wars have occurred; pain has

been the cost of progress. But man has persevered. Society is obviously an imperfect production, but each generation changes its direction just a little, and most of the time it works.

As a professor and father of seven, I have watched this new generation and concluded that *most* of them are fine. A minority are not. The trouble is that that minority genuinely threatens to tyrannize the majority and take over. I dislike that minority; I am aghast that the majority "takes" it and allows itself to be used; I am appalled that I have participated thus far in condoning it. I speak partly as a historian, partly as a father and partly as one fed up, middle-aged and angry member of the so-called "Establishment"— which, by the way, is nothing but a euphemism for "society."

Egocentric Boors

Common courtesy and a regard for the opinions of others is not merely a decoration on the pie crust of society, it is the heart of the pie. Too many "youngsters" are egocentric boors. They will not listen, they will only shout down. They will not discuss but, like four-year-olds, they throw rocks and shout.

Wisdom is not precocity; it is an amalgam of experience, reading, thought and the slow development of perception. While age is no guarantor of wisdom, whatever else the young are, they are not wise, precisely because they are young. Too many of them mistake glibness for wisdom and emotion for thought.

Arrogance is obnoxious; it is also destructive. Society has classically ostracized arrogance when it is without the backing of demonstrable accomplishment. Why, then, do we tolerate arrogant slobs who occupy our homes, our administration buildings, our streets and parks, urinating on our beliefs and defiling our premises? It is not the police we need, it is an expression of our disgust and disdain. Yet we do more than permit it, we dignify it with introspective flagellation. Somehow it is *our* fault. Balderdash again!

Sensitivity is not the property of the young, nor was it invented in 1960. The young of any generation have felt the same impulse to grow, to reach out, to touch stars, to live freely and to let the mind loose along unexplored corridors. Young men and young women have always stood on the same hill and felt the same vague sense of restraint that separated them from the ultimate experience, the sudden and complete expansion of the mind and the final fulfillment. It is one of the oldest, sweetest and most bitter experiences of mankind.

Today's young people did not invent it; they do not own it. And what they seek to attain all mankind has sought to attain throughout the ages. Shall we, therefore, approve the presumed attainment of it through violence, heroin, speed, LSD and other drugs? And shall we, permissively, let them poison themselves simply because we brought them into this world? Again, it is not police raids and tougher laws that we need; it is merely strength. The strength to explain, in our potty, middle-aged way, that what they seek, we sought; that it is somewhere but sure as hell not in drugs; that, in the meanwhile, they will goddam well cease and desist. And this we must explain early and hard—and then police it ourselves.

Society, "the Establishment," is not a foreign thing we seek to impose on the young. *We* know it is far from perfect. We did not make it; we have only sought to change it. The fact that we have been only minimally successful is the story of *all* generations, as it will be the story of the generation coming up. Yet we *have* worked a number of wonders with it. We *have* changed it. We are deeply concerned about our failures. We have not solved the racial problem, but we have at least faced it; we are terribly worried about the degradation of our environment, about injustices, inequities, the military-industrial complex and bureaucracy. But we *have* attacked these things. All our lives we have taken arms against our sea of troubles—and fought effectively. But we also have fought with a *rational* knowledge of the strength of our adversary; and, above all, we have known that the war is one of attrition in which the "unconditional surrender" of the forces of evil is not about to occur tomorrow. We win, if we win at all, slowly and painfully. That is the kind of war society has always fought because man and society are what they are.

———— • ————

"As a professor I meet the activists and revolutionaries of this new generation every day. They are not only boorish, they are inexcusably ignorant."

———— • ————

Knowing this, why do we listen subserviently to the violent tacticians of the new generation? Either they have total victory by Wednesday next or burn down our carefully built barricades in adolescent pique; either they win now or flee off to a commune and quit; either they solve all problems this week or join a wrecking crew of paranoids.

Youth has always been characterized by impatient idealism. If it were not, there would be *no* change. But impatient idealism does not extend to guns, fire bombs, riots, vicious arrogance and instant gratification. That is not idealism; it is childish tyranny. And the worst of it is that we (professors and faculties in particular), go along in a paroxysm of self-abnegation

and apology, abdicate, apologize as if we had personally created the ills of the world and thus lend ourselves to chaos. We are the led, not the leaders. And we are fools.

Ignorant Youth

As a professor I meet the activists and revolutionaries of this new generation every day. They are not only boorish, they are inexcusably ignorant. If you want to make a revolution, do you not study the ways to do it? Of course not! Che Guevara becomes their hero. He failed; he died in the jungles of Bolivia with an army of six. His every move was a miscalculation and a mistake. Mao Tse-tung and Ho Chi Minh [Communist Chinese and Vietnamese leaders] led revolutions based on a peasantry and an overwhelmingly ancient rural economy. *They* are the pattern-makers for the SDS [Students for a Democratic Society]and the student militants. I have yet to talk to an "activist" who has read Crane Brinton's classic, *The Anatomy of Revolution*, or who is familiar with the works of Jefferson, Washington, Paine, Adams, or even Marx or Engels. And I have yet to talk to a student militant who has read about racism elsewhere and/or who understands, even primitively, the long and wondrous struggle of the NAACP [National Association for the Advancement of Colored People] and the genius of Martin Luther King, Jr., whose name they invariably take in vain.

An old and scarred member of the wars of organized labor in the U.S. in the 1930's recently remarked to me: "These 'radicals' couldn't organize well enough to produce a sensible platform, let alone revolt their way out of a paper bag." But they can, because we let them, destroy our universities, make our parks untenable, make a shambles of our streets and insult our flag. I am *not* a conservative, I am a liberal. I am a concerned and fairly perceptive teacher and parent. I am neither blind to the ills of our society nor dedicated to the status quo.

I assert that we are in trouble with this younger generation not because we have failed our country, not because of affluence or stupidity, not because we are antediluvian, not because we are middle-class materialists, but simply because we have failed to keep that generation in its place and have failed to put them back there when they got out of it. We have the power, we do not have the will; we have the right, we have not exercised it.

To the extent that we now rely on the police, mace, the National Guard, tear gas, steel fences and a wringing of hands, we will fail. What we need is a reappraisal of our own middle-class selves, our worth and our hard-won progress. We need to use disdain, not mace; we need to reassess a weapon we came by the hard way—firm authority as parents, teachers, businessmen, workers and politicians.

The vast majority of our children from one to twenty are fine kids. We need to back up this majority with authority and with the firm conviction that we owe it to them and to ourselves. Enough of apology, enough of analysis, enough of our abdication of our responsibility, enough of the denial of our own maturity and good sense.

University Reforms

The best place to start is at home. But the most practical and effective place, right now, is our campuses. This does not mean a flood of angry edicts, a sudden clampdown, a "new" policy. It simply means that faculties should stop playing chicken, that demonstrators should be met not with police but with expulsions. The power to expel (strangely unused) has been the legitimate recourse of universities since 1209.

More importantly, it means that at freshman orientation, whatever form it takes, the administration should set forth the ground rules—not belligerently but forthrightly.

A university is the microcosm of society itself. It cannot function without rules for conduct. It cannot, as society cannot, legislate morals. It is dealing with young men and women of eighteen to twenty-two. But it can and *must* promulgate rules. It cannot function without order; therefore, those who disrupt order must leave. It cannot permit the students to determine when, what and where they shall be taught; it cannot permit the occupation of its premises, in violation both of the law and its regulations, by "militants."

There is room within the university complex for basic student participation, but there is *no* room for slobs, disruption and violence. Therefore, the first obligation of the administration is to lay down the rules, early in the game, clearly and positively, and to attach to this statement the penalty for violation. It is profoundly simple, and the failure to state it in advance is the salient failure of university administrators in this age.

Expulsion is a dreaded verdict. The administration need not play Torquemada; it merely needs to make it clear, quite dispassionately, that expulsion is the inevitable consequence of the violation of the rules. And among the rules, even though it seems gratuitous, should be these:

1. Violence—armed or otherwise—the forceful occupation of buildings; the intimidation by covert or overt act of any student or faculty member or administrative personnel; the occupation of any university property, field, park, building, lot or other place, shall be cause for expulsion.

2. The disruption of any class, directly or indirect-

ly by voice or presence; or the destruction of any university property, shall be cause for expulsion.

These two simple and clear-cut rules, with penalty attached, should be promulgated to every freshman as part of his general orientation and should be circulated by the means every university has to all upper classmen.

This is neither new nor revolutionary. It is merely the reassertion of an old, accepted and necessary right of the administration of *any* such institution. And the faculty should be informed, firmly, of this reassertion *before* trouble starts. This does *not* constitute provocation. It is one of the oldest rights and necessities of the university community. The failure of university administrators to use it is one of the mysteries of our permissive age, and the blame must fall largely on faculties because they have consistently pressured administrators not to act.

And suppose the students refuse to recognize expulsions, suppose they march, riot, strike. The police? No. The matter, by prearrangement, publicly stated, should then pass to the courts. If buildings are occupied, the court enjoins the participating students; it has the lawful power to declare them in contempt. If violence ensues, it is in violation of the court's order. Courts are not subject to pressures, not part of the action. And what militant will shout obscenities in court with contempt hanging over his head?

Too simple? Not at all. Merely an old process which we seem to have forgotten. It is too direct for those of us who seek to employ Freudian analysis, too positive for "academic senates" who long for philosophical debate and too prosaic for those who seek orgiastic self-condemnation.

This is a country full of decent, worried people like myself. It is also a country full of people fed up with nonsense. Those of us over thirty, tax-ridden, harried, confused, weary, need to reassert our hard-won prerogatives. It is our country too. We have fought for it, bled for it, dreamed for it, and we love it. It is time to reclaim it.

For Further Reading

Peter Collier and David Horowitz, *Destructive Generation: Second Thoughts About the Sixties.* New York: Summit Books, 1989.

Todd Gitlin, *The Sixties: Years of Hope, Days of Rage.* New York: Bantam Books, 1987.

David Harris, *Dreams Die Hard.* New York: St. Martin's/Marek, 1982.

James Kunen, *The Strawberry Statement: Notes of a College Revolutionary.* New York: Random House, 1969.

W.J. Rorabaugh, *Berkeley at War.* New York: Oxford University Press, 1989.

Irwin Unger, *The Movement: A History of the American New Left, 1959–1972.* New York: Dodd, Mead, 1974.

From Nixon to Reagan

VIEWPOINT 38A

America Needs an Equal Rights Amendment (1970)

Margaret M. Heckler (b. 1931)

A constitutional amendment guaranteeing equal rights to men and women was proposed to Congress as early as 1923, but it was not until 1970 that Congress held hearings on the matter. The following viewpoint is taken from a statement made by Margaret M. Heckler before the U.S. Senate in support of an Equal Rights Amendment. Heckler was a Republican representative from Massachusetts, a position she would hold for sixteen years. From 1983 to 1985 she served in President Ronald Reagan's cabinet as secretary of health and human services, and she was later appointed by Reagan to be U.S. ambassador to Ireland.

What do most American women want, according to Heckler? What evidence of sex discrimination does she present? In her view, why is the passage of the Equal Rights Amendment urgent?

I t is assumed today by many persons that women were granted equality with the passage of the 14th amendment, ratified in 1868. Only 50 years later, however, was woman suffrage guaranteed by the ratification of the 19th amendment. Half a century of waiting for the vote required a great deal of patience. In the temper of these turbulent times, I do not believe that total equality of opportunity for women can be further postponed.

Thus I speak out in support of the equal rights amendment—a measure that has been before each Congress since 1923. The fast pace of life in the world today fosters impatience. And when much is promised, failure to deliver becomes a matter of critical importance.

The Crusade for Equality

I am sure that every woman who has been in the position of "job seeker" identifies in some small measure with the fundamental complaints that have generated the crusade for equality in employment for women. The 42 percent of working women who are heads of household takes a serious economic interest

Margaret M. Heckler, testimony before the Senate Subcommittee on Constitutional Amendments, Committee on the Judiciary, 91st Cong., 2nd sess., May 5, 1970.

in fair job opportunity, a basic goal in the cause for women's rights. And the women who have contributed their full share to social security, yet who receive the sum allotted widows, certainly have cause for contemplation.

The average woman in America has no seething desire to smoke cigars or to burn the bra—but she does seek equal recognition of her status as a citizen before the courts of law, and she does seek fair and just recognition of her qualifications in the employment market. The American working woman does not want to be limited in advancement by virtue of her sex. She does not want to be prohibited from the job she desires or from the overtime work she needs by "protective" legislation.

These types of discrimination must be stopped, and the forthright means of halting discrimination against women is passage of the equal rights amendment at the earliest possible time. In fact, I have heard it said quite often that the only discrimination that is still fashionable is discrimination against women.

Perhaps, as some say, it is derived from a protective inclination on the part of men. But women seek recognition as individual human beings with abilities useful to society—rather than shelter or protection from the real world.

John Gardner has said that our Nation's most underdeveloped resource is womanpower. The old saying "you can't keep a good man down" might well serve as a warning. It is safe to say, I think, that women are unlikely to stay down and out of the field of competition for much longer.

Legal remedies are clearly in order, and the equal rights amendment is especially timely. Although changes in social attitudes cannot be legislated, they are guided by the formulation of our Federal laws. This constitutional amendment must be passed so that discriminatory legislation will be overturned. That custom and attitude be subject to a faster pace of evolution is essential if we are to avoid revolution on the part of qualified women who seek equality in the employment world.

The Status of American Women

Time and again I have heard American men question the fact of discrimination against women in America. "American women," they say, "enjoy greater freedom than women of any other nation." This may be true with regard to freedom from kitchen labor—because the average American housewife enjoys a considerable degree of automation in her kitchen. But once she seeks to fill her leisure time gained from automated kitchen equipment by entering the male world of employment, the picture changes. Many countries we consider "underprivileged" far surpass America in quality and availability of child care available to working mothers, in enlightened attitudes about employment leave for pregnancy, and in guiding women into the professions.

Since World War II, nearly 14 million American women have joined the labor force—double the number of men. Forty percent of our Nation's labor force is now composed of women. Yet less than 3 percent of our Nation's attorneys are women, only about 7 percent of our doctors, and 9 percent of our scientists are women. Only a slightly higher percentage of our graduate students in these fields of study are women, despite the fact that women characteristically score better on entrance examinations. The average woman college graduate's annual earnings ($6,694) exceed by just a fraction the annual earnings of an average male educated only through the eighth grade ($6,580). An average male college graduate, however, may be expected to earn almost twice as much as the female—$11,795. Twenty percent of the women with 4 years of college training can find employment only in clerical, sales, or factory jobs. The equal pay provision [a 1963 amendment] of the Fair Labor Standards Act does not include administrative, executive, or professional positions—a loophole which permits the talents and training of highly qualified women to be obtained more cheaply than those of comparable qualified men.

---•---

"The equal rights amendment is necessary to establish unequivocally the American commitment to full and equal recognition of the rights of all its citizens."

---•---

Of the 7.5 million American college students enrolled in 1968, at least 40 percent were women. American parents are struggling to educate their daughters as well as their sons—and are sending them to the best colleges they can possibly afford. As many of these mothers attend commencement exercises this summer, their hearts will swell with pride as their daughters receive college degrees—and these mothers may realize their daughters will have aspirations for exceeding their own horizons.

Few of the fathers or mothers, enrolling their daughters in college several years ago, were at the time aware of the obstacles to opportunity their daughters would face. But today they are becoming aware that opportunity for their daughters is only half of that available to their sons. And they are justifiably indignant. Young women graduating with degrees in business administration take positions as clerks while their male counterparts become man-

agement trainees. Women graduating from law school are often forced to become legal secretaries, while male graduates from the same class survey a panorama of exciting possibilities.

The Nation's Needs

To frustrate the aspirations of the competent young women graduating from our institutions of higher learning would be a dangerous and foolish thing. The youth of today are inspired with a passion to improve the quality of life around us—an admirable and essential goal, indeed. The job is a mammoth one, however; and it would be ill-advised to assume that the role of women in the crusade of the future will not be a significant one. To the contrary, never before has our Nation and our world cried out for talent and creative energy with greater need. To deny full participation of the resources of women, who compose over half the population of our country, would be a serious form of neglect. The contributions of women have always been intrinsic in our national development. With the increasing complexity of our world, it becomes all the more essential to tap every conceivable resource at our command.

The time is thus ripe for passage of the equal rights amendment. The women of America are demanding full rights and full responsibilities in developing their individual potential as human beings in relationship to the world as well as to the home and in contributing in an active way to the improvement of society.

In this day of the urban crisis, when we seem to be running out of clean air and water, when the quantity of our rubbish defies our current disposal methods, when crime on the streets is rampant, when our world commitments seem at odds with our obligations here at home, when breaking the cycle of ongoing poverty requires new and innovative approaches, when increased lifespan generates a whole new series of gerontological problems—in these complicated and critical times, our Nation needs the fully developed resources of all our citizens—both men and women—in order to meet the demands of society today.

Women are not requesting special privilege—but rather a full measure of responsibility, a fair share of the load in the effort to improve life in America. The upcoming generation is no longer asking for full opportunity to contribute, however—they are demanding this opportunity.

The equal rights amendment is necessary to establish unequivocally the American commitment to full and equal recognition of the rights of all its citizens. Stopgap measures and delays will no longer be acceptable—firm guarantees are now required. The seventies mark an era of great promise if the untapped resource of womanpower is brought forth into the open and allowed to flourish so that women may take their rightful place in the mainstream of American life. Both men and women have a great deal to gain.

VIEWPOINT 38B

An Equal Rights Amendment Would Be Harmful (1970)

Myra Wolfgang (1914?–1976)

In 1972 Congress passed an amendment to the Constitution stating, "Equality of rights under the law shall not be denied or abridged by the United States or any State on the basis of sex." After almost a decade of campaigning on the state level, however, supporters of the Equal Rights Amendment (ERA) were unable to attain ratification by the necessary 38 state legislatures. Opposition to the amendment came from a number of conservative organizations and leaders, as well as some labor movement leaders who objected that the proposed amendment might abolish needed protective job legislation for women. Such arguments are included in the following viewpoint by Myra Wolfgang, taken from Senate hearings on the Equal Rights Amendment in May 1970. Wolfgang, a union official representing hotel and restaurant employees in Detroit, Michigan, argues that while there is much wrongful discrimination against women, the proposed amendment would do working women more harm than good.

What specific objections does Wolfgang have to the Equal Rights Amendment? How does she characterize the feminist movement? Why do women sometimes need special protective legislation, according to Wolfgang?

M y name is Myra Wolfgang. I reside in the city of Detroit. I am the international vice president of the Hotel and Restaurant Employees Union, AFL–CIO, and also the secretary-treasurer of its Detroit local. I bring to this hearing 35 years of experience in representing the interests of service workers, both organized, and may I hasten to add, unorganized as well. I am a member of the Michigan Minimum Wage Board representing service employees thereon. I have been a member of the mayor's committee on human relations, and . . . I am a member of the current Governor's commission on the status of women and was a member of the Gov-

Myra Wolfgang, testimony before the Senate Subcommittee on Constitutional Amendments, Committee on the Judiciary, 91st Cong., 2nd sess., May 6, 1970.

ernor's commission under the previous two administrations. I am quite proud of the fact that I made the suggestion to Gov. John Swainson that we have a commission on the status of women, and Michigan was the first State to have such a commission.

Service Workers

The service industries which I represent comprise more than 5.5 million women workers. There are an additional 5 million women employed in wholesale and retail trades industries. I represent unskilled and untrained women workers, the majority of whom are not organized into trade unions. They also are not burdened with the necessity of holding philosophical discussions on whether women should or should not be in the work force. They are in the work force because of dire, economic necessity and have no choice in the matter.

My concern with the equal rights amendment, Senator, is not an academic one. It embodies the problems that I work with day in and day out, year in and year out. My concern is for the widowed, divorced mothers of children who are the heads of their families and earn less than $3,500 a year working as maids, laundry workers, hospital cleaners, or dishwashers. And there are millions of such women in the work force. Now is as good a time as any to remind you that only 1 out of 10 women in the work force has had 4 or more years of college, so I am not speaking of, or representing, the illusive "bird in the gilded cage." I speak for "Tillie the Toiler."

I am opposed to enactment of the equal rights amendment. I recognize that the impetus for the passage of the equal rights amendment is the result of a growing anger amongst women over job discrimination, social and political discrimination, and many outmoded cultural habits of our way of life.

And the anger is justified, for certainly discrimination against women exists. I do not believe, however, that passage of the equal rights amendment will satisfy, or is the solution to, the problem. The problem of discrimination against women will not be solved by an equal rights amendment to the Constitution; conversely, the amendment will create a whole new series of problems. It will neither bring about equal pay for equal work, nor guarantee job promotion free from discrimination. It will not compel the partner of a senior law firm to hire a woman lawyer if he has prejudice against a woman lawyer. And may I point out at this time that if that law firm employs fewer than 25 persons, they are not even covered by title VII of the Civil Rights Act. And I would suggest that would be a good place to start a fight against law firms that won't hire lady lawyers.

The amendment is excessively sweeping in scope, reaching into the work force, into family and social relationships, and other institutions, in which, incidentally, "equality" cannot always be achieved through "identity." Differences in laws are not necessarily discriminatory, nor should all laws containing different provisions for men and women be abolished, as the equal rights amendment would do.

Being opposed, as I am, to the equal rights amendment certainly does not mean that I am opposed to equality. The campaign for an equal rights amendment, in many instances, has become a field day for sloganeers and has become as jingoistic as the "right to work" law campaign did. The "right to work" laws do not guarantee a job, any more than the equal rights amendment will guarantee equality. To assume that it would is as invalid as to assume that because women have suffrage they are independent.

Threat to Labor Legislation

Representing service workers gives me a special concern over the threat that an equal rights amendment would present to minimum labor standards legislation. I am sure you are aware of the influence of such legislation upon working conditions. And I am sure you are aware that many such laws apply to women only.

They are varied and they are in the field of minimum wages, hours of work, rest periods, weight lifting, childbirth legislation, et cetera.

These State laws are outmoded and many of them are discriminatory. They should be amended where they are. They should be strengthened and they should be handled on a case-by-case basis.

It is difficult to unite women against vague philosophies, so the new feminists look for a focus in the law. Thus, the revived interest in the equal rights amendment. The feminist movement in the main is middle class, professional woman, college girl oriented. . . .

Differences Between Men and Women

Some feminist groups have concluded that since only females reproduce—and to be a mother is to be a "slave eternal"—that nothing short of the destruction of the family and the end of internal reproduction will do. Having discovered "artificial insemination," all that is missing now, in order to do away with women entirely, is discovering an artificial womb.

You will be hearing, I am sure, from many who will contend that there are no real differences between men and women, other than those enforced by culture. Has culture created the differences in the size of the hands, in muscular mass, in respiratory capacity? Of course not. The differences are physical.

Let me add some more. Women on the average—these are averages, Senator—are 85 percent as heavy as men and have only 60 percent as much physical strength. Therefore, they cannot lift as heavy weights.

They cannot direct as much weight or have the same strength for pushing or pulling of loads.

One can take any cell from a human being and determine whether it came from a male or a female. This does not suggest superiority or inferiority among the sexes, it emphasizes differences. Because of the physical—and I emphasize physical—differences between men and women, the question of protective legislation for women must be reviewed. In addition, the dual role of women in our modern society makes protective legislation necessary.

The working mother has no "wife" to care for her or her children. She assumes the role of home maker and worker and must perform both these roles in a 24-hour period. Even in the two-parent households, there is an unequal division of domestic chores. While much could be done to ease the burden of the working woman by men assuming the fair and equal share of domestic chores, they are not prepared to do so. And I am not prepared to become confused with what should be and what is.

————— • —————

"I oppose the equal rights amendment since the equality it may achieve may well be equality of mistreatment."

————— • —————

If the community does not take action through protective legislation to enable women to work outside the home, then the expressed desire for equal rights is an empty promise and a myth. The equal rights amendment would make it unconstitutional to enact and would repeal legislation embodying this protection for working women. You must ask yourself this question: Should women workers be left without any legislation because of State legislature's failure and unwillingness to enact such legislation for men?

The elimination of laws regulating hours women may work permits employers to force them to work excessive overtime, endangering not only their health and safety, but disrupting the entire family relationship.

The women in the work force who are in the greatest need of the protection of maximum hour legislation are in no position to fight for themselves. . . .

Unanswered Questions

In this mad whirl toward equality and sameness one question remains unanswered: Who will take care of the children, the home, cleaning, the laundry, and the cooking? Can we extend this equality into the home? Obviously not, since the proponents of the equal rights amendment are quick to point out the amendment would restrict only governmental action and would not apply to purely private action. . . .

I am aware of the recent position taken by the Citizens Advisory Council on the Status of Women [a committee appointed by and advising the president] in support of the equal rights amendment. Since it differs with the 1963 report of President Kennedy's Commission on the Status of Women, what has occurred to explain this change? You know, as it is said, in order to know the players, you have to have a scorecard. Well, have women changed since 1963? No. Have the 5th and 14th amendments to the Constitution been changed, repealed, or amended since 1963? The only thing that has changed is the personnel of the Citizens Advisory Council. The new Council was appointed last August and consists of business and professional women whose knowledge of proper labor standards for workers is negligible. And if you don't believe me, ask the domestics that work in their homes. Not one labor representative is on that Council.

You have been reminded in strong and ominous tones, and I was here yesterday and heard it, that women represent the majority of the voters. That is true. But there is no more unanimity of opinion among women than there is amongst men. Indeed, a woman on welfare in Harlem, a unionized laundry-worker in California, and an elderly socialite from Philadelphia may be of the same sex and they may be wives and mothers, but they have little in common to cause them to be of one opinion.

Whatever happens to the structure of opportunity, women are increasingly motivated to work—and they want to work short hours on schedules that meet their needs as wives and mothers. They want fewer hours a week because emancipation, while it has released them for work, has not released them from home and family responsibilities.

I oppose the equal rights amendment since the equality it may achieve may well be equality of mistreatment.

For Further Reading

Flora Davis, *Moving the Mountain: The Women's Movement in America Since 1960.* New York: Simon and Schuster, 1991.

Mary A. Delsman, *Everything You Need to Know About ERA.* Riverside, CA: Meranza Press, 1975.

Betty Friedan, *The Second Stage.* New York: Summit Books, 1981.

William L. O'Neill, *Feminism in America: A History.* New Brunswick, NJ: Transaction, 1989.

Jean Maddern Pitrone, *Myra: The Life and Times of Myra Wolfgang.* Wyandotte, MI: Calibre Books, 1980.

Barbara Sinclair, *The Women's Movement.* New York: Harper & Row, 1983.

VIEWPOINT 39A

A Defense of the Nixon Presidency (1973)

Richard M. Nixon (1913–1994)

In the 1970s a series of political scandals involving Richard M. Nixon, president of the United States from 1969 to 1974, caused a national crisis. The focal point of the scandals was a burglary at the Democratic Party National Headquarters at the Watergate apartment complex in Washington, D.C., on June 17, 1972. Although the seven burglars captured included two former White House aides and a member of Nixon's reelection committee, the president denied any administration involvement or knowledge, and coasted to reelection victory in November 1972. However, questions persisted. In February 1973 the U.S. Senate established the Special Committee on Presidential Campaign Activities (also known as the Watergate Committee). Chaired by Sam J. Ervin of North Carolina, the special committee began televised hearings that May. Over the next several months the American public heard numerous disclosures by presidential aides about Nixon's use of government agencies to harass opponents, the existence of an administration "enemies list," and evidence of White House involvement in covering up the Watergate burglary. One of the key revelations of the hearings was the existence of a White House taping system that had secretly recorded conversations made in the president's Oval Office. Nixon, citing "executive privilege," refused to turn over the tapes to the committee or to the special prosecutor he had appointed to investigate the affair.

The following viewpoint is taken from a speech Nixon made on nationwide television on August 15, 1973. In his speech Nixon reiterates his previous denials of personal involvement in a Watergate coverup or other misdeeds, defends his withholding of the tapes and his presidency in general, and calls for Americans not to focus exclusively on Watergate at the expense of other problems facing the nation.

What main points about his own Watergate involvement does Nixon stress? On what grounds does Nixon base his refusal to release the tapes? What comments does he make about the protest movements of the 1960s? How does he connect them to Watergate?

Now that most of the major witnesses in the Watergate phase of the Senate committee hearings on campaign practices have been heard, the time has come for me to speak out about the charges made and to provide a perspective on the issue for the American people.

For over four months Watergate has dominated the news media. During the past three months the three major networks have devoted an average of over 22 hours of television time each week to this subject. The Senate committee has heard over two million words of testimony.

This investigation began as an effort to discover the facts about the break-in and bugging at the Democratic national headquarters and other campaign abuses.

But as the weeks have gone by, it has become clear that both the hearings themselves and some of the commentaries on them have become increasingly absorbed in an effort to implicate the President personally in the illegal activities that took place.

Because the abuses occurred during my Administration, and in the campaign for my re-election, I accept full responsibility for them. I regret that these events took place. And I do not question the right of a Senate committee to investigate charges made against the President to the extent that this is relevant to legislative duties.

Defending the Presidency

However, it is my Constitutional responsibility to defend the integrity of this great office against false charges. I also believe that it is important to address the overriding question of what we as a nation can learn from this experience, and what we should now do. I intend to discuss both of these subjects tonight.

The record of the Senate hearings is lengthy. The facts are complicated, the evidence conflicting. It would not be right for me to try to sort out the evidence, to rebut specific witnesses, or to pronounce my own judgment about their credibility. That is for the committee and for the courts.

I shall not attempt to deal tonight with the various charges in detail. Rather, I shall attempt to put the events in perspective from the standpoint of the Presidency.

On May 22, before the major witnesses had testified, I issued a detailed statement addressing the charges that had been made against the President.

I have today issued another written statement, which addresses the charges that have been made since then as they relate to my own conduct, and which describes the efforts that I made to discover the facts about the matter.

On May 22, I stated in very specific terms—and I state again to every one of you listening tonight—these facts: I had no prior knowledge of the Watergate break-in; I neither took part in nor knew about

Excerpted from Richard M. Nixon's speech to the American people on nationwide television, August 15, 1973. The complete speech is reprinted in *Vital Speeches of the Day*, September 1, 1973.

any of the subsequent cover-up activities; I neither authorized nor encouraged subordinates to engage in illegal or improper campaign tactics.

That was and that is the simple truth. In all of the millions of words of testimony, there is not the slightest suggestion that I had any knowledge of the planning for the Watergate break-in. As for the cover-up, my statement has been challenged by only 1 of the 35 witnesses who appeared—a witness [John Dean] who offered no evidence beyond his own impressions, and whose testimony has been contradicted by every other witness in a position to know the facts.

Tonight, let me explain to you what I did about Watergate after the break-in occurred, so that you can better understand the fact that I also had no knowledge of the so-called cover-up.

From the time when the break-in occurred, I pressed repeatedly to know the facts, and particularly whether there was any involvement of anyone at the White House. I considered two things essential:

First, that the investigation should be thorough and above-board; and second, that if there were any higher involvement, we should get the facts out first. As I said at my August 29 press conference last year, "What really hurts in matters of this sort is not the fact that they occur, because overzealous people in campaigns do things that are wrong. What really hurts is if you try to cover it up." I believed that then, and certainly the experience of this last year has proved to be true.

Intensive Investigations

I knew that the Justice Department and the F.B.I. were conducting intensive investigations—as I had insisted that they should. The White House counsel, John Dean, was assigned to monitor these investigations, and particularly to check into any possible White House involvement. Throughout the summer of 1972, I continued to press the question, and I continued to get the same answer: I was told again and again that there was no indication that any persons were involved other than the seven who were known to have planned and carried out the operation, and who were subsequently indicted and convicted.

On Sept. 12 at a meeting that I held with the Cabinet, the senior White House staff and a number of legislative leaders, Attorney General [Richard] Kleindienst reported on the investigation. He told us it had been the most extensive investigation since the assassination of President Kennedy, and that it has established that only those seven were involved.

On Sept. 15, the day the seven were indicted, I met with John Dean, the White House counsel. He gave me no reason whatever to believe that any others were guilty; I assumed that the indictments of only the seven by the grand jury confirmed the reports he had been giving to that effect throughout the summer.

On Feb. 16, I met with Acting Director [Patrick] Gray prior to submitting his name to the Senate for confirmation as permanent director of the F.B.I. I stressed to him that he would be questioned closely about the F.B.I.'s conduct of the Watergate investigation. I asked him if he still had full confidence in it. He replied that he did; that he was proud of its thoroughness and that he could defend it with enthusiasm before the committee.

Because I trusted the agencies conducting the investigations, because I believed the reports I was getting, I did not believe the newspaper accounts that suggested a cover-up. I was convinced there was no cover-up, because I was convinced that no one had anything to cover up.

It was not until March 21 of this year that I received new information from the White House counsel that led me to conclude that the reports I had been getting for over nine months were not true. On that day, I launched an intensive effort of my own to get the facts and to get the facts out. Whatever the facts might be, I wanted the White House to be the first to make them public.

———— • ————

"A continued, backward-looking obsession with Watergate is causing this nation to neglect matters of far greater importance to all of the American people."

———— • ————

At first I entrusted the task of getting me the facts to Mr. Dean. When, after spending a week at Camp David, he failed to produce the written report I had asked for, I turned to John Ehrlichman and to the Attorney General—while also making independent inquiries of my own. By mid-April I had received Mr. Ehrlichman's report, and also one from the Attorney General based on new information uncovered by the Justice Department.

These reports made it clear to me that the situation was far more serious than I had imagined. It at once became evident to me that the responsibility for the investigation in the case should be given to the Criminal Division of the Justice Department. I turned over all the information I had to the head of that department, Assistant Attorney General Henry Petersen, a career Government employee with an impeccable nonpartisan record, and I instructed him to pursue the matter thoroughly. I ordered all members of the Administration to testify fully before the grand jury.

And with my concurrence, on May 18 Attorney General [Elliot] Richardson appointed a special prosecutor to handle the matter, and the case is now before the grand jury.

Far from trying to hide the facts, my effort throughout has been to discover the facts—and to lay those facts before the appropriate law-enforcement authorities so that justice could be done and the guilty dealt with.

I relied on the best law-enforcement agencies in the country to find and report the truth. I believed they had done so—just as they believed they had done so.

The White House Tapes

Many have urged that in order to help prove the truth of what I have said, I should turn over to the special prosecutor and the Senate committee recordings of conversations that I held in my office or my telephone.

However, a much more important principle is involved in this question than what the tapes might prove about Watergate.

Each day a President of the United States is required to make difficult decisions on grave issues. It is absolutely necessary, if the President is to be able to do his job as the country expects, that he be able to talk openly and candidly with his advisers about issues and individuals. This kind of frank discussion is only possible when those who take part in it know that what they say is in strictest confidence.

The Presidency is not the only office that requires confidentiality. A member of Congress must be able to talk in confidence with his assistants. Judges must be able to confer in confidence with their law clerks and with each other. For very good reasons, no branch of government has ever compelled disclosure of confidential conversations between officers of other branches of government and their advisers about government business.

This need for confidence is not confined to Government officials. The law has long recognized that there are kinds of conversations that are entitled to be kept confidential, even at the cost of doing without critical evidence in a legal proceeding. This rule applies, for example, to conversations between a lawyer and a client, between a priest and a penitent, and between a husband and a wife. In each case it is thought so important that the parties be able to talk freely to each other that for hundreds of years the law has said that these conversations are "privileged" and that their disclosure cannot be compelled in a court.

The Need for Confidentiality

It is even more important that the confidentiality of conversations between a President and his advisers be protected. This is no mere luxury, to be dispensed with whenever a particular issue raises sufficient uproar. It is absolutely essential to the conduct of the Presidency, in this and in all future Administrations.

If I were to make public these tapes, containing as they do blunt and candid remarks on many different subjects, the confidentiality of the Office of the President would always be suspect from now on. It would make no difference whether it was to serve the interests of a court, of a Senate committee or the President himself—the same damage would be done to the principle, and that damage would be irreparable. Persons talking with the President would never again be sure that recordings or notes of what they said would not suddenly be made public. No one would want to advance tentative ideas that might later seem unsound. No diplomat would want to speak candidly in those sensitive negotiations which could bring peace or avoid war. No Senator or Congressman would want to talk frankly about the Congressional horse-trading that might get a vital bill passed. No one would want to speak bluntly about public figures, here and abroad.

That is why I shall continue to oppose efforts which would set a precedent that would cripple all future Presidents by inhibiting conversations between them and those they look to for advice. This principle of confidentiality of Presidential conversations is at stake in the question of these tapes. I must and I shall oppose any efforts to destroy this principle, which is so vital to the conduct of this great office.

The Meaning of Watergate

Turning now to the basic issues which have been raised by Watergate, I recognize that merely answering the charges that have been made against the President is not enough. The word "Watergate" has come to represent a much broader set of concerns.

To most of us, "Watergate" has come to mean not just a burglary and bugging of party headquarters, but a whole series of acts that either represent or appear to represent an abuse of trust. It has come to stand for excessive partisanship, for "enemy lists," for efforts to use the great institutions of Government for partisan political purposes.

For many Americans, the term "Watergate" also has come to include a number of national security matters that have been brought into the investigation, such as those involved in my efforts to stop massive leaks of vital diplomatic and military secrets, and to counter the wave of bombings and burnings and other violent assaults of just a few years ago.

Let me speak first of the political abuses.

I know from long experience that a political campaign is always a hard and a tough contest. A candidate for high office has an obligation to his party, to his

supporters, and to the cause he represents. He must always put forth his best efforts to win. But he also has an obligation to the country to conduct that contest within the law and within the limits of decency.

No political campaign ever justifies obstructing justice, or harassing individuals, or compromising those great agencies of Government that should and must be above politics. To the extent that these things were done in the 1972 campaign, they were serious abuses. And I deplore them.

Practices of that kind do not represent what I believe Government should be, or what I believe politics should be. In a free society, the institutions of Government belong to the people. They must never be used against the people.

And in the future, my Administration will be more vigilant in ensuring that such abuses do not take place, and that officials at every level understand that they are not to take place.

And I reject the cynical view that politics is inevitably or even usually a dirty business. Let us not allow what a few overzealous people did in Watergate to tar the reputation of the millions of dedicated Americans of both parties who fought hard but clean for the candidates of their choice in 1972. By their unselfish efforts, these people make our system work and they keep America free.

I pledge to you tonight that I will do all that I can to ensure that one of the results of Watergate is a new level of political decency and integrity in America—and in which what has been wrong in our politics no longer corrupts or demeans what is right in our politics.

National Security

Let me turn now to the difficult questions that arise in protecting the national security.

It is important to recognize that these are difficult questions and that reasonable and patriotic men and women may differ on how they should be answered.

Only last year, the Supreme Court said that implicit in the President's constitutional duty is "the power to protect our Government against those who would subvert or overthrow it by unlawful means." How to carry out this duty is often a delicate question to which there is no easy answer.

For example, every President since World War II has believed that in internal security matters the President has the power to authorize wiretaps without first obtaining a search warrant.

An act of Congress in 1968 had seemed to recognize such power. Last year the Supreme Court held to the contrary. And my Administration is of course now complying with that Supreme Court decision. But until the Supreme Court spoke, I had been acting, as did my predecessors—President Truman,

President Eisenhower, President Kennedy, President Johnson—in a reasonable belief that in certain circumstances the Constitution permitted and sometimes even required such measures to protect the national security in the public interest.

Although it is the President's duty to protect the security of the country, we of course must be extremely careful in the way we go about this—for if we lose our liberties we will have little use for security. Instances have now come to light in which a zeal for security did go too far and did interfere impermissibly with individual liberty.

It is essential that such mistakes not be repeated. But it is also essential that we do not overreact to particular mistakes by tying the President's hands in a way that would risk sacrificing our security, and with it our liberties.

I shall continue to meet my constitutional responsibility to protect the security of this nation so that Americans may enjoy their freedom. But I shall and can do so by constitutional means, in ways that will not threaten that freedom.

Historical Perspective

As we look at Watergate in a longer perspective, we can see that its abuses resulted from the assumption by those involved that their case placed them beyond the reach of those rules that apply to other persons and that hold a free society together.

That attitude can never be tolerated in our country. However, it did not suddenly develop in the year 1972. It became fashionable in the 1960s, as individuals and groups increasingly asserted the right to take the law in their own hands, insisting that their purposes represented a higher morality. Then, their attitude was praised in the press and even from some of our pulpits as evidence of a new idealism. Those of us who insisted on the old restraints, who warned of the overriding importance of operating within the law and by the rules, were accused of being reactionaries.

That same attitude brought a rising spiral of violence and fear of riots and arson and bombings, all in the name of peace and in the name of justice. Political discussion turned into savage debate. Free speech was brutally suppressed as hecklers shouted down or even physically assaulted those with whom they disagreed. Serious people raised serious questions about whether we could survive as a free democracy.

The notion that the end justifies the means proved contagious. Thus it is not surprising, even though it is deplorable, that some persons in 1972 adopted the morality that they themselves had rightly condemned and committed acts that have no place in our political system.

Those acts cannot be defended. Those who were guilty of abuses must be punished. But ultimately the answer does not lie merely in the jailing of a few overzealous persons who mistakenly thought their cause justified their violations of the law.

Rather, it lies in a commitment by all of us to show a renewed respect for the mutual restraints that are the mark of a free and civilized society. It requires that we learn once again to work together, if not united in all of our purposes, then at least united in respect for the system by which our conflicts are peacefully resolved and our liberties maintained.

If there are laws we disagree with, let us work to change them—but let us obey them until they are changed. If we have disagreements over Government policies, let us work those out in a decent and civilized way, within the law, and with respect for our differences.

We must recognize that one excess begets another, and that the extremes of violence and discord in the 1960s contributed to the extremes of Watergate.

Both are wrong. Both should be condemned. No individual, no group and no political party has a corner on the market in morality in America.

If we learn the important lessons of Watergate, if we do what is necessary to prevent such abuses in the future—on both sides—we can emerge from this experience a better and a stronger nation.

Other Problems Facing the Nation

Let me turn now to an issue that is important above all else, and that is critically affecting your life today and will affect your life and your children's in the years to come.

After 12 weeks and 2 million words of televised testimony, we have reached a point at which a continued, backward-looking obsession with Watergate is causing this nation to neglect matters of far greater importance to all of the American people.

We must not stay so mired in Watergate that we fail to respond to challenges of surpassing importance to America and the world. We cannot let an obsession with the past destroy our hopes for the future.

Legislation vital to your health and well-being sits unattended on the Congressional calendar. Confidence at home and abroad in our economy, our currency and our foreign policy is being sapped by uncertainty. Critical negotiations are taking place on strategic weapons, on troop levels in Europe that can affect the security of this nation and the peace of the world long after Watergate is forgotten. Vital events are taking place in Southeast Asia which could lead to a tragedy for the cause of peace.

These are matters that cannot wait. They cry out for action now. And either we, your elected representatives here in Washington, ought to get on with the jobs that need to be done—for you—or every one of you ought to be demanding to know why.

The time has come to turn Watergate over to the courts, where the questions of guilt or innocence belong. The time has come for the rest of us to get on with the urgent business of our nation.

Last November, the American people were given the clearest choice of this century. Your votes were a mandate, which I accepted, to complete the initiatives we began in my first term and to fulfill the promises I made for my second term.

This Administration was elected to control inflation, to reduce the power and size of government, to cut the cost of government so that you can cut the cost of living, to preserve and defend those fundamental values that have made America great, to keep the nation's military strength second to none, to achieve peace with honor in Southeast Asia and to bring home our prisoners of war, and to build a new prosperity, without inflation and without war, to create a structure of peace in the world that would endure long after we are gone.

These are great goals. They are worthy of a great people. And I would not be true to your trust if I let myself be turned aside from achieving those goals.

If you share my belief in these goals—if you want the mandate you gave this Administration to be carried out—then I ask for your help to insure that those who would exploit Watergate in order to keep us from doing what we were elected to do will not succeed.

I ask tonight for your understanding, so that as a nation we can learn the lessons of Watergate, and gain from that experience.

I ask for your help in reaffirming our dedication to the principles of decency, honor and respect for the institutions that have sustained our progress through these past two centuries.

And I ask for your support, in getting on once again with meeting your problems, improving your life and building your future.

With your help, with God's help, we will achieve these great goals for America.

VIEWPOINT 39B

President Nixon Should Be Impeached (1973, 1974)

Barbara W. Tuchman (1912–1989)
and the House Judiciary Committee

As the Watergate scandal surrounding Richard M. Nixon deepened in 1973 and 1974, an increasing number of people called for the impeachment of the president—something that Congress had done only

once in U.S. history. The first section of the following two-part viewpoint is an editorial written in August 1973 by Barbara W. Tuchman, an author and Pulitzer Prize–winning historian. She argues that, regardless of whether a "smoking gun" reveals Nixon's personal involvement in a Watergate cover-up, his administration has been associated with enough political scandals and controversial policies (including the secret bombing of Cambodia in 1969) to discredit it in the eyes of the American people. She urges Congress to use the constitutional mechanism of impeachment. Part II presents the three articles of impeachment voted on by the House Judiciary Committee in July 1974, charging Nixon with obstruction of justice in the Watergate coverup, abuse of his presidential powers, and refusal to comply with subpoenas calling for the release of White House tapes.

The impeachment process initiated by the House Judiciary Committee was never completed. On August 8, 1974, Nixon became the first president in U.S. history to resign from office. On September 8, 1974, Nixon's successor, Gerald Ford (whom Nixon had appointed vice president following the October 1973 resignation of Spiro T. Agnew in an unrelated political scandal), pardoned Nixon for any crimes he might have committed in the Watergate affair.

How does the United States risk dictatorship, according to Tuchman? How do the charges of the articles of impeachment compare with Nixon's assertions made in the opposing viewpoint? Which charge(s) do you find the most serious? Why?

I

The Democratic party, fearing the advantage that incumbency would give [then–Vice President Spiro T.] Agnew in 1976, shrinks from the idea of impeachment. So do the Republicans, fearing the blow to their party. All of us shrink from the tensions and antagonisms that a trial of the President would generate. Yet this is the only means of terminating a misconducted Presidency that our system provides.

If it is the sole means, then we should be prepared to undertake it, no matter how uncomfortable or inexpedient. Political expediency should not take precedence over decency in government.

Fear of the remedy can be more dangerous in ultimate consequences than if we were to show ourselves capable of the nerve and the will to use a con-

From Barbara W. Tuchman, "A Fear of the Remedy," *New York Times*, August 7, 1973; ©1973 by Barbara W. Tuchman. Reprinted by permission of Russell & Volkening, Inc., as agents for the author's estate. From House Committee on the Judiciary, *Report on the Impeachment of Richard M. Nixon, President of the United States*, 93rd Cong., 2nd sess., August 20, 1974.

stitutional process when circumstances demand it. The show itself, if realistic, could well bring about the best solution: a voluntary termination of Mr. Nixon's Presidency. This would be a boon to the country because the Nixon Administration is already Humpty Dumpty; it cannot be put together again credibly enough to govern effectively.

The present crisis in Government will not be resolved on the basis of whether or not Mr. Nixon can be legally proved to have personally shared in obstructing justice in the Watergate case. His Administration has been shown to be pervaded by so much other malfeasance that the Watergate break-in is no more than an incident. To confine the issue to that narrow ground seems a serious error. Forget the tapes. What we are dealing with here is fundamental immorality.

The Nixon Administration

The Nixon Administration, like any other, is an entity, a whole, for which he is responsible and from which he is indivisible. Its personnel, including those now under indictment, were selected and appointed by him, its conduct determined by him, its principles—or lack of them—derived from him. Enough illegal, unconstitutional and immoral acts have already been revealed and even acknowledged to constitute impeachable grounds. The Domestic Intelligence Program of 1970, authorized by the President, and "mindboggling" in its violation of the citizen's rights, would alone be sufficient to disqualify him from office. Indeed this item is the core of the problem for it indicates not only the Administration's disregard for, but what almost seems its ignorance of the Bill of Rights.

———— • ————

"Richard M. Nixon has acted in a manner contrary to his trust as President and subversive of constitutional government, . . . to the manifest injury of the people of the United States."

———— • ————

The Dirty Tricks Department with its forgeries and frame-ups, burglaries and proposed firebombings, operated right out of the White House under the supervision of the President's personal appointees. Is he separable from them? Key members of the Committee to Re-Elect the President, who have already pleaded guilty to perjury and conspiracy to obstruct justice, were lent by or transferred from the White House. Is Mr. Nixon separable from them? Two of his former Cabinet officers are now awaiting judicial trial. Is he separable from them? His two closest advisers, his director of the F.B.I., his second nominee as Attorney General, have all resigned under the pressure of mounting disclosures. Is he separable from them? Corrupt practice in the form of selling Government favor to big business from I.T.T. and the milk lobby down have been his Administration's normal habit. Is he separable from that—or from the use of the taxpayer's money to improve his private homes?

Finally, under his authorization, the Pentagon carried on a secret and falsified bombing of Cambodia and lied about it to Congress, while the President himself lied to this country about respecting Cambodia's neutrality. There will be no end to the revelations of misconduct because misconduct was standard operating procedure.

In the light of this record, the question whether Mr. Nixon did or did not verbally implicate himself in the coverup of Watergate is not of the essence. The acts that needed covering and the process of covering were performed by members of his Administration.

Risks of Dictatorship

The lesson being taught to the country by Senator [Sam] Ervin and his colleagues is an education itself. Next to letting the people know, the prosecution and legal punishment of individuals is secondary. Yet I wish the Senate select committee would enlarge its focus because the emphasis on documentary or tape-recorded proof contains perils. If, as is conceivable, the proof fails, we will be left with a Government too compromised ever to be trusted and too damaged to recover authority. In such case an impotent or paralyzed Government will, like Taiwan president Chiang Kai-shek's, harden its monarchial or dictatorial tendencies, already well developed in the Nixon regime. Worse, we will have demonstrated for the benefit of Mr. Nixon's successors what measure of cynicism and what deprivation of their liberties the American people are ready to tolerate. From there the slide into dictatorship is easy.

At this time in world history when totalitarian government is in command of the two other largest powers, it is imperative for the United States to preserve and restore to original principles our constitutional structure. The necessary step is for Congress and the American public to grasp the nettle of impeachment if we must.

II

The Committee on the Judiciary, to whom was referred the consideration of recommendations concerning the exercise of the constitutional power to impeach Richard M. Nixon, President of the United States, having considered the same, reports thereon pursuant to H. Res. 803 as follows and recommends that the House exercise its constitutional power to impeach Richard M. Nixon, President of the United States, and that articles of impeachment be exhibited to the Senate as follows:

Resolution

Impeaching Richard M. Nixon, President of the United States, of high crimes and misdemeanors.

Resolved, That Richard M. Nixon, President of the United States, is impeached for high crimes and misdemeanors, and that the following articles of impeachment be exhibited to the Senate:

Articles of impeachment exhibited by the House of Representatives of the United States of America in the name of itself and of all of the people of the United States of America, against Richard M. Nixon, President of the United States of America, in maintenance and support of its impeachment against him for high crimes and misdemeanors.

Article I

In his conduct of the office of President of the United States, Richard M. Nixon, in violation of his constitutional oath faithfully to execute the office of President of the United States and, to the best of his ability, preserve, protect, and defend the Constitution of the United States, and in violation of his constitutional duty to take care that the laws be faithfully executed, has prevented, obstructed, and impeded the administration of justice, in that:

On June 17, 1972, and prior thereto, agents of the Committee for the Re-election of the President committed unlawful entry of the headquarters of the Democratic National Committee in Washington, District of Columbia, for the purpose of securing political intelligence. Subsequent thereto, Richard M. Nixon, using the powers of his high office, engaged personally and through his subordinates and agents, in a course of conduct or plan designed to delay, impede, and obstruct the investigation of such unlawful entry; to cover up, conceal and protect those responsible; and to conceal the existence and scope of other unlawful covert activities.

The means used to implement this course of conduct or plan included one or more of the following:

(1) making or causing to be made false or misleading statements to lawfully authorized investigative officers and employees of the United States;

(2) withholding relevant and material evidence or information from lawfully authorized investigative officers and employees of the United States;

(3) approving, condoning, acquiescing in, and counseling witnesses with respect to the giving of false or misleading statements to lawfully authorized inves-

tigative officers and employees of the United States and false or misleading testimony in duly instituted judicial and congressional proceedings;

(4) interfering or endeavoring to interfere with the conduct of investigations by the Department of Justice of the United States, the Federal Bureau of Investigation, the Office of Watergate Special Prosecution Force, and Congressional Committees;

(5) approving, condoning, and acquiescing in, the surreptitious payment of substantial sums of money for the purpose of obtaining the silence or influencing the testimony of witnesses, potential witnesses, or individuals who participated in such unlawful entry and other illegal activities;

(6) endeavoring to misuse the Central Intelligence Agency, an agency of the United States;

(7) disseminating information received from officers of the Department of Justice of the United States to subjects of investigations conducted by lawfully authorized investigative officers and employees of the United States, for the purpose of aiding and assisting such subjects in their attempts to avoid criminal liability;

(8) making false or misleading public statements for the purpose of deceiving the people of the United States into believing that a thorough and complete investigation had been conducted with respect to allegations of misconduct on the part of personnel of the executive branch of the United States and personnel of the Committee for the Re-election of the President, and that there was no involvement of such personnel in such misconduct; or

(9) endeavoring to cause prospective defendants, and individuals duly tried and convicted, to expect favored treatment and consideration in return for their silence or false testimony, or rewarding individuals for their silence or false testimony.

In all of this, Richard M. Nixon has acted in a manner contrary to his trust as President and subversive of constitutional government, to the great prejudice of the cause of law and justice and to the manifest injury of the people of the United States.

Wherefore Richard M. Nixon, by such conduct, warrants impeachment and trial, and removal from office.

Article II

Using the powers of the office of President of the United States, Richard M. Nixon, in violation of his constitutional oath faithfully to execute the office of President of the United States and, to the best of his ability, preserve, protect, and defend the Constitution of the United States, and in disregard of his constitutional duty to take care that the laws be faithfully executed, has repeatedly engaged in conduct violating the constitutional rights of citizens, impairing the due and proper administration of justice and the conduct of lawful inquiries, or contravening the laws governing agencies of the executive branch and the purposes of these agencies.

This conduct has included one or more of the following:

(1) He has, acting personally and through his subordinates and agents, endeavored to obtain from the Internal Revenue Service, in violation of the constitutional rights of citizens, confidential information contained in income tax returns for purposes not authorized by law, and to cause, in violation of the constitutional rights of citizens, income tax audits or other income tax investigations to be initiated or conducted in a discriminatory manner.

(2) He misused the Federal Bureau of Investigation, the Secret Service, and other executive personnel, in violation or disregard of the constitutional rights of citizens, by directing or authorizing such agencies or personnel to conduct or continue electronic surveillance or other investigations for purposes unrelated to national security, the enforcement of laws, or any other lawful function of his office; he did direct, authorize, or permit the use of information obtained thereby for purposes unrelated to national security, the enforcement of laws, or any other lawful function of his office; and he did direct the concealment of certain records made by the Federal Bureau of Investigation of electronic surveillance.

(3) He has, acting personally and through his subordinates and agents, in violation or disregard of the constitutional rights of citizens, authorized and permitted to be maintained a secret investigative unit within the office of the President, financed in part with money derived from campaign contributions, which unlawfully utilized the resources of the Central Intelligence Agency, engaged in covert and unlawful activities, and attempted to prejudice the constitutional right of an accused to a fair trial.

(4) He has failed to take care that the laws were faithfully executed by failing to act when he knew or had reason to know that his close subordinates endeavored to impede and frustrate lawful inquiries by duly constituted executive, judicial, and legislative entities concerning the unlawful entry into the headquarters of the Democratic National Committee, and the cover-up thereof, and concerning other unlawful activities, including those relating to the confirmation of Richard Kleindienst as Attorney General of the United States, the electronic surveillance of private citizens, the break-in into the offices of Dr. Lewis Fielding, and the campaign financing practices of the Committee to Re-elect the President.

(5) In disregard of the rule of law, he knowingly misused the executive power by interfering with agencies of the executive branch, including the Federal Bureau of Investigation, the Criminal Division, and the Office of Watergate Special Prosecution Force, of the Department of Justice, and the Central Intelligence Agency, in violation of his duty to take care that the laws be faithfully executed.

In all of this, Richard M. Nixon has acted in a manner contrary to his trust as President and subversive of constitutional government, to the great prejudice of the cause of law and justice and to the manifest injury of the people of the United States.

Wherefore Richard M. Nixon, by such conduct, warrants impeachment and trial, and removal from office.

Article III

In his conduct of the office of President of the United States, Richard M. Nixon, contrary to his oath faithfully to execute the office of President of the United States and, to the best of his ability, preserve, protect, and defend the Constitution of the United States, and in violation of his constitutional duty to take care that the laws be faithfully executed, has failed without lawful cause or excuse to produce papers and things as directed by duly authorized subpoenas issued by the Committee on the Judiciary of the House of Representatives on April 11, 1974, May 15, 1974, May 30, 1974, and June 24, 1974, and willfully disobeyed such subpoenas. The subpoenaed papers and things were deemed necessary by the Committee in order to resolve by direct evidence fundamental, factual questions relating to Presidential direction, knowledge, or approval of actions demonstrated by other evidence to be substantial grounds for impeachment of the President. In refusing to produce these papers and things, Richard M. Nixon, substituting his judgment as to what materials were necessary for the inquiry, interposed the powers of the Presidency against the lawful subpoenas of the House of Representatives, thereby assuming to himself functions and judgments necessary to the exercise of the sole power of impeachment vested by the Constitution in the House of Representatives.

In all of this, Richard M. Nixon has acted in a manner contrary to his trust as President and subversive of constitutional government, to the great prejudice of the cause of law and justice, and to the manifest injury of the people of the United States.

Wherefore Richard M. Nixon, by such conduct, warrants impeachment and trial, and removal from office.

For Further Reading

Carl Bernstein and Bob Woodward, *All the President's Men.* New York: Simon and Schuster, 1974.

Stanley L. Kutler, *The Wars of Watergate: The Last Crisis of Richard Nixon.* New York: Knopf, 1990.

Richard Nixon, *RN: The Memoirs of Richard Nixon.* New York: Grosset & Dunlap, 1978.

Herbert Parmet, *Richard Nixon and His America*. Boston: Little, Brown, 1990.

Theodore H. White, *Breach of Faith: The Fall of Richard Nixon*. New York: Atheneum, 1975.

Viewpoint 40A

America Is Facing a Crisis of Confidence (1979)

Jimmy Carter (b. 1924)

Jimmy Carter, a former governor of Georgia, won election to the presidency in 1976, following a post-Watergate campaign during which he pledged to restore trust in government. His popularity waned during his presidency, however, as he struggled with a variety of domestic and international problems. One major area of concern was energy. America in 1978 imported 40 percent of its oil, buying much of it from countries in the turbulent Middle East. In 1979 gasoline shortages developed after the American-supported government of Iran fell to Islamic revolutionaries, who then cut off oil exports to the United States.

The following viewpoint is taken from a televised speech Carter delivered to the nation on July 15, 1979. After recounting some advice he had received from Americans from various segments of society during the previous ten days, Carter argues that the energy crisis is part of a deeper problem—a national "crisis of confidence" in a country struggling to regain trust in its institutions and learning to live in a new era of limits. He argues that the Vietnam War, Watergate, and other developments have caused many people to be disillusioned about the strength and legitimacy of the American government. Carter concludes by listing his recommendations for reducing the nation's dependence on foreign energy supplies, which he argues will also help renew America's confidence and sense of purpose.

What does Carter mean by a "crisis of confidence"? What in his view are the causes of this crisis? Between what "two paths" must America choose, according to Carter?

G ood evening.
      This is a special night for me. Exactly 3 years ago, on July 15, 1976, I accepted the nomination of my party to run for President of the United States. I promised you a President who is not

From *Public Papers of the Presidents of the United States: Jimmy Carter, 1979*, vol. 2 (Washington, DC: National Archives and Records Service, 1980).

isolated from the people, who feels your pain, and who shares your dreams and who draws his strength and his wisdom from you.

During the past 3 years I've spoken to you on many occasions about national concerns, the energy crisis, reorganizing the Government, our Nation's economy, and issues of war and especially peace. But over those years the subjects of the speeches, the talks, and the press conferences have become increasingly narrow, focused more and more on what the isolated world of Washington thinks is important. Gradually, you've heard more and more about what the Government thinks or what the Government should be doing and less and less about our Nation's hopes, our dreams, and our vision of the future.

Ten days ago I had planned to speak to you again about a very important subject—energy. For the fifth time I would have described the urgency of the problem and laid out a series of legislative recommendations to the Congress. But as I was preparing to speak, I began to ask myself the same question that I now know has been troubling many of you. Why have we not been able to get together as a nation to resolve our serious energy problem?

Listening to America

It's clear that the true problems of our Nation are much deeper—deeper than gasoline lines or energy shortages, deeper even than inflation or recession. And I realize more than ever that as President I need your help. So, I decided to reach out and listen to the voices of America.

I invited to Camp David people from almost every segment of our society—business and labor, teachers and preachers, Governors, mayors, and private citizens. And then I left Camp David to listen to other Americans, men and women like you. It has been an extraordinary 10 days, and I want to share with you what I've heard.

First of all, I got a lot of personal advice. Let me quote a few of the typical comments that I wrote down.

This from a southern Governor: "Mr. President, you are not leading this Nation—you're just managing the Government."

"You don't see the people enough anymore."

"Some of your Cabinet members don't seem loyal. There is not enough discipline among your disciples."

"Don't talk to us about politics or the mechanics of government, but about an understanding of our common good."

"Mr. President, we're in trouble. Talk to us about blood and sweat and tears."

"If you lead, Mr. President, we will follow."

Many people talked about themselves and about the condition of our Nation. This from a young woman in Pennsylvania: "I feel so far from government. I feel like ordinary people are excluded from political power."

And this from a young Chicano: "Some of us have suffered from recession all our lives."

"Some people have wasted energy, but others haven't had anything to waste."

And this from a religious leader: "No material shortage can touch the important things like God's love for us or our love for one another."

And I like this one particularly from a black woman who happens to be the mayor of a small Mississippi town: "The big-shots are not the only ones who are important. Remember, you can't sell anything on Wall Street unless someone digs it up somewhere else first."

This kind of summarized a lot of other statements: "Mr. President, we are confronted with a moral and a spiritual crisis."

Several of our discussions were on energy, and I have a notebook full of comments and advice. I'll read just a few.

"We can't go on consuming 40 percent more energy than we produce. When we import oil we are also importing inflation plus unemployment."

"We've got to use what we have. The Middle East has only 5 percent of the world's energy, but the United States has 24 percent."

And this is one of the most vivid statements: "Our neck is stretched over the fence and OPEC [Organization of Petroleum Exporting Countries] has a knife."

"The erosion of our confidence in the future is threatening to destroy the social and the political fabric of America."

"There will be other cartels and other shortages. American wisdom and courage right now can set a path to follow in the future."

This was a good one: "Be bold, Mr. President. We may make mistakes, but we are ready to experiment."

And this one from a labor leader got to the heart of it: "The real issue is freedom. We must deal with the energy problem on a war footing."

And the last that I'll read: "When we enter the moral equivalent of war, Mr. President, don't issue us BB guns."

These 10 days confirmed my belief in the decency and the strength and the wisdom of the American people, but it also bore out some of my long-standing concerns about our Nation's underlying problems.

I know, of course, being President, that government actions and legislation can be very important. That's why I've worked hard to put my campaign promises into law—and I have to admit, with just mixed success. But after listening to the American people I have been reminded again that all the legislation in the world can't fix what's wrong with America. So, I want to speak to you first tonight about a subject even more serious than energy or inflation. I want to talk to you right now about a fundamental threat to American democracy.

I do not mean our political and civil liberties. They will endure. And I do not refer to the outward strength of America, a nation that is at peace tonight everywhere in the world, with unmatched economic power and military might.

A Crisis of Confidence

The threat is nearly invisible in ordinary ways. It is a crisis of confidence. It is a crisis that strikes at the very heart and soul and spirit of our national will. We can see this crisis in the growing doubt about the meaning of our own lives and in the loss of a unity of purpose for our Nation.

The erosion of our confidence in the future is threatening to destroy the social and the political fabric of America.

The confidence that we have always had as a people is not simply some romantic dream or a proverb in a dusty book that we read just on the Fourth of July. It is the idea which founded our Nation and has guided our development as a people. Confidence in the future has supported everything else—public institutions and private enterprise, our own families, and the very Constitution of the United States. Confidence has defined our course and has served as a link between generations. We've always believed in something called progress. We've always had a faith that the days of our children would be better than our own.

Our people are losing that faith, not only in government itself but in the ability as citizens to serve as the ultimate rulers and shapers of our democracy. As a people we know our past and we are proud of it. Our progress has been part of the living history of America, even the world. We always believed that we were part of a great movement of humanity itself called democracy, involved in the search for freedom, and that belief has always strengthened us in our purpose. But just as we are losing our confidence in the future, we are also beginning to close the door on our past.

In a nation that was proud of hard work, strong families, close-knit communities, and our faith in God, too many of us now tend to worship self-indulgence and consumption. Human identity is no longer defined by what one does, but by what one owns. But we've discovered that owning things and consuming things does not satisfy our longing for meaning. We've learned that piling up material goods cannot fill the emptiness of lives which have no confidence or purpose.

The symptoms of this crisis of the American spirit are all around us. For the first time in the history of our country a majority of our people believe that the next 5 years will be worse than the past 5 years. Two-thirds of our people do not even vote. The productivity of American workers is actually dropping, and the willingness of Americans to save for the future has fallen below that of all other people in the Western world.

As you know, there is a growing disrespect for government and for churches and for schools, the news media, and other institutions. This is not a message of happiness or reassurance, but it is the truth and it is a warning.

America's Wounds

These changes did not happen overnight. They've come upon us gradually over the last generation, years that were filled with shocks and tragedy.

We were sure that ours was a nation of the ballot, not the bullet, until the murders of John Kennedy and Robert Kennedy and Martin Luther King, Jr. We were taught that our armies were always invincible and our causes were always just, only to suffer the agony of Vietnam. We respected the Presidency as a place of honor until the shock of Watergate.

We remember when the phrase "sound as a dollar" was an expression of absolute dependability, until 10 years of inflation began to shrink our dollar and our savings. We believed that our Nation's resources were limitless until 1973, when we had to face a growing dependence on foreign oil.

These wounds are still very deep. They have never been healed.

Looking for a way out of this crisis, our people have turned to the Federal Government and found it isolated from the mainstream of our Nation's life. Washington, D.C., has become an island. The gap between our citizens and our Government has never been so wide. The people are looking for honest answers, not easy answers; clear leadership, not false claims and evasiveness and politics as usual.

What you see too often in Washington and elsewhere around the country is a system of government that seems incapable of action. You see a Congress twisted and pulled in every direction by hundreds of well-financed and powerful special interests. You see every extreme position defended to the last vote, almost to the last breath by one unyielding group or another. You often see a balanced and a fair approach

that demands sacrifice, a little sacrifice from everyone, abandoned like an orphan without support and without friends.

Often you see paralysis and stagnation and drift. You don't like it, and neither do I. What can we do?

Restoring Faith

First of all, we must face the truth, and then we can change our course. We simply must have faith in each other, faith in our ability to govern ourselves, and faith in the future of this Nation. Restoring that faith and that confidence to America is now the most important task we face. It is a true challenge of this generation of Americans.

One of the visitors to Camp David last week put it this way: "We've got to stop crying and start sweating, stop talking and start walking, stop cursing and start praying. The strength we need will not come from the White House, but from every house in America."

We know the strength of America. We are strong. We can regain our unity. We can regain our confidence. We are the heirs of generations who survived threats much more powerful and awesome than those that challenge us now. Our fathers and mothers were strong men and women who shaped a new society during the Great Depression, who fought world wars, and who carved out a new charter of peace for the world

We ourselves are the same Americans who just 10 years ago put a man on the Moon. We are the generation that dedicated our society to the pursuit of human rights and equality. And we are the generation that will win the war on the energy problem and in that process rebuild the unity and confidence of America.

Two Paths

We are at a turning point in our history. There are two paths to choose. One is a path I've warned about tonight, the path that leads to fragmentation and self-interest. Down that road lies a mistaken idea of freedom, the right to grasp for ourselves some advantage over others. That path would be one of constant conflict between narrow interests ending in chaos and immobility. It is a certain route to failure.

All the traditions of our past, all the lessons of our heritage, all the promises of our future point to another path, the path of common purpose and the restoration of American values. That path leads to true freedom for our Nation and ourselves. We can take the first steps down that path as we begin to solve our energy problem. Energy will be the immediate test of our ability to unite this Nation and it can also be the standard around which we rally.

In little more than two decades we have gone from

a position of energy independence to one in which almost half the oil we use comes from foreign countries, at prices that are going through the roof. Our excessive dependence on OPEC has already taken a tremendous toll on our economy and our people.

This is the direct cause of the long lines which have made millions of you spend aggravating hours waiting for gasoline. It is a cause of the increased inflation and unemployment that we now face. This intolerable dependence on foreign oil threatens our economic independence and the very security of our Nation.

A New Energy Policy

Point one: I am tonight setting a clear goal for the energy policy of the United States. Beginning this moment, this Nation will never use more foreign oil than we did in 1977—never. From now on, every new addition to our demand for energy will be met from our own production and our own conservation. . . .

Point two: To ensure that we meet these targets, I will use my Presidential authority to set import quotas. I am announcing tonight that for 1979 and 1980, I will forbid the entry into this country of one drop of foreign oil more than these goals allow. . . .

Point three: To give us energy security, I am asking for the most massive peacetime commitment of funds and resources in our nation's history to develop America's own alternative sources of fuel—from coal, from oil shale, from plant products for gasohol, from unconventional gas, from the sun. . . .

Point four: I am asking Congress to mandate, to require as a matter of law, that our Nation's utility companies cut their massive use of oil by 50 percent within the next decade and switch to other fuels, especially coal, our most abundant energy source.

Point five: To make absolutely certain that nothing stands in the way of achieving these goals, I will urge Congress to create an Energy Mobilization Board which, like the War Production Board in World War II, will have the responsibility and authority to cut through the red tape, the delays, and the endless roadblocks to completing key energy projects.

We will protect our environment. But when this Nation critically needs a refinery or a pipeline, we will build it.

Point six: I am proposing a bold conservation program to involve every state, county and city and every average American in our energy battle. This effort will permit you to build conservation into your home and your lives at a cost you can afford.

I ask Congress to give me authority for mandatory conservation and for standby gasoline rationing. To further conserve energy, I am proposing tonight an extra $10 billion over the next decade to strengthen our public transportation systems, and I am asking you for your good and for your Nation's security to take no unnecessary trips, to use car pools or public transportation whenever you can, to park your car one extra day per week, to obey the speed limit and to set your thermostats to save fuel. . . .

Every gallon of oil each one of us saves is a new form of production. It gives us more freedom, more confidence, that much more control over our own lives.

So the solution of our energy crisis can also help us to conquer the crisis of the spirit in our country. It can rekindle our sense of unity, our confidence in the future, and give our nation and all of us individually a new sense of purpose.

VIEWPOINT 40B

The American Spirit Remains Strong (1980)

Ronald Reagan (b. 1911)

The 1980 presidential election featured as its two major candidates Jimmy Carter, the incumbent, and Ronald Reagan, a former motion picture actor and governor of California. Reagan, who had sought the Republican nomination in 1968 and 1976 before succeeding on his third attempt, was a leading figure of the conservative wing of the Republican Party. In the following viewpoint, excerpted from his acceptance speech at the 1980 Republican National Convention, Reagan expounds on conservative themes that would help him win the 1980 and 1984 presidential elections.

Reagan argues in his 1980 speech that the source of many of America's problems is the federal government itself, which he claims has burdened the American people with high taxes and cumbersome regulations. He advocates cutting both taxes and government programs. The solution to the nation's chronic energy shortages, he asserts as one example, is to reduce government regulation and encourage the increased domestic production of oil, coal, and other energy sources. Reagan attacks his electoral opponent, Carter, both directly, on his ineffective policies and leadership, and indirectly, on his failure to appreciate and inspire American confidence.

How do Reagan's views of the fundamental problems facing America differ from those of Jimmy Carter, author of viewpoint 40A? What does Reagan promise to accomplish as president? Based on these viewpoints, do you think Reagan and Carter have opposing views on whether the "American spirit" is strong? Why or why not?

From Ronald Reagan's acceptance speech at the Republican National Convention, Detroit, Michigan, July 17, 1980. The complete speech is reprinted in *Vital Speeches of the Day*, August 15, 1980.

With a deep awareness of the responsibility conferred by your trust, I accept your nomination for the Presidency of the United States. I do so with deep gratitude.

I am very proud of our party tonight. This convention has shown to all America a party united, with positive programs for solving the nation's problems; a party ready to build a new consensus with all those across the land who share a community of values embodied in these words: family, work, neighborhood, peace, and freedom. . . .

More than anything else, I want my candidacy to unify our country, to renew the American spirit and sense of purpose. I want to carry our message to every American, regardless of party affiliation, who is a member of this community, of shared values.

Never before in our history have Americans been called upon to face three grave threats to our very existence, any one of which could destroy us. We face a disintegrating economy, a weakened defense, and an energy policy based on the sharing of scarcity.

A Failure of Leadership

The major issue of this campaign is the direct political, personal, and moral responsibility of Democratic Party leadership—in the White House and in Congress—for this unprecedented calamity which has befallen us. They tell us they have done the most that could humanly be done. They say that the United States has had its days in the sun, that our nation has passed its zenith. They expect you to tell your children that the American people no longer have the will to cope with their problems, that the future will be one of sacrifice and few opportunities.

My fellow citizens, I utterly reject that view. The American people, the most generous on earth, who created the highest standard of living, are not going to accept the notion that we can only make a better world for others by moving backward ourselves. Those who believe we can have no business leading the nation.

I will not stand by and watch this great country destroy itself under mediocre leadership that drifts from one crisis to the next, eroding our national will and purpose. We have come together here because the American people deserve better from those to whom they entrust our nation's highest office, and we stand united in our resolve to do something about it. . . .

[In 1863] Abraham Lincoln called upon the people of all America to renew their dedication and their commitment to a government of, for, and by the people.

Isn't it time once again to renew our compact of freedom, to pledge to each other all that is best in our lives, all that gives meaning to them—for the sake of this, our beloved and blessed land?

A New Beginning

Together, let us make this a new beginning. Let us make a commitment to care for the needy, to teach our children the values and the virtues handed down to us by our families, to have the courage to defend those values and the willingness to sacrifice for them.

Let us pledge to restore, in our time, the American spirit of voluntary service, of cooperation, of private and community initiative, a spirit that flows like a deep and mighty river through the history of our nation.

As your nominee, I pledge to restore to the federal government the capacity to do the people's work without dominating their lives. I pledge to you a government that will not only work well, but wisely, its ability to act tempered by prudence, and its willingness to do good balanced by the knowledge that government is never more dangerous than when our desire to have it help us blinds us to its great power to harm us. . . .

The Energy Crisis

Those who preside over the worst energy shortage in our history tell us to use less, so that we will run out of oil, gasoline, and natural gas a little more slowly. Conservation is desirable, of course, for we must not waste energy. But conservation is not the sole answer to our energy needs.

America must get to work producing more energy. The Republican program for solving economic problems is based on growth and productivity.

Large amounts of oil and natural gas lie beneath our land and off our shores, untouched because the present Administration seems to believe the American people would rather see more regulation, taxes, and controls than more energy.

Coal offers great potential. So does nuclear energy produced under rigorous safety standards. It could supply electricity for thousands of industries and millions of jobs and homes. It must not be thwarted by a tiny minority opposed to economic growth, which often finds friendly ears in regulatory agencies for its obstructionist campaigns.

Make no mistake. We will not permit the safety of our people or our environmental heritage to be jeopardized. But we are going to reaffirm that the economic prosperity of our people is a fundamental part of our environment.

Our problems are both acute and chronic, yet all we hear from those in positions of leadership are the same tired proposals for more government tinkering, more meddling, and more control—all of which led us to this state in the first place. . . .

Reducing Government

We Republicans believe it is essential that we maintain both the forward momentum of economic growth and the strength of the safety net beneath those in society who need help. We also believe it is essential that the integrity of all aspects of Social Security be preserved.

Beyond these essentials, I believe it is clear our federal government is overgrown and overweight. Indeed, it is time for our government to go on a diet. Therefore, my first act as Chief Executive will be to impose an immediate and thorough freeze on federal hiring. Then, we are going to enlist the very best minds from business, labor, and whatever quarter we can to conduct a detailed review of every department, bureau, and agency that lives by federal appropriation. We are also going to enlist the help and ideas of many dedicated and hard-working government employees at all levels who want a more efficient government as much as the rest of us do. I know that many are demoralized by the confusion and waste they confront in their work as a result of failed and failing policies.

Our instructions to the groups we enlist will be simple and direct. We will remind them that government programs exist at the sufferance of the American taxpayer and are paid for with money earned by working men and women. Any program that represents a waste of their money—a theft from their pocketbooks—must have that waste eliminated, or the program must go: by Executive Order where possible, by Congressional action where necessary. Everything that can be run more effectively by state and local government, we shall turn over to state and local government, along with the funding sources to pay for it. We are going to put an end to the money merry-go-round where our money becomes Washington's money, to be spent by the states and cities only if they spend it exactly the way the federal bureaucrats tell them to.

•

"The American spirit is still there, ready to blaze into life."

•

I will not accept the excuse that the federal government has grown so big and powerful that it is beyond the control of any President, any Administration or Congress. We are going to put an end to the notion that the American taxpayer exists to fund the federal government. The federal government exists to serve the American people and to be accountable to the American people. On January 20th, we are going to reestablish that truth.

Also on that date we are going to initiate action to get substantial relief for our taxpaying citizens and action to put people back to work. None of this will be based on any new form of monetary tinkering or fiscal sleight of hand. We will simply apply to government the common sense we all use in our daily lives.

Work and family are at the center of our lives, the foundation of our dignity as a free people. When we deprive people of what they have earned, or take away their jobs, we destroy their dignity and undermine their families. We cannot support our families unless there are jobs, and we cannot have jobs unless people have both money to invest and the faith to invest it.

These are concepts that stem from the foundation of an economic system that for more than two hundred years has helped us master a continent, create a previously undreamed-of prosperity for our people, and feed millions of others around the globe. That system will continue to serve us in the future, if our government will stop ignoring the basic values on which it was built and stop betraying the trust and goodwill of the American workers who keep it going.

The Tax Burden

The American people are carrying the heaviest peacetime tax burden in our nation's history—and it will grow even heavier, under present law, next January. This burden is crushing our ability and incentive to save, invest and produce. We are taxing ourselves into economic exhaustion and stagnation.

This must stop. We must halt this fiscal self-destruction and restore sanity to our economic system.

I have long advocated a 30 percent reduction in income tax rates over a period of three years. This phased tax reduction would begin with a 10 percent "down payment" tax cut in 1981, which the Republicans in Congress and I have already proposed.

A phased reduction of tax rates would go a long way toward easing the heavy burden on the American people. . . .

When I talk of tax cuts, I am reminded that every major tax cut in this century has strengthened the economy, generated renewed productivity, and ended up yielding new revenues for the government by creating new investment, new jobs, and more commerce among our people. . . .

Thanks to the economic policies of the Democratic Party, millions of Americans find themselves out of work. Millions more have never even had a fair chance to learn new skills, hold a decent job, seize the opportunity to climb the ladder and secure for themselves and their families a share in the prosperity of his nation.

It is time to put America back to work, to make our cities and towns resound with the confident voices of men and women of all races, nationalities, and faiths bringing home to their families a decent paycheck they can cash for honest money.

For those who have abandoned hope, we'll restore hope, and we'll welcome them into a great national crusade to make America great again! . . .

Meeting the American People

This evening marks the last step—save one—of a campaign that has taken Nancy and me from one end of this great land to the other, over many months and thousands and thousands of miles. There are those who question the way we choose a President, who say that our process imposes difficult and exhausting burdens on those who seek the office. I have not found it so.

It is impossible to capture in words the splendor of this vast continent which God has granted as our portion of His creation. There are no words to express the extraordinary strength and character of this breed of people we call Americans.

Everywhere we have met thousands of Democrats, Independents, and Republicans from all economic conditions and walks of life bound together in that community of shared values of family, work, neighborhood, peace, and freedom. They are concerned, yes, but they are not frightened. They are disturbed, but not dismayed. They are the kind of men and women Tom Paine had in mind when he wrote—during the darkest days of the American Revolution—"We have it in our power to begin the world over again."

Nearly one hundred and fifty years after Tom Paine wrote those words, an American President told the generation of the Great Depression that it had "a rendezvous with destiny." I believe this generation of Americans today also has a rendezvous with destiny.

The American Spirit

Tonight, let us dedicate ourselves to renewing the American Compact. I ask you not simply to "Trust me," but to trust your values—our values—and to hold me responsible for living up to them. I ask you to trust the American spirit which knows no ethnic, religious, social, political, regional, or economic boundaries, the spirit that burned with zeal in the hearts of millions of immigrants from every corner of the earth who came here in search of freedom.

Some say that spirit no longer exists. But I have seen it—I have felt it—all across the land, in the big cities, in the small towns, in rural America. The American spirit is still there, ready to blaze into life if you and I are willing to do what has to be done, the

practical, down-to-earth things that will stimulate our economy, increase productivity, and put America back to work.

The time is now to limit federal spending, to insist on a stable monetary reform, and to free ourselves from imported oil.

The time is now to resolve that the basis of a firm and principled foreign policy is one that takes the world as it is and seeks to change it by leadership and example, not by lecture and harangue.

The time is now to say that while we shall seek new friendships and expand and improve others, we shall not do so by breaking our word or casting aside old friends and allies.

And the time is now to redeem promises once made to the American people by another candidate, in another time and place. He said:

"For three long years I have been going up and down this country preaching that government—federal, state, and local—costs too much. I shall not stop that preaching. As an immediate program of action, we must abolish useless offices. We must eliminate unnecessary functions of government. . . .

"We must consolidate subdivisions of government and, like the private citizen, give up luxuries which we can no longer afford.

"I propose to you, my friends, and through you, that government of all kinds, big and little, be made solvent, and that an example be set by the President of the United States and his cabinet."

So said Franklin Delano Roosevelt in his acceptance speech to the Democratic National Convention in July 1932.

The time is now, my fellow Americans, to recapture our destiny, to take it into our own hands. But to do this will take many of us, working together. I ask you tonight to volunteer your help in this cause, so we can carry our message throughout the land.

Yes, isn't now the time that we, the people, carry out these unkept promises? Let us pledge to each other and to all America on this July day forty-eight years later that we intend to do just that.

I've thought of something that is not part of my speech, and I'm worried about whether I should do it.

Can we doubt that only a Divine Providence placed this land, this island of freedom, here as a refuge for all those people in the world who yearn to breathe freely: Jews and Christians enduring persecution behind the Iron Curtain, the boat people of Southeast Asia, of Cuba and Haiti, the victims of the drought in Africa, the freedom fighters of Afghanistan, and our own countrymen held in savage captivity?

I'll confess that I've been a little afraid to suggest what I'm going to suggest—I'm more afraid not to: that we begin our crusade joined together in a moment of silent prayer. God bless America.

For Further Reading

Robert N. Bellah, *Habits of the Heart.* Berkeley: University of California Press, 1985.

Lou Cannon, *Reagan.* New York: Putnam, 1982.

Barry Commoner, *The Politics of Energy.* New York: Knopf, 1979.

Garland A. Haas, *Jimmy Carter and the Politics of Frustration.* Jefferson, NC: McFarland & Co., 1992.

Haynes Johnson, *In the Absence of Power: Governing America.* New York: Viking Press, 1980.

Garry Wills, *Reagan's America: Innocents at Home.* New York: Penguin Books, 1988.

The End of the Cold War

VIEWPOINT 41A

The End of the Cold War Marked a Great Triumph for the United States (1992)

John Lewis Gaddis (b. 1941)

The Cold War between the United States and the Soviet Union, perhaps the single most significant factor of American history following World War II, ended in the late 1980s and early 1990s with the dismantling of the Berlin Wall in Germany in 1989 and the collapse of the Soviet Union in 1991. The significance of the Cold War and its close continues to be debated by historians. One perspective comes from John Lewis Gaddis, director of the Contemporary History Institute at Ohio University in Athens and the author of numerous books on the Cold War, including *Strategies of Containment* and *The Long Peace*. In the following viewpoint, excerpted from an essay published in 1992, Gaddis examines the Cold War in retrospect, noting that it was a period of relative peace compared to the conflicts that had preceded it. He disagrees with historians who have argued that the Cold War was simply a struggle between two great powers or an example of American militarism. The Cold War was an ideological confrontation between the democracy of the United States and the communism of the Soviet Union, Gaddis states, and it ended when the ideological underpinnings of the Soviet Union collapsed.

What defense does Gaddis make of President Harry S. Truman and his decisions at the beginning of the Cold War? How have many scholars been mistaken in their analyses of the Cold War, according to Gaddis? How, in his opinion, did nuclear weapons affect the development of the Cold War?

John Lewis Gaddis, "The Cold War, the Long Peace, and the Future," *Diplomatic History* 16 (Spring 1992). Reprinted with permission.

When the fictional dictator Big Brother proclaimed the propaganda slogan "War Is Peace" in George Orwell's novel *1984*, first published in 1948, he turned out to be a better prophet than anyone, including his creator, could ever have imagined. For we can now see that the Cold War, the most dangerous, bitter, and protracted rivalry between Great Powers in modern history, did in time become the most protracted period of freedom from Great Power war in modern history. Whether or not one approves of the *means* by which this happened, whether or not one even agrees on the *way* in which it happened, the simple fact is that the Cold War did evolve into a Long Peace. Whether the Long Peace can survive the end of the Cold War is, however, quite another matter.

The Cold War was many things to many people. It was a division of the world into two hostile camps. It was a polarization of Europe in general, and of Germany in particular, into antagonistic spheres of influence. It was an ideological contest, some said between capitalism and communism, others said between democracy and authoritarianism. It was a competition for the allegiance of, and for influence over, the so-called Third World. It was a game of wits played out by massive intelligence organizations behind the scenes. It was a struggle that took place within each of its major adversaries as supporters and opponents of confrontation confronted one another. It was a contest that shaped culture, the social and natural sciences, and the writing of history. It was an arms race that held out the possibility—because it generated the capability—of ending civilization altogether. And it was a rivalry that even extended, at one point, beyond the bounds of earth itself, as human beings for the first time left their planet, but for a set of reasons that are likely to seem as parochial to future generations as those that impelled Ferdinand and Isabella to finance Columbus when he first set out for the New World five hundred years ago.

The new world of the post–Cold War era is likely to have few, if any, of these characteristics: that is an indication of how much things have already changed since the Cold War ended. We are at one of those rare points of "punctuation" in history at which old patterns of stability have broken up and new ones have not yet emerged to take their place. Historians will certainly regard the years 1989–1991 as a turning point comparable in importance to the years 1789–1794, or 1917–1918, or 1945–1947; precisely what has "turned," however, is much less certain. We know that a series of geopolitical earthquakes has taken place, but it is not yet clear how these upheavals have rearranged the landscape that lies before us. . . .

No one can foretell, with any assurance, [what] is going to happen. But now that we can at last view the Cold War from beginning to end, it ought to be possible to get a clearer sense than we have had of what that conflict was all about, and to use that knowledge as a basis for attempting to anticipate what is to follow it. Projecting patterns from the past is, to be sure, an imperfect way of seeing into the future. But barring prophecy—whether of divine, ideological, or astrological inspiration—it is the only such means we have: history has always been a less than perfect teacher. This essay deals, therefore, with patterns and probabilities. It makes no assumptions about "laws" of history or the alleged certainties that flow from them. It should, as a consequence, be read with all the caution the phrase caveat emptor has always implied. But one has to start somewhere.

When President Harry S. Truman told the Congress of the United States on 12 March 1947 that the world faced a struggle between two ways of life, one based on the will of the majority and the other based on the will of a minority forcibly imposed upon the majority, he had more than one purpose in mind. The immediate aim, of course, was to prod parsimonious legislators into approving economic and military assistance to Greece and Turkey, and a certain amount of rhetorical dramatization served that end. But President Truman also probably believed what he said, and most Americans and Europeans, at the time, probably agreed with him. Otherwise, the United States would hardly have been able to abandon its historic policy of peacetime isolationism and commit itself, not only to the Truman Doctrine, but to the much more ambitious Marshall Plan and eventually the North Atlantic Treaty Organization as well. Those plans worked, in turn, because most Europeans wanted them to. The danger at the time seemed to be real, and few people at the time had any difficulty in explaining what it was: freedom was under attack, and authoritarianism was threatening it.

———— • ————

"The idea of freedom proved more durable than the practice of authoritarianism, and as a consequence, the Cold War ended."

———— • ————

In the years that followed, though, it became fashionable in academic circles to discount this argument. The Cold War, for many scholars, was not about ideology at all, but rather balances of power and spheres of influence; hence it differed little from other Great Power rivalries in modern and even ancient history. Others saw the Cold War as reflecting the demands of an unprecedentedly powerful American military-industrial complex that had set out to impose its hegemony over the rest of the earth. Students of Cold War origins never entirely neglected issues of ideology and principle, but few of them were prepared to say, as Truman had, that that conflict was *primarily* about the difference between freedom and its absence. Such a view seemed too naïve, too simplistic, and, above all, too self-righteous: politicians might say that kind of thing from public platforms, but professors in the classroom and in their scholarly monographs should not.

What the Cold War Was About

As a result, it was left to the people of Eastern Europe and now the Soviet Union itself—through their own spontaneous but collective actions over the past three years—to remind us of a fact that many of us had become too sophisticated to see, which is that the Cold War really was about the imposition of autocracy and the denial of freedom. That conflict came to an end only when it became clear that authoritarianism could no longer be imposed and freedom could no longer be denied. That fact ought to make us look more seriously at how ideology contributed to the coming of the Cold War in the first place.

Much of twentieth-century history has revolved around the testing a single idea: that one could transform the conduct of politics, government, and even human behavior itself into a "science" which would allow not only predicting the future but even, within certain limits, determining it. This search for a "science" of politics grew out of the revolution that had long since occurred in physics and biology: if scientific laws worked so well in predicting motions of the planets, the argument ran, why should similar laws not govern history, economics, and politics? Karl Marx certainly had such an approach in mind in the 1840s when he worked out his theory of dialectical materialism, which explicitly linked political and social consciousness to irreversible processes of economic development; his collaborator Friedrich Engels insisted in 1880 that the progression from feudalism through capitalism to socialism and ultimately communism was as certain as was the Darwinian process of natural selection.

This movement to transform politics into a science began, it is important to emphasize, with the best of intentions: its goal was to improve the human condition by making human behavior rational, enlightened, and predictable. And it arose as a direct response to abuses, excesses, and inequities that had grown out of the concept of freedom itself, as manifested in the mid-nineteenth century *laissez-faire* capitalism Marx had so strongly condemned.

But the idea of a "science" of politics was flawed from the beginning for the simple reason that human beings do not behave like the objects science studies. People are not laboratory mice; it is impossible to isolate them from the environment that surrounds them. They make judgments, whether rational or irrational, about the probable consequences of their actions, and they can change these actions accordingly. They learn from experience: the inheritance of acquired characteristics may not work in biology, the historian E. H. Carr once pointed out, but it does in history. As a result, people rarely act with the predictability of molecules combining in test tubes, or ball bearings rolling down inclined planes, or even the "dependent variables" that figure so prominently in the writings—and, increasingly, the equations—of our contemporary social scientists.

It was precisely frustration with this irritating unpredictability of human beings that led Lenin at the beginning of this century to invert Marx and make the state the instrument that was supposed to secure human freedom, rather than the obstacle that stood in the way of it. But that same problem of human intractability in turn caused Stalin to invert Lenin and make the state, its survival, and its total control of all its surroundings an end in itself, with a consequent denial of freedom that was as absolute as any autocrat has ever managed to achieve. A movement that had set out in 1848 to free the workers of the world from their chains had wound up, by 1948 and through the logic of its "scientific" approach to politics, insisting that the condition of being in chains was one of perfect freedom.

Anyone contemplating the situation in Europe at the end of World War II would have had good reason, therefore, to regard the very nature of Stalin's regime as a threat, and to fear its possible expansion. That expansion had already taken place in Eastern Europe and the Balkans, not so much because of Stalinism's accomplishments in and of themselves, but rather because of the opportunity created for it by the foolish behavior of the Europeans in allowing another flight from freedom—fascism—to take root among them. In one of history's many paradoxes, a successful, necessary, and wholly legitimate war against fascism created conditions more favorable to the spread of communism than that ideology could ever have managed on its own.

A Real Danger

The dangers Truman warned against in 1947, hence, were real enough. There is such a thing as bending before what one mistakenly believes to be the "wave of the future": fascism had gained its foothold in Europe by just these means. Many Europeans saw communism as such a wave following Hitler's defeat, not because they approved of that ideology, and not because they really expected the Red Army to drive all the way to the English Channel and the Pyrenees; the problem rather was that Europe had fallen into a demoralization so deep and so pervasive that Communists might have found paths to power there by constitutional means, much as the Nazis had done in Germany in 1933. Had that happened there is little reason to believe that constitutional procedures would have survived, any more than they did under Hitler; certainly the experiences of Poland, Romania, Hungary, and, after February 1948, Czechoslovakia do not suggest otherwise. Stalin's system could have spread throughout Europe without Stalin having to lift a finger: that was the threat. The actions the United States took, through the Truman Doctrine, the Marshall Plan, and NATO, were seen at the time and I think will be seen by future historians as having restored self-confidence among the Europeans, as having preserved the idea of freedom in Europe by a narrow and precarious margin at a time when Europeans themselves, reeling from the effects of two world wars, had almost given up on it.

To be sure, some historians have claimed that Europe might have saved itself even if the Americans had done nothing. There is no way now to prove that they are wrong. But few Europeans saw things this way at the time, and that brings us to one of the most important distinctions that has to be made if we are to understand the origins, evolution, and subsequent end of the Cold War: it is that the expansion of American and Soviet influence into Europe—the processes that really began that conflict—did not take place in the same way and with the same results. The Soviet Union, acting from primarily defensive motives, imposed its sphere of influence directly on Eastern Europe and the Balkans, against the will of the people who lived there. The United States, also acting for defensive reasons, responded to invitations from desperate governments in Western Europe, the Mediterranean, and even the Middle East to create countervailing spheres of influence in those regions. Compared to the alternative, American hegemony—for there is no denying that such a thing did develop—definitely seemed the lesser of two evils.

This distinction between imposition and invitation—too easily lost sight of in too much of the writing that has been done about Cold War history—proved to be critical in determining not only the shape but also the ultimate outcome of the Cold War. The system the United States built in Western Europe quickly won legitimacy in the form of widespread popular support. The Warsaw Pact and the other instruments of Soviet control in Eastern Europe never did. This happened because Europeans at the time understood the difference between authoritarianism and its absence, just as more recent Europeans and now citizens of the former Soviet Union itself have come to understand it. Survivors of World War II had no more desire to embrace the Stalinist model of "scientific" politics than their children and grandchildren have had to remain under it. Moscow's authority in Eastern Europe turned out to be a hollow shell, kept in place only by the sheer weight of Soviet military power. Once it became apparent, in the late 1980s, that Mikhail Gorbachev's government was no longer willing (or able) to prop it up, the system Stalin had imposed upon half of Europe almost half a century earlier collapsed like a house of cards.

The way the Cold War ended, therefore, was directly related to the way in which it had begun. Perhaps Harry Truman had it right after all: the struggle really was, ultimately, about two ways of life, one that abandoned freedom in its effort to rationalize politics, and another that was content to leave politics as the irrational process that it normally is, thereby preserving freedom. The idea of freedom proved more durable than the practice of authoritarianism, and as a consequence, the Cold War ended.

The Nuclear Threat

The Cold War did, however, go on for an extraordinarily long period of time, during which the world confronted extraordinary perils. . . . How close we came to not surviving we will probably never know; but few people who lived through the Cold War took survival for granted during most of its history. The vision of a future filled with smoking, radiating ruins was hardly confined to writers of science fiction and makers of doomsday films; it was a constant presence in the consciousness of several generations after 1945, and the fact that that vision has now receded is of the utmost importance.

I do not mean to imply by this that the nuclear threat itself has gone away. With the proliferation of lethal technology to more and more nations possessing less and less wisdom, the probability that someone may actually use a nuclear weapon someday against someone else could well be increasing. But although horrible enough, such an event would be far from what most people feared during most of the Cold War, which was the prospect of thousands of Soviet and American nuclear warheads raining down upon the territories of the United States, the USSR, and much of the rest of the world. The use of one or two nuclear weapons, in the post–Cold War world, would not end the world as we have known it. During the Cold War, it might have.

Nuclear weapons have evolved from their initial status in our minds as the ultimate instrument of the Apocalypse to, first, a means of deterrence, and then a method of reassurance, and then an object for negotiation, and then an inconvenience to be circumvented, and finally an embarrassment of such magnitude that old Cold War antagonists now race to divest themselves of what they once raced each other so avidly to possess. From having worried about how nuclear weapons could destroy us we have progressed to worrying about how we can safely destroy them, and that is undeniably progress.

How, though, did this happen? How did we get from the world of Dr. Strangelove and "The Day After" to what would have seemed—not so long ago—an even more improbable world in which the leaders of former Soviet republics, including Russia itself, report dutifully to a peripatetic American Secretary of State on how they propose to spend funds allocated by the United States Congress for the purpose of dismantling and disposing of the once formidable Soviet nuclear arsenal?

Nuclear weapons have for so long been the subject of our nightmares—but sometimes also of our delusions of power—that it is difficult to answer this question dispassionately. We have tended to want to see these devices either as a Good Thing or a Bad Thing, and hence we have talked past one another most of the time. But the role of nuclear weapons in Cold War history was neither wholly good nor bad, which is to say, it was more interesting than either the supporters or the critics of these weapons have made it out to be.

The Benefits of Nuclear Weapons

Nuclear weapons were, of course, a very bad thing for the people of Hiroshima and Nagasaki; but those Americans and Japanese spared the necessity of additional killing as a result of their use might be pardoned for seeing some good in them. Nuclear weapons were a bad thing in that they greatly intensified the fears the principal Cold War adversaries had of one another, and that much of the rest of the world had of both of them. But they were a good thing in that they induced caution on the part of these two Great Powers, discouraging irresponsible behavior of the kind that almost all Great Powers in the past have sooner or later engaged in. Nuclear weapons were a bad thing in that they held the world hostage to what now seems the absurd concept of mutual assured destruction, but they were a good thing in that they probably perpetuated the reputations of the United States and the Soviet Union as superpowers, thereby allowing them to "manage" a world that might have been less predictable and more dangerous had Washington and Moscow not performed that function. Nuclear weapons were a bad thing in that they stretched out the length of the Cold War by making the costs of being a superpower bearable on both sides and for both alliances: if the contest had had to be conducted only with more expensive conventional forces, it might have ended long ago. But nuclear weapons were a good thing in that they allowed for the passage of time, and hence for the education of two competitors who eventually came to see that they did not have all that much to compete about in the first place.

It is important to remember, though, that the peaceful end to the Cold War we have just witnessed is not the *only* conceivable way the Cold War could have ended. In adding up that conflict's costs, we would do well to recognize that the time it took to conclude the struggle was not time entirely wasted. That time—and those costs—appear to us excessive in retrospect, but future historians may see those expenditures as long-term investments in ensuring that the Cold War ended peacefully. For what we wound up doing with nuclear weapons was buying time—the time necessary for the authoritarian approach to politics to defeat itself by nonmilitary means. And the passage of time, even if purchased at an exorbitant price, has at last begun to pay dividends.

One of those dividends is that, now that the Cold War has finally ended, we can see just how useless nuclear weapons really are for most purposes most of the time. President [George] Bush, in his television address of 27 September 1991, wiped out more nuclear warheads in a single unilateral gesture than decades of negotiations over arms control have managed to remove, and President Gorbachev quickly offered to go even further. But these decisions do not necessarily mean that the weapons whose numbers both leaders have promised to reduce, and in some categories to eliminate altogether, never had any useful purpose. It could be that their purpose— ensuring a peaceful end to the Cold War—simply took a long time to achieve.

VIEWPOINT 41B

The End of the Cold War Was Not a Great Triumph for the United States (1992)

Ronald Steel (b. 1931)

The liberation of Eastern European countries from Soviet Union control in 1989 and the collapse

Ronald Steel, "The End and the Beginning," *Diplomatic History* 16 (Spring 1992). Reprinted with permission.

of the Soviet Union itself in 1991 were both hailed by many observers as a triumph for the United States and vindication of its foreign policies following World War II. A somewhat different perspective on the end of the Cold War is taken by Ronald Steel, a professor of international relations at the University of Southern California who has written several books on the Cold War and American foreign policy, including *Walter Lippmann and the American Century*. In the following viewpoint, taken from a 1992 essay, Steel argues that the Cold War had evolved into a rather comfortable situation for the United States, giving it unprecedented influence and power throughout the world as well as a rationale for high military spending that helped shape its economy. He writes that the Cold War's sudden ending, which he believes was totally unforeseen by the architects of American foreign policy, will result in the loss of American power and prestige as well as disruptions in the U.S. economy and domestic scene.

Why did the Cold War last as long as it did, according to Steel? What criticisms does Steel make of U.S. foreign policy during the Cold War? How does Steel respond to those who argue that the United States is the world's sole remaining superpower? Does Steel believe the Cold War was a contest between freedom and authoritarianism, as suggested by John Lewis Gaddis in the opposing viewpoint?

During the darkest periods of the Cold War, parallels were sometimes drawn to World War I. Armed conflict, it was said, could break out, as it had in 1914, through miscalculation, rhetorical posturing, and the technological imperatives of the new weaponry. What was not imagined, however, was that the Cold War might suddenly come to an end in a way strikingly similar to that in which the war had ended on the eastern front in 1918: through the internal collapse and unconditional withdrawal of one of the belligerents. That one of the two superpowers might simply retire from the contest, that it would lose its empire and its internal cohesion, seemed no less improbable seventy-five years ago than, in a different context, does the demise of its successor today.

The collapse of the Russian state, which allowed the Bolsheviks to seize power, and the withdrawal of Russia from the war after the surrender at Brest-Litovsk, resulted from the rigidities of autocratic rule, the costs of fighting an interminable war, and the loss of faith by the nation's elite in the system itself. After the event, what had hitherto seemed unthinkable became strikingly obvious: Of course the Russian state, so outwardly formidable and unyielding, was merely a shell. Beneath the façade of invincibility, however, it was ripe for disintegration. It was almost inevitable, considering the toll of war, that the Romanov dynasty would fall. Was this not evident?

Yet, of course, it was not evident at the time because virtually no one in a position of power wanted to believe it. The Allies sought Russian help in the war with Germany, and thus it fit their purposes to assume that its government was strong and its people united in a common purpose. Because the Allies needed a partner equal to the fervor of their endeavor, they suffered from a self-willed political blindness.

Now this all seems abundantly clear. But are there not clear parallels between the years 1917 and 1918 and the period 1989–1991? In both cases political leaders were stunned by a course of events in Russia for which their analyses and assumptions had not prepared them. They had viewed Russia through the lenses of their own preoccupations. As in World War I, Western policy in the Cold War was based on assumptions repudiated by events. Soviet Russia was clearly not the adversary that American policymakers thought it was: not in internal cohesion, not in military strength, and probably not even in geopolitical ambitions. To an important degree the United States was involved in a deadly struggle with a phantom Russia, just as Russian leaders—themselves bedeviled by suspicion, fear, and ideology—were with a phantom America.

An Unforeseen Ending

The Cold War was not supposed to have ended as it did, with the demise of the Soviet empire in Europe, the dissolution of the Soviet state, and the repudiation of communism itself by those thought to be its most ardent adherents. Such a situation normally results from a catastrophic defeat in war. According to the Cold War scenario, over a period of several more decades the conflict would gradually be reduced as the two superpowers worked out mutually beneficial arms control arrangements to lessen the cost of maintaining their respective spheres of influence. In effect, the Cold War was not supposed to end at all. The advantages it offered to both major contestants were so manifest, and its cost seemingly so manageable, that there seemed little incentive on either side to end it. Indeed, a political negotiation to end the Cold War in Europe, its focal point, had from the beginning been firmly rejected by American policymakers.

For these reasons, the way that the Cold War ended requires us to make a fundamental reassessment of the assumptions on which American actions were based. Unquestionably, the Soviet Union was far weaker ideologically, politically, structurally, and, of course, economically, than was generally assumed. Some of these assumptions were based on fear and

exaggeration, others seemed spun out of thin air to serve political purposes. Among the most fatuous of these was the theory advanced by one of Ronald Reagan's academic advisers, that totalitarianism by its very nature was irreversible. The purpose of this theory was to justify American support of rightist authoritarian regimes; its rationale was that these regimes, unlike Communist ones, might one day evolve into democratic ones. Adherence to such exaggerated, self-serving, and even delusional assumptions about what was generically labeled the "Communist threat" clouded our understanding of what was happening in the Soviet Union, impeded the course of orderly change, and inflicted terrible misery on the Cold War arenas of the Third World, where the contest between "good" and "bad" forms of authoritarianism was taking place.

---•---

"The end of the Cold War means a dramatic decline in the ability of the United States to determine the course of events."

---•---

The problem has not been one merely of a self-blinding dogma. The enormous apparatus of government intelligence and spy operations, of generously endowed think tanks and research institutes, and of the entire discipline of "strategic studies" failed to anticipate or even intellectually to prepare the ground for an understanding of what is arguably the most momentous political event of this century. In understanding the collapse of communism and the Soviet state, the strategists in government, at universities, and in the well-financed limbo in between have been virtually irrelevant.

In part, this is a failure of American social science, with its blind faith in quantification, its indifference to history and political culture, and its aggressive ethnocentrism. In a larger sense, it is also a failure of political intelligence, a failure to penetrate into the realities of an adversarial society. Americans saw the Soviet Union that they wanted to see: a society of automatons mesmerized by a messianic ideology and intent on applying all of its energies to gaining Soviet domination over the entire world.

Origins of the Cold War

This was the Soviet Union of George Kennan's "Long Telegram," which, lacking the nuances of his later writings, combined concerns over both totalitarianism and communism to portray a state that was relentlessly expansionist and implacably hostile to the West. This is the state found, in exaggerated form, in NSC-68 [National Security Council Document Number 68] of 1950, which, in calling for a vast expansion of U.S. military power, declared that "the Soviet Union, unlike previous aspirants to hegemony, is animated by a new fanatic faith, antithetical to our own, and seeks to impose its absolute authority over the rest of the world.". . .

One does not have to be a revisionist to recognize that Washington's interpretation of a global military and ideological struggle for dominance corresponded more to postwar America's ambitions and capacities than to the ability of the Soviet Union to control politically significant areas outside of Eastern Europe. Even without Soviet activism the United States would have dominated the post–World War II world—but not to the degree that it did. The Soviets, with their brutal methods and hostile behavior, provided the challenge that permitted American policymakers to block a retreat to prewar passivity and to engage the nation's formidable energies in a global vocation. Soviet power and ruthlessness in Eastern Europe were real enough, and required an American response in the West. But Soviet brutality was also fortuitous, for it permitted an engagement, and a global extension, of American power that otherwise could not have been justified domestically. The Cold War served a useful political function for both Soviet and American policymakers. If it provided the United States with a global vocation, it also elevated to theoretically equal world status an economically backward and politically primitive Soviet state.

We now know more about the Soviet Union than we did before: its inner weakness, both material and psychological, its vulnerability, and the structure of lies, intimidation, and apathy on which rule by the Communist party bureaucracy rested. This was not a state inspired by a proselytizing ideology, as so many of our political leaders and ostensible experts told us, but rather one sustained by habit, a custom of deference to authority, the lack of a democratic tradition, and the absence of a realistic alternative. The Soviet people did not embrace communism, or outside the Russian core even the union itself; they merely acquiesced in it.

American diplomacy during the Cold War would have been more successful, and its instruments less politically costly, had it confined itself to its supposed goal: the containment of Soviet military power. The forcible imposition of Soviet control on the peoples of Eastern Europe, Moscow's potential threat to the great industrial centers of Western Europe and Japan, the arsenal of nuclear weapons that could be used to intimidate the United States and its European allies—these needed to be checked by the only military power capable of doing so. Even though the

Russians, as Kennan . . . and others had long insisted, showed no intention of using military force against Western Europe, it was prudent to deny them opportunities for exerting political pressure. The scale of the military effort on both sides was, however, grossly disproportionate to the political situation, which was, in fact, quite stable. Neither side had the least interest in disturbing the political equilibrium by force. Europe, for all of the excessive arms that the two sides ranged against one another, was the quietest frontier of the Cold War.

The Cold War and the Third World

The reason that the Cold War produced such violence, entailed such cost, and periodically threatened to go out of control was not because of containment in Europe, but because of the links made between communism and radical social upheavals in the Third World. It was the attempt to control such social change, particularly in the former colonial areas, that transformed the Cold War from a dispute over the political orientation of Eastern Europe into a global conflict. The stated justification for U.S. intervention in the Third World was that the Soviet Union was the chief inspiration for such change and would be its primary beneficiary. This was the formula used to justify the interventions, either covert or overt, within the self-declared spheres of influence, notably Cuba, the Dominican Republic, Panama, Guatemala, El Salvador, Brazil and Chile—and also in Africa and Asia, notably Angola, the former Congo, Indonesia, Korea, and Vietnam.

That the expansion of the European quarrel to a global level would also enable the United States greatly to expand its military and political reach enhanced its appeal to American foreign policy elites eager to embrace the nation's new opportunities. The collapse of the former centers of global power—Britain and France no less than Germany and Japan—made this expansion not only easier but also seemingly necessary and inevitable. Thus, the Cold War was not simply a response to Soviet expansion, the containment of its geopolitical ambitions in Europe, but the framework by which American policymakers were able to extend globally the reach of American power and influence.

Without the Soviet factor such a policy would never have been able to achieve the widescale public support it required. The smothering of domestic dissent, as evidenced in the loyalty programs of the late 1940s and the 1950s, and a climate of fear intensified by the Korean War, made possible the vast expansion of the American security state. Thus, an understanding of the Cold War must be found not only in the ambitions, real or hypothetical, of the Soviet Union but also in the anxieties and ambitions of American policymakers suddenly confronted with a world, so different from that of a decade earlier, when opportunities seemed unlimited. That expansionism was simply the other side of the coin of containment was one of the ironies of the Cold War.

The two strands of Soviet containment and global expansion were there almost from the beginning and were linked in the Truman Doctrine of 1947. At the time a number of centrists objected to this linkage, including [influential political columnist Walter] Lippmann, who, even while approving an aid program to Greece and Turkey, warned against the globalist implications of an avowedly counterrevolutionary policy. But the exigencies of the Cold War, particularly over the political and economic control of Germany, and its spread to Asia with the triumph of the Communists in China and the expansion of the civil war in Korea, effectively transformed the containment of Soviet military power in Europe into a global struggle against what was glibly, but for policymakers usefully, termed the "international Communist conspiracy."

Although the Cold War was waged on many fronts and took a terrible toll in resources and human lives, it was, with one major exception, kept within bounds that the United States and the Soviet Union considered tolerable. That exception was, of course, the Cuban missile crisis of 1962: a near-catastrophic confrontation resulting from miscalculation, bravado, expediency, and duplicity on a scale that frightened both sides. After that crisis, the two antagonists made sure that their competition for advantage and influence was waged through either proxy or semicolonial wars. The American war in Vietnam and the Soviet war in Afghanistan were aspects of the Cold War: Each superpower justified its intervention as directed toward the containment (not only military, but also psychological) of the other; both sought to preserve spheres of influence. But these two conflicts also bore strong resemblance to the colonial wars that the French had fought in Indochina and North Africa and that Russian tsars had waged in central Asia.

Why Did the Cold War Last

What one must ask about the Cold War is not why it ended so soon but why it lasted so long. There were a number of reasons for its longevity: the preference of the Europeans and the Japanese to grow rich rather than to resume the game of power politics; the eagerness of both the United States and the Soviet Union to inherit those roles; the transformation of the Soviet-American geopolitical quarrel into an ideological one that respected no frontiers; and the utility of the conflict in establishing Soviet or American hegemony within their respective areas. Without the Cold War, U.S. and Russian positions, especially within Europe, would have been significantly weaker.

Most important, in the European context, the Cold War offered a solution of sorts to the perennial German problem. Partition had at last made it possible for the Europeans to live without serious anxiety about German power and to build in the West a European construction that Germany would neither threaten nor dominate. So long as the Soviets stood in the way of unification, there was no longer a German problem in the old sense. Even the Germans did not seem to be particularly troubled by their partition. They had found a new place of honor and respectability in the West with which they were quite satisfied. And during the long course of the Cold War they had at last achieved a democratic transformation of their society. Further, within the Soviet empire the Cold War was keeping deadly East European tribal hatreds in check. By the mid-1960s, with Western Europe moving gradually toward integration under the comforting and inexpensive umbrella of American protection, the Cold War had become quite institutionalized.

The Cold War had, in fact, developed into an eminently workable international system. It was predictable, economically manageable, politically useful, and militarily unthreatening. This was so because the Soviets, too, had developed a vested interest in its preservation. The Americans kept the Germans in check, and the Europeans kept the Americans in check. The Cold War allowed the Japanese to gain extraordinary economic power as America expended its resources on potlatch objectives, and it gave the Soviets, despite their primitive economy and retrograde social structure, the attributes of a Great Power. For all practical purposes it permitted the Americans to control the foreign policies of their major allies (and potential challengers): the Europeans and the Japanese. And it gave the Chinese a privileged position as the "good" Communists who would antagonize the Russians on their Asian flanks. Despite its considerable costs, the Cold War thus provided something desirable for all of the major participants. No nation had a compelling interest in ending it. From an American perspective it had a particular appeal. The Soviets were unquestionably the weaker power and posed no serious threat to American interests. As one astute critic has written: "The purpose of the Cold War was not victory but the maintenance of a controlled contest."

Decline of U.S. Influence

The demise of the Cold War system inevitably means a sharp reduction of the influence of the two major adversaries. While this is obvious in the case of the former Soviet Union, it is no less true of the

United States. To a far greater degree than has generally been realized, American political influence has rested significantly on the Cold War. It was concern over the reality of Soviet power and the uncertainty of Soviet ambitions that induced the Europeans and the Japanese to put their security in American hands, to play a historically passive role in world affairs. So long as fear of Soviet power was real, the most prudent, as well as the most economic, course for these countries was to rely on American leadership. For this they paid a certain price, both economic and political, of deference to the United States, whether in the form of trade concessions, financing of the U.S. treasury's deficits, purchases of U.S.-made military equipment, or allowing Washington alone to negotiate with Moscow.

So long as such deference seemed necessary, it was largely unchallenged by the allies, with the exception, of course, of Gaullist France in the 1960s. But the retreat of the Soviet Union from the contest, indeed the disappearance of that state itself, has dramatically altered the balance within the former Cold War coalition led by the United States. Today, the United States—in part because of exaggerated Cold War preoccupations, in part because of irresponsible fiscal and economic policies of its own making—has lost both its economic and its political freedom of action. Washington cannot finance its unquenchable deficits without the willingness of the Europeans and the Japanese to buy treasury bonds; it cannot undertake large-scale military interventions without their financial contributions, as the Gulf war of early 1991 demonstrated. The United States fought the Cold War, but today it is the Western Europeans who are financing, organizing, and influencing the political future of what was once the Soviet Cold War empire.

Unavoidably, the end of the Cold War means a dramatic decline in the ability of the United States to determine the course of events. This has not yet become fully apparent to foreign policy elites. Some, in the wake of the U.S.-initiated and mostly U.S.-fought Gulf war, and of the collapse of the Soviet Union, refer to the United States as the only superpower. To be a "superpower" in a world where the

instruments of power are either restricted by economic dependency or directed against a foe that has largely ceased to exist, however, is to render the term meaningless. It took two to fight the Cold War, two to ensure abdication by the lesser players, two to give American leaders a sense of mission and freedom of action, two to justify the suppression of American domestic social and economic needs to the exigencies of a Great Power struggle.

Two have been reduced to one, and the contest has shifted to other arenas. It is no longer between the United States and the Soviet Union, no longer over the pretensions of ideology, no longer waged by military interventions or by the accumulation of nuclear weaponry. With the end of the Cold War, the United States will be forced to adjust to a competition where its familiar instruments are inapplicable and where its allies and dependencies are increasingly rivals. It is not merely the end of the Cold War, but a dramatic reshifting of the world power balance. For the American economy, distorted by a half-century of reliance on military spending, for American political elites, who had come to believe that they were "born to lead," and for an American public, deprived of an enemy to justify its sacrifices, the experience will be a wrenching and possibly threatening one.

For Further Reading

Michael R. Beschloss and Strobe Talbott, *At the Highest Levels: The Inside Story of the End of the Cold War.* Boston: Little, Brown, 1993.

John Lewis Gaddis, *The United States and the End of the Cold War.* New York: Oxford University Press, 1992.

Michelle Stenehjem Gerber, *On the Home Front: The Cold War Legacy of the Hanford Nuclear Site.* Lincoln: University of Nebraska Press, 1992.

Don Oberdorfer, *The Turn: From the Cold War to a New Era.* New York: Poseidon Press, 1991.

Tobin Siebers, *Cold War Criticism and the Politics of Skepticism.* New York: Oxford University Press, 1993.

Ronald Steel, *Temptations of a Superpower.* Cambridge, MA: Harvard University Press, 1995.

Martin Walker, *The Cold War: A History.* New York: Henry Holt, 1994.

INDEX